How Law Works

Collected Articles and New Essays

Thomas Hemnes

Series in Law

VERNON PRESS

www.vernonpress.com

In the Americas:
Vernon Press
1000 N West Street, Suite 1200
Wilmington, Delaware, 19801
United States

In the rest of the world:
Vernon Press
C/Sancti Espiritu 17,
Malaga, 29006
Spain

Series in Law

Library of Congress Control Number: 2020939831

ISBN: 978-1-62273-826-7

Cover design by Vernon Press. Cover image by Joe Moore.

To my wife Carole, who has put up with my academic avocation over all these years; to our children (children no more!) Anna, Abigail, and Jonathan; to our grandchildren, who might one day wonder why on earth Grandpa was typing all the time; to those friends and colleagues whose opinions of this work I value most highly; and to that future reader who wonders what lawyers were thinking when the digital age dawned.

Contents

List of Figures and Tables

Table of Abbreviations

BLC	Bankrupt Licensors Coalition
CAFC	Court of Appeals for the Federal Circuit
CBEMA	Computer and Business Equipment Manufacturers Association
CCPA	California Consumer Privacy Act
CISG	UN Convention on International Sales of Goods
COPPA	Children's Online Privacy Protection Act
CTM	Community Trademark
EU	European Union
FACTA	The Fair and Accurate Credit Transactions Act of 2003
FCRA	Fair Credit Reporting Act
FTC	Federal Trade Commission
GDPR	General Data Protection Regulation
GLB	Gramm-Leach-Bliley Act
GNP	Gross National Product
GTC	GTC Law Group PC & Affiliates
HIPPA	Health Insurance Portability and Accountability Act
IP	Intellectual Property
TRIPS	Agreement on Trade-Related Aspects of Intellectual Property Rights
UCC	Uniform Commercial Code
UCITA	Uniform Computer Information Transactions Act
UK	United Kingdom
USPTO	United States Patent and Trademark Office

Foreword

It's fairly typical, I think, for a busy practitioner to take a quick look back as the welter of issues, problems, clients, and projects whizzes by. The thought is reflexive: "Wow, this (deal, case, legal field) is important, something new; or, this (deal, case, etc.) would have been different back in the day." But the harsh edge of the lawyer's life is this: in a business where you literally sell your time, you often have precious little to yourself. And so the passing intention to take a look back glides by, lost in the oncoming rush of whatever your clients cook up next.

Well, much to my delight and benefit (and yours too), Tom Hemnes decided to take the road less traveled. He has committed a valuable act of follow-through and retrospective: this book. What many professionals think they might one day do, Tom has done. He got off the professional freeway often enough and long enough to slow down to the writer's pace. He put the words down on paper about some of the issues he's wondered over in the field of IP law these past forty years or so. And about law practice, its ways and means. And about a few other topics to which he has given thought and attention.

I was a newly hatched law professor when I first met Tom Hemnes at an IP-related event in Boston. Since that time, I've learned that if he is interested in something, and puts that interest to work with attention, what he has to say is something I want to hear. It started with copyright protection of software, which was, when we met (c. 1990), a hot topic in Boston, Silicon Valley, and any place that cared about the software industry. But I soon saw that Tom was interested not in just one issue, or even one field of law; he had an interest in all the areas of law his practice touched on, and a number of others besides. I came to realize that Tom was blessed with a nimble and inquiring mind, and he liked to think things through until he was satisfied. We had an affinity, because this is what I was being paid to do.

You will see the imprint of this lively mind in the chapters that follow. They all hold interest, and are all worth a thorough read. You have to appreciate an author who guides you through a nuanced dissection of law firm paralegal economics and then glides into a discussion of John Rawls and Robert Nozick, whose philosophizing marked one of the twentieth century's great substantive contributions to Harvard University's Department of Philosophy. There are equally interesting discussions in this volume of feudal land tenure law, the intricacies of the merger, and idea/expression concepts in copyright law — and a host of other ideas and topics as well.

But Tom is a lawyer, and for me, the most appealing parts of this book are when he turns his wide-ranging analytic powers on the nature and operation of IP law. Put simply, I just enjoy watching Tom think about this intricate field. Take as one of many potential examples Tom's explanation of the difference between a material object (a sculpture in his example) and an IP right covering the object:

> Copyright law declares that the sculptor has created not just a sculpture (achievement enough in itself!) but a "work," which is a Platonic abstraction that is embodied in the sculpture as a "copy," but exists independently of the particular sculpture, hovering, one might say, above and beyond it. (p. 294)

This is not only philosophically grounded (hard to beat Plato); it is an excellent visual metaphor that reveals the presence of an experienced and thoughtful IP practitioner. Clients live mostly in the world of things, but IP lawyers are instead professional metaphysicians. They live in a world of expansible conceptual categories or sets, where material objects are just elements of the sets. Or candidate elements anyway. A good portion of the IP lawyer's job is to argue that item X is, or is not, an element of the (IP protected) set. It helps to have a clear head when working as a professional metaphysician in this fashion, partly because all lawyers (or at least senior lawyers) are parttime educators. This kind of brief sketch of how the law will see the client's case is absolutely essential. The clients may want to dive right into "what will it cost, and will we win?" but Instructor Hemnes knows from experience that the answer to the clients' pressing questions will not make sense until he explains the risk factors and contingencies in the case. For these, he needs the client to understand the issues from the law's point of view. The idea that an IP right "exists independently" of the material objects captures this. And the suggestion to see a penumbra of rights "above and beyond" the object — that's inspired. It is an excellent visual metaphor that helps people begin to view the world in the slightly orthogonal manner of the IP specialist. I personally speak of IP rights and transactions as existing "behind" or "in the background of" the world of things, but "above and beyond" works just as well.

Aside from the evident imprint of a master craftsperson, there are some other elements to this book that I found particularly distinctive. For myself, the most valuable part of the book is the middle chapters on private law topics. In Chapter 4, Author Tom speaks of "the plasticity of the common law," a wonderful phrase that captures a facet of IP law often overlooked by the academy: the place of IP rights in a private law system. As Tom puts it, also in Chapter 4:

> [T]he instinct of intellectual property law and lawyers . . . is to give the intellectual property rights holder the greatest possible freedom in constructing, subdividing, and exploiting the intellectual property rights. In other words, restraints on alienation and downstream restrictions on the use of chattels are anathema to the common law, but the norm in the context of intellectual property licensing. (p. 183)

Trust a lawyer who has seen his share of deals to drive this point home. As much as every IP right issued by the government and backed by the courts embodies numerous policy tradeoffs, in the hands of a business person, it has an entirely different appearance. As Tom says, this can cause problems. While post-contracting restrictions can add value in a private deal, they may impose costs on third parties. And so, even in this bastion of private ordering, the public policy issues enfolded into every IP right may well show themselves again.

But there is a bigger picture here. IP rights support and contribute to all kinds of business arrangements. The IP rights (and licenses) covered here in Chapter 4 may wind up in bankruptcy proceedings, but they started as leverage or strategic components in business deals of one kind or another. The "open source" contracts Tom describes in Chapter 3 ("Abracadabra") represent clever private law solutions to a perceived *excess* of IP rights. And so on through the book.

The problem with scholars who teach full time is they don't see enough of the private deals that pervade this volume. So they miss the private law role of IP rights and focus only on the headline-grabbing policy issues emanating from IP: incentive and monopoly, public access versus private appropriation. In this manner, they are apt to miss an entire dimension of what makes IP rights important. Studying deals also makes something else clear: to business people, IP is an asset like any other. It can be bought, sold, mortgaged, pledged, and so on, in the same fashion as a truck or a piece of machinery. The private law perspective could thus add a touch of humility to the field as well. (And perhaps, he said coyly, this explains why it's overlooked.)

I will close with this same theme of humility. Tom reminds us to have faith in the versatility of lawyers and basic common law tools. It's a faith not based on the need or even expectation that government will always get the issues right. The faith stems from the adaptability of business people, helped along by the kind of experienced and savvy legal advisor Tom represents. The flaming debates over the proper copyright doctrine for software user interfaces stand as a good example. To hear the oral arguments in the *Lotus v. Borland* case, some years ago now, or dip into the IP journals and law reports of the time, one would think a decision was at hand having a momentous potential impact. In the event, however, Tom reminds us that the issue is more or less a dead letter today. Anyone today who hangs out a shingle saying "software interface IP lawyer" will have a dusty shingle before she has many clients. Between the ease of crafting an interface, usually out of widely shared public domain elements, and the consolidation of many parts of the industry (online platforms, enterprise databases, popular mobile apps, etc.), there is not much contestation over interfaces anymore.

At the end of the day, this is good news. Maybe, as Tom hints, the high hopes and soaring aspirations of us "there at the beginning" of the digital era in IP were never fully realized. Maybe IP in the digital era was not really such an earth-shattering locus of policy. But on the other hand, this has conveniently limited the damage we have done as well. It will be for future economic historians to definitively survey the impact of IP policy on the dawn of the digital era. But even before that final verdict, Tom and his cohorts, including me, can say with some authority, "At least we didn't kill it. Plenty of good software available today." And maybe more important, to those who enjoy the metaphysical intricacy of the IP field, we can say, "we had fun at it too." If you, like me, think this is worth something, read on. You'll find an experienced voice that has traversed some fascinating mysteries of the law and elsewhere, and emerged with some wise and insightful thoughts. We should be grateful that Tom took the time to look backward and pull these thoughts together. I know I am.

Robert Merges, UC Berkeley Law School

Acknowledgments

I owe a debt of gratitude to the many colleagues with whom I worked to pull together these assembled articles. Some were named as co-authors with me; others are gratefully acknowledged in the credits for each of the articles. The errors are all mine, but the depth and quality of research is largely theirs.

A further debt of gratitude to the gifted lawyers at Foley Hoag who mentored me during my formative years: Hans Loeser, Ken Fish, Mark Clark, David Walker, and Jerry Preston, to name a few and to omit too many. Foley imbued the values of excellence, respect for the law, respect for others, and ethics that all of us carry with us, whether still at Foley or as part of the Foley diaspora, where we strive to continue these traditions.

And thanks also to my partners and shareholders, both at Foley and at GTC Law Group, who have tolerated my taste for the unremunerative researches and writings that make up this work.

Pulling together these articles, which were published over a forty-year period in who knows how many formats, and then conforming them to the publisher's requirements, was an ordeal that I would not wish on anybody, but that I did wish on the publishing experts Bridget Leahy and Hannah Fischer. I could never have done it without their dedicated work. And then indexing and re-indexing a manuscript that ballooned to almost 1000 typed pages was a further task that fell to Chris Crane. Without Bridget, Hannah, and Chris, this whole project would have foundered on the shoals of my shallow patience. Thank you, all.

Acknowledgements

Introduction

The original plan for this book was to collect in one place legal articles chronicling the dawn of the digital age. This was a period of time that began when the practice of law was so hide-bound that Oliver Wendell Holmes would have felt perfectly at home had he walked into Foley, Hoag & Eliot, the Boston law firm I joined in 1975. It was a comfortable old profession with partners, associates, personal secretaries, typewriters, and yellow pads. Legal advertising was considered champerty, and the very largest firms had perhaps 200 lawyers. In only a few years, the legal profession had morphed into an industry boasting 2000-member profit-driven firms, secretaries replaced by voice recognition software, and personal injury lawyers whose blaring ads dominate daytime TV. And the law itself struggled to make legal sense of the digital technologies that drove this transformation — first video games, then computer software, social networking, big data, and finally, privacy. The collected articles chronicle and analyze these developments.

During the collection process, it became obvious that the articles could be assembled around several interwoven themes. It also became obvious that some of what I had thought when the articles were written cried out for reconsideration — it might be said that I saw an opportunity to take advantage of the principle that hindsight is 20/20. This spawned the new essays introducing each thematic chapter and improved the work's title from "Collected Articles" (boring!) to the more intriguing "How Law Works."

One of the largest and most enduring issues the articles address is the question of how legal reasoning works, and more specifically, the relationship between language and legal analysis. A lawyer's tool is language, and the law is embodied in words. This suggests that something might be learned about how the law works from studies of how language — the stuff of which law is made — works. The philosophy of language, and in particular ordinary language philosophy, was a core discipline when I was an undergraduate and graduate student in philosophy. In law school, I was convinced that it had much to offer in understanding how law works. This led to the Note I wrote and published in the *Harvard Law Review* in 1974 that is the springboard for Chapter 2. It was also central to the discussion in Chapter 3 of the "idea/expression dichotomy" in copyright law that was central to considerations of the scope of copyright protection of computer software.

The question of the relation between language and the law has become particularly relevant at a time when politicians want to appoint judges who are "strict constructionists" and believe — or purport to believe — that the words in the Constitution or a statute supplant the exercise of judgment. Like today's "strict constructionists," as a law student, I believed that a minute examination of Constitutional language would avoid — or at least limit — the unfettered exercise of judicial judgment, which seemed rudderless to me, a 25-year-old who was steeped in logical analysis. The second and third chapters raise the question of whether I was right about this. If not, then "strict construction" misapprehends the way language works — and, as a creature of language, the way law works. If not, then words provide a vocabulary in which one can express a conclusion; but they do not, without more, dictate the conclusion.

Another recurring theme is the way lawyers work and the purposes served by the law and law firms. Chapter 1 considers the economic organization of business law firms, which changed dramatically in the decades covered by this book. It also touches on the use of legal practice to resolve disputes. Chapters 3 and 4 show how lawyers and judges used the legal tools at hand to create the legal and contractual environment in which the computer software industry prospered, and how lawyers' zeal to protect their clients often overshot the mark from the standpoint of the software industry as a whole.

Chapters 5 and 7 raise the question of whether intellectual property and its near cousin personal data can be considered property at all. That intellectual property, at least, should be protected as property, was comprehensively argued by Professor Merges in his landmark book *Justifying Intellectual Property*, but the fact that the question required such a book is telling. Although it has become a staple of modern commerce, fueling the enormous value of such companies as Google, Amazon, Facebook, Microsoft, Oracle, and Adobe, neither intellectual property nor data ever fit neatly into the traditional categories of property. They are not goods; they are not real estate. At one time, when computer software was stored on floppy disks and sold in boxes, one might have compared it with movies or books, in that it was an intangible property "fixed in a tangible medium of expression." But even this anchor has slipped its hold, as software becomes "software as a service," and most data is lodged in the "cloud." Taking a security interest in software or the assets of a data-driven company begins to assume the difficulty one would have in taking a security interest in a law firm: the real value is in the programmers and the institution standing behind the service, or in the individuals using the service and donating their data to it, and they are not easily made subject to repossession and sale. And trademarks protect both the interest of their putative owners and also the interest of the public who relies on them. Intellectual property is, one might say, the platypus of property law: it has some, but not all, of the features of personal property and real estate, but it also can seem more like a service or a public good.

I've presented this high-minded stuff in the context of a series of articles on some of the nuts and bolts of intellectual property law, especially as applied to computer software and personal data. I hope to deliver some big ideas in small, more easily digested packages. I also hope that some readers may find practical value in the nitty-gritty discussions, especially of mundane things, such as whether a license agreement can bind downstream purchasers, how to find a safe trademark, and how to make an indemnification clause realistic and workable.

As I look back on these articles — many of them from a standpoint many decades later — I am struck by a sense of paradise lost. The story begins in 1974, before cellphones, before personal computers, before there was word processing. I wrote the Note discussed in Chapter 2 on an Olympia portable manual typewriter, referencing a pile of hardbound books. The manuscript was then sent to the *Review*'s printer for typesetting. The printer returned long galleys with big margins in which the editors were expected to rip the draft to pieces and then write improvements using pencils and erasers and a set of proofreading symbols like the single loop for deletions and inverted "y" for insertions. This was the language of editing; we were proficient in it. The edited galleys were then sent back to the printer to typeset the edits and then sent back to us for more proofing and editing. The *Review* had been drafted and edited this way for as long as anyone could remember.

This was all about to change. The digital age was just dawning, creating a very heady legal environment for those of us involved in intellectual property law. What had once been a backwater of legal practice — the place of patent engineers and others practicing areas of law that, with the occasional exception of copyright, were not even taught in the "major" law schools — was suddenly front and center in commercial life. Law firms, mine included, scrambled to build expertise and capture the lucrative business associated with intellectual property litigation and transactions. We thought we were building a brave new world in which international cooperation, technology, and digital access would transcend the national boundaries that had so poisoned the first half of the twentieth century. We believed that the resolution of issues like the scope of copyright in computer programs and the consistent international protection of intellectual property would be as critical to this new world's health and success as the consolidation of the European Union following the collapse of the Soviet Union.

The story since then has grown much darker. The promise of the digital age has given way to fears of loss of privacy, social disintegration, and corrosive political manipulation. Sadly, the same digital technologies that gave us such high hopes are now the source of our loss, much as the great technologies of the previous century — electricity, steam power, transportation — have produced the nightmare of global warming. It has been for me, and for many in my generation, a disheartening decline from the hopes and dreams that many of us had shared.

My editors and peer reviewers have expended some worry over the audience for this tome. Many wish that the book would have a single audience: law students, law professors, lowly laborers in the legal vineyard trying to figure out the best way to draft an indemnity clause. Any of these might find value in parts of the book, but I have failed utterly at the goal of distillation.

My great hope is that there might be someone years, decades, or longer in the future, picking this dusty volume off the shelf in a library — if there are such things then — who might wonder what was going on in legal and social thought during that period of time when the digital world was spawned. The last is, I think, my most valued reader. Here is a record of what I, at least, was thinking about when the world moved from an industrial society to a new age when digital data overwhelmed all else. I fancy that I lived through a time of historic ephemera when the early Internet and early websites were lost to history, but when a new world of data, AI, social media, and disconnection through connection, were formed. If this volume can provide some small record of that time, it will have served a valuable purpose.

I begin, though, with an article on legal practice and its evolution from the guild structure I joined as a young associate to today's brutally capitalistic model.

Chapter 1

The Practice of Profits

"Paralegal Profitability Analysis" (1984)

Profitability was not always central to law firm management, status, and prestige. When I joined Foley Hoag & Eliot in 1975, law firms saw themselves as professional organizations, not businesses. One signed onto them for life and expected a comfortable living eventually, after serving a lengthy apprenticeship as an associate. Associates were paid a pittance, which meant that they could be trained slowly over the course of years. Legal practice among the major firms was a guild that paid its apprentices (associates) the "going rate," that resisted competition from within or without, and that offered its members a comfortable living with respect in the community. For a partner in one firm to resign and take a position with another was all but unthinkable. Law firm advertising was illegal; solicitation of clients already represented by another firm was considered unethical. As associates, we were advised that if we were at a cocktail party and someone mentioned that another firm represented them, the proper response was that they are an excellent firm and that we were sure they would be well represented there. Soliciting the client in such a circumstance was an offense that risked embarrassment to the senior partners and admonishment to the associate.

The traditional dignity of the legal profession was lost by, say, 1990.[1] Three great factors contributed to the loss: lawyer advertising, extreme increases in associate pay, and accelerating income inequality in the society at large, fueled by reductions in the top marginal tax brackets. In 1977, just two years after I had signed on with Foley, the Supreme Court held, in the case *Bates v. State Bar of Arizona,* that lawyer advertising was commercial speech protected by the First

[1] I refer throughout to the practice of law in medium to large law firms. The practice of law in the public sector, in charitable work, and in personal injury representation was impacted very differently by thc factors discussed in text.

Amendment to the U.S. Constitution.[2] The legalization of lawyer advertising fundamentally corroded the sense of professionalism and associated dignity of the practice of law — as anyone who sees TV advertisements for lawyers can appreciate. Lawyers became just one other kind of huckster, pitching their wares to people who may or may not need them. Every encounter with a potential client was a marketing opportunity, and every partner with a book of business a target for recruitment.

As mentioned, a third factor was the marginal tax rate. When I started practicing, the top marginal tax rate on ordinary income — that is, what lawyers make — was 70 percent, and capital gains were taxed at 36.5 percent. By 1990 the top rate on both ordinary income and capital gains had dropped to 28 percent. When I started, I distinctly recall partners at Foley commenting that there's not much point in working for the last marginal dollar when the government is going to take 70 percent of it. In other words, the tax rate had a profound cultural and lifestyle impact on professionals like lawyers: it provided an incentive to pay attention to things other than making money, such as professional development, associate training, and pro-bono (a very big thing then). Even sabbaticals for lawyers were a hot topic of discussion when I started. Nor did this mean that lawyers were relatively poor: the partners at Foley and other successful firms lived about as well as partners do today; it just cost them less because they weren't competing with bankers and venture capitalists making vastly more for things like summer homes and nice houses in Weston. Everybody was in about the same boat.

The sharp reductions in marginal tax rates initiated by Reagan changed all this. Suddenly, it was possible to keep three-fourths of that marginal dollar, and

---

[2] 433 U.S. 350 (1977). A very similar corrosion afflicted the medical profession, in part as a result of another Supreme Court opinion, *Virginia State Pharmacy Board v. Virginia Citizens Consumer Council*, 425 U.S.748 (1976), in which the Court held that the First Amendment protected pharmacists' advertising the price of prescription drugs. Most physicians suffer the consequences of the prescription drug ads, with patients demanding inappropriate treatments or, worse yet, receiving such treatments from doctors who simply can't withstand the anger when they refuse to prescribe something the patient has seen advertised. In recent years the ads cost over $5 billion yearly, in all likelihood causing overprescription that contributes to the extreme cost of medical care in the United States in comparison with the rest of the world, in which such advertising is usually banned. Plus, the ads are a depressing nuisance; it's such a relief when we're out of the country and not subjected to them. Both of these decisions were written by Justice Blackmun, author of *Roe v. Wade* 410 U.S. 113 (1973) . One might easily wonder how the politics and culture of the United States would have been different if these three decisions had not been rendered.

pie-in-the-sky incomes for law partners — or investment bankers or CEOs — seemed achievable. Furthermore, maintaining a comfortable lifestyle required keeping pace with the investment bankers, CEOs, and their ilk. To use a small example, a partner in a Boston law firm in 1970 could afford a place on the Vineyard or in Vermont — or both — without a multimillion-dollar income. In 2016 he or she would be competing for the same resource with hedge fund managers and CEOs whose incomes had climbed to unheard-of levels.

During the same period, associate salaries, which for decades had been essentially fixed, began to escalate. Several factors were supporting this dramatic increase. A dominant factor was simple demand for labor-intensive legal services, and thus for legal talent, especially among the "top" firms. Especially labor-intensive were litigation, particularly the discovery process in litigation, merger and acquisition (M&A) work, and public offerings. Environmental and employment regulation also played their roles, together with the internationalization of legal practice. Until the 1970s or 1980s, legal practice had been largely parochial, but in the late twentieth century, law firms like Baker MacKenzie and Clifford Chance rapidly expanded internationally and were quickly joined by any ambitious US firm hoping to "keep up with the Joneses." As a result of these and other factors, the size of law firms, in terms of numbers of lawyers, dramatically expanded during the 1970s and 1980s. To use a couple of examples, Latham & Watkins, today reputed to be the highest-grossing firm in the world, had 19 attorneys in 1960, 46 in 1970, and currently has 2200 attorneys. Had its size increased with the rate of inflation, it would have perhaps 200 attorneys today, not over 2000. Skadden Arps was, when I started practicing, considered a second-rate New York firm, but its commitment to M&A work combined with a merger mania during the 1980s to make it one of the most prominent firms in the United States, with some 1700 attorneys in 2017 (down from a high of 1900 a couple of years earlier). In 1970 a firm of 2000 would have been unheard of; today, there are many dozens of such firms.

The inflation in law firm size fed inflation in starting salaries as the major firms competed to fill their ranks with associates from top law schools. Making matters worse, investment banking, venture capital, and private equity firms, all of whom had money to burn, developed a taste for in-house legal talent and began bidding up the price. When I started in 1975, the "going rate" in Boston (informally set by tacit consent of all the major firms) was $14,500/year. By 1989 it had climbed to the vicinity of $70,000; by 2000, it was up to $125,000, and today it is $160,000–180,000. During the same period, $100 inflated to $448, implying that the $14,500 salary when I started should have become $64,960, not $180,000.[3] I distinctly recall that Foley's partners were traumatized by these increases, but felt that they had to keep pace or risk losing their access to top legal talent. To give a sense of the change, when I joined Foley, the firm didn't even interview at law schools but sent a letter to the *Harvard Law Review* indicating how many people it was interested in hiring the next year. The other option was Munger Tolles in Los Angeles. Both were attractive not because of their rates of pay, but because of their reputations for liberalism, commitment to social causes, and willingness to promote associates to partner much more quickly than their competitors (6 years for Foley when I joined vs. 10 or 12 for firms like Ropes & Gray). In other words, it was a classic case of a regulated industry (regulated in this case by consent), like airlines when they were regulated: competition was not over price, but over amenities. Huge increases in salaries changed all this: the goal was to make the most money, regardless of the amenities. A position as an associate was expected to last but a few years, followed by a lateral move, hoping to achieve still more income. Long-term stability was a thing of the past.

Partners in law firms were squeezed between dramatically increasing associate salaries, competition with investment bankers for coveted real estate, and their own inflating expectations. The triple solutions were to build the "top line" through marketing and lateral recruitment, increase hourly rates, and demand ever more billable hours from the overcompensated associates. The guild that had persisted for many years before collapsed under the "creative destruction" of "market capitalism." Law firms became businesses; associates became exploitable assets; partners became shareholders; and the dignity of an ancient profession was dissolved by the ruthless solvent of money.

To come back to the article I wrote about paralegal profitability: the chronic complaint about paralegals was that they were not "profitable." I resisted the idea that paralegals should be a "profit center," but my article was premised on the proposition that, more broadly construed, paralegals were profitable and contributed to the business success of a law firm. It was, I'm quite sure, mathematically correct, but it was also socially misdirected. The larger problem was the reduction of legal practice to a business, which I didn't question.

A few comments on the larger problem. For many years there has been a pervasive acceptance of the proposition that the law, law firms, business enterprises, laws, and society, in general, should be dedicated to the

---

[3] See Harrison Barnes, "A History of Legal Market Conditions and Attorney Lateral Hiring," BCG Attorney Search, http://www.bcgsearch.com/article/900042956/A-History-of-Legal-Market-Conditions-and-Attorney-Lateral-Hiring/#.

maximization of economic efficiency and economic growth. Law itself was understood and judged in economic terms; the "law and economics" movement sought to make law the instrument of economics.[4] Inefficiency, in the economic sense, is bad; increasing the GNP is good; the economic optimum is to be pursued at all costs. Few people question the premise. And it is certainly true that economic efficiencies are associated with lower prices and higher standards of living (measured economically). But what of the intangibles, the unpriceables? How can one weigh the value of a secure if modestly compensated job against the value of an insecure but higher paid job? Are today's associates in law firms happier, more content, more fulfilled (pick your adjective) than we were at $14,500/year? This seems to be the question that is finally being asked politically, although the outcome so far — protectionism fueled by xenophobia and racism — is not something I'd trade for the preceding decades of capitalistic efficiency and personal insecurity.

Yes, the old guild system was monopolistic; it was parochial; it did not maximize value in an economic sense. But it had many values that the current model has lost. I would like to think that there may be a parable at least in the history of what happened to the legal profession, and that the parable might suggest some means of recovery for the society at large. Returning to a marginal tax rate that is high enough to discourage unbridled competition for the highest wage would be a good start. Eliminating the "carried charge" and similar tax preferences for investment income is another. And how about universal health care and publicly funded higher education as a means of eliminating two of the greatest sources of anxiety? Finally, let's find a way to bring back labor unions so that working people have someone to listen to other than Fox News. The influence and importance that labor unions had during the glory years of the United States — the 1940s, '50s, and '60s — is remarkable, and one of the greatest losses in the present day. These are not new ideas, but perhaps the time to reconsider some of them is well overdue. I ask the reader to indulge this political digression.

I conclude this introduction with reflections on another innovation in legal practice, namely the unholy intersection of the discovery principles in the Federal Rules of Civil Procedure with the digital world. We learned in law school, during the first weeks of Civil Procedure class, that the Rules of Civil Procedure were a needed reform that replaced the formalities and injustices of the ancient "writ" system. The Rules of Civil Procedure were designed to

---

4 As evidenced by such eminences as Richard Posner; see Richard A. Posner, "The Law and Economics Movement," *The American Economic Review* 77, no. 2 (1987).

ferret out the facts and base decisions upon the truth rather than "litigation by ambush." Discovery — the production of documents, interrogatories, requests for admissions, depositions — would determine what "really" happened so that the court or jury could render fact-based rulings. Litigation was imagined as a kind of scientific excavation of the ruins of a relationship, akin to an archeological dig. Bear in mind that this reform was cooked up in the 1920s, when most business records took the form of a handful of hard-copy contracts and ledgers, if that. Not so today, when business records that are subject to discovery consist of thousands upon thousands of electronically captured communications, which inevitably contain some damaging utterance or other on either side of the dispute — which, as often as not, has nothing to do with the "truth" and more to do with foolishness on the part of an employee with an overactive email account. The current effect of the Rules is to convert most litigation into a war of attrition, in which whichever party can marshal the resources to withstand months if not years of staggeringly expensive email production, document production, depositions, and interrogatories, will prevail. Judges rarely control the discovery process, knowing full well that eventually one party or the other will send up a white flag and settle to staunch the bleeding. If the old writ system allowed formalism to preclude justice, the new system enlists cost and happenstance to an equally unjust effect. It is rare in either case that the truth is uncovered.

I submit that the Rules of Civil Procedure fundamentally misunderstand the purpose of most civil litigation. Its purpose is to resolve private disputes, not to determine the truth in some metaphysical sense. The Rules are premised on the proposition that litigation should determine the truth based on evidence, and that decision should be based on the truth. In most cases, there are no material facts in dispute. The debtor didn't pay her installments; the contract and law say that the lender can repossess the car. And in situations where there is a dispute of fact — did the contract deliverable meet the specifications? — the "facts" are inevitably obscured by the same problems that make archeological excavations subject to wildly differing interpretations, depending so often on the vagaries of what is or is not preserved in the archeological record and its interpretation when it is found.

A personal anecdote illustrates the point. When I began practicing law, there was something called the "motions session" in the Massachusetts Superior Court. Any attorney could "mark up" a motion — say, a motion for a preliminary injunction or temporary restraining order to prevent somebody from doing something like walking off with collateral for a loan. A motion could be "marked up" for hearing on a particular day. The Superior Court judge, many of whom were experienced attorneys, heard all motions that had been marked up for the day. There were no witnesses; one could file affidavits in support of motions; as it was said, filing a brief was considered cheating. The judge usually ruled from the bench after hearing the argument of counsel.

I distinctly recall one session in the Dedham Superior Court when I had marked up a motion for an order for a sheriff to repossess a car from a teacher for failure to make installment payments (yes, when I started practicing law, I was sometimes "repo man"). My motion was supported by an affidavit from GMAC, the lender, stating that the borrower was in default, that demand had been made, and that payment had not been made. No one appeared for the debtor. Often, but not always, the motions were heard *ex parte,* with no opposing counsel present. There were no facts in dispute, but what was in dispute is whether the court should enter an order permitting GMAC to repossess the car from that teacher on that day.

It happened to be a week or two before Christmas. What was before this judge was not a question of fact; it was a question of governance by one of our three branches of government. There sat a judge of the Massachusetts Superior Court, with the power to issue an order to take this teacher's means of transportation away from her and to enforce that order with armed representatives of the state if necessary. There sat a woman who had borrowed money to buy a car and promised to relinquish it if she didn't pay. It was not a question of fact; it was a question of justice. What's fair; what's reasonable, what tempers justice? These are the questions the judge in the Dedham Superior court had to ask himself that winter day many years ago. The facts weren't irrelevant, but they were not, and seldom are, decisive.[5]

The judge denied my motion, without prejudice to refiling later — after Christmas. I would have to say that justice was done.

It was rough justice, but for the most part, it worked. Sadly, the motion session is gone. It's been supplanted in the Massachusetts Superior Court by a process derived from the federal courts in which every case is assigned to a particular judge, and it is up to the judge to decide whether and when to hear a motion. The new process is slow and opaque. The theory is that cases will be decided on the merits by judges who are familiar with the case. The practice is that as often as not, cases and issues languish for months, and the judges prefer not to decide anything to increase pressure on the parties to settle. Settlements can't be appealed, and the judge can't be embarrassed by a reversal. Litigants are frustrated and maddened by the delays.

---

[5] There is an unfortunate impulse to make the exercise of judicial power a mechanical exercise — "applying the law to the facts," as one might apply a hammer to a nail. This is discussed in greater length in Chapter 2 in connection with "strict constructionism."

The law is an imperfect but reasonably good replacement for direct conflict, for the vendetta, for revenge, for getting even. It is a terrible vehicle for "determining the truth." European courts, and the courts in most other countries, get along quite well without extensive discovery. Admittedly, their courts do not serve the higher political functions our courts sometimes perform. It is difficult to imagine *Brown v. Board of Education* in a French or German court.[6] It is worth considering, though, that the vast majority of disputes that find their way into the courts are not matters of broad social concern. They are small, private matters, insignificant to anybody but the persons involved in them. These litigants want to be "heard," and whether they like the outcome or not, they will benefit if their disputes are put behind them. Judge Judy is closer to what is needed than the Rules of Civil Procedure; the Motions Session dispensed justice better than the most thorough discovery production under the Federal Rules or their state equivalents.

[6] There are exceptions. The EU Court of Justice recently took a controversial social step in validating prohibitions on head scarves in places of business against claims of inherent discrimination. *Achbita v. G4S Secure Solutions NV* (C-157/15) EU:C:2017:203 (March 13, 2017).

Paralegal Profitability Analysis*

It is stylish for lawyers, particularly members of large law firms, to say that their services should be provided in a more "businesslike" manner. In many cases, this concern manifests itself in healthy attention to accounts receivable, cost control and other fundamentals of sound business management. Ironically, though, this concern can also lead to counterproductive decisions based on an oversimplified concept of profitability. The pitfalls of the "businesslike" approach are nowhere more evident than in the management of paralegals.

Paralegals are a relatively new phenomenon. Virtually unheard of 20 years ago,[1] there are today law firms in which the number of paralegals rivals, or in some cases even exceeds, the number of attorneys. More typically, the ratio of attorneys to paralegals would be about five or six to one, so that a firm of, say, 100 lawyers might employ 15 to 20 paralegals.[2]

The growth in paralegal numbers reflects the convergence of many factors. An important one is the decline of the personal secretary. Not too many years ago, any lawyer would expect to have a secretary of his own within a very few years after starting practice. The personal secretary frequently perceived her job as a lifetime commitment, and over time she would develop substantial expertise in the areas of the attorney's practice. Thus, for example, the secretary to an attorney who concentrated his practice in estate planning would be expected to know how to prepare straightforward wills and trusts, the secretary to a tax lawyer would be skilled at the preparation and filing of tax returns, and the secretary for a litigator would become adept at document indexing and production.

Word processing, the copying machine, and escalating salaries for service employees changed all this. As automation of the basic secretarial functions dramatically increased secretarial productivity, it became impossible to justify the expense of a secretary for every lawyer. Furthermore, the secretary's job was broken into discrete components, and the components were divided between word processors, secretaries, photocopying departments, and others. This weakened the traditional bond between the secretary and her attorney

---

* *Law Office Economics & Management*, Summer 1984.

[1] This is not true in England, where "legal executives," who are comparable to highly experienced paralegals, have been in use for many years.

[2] The higher ratios tend to be found in firms which specialize in areas of the law requiring the control of very large numbers of documents, for example, antitrust litigation.

and between the secretary and the attorney's area of expertise. Secretarial turnover increased, secretarial expertise decreased and the ability of a secretary to index documents, draft wills, and prepare tax returns, and to fit such work into the interstices between her basic typing and filing responsibilities, declined. Paralegals — nonlawyers having substantive legal expertise — became necessary to fill the gap.

A second and equally compelling force driving the rise of paralegals was the relentless escalation of attorneys' hourly rates. To an extent not previously known, attorneys began to feel pressure from clients against further increases in rates. The rise of the "in-house" counsel, a central part of whose role frequently includes the limitation of outside counsel fees, contributed importantly to the resistance to further fee increases. Law firms quickly perceived that a lower average hourly rate would improve their client relations. One way to hold down the average hourly rates as to "unbundle" services, charging for items that previously had been packed into the attorney's hourly rate. Functions such as drafting simple documents and document indexing were a prime target for such unbundling. Of course, it would be difficult to charge for such services if they were performed by the attorney's secretary. But not if they were performed by a specialist. The solution was, once again, the paralegal.

In all of the above respects, the paralegal represented a reaction to market forces. As a result, attorneys suffer a nagging doubt whether paralegals are truly "profitable." The question of profitability is one that any manager of paralegals repeatedly confronts in connection with hiring decisions, salary reviews, and fringe benefit adjustments.

The question of profitability can be particularly vexing because it is difficult to argue that paralegals, if considered in isolation, represent a very good return on investment. A few representative calculations will quickly demonstrate the problem. The typical paralegal in a city like Boston might earn about $18,000 per year in salary. His or her fringe benefits, valued at 50 percent of salary, would add another $9,000. The paralegal would probably share a secretary with another paralegal or with an attorney, or perhaps with a group of attorneys or paralegals. Suppose that the paralegal's allocated share of secretarial overhead would be about $10,000 per year. The paralegal also contributes to general overhead when office space, library facilities, supplies, and such are considered. At current rates, these might easily total $10,000 to $15,000 per year. In all, the actual expense of a middle-level paralegal exceeds $50,000 per year — $55,000 would be a reasonable working hypothesis for a downtown Boston law firm.

Could our typical paralegal generate enough income to cover this yearly expense and generate a modest profit as well? In Boston, paralegal hourly rates range from about $25 per hour to $60 per hour. The paralegal making $18,000 per year would command an hourly rate in the vicinity of $40 to $45 per hour. This hourly rate must be reduced by the law firm's collection rate on hours recorded. For most firms, a collection rate of 85–90 percent would be good for paralegals. Thus, the effective hourly rate for the paralegal would be about $35 per hour. Dividing this rate into the yearly expense of $55,000 yields 1,571 hours per year of billable effort, or about 6.83 hours per working day,[3] just to break even.

Anyone in the field knows that averaging this many billable hours in a 7.5-hour working day would be a considerable achievement. Even if every minute of a 7.5-hour working day were billed, the paralegal's total yearly revenues would, on the assumptions described above, be only 7.5 × 230 × 35 = $60,375 per year. This would represent a profit of about $5,000 on an "investment" of $55,000 in additional expense to the firm — a very poor return in a profession historically accustomed to a return close to 100 percent per year on "investment" in associate salaries. In actual fact, paralegal billable hours usually average well under 1,571 per year, and paralegal "losses" therefore seem inevitable.

It is, of course, possible to mince these figures. One can argue, for example, that paralegals can be squeezed into the nooks and crannies left over after attorneys and administrative staff have taken the better or at least less negotiable office spaces, and that for this reason, it is inappropriate to allocate any more than a nominal amount of office space overhead to the paralegals. Some firms do not assign secretaries to paralegals. Others require their paralegals to share offices. All such measures can make the calculations described above come out better.

However, such measures may produce chimerical gains. As one reduces overhead by making a paralegal's access to secretarial services less ready, one increases the amount of non-billable time spent by the paralegal and thus reduces his or her effective hourly rate. Sharing offices is another potentially false economy since it has obvious and deleterious effects on morale and productivity. Except in unusual situations in which fleets of paralegals can be employed without offices (for example, on the client's premises) and without secretarial assistance (for example, sorting documents), the conclusion seems inevitable that paralegal revenues will not exceed expenses by an

---

[3] Based on a working year of 230 days. This assumes three weeks of vacation, 5 sick days and 10 holidays. For persons with 4 weeks of yearly vacation the daily rate of effort would be 6.98 hours.

economically significant margin. This sort of analysis leads many law firms to perceive paralegals as, at best, a necessary evil.

Is such a conclusion justified? The analysis rests on the premise that paralegal profitability may and indeed should be measured separately for its contribution to the firm's profits. I will call this the "profit center" theory. The theory has a potent superficial appeal. However, its effective application depends entirely on the assumption that any group or individual in a professional service firm may be separately analyzed for profitability and that the profitability of the firm as a whole is the arithmetic sum of such groups' or individuals' profitabilities. This assumption is frequently erroneous, as will be seen.

A simple example will serve to highlight the problems with the theory. Consider what would happen if one attempted to use it to determine whether a secretary is profitable for a sole practitioner. A secretary might cost $30,000 per year, including salary, fringe benefits, a workspace, and necessary furniture and equipment. None of the secretary's time will ever be billed to a client. The secretary's gross revenues will, therefore, always be 0. Considered as a "profit center," the secretary will inevitably appear not to be a profitable addition to a lawyer's practice. Indeed, this analysis would lead to the conclusion that a secretary would never be a profitable addition to any practice, be it the sole practitioner or the major big-city law firm.

The profit center analysis is obviously of little value when applied to a secretary or a group of secretaries. Why? The reason is that the secretary's contribution cannot be considered in isolation from the effect that the secretary's work has on the lawyer's billable dollars. To borrow a phrase from traditional economics, the secretary has *externalities.* The secretary enhances the revenue-producing capacity of the lawyer for whom the secretary works. Without the secretary, the lawyer would spend most of his or her time typing, filing, answering the telephone, and so forth. All of this time would either go unbilled or would depress dramatically the average hourly rate which the lawyer could charge for services. The secretary thus increases the lawyer's *effective* hourly rate. Any analysis of the secretary's "profitability" — how much more the attorney makes with her than he would without her — which fails to take these externalities into effect is wholly inadequate.

It is possible, in a rough and ready way, to quantify externalities. Consider, for another moment, our sole legal practitioner and his or her secretary. How does the solo decide in the first place whether the time has come when a secretary should be hired? Suppose the practitioner can collect fees at an optimal effective rate (after bad debts, write-downs, etc.) of $100.00/hr. If the attorney spends more than 300 hours per year[4] doing filing, typing, phone answering, and other nonbillable work, and if the attorney has 300 hours per year of additional billable work which could be done but for filing, typing and so on, then hiring a secretary will result in an increase in profits. The result follows, even though, considered alone, the secretary is not and cannot be "profitable" — that is, the yearly expense ($30,000) will always exceed revenues (0). Stated algebraically, the secretary increases the sole practitioner's net income if the secretary's yearly expense divided by the lawyer's hourly rate is less than *the number of hours of non-billable work that the secretary's presence can convert into billable work in each year:*

Formula I

$$\text{yearly expense} < (\text{hours of secretarial work}) \times (\text{lawyer's hourly rate})$$

or

$$\frac{\text{yearly expense}}{\text{lawyer's hourly rate}} < \text{hours of secretarial work}$$

Formula I can serve as a model for paralegal profitability as well. For the reasons described at the beginning of this article, some of the work performed by a paralegal would otherwise be performed by a secretary; another portion of the paralegal's work would be performed by a lawyer if the lawyer had no paralegal. It is fair to say that in the absence of a paralegal, the secretarial portion of this work would not be billed at all. Some of the lawyer's portion of the work would probably be billed, but at something less than the lawyer's maximum effective (optional) hourly rate.[5] The paralegal's effect on lawyers' billable time is thus less dramatic than a secretary's. To return to our example of the sole practitioner, suppose that his or her optional hourly rate for "lawyer work" is $100/hour. Suppose further that in the absence of a paralegal, the solo does some work (e.g., document indexing), which cannot be billed at more than an effective paralegal rate of $40/hr. and other work (no-charge work), which cannot be billed at all. If the solo hires a paralegal and has enough "lawyer work" in inventory to convert all the time otherwise spent on document indexing, no-charge matters, and the like into "lawyer work" collectible at $100

---

[4] That is, $30,000 per year / $100 per hour.

[5] I will refer to the effective hourly rate of attorneys doing paralegal work as the LP rate. It falls somewhere between the optimal lawyer's rate and the optimal paralegal rate.

per hour, then the solo can improve revenue-generating activities by $60 per hour for each billable hour worked by the paralegal and by $100 per hour for each no-charge hour taken over by the paralegal.

The paralegal thus has three "externalities":

i. reducing secretarial requirements;

ii. freeing the lawyer from doing work billable at a comparatively low effective hourly rate; and

iii. freeing the lawyer from no-charge work.

The paralegal's total contribution to firm profits is the sum of four amounts:

i. the paralegal's revenues;

ii. the savings in secretarial or other administrative expense caused by the paralegal;

iii. the increase in attorneys' effective hourly rates caused by moving "paralegal" work from attorneys to paralegals; and

iv. the increase in attorneys' billable hours by moving no-charge work from attorneys to paralegals.

A paralegal will be profitable when the sum of these amounts exceeds the paralegal's expense. Using the secretarial formula above as a model, one can express algebraically the situation in which the paralegal is profitable as follows:

Formula II[6]

Para yearly cost < (para billable hrs) × (para rate) (+ para hrs worked by attys converted into atty billable hrs) × [(atty rate) – (para rate)] + (no-charge hours

---

[6] This formula could be further refined by including a separate cost item to represent the additional lawyer time required to manage paralegals. However, in the interest of simplicity, I have assumed that this time has been included in the paralegal expense as part of general overhead. It is the experience of this writer that the cost in attorney hours to manage a group of 15 to 20 paralegals is on average less than 6 percent of their contribution to overall profitability.

worked by attys converted into atty billable hrs) × (atty rate) + savings in secretarial expense.

$$\text{Para yearly cost} < (\text{PBH}^*\text{PR}) + \text{A}+\text{B}+\text{C}$$

where:

$$\text{PBH} = \text{Paralegal billable hours}$$

$$\text{PR} = \text{Paralegal hourly rate}$$

$$\text{AR} = \text{Attorney hourly rate}$$

$$\text{A} = (\text{para hrs worked by attys converted into atty billable hrs}) \times [(\text{AR} - \text{PR})]$$

$$\text{B} = (\text{no-charge hours worked by attys converted into atty billable hrs}) \times (\text{AR})$$

$$\text{C} = \text{savings in secretarial expense}$$

Formula II contains many uncertainties. For example, it is guesswork to apportion a paralegal's hours between those which would otherwise be performed by an attorney and those which would be performed by a secretary or by some other member of the firm's administrative staff. However, it is possible with much less uncertainty to bracket these imponderables between more certain limits. The limits may be represented by different paralegal types.

At one end of the spectrum, one can propose a paralegal, all of whose billable and no-charge hours would, in the paralegal's absence, be performed by an attorney at an effective rate close to the paralegal rate. This is, in fact, true for experienced paralegals in areas such as tax and estate planning. A paralegal having these characteristics maximizes the paralegal's improvement of the lawyer's effective hourly rate and minimizes the paralegal's effect on secretarial expense (i.e., the savings in secretarial time effected by the paralegal). On this assumption, Formula II becomes:

Formula III

$$\text{Para yearly cost} < \text{PBH}^*\text{PR} + \text{PBH}^*(\text{AR} - \text{PR}) + (\text{PNCH})(\text{AR})$$

Where PNCH = paralegal no-charge hours

or

$$\text{Para yearly cost} < (\text{PBH})\ (\text{PR} + \text{AR} - \text{PR}) + (\text{PNCH})(\text{AR})$$

or

$$\text{Para yearly cost} < (\text{PBH})\ (\text{AR}) + (\text{PNCH})(\text{AR})$$

or

$$\text{Para yearly cost} < (\text{AR})\ (\text{PBH} + \text{PNCH})$$

or

$$\text{Para yearly cost} < (\text{AR})\ (\text{para total hrs})$$

or

$$\text{Para yearly cost/atty rate} < \text{para total hrs}$$ [7]

Formula III has surprising implications. As calculated above, the typical paralegal's yearly cost in the Boston area is in the vicinity of $55,000 per year. In a major law firm in Boston, the effective rate at which attorneys can, on average, charge for genuine "attorney" work averages close to, or perhaps a little higher than, $100 per hour.[8] Plugging these approximate figures into Formula III, one finds that the break-even point is approximately 550 total hours per year. That is, if a paralegal who costs about $55,000 per year can convert 550 attorney hours otherwise billable at an effective paralegal rate of, say, $40 per hour, or not billable at all, into 550 attorney hours billable at $100 per hour, the paralegal will have covered his or her expense. All of the paralegal's hours above 550 per year will go "straight to the bottom line." To the extent that the additional paralegal hours further free up attorney time for the more highly compensable "attorney" work, the effective rate of profit generation above 550 yearly hours will be at the lawyer rate — about $100 per hour, based on the ballpark estimates used in this article. The increase in net profits attributable to a paralegal who can free up 1,500 hours per year of attorney time in this way would be $95,000.[9]

Net profitability of $50,000 to $100,000 per year is not an unrealistic estimate for paralegals in areas such as trusts and estates or income tax preparation, where the ability of even highly experienced legal secretaries to perform similar services is limited, but where lawyers as a practical matter cannot charge clients at an optimal lawyer's rate for the more elementary or repetitive

---

[7] For this type of paralegal, the paralegal's hourly rate factors out because it is assumed that the work done by the paralegal, if done by the lawyer, would be billed out at an effective rate equal to the paralegal rate.

[8] The rate is considerably higher for more senior attorneys. It is reasonable to expect, though, that more junior attorneys would otherwise perform most of the work done by a Formula III paralegal.

[9] (1,500 billable hrs – 550 break-even hours) ($100).

parts of the practice. This would include the preparation of simple estate plans or the preparation and filing of income tax returns.

Before examining a paralegal at the opposite end of the spectrum, compare these results with the conclusions the "profit center" theory would produce. On that theory, the Formula III paralegal is a net loss at 1,500 hours per year, even if all of the hours are billable. The paralegal's expenses are $55,000, and his or her total individual revenues would be at most (1,500 hrs) ($35/hr), or $52,500. A firm which, as the result of such a calculation, decided not to hire a Formula III paralegal would miss out on an opportunity to increase its net profits by almost $100,000 per year.

Not every paralegal is as valuable as the type just described. At the opposite extreme, one would find paralegals who are much less efficient than attorneys, even when the attorneys are performing "paralegal" tasks. Such paralegals may also be less efficient than attorneys in performing no-charge work. Reflecting the attorney's greater efficiency, an attorney might charge his or her time at a higher effective rate than such a paralegal, even when the attorney is performing "paralegal" work.[10] Finally, it would be consistent with the characteristics we are giving this paralegal that a portion of his or her work would, in the paralegal's absence, be taken over by secretaries or other administrative (i.e., non-billing) personnel.

Suppose that this opposite-extreme paralegal is only one-half as efficient as an attorney in performing either billable or nonbillable work. Suppose further that the paralegal reduces administrative expense by about one-fifth of the yearly cost of one secretary (while at the same time continuing to use about one-third of a secretary). On these assumptions, Formula I becomes:

Formula IV

Para yearly cost < (para billable hrs) (para rate) + 1/2 (para billable hrs) (atty rate – LP rate) + 1/2 (para no-charge hrs) (atty rate) + 1/5 yearly sec'y expense

Assuming a yearly secretarial expense of $30,000:

Para yearly cost – $6,000 < (PBH) (para rate + 1/2 (atty rate – LP rate)] + (PNCH) (1/2 (atty rate)]

---

[10] I've already dubbed this the "LP" rate.

The solution to this inequation depends on the ratio between paralegal billable (PBH) and no-charge hours (PNCH) as well as the relationship between the effective hourly rates for lawyers, for paralegals, and for lawyers doing paralegal work. We have already assumed that in the Boston market, a lawyer's effective rate is about $100 per hour, and a paralegal's effective rate is about $35 per hour. The LP rate is bound to be somewhere between these two — say, about $60 per hour. Using these estimates, together with the assumed $55,000 per year cost of a paralegal, Formula IV can be significantly simplified:

$$\$55{,}000 - \$6{,}000 < (\text{PBH})\ [35 + 1/2\ (100 - 60)] + (\text{PNCH})\ [1/2\ (100)]$$

or

$$\$49{,}000 < (\text{PBH})\ (55) + (\text{PNCH})\ (50)$$

Note the effect of the LP rate on this formula. We have assumed the LP rate is $60 per hour; on this hypothesis, the paralegal's billable hours are worth about $5.00 more per hour to the firm than his or her no-charge hours. On the other hand, if one assumed that the LP rate is $80 per hour, the paralegal's billable hours would be about $5.00 less valuable per hour than his or her no-charge hours. Since these amounts are estimates at best, a further simplification is possible. On the assumption that the LP rate is $70 per hour, Formula III becomes:

$$\$49{,}000 < (\text{PBH})\ (50) + (\text{PNCH})\ (50)$$

or

$$\$49{,}000 < 50\ (\text{PBH} + \text{PNCH})$$

or

$$\frac{\$49{,}000}{50} < \text{PBH} + \text{PNCH}$$

or

$$980 < \text{PBH} + \text{PNCH}$$

or

$$980 < \text{Paralegal total hours}$$

This means that, on our simplifying assumptions, the break-even point for a Formula IV paralegal is about 980 total hours per year.

It is again instructive to compare this break-even point with the conclusion which the "profit center" analysis would lead to. Suppose that one-fourth of the 980 total hours, or 245 hours, were spent on no-charge work. These hours would be disregarded on the profit center analysis, leaving only 735 hours for consideration. We have assumed an effective paralegal hourly rate of $35 per hour. Applying this rate to the paralegal's 735 hours yields annual billings of 35 x 735 = $25,725. The yearly cost of a Formula IV paralegal is $49,000 per year. Thus, at 735 billable and 245 no-charge hours per year, the paralegal would be seen as losing about $23,725 per year. While Formula IV is subject to many uncertainties, it is clear that the profit center theory falls far short of the mark in estimating the contribution to firm profits made by what we have called a "Formula IV" paralegal.[11]

How much more would a firm which has paralegals make than one which does not have them? The answer requires some educated guesswork, but Formulas III and IV can be used to bracket the answer. On Formula III, the break-even point is about 550 total hours per year, and the rate of profit return for hours above that point is equal to the lawyer's optimal effective hourly rate — assumed for our purposes to be about $100 per hour. On Formula IV, the break-even point was about 980 total hours per year, and the rate of profit return for hours above that point is about half of the lawyer's optimal hourly rate — on our assumptions, about $50 per hour. In·a typical law firm, the complement of paralegals will range all the way from Formula III to Formula IV types. Formula IV types may be somewhat more abundant. If one, therefore, seeks an average weighted toward the Formula IV end of the scale, the "typical" paralegal might have a break-even point at about 700 hours per year and a profitability rate of about $70 per hour for hours in excess of that number (assuming, of course, that the paralegal continues to convert lawyer time billable at a comparatively low hourly rate into time billable at the optimal rate). It is the experience of this writer that paralegals can be expected to average between 1,400 and 1,800 hours per year, with exceptional cases beyond each of these extremes. If one chooses 1,500 hours per year as a conservative estimate, the profitability of a typical paralegal will be approximately (1,500 – 700) x 70 = $56,000 per year. That is, a firm having a paralegal will make about $56,000 more per year than a firm lacking one. For a

---

[11] The profit center analysis makes two errors in particular. First, it fails to recognize the improvement in the effective billing rate for attorneys which follows from shifting "paralegal work" away from attorneys. Second, it fails to recognize the increase in attorney billable hours that will result from shifting no-charge work from attorneys to paralegals.

firm of 100 lawyers with 15 to 20 paralegals, the paralegal contribution to profitability could approach $1 million per year--not bad for a necessary evil. Of necessity, the approach to analyzing paralegal profitability described above is highly generalized and cannot be considered a prediction of what profits would be in an actual firm, or regarding a particular paralegal. However, the formulas do suggest several generalizations about the management of paralegals, which the "profit center" approach would almost certainly overlook. Some of these are:

1. The key to paralegal profitability is the ability of the paralegal to take on work which attorneys would otherwise perform at an effective hourly rate lower than the attorneys' optimum rate, and the ability of attorneys to convert these freed-up hours into optimal rate hours.

2. The profits generated by a paralegal program are comparatively insensitive to the distribution of paralegal work between billable and no-charge hours.

3. The threshold for hiring a paralegal is about 2 or 3 times as high as the threshold for hiring a secretary. That is, in a well-run firm, attorneys will collectively perform about 550 to 1,000 hours of paralegal work per year before a new paralegal is hired. In the same well-run firm, attorneys will collectively perform about 300 hours of secretarial work per year before a new secretary (or another administrative staff member) is hired.

The study of paralegal profitability demonstrates a principle. You cannot carve up a law firm, or any other professional service firm, into arbitrary "profit centers" — be they departments, types of professionals, geographical locations, or whatever — and expect each piece to return a profit, or, worse yet, eliminate every piece that does not produce through its own revenues an excess over expense. Professional service firms are by their nature interdependent: the abilities, expertise, and availability of each member necessarily affect the income production of the other members.

One of the hottest topics in any law firm is the question of how to value the contributions of the principals. The concept of externalities applies here, as well. Consider, for example, a lawyer who has considerable expertise in an unusual area of the law, who is willing to put his or her expertise to "library" use by a willingness to tolerate interruption to answer questions in the area of expertise, but whose hours and client dollars are not high. How does one measure such a person's contribution to the firm? Contrast this person with the one who perhaps bills a large number of hours, but is seldom available to pitch in when needed and who, if he or she has special expertise, does not often find time to share it with others in the firm. Contrast finally the chronic malcontent who usually has him or herself and others upset about something, and has the firm's administration spending no-charge time either worrying about it or trying to fix it.

Like the paralegal, the first and last of these "types" have externalities. The expert who is willing to tolerate interruptions to share his or her expertise will tend to increase the average effective billing rates of the persons he or she is helping. In a law firm, the lack of such externalities will be seen in the inability to charge clients at optimal hourly rates — for time spent in researching obscure questions which, to an expert, may have obvious answers. The person who is unwilling to share expertise will be less valuable to the firm than the one with an equal number of billable hours and client dollars but who is willing to share. Finally, the chronic malcontent has what might be termed negative externalities. He or she will tend to diminish morale, reduce others' billable effectiveness, and consume inordinate amounts of no-charge administrative time: all factors which deserve to be counted against his or her income.

This brings us to the general topic with which our discussion began. What is a businesslike way to run a law firm? It obviously requires more than dividing the firm into the smallest possible pieces, expecting each of the pieces to prove viable on its own. The key is to fit personnel into positions in which they will contribute to the profitability of the organic whole--positions, to use the terminology of this article, in which their "externalities" will be used to full advantage. Despite all the formulae appearing above, this process of management is not susceptible to precise quantification or simple prescription. It is a matter of perceiving where a firm has gaps in its expertise or other revenue-related capacities, and which individuals are right to fill the gaps. The needs are sometimes obvious, but finding the right person to meet them — that is, a person who will make his or her abilities useful to others in the firm — can be notoriously difficult. The ability to make these matches is a sure indication of effective management in the professional service firm.

Chapter 2

Angular Momentum

"Note: The Speech and Press Clause of the First Amendment as Ordinary Language" (1974)

"The first thing we do, let's kill all the lawyers." It is said that Dick the Butcher's famous line in *Henry IV, Part II,* has been misinterpreted — it was, it is argued, meant by Shakespeare as a compliment to the lawyers, who would have impeded Dick's rebel plan to depose the King. But the misinterpretation has stuck, and the line has become a shorthand for the ordinary man's dislike of the legal profession. Sure, there are jokes about doctors, but as a lawyer, one has to be prepared to be the butt of jokes and to ride them out as gracefully.

What gets us this reputation? I believe it is rooted in the manipulation of language, which is at the core of a lawyer's skill and training. For lawyers, or good ones at least, words and their meaning are malleable objects that can be molded to suit a purpose, which may or may not coincide with what others thought they meant. "He twisted my words!" is the core complaint about us. When a lawyer knocks a word off its assumed perch, she violates the listener's sense of himself as an inhabitant of a secure community defined by shared meaning. This can be profoundly unsettling. It is no mistake that "community" and "communication" have the same root: something in common. Take that away, and community is lost; take away community, and the self stands naked and exposed.

The relationship among words, meaning, and their context was the core focus of "ordinary language philosophy." Ordinary language philosophy was in vogue when I was an undergraduate in philosophy. One of its fundamental tenets is that words have meaning only in a social context; remove them from that context, and they come adrift. In Wittgenstein's celebrated example,[1] a builder says "block," and his assistant brings a block; the builder says "pillar,"

[1] "[Imagine a language that] is meant to serve for communication between a builder *A* and an assistant *B.* A is building with building stones: there are blocks, pillars, slabs, and beams. *B* has to pass the stones, in the order in which *A* needs them. For this purpose they use a language consisting of the words 'block,' 'pillar,' 'slab,' and 'beam.' *A* calls them out; *B* brings the stone which he has learnt to bring at such-and-such a call. Conceive this as a complete primitive language." (L. Wittgenstein, *Philosophical Investigations,* §2).

and the assistant brings a pillar. So in this context, the word "block" means something like "bring me a block." But one can imagine another context in which the word "block" means "I'm out of blocks," or even "block that pillar."[2] Context is all in ordinary language philosophy. The builder and his assistant understand each other solely in the context of their jobs. Take the words out of that context, and their meaning is lost.[3]

---

[2] Here is an actual example of what Wittgenstein calls a "complete primitive language." In our building we have "regular" elevators and a small elevator for those with mobility issues or others who must avoid the entryway stairs. The "regular" elevators have two buttons outside the elevator door on each floor, labeled "up" and "down," as elevators typically have. Pushing the "up" button tells the elevator you want to go up to a floor above the one you are on. If the elevator is above you it comes down to pick you up and then proceeds to the higher floor; if it is below you it goes up, picks you up, and continues upward. Not so the stair-avoiding elevator. It also has two buttons by each door labeled "up" and "down" and two buttons inside the elevator, also labeled "up" and "down." In its case, pushing an "up" button tells the elevator to go up, regardless which floor you happen to be on or whether you are inside or outside the elevator. So if you are on floor #2 and want to go down to floor #1 you must push "up" to bring the elevator "up" to you. Then when you are inside the elevator you must push the "down" button to go "down" to floor #1. Each elevator "speaks" a "language" comprising two words, "up" and "down." But to understand what the words "mean" you have to understand how the elevators work. It takes a while to get it right. Once a person was confused enough that he got stuck in the stair-avoiding elevator, panicked, and called 911. He had to be rescued by the Boston fire department, who broke down one of the elevator doors to rescue him. They evidently didn't speak "Elevator" either.

[3] This principle is not limited to language; it seems true of other forms of expression as well. In *How Do We Look*, the classicist Mary Beard teaches repeatedly that "a lot depends on the context in which we see [images of human figures]; and a lot depends on *who's* looking." M. Beard, *How Do We Look*, at p. 120 (New York: Liveright Publishing 2018; emphasis in the original). One notable example is the use that the artist and suffragist Christiana Herrington made in 1915 of the Ajanta cave art, which was created some 1500–2200 years ago in India by or for Buddhist monks. "When [Herrington] looked at their colour, their perspective, their careful lines and composition what she saw was the Indian equivalent of Italian Renaissance art; and she sometimes even called the caves a 'picture gallery.'" Id. at 126. She then repurposed "the most beautiful vignettes" in a "single lavish volume," "almost as if they were easel paintings," and in doing so "she was translating the images of a Buddhist religious site into the heritage of world art." Beard notes that in their original form, in which episodes from the Buddha's life "are not arranged in any obvious logical order," the images are "about as far from the clear simplicity of Herrington's versions as you could imagine." And this is because in the original the images served a completely different purpose, which was to force the viewers to "identify, find and re-find the stories of the Buddha for themselves," thus to "*do religious work.*" Id. at 128 (emphasis in the original). The individual images were the

If not lost, the meaning is at least changed. Language has something akin to the angular momentum of a spinning top. In a given social context, it resists deflection, but if a word is pushed into a new context, it will veer away from its original meaning, conserving, so to speak, its linguistic angular momentum. A good lawyer, like a skilled acrobatic pilot, can use that angular momentum to her advantage, using context to cause a word that originally pointed North to point East or West. This is how lawyers "twist words" to the profound discomfort of the layperson whose words have stayed the same but have been deprived of their assumed meaning.

Another tenet of ordinary language philosophy is that language often performs a function; to use John Austin's phrase, when language performs a function, we have a "performative utterance."[4] When two people say "I do" at a wedding ceremony, they are not describing or indicating or denoting something; they are quite literally doing something: getting married, an act of great legal and personal consequence. Much of what lawyers say and do is performative, not descriptive, and the function that language performs for lawyers is intimately connected with its legal context, purpose, and effect. Outside of a wedding ceremony, saying "I do" does not marry anyone; inside the ceremony, it does.

The "Note" that is the sole entry in this chapter was my effort to apply some of the insights of ordinary language philosophy to a legal document — namely, the US Constitution. The Note was surely one of the oddest pieces ever published in the *Harvard Law Review*. The basic idea of the Note was that there must have been a reason why the founders expressed the free expression right found in the First Amendment differently from the similar right found in Article 1, Section 6. The First Amendment says, "Congress shall make no law . . . abridging the freedom of speech, or of the press." Article 1, Section 6 states, ". . . and for any Speech or Debate in either House [of Congress] they [Senators and Representatives] shall not be questioned in any other Place." The argument was that the language of the First Amendment — "freedom of . . ." — focused on a general quality of speech in general, in which individual speeches might be prohibited or punished as long as the general quality was not impaired, while the language for Congress applied to

---

same in Herrington's book as in the caves, but the instructive work they performed — their purpose and effect — was completely different.

[4] J. Austin, "Performative Utterances," collected in J. L. Austin, *Philosophical Papers*, 2d ed. (Oxford: Oxford University Press, 1970).

Congressional statements one by one. I think there's probably something to that, and I'm sure members of Congress would think so.[5]

The Note also raised the question of how judicial "balancing" works to reach an interpretative result. The great Constitutional scholar Paul Freund taught that Constitutional law was a question of balancing not right against wrong, but right against right. Okay, but how does that "balancing" occur? How does one assign weight to one right or another, and where does one position the fulcrum in the scales of justice? At the center? But how is the center defined; how are distances to the two sides and their weights measured? It bothered me as a young man that in the law, there was no equivalent to logical proof from unimpeachable axioms, as in Euclidean geometry. Stated another way, if deciding cases requires an exercise of judgment, how is judgment informed and exercised? I thought that the language of the Framers could be taken as a kind of axiom and that its proper interpretation would dictate results, at least within a more narrow range than would be the case if the precise language were disregarded entirely.

I'm embarrassed now that the Note bears many points of similarity with today's "strict constructionists." The Note was surprisingly prescient about the type of reasoning found in much later cases, such as the Supreme Court's decision in *District of Columbia v. Heller*,[6] which held that the District of Columbia's laws regulating the possession of loaded firearms in a home violated the Second Amendment. Justice Scalia's opinion could almost be considered an example of ordinary language analysis. He begins, "In interpreting this text, we are guided by the principle that [t]he Constitution was written to be understood by the voters; its words and phrases were used in their normal and ordinary as distinguished from technical meaning."[7] He then launches a thirty-page exegesis of the meaning in 1791 of each of the terms in the Second Amendment, worthy of a Talmudic analysis of the Torah.

---

[5] Unfortunately, the Note carried a lot of academic clap-trap in the form of discussion of the "meta-interpretation" of the First Amendment, which distracts from the basic point. Paul Freund read the piece prior to its publication and told me and my editors that he thought it might contain a genuine insight, but he questioned whether all the rigamarole I used to get there was necessary. Fair point indeed.

[6] 554 U.S. 570 (2008)

[7] Id. at 576. Remarkably, an amicus brief was actually filed in the case by a team of linguists. See https://www.scotusblog.com/wp-content/uploads/2008/01/07-290_amicus_linguists1.pdf. Justice Scalia draws on it, but begs to differ in its conclusions.

The clauses in the Second Amendment[8] that Scalia parses concern a "well regulated Militia," why it is "necessary to the security of a free State," whether a "right of the people" uses "people" as a collective or individual noun, what it means to "keep and bear Arms," and, most centrally, what on earth "Arms" might have meant in 1791. He concludes: "Putting all of these textual elements together, we find that they guarantee the individual right to possess and carry weapons in case of confrontation."[9] After acknowledging that the Second Amendment's reference to a "Militia" was central to the historical tyranny-resisting purpose with which the Second Amendment was written,[10] he dismisses this as merely a "prologue" to a statement of the "ancient right" to "bear Arms."[11]

Having labored to establish what the eighteenth-century drafters meant by a right to "bear Arms," Scalia declares it "bordering on frivolous" to suggest that "Arms" means the ones in existence in the eighteenth century, and then extends the Second Amendment's protection to "all instruments that constitute bearable arms, even those that were not in existence at the time of the founding"[12] and, in particular, "the class of 'arms' that is overwhelmingly chosen by American society [for self-defense],"[13] namely, handguns. By these sleights of hand, the eighteenth-century militia's right to "bear" arms becomes the twenty-first-century DC resident's right to own "bearable" arms, which conveniently allows Scalia to land where he wants: a right to handgun ownership.

Justice Stevens's lengthy dissent[14] accepts the premise that we must puzzle out why the drafters chose the language they did but reach a conclusion opposite Scalia's. Considering multiple alternative formulations related to a right to weaponry, including some that were not used that seemed expressly to contemplate an individual's right to have them for protection of home and

---

[8] Here it is, clothed in its opaque syntax: "A well regulated Militia, being necessary to the security of a free State, the right of the people to keep and bear Arms, shall not be infringed."

[9] 554 U.S. at 592.

[10] See Id. 595–99.

[11] More properly the prologue stated the social context in which the words achieved their purpose. But imagine if Scalia had concluded that the Second Amendment's purpose was to facilitate armed insurrection against the federal government by militias. Little wonder he decided that reference to "a well regulated militia" was "mere prologue," without Constitutional effect.

[12] Id. at 582.

[13] Id. at 628.

[14] 554 U.S. 636 et seq.

hearth, Stevens concludes that the phrase "bear Arms" was understood in a military context, linking it to the preamble's militias.[15]

Stevens's analysis seems the fairer of the two, in its insistence that the preamble means something and in its avoidance of Scalia's alchemic transmutation of "bear Arms" into "bearable arms" and then "bearable arms" into handguns — all of which seems a little too convenient. But one is left with the impression that we really don't know — and in some fundamental sense can't know[16] — exactly why the Founders chose the Second Amendment's formulation or exactly what they meant by the words they chose, except that they were good enough at the time to resolve one element of the conflict between Federalists and Anti-Federalists.

The Second Amendment was drafted in the hothouse environment of the First Congress, following the adoption of the Constitution, with Federalists and Anti-Federalists at loggerheads over the power of the newly created federal government. In such an environment, words can work in ways that differ from their use in less charged environments. Language has both a macro and a micro context. The macro context is the way that words and phrases are generally used by native speakers. The micro context is the function that the words and phrases perform in a given social interaction. Given the right context, the most innocent word can be offensive and the most offensive word innocent. The greater the intimacy of a situation, the more words become burdened with meanings that are unknown to the society at large. Spouses know this above all others, but it is also true of intense negotiations, which can and often do take on an intimacy of their own. The solution to a dispute is often a choice of words that are vague enough that each party can impart its own meaning to them. Effective dispute resolution entails the modulation of ambiguity.[17] So the language of the Second Amendment, or any other part of the Constitution and Bill of Rights, may well have been hit upon precisely because it was vague enough to bridge otherwise impossible divides.

---

[15] Id. at 637.

[16] At the risk of sticking my neck out an inch too far, one might say that the current social context is akin to Kant's *a priori* knowledge, creating a lens that inevitably colors and reshapes the *a posteriori* words on a page. We cannot understand but through that lens. See generally I. Kant, *Critique of Pure Reason*, trans. N. K. Smith (1781; New York: Macmillan & Co., 1929).

[17] One suspects that this was true of the choice of "high crimes and misdemeanors" as the criteria for impeachment, which was hotly debated in the impeachment of President Trump. These words may well have been chosen because they lacked definite meaning, which enabled their enactment by otherwise unreconciled factions.

But Scalia and other "strict constructionists" want us to believe that the words of the Constitution or a statute are little signposts, pointing the way to a decision, without the necessity for what he dismissively calls Justice Breyer's "judge-empowering, 'interest-balancing' inquiry."[18] This is false modesty spoken by a linguistic acrobat who could make words fly through the air with the greatest of ease to reach his desired landing spot. One cannot escape the conclusion that Scalia's decision was no more dictated by the language of the Second Amendment than was Justice Stevens's dissent in the same case.

Restraining judicial discretion was exactly what concerned me when I wrote the Note in 1974. In retrospect, the Note seems sophomoric, but I take some comfort in the fact that, although I urged close attention to language in the Note, in the end, I acknowledged that some balancing, interpretation, modification, whatever we want to call it, is inevitable if one is to try to adapt an ancient text like the Constitution to the context of modern life. At my now much more mature age, I realize that all the answers cannot be distilled from the Constitution's language, any more than all the theorems of mathematics can be derived from a set of axioms.[19] We are left with the fact that the original "meanings" of words in the Constitution, when separated from their original context, can be as opaque as Mayan or Egyptian hieroglyphs or the words "block" and "pillar" in Wittgenstein's "language game." Yes, we can understand quite a lot about what they meant to the Mayans or Egyptians, just as Justice Scalia and Stevens provide comprehensive accounts of what "keep and bear Arms" may have meant in 1789: this stele recounts a battle; that wall painting depicts a domestic scene; Madison was trying to assuage the Anti-Federalists. But we don't know why this formulation, as opposed to that, was enough to reach an agreement, and it asks too much of the poor little words to expect them to inform judgment 220 years later when faced with the question whether the District of Columbia can ban handguns.

This brings us finally to Justice Breyer's dissent[20]. While joining Stevens's dissent, Breyer accepts that there may be something to Scalia's argument that the Second Amendment included a concern about personal protection. In other words, the Second Amendment doesn't just say one thing; it says many things to different people, which may be why it was sufficient to reconcile

---

[18] 544 U.S. at 634–35.

[19] This is of course Gödel's incompleteness theorem. If it is true, as Gödel demonstrated, that all mathematical truths cannot be proven by an axiomatic system, how much more true it must be that all just Constitutional decisions cannot be deduced from the ancient language of the document itself.

[20] Id at 681.

differences in 1789. Then he considers what Paul Freund called balancing right against right: the right to bear arms, whatever that means, against the right of the District of Columbia to protect its citizens, concluding that the DC law represented a reasonable accommodation of the two competing rights. Breyer's dissent has the overwhelming virtue of candor. He does not pretend to be guided solely by the Second Amendment's words nor to be able to avoid exercising judgment, which is, after all, what judges are paid to do.

Breyer does not, of course, answer the questions of how judgment is to be formed, or how a judge is to strike a balance between competing rights. This problem has become ever more pressing in the wake of cases like *Bush v. Gore*[21] and the packing of the federal judiciary with "movement conservatives" who imagine that human rights were fixed in stony words in 1789 and that they can adjudicate using those words without exercising modern judgment.

I'm not sure I know the answer to the question of how judgment is exercised much better now than I did in 1975; I'm not sure anyone does. It is usually possible to identify, much as Justice Breyer did, what is at stake in a ruling, and what is at stake is often highly complex and multi-dimensional: the language of a Constitutional provision or statute, respect for precedent, impact on the present, deference to other branches and organs of government, maintaining the independence of the judiciary without overstepping its power, federalism, the conduct of the parties, procedural posture, the implications of any new precedent, whether there could be an appearance of impropriety or bias. The list goes on and on, without any *a priori* means of assigning relative weight to each element. It is easy to understand why one might want to condense it all into the simple question of what this or that word or phrase meant originally and leave it at that. What I am now quite certain of, though, is that this effort at condensation often results in something more like evaporation, in which meaning can seem to vaporize into thin air.

In the next chapter, we will see how judges and lawyers struggled when the language of copyright did not quite fit the new world of computer software and video games. But first, the *Law Review* "Note" to set the stage.

---

[21] 531 U.S. 98 (2000).

Note: The Speech and Press Clause of the First Amendment as Ordinary Language*

This Note pursues two ends, one through the other. Its ultimate purpose is to encourage close attention to the precise language of constitutional provisions[1] by subjecting the speech and press clause of the first amendment to analysis like that of ordinary language philosophy.[2] Its mediate purpose is to provide, through analysis of the language of the speech and press clause, a new approach to its interpretation.

At the outset, a distinction should be drawn between the question of how one should approach a case involving first amendment issues, and the question of what the proper decision should be. Following a customary locution in philosophy, one may call an answer to the second question an interpretation of the first amendment, and an answer to the first question a meta-interpretation of the first amendment. The meta-interpretation looks to method, the interpretation to result.[3] This Note develops and defends a new meta-interpretation of the first amendment's speech and press clause.

---

* *87 Harv. L. Rev.* 374 (1973).

[1] Many theorists believe that little enlightenment can be derived from the first amendment's exact language. See, e.g., *Dennis v. United States*, 341 U.S. 494, 523 (1950) (Frankfurter, J., concurring); T. Emerson, *Toward a General Theory of the First Amendment* (1966), vii; Chafee, "Book Review," 62 *Harv. L. Rev.* 891, 897–98 (1949).

[2] It would be misleading to dub this Note an exercise in ordinary language philosophy, for at least two reasons. First, the Note builds a theoretical framework for the first amendment, whereas ordinary language philosophers usually disclaim theorizing pretensions. See Quinton, "Contemporary British Philosophy," in *Wittgenstein: The Philosophical Investigations: A Collection of Critical Essays* (ed. G. Pitcher, 1966), 21. Second, ordinary language philosophy must be understood as a reaction against the prevailing denotation theory of meaning; see, e.g., G. Frege, "On Sense and Reference," in *Translations from the Philosophical Writings of Gottlob Frege* (ed. P. Geach and M. Black, 1960), 56, while this Note appears in a different historical context. For descriptions of ordinary language philosophy, see J. Austin, "A Plea for Excuses," in *Philosophical Papers* (ed. J. Urmson and G. Warnock, 1970), 175; S. Cavell "Austin at Criticism," in *Must We Mean What We Say?* (1969), 97; Quinton, *supra*. See generally L. Wittgenstein, *Philosophical Investigations* (3d ed., 1958).

[3] For example, faced with a First Amendment question, one commentator might interpret the amendment by speculating about the social purposes which underlie its language, whereas another commentator might concern himself solely with the historical intention of its authors. They disagree over the first amendment's meta-interpretation. On the other

I. Present meta-interpretations of the speech and press clause

There are at present two competing meta-interpretations of the first amendment's speech and press clause: "interest balancing" and "defining."[4] On the interest-balancing meta-interpretation, one determines the scope of first amendment protection by weighing the importance of the disputed communication against any other constitutional interests it threatens. On the defining meta-interpretation, the scope of first amendment protection is delimited by carefully defining the first amendment reference to "speech" and "the press."

Although balancing's first appearance in a Supreme Court decision is usually ascribed to *Schneider v. State,*[5] Justice Brandeis had balanced first amendment interests in *Whitney v. California.*[6] The clearest judicial statements of the interest balancing method are Chief Justice Vinson's opinion for the Court in *American Communications Association v. Douds*[7] and Justice

---

hand, if, after balancing social interests, one commentator approves loyalty oaths while another disapproves them, they disagree over the first amendment's interpretation. The distinction between meta-interpretation and interpretation is not always made and is not necessary for all purposes. See note 4 *infra.*

[4] Commentators sometimes do not distinguish these meta-interpretations from particular tests. Justice Brennan, for example, lumped the balancing "test" together with two other "tests," redeeming social value; see *Roth v. United States,* 354 U.S. 476, 484 (1957); and clear and present danger, see *Schenck v. United States,* 249 U.S. 47, 52 (1919). See Brennan, "The Supreme Court and the Meiklejohn Interpretation of the First Amendment," 79 *Harv. L. Rev.* 1, 5–9 (1965). See also T. Emerson, *supra* note 1, at 48–58. One should distinguish a holding that a statute strikes a proper balance — an interpretation — from an approach that balances interests — a meta-interpretation. It is the latter with which this Note will concern itself. However, there is nothing sacrosanct about the distinction; compared to the holding in a particular case, the clear and present danger test seems more like a method, but compared to the method of interest balancing it seems more like a result of balancing. The distinction urged in text is intended only to focus attention on methods of reaching results, rather than on specific results.

[5] 308 U.S. 147 (1939); see, e.g., Frantz, "The First Amendment in the Balance," 71 *Yale L. J.* 1424, 1425 (1962).

[6] [A]lthough the rights of free speech and assembly are fundamental, they are not in their nature absolute. Their exercise is subject to restriction, if the particular restriction proposed is required in order to protect the State from destruction or from serious injury, political, economic, or moral.

Whitney v. California, 274 U.S. 357, 373 (1926) (concurring opinion).

[7] 339 U.S. 382 (1950).

Frankfurter's concurring opinion in *Dennis v. United States.*[8] In *Dennis,* Justice Frankfurter justified the interest balancing method as follows:[9]

> The demands of free speech in a democratic society, as well as the interest in national security, are better served by candid and informed weighing of the competing interests, within the confines of the judicial process, than by announcing dogmas too inflexible for the non-Euclidian problems to be solved.

The method applies as well to cases involving other governmental interests.[10]

What stands behind the interest balancing approach is the perception that the first amendment in form brings, within the ambit of its protection, conduct that threatens the enjoyment of other rights secured by the Constitution. Thus, it is not enough merely to inquire whether conduct burdened by law[11] is the exercise of speech or the press; it is also necessary to inquire whether the conduct treads upon other constitutional interests. As Professor Freund notes, the Court's business is the balancing of rights against rights.[12] The damage to public safety or privacy must be considered in deciding a first amendment case because otherwise, the purpose of the Constitution could not be fully realized.[13] Interest balancing is perhaps the most natural meta-interpretation of the first amendment since it is consistent

---

[8] 341 U.S. 494 (1951).

[9] Id. at 524–25.

[10] See Frantz, *supra* note 5, at 1429-34. For example, in *Douds,* Chief Justice Vinson balanced first amendment interests against those in public order. See 339 U.S. at 399-400. For a recent opinion engaging in balancing, see *Branzburg v. Hayes,* 408 U.S. 665 (1972). For a recent commentator using balancing, see "The Supreme Court, 1970 Term," 85 *Harv. L. Rev.* 38, 199 (1971).

[11] This Note will not give a detailed analysis of differences in the impact of the first amendment upon state and federal laws. See note 52 *infra.*

[12] P. Freund, "Constitutional Dilemmas," in *On Law and Justice* (1968), 35–36.

[13] The true meaning of freedom of speech seems to be this. One of the most important purposes of society and government is the discovery and spread of truth on subjects of general concern. This is possible only through absolutely unlimited discussion. . . . Nevertheless, there are other purposes of government, such as order, the training of the young, protection against external aggression. Unlimited discussion sometimes interferes with these purposes, which must then be balanced against freedom of speech, but freedom of speech ought to weigh very heavily in the scale. The First Amendment gives binding force to this principle of political wisdom.
Z. Chafee, *Free Speech in the United States* (Athenium ed., 1941), 31.

with a method to which lawyers and judges have grown accustomed in other areas of the law.[14]

Not surprisingly, the first critic of the method of interest balancing was not a member of the legal profession, but rather the philosopher-educator, Alexander Meiklejohn. Emboldened by the absolute quality of the first amendment's language, Meiklejohn urged that arguments about expediency (his characterization of interest balancing) are improper in a case involving a burden on speech or the press because the Constitution has already "struck the balance" between speech and public safety, and has determined that the free exchange of ideas is always expedient.[15] The elder Justice Harlan had presaged Meiklejohn. In objecting to a state judgment upon an information for contempt, Justice Harlan declared:[16]

> The public welfare cannot override constitutional privileges, and if the rights of free speech and of a free press are, in their essence, attributes of national citizenship, as I think they are, then neither Congress nor any state since adoption of the Fourteenth Amendment can, by legislative enactments or by judicial action, impair or abridge them.

However, Justice Black was the first Supreme Court Justice who consistently propounded an absolute meta-interpretation of the first amendment.[17]

Without more, insistence upon the absolute quality of the first amendment would not allow such standard exceptions as the laws of defamation and

---

[14] The due process clauses of the fifth and fourteenth amendments veritably invite a balancing of interests. The concept also appears prominently in conflict of laws. See R. Cramton and D. Currie, *Conflict of Laws: Cases — Comments — Questions* (1968), 208–334. The method taught for deciding whether, for example, a statute of frauds is procedural or substantive for purposes of the Federal Rules of Civil Procedure is to look behind the words to the interests or policies which the procedural-substantive distinction pursues. See R. Field and B. Kaplan, *Materials for a Basic Course in Civil Procedure* (3d ed., 1973) 1–12.

[15] A. Meiklejohn, *Free Speech and Its Relation to Self-Government* (1948), 65–66. See also T. Emerson, *supra* note 1, at 115–16; Frantz, *supra* note 5, at 1441.

[16] *Patterson v. Colorado*, 205 U.S. 454, 465 (1906) (dissenting opinion).

[17] H. Black, "The Bill of Rights," 35 *N. Y. U. L. Rev.* 865, 879 (1960):

Of course the decision to provide a constitutional safeguard for a particular right, such as . . . the right of free speech protection of the First [Amendment], involves a balancing of conflicting interests. . . . I believe, however, that the Framers themselves did this balancing when they wrote the Constitution and the Bill of Rights.

incitement to riot.[18] Advocates of an absolute first amendment avoid radical disagreement with the case law, however, by narrowing, for first amendment purposes, the definition of "speech" and "the press." Meiklejohn, for example, believes that "speech" includes only the public discussion of issues that are of civic importance.[19] A more common approach is to distinguish speech from conduct.[20]

Theorists such as Meiklejohn justify the distinctions they draw between protected and unprotected speech on the basis of political theory. Meiklejohn believes that the Constitution embodies a system of self-government, which necessarily requires the free exchange of ideas that the first amendment protects. The first amendment is, therefore, a repository of the governing powers of the people, not of privileges granted them.[21] Another respected theorist, Professor Emerson, believes that the speech and press clause of the first amendment denotes the theoretical preconditions for self-government.[22] However, Emerson's conception of the theoretical scope of freedom of speech goes beyond Meiklejohn's to include the right to self-expression, even on issues of purely personal concern.[23] But the essential point is that the meta-interpretations of Meiklejohn and Emerson find it appropriate to justify a first amendment decision by reference to political theory, which is used to define what constitutes "speech."[24] One may therefore characterize this second

---

[18] Cf. A. Meiklejohn, *supra* note 15, at 18. See generally *Konigsberg v. State Bar*, 366 U.S. 36, 49–51 & n.10 (1961) (listing exceptions to first amendment protection).

[19] See A. Meiklejohn, *supra* note 15, ch. 1, especially 18–19, 22–27.

[20] See *Giboney v. Empire Storage & Ice Co.*, 336 U.S. 490, 498 (1948) (Black, J.); T. Emerson, *supra* note 1, at 60–61. See also note 24 *infra*. Balancers criticizing the defining method generally overlook this limitation on what constitutes "speech" and "the press." See, e.g., *Konigsberg v. State Bar*, 366 U.S. 36, 49 n.10 (1960).

[21] A. Meiklejohn, *supra* note 15, at 93–94.

[22] T. Emerson, *supra* note 1 at 59. Members of the Court have observed that the first amendment protects the theoretical preconditions for self-government. See *United States v. Carolene Prods. Co.*, 304 U.S. 144, 152–53 n.4 (1938) (Stone, J.); *Gilbert v. Minnesota*, 254 U.S. 325, 337–38 (1920) (Brandeis, J., dissenting). See also P. Freund, *The Supreme Court of the United States* (1961) 81–87.

[23] T. Emerson, *supra* note 1, at 4–7; cf. A. Meiklejohn, *supra* note 15, at 91.

[24] Justice Black's position is different from that of Meiklejoh or Emerson in one important respect. His distinction between speech and conduct, see, e.g., *Konigsberg v. State Bar*, 366 U.S. 36, 64 (1961) (dissenting opinion)); *Giboney v. Empire Storage & Ice Co.*, 336 U.S. 490, 498 (1948) is essentially similar to Emerson's "consideration of whether the conduct partakes of the Essential qualities of expression or action," T. Emerson, supra note 1 at 61. But Justice Black concentrates on the intention of the framers rather than on political theory to justify the distinction. Compare Black, supra

meta-interpretation as the defining method.[25] Definers maintain that all "speech" is protected absolutely by the first amendment.[26]

Despite its frequent appearance in the concurring and dissenting opinions of Justice Black, the defining approach simpliciter has never commanded a majority of the Supreme Court.[27] It has been argued, however, that in *New York Times Co. v. Sullivan*[28] and *Garrison v. Louisiana*,[29] the Court endorsed Meiklejohn's view by distinguishing speeches or publications about public affairs from those about private affairs.[30] These cases do not, however, agree with Meiklejohn's absolute protection of speech in the public domain: an

---

note 171 at 867–70, with T. Emerson, supra, ch. 1. For criticism of Justice Black's distinction between speech and conduct, see A. Meiklejohn, *supra* note 15, at 42–43.

[25] A similar characterization appears in T. Emerson, supra note 1, at 56–58, and in Frantz, *supra* note 5, at 1435.

[26] See T. Emerson, *supra* note 1, at 56–58; A. Meiklejohn *supra* note 15, at 17.

[27] It is arguable that the Supreme Court adopted a defining approach in *Roth v. United States*, 354 U.S. 476 (1957), when it held that obscenity was not "speech" for purposes of the first amendment. Id. at 484; cf. *Beauharnais v. Illinois*, 343 U.S. 250, 266 (1952) (group libel); *Chaplinsky v. New Hampshire*, 315 U.S. 568, 572 (1942) (fighting words). However, in subsequent obscenity cases, the Court appears to have covertly reintroduced a balancing approach. See *Miller v. California*, 93 S. Ct. 2607 (1973), noted in "The Supreme Court, 1972 Term," 87 *Harv. L. Rev.* 55, 160 (1973); *Memoirs v. Massachusetts*, 383 U.S. 4I3 (1966), noted in "The Supreme Court, 1965 Term," 80 *Harv. L. Rev.* 123, 186 (1966). Furthermore, *Roth* itself may have rested on balancing-like considerations. See "The Supreme Court, 1972 Term," *supra*, at 165–66.

[28] 376 U.S. 254 (1964).

[29] 379 U.S. 64 (1964).

[30] See Brennan, *supra* note 4, at 18; Kalven, "The *New York Times* Case: A Note on 'The Central Meaning of the First Amendment,'" 1964 *Sup. Ct. Rev.* 191, 208. See also *Red Lion Broadcasting Co. v. FCC*, 395 U.S. 367, 390 (1969). In *Rosenbloom v. Metromedia, Inc.*, 403 U.S. 29, (1971), noted in "The Supreme Court, 1970 Term," 85 *Harv. L. Rev.* 38, 222 (1971), the Court extended *Sullivan* to protect the reporting of events of public concern even where the plaintiff, an obscure defendant of an obscenity prosecution, was neither a "public official," see *New York Times Co. v. Sullivan*, 376 U.S. 254, 279-80 (1964), nor a "public figure," see *Curtis Publishing Co. v. Butts*, 388 U.S. 130, 155 (1967). *Rosenbloom* demonstrates the difficulty in drawing the line that Meiklejohn suggests between events of public and private concern. It has been argued that *Rosenbloom* was in fact "taking a significant step toward the absolute immunization of the news media from libel judgments." "The Supreme Court, 1970 Term," *supra*, at 222. If this interpretation is correct, *Rosenbloom* does not rest on Meiklejohn's distinction.

exception is drawn to the protection where false defamation results from actual malice or reckless disregard of the facts.[31]

Neither the defining nor the interest balancing meta-interpretation survives critical scrutiny. The essential precept of interest balancing is unexceptionable: the judge must do justice in the case before him by weighing all the facts together with the constitutional interests represented by the parties. In practice, however, interest balancing opens a broad door through which the judge's personal prejudices and misconceptions pass along with his legitimate and constitutional concerns. Where judges must determine, for example, whether criminal syndicalism represents a clear and present danger,[32] the potential for abuse is manifest.[33]

Furthermore, when a decision cannot be criticized on the ground of bias, a commentator can only assert that the judge struck a balance that he would not have. In theory, any balance is a possibility, and criticism becomes counterassertion. Interest balancing is also characteristically vague, leaving judges, prosecutors, police, other governmental officials, and citizens essentially without guidelines.[34] Moreover, any real balancing would be prohibitively time-consuming;[35] for example, for a court seriously to consider the danger to government of "criminal syndicalism," it would have to determine such facts as the numbers of criminal anarchists, their finances, and the success of their organizing efforts. Anything less would pretend to balance real interests, but would, in fact, substitute a spurious judicial notice of the most controversial facts. There is, finally, the definers' objection that it is unjustifiable for a judge to balance the rights guaranteed by the speech and press clause against other governmental "interests" because it was the very purpose of the first amendment to strike a balance, once and for all.[36]

Defining attracts theorists like Meiklejohn and Emerson, and jurists like Justice Black, precisely because it appears to bridle the judicial discretion that animates the major criticisms of interest balancing. Defining has problems of its own, however. In the first place, although neat distinctions between protected and unprotected speech derive effortlessly from political theory,

---

31 *Garrison v. Louisiana*, 379 U.S. 64, 75 (1964). Justice Brennan argues that this exception is consistent with Professor Meiklejohn's interpretation. See Brennan, *supra* note 4, at 19.

32 See, e.g., *Whitney v. California*, 274 U.S. 357 (1927).

33 Cf. Frantz, *supra* note 5, at 1441–42.

34 T. Emerson, *supra* note 1, at 55–56.

35 Id.

36 See note 15 *supra*.

their application to actual cases is highly problematic. For example, Meiklejohn distinguishes between the discussion of public and private issues. But a public speech claiming that the President is an adulterer surely touches private issues, although it also raises a question as to the President's moral qualification for his office. As Professor Chafee remarked, "The truth is that there are public aspects to practically every subject."

Moreover, when one considers how a judge might determine whether a speech is on public or private matters, the insulation of the defining method from the very balancing that definers purport to eschew is thrown into question. It is reasonable to assume that in the above example, a judge could only decide the question of first amendment protection by looking to the policy underlying the distinction between public and private speech.[37] Thus, he would have to inquire whether the President's morals are so important a public consideration that it would outweigh the personal impact of the speech. Yet this is precisely the approach a balancer would use[38] with greater candor.

Meta-interpretation of the first amendment has thus reached an impasse. Balancers surely controvert the absolute appearance of its language when they restrike the balance agreed to by the Framers, but the definers must also resort to balancing in applying their theoretical distinctions to actual cases. There is a reason for the central importance of balancing under either meta-

[37] See note 14 *supra.*

[38] See "Note, The First Amendment Overbreadth Doctrine," 83 *Harv. L. Rev.* 844, 915 (1970). To the foregoing criticisms Chafee adds that, as a tactical matter, one interested in safeguarding freedom of speech and press is better advised to argue on the balancers' level of policy than on the definers' level of theory and logic, legislators and judges being practical men who must run a country, not philosophize about it. Chafee, *supra* note 1, at 894. Furthermore, Chafee argues that the framers did not have the clear understanding which Meiklejohn enjoyed of the theoretical scope of these freedoms. It is, therefore, incorrect to say that the first amendment stands for the preconditions for Meiklejohn's system of self-government: the framers had no idea what that system was. Id. at 898. See also Levy, *Legacy of Suppression* (1960), 190–91. It is not, of course, necessary for definers to argue that their theory of free expression is identical to the Framers'; it is possible, for example, to postulate a continuing social contract, whose precise content changes over time. On this view, the speech and press clause protects whatever freedom is necessary for society at a particular time. See, e.g., A. Meiklejohn, *supra* note 15, at 13–14.

interpretation.[39] Both the balancers and the definers believe that it is particular acts — speeches and publications — and particular actors — speakers and publishers — that have first amendment protection. The disagreements only arise over the categories of activity protected and the absolute nature of the protection. Since it is impossible that all speeches should be protected by the first amendment, and since there are no independent criteria for determining what may properly be called a "protected speech," it becomes necessary to limit the category of protected speeches by reference to the interests against protecting all speeches. Given their shared assumption, therefore, both definers and balancers are inevitably committed to balancing — whether directly or in terms of the policies behind the protected-unprotected theoretical distinction — in order to determine the scope of first amendment protection.

II. The speech and press clause as ordinary language

It is the purpose of this section to introduce a meta-interpretation of the first amendment that displaces the centrality of balancing in determining the contours of first amendment interests. By attending to the language of the first amendment, one may both postpone and focus the balancing that is still necessary for accommodating the first amendment to other constitutional interests.

The proposed meta-interpretation is based on the way native speakers of English would follow a rule that shares the first amendment's grammatical

---

[39] Professor Fried has argued that there are different levels of generality at which balancing can proceed. Fried, "Two Concepts of Interests: Some Reflections on the Supreme Court's Balancing Test," 76 *Harv. L. Rev.* 755 *passim* (1963). On a lower level, the issues are framed in terms of "bare demands for satisfaction," id. at 756, which leads to a "necessarily particularistic balance of interests," id. at 765. The balancing meta-interpretation may be identified with this level. On a higher level, the interests are "viewed as competences," id. at 763, and a decision formulates "rules defining the limits of the respective competences," id. at 773. While Fried characterizes the latter as a balancing approach, it is similar to the litigation that would be necessary under the defining approach. It is thus possible to argue that balancing and defining are merely two levels for the application of the same technique. This conclusion appears to be supported by opinions like Justice Harlan's in *Konigsberg v. State Bar*, 366 U.S. 36 (1961), which appears to share the definers' assumption that activity within the language of the first amendment may not be burdened, but candidly determines what activity is within the language on the basis of a particularistic balancing of interests. See id. at 49–50.

form.[40] Imagine a bandage manufacturer, *M*, attempting to follow a set of standards promulgated by the Red Cross, which includes the following:

> Standard A: Manufacturers should design no bandage which interferes with the freedom of movement of the limbs.

Shortly after *M* has marketed a new bandage a customer writes, complaining that he is unable to hammer nails when he is wearing *M*'s bandage. Has the letter provided *M* with enough information to decide whether the design complies with Standard A? Although driving a nail is a movement of the arm, this customer's complaint does not necessarily imply that *M* has designed the bandage improperly. It does, however, raise the issue. To settle it, *M* would first inquire whether this customer is an isolated case, or whether, in fact, no one can drive nails when he is wearing the new bandage. If this were not the only complaint, *M* would next inquire whether there are many other movements that the new bandage inhibits or prevents. Very likely, he would call in persons wearing the bandage and ask them to swing their arms, noticing whether they flinched or hesitated. If they flinched whatever way they swung their arms, or if the bandage interfered with several activities of the arm, *M* would conclude that the bandage did not meet Standard A. But note that Standard A does not mean that every person must be able to perform every movement of his arm; it does not "protect" movements one at a time. It means, rather, that the bandage must not prevent too many movements, nor crimp movement so randomly or generally as to give rise to a worry, a hesitation, every time a limb is moved. One can conclude that freedom of movement is a *quality* that movement in general enjoys or lacks.

---

[40] In this Note "grammatical form" will be used where one might otherwise say "wording." The reason is that calling the linguistic form in which a provision is expressed "wording" would carry the implication that the same provision could be made with different "wording." On the contrary, it is a premise of this Note's analysis that native speakers of English will ordinarily follow a provision differently depending upon the precise way in which it is expressed, and that the form in which a provision is expressed will therefore reveal the manner in which its author expected it to be followed. "Grammatical form" is an effort to convey the rule-like connection between the way a provision is expressed and the way it is ordinarily followed. Cf. L. Wittgenstein, *supra* note 2, at 85 (rules for the use of language are obeyed "blindly"). See also S. Cavell, *The Availability of Wittgenstein's Later Philosophy*, *supra* note 2, at 62–65 (in examining language one examines the possibility of phenomena); L. Wittgenstein, *supra*, at 59 (example of a "grammatical investigation").

Standard A thus protects that quality of movement, not particular instances of movement.[41] Contrast *M*'s method of following a standard in this form:

> Standard B: Manufacturers should design no bandage which interferes with any movement of the limbs.

Again, *M* markets a new bandage and receives a customer's letter, complaining that he is unable to hammer nails when he is wearing *M*'s bandage. In this case, the customer's complaint not only raises, but also settles, the question of substandard bandage design. Additional inquiry would only be necessary if there were some question of whether the customer's complaint referred to a movement of the arm within the meaning of Standard B. If, for example, the customer complained that the bandage caused difficulty when her husband moved her arm for her, *M* might say that the bandage is not defective because it was her husband who moved her arm. In short, Standard B "protects" movements of limbs one at a time, so long as the movements are within its contemplation.

Since the first amendment provision, "Congress shall make no law . . . abridging the freedom of speech, or of the press," has the same grammatical form as Standard A, the same sort of considerations are relevant in following it as were relevant in following Standard A. Thus, in a first amendment case, the issue of first amendment violation is raised by a burden placed upon a speech or a publication. But this complaint does not settle the question. To settle it, one must inquire into the amount of speech and publication that the statute burdens and the effect of the statute upon the quality of speaking and publishing generally.[42] By this method, the scope of the first amendment may

---

41 For another example of this use of the phrase "freedom of . . ." to refer to a quality, consider the following excerpt from the debates over the adoption of the Bill of Rights in the House of Representatives. On a motion intended to limit debate after a day-long controversy regarding a proposal to amend what became the first amendment to include the phrase "to instruct their Representatives," Mr. Page begged the gentlemen to consider that the motion tended to deprive the members of that freedom of debate which they had heretofore been indulged in. . . .

I. Annals of Cong. 777 (1789) (published as I Debates of Congress).

42 This Note will not attempt to solve all the practical difficulties a court would face in using the methods proposed in text. While it would be natural for the manufacturer *M* to conduct experiments and surveys in order to determine whether he is in compliance with Standard A, see *supra*; such procedures present both practical and legal problems for the trial judge attempting to determine the impact of a statute on the freedom of speech. Of course, it would be open to the parties to bring studies of the impact of

be preliminarily ascertained on the basis of criteria that are independent of a consideration of the countervailing constitutional interests.[43]

The meta-interpretation of the speech and press clause as ordinary language reveals that both balancers and definers had replaced the logic of Standard A with that of Standard B.[44] Both balancers and definers assumed

---

governmental action affecting expression to the attention of the judge. Where such studies are not forthcoming, however, judicial notice of the quality of speaking generally may be the only resort; such judicial notice opens a serious danger of excessive discretion and bias. Cf. *supra*. See also note 50 *infra*.

43 In utilizing independent criteria for the use of the phrase "the freedom of . . . ," this Note's proposals for a new meta-interpretation are not intended to obviate the need for judicial line drawing. On the contrary, adjudication under the proposed meta-interpretation would be necessary in order to create tests for the threshold at which imposition on speaking and publishing becomes an abridgment of "the freedom of" speech. Such tests would represent an interpretation of the amendment which had been formed by the method of the proposed meta-interpretation.

44 It is not difficult to imagine how the confusion of Standards A and B comes about. A major source is the lawyer's rhetorical attraction to parallel form. For example, so cautious a reasoner as Chief Justice Hughes wrote:

> The greater the importance of safeguarding the community from incitements to the overthrow of our institutions by force and violence, the more imperative is the need to preserve inviolate the constitutional rights of free speech, free press, and free assembly in order to maintain the opportunity for free political discussion.

De Jonge v. Oregon, 299 U.S. 353,365 (1937). By writing in this manner, the Chief Justice lost the difference between (general) freedom of speech and (an individual's) freedom to speak. One of the lessons of ordinary language philosophy is to be suspicious of the assumption that meaning survives facile transformations of grammatical form. Compare:

a) The Court ignored the action of the Washington court.
b) The Court's ignorance of the action of the Washington court. . . .

with:

c) The Court continued the case until October.
d) The Court's continuance of the case until October. . . .

Meaning survives the change from c) to d), but not the change from a) to b).
A second reason for the replacement of the logic of Standard A with that of Standard B derives from a conception of the judicial function. The Court believes that it should only decide constitutional issues when the decision cannot be based on some other ground. See *Ashwander v. TVA*, 297 U.S. 288, 345–48 (1936) (Brandeis, J., concurring). Furthermore, there is a sense that courts are only competent to decide "flesh and blood controversies" before them. See A. Bickel, *The Least Dangerous Branch* (1962), 115–16. For these reasons the "Court has generally insisted that parties rely only on constitutional rights which are personal to themselves." *NAACP v. Alabama*, 357 U.S.

that the first amendment protects speeches and publications individually. Similarly, the essential inquiry under Standard B was whether the movement complained of was "protected" by the standard. But the first amendment no more protects particular speeches than Standard A protects particular movements. Speeches are protected by the first amendment only indirectly when their inhibition would diminish the free quality of speech in general.[45]

However, a variation upon the manufacturer example will demonstrate that this is as far as the language alone can carry analysis. Suppose that Standard A′ does not appear in a set of standards for all bandages, but in a set of standards for athletic braces. After *M* has marketed a new knee brace, a football player complains that when he is wearing the brace, he is greatly

---

449, 459 (1958). Since Standard B "protects" movements one at a time, it is natural for courts to read the speech and press clause as if it were in the form of Standard B.

[45] The proposed meta-interpretation thus explains the importance in first amendment adjudication of inquiring into the chilling effect governmental action may have on the freedom of expression. See "Note, The Chilling Effect in Constitutional Law," 69 *Colum. L. Rev.* 808 (1969); "Note, The First Amendment Overbreadth Doctrine," 83 *Harv. L. Rev.* 844, 852–58 (1970). But see *Broadrick v. Oklahoma,* 93 S. Ct. 2908, 2917–19 (1973) (requiring "substantial" overbreadth), noted in "The Supreme Court, 1972 Term," 87 *Harv. L. Rev.* 55, 141 (1973); *California v. LaRue,* 409 U.S. 109 (1972) (twenty-first amendment supersedes first amendment), noted in "The Supreme Court, 1972 Term," 87 *Harv. L. Rev.* 55, 133 (1973). The rhetoric in chilling effect cases is very nearly congruent to the considerations which are appropriate on the proposed meta-interpretation. In *New York Times Co. v. Sullivan,* 376 U.S. 254 (1964), Justice Brennan wrote:

> The fear of damage awards under a rule such as that invoked by the Alabama courts here may be markedly more inhibiting than the fear of prosecution under a criminal statute. . . . [T]he pall of fear and timidity imposed upon those who would give voice to public criticism is an atmosphere in which the First Amendment freedoms cannot survive.

Id. at 277–78. See also *Keyishian v. Board of Regents,* 385 U.S. 589, 601 (1967).

The justiciability of the chilling effect of governmental surveillance was thrown into question in *Laird v. Tatum,* 408 U.S. 1 (1972). However, the Court in *Laird* did not clearly distinguish the ripeness of respondents' claim that first amendment freedom had been chilled from the claim's justiciability. See "The Supreme Court, 197I Term," 86 *Harv. L. Rev.* 50, 130 (1972). Furthermore, the existence of a pervasive system of governmental surveillance throws the sort of pall over political debate which on the proposed meta-interpretation it is the purpose of the first amendment to prevent. See "Note, Judicial Review of Military Surveillance of Civilians: Big Brother Wears Modern Army Green," 72 *Colum. L. Rev.* 1009, 1047 (1972). See also F. Askin, "Police Dossiers and Emerging Principles of First Amendment Adjudication," 22 *Stan. L. Rev.* 196 (1970), and cases cited therein.

inhibited in punt kicking. *M* determines that this is not an isolated instance, but rather a common complaint. He also determines that people wearing the brace can move their leg in an uninhibited manner, as long as they do not try to kick punts. Under Standard A, which appeared in a set of standards for all bandages, it might be reasonable to conclude that the standard had been met despite the punt kickers' complaints, since punt kicking constitutes such a minor proportion of all the possible movements of the leg. But under Standard A′, the universe of possible leg movements is narrowed to athletic activities. Within this universe, an inhibition upon punt kicking constitutes a greater proportion of the whole, and assumes a special significance that may imply that *M*'s bandage has failed to meet Standard A′. But note that the special significance of inhibitions on athletic activities arose not from the language of Standard A′ (which is identical to the language of Standard A), but from its apparent purpose to protect the freedom of athletic activities.

In following the rule of the speech and press clause, one should consider purpose in the same way. Suppose, for example, that Congress passes a law that prohibits antigovernment speeches on the Fourth of July. One could initially object to such a law on the ground that many important speeches occur on the Fourth of July, and also on the ground that the law violates equal protection.[46] But these considerations do not exhaust the objections to such a law, because it seems to be the very purpose of the first amendment to protect the nation's democratic processes by allowing criticism of the government on occasions when one might be expected to find an audience. To reach this result, however, it has been necessary to look behind the amendment's language to its political purposes.[47]

In sum, the meta-interpretation of the first amendment that derives from its language has two effects. First, it directs attention to a consideration that is entirely overlooked by the balancers and definers: the impact of governmental action on the quality of freedom that speech generally has or lacks. Second, it does not discard the necessity of looking behind the amendment's words to its purposes; rather, it limits and directs their use. Limits, because there is a range of cases that can be disposed of on the ground that the challenged

---

[46] See also note 49 *infra.*

[47] The proposed meta-interpretation thus incorporates the debates among definers as to the purposes of the first amendment. If one is convinced by Meiklejohn that protection of a system of self-government is the only purpose of the first amendment, a system of restraint on the private distribution of obscene literature would not seem to threaten the freedom of political speech in general. On Emerson's theory, see id., such a system of restraint would threaten the freedom of personal expression.

governmental action does not inhibit the general freedom of speech.[48] Directs, because one looks to purpose only in order to determine the range of speech to be considered in assessing the impact of governmental action on the freedom of speech. In the preceding Fourth of July hypothetical, for example, the first amendment purpose of protecting the vitality of democratic processes leads one to inquire into the statute's impact on the general quality of freedom of political speech, and in this narrowed range of consideration speeches on the Fourth of July assume a special significance. Thus, a statute inhibiting them may be an abridgment of political speech, even if not of speech in general.

Although one could join the definers in arguing that a first amendment claim, as defined by this Note, should be absolute, it is more realistic to admit the ultimate necessity of judging the impact of first amendment claims on other constitutional interests with which they may be in conflict.[49] Thus,

---

[48] Examples of such actions are a governmental prosecution against a person who has used "fighting words," see *Chaplinsky v. New Hampshire*, 315 U.S. 568 (1942), and entertainment of a suit for malicious defamation, see *New York Times Co. v. Sullivan*, 376 U.S. 254, 279-80 (1964) (dictum). Neither sort of utterance significantly contributes to any realm of expression or discussion; neither, therefore, presents a valid first amendment claim. However, in fashioning rules excising such utterances from first amendment protection, judges should be sensitive to the possibility that too broad a rule will chill other speech as well. See generally "Note, The First Amendment Overbreadth Doctrine," 85 *Harv. L. Rev.* 844 (1970). Such problems are particularly acute in the obscenity area. See *Paris Adult Theatre I v. Slaton*, 93 S. Ct. 2628, 2647–51 (1973) (Brennan, J., dissenting).
In addition to the standard exceptions to first amendment protection, see *Konigsberg v. State Bar*, 366 U.S. 36, 49 n.10 (1961)), on the proposed meta-interpretation there would be no valid first amendment claim against a law which, for example, prohibited one obscure person from speaking, unless it could be shown that others feared that similar laws might subsequently be passed against them. For this reason the proposed meta-interpretation appears to afford less protection than current first amendment doctrine. However, it must be borne in mind that a law such as the one described would surely be challengeable under such other constitutional provisions as the equal protection, due process, and bill of attainder clauses, even if the first amendment did not exist.

[49] By acquiescing in the necessity of balancing, the proposed meta-interpretation does not preclude the abuses of judicial discretion, which are identified with the balancing approach. In fact, the proposal could prove dangerous to first amendment freedom because it gives a judge who is hostile to first amendment claims two chances to hold against them: one, when the validity of the claim is ascertained; the other, when a valid claim is balanced against competing constitutional interests. However, it is unlikely that any meta-interpretation could foreclose the possibility of such misuse, and for a judge

relying as it does on the mere language of the first amendment, the proposed meta-interpretation is not a decision procedure for those cases in which the amendment's language, or its language together with its purposes, leads to conclusions that conflict with other constitutional provisions. In this respect, the proposed meta-interpretation is weaker than the interest-balancing and defining approaches, both of which purport to be decision procedures for cases involving both first amendment and competing claims. The proposed meta-interpretation does, however, provide a procedure for establishing the validity of a first amendment claim independently of a consideration of competing claims.[50] And when it has been established that a governmental action[51] abridges the general freedom of a particular kind of speech, it should not be as easy to find an overriding governmental interest as it has been with the first amendment interest defined as one person's right to give a particular speech.[52]

---

who is sensitive to the first amendment, the proposed meta-interpretation can provide insight into the first amendment concern which arises when no particular speech or speaker is censored or punished, but speech in general is affected by governmental action. See note 46 *supra;* note 51 *infra.*

[50] On the proposed meta-interpretation, the validity of the first amendment claim in Red Lion Broadcasting Co. v. FCC, 395 U.S. 367 (1969), supporting the Federal Communications Commission's fairness doctrine, see id. at 377, for example, is manifest. Broadcasters had objected that the regulations abridged their freedom of speech and of the press. Rejecting their claims, the Court held that "[i]t is the purpose of the First Amendment to preserve an uninhibited marketplace of ideas," id. at 390, and that the regulations promulgated pursuant to the fairness doctrine" enhance rather than abridge the freedoms of speech and press," id. at 375. This holding is entirely consonant with the proposed meta-interpretation, which eschews particular persons' rights to give speeches or to publish in favor of a concern with the free quality of speech and publication. See also 'Note, The First Amendment and the 'Abridgeable' Right of Self-Expression, 72 *Colum. L. Rev.* 1249 (1972). But see *Columbia Broadcasting Sys., Inc. v. Democratic Nat'l Comm* 412 U.S. 94 (1973).

[51] Since the first amendment has been made applicable to the states through the due process clause of the fourteenth amendment, see, e.g., *Edwards v. South Carolina*, 372 U.S. 229, 235 (1963); *Whitney v. California*, 274 U.S. 357, 373 (1926) (Brandeis, J., concurring); *Gitlow v. New York*, 268 U.S. 652, 666 (1925), it is arguable that the proposed meta-interpretation should be used only where federal statutes are challenged on first amendment grounds. Cf. note 14 *supra.* However, the insights into the nature of first amendment interests provided by the proposed meta-interpretation would be relevant to the balancing approach which is natural in litigation under the due process clause.

[52] An example will help to clarify this last advantage. In *Feiner v. New York*, 340 U.S. 315 (1951), the petitioner was convicted of disorderly conduct for refusing to stop speaking

III. The historical validity of the proposed meta-interpretation

The meta-interpretation that this Note has proposed may properly be considered a theory of how the Framers expected the speech and press clause to be followed. It is the first purpose of this section to demonstrate the proposal's consistency with historical analysis of the amendment. The second purpose is to meet the objection that the grammatical form of the amendment was a matter of too little importance to the Framers to form the basis of a meta-interpretation.

The proposed meta-interpretation is consistent with the popular view that the primary historical purpose of the first amendment was to abolish the distinction at common law between prior restraints and subsequent punishments, and in particular, to render the common law of seditious libel unconstitutional.[53] The validity of a first amendment claim against criminal liability for criticism of the government could be readily established under the

---

to a crowd of seventy-five to eighty which had become restive as the result of his speech. In respecting the community's interest "in maintaining peace and order on its streets," the Court commented, "We cannot say that the preservation of that interest here encroaches on the constitutional rights of this petitioner." Id. at 320. Thus, the Court framed the balance in terms of the right of this person to deliver a particular speech versus the right of the community to preserve peace and order. In such terms, it is difficult to imagine how the petitioner could ever prevail; one seems to purchase public tranquility at the cost of but one speech.

Under the proposed meta-interpretation, the outlines of the "interest" represented by the petitioner were somewhat different. The state sought to proscribe speeches which occasion a hostile reaction in their audiences. Feiner's was not merely any speech, but a political speech, protesting the cancellation of a former assistant attorney general's speech on racial discrimination and civil liberties. The question therefore becomes: does the rule advocated by the state restrict the freedom of political speech? Important considerations are the frequency with which political speeches arouse hostile reactions in their audiences, and the relative importance of street corner megaphone speeches like the petitioner's to political expression generally. In this context, the petitioner was not arguing for his right to have given that speech, but was representing the importance of street corner speeches to the freedom of political speech generally. There is a first amendment interest at stake only if the petitioner convinces the court of the importance of such speeches. But when the first amendment interest at stake in the litigation is determined in this way, the contest with the community's interest in public order is closer. One is not exchanging this one speech for public order; rather, one is exchanging a significant diminution in the free quality of political debate for the public order.

53 See, e.g., Z. Chafee, *supra note* 13, at 18–22. For a discussion of prior works reaching this conclusion, see L. Levy, *supra note* 24, at 1–3.

proposed meta-interpretation since such liability would surely inhibit the freedom with which men speak about affairs of state.

Professor Leonard Levy has argued persuasively, however, that the Framers had no intention of abolishing the common law of seditious libel by means of the first amendment.[54] Levy demonstrates that libertarian theory at the time of the drafting of the first amendment perceived no tension between protecting the freedom of speech and punishing libels against the state,[55] that the constitutions of eight states proclaimed in one breath the freedom of speech and in the next acknowledged the common law of seditious libel,[56] and that influential figures such as James Wilson embraced the distinction between prior restraint and subsequent punishment.[57] Faced with such overwhelming evidence, Levy finds himself "reluctantly forced to conclude" that the authors of the first amendment did not understand it to sweep away the law of seditious libel.[58]

---

[54] L. Levy, *supra note* 39.

[55] Id. at 104. Levy acknowledges at least three theorists who recognized the tension, however. See id. at 115–20 ("Cato"), 149–51 ("Father of Candor"), 164–65 (Furneaux).

[56] L. Levy, *supra note* 39, at 191–92.

[57] Id. at 201-02.

[58] Id. at vii; see id. at 236-37. But see Z. Chafee, *supra* note 13, at 18–22. Justice Black reiterated the Chafee interpretation despite the Government's argument to the contrary in *Communist Party v. Subversive Activities Control Bd.*, 367 U.S. 1, 159–60 n.46 (1961) (dissenting opinion). Levy himself admits that there is not enough evidence available "to justify cocksure conclusions." L. Levy, *supra* note 39, at 236. Perhaps the profoundest gap in his reconstruction of opinion on the freedom of speech, and the point emphasized by scholars who had reached conclusions opposite to Levy's, see, e.g., Z. Chafee, *supra* note 13, at 27–30, is his explanation of the torrent of constitutional objection voiced against the Sedition Act. L. Levy, *supra,* at 245-48. For all the rhetoric about the virtues of free press and speech, Americans for the most part ignored the impact of the first amendment on the common law of seditious libel until the Sedition Act in 1795, Id. at 217. Levy believes that, with the advent of the Sedition Act, a new understanding of the freedom of speech took root, matured, and flowered overnight into theory, fertilized only by the political stance of the Jeffersonians:

> For the first time our public men of the generation of the Framers expressed themselves with force, clarity, and elaborate detail on the meaning and limitations of freedom of speech and press. . . . A full discussion of all these matters may be based on an analysis of the controversy over the Sedition Act.
>
> But as a revelation of prior opinion, the debate of 1798 and after is suspect.

Views expressed during that acrimonious time are untrustworthy because they were distinctly ad hoc in character and because partisans were even less motivated by principle and precedent than usual. They argued from personal and party interests.

The Framers' conviction that the first amendment did not throw into question the constitutionality of the common law of seditious libel appears to be at odds with the proposed meta-interpretation, under which seditious libel would be open to the most serious constitutional objection. However, the apparent inconsistency between Levy's work and this Note is dispelled when it is realized that the Framers could have been both concerned with the quality of freedom of speech and convinced that only prior restraints posed a threat to that quality. That is, the Framers may have followed the proposed meta-interpretation, but disagreed with modern opinion[59] as to the first amendment's interpretation when applied to subsequent punishments.

This Note's conclusions and Levy's may also argue past one another. Levy is preeminently concerned with grasping the Framers' theoretical understanding of the scope of freedom of speech and the press.[60] An analysis of the amendment's language, on the other hand, attempts to grasp the Framers' concerns in drafting the amendment. It is possible that the Framers' theoretical understanding lagged behind their practical concern with the free quality of speech. Levy notes the general silence of the Framers as to the impact of the first amendment on the common law of seditious libel to support his conclusion that they intended to protect only what was protected under the contemporary theoretical understanding.[61] Instead, why not conclude from their silence that seditious libel and its theory simply were not on their minds when they drafted the Bill of Rights? The language suggests that what really was on their minds was the quality of freedom that speech and the press could and sometimes did enjoy,[62] rather than a background of

---

Id. at 245–46. It may be true that the threat of political disaster inspires constitutional revision, but it is implausible that an act which was entirely consonant with previous constitutional understanding should have produced the outrage that the Sedition Art evoked. Although the argument for interpreting the framers' understanding of the first amendment as outlawing the common law of seditious libel is admittedly "suspect" when based on politically motivated declarations coming long after the fact, it is not defunct. The Jeffersonian response to the Sedition Act does not have the flavor of a concocted rationalization for a political purpose, but rather the flavor of expectations disappointed. The indignation at least opens a crack in the solid mass of Levy's evidence through which the analysis of the first amendment's language may shed some light.

59 See, e.g., Z. Chafee, *supra note* 13, at 19–30.

60 See L. Levy, *supra note* 39, at 309.

61 See id. at 214–17.

62 That speech and the press had the aspect of freedom in colonial times Levy himself admits:

case law as interpreted by Blackstone.[63] Indeed, it is natural to assume that the Framers' concerns following a revolution represented a break with the past, not merely a codification of the status quo. Thus, it was not until the advent of the Sedition Act that some of the Framers, notably Madison,[64] were forced to articulate the inconsistency of subsequent restraints with that quality of freedom protected by the First Amendment.[65]

An anticipated historical objection to this Note's analysis is that the Framers had so little regard for the precise language of the speech and press clause that it is unjustifiable to derive a meta-interpretation from it.[66] Not surprisingly, the sparse history of the drafting of the Bill of Rights provides little enlightenment as to the reasons for the specific wording of the amendment.[67] It is clear, however,

---

> In England and her colonies, the king's subjects were so interested in politics and so convinced by their glorious, if largely rhetorical, traditions of freedom that an astonishing degree of discussion existed, considering the restraints.

Id. at 17. Levy remarks, however, that

> Nevertheless it would be an exaggeration to say that speech and press were free as a matter of common experience, although fettered by the law.

Id. To appreciate the extent of the freedom of colonial speech and press, see Chafee, *supra note* 1, at 898.

63 For the framers' reliance on Blackstone's theories, see L. Levy, *supra note* 24, at 201–09.

64 Id. at 247.

65 Commentators on Levy's book have raised similar objections. Murphy, for example, writes:

> Critics have raised serious questions concerning the implications drawn from this evidence. There was almost certainly a wide degree of freedom of expression in colonial and early national America. Granting the existence of the narrow common law definition of seditious libel, it was nevertheless true that "that the people were willing to run the risk of prosecution for uttering unpopular opinions suggests that there was a 'popular' concept of liberty of expression, no matter how unarticulated in terms of theoretical definition, which clashed with the legal definition."

P. Murphy, *The Meaning of Free Speech* (1972), 13, quoting Smith, "Book Review," 20 *Wm. & Mary Q.* (3d ser.) 158–59 (1963). See also note 59 *supra*.

66 See, e.g., Chafee, *supra* note 11 at 897–98.

67 See L. Levy, *supra* note 391 at 221. When Madison first proposed various amendments to the Constitution to the House of Representatives on May 5, 1789, what eventually became the speech and press clauses of the first amendment appeared as an addition to the provisions of Article 11, §9, protecting against abuses of federal power:

Fourthly. That in article 1st, section 9, between clauses 3 and 4, be inserted these clauses, to wit: . . .

> The people shall not be deprived or abridged of their right to speak, to write, or to publish their sentiments; and the freedom of the press, as one of the great bulwarks of liberty, shall be inviolable.

that the Framers faced a choice concerning the language to be used.[68] The wording of the protection was evidently of some concern to the Framers — the Committee of Eleven changed it[69] — and, faced with the choice between its various prior expressions,[70] they chose the language that now confronts us.

The conclusion that a conscious choice underlies the present language of the first amendment is reinforced by the history of the speech or debate clause of the Constitution.[71] It appears that this clause was intended to protect roughly the same interests, for a more limited group of people, that the speech and press clause of the first amendment protects. After considering numerous proposals, the Framers adopted the present wording of the speech or debate clause.[72] That

---

I Annals of Cong. 451 (1789) (published as I Debates of Congress). The language was changed to its current form, "freedom of speech, and of the press," by the Committee of Eleven to which Madison's amendments were referred on July 21. 2 B. Schwartz, *The Bill of Rights: A Documentary History* (1971), 1050. There is no explanation for the change and the language was not altered or questioned thereafter. The debate over the amendment in the House is not helpful, since the members addressed themselves exclusively to motions, first, to delete the clause guaranteeing the right of the people peaceably to assemble and, second, to insert the words, "to instruct their representatives." I. Annals of Cong. 759–76 (1789) (published as I Debates of Congress). The latter can refer syntactically only to the right to assemble; the attention of the congressmen was therefore drawn primarily to the assembly clause by the proposed changes. For a summary of the successive versions of the first amendment, see G. Anastaplo, *The Constitutionalist,* App. A (1971). For collections of various drafts of the Bill of Rights, see E. Dumbauld, *The Bill of Rights and What it Means Today* (1957) 206–22; L. Levy, *supra* note 39, at 280 and n.68.

68 Precursors of the first amendment's speech and press clause do not uniformly employ the present language. The Massachusetts Body of Liberties (1641), for example, provides:

> Section 12: Every man whether Inhabitant or fforreiner, free or not free, shall have libertie to come to any publique Court, Councel, or Towne meeting, and either by speech or writeing to move any lawfull, seasonable, and materiall question, or to present any necessary motion, complaint, petition, Bill or information. . . .

The Colonial Laws of Massachusetts (ed. W. Whitmore, 1889), 35. And Madison's original version, see note 68 supra, uses the phrase, "right to speak," together with "freedom of the press." It might be argued that the various versions were merely alternative methods of expressing the same thought. However, because two provisions protect roughly the same activities, they need not be intended to protect them in exactly the same way. Indeed, Standards A and B protect roughly the same thing, but one follows their commands differently.

69 See note 68 *supra.*

70 For various provisions in state constitutions and bills of rights guaranteeing freedom of expression, see B. Schwartz, *supra note* 68, *passim* (1971).

71 U.S. Const. art. I, §6.

72 In the Articles of Confederation, Article 5 provided as follows:

clause — "and for any Speech or Debate in either House, they [Senators and Representatives shall not be questioned in any other Place" — is in form similar to Standard B, which protects movements one at a time.

If one accepts the difference between the way one follows Standards A and B, one can explain why the Framers implemented their concern with free speech differently in Article I, section 6, than they did in the first amendment. No matter how great a danger or offense a particular legislative speech may occasion, it is crucially important that every member of Congress be able to make it without fear of retaliation. By contrast, one may tolerate impositions upon some speeches among the general populace, so long as the free trade in ideas is not generally burdened by the government. Therefore, the Framers protected every speech or debate in Congress by means of Article I, section 6, and protected only the quality of freedom of expression outside of Congress by means of the first amendment.

If this explanation for the difference between the language of the first amendment and Article I, section 6, is correct, one may infer that the Framers sensed the difference between following a rule in the form of Standard A and a rule in the form of Standard B, and that they intentionally drafted the speech and press clause in the form of Standard A. It follows, then, that the first amendment guarantees that the general quality of freedom of speech and publication may not be impaired, but does not protect particular speeches or publications.

> Freedom of speech and debate in Congress shall not be impeached or questioned in any court, or place out of Congress. . . .

Similarly, the Pinckney plan presented to the Constitutional Convention provided:

> In each House a Majority shall constitute a Quorum to do business — Freedom of Speech and Debate in the legislature shall not be impeached or Questioned in any place out of it. . . .

3 *Records of the Federal Convention of 1787* (ed. M. Farrand, 1911), 597. Toward the end of the Convention the same language was referred to the Committee of Style and Arrangement, which without explanation changed it to the language of the current provision. 2 id. at 567, 593.

It is interesting to note that Meiklejohn's meta-interpretation leads him to equate the protection of Article 1, §6, and the speech and press clause:

> In these respects, the Constitution gives to all "the people" the same protection of freedom which, under Article 1, sec. 6(1), it provides for their legislative agents. . . . Just as our agents must be free in their use of their delegated powers, so the people must be free in the exercise of their reserved powers.

Meiklejohn, "The First Amendment as an Absolute," *1961 Sup. Ct. Rev.* 245, 256.

Chapter 3

Abracadabra

"The Adaptation of Copyright Law to Video Games" (1982)

"Three Common Fallacies in the User Interface Copyright Debate" (1990)

"The User Interface: Copyright? Or a Right to Copy?" (1990)

"Novelty, Scope, and the Shared Geometry of Patent and Copyright Protection" (1990)

According to Wikipedia, *Computer Space* was the first video game; it was released in 1970. Atari introduced *Pong* in arcades in 1974, *Pac-Man* was released in Japan in 1980, and *Tetris* hit the marketplace in 1984. Where there's money, there's litigation, and lawsuits between the video game proprietors began soon afterward.

The resulting body of law provided a valuable study in the question of how judges reach decisions in an area in which the standard rules — the "black letter law" — do not easily apply, and whether and to what extent the words that seem to resolve legal issues in one context are useful tools when the context has changed. The video game cases were "early movers" in this field, followed in quick succession by cases dealing more directly with the application of copyright law to computer software more generally. The specific question in both the video game and the software cases had to do with what judges and lawyers are fond of calling the "idea–expression dichotomy" in copyright law. The expression springs from the Supreme Court's decision in the celebrated case *Mazer v. Stein*,[1] in which the Court upheld copyright in the design (a human figure) of lamp bases, notwithstanding their utilitarian use: "Unlike a patent, a copyright gives no exclusive right to the art disclosed; protection is given only to the expression of the idea — not the idea itself. . . . The dichotomy of protection for the aesthetic is not beauty and utility but art for the copyright and the invention of original and ornamental design for design patents."[2] The current Copyright

---

[1] 347 U.S. 201 (1954).
[2] Id. at 217–18.

Act has a much longer list of things that copyright does not reach: "In no case does copyright protection for an original work of authorship extend to any idea, procedure, process, system, method of operation, concept, principle, or discovery, regardless of the form in which it is described, explained, illustrated, or embodied in such work."[3] This longer list is, however, routinely discarded in copyright case law and discussion in favor of the simpler "dichotomy" of "idea" and "expression."

Thus, it is said that everything falls into one of two buckets: either an "idea" or an "expression," and never the twain shall meet. In the context of games, the mantra was that "copyright does not protect games" because "rules of play" fall neatly into the "idea" bucket and therefore are not protected by copyright.

These propositions lost their moorings in the context of video games. In the previously "leading" cases, the rules of play were either unoriginal or so trivially simple as to merit no protection. Their pictorial and graphic elements were plainly distinguished from the rules and, what's more, closely resembled traditional graphic objects of copyright protection and therefore constituted copyrightable "expression."[4] By contrast, in video games such as *Pac-Man*, *Space Invaders*, *Tetris*, and *Pong*, the "rules of play" were largely new and extremely difficult to distinguish from the graphic features. Take *Tetris* as an example: Can one separate the shapes of the objects from the rules of their stacking? This put great pressure on the "black letter law" because the words used to identify "ideas" and "expressions" in earlier games proved useless in the context of video games. It was as if one were trying to drive a Phillips-head screw with a flat-head screwdriver.

We are back to Wittgenstein's builders here. Like the words "block" and "slab" in Wittgenstein's language game, "idea" and "expression" work well enough a case like *Mazer v. Stein*, where the "idea" is to have a lamp base

---

[3] 17. U.S.C. §102(b). Without providing specific justification for the specific words in this list in Section 102(b), the legislative history cites *Mazer v. Stein* to justify the Act's requirement in its definition of "pictorial, graphic and sculptural works" that "the design of a useful article, as defined in this section, shall be considered a pictorial, graphic, or sculptural work only if, and only to the extent that, such design incorporates pictorial, graphic, or sculptural features that can be identified separately from, and are capable of existing independently of, the utilitarian aspects of the article." See Report (of the House Judiciary Committee) No. 94-1476, at 53–57 (94th Congress, 2d Session, 1976). This concept is consistent with the Act's thoroughgoing Platonism, by which the copyrighted "work," really a Platonic Form, is defined as being separate from and existing independently of any particular embodiment of it.

[4] Descriptions of the "leading cases" can be found *infra*.

shaped like a human and its "expression" is the particular human form embodied in a particular lamp base. Adding a high-falutin' word like "dichotomy" cloaks the distinction with intellectual respectability, making the words seem precision instruments easily identifying what is or is not copyrightable. But in a new context such as video games, the words turn out to be worse than useless: like a magic wand or talisman that has suddenly lost its power, they don't actually help decide anything, but by force of judicial precedent, they demand use and application. It's as if Wittgenstein's builders were plunked down in an alien environment — plumbing, say — containing nothing they could have identified as "blocks" and "slabs" but had no other words with which to communicate and were in fact required, perhaps by the law or their private custom, to use one word or the other. Confronted with plungers, pipe wrenches, PVC pipes, and ball valves, and with only two words at their disposal, how would they communicate or work together?

Sophisticated jurists are well aware of this problem. The greatest of them, Learned Hand,[5] said it best in the venerable case *Nichols v. Universal Pictures Corp*[6]:

> Upon any work, and especially upon a play, a great number of patterns of increasing generality will fit equally well, as more and more of the incident is left out. The last may perhaps be no more than the most general statement of what the play is about, and at times might consist only of its title; but there is a point in this series of abstractions where they are no longer protected, since otherwise the playwright could prevent the use of his "ideas," to which, apart from their expression, his property is never extended. . . . Nobody has ever been able to fix that boundary, and nobody ever can.

In other words, there is no clear boundary between "idea" and "expression," and one can stare at the words all day without finding an answer to the question of what copyright protects and what is left either to the public

---

[5] It didn't hurt that Hand was equipped with an undergraduate degree in philosophy from Harvard. I presumptuously take pleasure in having the same background myself.

[6] 45 F.2d 119 (2d Cir. 1930). Sadly, and predictably, Hand's sophistication has be translated into the "abstractions test," as if lawyers and judges could deploy a kind of legal litmus paper that would turn blue or red depending on whether a thing was "idea" or "expression." I believe it would not do a disservice to Hand to say that this simplification of his thought would have appalled him. The whole point of his analysis was that there is no test – as he said, nobody can fix the boundary.

domain or to the domain of patents. But this begs the question, if the words do not and cannot answer the question, how can the scope of copyright protection be decided? Or, more generally, how can there be a reasoned basis for any judicial decision?[7]

One of the striking features in Hand's *Nichols* opinion is his sophistication and humor in describing the copyrighted and accused works, *Abie's Irish Rose* and the allegedly infringing movie, *The Cohens and the Kellys,* and the extent to which he draws on his own command of the liberal arts to inform his decision about the scope of copyright. Hand discusses Shakespeare's *Twelfth Night,* considering whether and how its plot or characters might be infringed if copyright in it subsisted; he digresses into Einstein's theory of relativity and Darwin's *On the Origin of Species.* He addresses directly the policy question to be decided: whether the extension of copyright to the plot and characters of *Abie's Irish Rose* would confer an unreasonable "monopoly" on the topic of "a quarrel between a Jewish and an Irish father, the marriage of their children, the birth of grandchildren and a reconciliation," concluding "We have to decide how much [the plaintiff's copyright covers], and while we are as aware as any one that the line, wherever it is drawn, will seem arbitrary, that is no excuse for not drawing it; it is a question such as courts must answer in nearly all cases. Whatever may be the difficulties a priori, we have no question on which side of the line this case falls. A comedy based upon conflicts between Irish and Jews, into which the marriage of their children enters, is no more susceptible of copyright than the outline of Romeo and Juliet."[8] Using another phrase not found in the Copyright Act, but sometimes instructive and helpful, the tableau of hostile ethnic families tragically linked by young lovers would be considered a *scène à faire*: a common dramatic structure around which many dramatic works have been built. These are the raw materials of dramatic invention, used by every author. And, where all else fails, a court can decide that the accused's borrowing was a "fair use" because it "transformed" the original in a way that was of benefit to society.[9]

---

[7] As noted in Chapter 2, one suspects that the judicial "originalists," like me when I wrote the *Harvard Law Review* note, yearn for a linguistic formula that constrains or at least powerfully informs judicial decision making.

[8] Ibid.

[9] See *Campbell v. Acuff Rose, Inc.*, 510 U.S. 569 (1994). A particularly telling example of the application of the doctrine of fair use to justify the most comprehensive copying is the Second Circuit's decision in *The Authors Guild, Inc. v. Google, Inc.*, 721 F. 3d 132 (2d Cir. 2013), which quite explicitly grounded its decision on the public benefit of the Google search engine.

Hand thus places his decision in the context in which it arose: literature, plays, and motion pictures, and considers the impact his decision will have on other playwrights or screenwriters. His conclusion allows anyone to be able to make another play or movie about ethnic conflict without fear of copyright retribution. His decision is informed not by the words "idea" and "expression," but by a deep knowledge of the subject matter and consideration of the impact his ruling will have on the field. At the conclusion of his opinion, he disfavors the expert testimony that had been adduced during the trial, in effect, as a waste of time. And surely it had been when the jurist was none other than Learned Hand.

Another fine example of the policy behind the "idea–expression dichotomy" is the drafting of legal agreements. Faced with the need to draft an agreement, the first question any lawyer asks is, "Do I have an example of a similar contract, or can I get one?" With a precedent in hand, the lawyer will copy as much of the precedential form as possible, for several basic reasons. First, standard forms accrete language like scar tissue. Whenever something goes wrong in a transaction, the form will be revised to try to keep it from going wrong in the future. There may be no record of the injury giving rise to the scar language, but removing the language carries the risk of exposing the next transaction to a repeat of the original injury. Second, to the extent that a form is used by others, the form will reflect the "standard of care" for the type of transaction. Third, and perhaps most compellingly, drafting from scratch without reference to precedential agreements and language would both be extremely costly and also likely to miss issues that the standard forms address: it is very hard to think of everything.

For all these reasons, when lawyers draft agreements, they completely disregard copyright. Lawyers crib from each others' documents enthusiastically and continuously. There is no question that the expression in a detailed legal agreement would be considered copyrightable authorship in any other context, but lawyers don't give the slightest thought to the question of who might be the author and whether a license would be necessary to "borrow" from it. Short of taking a form book and republishing it verbatim as one's own (which is not the practice of law; it's the business of publishing), the legal profession has never tried to stop the practice of basing one agreement on a precedential agreement.

If a lawyer bothered to consider the question, she might say that virtually every clause in a legal agreement is an uncopyrightable "idea," or a *scène à faire.*[10] Any other conclusion would require lawyers to investigate the copyright provenance of every document they reference before writing a contract. Such a result would make the practice of law, already hugely expensive, incomparably more expensive, not to mention borderline incompetent if lawyers were making up documents out of thin air as they go along. The problem here is not that the law is unclear — there is no question that a legal document is copyrightable authorship to the extent it is original.[11] The problem is that in the context of legal practice, copyrightable expression must, as a practical matter, be reduced to the narrowest possible range if absurd results are to be avoided.

One might almost say that when it comes to copyrightable expression, familiarity breeds contempt. The better one understands an art, and can practice it, the more one realizes that much of what the author does is to practice a learned skill that has rules that all practitioners follow. And most creative people operate within groups that cross-fertilize with a welter of new ideas that are shared, exchanged, and developed within the group.[12] Improvisational music can seem wonderfully original, but any jazz musician can tell you that he or she is following a set of rules: resolution to a tonic through the circle of fifths, using the pentatonic scale or a seven-tone scale in an Ionian or Mixolydian mode, the 12-bar blues or AABA song form — and on and on.[13] Painters understand and use the color wheel when mixing and applying their colors, and the rules of perspective, shading, and form, whether in abstractions or representational art. Writers of television scripts understand

---

[10] One might argue that each contract is the product of evolutionary change, and one can no more find the original author of a contract than, short of creationism, one can find the original creator of a particular species. There is a difference though: each contractual iteration has an author, and that author in principle holds copyright in whatever he or she added that was not found in the predecessor. It is fair to say that lawyers never trouble themselves to consider who the author of the version they are cribbing from was, much less what that author may have contributed.

[11] See, e.g., *William A. Graham Co. v. Houghey*, 430 F. Supp 2d 258 (E.D. Pa. 2006) (holding that certain "Standard Paragraphs" contained in a manual for insurance brokers were subject to copyright and were infringed when a broker copied the paragraphs without permission in working for new employer). Notably, the defendants in this case were not lawyers using the form paragraphs to practice law.

[12] See J. Silbey, *The Eureca Myth* (2014).

[13] Improvisational jazz is another art in which copyright is completely disregarded. Any improvisation on a jazz standard could be considered an infringing derivative work without the permission of the copyright holder, but to the author's knowledge no such claim has ever been lodged.

and follow the Aristotelian principles of comedy and tragedy,[14] and poets, even those as unconventional as e e cummings, follow rules of meter, rhyme, and form. All of these structures would undoubtedly be recognized as uncopyrightable "ideas," at least by courts familiar with the genres. Nobody plays 13-bar blues.

Writing computer software has much in common with drafting contracts. Contracts and software programs can both be understood as algorithms that translate inputs into outputs. If you default, then this happens. If your deliverable is accepted, then that happens. Both contracts and software often reference and rely on elements that lie outside the four corners of the contract or program (notwithstanding "integration" clauses in the contracts). A standard clause in a security agreement is an example: "In the event of a default, the secured party shall have the rights of a foreclosing creditor under Article 9 of the UCC." In programming terms, this is a call to a library of rights, just as computer programs include "calls" to "libraries" of code lying outside the four corners of the particular program. And, most tellingly, when a programmer has at hand a routine that correctly employs an algorithm or solves a programming problem, the programmer will be loathe to try to rewrite the same thing with different code. Also, like lawyers, computer programmers do not code from scratch. Many tried-and-true code routines are widely available on the Web in common programming languages like Java, and it would be foolish for a programmer to attempt to re-create their functionality from scratch. This insight is fundamental to the "open source" movement, which employs the "copyleft" concept to implement the principle of group sourcing. One might say that legal drafting has been open source for a very much longer period of time.

One might expect, then, that caselaw applying copyright to computer programs would consider the impact their decisions would have on the realities of computer programming at least as much as trying to divine what is "idea" and what is "expression" in a computer program, just as Hand considered the impact on writers in considering the scope of copyright in *Abie's Irish Rose*. Alas, this has not been the case. As chronicled in the articles in this chapter, the courts instead struggled mightily to make sense of the "idea–expression dichotomy" in the digital world, coming up with such absurdities as the "abstraction-filtration-comparison test" for copyright

---

[14] To use one example, virtually every episode of *Curb Your Enthusiasm* employs the principle of Aristotelian comedy involving a mistake that has consequences, committed by less-then-noble personages, that is resolved at the end — omitting, however, the multiple marriages Shakespeare provides, in closer alliance with Aristotle, in his comedies.

infringement.[15] From the name, one would have thought that it was a manual for a high school chemistry lab rather than a means of regulating and promoting an important commercial industry.

As already noted, the first paper in this chapter addresses the question of what happens when courts consider copyright protection in a field, video games, with which they are not familiar; indeed, they are largely ignorant. The predictable result, where the courts had no idea what the creators of the games would consider raw material that anybody could use, was overprotection for the early games. The two papers I published in 1990 continue in this vein, arguing that the software industry was pushing too far in the direction of protection, particularly for the "user interface" of computer programs, where the programs met the people using them.

These papers were written during a heady time in the software/personal computer industry. It was all new territory, and everyone had the sense — fairly accurately — that new law was about to be made and the further sense — fairly inaccurately — that a great deal depended on the direction the law would take. Would the law allow such broad protection for all elements of computer programs that innovation would be stifled, or would protection be so curtailed that investment in innovation would be equally discouraged?

As it turned out, the question of copyright in "user interface" was never definitively resolved, and the fact that it was never resolved did not deter in the slightest the success of the software industry. In 1995, the First Circuit in *Lotus v. Borland*[16] held that fundamental aspects of "user interface" are not copyrightable subject matter.[17] Other circuits, notably the Third Circuit in the 1986 case *Whelan v. Jaslow,*[18] had reached an opposite conclusion. In 1996 the Supreme Court split 4–4 in the appeal of the *Lotus v. Borland* case,[19] and the inconsistency among the circuits was never resolved.

---

[15] *Computer Associates v. Altai, Inc.*, 982 F.2d 693, (2d Cir. 1992).

[16] *Lotus Dev. Corp. v. Borland Int'l,* Inc., 49 F.3d 807 (1995).

[17] I represented one of the original defendants in a series of lawsuits brought by Lotus against companies it believed to be infringing rights in its seminal computer program, Lotus 1-2-3. The case against my client, Mosiac Software, never went to judgment, the client having been exhausted by the cost of discovery. Sadly the First Circuit's decision in *Borland v. Lotus* largely vindicated Mosaic's position that the "user interface" of Lotus 1-2-3 was not copyrightable subject matter. On the impediments to justice under the Rules of Civil Procedure, see the discussion of the legal process in chapter 1.

[18] *Whelan Assocs., Inc. v. Jaslow Dental Laboratory, Inc.,* 797 F.2d 1222 (3d Cir. 1986),

[19] *Lotus Dev. Corp. v. Borland Int'l, Inc.,* 516 U.S. 233 (1996).

There is something to be learned from the fact that the sky hasn't fallen as a result; the software industry remains alive and well, and we seem to get along just fine not knowing the Whole Answer. There are a couple of possible explanations for why. At a very general level, one might say that in the realm of commerce, very widely placed legal guide rails are more than sufficient; indeed, they may be preferable to minutely circumscribed areas for operation that require attention to legal and regulatory detail, or worse yet, investment in litigation, at the expense of innovation and development. In computer software, it is perhaps enough to know that you can't copy wholesale entire computer programs without the permission of the copyright owner, but you can make programs that perform highly analogous tasks. Despite the uncertainty left in the caselaw, copyright litigation over computer programs seems to have abated since the early days of the 1980s and 1990s.

A second, and related, reason is that the companies involved in the field fill in the wide gaps left in the decided law through the medium of contracts — for computer software, licensing agreements. Computer licensing agreements have taken on the character of an enormous body of private law that is enforced, or at least announced, through the ubiquitous "Accept" buttons associated with virtually every computer program that is not covered by a negotiated agreement. The proprietors of computer software, when left to their own devices to create their own law in this way, oftentimes get the bit in their teeth and go much further in asserting rights in their products than seems healthy for the industry — just as they did in asserting rights in software in the 1980s. But, lastly, there has been an important antidote in a second thread in the history of the software industry, namely the open source movement. The open source movement, which originally pitted ideologues like Richard Stallman against the likes of Mitch Kapor and Bill Gates, can be considered a private antidote to the inclination of software companies and courts to assert or grant excessive protection to computer programs. Proponents of open source are usually persons steeped in the programming culture, who, with considerable justification, see writing computer programs as a collective enterprise, not a proprietary one. To a remarkable extent, this movement has made inroads even in the largest corporations, especially those like IBM, whose revenues are not exclusively dependent on licensing computer software. The net effect of a broad swath of legal uncertainty over copyright protection combined with the private back-filling of software licensing and the open source movement has arguably reached something of a happy medium, in which the software industry has thrived with only occasional bouts of litigation.

Not so, however, when it comes to patents. The final paper in this set addresses the emerging question of whether and to what extent patent protection could also be extended to computer software, and how the principles underlying patent and copyright protection might be reconciled. Patenting software was quite a new concept at the time this article was written; many practitioners assumed that software was outside the realm of patent protection, being more in the nature of mathematical formulae or algorithms that traditionally were excluded from patents. One of the inventors of VisiCalc, Dan Bricklin, famously lamented that in 1979, when VisiCalc was shown to the public, he was advised that he had a 10-percent chance of patenting it. The Supreme Court's 1981 case of *Diamond v. Diehr*[20] opened the door to patenting software-driven inventions. Hot on its heels, the Court of Appeals for the Federal Circuit was created in 1982. For the first time, appeals of patent cases were heard by sympathetic patent attorneys sitting on the CAFC, and the survival rate for patents on appeal jumped from single digits in some circuits to fifty percent in the CAFC.[21] Under the tutelage of the CAFC, patenting software-based products became the norm, leading eventually to the controversial patenting of "business methods," which was finally curtailed by the Supreme Court in the *Alice* case in 2014.[22] If the lax rules governing copyright in computer software has contributed to the health of the industry, as argued above, the tight guidelines implied by multiple and overlapping patents has had the opposite effect, leading to large expenditures for both patent prosecution and litigation that, at least arguably, has not been a boon to the software industry.

In his seminal article *On the Complex Economics of Patent Scope* (1990), Rob Merges concluded that patent law works fairly well for industries such as pharmaceuticals, in which the inventions are by their nature not cumulative (i.e., one pharmaceutical's chemical structure or effectiveness rarely depends on the structure of another even when their therapeutic effects are similar — compare Tylenol and aspirin, for example), but not so well in technologies that are by their nature accretive or cumulative (Professor Merges's examples: aircraft and radio). In the latter case, one patentee's rights tend to interfere with another's development, particularly when the transaction costs of cross-licenses are too high or the personalities involved are opposed to licensing.

Computer software definitely falls into the cumulative camp. Like the clauses in a legal document, most programs accrete routines and algorithms whose original authors are lost in the mists of software history. The very most

---

[20] *Diamond v. Diehr*, 450 U.S. 175 (1981).

[21] My first case as a law clerk in the Third Circuit, in 1974, was a patent case. In handing me the briefs my predecessor's clerk said, "Remember, Tom, no patents are valid in the Third Circuit." This was almost the case; I believe the survival rate for patents there was on the order of three percent.

[22] *Alice Corp. v. CLS Bank Int'l.*, 573 U.S. 208 (2014).

successful regions for software development — Silicon Valley preeminently, Washington state, now Colorado, tomorrow, perhaps, Massachusetts[23] — are states in which noncompete clauses are largely unenforceable, permitting programmers to jump from one job to another, cross-fertilizing the field with learning and code derived from multiple sources. Copyright's limitations, manifest in principles such as *scènes à faire*, fair use, "merger," and even the idea–expression distinction, as well as the failure ever to resolve fundamental questions such as the scope of copyright in user interfaces, supplemented by the open source movement, fostered the development of the industry. The burst of copyright litigation over computer software in the 1980s died out not so much because the application of copyright to software became clear, but because it was never completely clarified, discouraging litigation whose outcome would be speculative at best.

The radical extension of patents into the software field compromised these practical gains in the field of copyright. Patent law includes nothing comparable to the copyright doctrines that moderate the otherwise stifling effect that broad intellectual property claims can have on a burgeoning new industry. The result was a kind of intellectual property land grab, reflected in the filing of thousands of patent applications extending to the furthest reaches of patent law — "anything under the sun that is made by man,"[24]which came to mean business methods and the software implementing them. The harm to the industry was widely recognized, first outside the United States, where patents on business methods were never allowed, and then finally by the Supreme Court in its *Alice* decision in 2010. Meanwhile, the industry itself, or at least the players in the industry with sufficient resources to build large patent portfolios, reacted by pooling and cross-licensing their patents, which was the patent law equivalent to the open source movement in copyright.[25]

---

[23] It is a remarkable fact that Massachusetts, whose famous universities well positioned it for a leadership role in software development, had been in the forefront of software development in the late twentieth century, with companies like Wang and Lotus based there, but quickly fell behind California and Washington state. One speculates that the enforceability of noncompete clauses in employment agreements had at least as much to do with this as the weather. Within the past year Massachusetts very belatedly enacted legislation severely limiting the enforceability of noncompete clauses. MGLA, Ch. 149, sec. 24L (effective October 1, 2018).

[24] *Diamond v. Chakrabarty*, 447 U.S. 303, 309 (1980) (holding a genetically modified bacterium patentable).

[25] The Antitrust Guidelines for the Licensing of Intellectual Property of the US Department of Justice and Federal Trade Commission, first recognized the pro-competitive benefits of patent pooling in 1995.

The Adaptation of Copyright Law to Video Games*

Video games are big business. The earliest games appeared in the early 1970s,[1] and by 1981 a single game, *Pac-Man,* had generated $150 million in sales over a thirteen-month period[2] and $1 billion in revenues for arcade operators in the course of a year.[3] Sales of another game, *Scramble,* totaled $20 million over a two-month period during 1981.[4] Games played in arcades have become so popular that the manufacturers have felt constrained to protest, perhaps too much, that the games are not "reprehensible diversions for idlers."[5]

As the video game business has grown, video game competition has grown as well. *Galactic Invaders* wars with *Galaxian*; *Asteroids* and *Meteors* collide; *Pac-Man* contends with *K.C. Munchkin.*[6] Video game owners and licensees are eager to stake out their market shares, resorting in part to suits and threats of suits to achieve their business goals. One video game purveyor, Atari, actually fielded a nationwide advertising campaign warning that it "registers the audiovisual works associated with its games," that it "considers its games proprietary," and that it will "vigorously [enforce] these copyrights."[7]

Despite the hopes of Atari and its kind that the courts will protect their market penetration, video games themselves are, in many ways, perversely unsuited to traditional forms of legal protection, particularly protection against copyright infringement. The owner of the copyright in a popular game such as *Pac-Man*

---

1 One of the first video games was *Pong,* which was introduced in 1972. *Washington Post,* Mar. 11, 1982, at DCl (District Weekly), col. 1.

2 See *Atari, Inc. v. North American Philips Consumer Elecs. Corp.*, 2 Copyright L. Rep. (CCH) ¶25,363, at 17,045–46 (N.D. Ill. Dec. 4, 1981), rev'd, 672 F.2d 607 (7th Cir.). cert. denied, 51 U.S.L.W. 3258 (U.S. Oct. 4, 1982).

3 See *Wall Street Journal,* Mar. 12, 1982, at 25, col. 3.

4 See *Stern Elecs., Inc. v. Kaufman,* 669 F.2d 852, 854 (2d Cir. 1982).

5 T. Lippman, "Warner's Atari Video Games are a Rocketship to Riches," *Washington Post,* Nov. 8, 1981, at Fl, col. 1.

6 See cases discussed infra text accompanying notes 85–90, 106–22, 124–42.

7 See the Atari advertisement appearing in the November 1981 issue of *Creative Computing,* at 99. Despite the amount of litigation on copyright in video games, surprisingly little has been written on the subject. However, a useful overview of the subject, including a detailed discussion of the interplay of the games and the computer software used to operate them, is Jones, "Video Game Litigation and the 1976 Copyright Act: The Idea of Games, the Expression of Aliens and the Underlying Computer Software," 1 *J. Copyright, Entertainment and Book Law* 17 (1982).

may be as jealous of its method and pattern of play as he is about the particular colors and shapes of the game's "gobbler" and "ghost monsters."[8] Furthermore, creation of the game's method of play may involve significant creativity of the type the Copyright Act is intended to protect.[9] But affording protection to the game's method of play is, at least superficially, inconsistent with venerable principles of copyright law, in particular, those stating that it does not protect "games," "methods of operation," "ideas," and "utilitarian" aspects of pictorial works.[10] The limits of copyright protection must therefore be stretched if they are to serve the interests of video game proprietors.

---

[8] See infra text accompanying notes 124–42 for a more detailed description of *Pac-Man* and its comparison with the similar game *K.C. Munchkin.*

[9] See infra text accompanying notes 212–15, 246–49; Copyright Act of 1976, 17 U.S.C. §§101–810 (1976 & Supp. V 1981). The Constitution empowers Congress to grant authors and inventors monopolies to "promote the Progress of Science and useful Arts. . . ." U.S. Const. art. I, §8, cl. 8. But the Constitution requires such monopolies to be "for limited Times." Id. If the author's monopoly over a copyrighted work or patented invention were not limited, it would stifle the very progress it is designed to foster. In the case of patents, Congress has chosen to limit severely their duration — a patent lasts only 17 years — while permitting the patent to preempt all other appropriation of the same "invention," no matter how expressed. See 35 U.S.C. §154 (Supp. V 1981). The duration of copyright protection is very long — more than the life of a man. See 17 U.S.C. §302 (1976 & Supp. V 1981) (for works created on or after January 1, 1978, copyright endures for the author's lifetime plus 50 years, unless the work is a work for hire or is an anonymous or pseudonymous work, in which case it endures for 75 years from the date of publication or 100 years from the date of creation, whichever is less). Nevertheless, the scope of copyright protection does not extend any further than the expression of ideas found in the copyrighted work. See infra note 10.

[10] The distinction between "ideas" and "expressions of ideas" is found in §102(b) of the Copyright Act which declares: "[i]n no case does copyright protection for an original work of authorship extend to any idea, procedure, process, system, method of operation, concept, principle, or discovery, regardless of the form in which it is described, explained, illustrated or embodied in such work." 17 U.S.C. §102(b) (1976 & Supp. V 1981). By implication, only the expression of ideas, of methods of operation, and the like receive protection. The policy that copyright does not protect ideas is a vestige of an historically much broader exception to copyright protection. See infra notes 216-25 and accompanying text. See generally B. Kaplan, *An Unhurried View of Copyright,* 1–38 (1967) (noting, at 14, that copyright once included only the exclusive right to copy the original text and did not include any right to derivative works).

Like a theorem of geometry, the proposition that copyright protects only the expression of ideas has corollaries. One is that copyright protects the design of a utilitarian work only to the extent that the design incorporates "pictorial, graphic, or sculptural features that can be identified separately from, and are capable of

Against the backdrop of the blackletter law that "copyright does not protect games," this paper will review recent decisions in which courts wrestled for the first time with copyright protection for video games.[11] It will be seen that

---

existing independently of, the utilitarian aspects of the article." 17 U.S.C. §101 (1976 & Supp. V 1981). A second is that copyright does not protect games. See 1 M. Nimmer, *Nimmer on Copyright* §2.18 [H][3] (1982) (citing *Chamberlin v. Uris Sales Corp.*, 56 F. Supp. 987 (S.D.N.Y. 1944), aff'd, 150 F.2d 512 (2d Cir. 1945)); see also *Morrissey v. Procter & Gamble Co.*, 379 F.2d 675 (1st Cir. 1967); *Affiliated Enters., Inc. v. Gruber*, 86 F.2d 958 (1st Cir. 1936). In practice, this seems to mean that copyright does not inhere in the rules for a game, although the more arbitrary aspects of the game, such as the graphics and pictorial design of a board game, may be afforded copyright protection. See infra text accompanying notes 20–27. One rationale for the dogma is that the rules of a game are its idea and copyright does not protect ideas, but only their expression. An alternative formulation, probably derived from *Baker v. Selden*, 101 U.S. 99 (1879), is that the rules of a game are "utilitarian" and therefore outside the scope of copyright protection. See generally 1 M. Nimmer, supra, §2.18. Related to this is the view that protection for a game's method of play or rules would require a patent. See 1 M. Nimmer, supra, §l.08[E], at 1-55 to 1-56. Although unusual, patent protection for a game is not unheard of. The Parker Brothers Company originally protected its rights in the game Monopoly by means of a patent. See *Anti-Monopoly, Inc. v. General Mills Fun Group*, 611 F.2d 296, 299 (9th Cir. 1979).

[11] All video games are based on complicated computer programs, usually embedded in a microprocessor chip. It is possible to copy a computer-based game by copying the underlying program. In *Data Cash Sys., Inc. v. JS&A Group, Inc.*, 628 F.2d 1038 (7th Cir. 1980), for example, the plaintiff alleged infringement of copyright in a computer program capable of playing chess. The court held that copyright in the program had been lost under the Copyright Act of 1909 by failure to place a copyright notice on the microprocessor chip embodying the program. Id at 1042–44. However, it is also possible to replicate significant features of a video game without copying the program used by the copyright holder to operate the game. As the court said in *Stern Elecs., Inc. v. Kaufman*:

> [Registering the program] would not have prevented a determined competitor from manufacturing a "knock-off" of "Scramble" that replicates precisely the sights and sounds of the game's audiovisual display. This could be done by writing a new computer program that would interact with the hardware components of a video game to produce on the screen the same images seen in "Scramble," accompanied by the same sounds. Such replication is possible because many different computer programs can produce the same "results," whether those results are an analysis of financial records or a sequence of images and sounds.

669 F.2d 852, 855 (2d Cir. 1982) (discussing copyright registration of video game "Scramble"). The underlying computer program may be protected by one or more of copyright, trade secret law, or (arguably) a patent. See Rilee, The Protection of

the early decisions swing widely between cases in which courts disregarded or paid only lip service to the established dogmas, resulting in extreme overprotection for the games, and other cases in which courts applied the blackletter rules so unbendingly that they provide little or no protection for the games. It will be argued that the courts' difficulty in finding a good fit between copyright law and the facts in video game cases is the direct result of three pitfalls of copyright adjudication: the surprisingly persistent fiction that "ideas" and "expressions" may be distinguished a priori without examining the context in which the subject works are created and the policies underlying copyright protection; the use of copyright to remedy trademark infringement and other forms of unfair competition; and the use of the "ordinary observer test"; as a prescription for copyright remedies rather than as a criterion for infringement. Some suggestions will be made for avoiding these pitfalls, both in video game cases and elsewhere. Based on the courts' struggle to adjust copyright law to video games, some conclusions will also be drawn about the process by which law reshapes itself in a new environment.

Background: Video games compared with "leading cases" establishing the blackletter law that copyright does not protect games

"Copyright does not protect games" is an example of a principle of law that may have grown larger and more rigid than the facts of the seminal cases warranted. For example, in *Chamberlin v. Uris Sales Corp.*,[12] the plaintiff claimed copyright in a game called *Acy-Ducy* and unsuccessfully attempted to enjoin the sale of the defendant's similar game. The proof showed that "the game, with some variations, is the old Maskee game of India, taught to plaintiff by his grandmother, when he was eight years of age."[13] The plaintiff alleged that he had added a few new twists to the old game, but these few twists did not

---

Property Rights in Computer Software, 19 *Pub. Ent. Advert. & Allied Fields L.Q.* 265, 269 (1980); Jones supra note 7, at 22–26, 44–48. A discussion of the various means for protection of the underlying program is beyond the scope of this article. All of the video game cases discussed in the text involve alleged infringement of copyright in a video game without alleged infringement or conversion of the copyright holder's rights (if any) in the computer program used to operate the game. Cf. *Williams Elecs., Inc. v. Artic Int'l,* 685 F.2d 870, 872, 876-77 (3d Cir. 1982) (infringement of computer program alleged).

[12] 56 F. Supp. 987 (S.D.N.Y. 1944), aff'd, 150 F.2d 512 (2d Cir. 1945), cited in 1 M. Nimmer, supra note 10, §2.18[H][3], at 2-212, n. 69.

[13] 56 F. Supp. at 988.

persuade the court that he deserved credit for an original work of authorship.[14] Furthermore, the court doubted whether the similarity of the defendant's rules and board to the plaintiff's proved that the defendant had copied the plaintiff's game, because each party's rules and board "applied to a well known game played by many for many years."[15] Thus, the court's holding could be explained on either of two grounds sufficient in themselves — that the game was not an original work of authorship or that copying had not been proven — without reaching the question of whether copyright can extend to a game under circumstances when these other elements of infringement are proven.

Another venerable game case is *Affiliated Enterprises, Inc. v. Gruber.*[16] In *Gruber,* the "game" was a very simple promotional device used to attract patrons to movie theaters and other establishments by offering prizes selected on the basis of names and numbers drawn out of a receptacle.[17] In denying relief, the court did not even reach the infringement issue because the plaintiff had failed properly to plead copyright infringement.[18] The court also dismissed the plaintiff's closely related unfair competition claim, commenting that protection of such an elementary principle for the distribution of prizes would grant "a monopoly to the plaintiff, preventing any other person from entering the field."[19] This case is often cited for the proposition that copyright does not protect games, but at most, the case holds that an action for unfair competition will not lie for copying an artless commercial gimmick.

Despite the limitations of these "leading" cases, the principle that copyright does not protect games has embedded itself in the law, subject to one major exception — graphic and pictorial aspects of games (such as the visual designs of game boards and playing cards) are said to be copyrightable, as long as their copyright does not create a monopoly on the "method of play."[20] An example of a recent case exemplifying the method-of-play/nonessential graphics distinction is *Durham Industries, Inc. v. Tomy Corp.*[21] Among other things, the case involved counter-claims by Tomy that

---

[14] See id. ("the parts claimed by plaintiff to be original with him have not been shown to be such.")

[15] Id.

[16] 86 F.2d 958 (1st Cir. 1936), cited in 1 M. Nimmer, supra note 10, §2.18[H][3], at 2-212, n. 70.

[17] See 86 F.2d at 959.

[18] See id. at 961.

[19] Id.

[20] 1 M. Nimmer, supra note 10, §2.18[H][3].

[21] 630 F.2d 905 (2d Cir. 1980).

Durham's game *Mickey Mouse Peanut Putter* infringed Tomy's copyright in a game called Pass the Nuts. The court found that Pass the Nuts and *Mickey Mouse Peanut Putter* were "mechanically identical and structurally similar," each involving the use of push-buttons to move an object from starting point to goal.[22] However, the court described Durham's artwork for each game as "totally different" from Tomy's.[23] Tomy's *Pass the Nuts* was "designed to make it appear as if a bear, a rabbit, a monkey and a squirrel are attempting to throw an acorn from the ground up to the top of a tree."[24] By contrast, Durham's *Mickey Mouse Peanut Putter* "features Mickey Mouse, Minnie Mouse, Donald Duck and Pluto engaged in a game of golf."[25] Tomy argued that its copyrights protected the "sculpture" of each game, but the court rejected this argument, holding that Tomy had failed to identify any "sculptural" features which were not also utilitarian.[26]

Cases such as *Durham Industries, Chamberlin,* and *Gruber* lend themselves readily to the distinctions between ideas and expressions (or games and their graphics) drawn by the statutory and blackletter copyright law. A first characteristic shared by the rules and methods of play of the games in these leading cases is that they either were in the public domain or displayed a dismally low level of originality. *Chamberlin* is the most extreme example because the copyright holder, in that case, failed completely to show any original work of authorship in the *Acy-Ducy* game he sought to protect. Lack of originality characterizes the games in the other leading cases as well. Using a steering wheel to direct a toy car along a road, using a series of levers to push an object toward a goal, and offering prizes on the basis of names or numbers selected out of a receptacle are such elementary ideas that one might

---

22 Id. at 914.

23 Id. By analogous reasoning, the court also concluded that Durham's game *Mickey Mouse Star Ship* had not infringed copyright in Tomy's *Drive Yourself Crazy.* Id.

24 Id.

25 Id.

26 Id. at 914–15. See 17 U.S.C. §101 (1976 & Supp. V 1981) (definition of "Pictorial, graphic and sculptural works") ("the design of a useful article [can be protected as such a] pictorial, graphic, or sculptural work only if, and only to the extent that, such design incorporates pictorial, graphic, or sculptural features that can be identified separately from, and are capable of existing independently of, the utilitarian aspects of the article.").

question whether they constitute "original works of authorship" appropriate for protection under the Copyright Act.[27]

A second characteristic is that, unlike the methods of play, the graphic elements in these games do reflect originality. Examples are the animals in *Pass the Nuts* and the familiar Walt Disney figures in *Mickey Mouse Peanut Putter*. Combining this with the lack of originality found in the games' rules, it is easy to conclude that copyright protection should extend to the games' graphics, but not to their methods of play.[28]

A third characteristic, related to the first, is that the plaintiffs in the leading cases failed to show (and, indeed, probably could not show) that they had made substantial investments in the games they sought to protect. One guesses that thinking up a lottery based on names and numbers picked out of a receptacle or inventing *Pass the Nuts* required little more than a few minutes of the author's time. The Copyright Act does not require any significant investment as a prerequisite to copyright protection. However, most plaintiffs in infringement cases seek injunctive relief, which requires a showing of irreparable harm. With good reason, courts routinely consider the size of the investment a plaintiff stands to lose in assessing the question of irreparable harm.[29] An injunction, in effect, confers a long-term monopoly[30] for the copyrighted work and any "substantially similar" work;[31] a court would therefore be reluctant to issue an injunction unless the plaintiff can show a substantial investment of time or money or both. As a practical matter, therefore, the size of a plaintiff's investment figures importantly in many copyright infringement actions.

A fourth characteristic, best seen in *Durham Industries*, is that the games in these leading cases easily lend themselves to, and become paradigms for, the seemingly self-evident distinction between the games' "utilitarian" aspects, including their methods of play, and their more arbitrary and

---

[27] See 17 U.S.C. §102(a) (1976 & Supp. V 1981) ("Copyright protection subsists . . . in original works of authorship fixed in any tangible medium of expression. . . ."). For a discussion of the relevance of originality to copyright, see infra notes 246–49 and accompanying text.

[28] See supra note 26 (quoting the distinction made in the Copyright Act at 17 U.S.C. §101 (1976 & Supp. V 1981) between the graphic and the utilitarian aspects of useful articles).

[29] See, e.g., *Atari, Inc. v. North American Philips Consumer Elecs. Corp.*, 672 F.2d 607 (7th Cir.), cert. denied, 51 U.S.L.W. 3258 (U.S. Oct. 4, 1982) .

[30] See supra note 9.

[31] For a discussion of "substantial similarity," see generally infra note 75 and infra text accompanying notes 232 & 289–302.

"pictorial" features. In Tomy's and Durham's games of moving objects toward goals using levers, for example, one can describe the way the games are played without referring to the bears, rabbits, and Disney cartoon characters Tomy and Durham employed to add interest and appeal to the simple structure of the games.

Video games place great pressure on the statutory and blackletter formulations because they have none of the above characteristics. Take first the question of originality in the games' methods of play.[32] The very idea of a video game did not exist until only a very few years ago,[33] and the games' methods of play have become extremely complicated. The *Durham Industries* court described *Pass the Nuts* in three sentences totaling sixty-four words.[34] In *Atari, Inc. v. North American Philips Consumer Electronics Corp.*,[35] the appellate court's description of the video game *Pac-Man* required six paragraphs totaling more than 700 words,[36] and its description of the competing game, *K.C. Munchkin* required at least equal verbal space.[37] Although not discussed explicitly in *North American Philips*, it was implicit that substantial portions of the games' methods of play were not in the public domain and were invented out of whole cloth by their authors.[38]

An additional distinction between video games and the games in the leading cases is that the authors of video games invest at least as much of their talent and originality in the creation of new rules and methods of play as in the games' more arbitrary audiovisual effects.[39] For this reason, the graphics/rules-of-play distinction that appears in the context of video games may save the chaff while discarding the wheat — it would protect the occasionally mundane aspects of the games such as the shapes of their characters and the beeping sounds they emit while throwing the games' original and intriguing rules into the public domain.

---

32 This Article is concerned primarily with nonmimicking video games such as *Pac-Man*, *K.C. Munchkin*, and *Galaxian*, all of which are described infra text accompanying notes 85–90, 124–42. Such games should be distinguished from video versions of public domain games such as baseball and basketball. For video versions of the latter games, originality in the basic rules of play is obviously lacking.

33 One of the first video games was introduced in 1972. See supra note 1.

34 See 630 F.2d at 914.

35 672 F.2d 607 (7th Cir.). cert. denied, 51 U.S.L.W. 3258 (U.S. Oct. 4, 1982).

36 See id. at 610–11.

37 See id. at 611–13.

38 See the lower court's discussion of the method by which the author created *K.C. Munchkin*. 2 Copyright L. Rep. (CCH) ¶25,363, at 17,047–48 (N.D. Ill. Dec. 4, 1981).

30 See id.

A third distinction is that video games can be costly and time-consuming to create. Atari invested more than $1.5 million in "licensing, developing, and advertising its 'Pac-Man' home video game."[40] In *Stern Electronics, Inc. v. Kaufman*,[41] the district court found that "[d]evelopment of a new game requires substantial investment and takes between eight months to a year."[42] Just as the cost of creation is substantial, the windfall to a successful infringer can be shocking. In *Stern Electronics*, for example, the plaintiff had $20 million in sales during the period from March 1981 to May 1981.[43] The defendant, who was able to sell its "knock-off' game for $650 less per game than the plaintiff,[44] threatened to divert to itself a significant portion of these lucrative sales. Such substantial investments by the copyright holders and potential windfalls for the infringers generate powerful equity arguments for granting speedy and broad injunctive relief to the copyright holders.

A final distinction between video games and the games in the leading cases is that in many video games, the rules of play are partially disguised (from a copyright standpoint) in the games' audiovisual elements. One of the rules of *Pac-Man*, for example, is that the "gobbler" may consume "monsters" if the "monsters" are blue.[45] Without careful analysis of the game, one would describe the color of the monsters as a graphic element of the game, rather than as part of a rule of play. Similarly, the district court in *North American Philips* described *K.C. Munchkin* as utilizing in its play "a practically infinite number of mazes," appearing on a video screen.[46] The mazes are certainly "graphic," but as the lower court had noted, they affect "play tactics and technique."[47]

---

[40] Id. at 17,046.

[41] 523 F. Supp. 635 (E.D.N.Y. 1981), aff'd, 669 F.2d 852 (2d Cir. 1982).

[42] 523 F. Supp. at 638.

[43] See id.

[44] Id. An illegal copying of a video game is "known in the trade as a 'knock-off.'" 669 F.2d at 855. The district court described counterfeit models as "knock-ups," rather than "knock-offs," perhaps confusing illicit reproduction in the biological and computer programming fields. The slip was rectified by the court of appeals, which otherwise affirmed.

[45] *North American Philips*, 672 F.2d at 611.

[46] 2 Copyright L. Rep. (CCH) ¶25,363, at 17,046; see also 672 F.2d at 611 n.1 (describing "an almost indefinite variety of mazes.").

[47] 2 Copyright L. Rep. (CCH) ¶25,363, at 17,046. The Copyright Act proscribes relief for "sculptural" features that cannot be "identified separately from, and are capable of existing independently of, the utilitarian aspects of the article." 17 U.S.C. §101 (1976 & Supp. V 1981) (definition of "Pictorial, graphic, and sculptural works"). If video games were considered graphic works, and if the rules of play were considered "utilitarian" for purposes of the Copyright Act, then copyright protection of video games could be

In sum, strong equities favor the video game copyright holder; originality is found in the games' rules, and a video game's rules tend to be embedded in its graphics. As will be seen, this combination of factors resulted in early and surprisingly broad protection for copyright in video games.

Cases applying copyright law to video games

Technical considerations[48]

Before addressing the interesting question of the scope and nature of copyright protection for video games, it will be necessary to discuss briefly the more dreary issues related to the statutory requirements of fixation and registration. These issues include whether copyright inheres in the game itself or in the computer program generating the game and how one goes about registering a copyright claim.

It has become virtually a requirement of sound legal practice for defendants in video game cases to include in their pleadings the argument that "the original work of authorship is the computer program," which directs play of the game,[49] and not the game itself. This argument has been uniformly unsuccessful. Every court addressing the issue has held that video games are entitled to copyright

---

very limited indeed. Cf. 1 M. Nimmer, supra note 10, §2.18[H][3]. However, courts invariably characterize video games as audiovisual works rather than as graphic works. See, e.g., North American Philips, 2 Copyright L. Rep. (CCH) ¶25,363, at 17,045; see also cases cited infra note 50; Copyright Act §102(a) (6), 17 U.S.C. §102(a) (6) (1976 & Supp. V 1981) (subject matter of copyright, "motion pictures and other audiovisual works"). Section 101 of the Copyright Act provides that:

> "Audiovisual works" are works that consist of a series of related images which are intrinsically intended to be shown by the use of machines or devices such as projectors, viewers, or electronic equipment, together with accompanying sounds, if any, regardless of the nature of the material objects, such as films or tapes, in which the works are embodied.

17 U.S.C. §101 (1976 & Supp. V 1981). Moreover, unlike the definition of pictorial works in §101 of the Copyright Act, 17 U.S.C. §101 (1976 & Supp. V 1981), §102 of the Act, 17 U.S.C. §102 (1976 & Supp. V, 1981) does not require the expression of an idea to be "capable of existing independently of" the idea itself. But see infra note 170 and text accompanying note 231.

[48] The issues of fixation and deposit requirements discussed in this section appear in more detail and from a different standpoint in Jones, supra note 7, at 27–35.

[49] *Atari, Inc. v. Amusement World, Inc.*, 547 F. Supp. 222,226 (D. Md. 1981).

protection as audiovisual works independent of the underlying programs.[50] In *Stern Electronics, Inc. v. Kaufman*,[51] for example, the Second Circuit held that the "visual and aural features of the audiovisual display are plainly original variations sufficient to render the display copyrightable even though the underlying written program has an independent existence and is itself eligible for copyright."[52] The court of appeals also noted that the defendants' argument overlooked the fact that original authorship occurred when "[s]omeone first conceived what the audiovisual display would look like and sound like,"[53] rather than at the later point when the program was written.[54]

A second refrain added to most defendants' pleadings is the argument that the audiovisual displays in video games lack the requirement of "fixation"[55] because the sequence of sounds and images varies each time the game is played, depending upon the player's actions.[56] This defense has also been unavailing. The court in *Stern Electronics* found that "the repeated appearance of the same sequence of numerous sights and sounds in each play of the game

---

[50] See, e.g., *Stern Elecs., Inc. v. Kaufman*, 669 F.2d 852, 856–57 (2d Cir. 1982); *Amusement World*, 547 F Supp. at 226–27; *Midway Mfg. Co. v. Dirkschneider*, 543 F. Supp. 466, 479–80 (D. Neb. 1981); see also supra note 47 (citing sections of the Copyright Act pertaining to audiovisual works).

[51] 669 F.2d 852 (2d Cir. 1982), aff'd 523 F. Supp. 635 (E.D.N.Y. 1981).

[52] 669 F.2d at 856.

[53] Id.

[54] The copyright holders in *Stern Electronics* did not register the computer program that operates the game, probably for two reasons. First, registration of the program would not protect the game because "it would not have prevented a determined competitor from manufacturing a 'knock-off' of 'Scramble' that replicates precisely the sights and sounds of the game's audiovisual display . . . by writing a new computer program . . . to produce on the screen the same images . . . accompanied by the same sounds." 669 F.2d at 855. Second, most owners of computer programs attempt to protect them as trade secrets because copyright does not protect the sequence of instructions to a computer which constitutes the program's value. See "Comment, Copyright Protection for Computer Programs," 47 Tenn. L. Rev. 787, 797–98, 802–03 (1980). An essential element of a tort action for misappropriation of a trade secret is that the information be a secret not within the public domain, and the deposit required for copyright registration can constitute a disclosure inconsistent with such secrecy. See *Warrington Assocs., Inc. v. Real-Teim Eng'g. Sys., Inc.*, 522 F. Supp. 367, 368–69 (N.D. Ill. 1981). But see *Williams Elecs., Inc. v. Artic Int'l Inc.*, 685 F.2d 870 (3d Cir. 1982) (instance in which copyright holder registered both audiovisual effects and program underlying a game; copyright protection given to the underlying computer program). See generally Jones, supra note 7, at 46–48.

[55] 17 U.S.C. §102(a) (1976 & Supp. V 1981).

[56] See, e.g., *Stern Elecs.*, 669 F.2d at 85556.

defeats" the argument based on the player's participation.[57] In *Atari, Inc. v. Amusement World, Inc.*,[58] the district court found the fixation requirement satisfied by the game's printed circuit board, "since the 'work,' the audiovisual presentation, can be communicated from the printed circuit board with the aid of the video game's display screen."[59] In *Amusement World,* the court summarily rejected a closely related challenge to video game copyrightability. The defendants argued that a "video tape of one game sequence" is not a "complete copy" of the work for purposes of the deposit requirements of the Copyright Act.[60] In rejecting this argument, the court reasoned that the videotape is "alternative identifying material"[61] which is an appropriate deposit, "[g]iven the bulkiness and cost of the actual video game. . . ."[62]

Although the courts' decisions on the foregoing issues seem unexceptionable, a more subtle question related to the concept of derivative works may lurk behind the issue of fixation. The video tape of a single play of a game such as *Scramble* is comparable to the video tape of a performance of a play. Each performance of a play will be somewhat different, depending as it does on the actors' performances, just as the play of a video game depends on the player's moves. If the performance is fixed in a tangible medium such as a film or videotape, it may be considered a derivative work that, under the Copyright Act, is separate from the underlying script.[63] Copyright in the derivative work is limited to the original elements in the derivative work not found in the original work.[64] Registration of a work is a prerequisite to suing for its

---

57 Id. at 856. The videotapes used for copyright deposit were by necessity tapes of particular plays of the game, because the actual sequence of images and sounds, and even the game's duration, vary each time the game is played depending upon the actions taken by the player. See id. at 855; see also *Williams Elecs.*, 685 F.2d at 873–75; *Midway Mfg. Co. v. Artic Int'l, Inc.*, 2 Copyright L. Rep. (CCH) ¶25,337, at 16,888 (N.D. Ill. June 2, 1981) ("When plaintiff applied for its copyright, it submitted two video tapes of the game Galaxian being played.").

58 547 F. Supp. 222 (D. Md. 1981).

59 Id. at 226.

60 Id.; see 17 U.S.C. §408 (1976 & Supp. V 1981).

61 37 C.F.R. §§202.20(d), 202.21 (1982).

62 547 F. Supp. at 227. The court did not inquire whether these "identifying materials" identified a derivative work — namely the performance of the game by a particular player. For another case rejecting a defendant's argument on the fixation and deposit issues, see *Williams Elecs., Inc. v. Artic Int'l, Inc.*, 685 F.2d 870, 873–75 (3d Cir. 1982).

63 See 17 U.S.C. §103 (1976 & Supp. V 1981).

64 See 17 U.S.C. §103(b) (1976 & Supp. V 1981); 1 M. Nimmer, supra note 10, §3.04 (Scope of Protection for a Derivative or Collective Work).

infringement,[65] and one might question whether registration of the limited original elements in a particular play of the game — a derivative work — provides a sufficient basis on which to sue for infringement of the unregistered underlying work. It is impossible to register every possible play of a game — the number is probably infinite — and the alternative of registering the computer programs which operate the games is unpalatable for the games' owners because it could jeopardize their protection of the programs as trade secrets.[66] Furthermore, as the *Stern Electronics* court of appeals noted,[67] registration of the program might not prevent the creation of similar audiovisual displays using different computer programs.

These dilemmas may have academic interest, but the purpose of copyright registration is to facilitate, not impede, the enforcement of copyrights. For this reason, it would be inconsistent with the scheme of the Copyright Act to imperil all protection for the games because of the logical impossibility of "fixing" and registering anything more than an example of a play of a game. The games are undeniably works of authorship and creativity to which copyright ought to accord some protection. As long as the registered materials provide a sufficient foundation on which to base a finding of substantial similarity between the copyrighted and accused works, objections to the precise form of registration (that the tape of a play of the game is a derivative work, that it does not constitute a "fixation" of the game itself, and the like) descend to the level of quibbles and have been quite properly rejected by the courts. The *Amusement World* court brushed aside these technicalities with an elegant rationale: it found that the tape of a play of a game should be considered "alternative identifying materials" sufficient to meet the registration requirements.[68]

There is, however, an important qualification to the *Amusement World* rationale. If the deposited tapes were insufficient to provide a basis for comparing the allegedly infringed work with the accused work, then the action for infringement would fail, not because of a defect in fixation or registration, but because the registrant would not be able to prove substantial similarity between the copyrighted and accused works. It is to the more substantive matter of the assessment of substantial similarity between video games that we will now turn.

---

[65] See 17 U.S.C. §411 (1976 & Supp. V 1981).

[66] See supra note 54.

[67] See 669 F.2d at 855.

[68] See 547 F. Supp. at 226.

Cases finding infringement

Of the earliest decisions applying copyright law to video games, the leading example is the district court opinion in *Stern Electronics, Inc. v. Kaufman.*[69] The plaintiff, Stern, held an exclusive North and South American sublicense for the video game *Scramble.*[70] The district court described Scramble as follows:

> Stern's video game, "Scramble" . . . presents on a screen a series of images projected by a cathode ray tube which depicts a spaceship simultaneously trying to navigate a mountainous airspace, destroy enemy fuel depots, evade deadly ground fire, and prevail in any aerial dogfight, while at the same time watching carefully over a diminishing fuel supply. In essence, the work is a movie in which the viewer participates in the action as the fearless pilot controlling the spaceship.[71]

Like other video games, Scramble had been registered with the Copyright Office as an audiovisual work, using a videotape of the game to satisfy the deposit requirements of the Copyright Act.[72]

One of the defendants, Omni Video Games, Inc., marketed a competing video game called *Scramble 2.*[73] The district court compared the two games as follows:

> At the hearing, this court viewed a videotape of plaintiff's "Scramble" and defendants' "Scramble 2." The sequence of images and sounds that appears on the screen when the game has started — the "play mode" — is virtually identical in the two games. The sequence of images that appears on the screen when the game is not being played — the "attract mode" — is slightly different. The Omni game's attract mode uses different wording than Stern's and begins in a different phase. These differences in the attract mode certainly indicate that the games are not identical, but the two games are substantially similar.[74]

---

[69] 523 F. Supp. 635 (E.D.N.Y. 1981), aff'd, 669 F.2d 852 (2d Cir. 1982).

[70] Id. at 637. The game had been created by a Japanese corporation, Konami Industry Co., Ltd. Id.

[71] Id. at 638–39.

[72] See 669 F.2d at 854; 17 U.S.C. §407(a) (1976 & Supp. V 1981). For a discussion of the Copyright Act registration and deposit requirements in the video game context, see supra notes 48–68 and accompanying text.

[73] See Stern Elecs., 523 F. Supp. at 637.

[74] Id. at 639.

Based on its finding of substantial similarity,[75] the district court found a probability that Stern would succeed on the merits and entered an order granting Stern sweeping injunctive relief. The court preliminarily enjoined Omni "from infringing in any manner plaintiff's copyright in the audiovisual work entitled 'Scramble.'"[76] The court also impounded "all of [the] defendants' 'Scramble 2' video games or any other copies of plaintiff's 'Scramble' audiovisual work that infringe plaintiff's copyright and are under defendants' control."[77] Finally, the court found that the defendants had infringed Stern's trademark rights in the mark "Scramble" and enjoined the defendants from further use of that mark.[78] From a defendant's point of view, the preliminary relief was calamitous.

Considering the potency of its remedies, the district court's decision on the nature and scope of Stern's copyright in the game *Scramble* is less than convincing. The court failed completely to address the question of whether the similarity it saw between *Scramble* and *Scramble 2* was the necessary consequence of their being based on the same idea, employing the same method of play. In particular, the court did not inquire whether any video game about the trials and tribulations of a spaceship moving through enemy territory would necessarily be at least as similar to Stern's game as *Scramble 2* was. If so, then there would be a strong argument that Stern was improperly seeking to protect the idea of a game involving a "space-ship" in enemy territory. The court based its holding that the games were substantially similar on its impression that the two games were similar in appearance rather than on an analysis of the difficult problem of applying the idea/expression distinction in the video game setting.[79]

---

[75] A work which is not identical to a copyrighted work can still infringe the copyrighted work if the two works are "substantially similar." See 3 M. Nimmer, supra note 10, §13.03[A]. See also infra text accompanying notes 232 and 289–302. The *Stern* court of appeals did not reach the issue of substantial similarity. See 669 F.2d at 857.

[76] 523 F. Supp. at 641–42.

[77] Id. at 642.

[78] See id. Although the first person to use a trademark generally has prior rights on the mark and Omni had been first to use the mark "Scramble," the court found for Stern on the ground that Omni's prior use had not been in good faith. See id. at 641; see also 669 F.2d at 857.

[79] See 523 F. Supp. at 639; see also infra text accompanying notes 211–15; cf. *Amusement World*, 2 Copyright L. Rep. (CCH) ¶25,347, at 16,961–62 ("[I]t is not enough to observe that there are a great number of similarities in expression between the two games. It is necessary to determine whether the similar forms of expression are forms of expression that simply cannot be avoided in any version of the basic idea").

Other early cases finding copyright infringement of video games posed similar issues of substantial similarity, and the courts' opinions in those cases contained analogous failures to address the idea/expression issue. For example, in *Atari, Inc. v. Armenia, Ltd.*,[80] plaintiff Atari charged that the defendants' video game *War of the Bugs* infringed Atari's copyright of its game *Centipedes*. Concluding that the two games were substantially similar, the court acknowledged that the similarity between the two games did not extend to "the color and shape of the objects and so on."[81] The points of similarity the court found were in such aspects as to how the "worms" "travel" and how the "shots" are "fired"[82] elements that could easily be characterized as "methods of operation" for purposes of section 102(b) of the Copyright Act.[83]

This finding might have led to the conclusion that Armenia had copied only the methods of operation for Atari's *Centipedes*, implying that no action for copyright infringement should lie.[84] As in *Stern Electronics*, however, exactly the opposite occurred. The *Armenia* court found for the plaintiff without even

---

[80] 2 Copyright L. Rep. (CCH) ¶25,328 (N.D. Ill. Nov. 3, 1981). The opinion, which is published as the transcript of a decision rendered from the bench, draws an interesting comparison between biological categories and the levels on which the two games were similar:

> I may say, if I may make a little homely example, if I were a biologist and the machines were animals, belonged to the animal kingdom in place of being machines and belonged to the material world, shall we say — and I were a biologist and there was a controversy concerning homeds [sic], I would have to find that both of these machines were homo sapiens; in other words, they were both, at least members of the same type or species.
>
> I think I would have to go further — I know I would have to go further from all of the evidence in front of me and find that they belonged to the same family.
>
> I would even have to go further but not as far as counsel for the plaintiff says — they are not identical twins. In fact, they are not twins at all, but, in my judgment, they are brothers.

Id. at 16,845. The court concluded:

> And having examined all of the evidence, as I have said, I find that the plaintiff has shown, first, that there is substantial similarity between the accused device or devices and the plaintiff's device or machine, or whatever you wish to call it, and so similar that the court in viewing them, except for the color and the shape of the objects and so on, they are very similar [sic].

Id.

[81] Id.

[82] Id.

[83] See 17 U.S.C. §102(b) (1976 & Supp. V 1981).

[84] See supra note 10 and accompanying text.

attempting to draw a distinction between the games' methods of play on the one hand and their more arbitrary graphic elements on the other. By failing to distinguish the games' rules from their graphics, the court's decision enjoining Armenia from selling *War of the Bugs* could be interpreted as granting Atari a long-term monopoly on bug games, just as *Stern Electronics* appears to grant Stern an equally long-term monopoly on spaceship games.

In other instances, allegations of video game infringement did not engage as vividly the problem of distinguishing idea and expression. In *Midway Mfg. Co. v. Dirkschneider*,[85] the plaintiff alleged infringement by the defendants of three games at once: *Galaxian* (by the defendants' *Galactic Invaders* and *Kamikaze III*), *Pac-Man* (by *Mighty Mouth*), and *Rally-X* (by *Rally-X*).[86] The court found that "[a] comparison of the defendants' games and the plaintiff's games shows that the games are virtually identical."[87] In support of this result, the court provided a convincing recitation of identical features, descending even to such particulars as to the way the wings of *Galaxian*'s and *Galactic Invaders*' aliens "extended upward in a stationary position" as the aliens "swoop[ed] down on the defense ship."[88] As in *Stern Electronics*, the *Dirkschneider* court also found a likelihood that defendants had infringed plaintiff's trademarks.[89] The court found that nonfunctional features of Midway's games, such as the shape and appearance of the characters in Midway's games, had acquired a secondary meaning so that "the ordinary consumer viewing the attract mode would likely think the game being advertised was the plaintiff's."[90]

A different form of infringement was alleged in *Midway Manufacturing Co. v. Artic International, Inc.*,[91] and, correspondingly, the court's holding shows a different sort of overbreadth. Defendant Artic allegedly marketed a speed-up

---

[85] 543 F. Supp. 466 (D. Neb. 1981).

[86] See id. at 472–77. The Dirkschneider court found fixation in the games' printed circuit boards, see id. at 480, and found the Copyright Act's deposit requirement satisfied by Atari's deposits of videotapes of "each of its games in their attract and play modes," id. at 480–81. Presaging *Amusement World*, *Dirkschneider* also recognized that ideas are not copyrightable, but found that "[t]he plaintiff's copyrights cover the plaintiff's audiovisual expression of various game ideas [including] the distinctive color and design of the space ships and other players, as well as the sounds accompanying the playing of the games." Id. at 480.

[87] Id. at 482.

[88] Id.

[89] See id. at 484–90.

[90] Id. at 488.

[91] 2 Copyright L. Rep. (CCH) ¶25,337 (N.D. Ill. June 2, 1981).

kit for plaintiff Midway's video game *Galaxian.*[92] Artic moved for summary judgment on the ground that it had "not copied plaintiff's work or induced others to copy that work."[93] Midway countered that "an infringement arises regardless of whether defendant itself has copied the protected work" and that "the sale of the speed-up kits enables others to make and perform unauthorized alterations of plaintiff's copyrighted material."[94] Midway's theory was that playing *Galaxian* with the speed-up kit produced visual images "substantially similar to the visual images originally copyrighted," thus "creating an unauthorized derivative work."[95] Midway did not allege that it marketed or intended to market any similar speed-up kits.

To approach this issue, the court examined at length the Copyright Act's policies of rewarding individuals for their "unique creative efforts" and of providing "an incentive for individuals to engage in artistic endeavors by forbidding any other person from copying their original expression of ideas."[96] The court omitted to mention the countervailing policy of limiting the scope of the protected rights so that other authors are not crowded out of arenas for the exercise of their creative efforts.[97] In its opinion denying the defendant's motion for summary judgment, the court said:

> As noted, the copyright law is designed to reward creative and artistic endeavors. It gives the author the exclusive right to distribute copies of that work and make derivative works from the original. If defendant's device is designed and used solely to modify plaintiff's visual image, then plainly defendant's device would only have value because of

---

[92] See id. at 16,884, 16,890–92. Midway also alleged that Artic sold "electronic devices that are intended to simulate Midway's Galaxian and Pac-Man games." Id. at 16,844. The court's opinion dealt, inter alia, with Artic's motion for summary judgment, and therefore assumed, for purposes of that motion, that Midway's allegations were true.

[93] Id. at 16,890.

[94] Id. The issue raised was similar to the contributory infringement issues in the Betamax case, *Universal City Studios, Inc. v. Sony Corp.*, 659 F.2d 963 (9th Cir. 1981), cert. granted, 102 S. Ct. 2926 (1982) (No. 81-1687). Only the district court decision in *Sony,* 480 F. Supp. 429 (C.D. Cal. 1979), aff'd in part and rev'd in part, 659 F.2d 963 (9th Cir. 1981), was available when the *Midway v. Artic* court rendered its opinion. See 2 Copyright L. Rep. (CCH) ¶25,337, at 16,892.

[95] 2 Copyright L. Rep. (CCH) ¶25,337, at 16,891.

[96] Id. at 16,890.

[97] Cf. *Nichols v. Universal Pictures Corp.*, 45 F.2d 119, 122 (2d Cir. 1930) (L. Hand, J.) (holding there was no copyright infringement when similarities between two plays were only in the ideas and not in the expression), cert. denied, 282 U.S. 902 (1931).

> plaintiff's particular copyrighted audiovisual work. Defendant, thus, by selling its device, reaps the benefits of plaintiff's artistic endeavor. Such conduct would be violative of §106(2) [of the Copyright Act].[98]

This dicta is remarkable in that it ignores the fact that Artic's speed-up kit was not sold as, and apparently could not be used as, a substitute for Midway's *Galaxian* game.[99] Thus, the sale of the speed-up kit could not have reduced Midway's *Galaxian* sales, even if, as the court hypothesized, the speed-up kit could only be used with the *Galaxian* game. Indeed, the speed-up kit could be expected to enhance *Galaxian* sales because the added challenge of greater speed probably made the game attractive to a broader segment of the video game market.

The *Galaxian* speed-up kit has a converse analogy in the field of literature. Difficult literary books such as James Joyce's *Ulysses* and *Finnegans Wake* have spawned commentaries such as Gilbert's *James Joyce's* Ulysses[100] and Tindall's *A Reader's Guide to* Finnegans Wake.[101] One might consider these commentaries to be Joyce slow-down kits. They explain Joyce's works in a way that makes them more accessible to the ordinary reader. Indeed, many readers might not purchase Joyce's books if such assistance were not available. Like the *Galaxian* speed-up kit, commentaries such as James Joyce's *Ulysses* are useful solely as a result of the underlying work. The commentaries have no value in connection with any other work. Thus, to use the *Midway v. Artic* court's phrase, the commentator's work "would only have value because of [the original author's] copyrighted . . . work," and the commentator thus "reaps the benefits of the [original author's] artistic endeavor."[102] Should one, therefore, conclude that

---

[98] 2 Copyright L. Rep. (CCH) ¶25,337, at 16,891. The court also said that "if defendant's device is one which enhances all video games, it would be anomalous to apply the copyright laws to inhibit its distribution." Id. Note that section 106(2) of the Copyright Act grants the owner of a copyright exclusive rights to prepare derivative works. See 17 U.S.C. §106(2) (1976 & Supp. V 1981).

[99] See id. at 16,884 (The speed-up kits were described as "devices that are designed to be inserted into Midway's *Galaxian* game to speed up and otherwise alter the play of the game").

[100] S. Gilbert, *James Joyce's* Ulysses (1930).

[101] W. Tindall, *A Reader's Guide to* Finnegans Wake (1969). Tindall's book reprints excerpts from *Finnegans Wake* with permission. See W. Tindall, supra, at iv. The author has examined the certificates of copyright registration for both the Gilbert and Tindall works. Neither is described in its certificate as a derivative work.

[102] 2 Copyright L. Rep. (CCH) ¶25,337, at 16,891.

literary commentators and critics must obtain the permission of the holders of copyright in the works on which they comment?

Both tradition and the Copyright Act hold that off-shoots such as commentary, criticism, and parody are not infringing,[103] despite the fact that such works are fundamentally parasitic on the work of the original author. The commentary must not paraphrase or quote so extensively that it becomes a substitute for the original,[104] but this consideration does not even arise in the case of the *Galaxian* speed-up kit because the purchaser of the speed-up kit cannot use it unless he also purchases a copy of the *Galaxian* game. If the *Midway v. Artic* court's analysis were applied to literature, all commentary, criticism, and parody would require a license from the original copyright holder. Not all criticism is friendly; not all parody is kind. One can imagine that authors would grant licenses for such works on a very selective basis indeed.

Cases finding no infringement

The dicta quoted above from *Midway v. Artic* is perhaps the most extreme example of the expanded copyright protection courts are willing to provide for the owners of video games. Similar disregard for the traditional bounds of copyright is, as we have seen, evident in *Stern Electronics v. Kaufman* and *Atari v. Armenia.*[105] Not all courts, however, have overlooked traditional principles in applying copyright to video games. One of the most thoughtful opinions attempting to apply those principles in this new context is *Atari, Inc. v. Amusement World, Inc.*[106] In *Amusement World,* Atari, again the plaintiff, and in this case, the owner of a video game called "Asteroids," sought to enjoin defendants "from manufacturing or distributing any product in violation of plaintiff's copyright."[107] In particular, Atari alleged that Amusement World's

---

[103] See 17 U.S.C. §107 (1976 & Supp. V 1981) ("the fair use of a copyrighted work . . . for purposes such as criticism [and] comment . . . is not an infringement of copyright"); L. Seltzer, *Exemptions and Fair Use in Copyright* 43–45 (1978); 3 Nimmer, supra note 10, §13.05[C]; Kaplan, supra note 10, at 68–69.

[104] See 17 U.S.C. §§107(3)–107(4) (1976 & Supp. V 1981) (factors bearing on question of fair use include "amount and substantiality of the portion used in relation to the copyrighted work as a whole" and "the effect of the use upon the potential market for or value of the copyrighted work").

[105] See supra notes 69–84 and accompanying text.

[106] 547 F. Supp. 222 (D. Md. 1981).

[107] Id. at 224.

video game *Meteors* was substantially similar to, and therefore an infringement of, Atari's *Asteroids.*[108]

The court did not satisfy itself with infringement analysis based on a superficial impression of the similarities between the games, nor did it focus on the conduct of the parties. Instead, it cataloged twenty-two "design features," which the games shared and nine respects in which the games differed.[109] The similarities identified by the court ranged from those as general as the fact that both games presented an "overhead view of the battle field"[110] to those as minute as the fact that "[t]here is a two-tone beeping noise in the background throughout the game, and the tempo of the noise increases as the game progresses."[111] The nine differences included, for example, the facts that '"Meteors' is in color, while 'Asteroids' is in black and white," "the rocks in 'Meteors' appear to tumble as they move across the screen," and "the pace of the 'Meteors' game is faster at all stages."[112]

The *Amusement World* court went beyond earlier decisions such as *Stern Electronics* and *Midway v. Artic* by examining carefully the questions whether the plaintiff was claiming copyright in an idea and whether the two games could be considered "substantially similar" without rending the delicate veil separating ideas from their expressions. The court first rejected the defendants' contention that Atari's copyright claim was void in its entirety because it attempted to monopolize "the idea of a video game in which the player fights his way through asteroids and spaceships."[113] In rejecting this contention, the court said:

> Thus, when plaintiff copyrighted his particular expression of the game, he did not prevent others from using the idea of a game with asteroids. He prevented only the copying of the arbitrary design features that makes [sic] plaintiff's expression of this idea unique. These design features consist of the symbols that appear on the display screen, the ways in which those symbols move around the screen, and the sounds emanating from the game cabinet. Defendants are entitled to use the idea of a video game involving asteroids, so long as they adopt a different expression of the idea — that is, a version of such a game that

---

108 See id.
109 Id. at 224–25.
110 Id. at 225.
111 Id. at 224.
112 Id. at 225.
113 Id. at 227.

uses symbols, movements, and sounds that are different from those used in plaintiff's game.[114]

The quoted passage is one of the more careful and explicit judicial efforts to apply the idea/expression dichotomy to video games, and it spelled defeat for Atari's infringement action. The court observed that the mere fact that "there are a great number of similarities in expression" between *Meteors* and *Asteroids* does not imply infringement of one by the other.[115] Instead, "[i]t is necessary to determine whether the similar forms of expression are forms of expression that simply cannot be avoided in any version of the basic idea of a video game involving space rocks."[116] The court held that "most of these similarities [between the two games] are inevitable, given the requirements of the idea of a game involving a spaceship combatting space rocks and given the technical demands of the medium of a video game."[117] On this ground, the court denied Atari's motion for a preliminary injunction and entered judgment for the defendant.[118]

Although the *Amusement World* court's readiness to tackle the idea/expression distinction is laudable, one might question whether the court's holding does not rest on an overbroad view of the idea of a space rocks game. In effect, the court assumed that every rule of play must be an "idea" for purposes of section 102(b) of the Copyright Act. It is worth asking whether this necessarily follows. An important attribute of "ideas" for purposes of section 102(b) appears to be generality.[119] Such generality is probably present in "the idea of a video game in which a player fights his way through asteroids and spaceships."[120] By comparison, some of the twenty-two points of similarity identified by the court are so particularized that they could more easily be said to involve the "expression" of the basic idea rather than an idea in themselves. Examples are the two-tone beeping noise, which increases in frequency as each game progresses, the "three sizes of rocks" employed by each game, and the pattern of asteroid decay in each game: "[w]hen hit, a large rock splits into two medium rocks, a medium rock splits into two small

[114] Id.

[115] Id. at 229.

[116] Id. (Footnote omitted).

[117] Id.

[118] See id. at 230.

[119] See infra text accompanying notes 229–31.

[120] *Amusement World*, 547 F. Supp. at 227.

ones, and a small rock disappears."[121] On the other hand, many other points of similarity, including, for instance, the player's control of one space ship under attack by enemy ships, the shared rule that "[w]hen a rock hits the player's spaceship, the ship is destroyed," and the joint feature that "[t]he player's ship and enemy ships shoot projectiles"[122] seem by their generality to be better candidates for the "idea" category.

These considerations suggest that although some aspects of *Meteors* may have infringed *Asteroids*' expression, in other respects, the games deserved to coexist. It is not unprecedented for courts to tailor relief in copyright infringement cases to the precise outlines of the area of infringement, and a selection of the most particularized items on the court's list of similarities could have been used to define an injunction limited to improperly copied "expression."[123] The *Amusement World* court, however, does not appear to have even considered such relief, and, by making a unitary finding of noninfringement, the court's holding blurs the very distinction between idea and expression that it had been so careful to draw in its opinion.

Few courts have held for the defendant in a case of alleged video game infringement. One is *Amusement World*, and another is the district court's opinion, subsequently reversed, in *Atari Inc. v. North American Philips Consumer Electronics Corp.*[124] In *North American Philips*, Atari and its co-plaintiff, Midway Manufacturing Co., alleged, among other things, that North American's game *K.C. Munchkin* infringed Atari's and Midway's rights in *Pac-Man.*[125] In a lengthy opinion, the district court denied plaintiffs' prayer for a

---

121 Id. at 224.

122 Id.

123 See *Breffort v. I Had a Ball Co.*, 271 F. Supp. 623, 625–26 (S.D.N.Y. 1967) (issuing an injunction against infringing plaintiff's work, but expressly excluding from the injunction certain noninfringing uses of music and lyrics); 3 M. Nimmer, supra note 10, §14.06[B], at 14–53 ("The defendant may be able to avoid a permanent injunction if the infringing portion of defendant's work can be removed without destroying the usefulness of the remainder of the work."). See generally infra text accompanying notes 303–15.

124 2 Copyright L. Rep. (CCH) ¶25,363 (N.D. Ill. Dec. 4, 1981), rev'd, 672 F.2d 607 (7th Cir.), cert. denied, 51 U.S.L.W. 3258 (U.S. Oct. 4, 1982). The court of appeals opinion is discussed infra text accompanying notes 161–209. Another case finding no infringement of the *Pac-Man* game is *Atari, Inc. v. Williams*, 2 Copyright L. Rep. (CCH) ¶25,412 (E.D. Cal. Dec. 28, 1981).

125 Atari holds an assignment of the exclusive right to copy *Pac-Man* in home video games; Midway holds similar rights to *Pac-Man* as a coin-operated arcade game. See 2 Copyright L. Rep. (CCH) ¶25,363, at 17,045. North America's game *K.C. Munchkin* was marketed as a home video game. See id.

preliminary injunction "barring defendants . . . from advertising, distributing, displaying, performing, selling, or offering for sale, the 'K.C. Munchkin' home video game, or in any other manner violating plaintiffs' exclusive rights under the copyright in the 'Pac-Man' audiovisual work."[126]

As in *Amusement World*, the district court opinion in *North American Philips* compared the two works in great detail. The court found both *Pac-Man* and *K.C. Munchkin* to be "maze-chase" games[127] — each game features on its video screen a maze or mazes.[128] The player in each game controls a "central character" which moves through the maze, gobbling "dots" as it moves[129]. A further similarity is that the central character in each game is subject to attack by other figures (called by the district court "munchers" for *K.C. Munchkin* and "goblins" for *Pac-Man*).[130] These attacking figures are not controlled by the player.[131] The object of each game is to score points by causing the central character to gobble the dots while at the same time avoiding the goblins or munchers.[132]

Based on these similarities, the court might have immediately concluded, as the courts did in *Stern Electronics* and *Armenia*,[133] that *Pac-Man* and *K.C. Munchkin* were "substantially similar." Like the *Amusement World* court,[134] however, the *North American Philips* court also cataloged and analyzed the area of dissimilarity. The maze in *K.C. Munchkin* is more rectangular with more horizontal passageways than the maze in *Pac-Man*.[135] *Pac-Man*'s central character is yellow and appears only in profile,[136] *K.C. Munchkin*'s is blue with horns and a smile that, under attack, turns to a frown. He shows himself both

---

126 Id. (quoting plaintiffs' prayers for relief). This requested relief was eventually entered, following the court of appeals reversal. See infra text accompanying note 197.

127 2 Copyright L. Rep. (CCH) ¶25,363, at 17,046.

128 In *K.C. Munchkin* there is "variability of mazes," whereas in *Pac-Man* the maze is fixed throughout the play. Id.

129 Id. at 17,046–47.

130 Id. The court of appeals terminology was somewhat different. It referred to the central character in both games as "goblins" and called the other figures in both games "monsters" or "ghost monsters." See infra text accompanying notes 175–78. The appellate court used its similarity of terminology to support its finding of infringement. See 672 F.2d at 617–18.

131 See 2 Copyright L. Rep. (CCH) ¶25,363, at 17,046.

132 In *Pac-Man*, points can also be scored by consuming goblins when they have turned blue. See id.

133 See supra text accompanying notes 69–84.

134 See supra text accompanying notes 106–23.

135 See 2 Copyright L. Rep. (CCH) ¶25,363, at 17,046.

136 See Id. at 17,046–47.

in profile and full-face.[137] The four "goblins" in *Pac-Man* have eyes and appendages. The "munchers" in *K.C. Munchki*n "are much 'spookier' than the goblins in Pac-Man," having vacant eyes and more dramatically animated, longer legs[138]. *K.C. Munchkin*'s munchers are colored red, green, and yellow, while *Pac-Man*'s are red, blue, turquoise, and orange.[139]

All of the foregoing differences might be characterized as involving only the "graphic" aspects of the games. The court also identified differences "from the point of view of play of the two games." In *Pac-Man,* the goblins move "upward out of a fixed center 'box' into the maze," while *K.C. Munchkin*'s "first mode of play shows the center of the maze as a box changing the open side by ninety degrees every two or three seconds."[140] There are several hundred stationary dots in *Pac-Man,* while *K.C. Munchkin* has but twelve dots that move. *K.C. Munchkin*'s dots also accelerate as their brethren are consumed until the last dot is moving as fast as the central character. As the court put it, the last dot "cannot be caught by overtaking it; it must be munched by strategy."[141] Another equally fundamental difference is that the *K.C. Munchkin* player can "draw on the screen whatever walls he wishes to cause in the maze, thus creating a continuously changing maze from game to game."[142]

On the equities, the district court opinion in North American Philips is unique among video game cases in the detail with which it examined the process by which the defendants created and marketed the accused work. It was admitted that Mr. Ed Averett, the creator of *K.C. Munchkin,* had seen and played *Pac-Man* before completing his design of *K.C. Munchkin.*[143] It was

---

137 See id.

138 Id.

139 See id.

140 Id. at 17,047.

141 Id.

142 Id.

143 See id. at 17,048. Mr. Averett had created another maze-chase game, *Take the Money and Run,* before starting work on *K.C. Munchkin* and presumably before seeing *Pac-Man.* See id. at 17,047, 17,050. The district court opinion suggests that some aspects of the earlier game may have been incorporated into *K.C. Munchkin.* See infra text accompanying note 158. Without explanation for its different finding of fact, the Court of Appeals stated, "Mr. Averett also played PAC-MAN at least once before beginning work on K.C. Munchkin." 672 F.2d at 613. The court's failure to explain the basis on which it reached this differing finding of fact is particularly troubling since the independent creation of *K.C. Munchkin*'s predecessor prior to the creation of *Pac-Man* was a fact explicitly relied on by the district court in reaching its noninfringement conclusion. See 2 Copyright L. Rep. (CCH) ¶25,363, at 17,050. See generally infra text accompanying note 179.

further admitted that the defendant North American had initially attempted to obtain a license for *Pac-Man* from the plaintiff Midway and asked Mr. Averett to develop *K.C. Munchkin* only after Midway had rebuffed its licensing overtures.[144] In anticipation of the plaintiffs' infringement claims, North American asked Averett to alter the shapes and colors of *K.C. Munchkin*'s central character and munchers "to get away from even a cosmetic similarity to the colors in 'Pac-Man.'"[145]

North American's and Averett's conduct in creating *K.C. Munchkin*, as described in the preceding paragraph, could cut either way. On the one hand, it was clear that the defendants avoided marketing a product identical to *Pac-Man*. On the other hand, one could argue that having failed to secure a license for *Pac-Man*, North American had tried to market a product as close to *Pac-Man* as possible, thus endeavoring to profit from *Pac-Man*'s obvious success without paying a royalty to *Pac-Man*'s owners.[146] One crucial difference, however, distinguishes the North American Philips defendants from those in cases such as *Stern Electronics* and *Dirkschneider*. That is the fact that North American took extraordinary measures to avoid creating the impression that its game and *Pac-Man* came from the same source. The court described these measures as follows:

> Internal instructions were issued within the company to avoid use of all trade names, trademarks, or trade definitions of others in connection with the game promotion. Specifically, instructions given were for the purpose of avoiding any reference to the "Pac-Man" game. On October 27 and November 27, 1981, memoranda were addressed to its sales force in which North American stressed that it did not want "others to misapply our game names and trademarks to their games. Likewise, we should not use other people's trademarks or game names to refer to our own games [sic]." The advertisements used referred to the "K. C. Munchkin" video game cartridge, its packaging for that cartridge, and the instruction manual; it did not include any material which could reasonably result in confusion with "Pac-Man."[147]

---

144 See 2 Copyright L. Rep. (CCH) ¶25,363, at 17,047.

145 Id. at 17,048.

146 The Seventh Circuit opinion made the latter inference. See 672 F.2d at 619.

147 2 Copyright L. Rep. ¶25,363, at 17,048. The opinion of the Court of Appeals omitted these facts entirely. See 672 F.2d 607 (7th Cir. 1982).

When an independent distributor, "Minnesota Fats, the Video King," advertised *K.C. Munchkin* as "a Pac-Man type game," a North American representative rapidly contacted Video King "for the purpose of attempting to get that company to delete any reference of [sic] 'Pac-Man' game in any future advertisement."[148] In sharp contrast, the defendants in *Stern Electronics* attempted in bad faith to establish a first use of the work "Scramble" and then called their product "Scramble 2," all in an obvious effort to trade off the goodwill of Stern's "Scramble."[149] Similarly, the defendants in *Dirkschneider* had chosen for one of their infringing games the same name plaintiff used — "Rally-X" — and otherwise infringed Atari's trademarks.[150] In these respects, the conduct of the defendants in *North American Philips* compares favorably with that of the defendants in *Stern Electronics* and *Dirkschneider* and may have helped to push the court away from a finding of infringement.

Following such an extensive review of relevant facts, the district court's analysis of the infringement issue is disappointing and unconvincing. The court acknowledged that "'[c]opying' proscribed by copyright law means more than tracing original [sic], line by line; to some extent it includes appropriation of artist's [sic] thought in creating his own form of expression."[151] This seems to acknowledge the accepted principle that a work can be "reproduce[d] . . . in copies" in violation of the owner's exclusive rights under section 106(1) of the Act[152] if the infringer makes a "substantially similar" copy. But the court next declares, "[s]ince plaintiffs cannot prove copying, they advance the theory that 'K.C. Munchkin' is substantially similar to 'Pac-Man.'"[153] This statement incorrectly suggests that a substantially similar work could infringe a copyrighted work even if it were proven that the substantially similar work had been created independently of the copyrighted

---

148 2 Copyright L. Rep. ¶25,363, at 17,049. The court properly observed that "[t]he advertisement by Minnesota Fats referring to 'K.C. Munchkin' as 'a Pac-Man type game' did not confuse one game with the other." Id. at 17,050. But cf. *Invicta Plastics (U.S.A.) Ltd. v. Mego Corp.*, 523 F. Supp. 619 (S.D.N.Y. 1981) (enjoining under the Lanham Act [Trade-Mark Act of 1946] July 5, 1946, ch. 540, 60 Stat. 427 [codified in scattered sections of 15 U.S.C.] even truthful comparisons of the defendant's games with the plaintiff's).

149 See Stern Elecs., 523 F. Supp. at 640–41; see also supra note 78 and accompanying text.

150 See supra notes 89–90 and accompanying text.

151 2 Copyright L. Rep. (CCH) ¶25,363, at 17,050.

152 17 U.S.C. §106(1) (1976 & Supp. V 1981).

153 2 Copyright L. Rep. (CCH) ¶25,363, at 17,050.

work.[154] The statement also overlooks the principle that "copying may be inferred where the defendant had access to the copyrighted work and the accused work is substantially similar to the copyrighted work."[155] Having gotten its copyright analysis off to a bad start, the court concluded:

> But evidence in this record shows that "K.C. Munchkin" is not substantially similar to "Pac-Man." In fact, it has been established in the proceeding that [the] defendants created their game from a source they had utilized before "Pac-Man" came into existence; the maze defendants utilized is different, and the way their game is played is different from plaintiffs' "Pac-Man."[156]

The court's conclusion thus repeats the error of its premise. If *K.C. Munchkin* was created before *Pac-Man* came into existence, then no prior access could be shown, and the question of substantial similarity would be irrelevant. On the other hand, the court's recitation of facts had stated: "Prior to embarking on the development of his game, Mr. Averett, in the company of a North American executive, saw a 'Pac-Man' in an Atlanta, Georgia airport arcade."[157] In context, this seems to mean that Averett saw *Pac-Man* before he started to develop *K.C. Munchkin,* but after he had created another maze-chase game called *Take the Money and Run,*[158] "whose maze configuration is rectangular and almost identical with that in 'K.C. Munchkin.'"[159] Thus, the plaintiffs had shown access, but only with respect to any parts of *K.C. Munchkin* created after Averett saw *Pac-Man* in the Atlanta airport.

Besides the court's failure to focus on the issue of access, its one-sentence analysis of the issue of substantial similarity is wholly inadequate. Because Averett had evidently created a maze-chase game, *Take the Money and Run,* before seeing *Pac-Man,* the case raised the issues: (i) whether some of the similarities between *K.C. Munchkin* and *Pac-Man* were created before Averett had access to *Pac-Man*; and (ii) if the answer to (i) is "yes," what relief, if any, should be accorded to the plaintiffs — should the marketing of *K.C.*

---

[154] Such a suggestion would directly contradict the principle that copyright infringement, unlike patent infringement, requires copying. See 3M. Nimmer, supra note 10, §13.01, at 13-3.

[155] North American Philips, 672 F.2d at 614.

[156] 2 Copyright L. Rep. (CCH) ¶25,363, at 17,050.

[157] Id. at 17,048.

[158] See id. at 17,047.

[159] Id.

Munchkin, in its entirety, be enjoined, or should the injunctive relief be limited to those elements created after Averett gained access to *Pac-Man.* The court did not so much as acknowledge the existence of these issues. Instead, it made a blanket finding that "evidence in this record shows that 'K.C. Munchkin' is not substantially similar to 'Pac-Man.'"[160]

The plaintiffs promptly appealed the district court's denial of their motion for a preliminary injunction. Considering the limitations of the district court's reasoning, it is not surprising that the appeal was successful. What is surprising, however, is that the court of appeals' careful exposition of copyright law did not provide the basis for a more compelling decision on the issue of infringement.

The seventh circuit opinion in *North American Philips*

The Seventh Circuit's opinion in *North American Philips* is undoubtedly the preeminent case to date on the issue of copyright protection for video games. The court's exposition of the standard principles of copyright law is thorough and accurate. The court properly begins by noting that "copying" may be proven by a combination of access and substantial similarity.[161] The court endorses the traditional view that substantial similarity should be assessed through the eyes of the "ordinary observer," stating, "the test is whether the accused work is so similar to the plaintiff's work that an ordinary reasonable person would conclude that the defendant unlawfully appropriated the plaintiff's protectible expression by taking material of substance and value."[162] The court states that its analysis should avoid "analytic dissection and expert testimony,"[163] focusing instead on the "total concept and feel" of the copyrighted work.[164] Finally, the court observes that, unlike a patent, copyright protects only the expression of the author's ideas and therefore "does not extend to games as such," but only to pictorial of graphic portions

---

[160] Id. at 17,050.

[161] See 672 F.2d at 614. The court did not, however, examine the factual question of the timing of the defendant's access as carefully as it might have. See infra text accompanying notes 179–84.

[162] Id. at 614. For criticism of the "ordinary observer" test, see infra text accompanying notes 282–302.

[163] Id. (quoting *Arnstein v. Porter,* 154 F.2d 464, 468 [2d Cir. 1946]).

[164] Id. (quoting *Roth Greeting Cards v. United Card Co.,* 429 F.2d 1106, 1110 [9th Cir. 1970]).

of games.[165] Thus, the court set for itself the task of attempting "to distill the protectible forms of expression in PAC-MAN from the game itself." [166]

To tackle this difficult question, the court employed two basic tools of copyright analysis. One is Learned Hand's famous "abstractions test":

> Upon any work, and especially upon a play, a great number of patterns of increasing generality will fit equally well, as more and more of the incident is left out. The last may perhaps be no more than the most general statement of what the play is about, and at times might consist only of its title; but there is a point in this series of abstractions where they are no longer protected, since otherwise the playwright could prevent the use of his "ideas," to which, apart from their expression, his property is never extended.[167]

The second is the concept of "scènes à faire," meaning "incidents, characters or settings which are as a practical matter indispensable, or at least standard, in the treatment of a given topic."[168] Scènes *à* faire do not enjoy protection, even if they are too particularized to be considered ideas. One reason for this rule is that, as the *North American Philips* court suggests, scènes à faire may be so closely connected with the underlying, unprotected idea that they become indistinguishable from it.[169] An additional reason may be that the author of the copyrighted work does not deserve credit and protection for aspects of his work that could have been copied from other works, even if he invented them without copying and even if the defendant actually copied them from the copyrighted work. Thus, the scènes à faire exception furthers the Copyright Act's policy of protecting only original works of authorship.[170]

---

[165] Id. at 615 (citing 1. M. Nimmer, supra note 10, §2.18[H][3], at 2-212, and *Stern Elecs.*, 669 F.2d at 856).

[166] Id.

[167] *Nichols v. Universal Pictures Corp.*, 45 F.2d 119, 121 (2d Cir. 1930), cert. denied, 282 U.S. 902 (1931), quoted in *North American Philips*, 672 F.2d at 615–16.

[168] *North American Philips*, 672 F.2d at 616 (quoting *Alexander v. Haley*, 460 F. Supp. 40, 45 [S.D.N.Y. 1978]).

[169] See id.

[170] See infra text accompanying notes 246–49. An additional element in the court's exposition of copyright law is the proposition that when expression and idea are indistinguishable, only verbatim copying will be protected. See *North American Philips*, 672 F.2d at 616–17. The court uses *Herbert Rosenthal Jewelry Corp. v. Kalpakian*, 446 F.2d 738 (9th Cir. 1971) as an example of this principle. Although the Kalpakian case has been cited for this proposition, see, e.g., *Sid & Marty Krofft*

Using these tools, the court found that many similarities between *Pac-Man* and *K.C. Munchkin* were not protected expression. The court described the "idea" of Pac-Man in "abstract" terms as follows:

> PAC-MAN is a maze-chase game in which the player scores points by guiding a central figure through various passageways of a maze and at the same time avoiding collision with certain opponents or pursuit figures which move independently about the maze. Under certain conditions, the central figure may temporarily become empowered to chase and overtake the opponents, thereby scoring bonus points.[171]

The court resolved to protect only the "audio component and the concrete details of the visual presentation [that] constitute the copyrightable expression of that game 'idea.'"[172] The court also identified certain "standard game devices" as unprotected scènes à faire. These included a "wrap around" feature,[173] the use of a maze, a scoring table, and dots that provide "a means by which a player's performance can be gauged and rewarded".[174]

Having carved out an unprotected domain of ideas and scènes à faire, the court nevertheless found infringement on the basis of *K.C. Munchkin*'s "substantial appropriation of the PAC-MAN characters."[175] This appropriation was found to inhere in each game's use of "goblins" and "ghost monsters," and in the "portrayal" of those characters, including their styles, movements and

---

Television Prods., Inc. v. McDonald's Corp., 562 F.2d 1157, 1167–68 (9th Cir. 1977), the Kalpakian opinion actually suggests the reverse. In *Kalpakian* the plaintiff claimed that the defendant had infringed the design of the plaintiff's copyrighted "jeweled bee pin." The court held for the defendant, commenting that "[w]hen the 'idea' and its 'expression' are thus inseparable, copying the 'expression' will not be barred, since protecting the 'expression' in such circumstances would confer a monopoly of the 'idea' upon the copyright owner free of the conditions and limitations imposed by the patent law." 446 F.2d at 742. On the other hand, this dicta may have exceeded the requirements for the court's holding, since the accused and copyrighted bee-pins were not identical. See id. at 741. See generally infra text accompanying notes 228–32.

171 *North American Philips*, 672 F.2d at 617.

172 Id.

173 Id. The "wrap around" feature is a method of operation by which the gobbler can exit via a "tunnel" at one side of the video screen and reappear on the opposite side of the screen.

174 Id.

175 Id.

qualities such as "role reversal" and "regeneration."[176] The court brushed aside the differences between the games, particularly the concept of moving dots, the variation in mazes, and certain changes in "facial features and colors of the characters,"[177] reasoning that the ordinary observer test requires a court to focus on "the overall similarity rather than minute differences," that "the nature of the alteration . . . only tends to emphasize the extent to which [the defendant] deliberately copied from the plaintiff's work," and that the "undiscriminating" audience for video games "would be disposed to overlook" minor differences in detail, since the "main attraction of a game such as PAC-MAN lies in the stimulation provided by the intensity of the competition."[178]

Taken by itself, the court of appeals opinion is convincing and generally consistent with the policies of the Copyright Act. On close examination, however, one finds that the court's legal analysis goes smoothly only because the court suppressed untidy facts. The appellate court's violence with the facts is most evident on the issue of access. On this issue, which had also stymied the district court, the court of appeals declared that "[after] view[ing] Pac-Man in an airport arcade [and] after discussing the strengths and weaknesses of the PAC-MAN game and its increasing popularity, [Mr. Averett and a North American Philips representative] decided to commence development of a modified version. . . ."[179] The court further said, "Mr. Averett also played PAC-MAN at least once before beginning work on K.C. Munchkin."[180] On these same issues, the district court had said, "[o]n at least one occasion before completing his design, [Mr. Averett] played a 'Pac-Man,'"[181] and in its conclusion said, "it has been established in this proceeding that defendants created their game from a source they had utilized before 'Pac-Man' came into existence. . . ."[182] As already noted, if the game *Take the Money and Run* was created before Mr. Averett had access to *Pac-Man,* then the plaintiffs had failed to prove prior access with respect to any features of *K.C. Munchkin* that were included in *Take the Money and Run.* Unlike the question of substantial

---

176 Id. at 618.

177 Id.

178 Id. at 618–19. The court further supported its finding that the plaintiff was likely to succeed on the merits on the ground that retailers and "clerks — "lay observers" — had described K.C. Munchkin as a "Pac-Man type game." Id. at 619; see also supra note 148 and accompanying text.

179 *North American Philips,* 672 F.2d at 613.

180 Id.

181 2 Copyright L. Rep. (CCH) ¶25,363, at 17,048.

102 Id. al 17,050.

similarity, for which the court of appeals may be "in as good a position as the district court to decide,"[183] the question of the time of Averett's access is an issue of fact on which the district court may be reversed only if clearly erroneous.[184] Incredibly, the court of appeals gave no explanation whatsoever for its statements of fact, which contradicted the findings of the lower court on the central issue of the time of Averett's access to *Pac-Man.*

In another part of its opinion, the court of appeals remarked that "[t]he parties stipulated . . . to access."[185] The parties had filed a three-page stipulation with the district court in connection with Atari's motion for a preliminary injunction. Contrary to the appellate panel's implication, the stipulation did not expressly state that the defendants had "access" for

---

[183] *North American Philips,* 672 F.2d at 614.

[184] See *Menominee Rubber Co. v. Gould, Inc.*, 657 F.2d 164, 166 (7th Cir. 1981), cited in *North American Philips,* 672 F.2d at 613. It is ironic that only ten months prior to its North American Philips decision, the Seventh Circuit had made it a point to hold that a preliminary injunction should not be issued without an evidentiary hearing to test the credibility of the plaintiff's witnesses. *See Swiderek v. Medeco Security Locks, Inc.*, 2 Copyright L. Rep. (CCH) ¶25,402 (7th Cir. May 26, 1981).

[185] *North American Philips,* 672 F.2d at 614. The text of the stipulation provided:

1. Validity of the copyright-in-suit is not contested for the purposes of this hearing.
2. The audiovisual work covered by the copyright-in-suit is a series of images which appear on the television screen of Midway's Pac-Man coin-operated video game and associated sounds.
3. The person at North American who was principally responsible for the design of the K.C. Munchkin game at issue here and the person in charge of home video product development for North American saw a Midway Pac-Man coin-operated video game at an airport in New York City in February, 1981. These persons have reported that they do not recall playing the Pac-Man game at that time.
4. The K.C. Munchkin game was designed thereafter, in Spring and Summer, 1981.
5. Before coming out with their K.C. Munchkin game, North American approached plaintiff Midway and inquired whether a license under the Pac-Man copyright for the home video market could be obtained.
6. Midway responded to North American that exclusive home video rights under the Pac-Man copyright had already been licensed to Atari, and therefore could not be licensed by Midway to North American.
7. The introduction of the K.C. Munchkin game was a careful, conscious decision by North American.
8. North American plans to ship quantities of the "K.C. Munchkin" game to distributors and dealers over the next six months.

copyright purposes. Instead, the stipulation recited a sequence of facts related to access. Taken together, and out of the context of the lower court's findings of *Take the Money and Run,* the sequence might have provided the basis for inferring access. However, drawing such an inference seems inappropriate when, as in this case, the lower court based its finding — that some of *K.C. Munchkin* was created before Averett's exposure to *Pac-Man* — on approximately two days of testimony during which both the plaintiff and the defendant presented several witnesses.[186] At the very least, this suggests that the court of appeals should have remanded the case to determine whether the stipulation should not have been withdrawn in light of the district court's findings, or whether, on the other hand, the district court's findings should be revised in light of the stipulation.[187]

On the question of the similarity between the two games, the comparison between the appellate and lower court's opinions is equally unsettling. The district court observed distinctive dissimilarities between the games' characters. The colors were different; *K.C. Munchkin*'s monsters were "spookier", and the central figure in *K.C. Munchkin* was more developed as a character, showing frowns and smiles.[188] None of these distinctions impressed the appellate panel, which believed (without adducing any proof) that the audience for video games "is fairly undiscriminating insofar as their concern about more subtle differences in artistic expression."[189] The court of appeals also assumed (again without proof) that "[t]he main attraction of a game such as PAC-MAN lies in the stimulation provided by the intensity of the competition."[190] If true, this assertion should have led to the conclusion that the significant differences in the way the games played would favor a finding that the games were not substantially similar. But the court of appeals instead held that similarities in "expression" are more significant from a copyright standpoint than are dissimilarities in play.[191] In all, one is left with the distinct impression that the court's finding of substantial similarity was based entirely

---

[186] This fact is based on the author's conversations with counsel for both parties to the North American Philips litigation.

[187] There is certainly a lesson to be learned here on the deleterious effect that stipulated facts can sometimes have on judicial performance. Presumably, the court of appeals was entitled to rely on facts stipulated by the parties. On the other hand, it is extraordinary to ignore the detailed findings of a judge who sat through two days of testimony.

[188] See supra text accompanying notes 135–39.

[189] North American Philips, 672 F.2d at 619.

[190] Id.

[191] See id.

on the court's uncritical impression of the similarities between the games. The court's conclusion of infringement thus seems to have been uninfluenced by its sophisticated copyright analysis based on the idea/expression distinction and the concept of scènes à faire.[192]

The appellate court's simplified and stylized version of the facts allowed it to push aside the really difficult aspect of the *K.C. Munchkin/Pac-Man* case: *K.C. Munchkin,* although superficially similar to *Pac-Man,* was, in some respects, a different game, created in part before its creator had ever seen *Pac-Man.* For this reason, Learned Hand's "abstraction" continuum did not apply — the amount of similarity between the games did not increase uniformly as the level of abstraction increased. At a highly abstract level, *K.C. Munchkin* and *Pac-Man* were similar: both were maze-chase games in which the player scores points by consuming dots and avoiding monsters. At a middle level, they were dissimilar — *K.C. Munchkin* had variable, programmable mazes, moving dots, and more need for "strategy." At a superficial level, they were again similar — according to the court of appeals, at least, the characters looked the same in each game. The court was not oblivious to the presence of this problem. It acknowledged that "[t]he defendants and the district court order stress that K.C. Munchkin plays differently because of the moving dots and the variety of maze configurations from which the player can choose."[193] The court dismissed this unsettling fact, however, in a blizzard of rhetoric. It declared that the "focus" of a copyright action is on "similarities in protectible expression"; that "no plagiarist can excuse the wrong by showing how much of his work he did not pirate"; and that "[i]t is irrelevant that K.C. Munchkin has other game modes which employ various maze configurations," because "[t)he only mode that concerns this court is the one that uses a display most similar to the one in PAC-MAN."[194] The court's tone in addressing the most substantial issue it faced thus had the sound of the prosecutor's summary in a murder trial. *K.C. Munchkin* was not merely the accused work, and North American Philips not merely the defendant in a civil proceeding brought by a multi-million dollar corporation: the defendant was a plagiarist, and all

---

[192] The court of appeals should not be faulted too harshly for this impressionistic approach, since it is consistent with a traditional ("ordinary observer") style of decision in copyright cases. The "ordinary observer" test employed by the court has the most august credentials, see infra text accompanying notes 282–87, but is subject to serious shortcomings, see infra text accompanying notes 298–302.

[193] *North American Philips,* 672 F.2d at 619.

[194] Id. Why this should be irrelevant is difficult to understand. At least, it suggests that only the similar game features should be enjoined, not that K.C. Munchkin is as a whole infringing.

aspects of *K.C. Munchkin* should be disregarded except those tending to prove its resemblance to *Pac-Man.*

Based on its sanitized reading of the facts, the court of appeals was able to direct the district court to enter an equally sterile preliminary injunction "against continued infringement of plaintiffs' copyright."[195] In the context of the court of appeals' opinion, this command required the defendant to be "enjoined from marketing K.C. Munchkin,"[196] and on March 5, 1982, the district court entered an order enjoining and restraining the defendants "from advertising, distributing, displaying, performing, selling or offering for sale a video game cartridge known as 'K.C. Munchkin', or in any other manner violating plaintiffs' exclusive rights under the copyright in the Pac-Man audiovisual work."[197] The Seventh Circuit panel declared pridefully that the injunction would "preserve the integrity of the copyright laws which seek to encourage individual effort and creativity by granting valuable enforceable rights."[198] The court awarded itself this ovation without pausing to measure the impact of its injunction on the effort and creativity of persons who, like Mr. Averett, create maze-chase games that will compete with, and possibly improve upon, *Pac-Man. Pac-Man* had sales of $150 million between October of 1980 and December 1981,[199] and *K.C. Munchkin* had been in production for that entire period of time — since August of 1980.[200] Under these circumstances, it is fictional for the appellate court to have concluded that the effort and creativity of the makers of *Pac-Man* would not be rewarded, and the "integrity of the copyright laws" would be lost, unless *K.C. Munchkin* was enjoined. The court's injunction may have protected the size of *Pac-Man* profits, but it surely was not necessary for their existence.

One can only surmise that the court's rhetorical flourishes served to assuage discomfort over its artificially uncomplicated holding. That holding was required by two assumptions: first, that *K.C. Munchkin* as a whole either

---

[195] Id. at 621.

[196] Id. at 620.

[197] See the district court's order on remand, *Atari, Inc. v. North American Philips Consumer Elecs. Corp.*, No. 81 C 6434 (N.D. Ill. March 5, 1982), reprinted in North American Philips Consumer Elecs. Corp., Petition for a Writ of Certiorari to the U.S. Court of Appeals for the Seventh Circuit app. E, at E1, *Atari, Inc. v. North American Philips Consumer Elecs. Corp.*, 672 F.2d 607 (7th Cir.), cert. denied, 51 U.S.L.W. 3258 (U.S. Oct. 4, 1982).

[198] *North American Philips*, 672 F.2d at 620.

[199] See supra note 2 and accompanying text.

[200] See *North American Philips*, 2 Copyright L. Rep. (CCH) ¶25,363, at 17,048.

infringed *Pac-Man* or did not, and second, that the plaintiff's rights in *Pac-Man* could only be protected by copyright. As will be discussed at length later in this article, neither of these assumptions is valid.[201] As one alternative, the court could have found that only certain aspects of *K.C. Munchkin* infringed *Pac-Man*. The court of appeals based its finding of infringement primarily on the similarities between the *Pac-Man* and *K.C. Munchkin* "characters."[202] It has sometimes been held that one may claim copyright infringement in the unauthorized copying of a character, even if in the accused work the character participates in a wholly different plot.[203] The typical remedy for "character infringement" is to enjoin the infringer's use of the infringing characters, while leaving the defendants free to employ different characters in the service of the same or a similar plot. Thus, a finding that *K.C. Munchkin*'s characters were "substantially similar" to *Pac-Man*'s, and therefore infringing would have required the defendants to change the appearance of *K.C. Munchkin*'s "muncher" and "monsters," while preserving for public enjoyment *K.C. Munchkin*'s programmable mazes, moving dots, and other unique features.

A problem in the character infringement approach is that the character must be "sufficiently developed to command copyright protection."[204] One might question whether the stylized, geometrical figures that constitute *Pac-Man*'s characters meet this criterion. Even if they do not, however, there is a second alternative to the appellate court's blanket finding of copyright infringement. If one accepts the district court's conclusion that *K.C. Munchkin* and *Pac-Man* were significantly different maze-chase games (so that Hand's continuum of abstractions does not apply), and if one further believes that the *Pac-Man* "characters" are too rudimentary to qualify for copyright protection, then the superficial similarities between the otherwise

[201] See infra text following note 263.

[202] The court said, "it is the substantial appropriation of the PAC-MAN characters that requires reversal of the district court." *North American Philips*, 672 F.2d at 617.

[203] See, e.g., *Goodis v. United Artists Television, Inc.*, 425 F.2d 397,406 (2d Cir. 1970); *Nichols v. Universal Pictures Corp*, 45 F.2d 119, 121 (2d Cir. 1939); *Warner Bros., Inc. v. American Broadcasting Cos.*, 530 F. Supp. 1187, 1193 (S.D.N.Y. 1982); *United Artists Corp. v. Ford Motor Co.*, 483 F. Supp. 89, 93 (S.D.N.Y. 1980); 3 M. Nimmer, supra note 10, §2.12, at 2-169. Kaplan has questioned the possibility of character infringement in its entirety, arguing that "literary characters, in plays as in novels, achieve their distinctness in large part by being made to react to the particular flux of incident in the particular milieu." B. Kaplan, supra note 10, at 51. He leaves the door open for infringement "as between pictorial characters," Id., but even there warns of "trouble in setting proper bounds to their protection." Id. at 52.

[204] 3 M. Nimmer, supra note 10, §2.12, at 2-171.

differing games suggest that the defendant's real offense may have been more in the nature of trademark infringement and unfair competition than in the nature of copyright infringement.[205] Indeed, *Pac-Man*'s central "gobbler" character has become a recognized symbol, apparently having great value[206] independent of its function in the game itself. Assuming that the plaintiffs in *North American Philips* could show that they began using the distinctive features of the *Pac-Man* characters before the defendant began to market *K.C. Munchkin*, a confusing similarity in appearance between *K.C. Munchkin*'s characters and *Pac-Man*'s could provide a basis for relief both at common law,[207] under state statutes,[208] and under section 43(a) of the Lanham Act.[209]

---

205 See Lanham Act §43; 15 U.S.C. §1125 (1976). At least one court has suggested that the criteria for trademark infringement may be the same as those for "substantial similarity" under the Copyright Act. See *Warner Bros. Inc. v. American Broadcasting Cos.*, 530 F. Supp. 1187, 1198 (S.D.N.Y. 1982). This equivalence may be true for the trademark issue of "confusing similarity" and the copyright issue of "substantial similarity." As discussed in the text, however, the policies of trademark protection are different from those of copyright protection. For this reason, a geometrical form such as *Pac-Man*'s central character (a circle with a v-shaped notch cut in it) might be too simple to enjoy protection as a "character" protected by copyright but may nevertheless be a "strong" trademark (analogous to such well-known marks as the McDonald arches, the Shell Oil Company shell, and the CBS "eye") because its very simplicity gives it distinctiveness and a propensity for immediate recognition. Strength of a mark refers to "its tendency to identify the goods sold under the mark as emanating from a particular . . . source." *McGregor-Doniger, Inc. v. Drizzle, Inc.*, 599 F.2d 1126, 1131 (2d Cir. 1979). Thus, if the threshold criteria of confusing substantial similarity is met by two figures, trademark law may protect them as "marks" while copyright law would not protect them as "characters." It has been expressly held that "ingredients" of products which are sold as entertainment, such as the Dallas Cowboys Cheerleaders' uniform, the Star Wars characters, and comic book characters such as "Aquaman" may be protected under §43(c) of the Lanham Act. See *D.C. Comics. Inc. v. Filmation Associates*, 486 F. Supp. 1273, 1277 (S.D.N.Y. 1980). For an example of a court finding trademark infringement in the appropriation of video game characters, see *Midway Mfg. Co. v. Dirkschneider*, 543 F. Supp. 466 (D. Neb. 1981) (discussed supra text following note 85).

206 Judging from the frequency and breadth of its use, its value is clear. There is, for example, a Pac-Man cartoon series, and the author recently discovered that there is even a Pac-Man ice cream bar. The bar is in the shape of the Pac-Man gobbler, and its shape and name are duly licensed to the ice cream manufacturer by Midway Manufacturing Corp., one of the plaintiffs in North American Philips.

207 See R. Callman, *The Law of Unfair Competition, Trademarks and Monopolies* §2.01 (4th ed. 1981). Note that the action could lie regardless of whether the plaintiffs had registered the character as trademark. See id. at §2.01, n. 2.

Such relief could prevent *North American Philips* from unfairly appropriating to its own advantage the goodwill associated with the famous *Pac-Man* "characters" while at the same time allowing the distribution of a maze-chase game having *K.C. Munchkin*'s unique playing features. Had the court of appeals focused on these considerations, its interpretation of the facts in its *North American Philips* opinion might have been less strained and its conclusion more convincing and just.

Some suggestions for improved copyright analysis

All of the opinions described above were rendered during the years 1981 and 1982.[210] During that brief span, the courts swung sharply between overbroad and overnarrow scope of protection for the games. In some early opinions (*Stern Electronics* district court opinion, *Armenia, Artic International,* and *Dirkschneider*), courts granted sweeping relief to the copyright claimants, often paying little or no attention to the traditional limitations on copyright protection for games. In other opinions (*Amusement World* and the *North American Philips* district court opinion), the older dogmas that copyright does not protect "ideas" and "games" were reasserted so strongly that the courts found noninfringement in the face of surprisingly numerous and specific points of identity between the copyrighted and allegedly infringing games. In other cases (*Stern Electronics* and *North American Philips* court of appeals opinions), the courts appeared to overextend copyright law to remedy trademark infringement. None of these opinions presents a convincing balance of the interests protected by copyright law.

In several video game cases, the courts' holdings on the issue of infringement were by no means foregone conclusions. *North American Philips* is perhaps the best example because, in a detailed opinion, the district court had found *Pac-*

---

[208] See, e.g., 1964 Uniform Deceptive Trade Practices Act §2, Ill. Rev. Stat., ch. 121 1/2, §312 (Supp. 1982) (claimed by Atari to have been violated by the North American Philips defendants).

[209] Section 43 of the Lanham Act, 15 U.S.C. §1125 (1976), is generally considered to be a grab-bag for types of unfair competition that may not fall into a recognized category of trademark infringement. See, e.g., *Berlitz School of Languages of America, Inc. v. Everest House*, 619 F.2d 211 (2d Cir. 1980); *Smith v. Chanel, Inc.*, 402 F.2d 562 (9th Cir. 1968).

[210] Two more recent video game copyright decisions, *Williams Elecs., Inc. v. Artic Int'l. Inc.*, 685 F.2d 870 (3d Cir. 1982), and *Midway Mfg. Co. v. Bandai-America, Inc.*, 546 F. Supp. 125 (D.N.J. 1982) were rendered while this article was being edited, and are referred to in several footnotes.

Man and *K.C. Munchkin* not substantially similar, only to have its finding on this issue of fact reversed by the court of appeals. Likewise, the points of similarity between the plaintiff's and defendant's games in *Amusement World* were so extensive that a reasonable person might easily have concluded that the defendant's game had infringed the plaintiff's, although the court, in a scholarly opinion, held otherwise. Despite the differing conclusions that could reasonably be reached from the facts both in *North American Philips* and *in Amusement World*, the outcome in both cases was a complete victory for one party over the other, like a verdict of guilty or not guilty.

It has already been remarked that the peculiar characteristics of video games could be expected to place great pressure on the established copyright dogmas that a distinction may be drawn between ideas and expressions, and that ideas, and more particularly games, should not enjoy copyright protection. The considerable variations of outcomes in the video game cases reflect the courts' efforts to respond to this pressure, sometimes giving in to the claims for protection too quickly, and at other times failing adequately to acknowledge them. Some back-and-forth movement of this kind is inevitable whenever the law seeks to mold itself to a new environment. It is the thesis of this article, however, that the swings of precedent in the early video game cases have been too wide. Their breadth, it is submitted, is the direct result of several largely unrecognized, but nevertheless pervasive, habits of copyright adjudication, all of which incline the courts to grant or deny relief on an all-or-nothing basis. The following sections of the article will describe how these habits have become pitfalls to the elaboration of copyright law in new settings such as video games. Suggestions for avoiding these pitfalls will also be made.

Ideas and expressions[211]

In video game cases such as the appellate court decisions in *Stern Electronics* and *North American Philips*, the courts' application of copyright law resulted in overbroad protection for the video games. The principle that is supposed to stand as a bulwark against such overbroad protection is that copyright does not protect "ideas." Unfortunately, the courts' employment of this concept in the video game cases has been inhibited in two ways, both of which make the idea/expression distinction at best a stilted instrument of policy. The first is that the courts have generally excluded or overlooked evidence extrinsic to the accused and copyrighted games that might have helped them decide what

---

[211] For a general discussion of the application of the idea/expression distinction to video games, see Jones, supra note 7, at 35–43.

forms of taking may be called the taking of "ideas." The second is that the courts have assumed that anything one might call a "rule of play" is an "idea" and, therefore, outside the scope of copyright protection. To these errors, we will now turn.

1. The idea/expression distinction, scènes à faire, and a sense of context

a. Copyright policy considerations

As has already been observed, the central problem of copyright law is to reconcile and balance interests in, on the one hand, rewarding individuals for their "unique creative efforts,"[212] and, on the other hand, making authors' "ideas freely accessible to the public so that they may be used for the intellectual advancement of mankind,"[213] thus promoting "the Progress of Science and useful Arts."[214] Some might question the contribution of video games to the intellectual advancement of mankind, but copyright protection is blind to such normative considerations[215] , and one of the most impressive aspects of the video game phenomenon is the burst of creativity this new medium has fostered. To inhibit such vigorous creative activity by threatening each variation and improvement of an initial work with costly infringement liability would be wholly inconsistent with the Copyright Act policy of promoting diversity and advancement. To expose video game authors to uncontrolled expropriation of the fruits of their labors by the marketing of knock-off games would be equally inconsistent with the Copyright Act policy of rewarding creative efforts.

The idea/expression distinction aspires to resolve, or at least to stand as a proxy for, these competing policy considerations. Copyright protects expression (thus rewarding authors) while thrusting ideas into the public domain (thus promoting science and the useful arts). Historically, the public domain encompassed far more territory than that bounded by the modern concept of

---

[212] *Midway Mfg. Co. v. Artic Int'l, Inc.*, Copyright L. Rep. (CCH) ¶25,337, at 16,890 (N.D. Ill. June 2, 1981).

[213] 3 M. Nimmer, supra note 10, §13.03[A], at 13–19; see L. Seltzer, *Exemptions and Fair Use in Copyright*, 3–17 (1978).

[214] U.S. Const. art. I, §8, cl. 8; see *Becker v. Loew's, Inc.*, 113 F.2d 889 (7th Cir. 1943); *Eichel v. Marcin*, 241 F. 404 (S.D.N.Y. 1917); 3 M. Nimmer, supra note 10, §13.03[A], at 13–18; supra note 9.

[215] See *Mitchell Bros. Film Group v. Cinema Adult Theater*, 604 F.2d 852 (5th Cir. 1979), cert. denied, 445 U.S. 917 (1980) (holding, inter alia, that obscene content is not a bar to copyrightability).

the copyright "idea."[216] The first genuine copyright legislation (following the overthrow of the Stationers' Company's monopoly) was the Statute of Anne,[217] enacted in 1709, which accorded to an author and his assigns "the sole liberty of printing and reprinting" a book.[218] In a series of cases decided between 1720 and 1785, the English courts held that translations, abridgments, and improved editions of informational works such as maps, histories, and dictionaries (all certainly "derivative" works in the modern sense)[219] did not infringe the earlier, copyrighted works on which they were based.[220] Justice Kaplan proposes two principles on which these cases may have been based. First, the courts would hold against infringement if the defendant had added to or improved upon the original work. In the case of an abridgment of Hawkesworth's *Voyages*, the defendant "was not only exculpated but congratulated for reducing Hawkesworth and preserving the substance in different language perhaps better than the original."[221] Second, the courts would hold against infringement if they found that the defendant's work did not "interfere unduly with the normal economic exploitation of the copyright."[222] Whatever the rationale, the effect of such cases was to restrict copyright infringement essentially to verbatim copying of the entire original work.

Nineteenth-century decisions in England and the United States preserved the rules that permitted translations and abridgments. However, the dike separating actionable verbatim copying from all other forms of taking suffered a steady erosion under the influence of expansive copyright legislation,[223] judicial elaboration of the concept of "substantial" taking, [224]and scholarly

---

216 This synopsis of copyright history is based on the account in B. Kaplan, supra note 10, at 1–38.

217 An act for the encouragement of learning, by vesting the copies of printed books in the author's [sic] or purchasers of such copies, during the times therein mentioned, 1709, 8 Anne, ch. 19.

218 Id.§1.

219 See 17 U.S.C. §101 (1976 & Supp. V. 1981) (definition of a "derivative work").

220 See B. Kaplan, supra note 10, at 9–17.

221 Id. at 12.

222 Id. at 17. This consideration has survived as one of the criteria for fair use in the Copyright Act. See 17 U.S.C. §107(4) (1976 & Supp. V 1981).

223 For example, an English statute on engravings prohibited copying "in whole or in part, by varying, adding to, or diminishing from the main design," B. Kaplan, supra note 10 at 20 (quoting from 8 Geo. 2, ch. 13, §1 (1735), and the 1870 amendment to the United States copyright laws extended protection to translations and dramatizations of copyrighted works. See Act of July 8, 1870, ch. 230, §86, 16 Stat. 186, 212 (discussed in B. Kaplan, supra note 10, at 32).

224 See B. Kaplan, supra note 10, at 20.

criticism of the early limitations on copyright protection.[225] The modern exception to liability for the taking of "ideas" appears to have emerged as a fall-back levee against the flood of unlimited protection, which otherwise would have ensued once a remedy for nonverbatim copying was recognized.

Reflecting these developments, our present Copyright Act reverses the historical presumption favoring all but verbatim copying. Section 102(b) of the Act extends protection to all aspects of an "original work of authorship" except "any idea, procedure, process, system, method of operation, concept, principle, or discovery" that is "described, explained, illustrated or embodied" in the work.[226] Thus, the logic of the Copyright Act is like a Venn diagram in which the "universe" includes all aspects of the work. Copyright protection extends to the whole universe except for the area within the universe carved out by the phrase "any idea, procedure, process, system, method of operation, concept, principle or discovery." Where, as in the case of video games, ideas are not easily distinguished from their expressions, the difficulty of identifying ideas combined with the logic of the Copyright Act (universal protection, except for ideas) foretells an area of protection that may expand beyond the bounds set by copyright policy.[227]

For convenience, courts typically use the word "idea" as a shorthand for the longer list in section 102(a).[228] Like any English word drafted into the service of the law, the word "idea" has acquired a special copyright meaning. It is a relatively narrow meaning, the contours of which can be perceived in certain

---

[225] See Justice Kaplan's comments on Justice Storey, B. Kaplan, supra note 10, at 28-29. See generally Kaplan's remarks on the reflection in the law of the cultural transformation from classical virtues (which emphasized the importance of imitation) to the romantic ideal (emphasizing new creation and individuality), id. at 22–25.

[226] 17 U.S.C. §102(b) (1976 & Supp. V 1981). For the designs of "useful articles" which also fall within the definition of "pictorial, graphic, and sculptural works," the Act conditions operation of this presumption on satisfaction of the requirement that the pictorial, graphic, and sculptural features of such works be "identified separately from, and . . . capable of existing independently of, the utilitarian aspects of the article." 17 U.S.C. §101 (1976 & Supp. V 1981) (definition of pictorial, graphic and sculptural works). However, all courts have characterized video games as audiovisual works, to which the limitation expressed in §101 for copyright in pictorial, graphic, and sculptural works which are also "useful articles" probably does not apply.

[227] This has been true in the video game cases despite the traditional rule that when ideas and expressions cannot be distinguished, copyright protects only against verbatim copying. See supra note 170.

[228] See 17 U.S.C. §102(a) (1976 & Supp. V 1981).

axioms of copyright protection. One such axiom is that, with rare exceptions,[229] the verbatim copying of an entire work constitutes infringement of the work.[230] Of necessity, a verbatim copy incorporates each and every "idea" in the original work and punishing the verbatim copier, therefore, punishes one form of copying of ideas. It is assumed, however, that an "idea" for copyright purposes is capable of expression in a way different from the way it was expressed in the original work. This assumption is by no means obvious,[231] but it forms the basis for reasoning that one may penalize the verbatim copier without unlawfully extending protection to the ideas in the original work.

A second axiom is that a work which is not a verbatim copy, but which is "substantially similar" to the original work, may also be an infringement. To be "substantially similar" to the original work, the infringing work must express the same things as the original work, albeit with different words, sounds, or images. The recognition that a "substantially similar" work may infringe the original therefore implies that capability of expression in more than one way is a necessary, but not a sufficient, condition for qualification as an "idea" for copyright purposes. To qualify as an idea, what has been expressed differently in the original and in the substantially similar work must also attain a minimum level of generality. This principle forms the basis for Learned Hand's famous "abstractions test."[232]

Combined, the logic of the Copyright Act (universal protection, except for ideas) and the narrow meaning of the copyright "idea" carry an important implication. If it is difficult to identify the ideas embodied in the copyrighted

---

[229] One exception is the verbatim copying of blank forms. See 37 C.F.R. §202.l(c) (1982): see also Baker v. Selden, 101 U.S. 99, 107 (1879) ("The conclusion to which we have come is, that blank account-books are not the subject of copyright"). However, even this exception has been questioned. See 1 M. Nimmer, supra note 10, §2.18[C]. Another exception may be the verbatim copying of a very elementary idea. See supra note 170 (jeweled bee pin).

[230] See *North American Philips*, 672 F.2d at 614, n. 6, 616 (implying that review is not required when copying is verbatim); supra note 170.

[231] Reverting to the ordinary meaning of "idea," one might question, for example, whether the "idea" of "To be or not to be" is capable of expression in different words. Could any paraphrase (e.g., "I can't decide whether to act or to remain passive") express the same idea? Cf. *Morrissey v. Proctor & Gamble Co.*, 379 F.2d 675, 678–79 (1st Cir. 1967) (holding that a rule which has a limited number of forms of expression is not copyrightable); *Sid & Marty Krofft Television Prods., Inc. v. McDonald's Corp.*, 562 F.2d 1157 (9th Cir. 1977). See generally B. Kaplan, supra note 10, at 45-56 (questioning idea/expression analysis as applied, for example, to the fine arts).

[232] See supra note 167 and accompanying text.

work, or if one cannot effectively separate the ideas from the expression, then the "ideas" exception becomes a null set, and copyright protection expands to include all aspects of the copyrighted work. In such circumstances, the idea/expression distinction, historically the next line of defense against overbroad protection once copyright actions for nonverbatim copying had been recognized, and the modern embodiment of the public policy favoring use and exploitation of copyrighted works, fails its purpose. This is exactly what seems to have happened in video game cases, particularly Stern Electronics (district court), Armenia, and Artic International, in which the courts did not even attempt to separate the games' ideas from their expressions and, as a result, granted the plaintiffs sweeping equitable relief. The task of separating ideas from expressions is particularly difficult with regard to video games, in which the rules of play are often embedded in, and are in some ways indistinguishable from, the games' graphics.[233] The results in cases such as Stern Electronics, Armenia, and Artic, are thus the predictable sum of adding the nature of the games to the logic of the Copyright Act.

Video game cases are not the only types of cases in which ideas are so difficult to separate from their expression that the distinction seems unhelpful as an arbiter of copyright policy. For graphic works such as paintings and sculptures, the distinction is especially inept; it is perhaps in recognition of this that Congress reversed the Act's logic for "pictorial, graphic, and sculptural works," granting their expression protection only if "capable of existing independently of" the "utilitarian" aspects of the work.[234] Justice Kaplan has argued persuasively that the identification of "ideas" in musical works, particularly modern works lacking in melody, is equally futile.[235] Arguably, it would be better to do without the distinction altogether.[236]

---

[233] It will be recalled that this is one of the differences between video games and the leading cases establishing the blackletter rule that copyright does not protect games. See supra notes 45–47 and accompanying text.

[234] 17 U.S.C. §101 (1976 & Supp. V 1981); see also B. Kaplan, supra note 10, at 54–56.

[235] See B. Kaplan, supra note 10, at 53.

[236] Perhaps a better approach would recognize that no single formulation can hope to strike the policy balance across the whole range of "works" by which humans reach out to each other through their senses, and would instead substitute a set of factors, shifting in importance as one moves from one type of work to another. Such factors would probably include the nature and substantiality of the taking, the purpose of the taking, and the impact of the taking on the market for the copyrighted work. These are similar to the Act's criteria for fair use, located in §107:

In determining whether the use made of such a work in any particular case is a fair use the factors to be considered shall include —

Considering that the Copyright Act is only six years old, and considering that there had been calls for a revision of copyright law for more than thirty years before its passage,[237] the thought of discarding the idea/expression distinction entirely must be considered a utopian dream at best. For the time being, we are stuck with the Act's use of the idea/expression dichotomy to modulate the scope of copyright protection, and we will have to make the best of it. Fortunately, the Act's list of idea-like elements is not one of these legal bugs encased in the amber of a statute.[238] The Act leaves plenty of room for the development of the idea of an "idea"; by framing discussion in terms of "ideas" and "expressions," the court's freedom of consideration is restricted, but not entirely lost.

---

1. the purpose and character of the use, including whether such use is of a commercial nature or is for nonprofit educational purposes;
2. the nature of the copyrighted work;
3. the amount and substantiality of the portion used in relation to the copyrighted work as a whole; and
4. the effect of the use upon the potential market for or value of the copyrighted work.

17 U.S.C. §107 (1976 & Supp. V 1981). For historical examples of the consideration of such factors, see B. Kaplan, supra note 10, at 11–21, discussing *Gray v. Russell*, 10 F. Cas. 1035, 1038–39 (C.C.D. Mass. 1839) (No. 5728) (Story, J.) (considering importance of part taken); *Wilkins v. Aikin*, 34 Eng. Rep. 163 (Ch. 1810) (discussing relevance of borrower's profit motive); *Dodsley v. Kinnersley*, 27 Eng. Rep. 270 (Ch. 1761) (discussing effect of infringing work on sales of copyrighted work). For limited borrowings which exceed the policy limits, the ideal act we are imagining might sanction the grant of royalties to the copyright holder as a less restrictive alternative to injunctive relief. In effect, the concept of substantial similarity would be subsumed into the doctrine of fair use.

237 Revisions of the Copyright Act of 1909 were under serious discussion at least since the 1940s. See, e.g., Chafee, "Reflections on the Law of Copyright" (pts. 1 & 2), 45 Colum. L. Rev. 503, 719 (1945).

238 Contrast §117 of the Act, as originally passed, which attempted to freeze the law of computer uses of copyrighted works at its 1977 state of development.

Notwithstanding the provisions of sections 106 through 116 and 118, this title does not afford to the owner of copyright in a work any greater or lesser rights with respect to the use of the work in conjunction with automatic systems capable of storing, processing, retrieving, or transferring information, or in conjunction with any similar device, machine, or process, than those afforded to works under the law, whether title 17 or the common law or statutes of a State, in effect on December 31, 1977, as held applicable and construed by a court in an action brought under this title.

Act of Oct. 19, 1976, Pub. L. No. 94-553, tit. I, §101, 90 Stat. 2541, 2565 (1976) (current version at 17 U.S.C. §117 [1976 & Supp. V 1981]).

One must, then, find ways to make ideas and expressions effectuate the desired policy even in those cases, like video game cases, in which they are not ideal intellectual tools. A careful examination of the way courts have used these tools in more traditional cases can provide some insight — both in showing techniques that may work for the more unusual cases and in showing why some standard techniques will not work.

b. Scènes à faire

One of the most important tools used to strike the policy balance in traditional cases is the concept of "scènes à faire." Using this device, courts inquire whether the copyrighted and allegedly infringing works are more similar to each other than they are to other works of the same genre. In a traditional case, such as the alleged infringement of a novel, courts dig into their own knowledge and experience to provide the necessary information about other works. *O'Neill v. Dell Publishing Co., Inc.*[239] is a good example. In *O'Neill,* the plaintiff claimed that his unpublished manuscript *Return to Nowhere*" had been infringed by the defendant's published book *Ghost Boat.* Both novels used the device of a submarine that mysteriously disappears, only to reappear at a much later time. The court immediately placed this theme in a literary context familiar both to the court and (presumably) to anyone reading the opinion:

> As the district court noted, *Return to Nowhere* uses the *Rip Van Winkle* theme of a sleep that lasts for years. Instead of taking place in the Catskill Mountains and being induced by strong drink quaffed during a game of "bowls" with little men, the sleep in *Return to Nowhere* takes place off the coast of Alaska when a submarine with its entire crew is trapped under a massive ice formation. Unlike old Rip, however, the submariners do not age as the years pass. When awakened from their frozen state, they are the same age as when the submarine dove under the ice pack on one Christmas Eve, 1942, to avoid Japanese destroyers.[240]

By drawing an analogy to the story of Rip Van Winkle, the court showed that the idea of a character who disappears and mysteriously returns at a later time was already in the public domain and not available for copyright

---

[239] 630 F.2d 685 (1st Cir. 1980). For another example, see *Warner Bros., Inc. v. American Broadcasting Cos.,* 530 F. Supp. 1187 (S.D.N.Y. 1982) (holding that the television show *The Greatest American Hero* does not infringe "Superman" based in part on comparison of those works with other works of the superhero genre).
[240] O'Neill, 630 F.2d at 687.

protection. After summarizing the plot of each book in some detail, the court affirmed the district court's summary judgment for the defendant, holding that the similarities between the two works were only on the level of unprotected ideas.[241]

A similar use of context appears in a more recent decision, *Warner Brothers, Inc. v. American Broadcasting Cos.*,[242] in which the court held that the television series *The Greatest American Hero* had not infringed copyright in the "Superman" comic books, television series, and movies. In that case, the central characters in the accused and infringing works shared many features: "Super-strength," "Super-hearing," "Super-vision," "Super-speed," "Super-breath," "Invulnerability," "The ability to Fly," an "Alter-ego," and a "Costume."[243] However, the court reviewed generally the literature of "superheroes," finding that many of them also had capes, tightfitting uniforms, role reversals, and so on. At most, the hero in *The Greatest American Hero* was only marginally more similar to Superman than it was to the other works of the superhero genre. The court, therefore, found for the defendant.

Courts often equate scènes à faire with the "idea" of the copyrighted and accused works.[244] This equation is an instance of legal fiction or at least legal exaggeration. For example, the cape typically worn by comic book superheroes has no discernable intrinsic connection with the idea of a creature having extraordinary powers. (By contrast, bulging muscles and a trim physique might claim such a connection.) The cape is more fairly described as a literary convention or device that probably has a historical rather than a logical explanation. Clearly, scènes à faire and ideas are often not synonymous, and thus recitation of the principle that ideas are not protected does not adequately explain denial of protection to scènes à faire. More plausible alternative explanations come to mind.

One is that the standard assumption that access plus substantial similarity implies copying does not obtain when the substantial similarity between the works lies in their use of conventional devices: the author of an accused work could have copied the devices from any number of sources, not only from the

---

[241] See id. at 690.

[242] 530 F. Supp. 1187 (S.D.N.Y. 1982). An additional factor supporting the court's finding of noninfringement is that the Hero series parodies Superman. As Kaplan has noted, parody often requires a high degree of similarity to be effective. See B. Kaplan, supra note 10, at 69.

[243] *Warner Bros.*, 530 F. Supp. at 1190-92.

[244] See, e.g., *North American Philips*, 672 F.2d at 616.

copyrighted work.[245] Suppose, though, that the plaintiff could prove beyond question that the defendant copied a device, such as the superhero cape, from the plaintiff's copyrighted work. Once again, infringement should not lie, for two reasons. First, the device cannot be used to distinguish the copyrighted work from others in the marketplace, because by definition, the device appears in works other than the copyrighted work. The purpose of protecting the market for copyrighted works would not be served by protecting a feature that is incapable of inducing a person to use the copyrighted work in preference to other, similar works. A second reason relates to the concept of originality.[246] In copyright, the requirement of originality is thought to be essentially trivial. The copyright registration — which is not reviewed substantially by the Copyright Office — constitutes prima facie evidence of originality,[247] and the burden is on the defendant to prove absence of originality.[248] The concept of scènes à faire, however, gives content to this otherwise trivial requirement. It would be incredible for an author (who presumably is reasonably widely read) to claim that he invented out of whole cloth a standard literary (or video game) device that he could have taken from

---

[245] See B. Kaplan, supra note 10, at 44.

[246] Both courts and commentators have been leery of introducing to copyright any doctrine as stringent as the criterion of novelty in patent law. Compare *Hein v. Harris,* 175 F. 875 (C.C.S.D.N.Y. 1910), aff'd, 183 F. 107 (2d Cir. 1910) (Hand, J., applying an "invention" test) with *Fred Fisher, Inc. v. Dillingham,* 298 F. 145 (S.D.N.Y. 1924) (Hand, J., avoiding a strict test of novelty). These cases are discussed in B. Kaplan, supra note 10, at 41–44. See also 3 M. NIMMER, supra note 10, §16.08[B], at 16–58. The courts have avoided such a doctrine with good reason — as Kaplan puts it, "[i]f [novelty] is a difficult, perhaps an illusory, measure in the field of mechanical improvements, how much harder would it be in literature or the other arts." B. Kaplan, supra note 10, at 43. Copyright "originality" differs from patent "novelty," in that the former requires only that the author did not copy from the prior art, whereas the latter requires that he could not have. See *Filmon Process Corp. v. Spellright Corp,* 274 F. Supp. 312, 313 (D.D.C. 1967) (patent law requires the applicant to be first inventor as well as an original one), aff'd, 404 F.2d 1351 (D.C. Cir. 1968); *Russel v. Trimfit, Inc.,* 428 F. Supp. 91, 93 (E.D. Pa. 1977) (copyright protects from copying only whereas patent protects from any infringement), aff'd, 568 F.2d 770 (3d Cir. 1978): *Fred Fisher, Inc.,* 298 F. at 150; see also B. Kaplan, supra note 10, at 43–44.

[247] See *Midway Mfg. Co. v. Bandai-America, Inc.,* 546 F. Supp. 125, 139 (D.N.J. 1982).

[248] See id.

any number of previously published works.[249] Thus, a court can deny relief under the scènes à faire concept without at the same time overtly expanding the concept of originality or upsetting the presumption of originality arising from registration.

Scènes à faire thus play a vital role in cases in which courts attempt to draw the line between actionable and permissible borrowing. The identification of standard literary devices for the copyrighted work's genre provides the context in which the author created his work and in which the work will be presented to its audience. With an eye on this context, the court may, with a steadier hand, draw a line between idea and expression responsive to copyright policy. The context gives the court a feel for what the author created, and for which he therefore deserves a reward. It also helps the court to judge what type of infringement would adversely affect sales of the work. One might say that in a case like O'Neill or Warner Brothers, the idea/expression distinction loses its arid metaphysical quality — what Kaplan calls its "abracadabra"[250] — and becomes tangible. If Hand's continuum frames the discussion of ideas and expressions, scènes à faire fill in the picture, adding perspective and horizon. At the same time, scènes à faire subtly expand the exception to copyright protection by intimating the more sensitive issues of originality and novelty. To use an old metaphor, when effectively used, scènes à faire put meat on the bare bones of the Copyright Act's idea/expression scheme.

If scènes à faire are so helpful in drawing the idea/expression line, why haven't they assisted courts in drawing that line in the video game context? The answer lies in the manner by which courts habitually acquaint themselves with the relevant context. As exemplified by *O'Neill,* for traditional literary works, courts examine the copyrighted and allegedly infringing works against the background of their own literary knowledge. Expert testimony and time-consuming testimony on "extrinsic" issues such as comparisons of the copyrighted and accused works with other works of a similar type are

---

[249] This is like the grounds on which Judge Hand held for the plaintiff in *Fred Fisher, Inc.*: he believed that the accused author, Jerome Kern, did not remember taking from the plaintiff's copyrighted song "Dardanella," but concluded that the taking must have been unconscious. See 298 F. at 147.

[250] B. Kaplan, supra note 10, at 56.

disfavored.[251] The *O'Neill* court rejected the plaintiff's request for additional discovery, commenting, "[i]t is difficult to understand how additional evidence, whatever it might be, could change the written words of the two novels."[252] The court concluded:

> Nor can the testimony of an expert provide what is clearly lacking. Although we may not be qualified literary critics, we are fitted by training and experience to compare literary works and determine whether they evidence substantial similarity. We share Learned Hand's feeling that, in this type of case, expert evidence ought generally to be excluded.[253]

The exclusion of extrinsic evidence and expert testimony is appropriate for traditional literary and audiovisual works because the court's own expertise provides the context within which the line between idea and expression may be assayed intelligently. One may question, however, whether courts are "fitted by training and experience to compare"[254] very new forms of expression such as video games. The wide swings of precedent in video game cases suggest that they are not. Missing in many video game opinions is a confident sense of the extent to which two video games are more or less similar to each other than they are to other video games.[255] Missing also is a sense of the "public domain" and "scènes à faire" for video games.[256] If, as has been suggested, context and scènes à faire help to give substance and particularity to the otherwise vacant concept of an "idea," then courts that

---

[251] See, e.g., *Nichols v. Universal Pictures Corp.*, 45 F.2d 119, 123 (2d Cir. 1930). But see *Franklin Mint Corp. v. Nat'l Wildlife Art Exchange, Inc.*, 575 F.2d 62, 66 (3d Cir.) (expert testimony admitted on conventions in ornithological art), cert. denied, 439 U.S. 880 (1978); *Sid & Marty Krofft Television Prods., Inc. v. McDonald's Corp.*, 562 F.2d 1157, 1164 (9th Cir. 1977) (commenting that "analytical dissection and expert testimony are appropriate" to determine whether ideas in two works are substantially similar).

[252] *O'Neill*, 630 F.2d at 690.

[253] Id.

[254] Id.

[255] But see *Midway Mfg. Co. v. Bandai-America Inc.*, 546 F. Supp. 125 (D.N.J. 1982), in which the court compares Midway's *Galaxian* game with a preexisting work, *Space Invaders*, and with Bandai's subsequent game, also called *Galaxian*. Compare id. at 144 with id. at 146–47.

[256] Cf. *North American Philips*, 672 F.2d at 617 ("Certain expressive matter in the Pac-Man work, however, should be treated as scènes à faire and receive protection only from virtually identical copying.")

lack a sense of context will have difficulty filling in a region of unprotected "ideas" for video games.[257] To return to the Venn diagram analogy, the "ideas" exception to the Copyright Act's otherwise universal protection becomes a null set, and the extreme overbreadth of the holdings in cases such as Stern Electronics and Armenia may result. To put it more simply, any two video games will appear similar to a judge who has seldom seen, much less played, a video game. To the video game connoisseur, which many of the players — the video game "audience" — seem to be, the same two games may exhibit intriguing differences. By analogy, if one rarely views TV soap operas, any two soap operas might seem highly and infringingly similar. Only persons who regularly watch soap operas seem to appreciate the unique features of each.

One may conclude that the protection for video games has often been overbroad, and that the occasional discussions of ideas in the video game cases have been hollow and unsatisfying in part because, on the one hand, the courts' experience with the games is too limited to take judicial notice of standard devices comparable to the *Rip Van Winkle* theme of literature and, on the other hand, the courts have been deterred by precedent and habit from supplementing their own knowledge with extrinsic evidence and expert testimony.

Several of the video game cases provide a notable exception to this trend, in that they carefully distill the unprotected ideas from the copyrighted video games and acknowledge that copyright protection cannot extend to those ideas. Thus, in *North American Philips* and in *Bandai-America,* the ideas in *Pac-Man* and *Galaxian* were abstracted and described.[258] These opinions are also unusual in their attempts to "consider the nature of the protected material and the context in which it appears"[259] as an additional step toward distinguishing ideas from protectible expression. It is perhaps from this sense of "context" that the court in *North American Philips* asserted that "[t]he main

---

[257] The only courts that seem to have successfully undertaken this task are the Seventh Circuit in the North American Philips case, see 672 F.2d at 617 (describing the abstract "idea" underlying the *Pac-Man* "maze chase" game, quoted supra in the text accompanying note 171), and the opinion of the District Court in *Bandai-America,* see 546 F. Supp. at 148 (describing the idea of Midway's *Galaxian* game: "it is an outer space video game in which the player controls a rocket ship defending itself against a swarm of computer-controlled attacking aliens who attempt to bomb and collide with the player's ship.").

[258] See supra text accompanying note 171 and supra note 257.

[259] *North American Philips,* 672 F.2d at 619; see also *Bandai-America,* 546 F. Supp. at 149.

attraction of a game such as Pac-Man lies in the stimulation provided by the intensity of the competition."[260]

It is submitted that in unusual contexts, such as video games, the admission of evidence, both expert and otherwise, about other works similar to the copyrighted and accused works, should become standard practice.[261] Such evidence would provide valuable information about the standard devices (scènes à faire) found in games similar to the ones involved in the suit at hand. Such evidence would also allow the courts to place their comparison of the copyrighted and allegedly infringing games into the context in which the games are actually created and played.[262] The routine use of such evidence would guard against over-broad copyright protection, and at the same time, facilitate a less metaphysical and more policy-oriented approach to infringement issues. Over time, as the courts' experience catches up with new medium, the need for such evidence can be expected to diminish.

2. Not all rules are copyright ideas

One may criticize all of the video game decisions rendered to date for their failure to provide convincing analyses of the issue of substantial similarity. Even decisions such as those in *Amusement World* and at the trial and appellate levels in *North American Philips*, which minutely compare the games in question, fail to explain why they drew where they did the line between ideas and expressions. However, the early decisions' reluctance to

---

260 *North American Philips*, 672 F.2d at 619; see supra notes 190–92 and accompanying text.

261 It is generally said that proving substantial similarity, to which such evidence would be directed, is part of the plaintiff's burden of proof in an infringement action. See 3 M. Nimmer, supra note 10, §13.0l[B], at 13-6. However, the nature of these issues would require the plaintiff to prove a negative — that the similarities between the accused and copyrighted works cannot be explained by a genre, scènes à faire, and the like. For this reason, the most telling evidence on either of these points is likely to be introduced by the defendant.

262 An example of the effective use of such testimony in a copyright case is *Franklin Mint Corp. v. Nat'l Wildlife Art Exchange, Inc.*, 575 F.2d 62 (3d Cir.) cert. denied, 439 U.S. 880 (1978), discussed supra note 251. In another case, *Midway Mfg. Co. v. Bandai-America, Inc.*, 546 F. Supp. 125 (D.N.J. 1982), the court liberally entertained evidence of games similar to those before it, but considered that evidence only on the narrow issue of copyright originality. See, e.g., id. at 151. The court did not expressly use the evidence of other works to identify unprotected scènes à faire, although it achieved the same effect by limiting its injunctive relief to the "original" elements of the copyrighted work (*Pac-Man*). See id. at 153.

apply dogmatically to video games the principle that "copyright does not protect games", is more justifiable. As a direct consequence of the fact that video games are a new field and that their creation requires enormous effort and expense,[263] original works of authorship are evident in the games' rules and methods of play. The authors of *K.C. Munchkin*, for example, invented out of whole cloth the programmable maze and the moving, accelerating dots, which are central to the play of *K.C. Munchkin*.[264] They also created such nonessential "graphic" or "pictorial" features of the game as the face on the central character and "spookier" goblins.[265]

The time and investment required to create a game like *Pac-Man* or *K.C. Munchkin*, coupled with the fact that creativity tends to be centered in the games' rules rather than their graphics, suggests that it may be appropriate for copyright protection to reach some aspects of the games' "methods of play." Any protection for method of play would be a departure from the blackletter law that copyright does not protect games. However, to protect only the shapes and facial expressions of the munchkins and munchers might be an inadequate inducement to, and reward for, the creation of a game such as *K.C. Munchkin* or *Pac-Man*. If the scope of protection is not broad enough to encourage the creation of new games, then creativity will be deterred just as surely as it will be deterred by overbroad protection of existing games.

It should be possible to extend copyright protection to some rule-like aspects of video games without doing great violence to the statutory principles that copyright does not protect "ideas" and "methods of operation." As noted above, an "idea" for copyright purposes must have a minimum level of generality. Not all of the rules and methods of play of a video game necessarily reach this level of generality. An example of a very particularized rule is the principle in the *Asteroids* game that, when hit, a large rock splits into two medium rocks, which, when hit, split into smaller rocks, which, when hit again, disappear.[266] For reasons already discussed at length,

---

[263] See supra text accompanying notes 39–44; see also the *North American Philips* district court's description of the creation of *K.C. Munchkin*, 2 Copyright L. Rep. (CCH) ¶ 5,363, at 17,046–48.

[264] See *North American Philips*, 2 Copyright L. Rep. (CCH) ¶25,363, at 17,046–47. The court's opinion notes that Mr. Averett had invested in an earlier maze-chase game called *Take the Money and Run*, see id. at 17,047, but the opinion does not indicate whether this game antedated *Pac-Man*, nor does it indicate whether any other maze-chase game had preceded the development of *Pac-Man*.

[265] See id. at 17,046–47; supra text accompanying notes 136–38 & 188.

[266] See supra text accompanying note 121.

deciding whether this rule ought to be protected requires some knowledge of similar games employing similar rules (i.e., knowledge of context), but it seems likely that such a rule might be protected without savaging the principle that copyright does not protect "ideas." In other words, not all rules and methods of play are necessarily "ideas" for copyright purposes.[267]

On the other hand, the broad statutory prohibition against any protection for "any idea, procedure, process, system, method of operation, concept, principle or discovery"[268] must not be short-changed. The purpose of copyright is to foster creativity, and this purpose will be achieved in the highest degree if protection is no broader than necessary to create an incentive for the creation of new works. In the context of video games, this suggests that, at most, only the most narrowly particular method of play or rule should qualify for copyright protection.

As discussed above, the Seventh Circuit in *North American Philips* thoughtfully applied the idea/expression distinction to the video games before it, considering doctrines such as scènes à faire and the policies underlying the Copyright Act. Yet the court's analysis ultimately failed, extending such broad protection to the plaintiffs' *Pac-Man* that it appeared to require many original features of the defendants' *K.C. Munchkin* game to be abandoned as well.[269] This result reflects two further difficulties in video game copyright adjudication that lead courts to create overbroad remedies on behalf of plaintiffs whose copyrights have been to some degree infringed: the use of copyright to remedy trademark infringement, and the "ordinary

---

[267] The Copyright Act proscribes protection for "sculptural" features that cannot be "identified separately from, [or be] capable of existing independently of, the utilitarian aspects of the article." 17 U.S.C. §101 (1976 & Supp. V 1981) (definition of pictorial, graphic, and sculptural works). If video games were considered graphic works, and if the rules of play were considered "utilitarian" for purposes of the Copyright Act, then copyright protection of video games could be very limited indeed. Cf. 1 M. Nimmer, supra note 10, §2.18[H][3][a]. Note, however, that courts invariably characterize video games as audiovisual works, and that 102(a) of the Copyright Act does not require the expression of an idea to be "capable of existing independently of" the idea itself. See supra text accompanying note 50; see also 1 M. Nimmer, supra note 10, §2.18[H][3][b].

[268] 17 U.S.C. §102(b) (1976 & Supp. V 1981).

[269] North American Philips has since introduced a new game, *K.C.'s Krazy Chase!,* which incorporates some aspects of the mazes developed for *K.C. Munchkin.* See Blanchet, "Drats! Avoid Them or You're Out of Luck, *Philadelphia Inquirer,* Nov. 7, 1982, at PS, col. 1.

observer test" as a prescription for remedies, rather than as a litmus test of infringement. To these errors, we will now turn.

Copyright infringement, inequitable conduct, and unfair competition

One of the lessons of the video game cases is that allegations of copyright infringement are often accompanied by circumstances suggesting trademark infringement or other unfair methods of competition. In *Stern Electronics*, the defendant had adopted "Scramble 2" as a mark for the game accused of violating Stern's copyright in the game *Scramble*. "Scramble 2" is not only so similar to "Scramble" that a buyer would assume that the products came from the same source; the use of the numeral "2" also suggests that the defendant's game was a later or better edition that should be purchased in preference to the plaintiff's game.[270] In *Dirkschneider*, the defendants had for one game adopted the plaintiff's mark (Rally-X) exactly and for another game had adopted a mark (Galactic Invaders) very similar to the plaintiff's (Galaxian). The court also found trademark infringement in the defendant's appropriation of the plaintiff's game characters.[271] With regard to *North American Philips*, a strong argument can be made that if the creators of *K.C. Munchkin* had transgressed, the wrong lay in their appropriation of *Pac-Man*'s characters, seen as trademarks, rather than in the infringement of *Pac-Man*'s copyright.[272]

If one judges by what the courts said in these cases, the trademark infringement issues seem to be treated as an afterthought at best,[273] riding on the coattails of the courts' copyright infringement holdings. In *Stern Electronics* and *Dirkschneider*, the courts addressed trademark issues only briefly toward the ends of the opinions; the *North American Philips* courts omitted altogether any explicit consideration of the Pac-Man characters as trademarks. Most

---

[270] It is generally said that trademark law serves two purposes: protecting the public against false designation of origin and protecting the goodwill of the person who is first to use the mark in connection with particular goods or services. The defendant's conduct in *Stern Electronics* was flagrantly inconsistent with both of these policies. It traded off the plaintiff's goodwill, and also carried the implication that the plaintiff's product was outmoded. See supra text accompanying note 78.

[271] See supra text accompanying notes 89–90.

[272] See supra text accompanying notes 204-10.

[273] See, e.g., *Williams Elecs., Inc. v. Artic Int'l, Inc.*, 685 F.2d 870, 871 (3d Cir. 1982), in which the court noted that "[t]he district court . . . severed plaintiff's claims of copyright infringement from its claims of trademark infringement and unfair competition. . . . These latter claims have not yet been adjudicated."

striking is the fact that no court in a video game case has found for the defendant on one type of infringement, but for the plaintiff on the other.

Rather than distinguish and separate their considerations of copyright and trademark issues, the courts have tended to decide both questions together,[274] often basing their decisions on an implicit characterization of the defendant as a "good guy" or a "bad guy."[275] Again, the practical effect of this habitual all-or-nothing approach is that good guys are exonerated and bad guys punished, even when such an outcome considered more dispassionately may seem oversimplified.

Equitable considerations about the quality of a litigant's conduct may be appropriate to consideration of alleged trademark infringement, but less so to alleged copyright infringements. Trademark law and section 43(a) of the Lanham Act[276] share the broad purposes of protecting a first user's exclusive right to profit from the goodwill he has generated and of protecting the public against "false designations of origin."[277] Thus, trademark law recognizes a right in the first user of a mark to make all of the profit derived from the goodwill associated with a mark and to prevent unfair or deceptive use of the

---

[274] Another example of a video game case in which trademark and copyright claims are joined is *Midway Mfg. Co. v. Bandai-America, Inc.*, 546 F. Supp. 125 (D.N.J. 1982). *Williams Electronics, Inc. v. Artic Int'l, Inc.*, 685 F.2d 870, 877 (3d Cir. 1982) is an exception because in that case the court severed the trademark and copyright issues.

[275] This apparent preoccupation with the parties' conduct might result in part from the fact that the defendants in several cases were guilty of highly inequitable practices. In *Stern Electronics*, for example, the defendants chose, under circumstances that showed bad faith, a confusingly similar mark for a work that was already dangerously similar to the plaintiffs' copyrighted works. See supra note 78 and text accompanying notes 78 and 149. In a close case, such conduct might easily tip the balance against the defendants, who will find it difficult under the circumstances to make high-minded public policy arguments about the evils of overbroad copyright protection. Conversely, policy justifications for conduct that may damage a plaintiff's economic interests will always be more persuasive when urged by a defendant whose conduct otherwise shows solicitude for the public good by avoiding confusing trademarks and other forms of unfair competition. See supra text accompanying notes 149–50.

[276] 15 U.S.C. §1125(a) (1976).

[277] See *Warner Bros. Co. v. American Broadcasting Cos.*, 530 F. Supp. 1187-95 (S.D.N.Y. 1982). Compare 15 U.S.C. §l 125(a) (1976) (statutory protection against false designations of origin) with 1 R. Callman, supra note 207, §1.24 (discussing protection of public from deception as one of the goals of trademark law). See generally 3 R. Callman, *The Law of Unfair Competition, Trademarks and Monopolies* §67.5 (3d ed. Supp. 1981) (explaining public policy bases for protection against trademark infringement and unfair competition).

same or confusingly similar marks by other persons. By contrast, protection for the economic interests of the copyright owner is more limited. The owner's profits are not an end in themselves, but only a means to the constitutional goal of encouraging the development of "science and the useful arts."[278] In a case such as *North American Philips,* the fact that the copyright holders made $150 million during a thirteen-month period when the accused work was also on the market[279] does not diminish the trademark interest in safeguarding the amount of the claimant's profits. By contrast, $150 million seems sufficient to reward and encourage the creation of a video game. The copyright policies may therefore be consistent with allowing the alleged infringement to continue.

The copyright concept of character infringement could function in some cases as a half-way house between copyright and trademark analysis. As discussed in connection with *North American Philips,* a court may find character infringement even if the accused work involves similar characters in an entirely different "idea," or plot, as long as the characters are "sufficiently developed to command copyright protection."[280] On the other hand, trademark protection is available for symbols and shapes that are too stylized and simplified to qualify for protection as copyrighted "characters." Indeed, the best trademarks tend to be very simple. By contrast, copyright focuses its protection on details; oversimplified features of a work are often geometrical and abstract, falling toward the "ideas" end of Hand's abstraction continuum. Trademark and unfair competition law thus provide protection both to types of creations (simplified marks) and in types of situations (where the plaintiff has been amply rewarded despite the alleged infringement) in which the argument for copyright protection might be comparatively weak.

Because the goals of trademark and copyright protection are so different, the courts should not permit the equitable considerations appropriate to trademark law unduly to influence their decisions on copyright issues. When the copyright issues are as unusual as they are in video game cases, any confusion of the two issues will inevitably interfere with the development of a consistent copyright analysis for video games. A more desirable alternative would be to provide separate remedies for trademark and copyright infringement.[281] In appropriate cases, this might be done by enjoining the defendant's use of the plaintiff's trademarks and granting damages for infringement or unfair competition, while at the same time holding (if true)

---

[278] See supra text accompanying notes 212–14.

[279] See supra text accompanying note 199–200.

[280] See supra text accompanying notes 202–09.

[281] See, e.g., *Midway Mfg. Co. v. Bandai-America. Inc.*, 546 F. Supp. at 154–55.

that part or all of the defendant's work is not "substantially similar" to the plaintiff's for copyright infringement purposes.

The ordinary observer test

The all-or-nothing character of relief in many copyright cases has already been associated with shortcomings in the application of the idea/expression distinction and with the use of copyright law to remedy trademark infringement. Perhaps the most potent source of all-or-nothing relief, however, is the "ordinary observer test" for substantial similarity. This test has had a variety of manifestations. In its purest and perhaps earliest form, it states that actionable copyright infringement may only be found if the ordinary, reasonable layperson would detect the plagiarism without the aid of critical analysis or expert testimony.[282] Two leading cases, *Arnstein v. Porter,*[283] and *Sid & Marty Krofft Television Productions, Inc. v. McDonald's Corp.*,[284] modified the original statement of the test by recognizing that expert testimony and "dissection" may be appropriate for some limited purposes. In Arnstein, the Second Circuit separated the question of copying from the question of infringement. The court held that when "there is evidence of access and similarities exist," "analysis (dissection) is relevant, and the testimony of experts may be received," to aid the trier of fact in determining whether "the similarities are sufficient to prove copying."[285] The court held, however, that once copying is established, the issue of "unlawful appropriation" must be decided by "the response of the ordinary lay [observer]; accordingly, on that issue, 'dissection' and expert testimony are irrelevant."[286] In *Krofft,* the Ninth Circuit appeared to lump together the questions of copying and infringement (applying the ordinary observer test to both), but allowed expert testimony and dissection for the limited purpose of

---

282 See *Harold Lloyd Corp. v. Witwer,* 65 F.2d 1, 18 (9th Cir. 1933). cited in 3 M. Nimmer, supra note 10, §13.03[E], at 13-40 to 13-41.
283 154 F.2d 464 (2d. Cir. 1946).
284 562 F.2d 1157 (9th Cir. 1977).
285 *Arnstein,* 154 F.2d at 468.
286 Id.

determining whether there was substantial similarity as to the "general idea" contained in the two works.[287]

Subject to variations like those in *Arnstein* and *Krofft*, and despite persistent criticism,[288] the courts have continued placing great emphasis on the uncritical reactions of the "ordinary lay observer." Although typically stated as a unitary "test" for substantial similarity,[289] the ordinary observer approach is a complex of several policy decisions about the nature of, and proper remedies for, copyright infringement. Fundamentally, it embodies a philosophy about the nature of copyright protection. That is, courts have emphasized the reactions of the lay observer because they have found that copyright is intended to protect the copyright holder's market, which, the courts assume, is comprised of "ordinary observers." The identification between the market for copyrighted work and the ordinary observer is so strong that the "ordinary observer test" is also referred to as the "audience

---

[287] *Krofft*, 562 F.2d at 1164–66. Nimmer criticizes *Krofft* on the ground that similarity in the works' "general ideas" is irrelevant to infringement, since copyright does not protect "general ideas" in any event. See 3 M. Nimmer, supra note 10, §13.03[E], at 13-49, n.121.3. In this, Nimmer is surely correct, although the mistake he identifies is so elementary that it is difficult to believe that the Ninth Circuit meant what it said. It seems more likely that the court meant to allow expert testimony to help bridge the gap between a basic work (perhaps a novel) and its derivatives (movies, plays). Considered in this way, the *Krofft* test is directed at the problem that mainly troubles Nimmer about the ordinary observer test — that the layman might not, without expert coaching, perceive that a difference between the copyrighted and accused works might be required by the technical demands of a different medium and might not, therefore, weigh against infringement. See 3 M. Nimmer, supra note 10, §13.03[E], at 13-45. Nimmer's point may be valid on the issue of proof of copying, but one might question why technically required differences should not weigh against infringement as much as whimsical differences. The author of the accused work put in the additional effort in either case, and it seems unfair to penalize him for meeting the technical demands of his medium. Ridden far enough, this train of thought can lead one to question why the author of, for example, a novel should not be required to write a screenplay before he acquires rights in the movie derived from his novel, particularly when extensive revision is required and the novel and movie share little more than title, character names, and highlights of plot. But this raises the general question of protection for derivative works, which is beyond the scope of this Article. See generally B. Kaplan, supra note 10, at 56–58; id. at 6–12 (historical nonprotection ofabridgements).

[288] See 3 M. Nimmer, supra note 10, §13.03[E], at 13.41–.46.

[289] See, e.g., *North American Philips*, 672 F.2d at 614.

test,"[290] reflecting the belief that the audience for a copyrighted work and the ordinary observer is essentially the same.

The test is invariably categorized as a method for determining whether the accused work infringes the copyrighted work. However, the test also carries implications about the proper remedies for infringement. This second dimension is not stated explicitly in the published opinions, but it may be perceived in the curious manner by which courts ask their hypothetical ordinary observer to compare the accused and infringed works. Courts say that infringement will be found only if the accused work's "general design, style and tone . . . is such that an average lay observer would be likely to recognize [it] as having been derived from [the copyrighted work]."[291] Pursuing this theme, courts remind themselves not to assess the two works "hypercritically or with meticulous scrutiny,"[292] but to determine instead "whether the accused work has captured the 'total concept and feel' of the copyrighted work."[293] The test thus requires the hypothetical ordinary observer to consider each work in its entirety so as to ascertain not its details but, so to speak, its gestalt.

This holistic approach to infringement is not a logically required implication of the selection of the ordinary observer as the principal judge of copyright infringement: surely, the lay observer is capable of judging whenever a chapter of an accused work is similar to a chapter of the copyrighted work. Whatever its origins, however, this explicit element of the test for infringement has come to bear a vital implicit message about the proper remedy for infringement. If the ordinary and reasonable person finds the accused and copyrighted works to vary in overall design, the defendant gets off scot-free, no matter how many details he may have borrowed from the plaintiff. If the ordinary person finds the works to be the same, the powerful equitable remedies of the Copyright Act (injunction, and impoundment or destruction of infringing copies) are oftentimes applied to the whole accused work, regardless of how many non-infringing elements it may also contain.[294]

---

290 See 3 M. immer, supra note 10, at §13.03[E].

291 *Jack Lenor Larsen, Inc. v. Dakotah, Inc.*, 452 F. Supp. 99, 100 (S.D.N.Y. 1978).

292 *Krofft*, 562 F.2d at 1164 (quoting *Stonesifer v. Twentieth Century-Fox Film Corp.*, 140 F.2d 579, 582 [9th Cir. 1944]).

293 *North American Philips*, 672 F.2d at 614 (quoting *Roth Greeting Cards v. United Card Co.*, 429 F.2d 1106, 1110 (9th Cir. 1970)).

294 *Midway Mfg. Co. v. Bandai-America, Inc.*, 546 F. Supp. 125 (D.N.J. 1982) is an exception to the generalization. In that case the court tailored the relief more carefully.

This implication about infringement remedies is the silent partner of the ordinary observer test for infringement itself.

The "ordinary observer" test is thus at once both an impressionistic approach to the issue of actionable infringement and a wholesale approach to the remedy for infringement. In each aspect, it serves useful purposes. In the first place, it is — and should be — a sine qua non for copyright infringement. The "ordinary observer" is, of course, a projection of the trier of fact (usually the judge himself).[295] If to his untrained but presumably impartial and perspicacious eye, the works do not appear to be similar, and if he is not led to believe that the accused work copied substantially from the copyrighted one, then it can be argued that the copying, if any, was either too slight or too subtle to be the proper subject of copyright protection. Copyright is designed in part to protect the income of an author's work. Often, the economic success of a work (a novel, a play, a movie, a television series, a how-to book) will depend on whether "ordinary" people like the judge or members of a jury will buy it, watch it, or use it. In such cases, copyright protects the market for the work among "ordinary observers," and if they would not perceive the accused work as a substitute for the original, then the economic harm potentially caused to the copyrighted work becomes attenuated, and the strength of the justification for banning the accused work diminishes.[296] Thus, for many works, there is sound justification in policy for stressing the ordinary observer's reaction.

The ordinary observer approach has secondary benefits as well. It encourages judicial economy and avoids interminable expert testimony. A procession of English professors (or computer programmers) on the witness stand, each competing with the other for the most precious comparison between the accused and copyrighted works, is a judge's nightmare that probably exerts a powerful disincentive against expert testimony and "dissection." The test may also afford a court a psychological advantage in the exercise of judicial discretion. As mentioned above, the test allows the judge to project his personality into the shell of the "ordinary observer." In that guise, the judge can exercise personal judgment — which is surely indispensable to his work —

---

[295] Indeed, every video game opinion to date has been rendered on a motion for a temporary restraining order or preliminary injunction, so that the trier of fact in every one of these cases has been a federal district court judge. For works such as video games, which have a profitable life measured in months rather than years, see *North American Philips*, 672 F.2d at 620, and *Stern Electronics*, 523 F. Supp. at 638, it is likely that the ordinary observer will always be the judge, since the fighting issue of market share will have disappeared before a trial can be had.

[296] See 3M. Nimmer, supra note 10, §13.05[A][4], at 13-64.

without relinquishing the court's outward appearance of impartiality. Thus, the test protects the judge against the dangers of stating openly, "I think these works are so similar I would as soon buy the accused one as the copyrighted one" and allows himself to say instead, "The court finds that an ordinary lay observer would as soon buy one as the other."[297]

The ordinary observer test's wholesale approach to relief may also help to deter infringement. If a would-be plagiarist knows that any borrowing from a copyrighted work could jeopardize his entire work, including even those portions that are original, he may be assisted in overcoming the temptation to profit from the success of others. Thus, the in terrorem effect of a wholesale approach may reduce the need for authors (who by reputation are impecunious) to file expensive lawsuits to protect their copyrighted works.

Despite these many advantages, the ordinary observer test has profound limitations. Nimmer, for example, argues that the test may fail to uncover instances of copying, such as the conversion of a novel into a derivative work such as a movie, in which "the immediate and spontaneous observations of a person untrained in the special requirements and techniques of the play, the novel, the short story, and the motion picture, may fail to note similarities which, if analyzed and dissected, would be only too apparent."[298] The application of the ordinary observer test in the video games cases suggests that in other circumstances, it may incline the court too much in the direction of finding infringement. The most avid video game users seem to be pre-teens and teenagers, not the middle-aged adults who occupy the federal bench and jury box. As discussed above in connection with scènes à faire, two games that appear similar (and perhaps equally pointless) to a distinguished member of the federal judiciary might, to the thirteen-year-old enthusiast, show stimulating and laudable diversity.

Furthermore, the games are created by computer programmers, a breed notorious for the opacity of its language and processes to the "ordinary observer." The "ordinary observer" — the judge — might not have a good sense as to whether one work was "copied" from another. He would need expert testimony to help resolve the issue.

---

[297] This psychological advantage may help to explain the prevalence of "ordinary observer" or "ordinary reasonable man" tests in many areas of the law. See 3 Nimmer, supra note 10, §13.03[E], at 13-43 (comparing the ordinary observer test in copyright with similar tests in torts and criminal law, among others).

[298] 3 M. Nimmer, supra note 10, §13.03[E], at 13-45. But see supra note 287.

As exemplified by *Amusement World* and by the court of appeals decision in *North American Philips,* the all-or-nothing relief implied by the ordinary observer test cuts across the line between idea and expression, no matter how carefully the court's opinion may have been to draw that line. This blurring is undesirable for several reasons. It can be unjust. In *Amusement World,* the copyright holder obtained no relief, even though some aspects of its game Asteroids had obviously been copied by the creator of the accused work *Meteors.* At the opposite extreme, the appellate decision in *North American Philips deprived* the defendants of any reward for their creation of the many unique features in *K.C. Munchkin* — features the district court had found to be challenging and, one infers, superior to similar features in *Pac-Man.*[299] Thus, the in terrorem effect of the wholesale approach tends to deter the creation of new video games and to foster monopolization by the first promoter of each type of game.[300]

Finally, the wholesale approach to infringement and relief can retard the development of a consistent body of law in any new area, such as copyright protection for video games. This effect is evident in the video game decisions rendered to date. If one considers together cases as diametrically opposed as, on the one hand, *Stern Electronics, Armenia,* and the *North American Philips* court of appeals opinion, and on the other hand, *Amusement World* and the *North American Philips* district court opinion, it is most difficult to advise a client what it may and may not do in creating and marketing video games. To borrow a phrase from physics, the test is dynamically unstable. A slight push one way or the other seems capable of toppling the entire case one way or the other. When the law is in such a state, the lawyer's only safe advice is to avoid similarity with existing games altogether. This is undoubtedly what the pioneers in the field would like, but it is wholly inconsistent with the Copyright Act's policy of distinguishing ideas and expressions, protecting the latter, and at the same time, opening the way for creativity in and development of the former.

These limitations suggest that, at least in untried situations such as video game cases, and especially in assessing requests for equitable relief, courts should relegate the ordinary observer test to a more limited role. In most cases, the similarity between the accused and copyrighted works, as seen by

---

299 See, e.g., the district court's comment that in K.C. Munchkin, unlike in *Pac-Man,* the last dot "cannot be caught by overtaking it, it must be munched by strategy." *North American Philips,* 2 Copyright L. Rep. (CCH) ¶25,163, at 17,047. See generally supra text accompanying notes 134-42.

300 See supra text following note 84.

the court (wearing its guise as "ordinary observer"), ought to remain the touchstone, the sine qua non for infringement.[301] The video game cases suggest, however, that additional questions must be answered before an ultimate finding of copyright infringement may be reached, and before relief may be entered. In some cases, such as the *North American Philips* court of appeals opinion, the superficial similarity that an ordinary observer would perceive between the games leads to the question of whether the infringement lay in the appropriation of the plaintiff's copyright or of its trademarks. In other cases, such as Stern Electronics, the preliminary finding of similarity between the games should have provided the basis for asking whether the similarity lay in the unprotected realm of ideas and scènes à faire. In still other cases, such as *Amusement World*, the finding that there was similarity, and that some of it lay in the realm of ideas, should not have precluded a consideration whether other elements of the accused work had improperly appropriated the copyrighted work's expression.

A better approach in each of these cases would have been to treat the ordinary observer's reaction as a preliminary inquiry. Both the question of copying and the ordinary observer test for substantial similarity should ideally be followed by consideration of several other issues. The analysis would include the following questions: (i) has copying or access been proved; (ii) would the ordinary observer consider the works to be similar; (iii) is the similarity confined to the trademark-like elements in the work; (iv) does the remaining similarity inhere in the works' ideas or in the expression of those ideas; (v) if the similarity is in the realm of copyrighted expression, can relief be entered that will remedy the appropriation of the copyrighted work's expression without interfering with the public interest in the exploitation of the work's ideas?

The suggestion of a program for discussion like the foregoing one is inevitably more stilted than a convincing legal opinion could or should be. It can serve, however, as a checklist for considerations that are relevant and important and that, if one judges from the video game cases, are often overlooked. In practice, it would yield remedies in copyright infringement cases, which are now more narrowly drawn but perhaps more frequently awarded than has been typical in the past. The following section of this article will consider whether such remedies are consistent with the Copyright Act.

---

[301] It might be necessary to make an exception even to this limited role for the ordinary observer in the instances in which the copying could be observed only by technical analysis of the copyist's medium. See 3 M. Nimmer, supra note 10, §13.03, at 13-45. But see supra note 287.

Targeting the remedy to the wrong

The moral of the preceding sections of this article is that habits of copyright adjudication have inclined the courts toward all-or-nothing remedies for infringement, and that such remedies are inimical to the policies underlying copyright protection. The alternative would be more carefully tailored infringement remedies. It is worth inquiring whether such remedies are feasible as a practical matter and whether support for them can be found in the remedial provisions of the Copyright Act.

Let us suppose we have the following case. The plaintiff alleges copyright infringement of a video game. The court has read this article and has taken to heart the recommendations made above. It has reached the following tentative conclusions: access has been proven, and the "ordinary observer" would find the accused and copyrighted works to be similar. The defendant has been guilty of trademark infringement, but after carefully excising the trademarks from the accused work, there remain elements similar to the copyrighted work. The court has heard both extrinsic evidence and expert testimony comparing these remaining elements with standard devices found in similar games. On the basis of the context provided by this evidence, the court finds that some of the remaining elements are unprotected "ideas," some are material created by the defendant, and others are "expression" subject to copyright protection and copied from the plaintiff's copyrighted work. What should the court do?

Relief can be patterned on one of three models. The court could find that the accused work as a whole infringes the copyrighted work. This would lead to an injunction banning further marketing of the accused work and ordering the destruction of all copies in the defendant's possession. Alternatively, the court could find infringement only with respect to the individual elements in the accused work that are similar to elements in the copyrighted work. This would suggest an injunction against further marketing of any work that included those elements and, possibly, ordering the destruction of any copies of the accused work in the defendant's possession that included those elements. Finally, the court could find the copying to be de minimus, accord the plaintiff no injunctive relief, but perhaps award the plaintiff nominal damages.

Perhaps the most important question is how large a portion of the accused work represents plagiarized material, and whether anything of value would remain if the copied portion were excised. If, on the one hand, the improperly copied material is a tiny fraction of the entire accused work, then no injunctive relief might be entered at all, because any injunction would impose an unfair hardship on the defendant. At the opposite extreme, there would be no point in attempting to salvage any part of a work that was plagiarized virtually in its entirety. The extraordinary copying described by the court in Dirkschneider may be an example of the latter extreme.[302]

In many cases, the copying can be expected to fall between these poles. Examples of video game cases in which the accused work was partially copied from the copyrighted work, but contained substantial amounts of other material that were either original or not subject to copyright protection, are *North American Philips* and *Amusement World.* In such cases, a strong argument can be made that relief that is targeted to the infringing elements is, in fact, mandated by the Copyright Act. Section 502 of the Act empowers the court to "grant temporary and final injunctions on such terms as it may deem reasonable to prevent or restrain infringements of a copyright."[303] This language plainly contemplates a flexible and "reasonable" application of injunctive relief. The destruction or impoundment of copies "made or used in violation of the copyright owner's exclusive rights" pursuant to section 503[304] seems more suited to eradication of the defendant's work as a whole, but even with regard to that language, there may be room for flexibility. Destruction or impoundment is not required by the Act: section 503 provides that the court "may" order such relief.

Furthermore, a video game, unlike a published book or record, can be modified without destroying the entire device. For example, a court might order the impoundment or destruction of the microchips that operate a game,[305] while allowing the defendant to keep the devices to which the chips are connected and to replace the chips with new chips embodying programs for games that do not include the game's infringing features. These statutory considerations thus support the view that, whenever possible, injunctive relief should be limited to the infringing elements in the accused work.[306]

Courts are fond of reciting that "no plagiarist can excuse the wrong by showing how much of the work he did not pirate,"[307] and it might be felt that limited forms of injunctive relief would not sufficiently punish an infringer. The Copyright Act suggests, however, that Congress wished to emphasize

---

[302] See supra text accompanying notes 85–90.

[303] 17 U.S.C. § 502(a) (1976 & Supp. V 1981).

[304] 17 U.S.C. § 503(a) (1976 & Supp. V 1981).

[305] See supra note 11.

[306] For an example of a video game case in which injunctive relief was limited to certain elements of the copyrighted and accused works, see *Midway Mfg. Co. v. Bandai-America, Inc.*, 546 F. Supp. 125 (D.N.J. 1982).

[307] *Sheldon v. Metro-Goldwyn Pictures Corp.*, 81 F.2d 49,56 (2d Cir.), cert. denied, 298 U.S. 669 (1936), quoted in *North American Philips*, 672 F.2d at 619.

damages and criminal penalties, not injunctions, as the preferred means of punishing infringement. For willful infringement, the Act provides startling statutory damages of up to $50,000, even if no actual damages can be shown,[308] and criminal penalties of up to $250,000 or five years imprisonment, or both.[309] Using these tools, a genuinely punitive blow can be dealt to any infringer even if injunctive relief is limited to the infringing elements of the accused work. Aside from the draconian statutory damage provisions, congressional intent that the Act's damage provisions be a preferred method of punishment is also seen in the Act's provisions for the allocation of an infringer's profits. Congress recognized that it may not, as a practical matter, be possible to determine what portion of a defendant's profits were "attributable to the infringement."[310] The Copyright Act has resolved this problem in favor of the plaintiff by requiring the plaintiff to prove only "the infringer's gross revenue," placing on the infringer the burden of proving "the elements of profit attributable to factors other than the copyrighted work."[311] One can conclude that Congress intended to punish infringers through damages, and, where appropriate, criminal prosecution, while leaving the door open to comparatively nonpunitive forms of injunctive relief.

Undoubtedly there will be cases in which the infringing elements in the accused work are so interwoven with the noninfringing elements that the court could not issue an injunction directed against only the infringing elements without rewriting the entire work. Such cases, however, are probably the exception rather than the rule, at least in the video game context.[312] If one judges by the meticulous detail with which the courts segregated and categorized infringing and noninfringing features in cases such as *Amusement World, Dirkschneider,* and the two *North American Philips* opinions, the identification of infringing features in an injunction should not be viewed as an impossible task. It might raise the specter of a defendant attempting to skirt around the edges of the list thereafter, but this risk is present whenever injunctive relief is entered. On balance, the risk of an end-run around the terms of the injunction seems a small price to pay for an outcome that is

---

308 See 17 U.S.C. § 504(c)(2) (1976 & Supp. V 1981).

309 See 17 U.S.C. § 506(a) (1976 & Supp. V 1981) (making willful infringement for commercial advantage or private financial gain a crime); Piracy and Counterfeiting Amendments Act of 1982, Pub. L. No. 97-180, §3, 96 Stat. 91, 93 (to be codified at 18 U.S.C. §2319) (specifying criminal penalties).

310 17 U.S.C. § 504(b) (l976 & Supp. V 1981).

311 Id.

312 In the fine arts, separately identifying the protected and copyrighted elements may be much more difficult, even impossible. See B. Kaplan, supra note 10, at 56.

otherwise more consistent with the rights of the parties and with the policies supporting copyright protection.

In sum, the interplay of the Copyright Act injunction and damage provisions strongly supports the conclusion that, whenever possible, courts should enter limited injunctive relief while at the same time punishing willful infringement by the imposition of statutory damages and by the liberal application of the Act's provisions regarding the measure of actual damages.

End Notes

Early in this article, video games were compared with the situations in the leading cases cited for the blackletter rule that "copyright does not protect games." There were many differences, all pointing toward greater protection for video games. Those differences forecast that the application of law to facts in video game cases would not be smooth sailing. The cases bore out that prediction. The courts could be seen struggling to accommodate the need for protection for the games to the proscriptions against protecting games, rules, and ideas. One finds in this struggle support for a few generalizations about the process by which the law shapes and transforms itself in a new environment. Some of these generalizations are widely accepted; others may be less so.

The first is that, in the absence of clear guidelines from precedent or statute, courts find it easier to decide cases by comparing the equitable nature of the parties' conduct than by interpreting the precedents and statutes in the new context. Thus, many of the seminal video game decisions, including particularly the early decisions in *Stern Electronics* and *Artic International*, but also including the Seventh Circuit's decision in *North American Philips*, focus on the relative merits of the conduct of the parties rather than on the copyright issues. This tendency provides the basis for the maxim that it is more important (particularly for a plaintiff) to argue the facts than the law. One might say that the equitable tail tends to wag the legal dog.

A second is that legal dogma often functions to limit equitable claims in the interest of public policy. The principle that copyright does not protect ideas is a good example of a legal rule performing this function. It serves to protect the salutary constitutional interest favoring the development of the useful arts. But it is usually asserted against the claims of a party who has been in some sense cheated. Plagiarism is not an agreeable occupation, and arguing that the creator of an accused work stole "only" the plaintiff's ideas hardly mitigates the perceived fault. The courts must recognize, however, the public interest behind which the "plagiarist" defends his conduct if the policies of the Copyright Act are to be served.

A third generalization, derived from the first two, is that a dramatic expansion of legally recognized rights can occur in any new setting where old dogmas cannot be applied with ease, where the plaintiff has a strong (even self-righteous) claim for protection, and where the defendant can be characterized as having "profited at the plaintiff's expense," been "unjustly enriched," "stolen the plaintiff's idea," or engaged in any other inequitable conduct. Again, video game cases such as *Stern Electronics* and *North American Philips* provide vivid examples of this process at work.

That courts are disposed to provide remedies for new wrongs is a lively creative force, without which the law would stagnate, and lawyers would probably go hungry. No set of formulas or suggestions can or should pretend to eliminate it. Courts can, however, take steps to soften the disruptive impact strong, equitable claims have on old legal rules. For one thing, they can spread the strain of new claims for protection over more than one legal right. By drawing on closely related areas of the law — in copyright cases, concepts such as character infringement, trademark, and unfair competition — the tendency to overstretch a single legal right by asking it to do too much work, and to remedy too many wrongs, might be avoided. Courts can also resist the temptations of an "all-or-nothing" approach. As the video game cases amply demonstrate, such an approach seldom fairly balances the claims of the parties and often interferes with the consistent and proportionate development of the law.

Three Common Fallacies in the User Interface Copyright Debate*

Both proponents and opponents of copyright protection for the "user interface" of computer software commonly assume the truth of the following three propositions: 1) §102(b) of the Copyright Act is an exception to the general rule that copying is wrongful; 2) the difficulty and expense of creating an interface support its copyrightability; and 3) the existence of multiple alternative interfaces implies that no one of them is an unprotected "idea." Each of these propositions is a fallacy.

Fallacy #1: §102(b) of the Copyright Act is an exception to the general rule that copying is wrongful

It is easy to fall into the trap of thinking that copying is a bad thing — a sort of tort — that copyright is designed to deter and remedy. Nothing could be further from the truth. Copying is the rule and not the exception, in our competitive society. Federal Express invents overnight delivery using a hub-and-spoke system and is promptly imitated by UPS, Purolator, and even the United States Postal Service.[1] Christian Dior shows his new line of dresses in Paris, and copies of them appear within weeks on the racks of US department stores. [2] Chanel expends energy and talent in creating a new fragrance, only to have imitations sold at a fraction of the price.[3] Stiffel no sooner designs a popular lamp than Sears offers its customers a duplicate.[4] Chrysler Corporation designs and builds a phenomenally successful line of "minivans,"

---

* Reprinted with permission from *The Computer Lawyer*, Volume 7, Number 2, February 1990. The author gratefully acknowledges the assistance of Laurie Woog. This article is adapted from a presentation given by the author at the University of Southern California Law Center's Tenth Annual Computer Law Institute in Los Angeles, May 1989.

[1] Such copying is entirely lawful. See *Holding Security Checking Co. v. Lorraine Co.*, 160 F. 467 (2d Cir. 1908) ("the law is settled that a method of doing business can be rejected as not being within the statutory classes" protected by patent law).

[2] This too is lawful. See *Russell v. Trimfit, Inc.*, 425 F. Supp. 91 (E.D. Pa. 1977). See *also Société Comptoir de L'Industrie Cotonnière Etablissements Boussac v. Alexander's Department Stores, Inc.*, 299 F.2d 33, 36 (2d Cir. 1962) ("'pirating' of the design is lawful and proper").

[3] *Smith v. Chanel, Inc.*, 402 F.2d 562, 563 (9th Cir. 1968).

[4] *Sears, Roebuck & Co. v. Stiffel Co.*, 376 U.S. 225, 231 (1964), reh'g denied, 376 US. 973 (1964) (holding Sears's·manufacture and sale of lamps almost identical to Stiffel's not actionable).

only to be imitated by Ford, General Motors, and the Japanese automakers. Short-order restaurants endeavor to make their french fries as much like McDonald's' as humanly possible. The copyists even advertise that their products are as close as possible to the originals.[5]

All of these forms of copying — and many more besides — are protected by federal and state law. The reason is that copying serves two fundamental purposes. First, it facilitates price competition. If others were not permitted to offer the same product or service, competition as to price would be confused and blunted by distinctions as to the goods or services offered. Where the competitor offers exactly the same thing, prices are driven down, and "efficiency" in the economic sense is maximized.

Second, copying transmits society's collective store of knowledge. We learn by imitation. Art students copy the works of the great masters. Auto manufacturers buy their competitors' products and disassemble them down to the last nut and bolt to learn improved techniques of design and construction. Young lawyers learn to draft agreements by "marking up" — that is, copying language out of — other agreements.

Without copying, it would be necessary for everyone to "reinvent the wheel" before marketing a product, writing a play, performing an experiment, producing a movie, preparing a contract or undertaking any other creative activity. This would be inefficient and undesirable. In computer parlance, working from scratch creates "bugs.[6] That is why lawyers work from forms and use "boilerplate": otherwise, they would be sure to repeat the mistakes of their forebears. It would be the unsuccessful manufacturer of a screwdriver that did not start with the assumption that his screwdrivers should look and feel just about like ones already on the market. If they did not, customers might not know how to use them, and the screwdrivers might not fit the screws they are supposed to be used with.

For these reasons, the law has jealously guarded the right to copy. As Learned Hand put it, a competitor may copy any product "slavishly down to the minutest detail."[7] In Justice Holmes's words, a competitor "has a *right* . . . to get

---

[5] See e.g., *Saxlehner v. Wagner,* 216 U.S. 375, 380 (1910) (Holmes, J.); *Société Comptoir,* note 2 supra, at 35; *Smith v. Chanel,* note 3 supra, at 563.

[6] It has been suggested that the OS/2 operating system contains many programming shortfalls precisely because it was created using "clean room" techniques that prevented its designers from avoiding their predecessors' mistakes.

[7] *Crescent Tool Co. v. Kilborn & Bishop Co.*, 247 F. 299, 301 (2nd Cir. 1917). Of course, the competitor may not pass off its good as those of another. Id.

whatever share they can in the popularity of [another company's] product by advertising that they are trying to make the same article, and think that they succeed."[8] One of the most forceful statements of the right to copy appears in the very recent Supreme Court decision in *Bonito Boats, Inc. v. Thunder Craft Boats, Inc.*: "imitation and refinement through imitation are both necessary to invention itself and the very lifeblood of a competitive economy."[9]

At issue in *Bonito Boats* was a Florida statute that made it unlawful to duplicate products using the "plug-molding" process. That process represents the most "slavish" copying imaginable. The competitor uses the originator's product to make a mold, and then uses the mold to make duplicates of the originator's product. In the Hand/Holmes tradition, the Court found that the Florida attempt to outlaw plug-molding "[erodes] the general rule of free competition."[10] The Court based its decision in part on the fact that (at least as to patentable subject matter) there is "a federal *right to* 'copy and to use,'"[11] and that "[t]hat which is published may be freely copied as a matter of federal *right*."[12]

Bonito Boats reflects a historical and deep-seated association between patents, copyrights and monopolies.[13] This association has been most pronounced in the field of patents. The beginning of modern patent law is usually traced to the "Statute of Monopolies," enacted in 1623. Far from being a grant of patent-like rights, the Statute of Monopolies was a Parliamentary effort to curb exclusive "patents" granted by the Crown. Similarly, the first true copyright statute, the Statute of Anne, enacted in 1710, was intended in part to limit the monopolistic rights of publishers.[14] Prior to that statute, the

---

[8] *Saxlehner v. Wagner*, 216 U.S. 375, 380 (1910) (emphasis added). ("[T]he plaintiff has no patent for the ['bitter'] water, and the defendants have a right to reproduce it as nearly as they can"). Id. at 380.

[9] 109 S. Ct. 971, 975 (1989).

[10] Id. at 983.

[11] Id. at 985 (referring to material covered by expired patents and by potentially patentable ideas that have been "fully exposed to the public") (emphasis added).

[12] Id. at 984, quoting *Bailey v. Logan Square Typographers, Inc.*, 441 F.2d 47, 51 (7th Cir. 1971) (emphasis added). The Court quoted similar language from *Inwood Labs., Inc. v. Ives Labs., Inc.*, 456 U.S. 844, 863 (1982) ("'[r]eproduction of a functional attribute is legitimate competitive activity,'" when an unpatented item is in general circulation). Bonito Boats at 984.

[13] Many patent attorneys chafe at the suggestion that a patent is a form of monopoly, preferring to think of it as a form of property instead. This effort to clothe the wolf in lamb's clothing, as *Bonito Boats* shows, has not spread to the Supreme Court.

[14] Nutshell, *Intellectual Property* 279.

common law had few rights in authors, and rights in published works were controlled by the unpopular "Stationers' Company's monopoly."[15]

The American colonists shared this hostility; indeed, the colonists had rebelled in part because of excessive monopolies granted by the Crown. There was a strong sentiment among the founding fathers that any power in the federal government to grant monopolies,[16] and in particular, monopolies in the nature of patents and copyrights, would be intolerable.[17] The most notable proponent of this view was Thomas Jefferson, who considered exclusive statutory monopolies such as patents to be an "embarrassment."[18] Jefferson was himself, of course, a redoubtable inventor and thus might judge which legal system would best foster innovation.

Jefferson eventually came around to the view that "[m]onopolies may be allowed to persons for their own productions & their own inventions in the arts," but only for limited times.[19] Thence the current constitutional provision, which empowers Congress "[T]o promote the Progress of Science and the Useful Arts, by securing for limited Times to Authors and Inventors the exclusive Right to their respective Writings and Discoveries."[20] It is noteworthy that, from both a constitutional and historical standpoint, the concern about excessive monopolization applies to patents and copyrights

---

15 B. Kaplan, *An Unhurried View of Copyright* 3 (1967) (hereinafter, *Unhurried View*).

16 James Madison felt that government was instituted to protect the "free use of their physical and mental faculties." A just government would "not permit citizens to suffer under arbitrary restrictions, exceptions, or monopolies." Madison on "Property," *National Gazette*, Mar. 29, 1792, cited in Adrienne Koch, *Jefferson and Madison: The Great Collaborators* 109 (New York: Oxford University Press, 1950). Jefferson felt similarly, writing in 1787 to Madison from Paris decrying the omission of certain concepts from the plans for a new government: "I will tell you now what I do not like. First, the omission of a Bill of Rights, providing . . . for freedom of religion, freedom of the press, . . . restriction of monopolies. . . ." Koch and William Peden, eds., *The Life and Selected Writings of Thomas Jefferson* 437 (New York: Random House, 1972).

17 Jefferson's contribution to the Constitutional provision governing patents and copyrights, Article I, §8, cl. 8, was reviewed by the Supreme Court in *Graham v. John Deere Co.*, 383 U.S. 1, 7–10 (1966).

18 Id. at 8–9.

19 Id., at 8, quoting Jefferson's August 1789 letter to Madison, as cited in *V Writings of Thomas Jefferson* 113 (Ford, ed. 1895)

20 U.S. Const., art. I, §8, cl. 8. Some delegates to the Constitutional Convention suggested an even greater governmental role in fostering the arts and sciences. Pinckney suggested Congress should have the power "to establish public institutions, rewards, and immunities for the promotion of agriculture, commerce, trades and manufacture." 3 *Notes of James Madison of the Federal Convention*, August 18, 1789, at 325.

equally. Particularly in a climate in which copyright has been extended to such utilitarian creations as computer software, the Constitution, therefore, demands that the same policy considerations inform both copyright and patent adjudication. Otherwise, all of the limitations that the courts have strived to impose on patents to guard against unwarranted or excessive monopolization might be lost through the medium of copyright protection.

The Patent Act implements the constitutional scheme — and protects the right to copy — in two ways. First, there is a high standard for patentability. If an invention is neither new nor nonobvious, it does not merit embarrassing Jefferson with yet another monopoly.[21] Second, the patent lasts only 17 years. At the end of that time, the invention (which must be fully disclosed in the patent itself) becomes available for all to copy and use.[22] The policy favoring copying is so strong that state statutes that purport to inhibit copying of an invention that does not meet the standard of patentability, or that purport to extend protection beyond the 17-year period, are preempted.[23]

Copyright has gone about the constitutional scheme in a different manner. Rather than pinning protection[24] of the right to copy on a high threshold for protection or on a short duration[25], the courts and Congress have severely limited the sorts of things that might be copyrighted at all. The current statute exempts from its protection "any idea, procedure, process, system, method of operation, concept, principle, or discovery, regardless of the form in which it is described, explained, illustrated, or embodied in such work." Section 102(b) was intended to codify the existing law regarding what might and might not be protected by copyright.[26] Thus, its compendious list must be understood and interpreted in light of historical and Constitutional limitations on excessive

---

[21] *Graham v. John Deere* at 9.

[22] *Bonito Boats*, supra, at 978.

[23] Id. at 978, discussing *Sears, Roebuck & Co. v. Stiffel Co.*, 376 U.S. 225 (1964); *Compco Corp. v. Day-Brite Lighting, Inc.*, 376 U.S. 234 (1964).

[24] It is usually said that copyright does not require newness (novelty), and that the copyright standard of originality is minimal. See *Sheldon v. Metro Goldwyn Pictures Corp.*, 81 F.2d 49 (2d Cir.), cert. denied, 298 U.S. 669 (1936) (L. Hand, J.). However, protection has been denied in certain circumstances that look suspiciously like lack of novelty. See, e.g., *Donald v. Zack Meyer's T.V Sales and Service*, 426 F.2d 1027 (5th Cir. 1979), cert. denied, 400 U.S. 992 (1971).

[25] The duration of copyright has always been lengthy; the current statute's lifetime of the author plus 50 years (or 75 years for a work made for hire) is essentially forever in the case of a computer program.

[26] HR. Rep. (Judiciary Committee) on the Copyright Act of 1976, No. 1476, 94th Cong., 2d Sess. 57, reprinted in 1976 U.S. Code Cong. and Admin. News 5670.

monopolies, which have produced the more general pro-competitive federal policy described above. The list also must be understood as incorporating the myriad of specific exceptions to copyright protection that have arisen under that policy. It excludes from protection the design of wearing apparel;[27] business forms;[28] type fonts;[29] the titles of books;[30] the results of architectural designs;[31] the formats and designs used in maps such as boundary symbols and keys,[32] any object in which the copyrightable "expression" is not capable of existing independently of its utilitarian function;[33] and all the other items that courts have held are not subject to copyright protection.

In short, copyright is but one small part of a much larger body of federal and state law that serves a variety of important policies. One policy is the provision of incentive and reward for invention. Others are the avoidance of stifling monopolies and the preservation of competition. The right to copy is a central feature of this body of law. Thus, it is fair to say that § 102(b) of the Copyright Act is the rule, to which copyright protection is a limited exception.

Fallacy #2: The difficulty and expense of creating an interface supports its copyrightability

The suggestion that a computer program's "user interface" should not be protected frequently runs up against the following line of reasoning: "The plaintiff expended substantial time and effort in creating an interface that is one of the main reasons for the success of the plaintiff's product. The defendant has imitated this interface at a fraction of the plaintiff's effort. If we do not protect the plaintiff's interface, there will be no incentive to create new and better interfaces, and society will consequently suffer. Therefore, the plaintiff's interface must be protected against imitation or unauthorized use by the defendant. The greater the protection, the greater the potential reward, and therefore the greater the innovation."

---

[27] See note 2 supra.

[28] *Baker v. Selden*, 101 U.S. 99 (1879).

[29] *Eltra Corp. v. Ringer*, 579 F.2d 294, 298 (4th Cir. 1978); see also H.R.Rep. 1476, note 26 supra. at 55 (a typeface is not a copyrightable "pictorial, graphic or sculptural work" within the meaning of the bill).

[30] *Becker v. Loew's, Inc.*, 133 F.2d 889, 891 (7th Cir. 1943).

[31] *DaSilva Construction Corp. v. Herrald*, 213 F. Supp. 184, 195-196 (MD. Fla. 1962).

[32] *United States v. Hamilton*, 583 F.2d 448 (9th Cir. 1978); see also *Andrews v. Guenther*, 60 F.2d 555 (S.D.N.Y. 1932).

[33] 17 U.S.C. §101 (definition of "pictorial, graphic and sculptural" works).

This line of reasoning rests on three fallacies, one philosophical, one legal, and one factual. The philosophical error is that the argument implicitly assumes that copyright is a matter of natural right: if you create something by your own labors, it is yours, and others may not use it without your permission.[34] This argument has a powerful emotional appeal that no plaintiff's lawyer has failed to exploit. It is, nevertheless, erroneous. As the Supreme Court observed in *Graham v. John Deere*, the "natural right" theory of intellectual property rights was rejected by Jefferson in favor of a "social and economic rationale"[35] under which protection is granted by society as an inducement to new creation. Thus, the protection is a means to an end, not an end in itself.[36] When protection would interfere with the creation of new works, it defeats the purpose and should be denied.

The fallacy of law is that the difficulty or expense of creating a thing makes it a proper subject of copyright or patent protection. There is no such legal principle. The most potent counterexample is the discovery of a law of nature. It probably can be fairly said that the effort, genius, and creativity required to discover new laws of nature is unrivaled in any other field of human endeavor. Einstein's $E=mc^2$ is the most famous example, but others abound.

In many cases, millions of dollars, years of effort, and unparalleled individual applications are required to make the most modest advance in human scientific knowledge. Nevertheless, the law accords no protection whatsoever against the exploitation of that discovery by others.[37] The reason

---

34 The Berne Convention tends to assume that a copyright is the "natural right" of an author. One might argue whether US's decision to comport with the requirements of Berne undermines the historical and constitutional rejection of the "natural rights" theory of copyright.

35 *Graham v. John Deere*, supra note 17, 383 U.S. at 8–9.

36 Jefferson felt that rights in intellectual property should be limited to their usefulness to society. One did not "lose" by sharing an idea. "He who receives an idea from me, receives instruction himself without lessening mine, as he who lights his taper at mine, receives light without darkening mine." The free movement of ideas was essential to man's development; therefore, "[i]nventions . . . cannot, in nature, be a subject of property. Society may give an exclusive right to the profits arising from them, as an encouragement to men to pursue ideas which may produce utility" but within limits. Letter of Thomas Jefferson to Isaac McPherson, cited in Federico, "Operation, of the Patent Act of 1790," 18 *J. of the Pat. Off. Soc'y* 237, 241–242 (April 1936).

37 *Diamond v. Diehr*, 450 U.S. 175, 185–186 (1981). A new discovery of e.g., a law of nature, can in principle be protected as a trade secret, but in fact few scientific discoveries are ever protected in this manner.

is that such discoveries are simply too important to the common good to allow their monopolization by any one owner.[38]

The fallacy of fact is twofold. It is, in the first place, an error to assume that financial incentives are necessary or even sufficient to motivate creative effort. Scientists devote their lives to the discovery of new laws of nature, without the slightest hope that they will have exclusive rights in the discoveries they publish.[39] What motivates them? Curiosity, a desire to be remembered as the discoverer of something valuable and important, and professional recognition are powerful motivators for many.

On the other hand, works that are motivated solely by a need to make money are frequently of inferior quality and value to the society at large. "Potboilers" are not, as a rule, the best examples of great literature. An occasional excellent book is written solely for the purpose of making money (U.S. Grant's *Memoirs* comes to mind), but it is probably outnumbered 100 to 1 by good books that were written in spite of the author's sure knowledge that they would not be best-sellers.

The second error of fact is the assumption that legal protection is necessary if one is to profit from an intellectual creation. Innovations in business methods such as the Federal Express method of express delivery, and designs such as Parisian fashions and the Chrysler minivans, are neither patentable nor copyrightable. Nevertheless, they can be enormously profitable.

It thus appears that business innovations and new nonpatentable designs are, in fact, regularly created, from which the innovators do get rich, even though there is no legal protection for them whatsoever. One important explanation for this is lead time. The first person to bring a new product to the market will have the jump on competitors; this jump can be extended by brand identification and product improvement, while the competitors are playing catch-up.[40]

---

[38] *Funk Bros. Seed Co. v. Kala Inoculant Co.*, 333 U.S. 127, 130 (1948) ("He who discovers a hitherto unknown phenomenon of nature has no claim to a monopoly of it which the law recognizes. If there is to be invention from such a discovery, it must come from the application of the law of nature to a new and useful end.")

[39] As noted above, a scientist could in principle protect a law of nature as a secret: Yet how many instances have there been of scientists choosing this route, rather than publishing and receiving credit for their discoveries?

[40] Stephen Breyer, "The Uneasy Case For Copyright: A Study of Copyright in Books, Photocopies, and Computer Programs," 84 *Harv. L. Rev.* 281, 299–301 (Dec. 1970).

This is not to say that legal protection is never required for financial reward. One of the key determinants is whether the creator provides any benefit or value other than the intellectual creation itself. In the case of an original Parisian dress, the designer's trademark has a high value. In the case of the Chrysler minivan, the particular implementation of the idea seems to be as significant as the basic idea itself. In the case of Federal Express, the clever idea for overnight delivery must be matched by near-perfect execution for the service to be a success.

On the other hand, once a book is published, the author has little else to offer a potential buyer; for this reason, unrestricted copying of a book effectively eliminates the author's possibility of meaningful recovery. The lead time an author of a book would have over copyists would probably be insufficient to return any substantial recovery to the author.[41] Similarly, an unlimited right to copy the programming code of an "off the shelf" computer program would probably deprive its owner of any meaningful recovery. But the title of a book (however clever) is not protected by copyright,[42] in part for fear of creating an overly broad impediment to the creation of future books, and in part, because the title alone will not sell the book: it has to read well also, just as the computer program must work well if it is to sell, even if it borrows the "user interface" of another program.

For present purposes, a vital question, therefore, is whether the creators of user interfaces are more like Chrysler with its minivan, or more like an author with his or her book, in their need for legal protection in order to earn a living. The evidence seems strong that they fall more into the Chrysler category. Like the overall concept of a minivan, the interface of a computer program is but one determinant of commercial success. The program must have features that consumers want, it must be relatively free of bugs, and it must be backed up with credible and effective support staff, to name but a few other determinants of the commercial success of a computer program. Unlike the copyist of a book, the copyist of a user interface must add new value to the underlying program in order to compete effectively with the creator of the interface.

The conclusion seems inevitable that the creators of computer program interfaces will be — and indeed have been — able to profit handsomely, without any legal protection for their programs' "look and feel" whatsoever, just as Chrysler has been able to profit handsomely without any protection

---

[41] See Breyer, note 40 supra, at 302 (referring to books with heavy fixed costs and lengthy prerecoupment periods).

[42] *Becker v. Loew's, Inc.*, 133 F.2d 889, 891 (7th Cir. 1943).

against other auto manufacturers marketing products that "look and feel" much like the Chrysler minivans.

Fallacy #3: The existence of multiple alternative interfaces implies that no one of them is an unprotected "idea"

The Copyright Act's list of the things that may not be protected by copyright is commonly referred to as "the idea/expression dichotomy." After a lifetime of unparalleled contribution to the law of intellectual property, Learned Hand declared, "[N]o principle can be stated as to when an imitator has gone beyond the 'idea,' and has borrowed its 'expression.'"[43] Similarly, in his *Unhurried View of Copyright* (which should be required reading for any court addressing a question of copyright protection), Benjamin Kaplan referred to the distinction between "idea" and "expression" as "abracadabra." However, accepting this supposed "dichotomy," courts and commentators labor endlessly to define what constitutes the "idea," and what the "expression" of a screen display, or of another element of a program's "user interface."

One of the most pernicious "tests" currently in vogue for distinguishing ideas and expressions is the "Doctrine of Merger." Under this supposed "doctrine," one asks whether there is only one way of doing whatever it is that the plaintiff has done. If so, then the "idea" and its "expression" are said to have "merged," and copyright protection is denied. If not, the plaintiff wins.[44] The plaintiff almost always wins.[45] A slightly less overbroad variant on the theme is to say that protection will be denied if there are only a few ways of "expressing" the "idea."[46]

---

[43] *Peter Pan Fabrics, Inc. v. Martin Weiner Corp.*, 274 F.2d 487, 489 (2d Cir. 1960).

[44] This so-called doctrine is usually traced to the "jeweled bee pin" case, *Herbert Rosenthal v. Kalpakian*, 446 F.2d 738 (9th Cir. 1971). In that rather poorly reasoned decision, the court denied protection for a pin that was in the shape of a bee, on the ground that there was only one way to make such a pin. The premise of this argument – that one can make a jeweled bee pin in only one way – seems so manifestly incorrect that one must question the validity of the court's holding.

[45] See *Whelan Assoc. v. Jaslow Dental Lab., Inc.*, 797 F.2d 1222, 1236 n.28 (3rd Cir. 1986), cert. denied, 479 U.S. 1031 (1987). The merger doctrine's resultant overbroad protection has been noted and questioned. See, e.g., Comment, "Does Form Follow Function? The Idea/Expression Dichotomy in Copyright Protection of Computer Software," 35 U.C.L.A. L. Rev. 723, 741 (April 1988) (noting that courts frequently find that alternative methods of expression exist "regardless of their impracticability."

[46] *Morrissey v. Procter & Gamble Co.*, 379 F.2d 675, 678 (1st Cir. 1967).

The problem with this bogus "doctrine" is that it begs the question. Is something that can be expressed in only one way necessarily an "idea" for purposes of copyright protection? Sometimes yes, sometimes no. "Its spring and the world is mudluscious/the goatfooted balloon man whistles far and wee." Could anyone honestly say that he or she had found another way to express what ee cummings expressed in this poetry? Does the fact that the idea can be expressed in only one way imply that cummings' poem may not be copyrighted? Of course not.

On the other hand, each expression of something that can be expressed in an unlimited number of ways is not necessarily "expression" for purposes of copyright protection. There are undoubtedly a vast number of ways of designing a dress,[47] or a building,[48] or of structuring the input formats of a computer program,[49] or of preparing an accounting form,[50] or of writing a conditional sales agreement,[51] yet no one of them is entitled to copyright protection. The "Doctrine of Merger" is hopelessly inadequate to explain or elucidate these results.

The fact is that for most copyrighted works, it is impossible to speak intelligently about their "ideas" as distinguished from their "expressions."[52] Not only is it impossible to make this distinction for many works, but it also is not necessary to do so. The Copyright Act does not state the "dichotomy"; it is entirely judge-made. While it may be a useful distinction for some works, different intellectual tools are likely to be required for most other works if courts are to succeed in implementing the underlying copyright and competitive policies.

A different vocabulary helps: focusing on the question of whether elements of an interface constitute "methods of operation" or "function" is probably more illuminating than inquiring whether they constitute "ideas." Even more importantly, though, the courts should more directly confront the underlying

---

[47] *Jack Adelman, Inc. v. Sonners and Gordon, Inc.*, 112 F. Supp. 187, 190 (S.D.N.Y. 1934); *Russell v. Trimfit, Inc.*, 478 F. Supp. 91 (E.D. Pa. 1977).

[48] *DaSilva Construction Corp.*, note 31 supra.

[49] See *Synercom Technology, Inc. v. University Computing Co.*, 462 F. Supp. 1003 (N.D. Tex. 1978).

[50] *Baker* v. *Selden*, 101 U.S. 99 (1879).

[51] *Donald v. Zack Meyer's T.V. Sales and Service*, note 24 supra.

[52] Kaplan found further support for this conclusion in modem music and visual art. It is senseless to attempt to distinguish intelligently between the "idea" and "expression" of a work of modern music that is lacking in melody, or of an abstract painting that is lacking in representation. Kaplan, *An Unhurried View*, 52–53.

policy questions. Some suggestions for improved copyright analysis are put forward below.

The debate without the fallacies

For the reasons described above, the argument that improvements and creativity require financial incentives, the emotional "natural rights" argument, and the "idea/expression dichotomy" are not useful tools in the debate over copyright protection for the "user interface" of computer programs. But if these are not useful tools, what are?

One must begin with thoughtful consideration of the policies of the Copyright Act in particular, and the federal law of competition, monopolization, and copying in general. There is nothing all that mysterious or difficult about these underlying policies or their application. One important policy, encountered in contexts as diverse as patent cases, trademark cases, and unfair competition cases, is the preservation of competition. Another is the encouragement of innovation. A third is reward to authors for their labors.

If there is a general rule that can be distilled from the patchwork of exceptions, judge-made rules, and constitutional policies incorporated into the Patent and Copyright Acts, it is this: legal protection should be granted only when it is necessary to provide financial reward to the innovator, and when it will not substantially diminish competition, innovation or other important goals. Thus, an author can make money from a published book only if there is protection against unauthorized copying. The same is true of programming code. On the other hand, legal protection has been denied whenever the innovator can obtain a substantial financial reward without it (e.g., innovative business methods) or when there is a substantial risk that protection would materially diminish competition and innovation (as would protection for laws of nature), interfere with the standard means of creating new products (as would protection for scènes à faire and legal forms),[53] or conflict with other social goals such as the readability of maps (as would protection for standard map symbols, formats, and designs).[54]

Applying these general principles to the user interface example, one must first inquire whether the persons who create user interfaces will be prevented from obtaining a recovery for their labors without legal protection. On this question, the balance tips against legal protection in most cases. The reason is that the interface is invariably sold as part of a computer program, and few

---

[53] *Donald v. Zack Meyer's T.V. Sales and Service,* notes 24 and 51, supra.

[54] *United States v. Hamilton,* 583 F.2d 448 (9th Cir. 1978).

consumers buy a program solely for its interface. The program must also operate well, and it must be backed up with a reputable company that can provide updates and other services. For these reasons, the company that creates a program with a new interface can profit from its investment even if the interface is unprotected.[55] The company's profits might not be as large as they would be if the interface were protected – but that is a good thing, not a bad thing: monopoly profits are disfavored in a competitive economy.

The second inquiry is the effect of copyright protection on competition. It seems virtually certain that copyright protection for interfaces favors monopolization by the most dominant software companies. The simple reason is that interfaces take time to learn, and once one learns a particular interface, one is reluctant to invest the additional effort required to learn another one. As a result, protection for the interface of a successful program creates a powerful barrier to entry. By contrast, the success of one novel does not threaten competition among novelists because readers are not reluctant to read novels having new characters and plots.

The third policy consideration is the effect of protection on innovation. It is frequently argued that broad protection for software interfaces is valuable because it will compel programmers to invent completely new interfaces that will be better than the existing ones. Without the broad protection, the industry will stagnate at a lower level than it might otherwise have attained.

The famous example of the "QWERTY" typewriter keyboard debunks this reasoning. As is widely known, the standard QWERTY keyboard was devised in the late nineteenth century as a means of preventing typewriter keys from jamming.[56] As a typewriter/human interface, the QWERTY keyboard is far from ideal. It loads most of the effort onto the left hand, its most frequently used keys are not in the center row, and it compels the typist to make awkward jumps and reaches between common letter combinations. QWERTY was never protected by patent, copyright or otherwise. It nevertheless became the standard, largely as the result of a nationwide string of typing schools established by the Remington typewriter company and the commercial success of its typewriters.

---

[55] To the extent that there are some independent persons or companies engaged solely in the creation of interface elements, they can protect their recovery through contract with the companies that market the combined program interface.

[56] For an excellent discussion of the history of the QWERTY keyboard, see C. Blanchard, *The Early Word Processors* (Research Rpt. 3, Educators: Project IV, Lake George, NY 1981). See, generally A. Dvorak, N, Merrick, W. Dealey, and G. Ford, *Typewriting Behavior* (American Book Co., 1936).

Despite QWERTY's wide acceptance, radically different and much more efficient keyboards have been devised and patented — most notably the "Dvorak simplified keyboard."[57] This proves two points. First, the lack of any legal protection for a standard "user interface" such as QWERTY does not prevent innovators from creating new and improved keyboard designs. Second, the existence of legal protection for an interface has little to do with the ability of its creator to earn a reward. QWERTY was never protected, but Remington and others made plenty of money selling typewriters. On the other hand, none of the patented or unpatented keyboard designs that followed QWERTY has achieved any commercial success.[58]

The "broad protection favors innovation" line of reasoning also makes a false assumption about the nature of development in the software industry. It assumes that important innovations in software interfaces are revolutionary and not evolutionary in nature. This is wrong. It is impossible to point to a single element of any current mass-market program's interface that did not have a progenitor in one or more prior programs. Software interfaces are a means of communication between programs and their users. Like other languages, they evolve over time. But each language depends on an accumulation of conventions about meaning and syntax that were established by prior languages. Extending copyright protection to any particular language would prevent others from building on its conventions of meaning and syntax and retard its evolutionary development.[59]

For all these reasons, courts should be reluctant to extend copyright protection to any part of a computer program that potential buyers would

---

[57] See Dvorak, August, and Dealey, "Simplified Keyboard Arrangement," U.S. Pat. Off. Ser. No. 612738 (1932). The world's record for typing speed (about 240 words per minute) was set on a Dvorak keyboard.

[58] Dvorak first patented his keyboard, and then dedicated it to the public domain in hopes of encouraging its dissemination. Other inventors have retained their patent claims. See, e.g., references in Dvorak patent, cited in note 57 supra.

[59] Drawing on the seminal work of Professors Robert Merges and Richard Nelson, one can describe computer software in general, and interfaces in particular, as a "cumulative" technology like aircraft, as opposed to an iterative one like pharmaceuticals. Each improvement in a cumulative technology necessarily accumulates and builds upon prior improvements. For such technologies, Merges and Nelson have found strong evidence that intellectual property protection can retard rather than enhance industry development. See Merges and Nelson, "On the Complex Economics of Patent Scope," 90 Colum. L. Rev. 839 (1990).

prefer not to re-learn before buying a competitive product.[60] Many user interface elements — command terms, syntax, organization of command terms in a menu, to name a few — fall into this category. By contrast, many other parts of computer programs — most notably the programming code itself — can be protected without serious harm to competition and innovation in the industry.

To draw the line between what will foster the creation of improved competitive programs and what will not, it will be necessary for courts to distinguish the needs of computer programmers and users from the needs of the authors and readers of more traditional literary works. It has been all too easy for courts to assume that the same copyright principles will protect the rights of authors and programmers alike. They will not. Software is radically different from books, poems and plays. The "interface" of a book is a natural language; the "interface" of software is an artificial language. A program is written in a different language from the language by which it "interfaces" with the user; a book is not. The purpose of a book is to be read and quoted; the purpose of software is to perform functions. A court that fails to accommodate these profound differences is bound to render decisions that are unhelpful at best, and disastrous at worst, for this important industry.

Knowledge of the industry must be combined with a thoughtful and candid balancing of the underlying policies. In balancing the policies, courts need not fear treading on ground already occupied by Congress. The Copyright Act's §102(b), its definition of "pictorial, graphic and sculptural" works, and traditional exclusions such as that of *Baker v. Selden*[61] and scènes à faire give courts extraordinary latitude to decide what should and should not be copyrightable, particularly in the case of works as utilitarian as computer programs. Courts should seize this opportunity to fashion principles that will advance the science and art of computer programming. Only in this way can the constitutional purpose of copyright protection be achieved.

---

[60] This consideration may explain the *Digital Communications* court's otherwise inexplicable distinction between the rule that one chooses an item from a menu by depressing the keys that correspond to letters in the command term that are capitalized on the screen, and the choice of which letters to capitalize. The rule has to be learned and remembered, whereas the capitalized letters can be read off of the screen. *Digital Communications Assoc., Inc. v. Softklone Distributing Corp.*, 659 F. Supp. 449, 459 (N.D. Ga. 1987).

[61] 101 U.S. 99 (1879).

The User Interface: Copyright? Or a Right to Copy?*

When readers of *BCS Update* were polled [in a Reader Forum], most opined that software developers should not be protected against copying of the "look and feel" of their programs (*BCS Update*, September 1989), but most of the judges who decide whether user interfaces can be monopolized by copyright seem to disagree. For example, Judge Keeton of the United States District Court in Boston recently decided that significant portions of the user interface of *Lotus 1-2-3* cannot be copied without permission. However, we think that the judges, by and large, are wrong because they have often relied on legalistic precepts that are generally questionable — and wholly fallacious when applied to software.

Fallacy No. 1: Copyright is the only law that applies

When courts recognize property rights, they effectively allow the owners of those rights to exercise monopolies of one sort or another. But these monopolies tend to be limited. For example, zoning laws limit what you can do with your land, and public easements invade your monopoly on the use of your land with sewer pipes and power lines.

Intellectual property rights — copyrights, patents, trademarks, and trade secret rights — are also limited, generally by the law of "fair competition." However, while the courts have long recognized that antitrust principles restrict the freedom with which a patent-holder or the owner of a trademark or trade secret may exercise what is otherwise a legally-protected monopoly, the courts are not accustomed to thinking about issues of industrial competitiveness when it comes to copyrights.

The reason for this may be that until the advent of copyright protection for software, it was rather silly to suppose that copyright could create a harmful monopoly in the industrial sense. After all, the Copyright Act itself withholds protection from "any idea, procedure, process, system, method of operation, concept, principle, or discovery." So long as the application of these principles prevented a Margaret Mitchell from monopolizing the "idea" of how a belle might cause a war-profiteer not to give a damn, it was absurd to suppose that any book — even a blockbuster like *Gone With the Wind* — could squeeze out competition, stifle innovation, and hurt consumers.

However, if the judges extend copyright protection to the user interface of a widely used spreadsheet, for example, the effects on competition are all too apparent. Would-be competitors will not only have to develop a better spreadsheet, but they will also have to convince users that their products are superior enough to justify the expense of learning (and training employees to use) a new, unfamiliar interface. This would be like telling Mitchell's progeny that, although they were free to market Reconstruction romances, they could do so only if they used their own substitute systems of punctuation, paragraphing, and pagination.

Thus, to develop meaningful limits on copyright protection for software, judges must now do what they have always done with other forms of intellectual property — consider not only the level of protection that is necessary to stimulate innovation, but also the effects of protection on that freedom of competition which is also essential to our economic well-being.

Fallacy No. 2: Copying is a "wrong" that copyright is designed to redress

It is easy to fall into the trap of thinking that all copying is bad — a "tort" that copyright is designed to deter and remedy. This is bunk. Copying is the rule and not the exception in our competitive society. Examples abound.

Federal Express invents overnight delivery using a hub-and-spoke system and is promptly imitated by UPS, Purolator, and even the United States Post Office. Christian Dior shows his new line of dresses in Paris, and "knock-offs" appear within weeks on department store racks. Chanel devises a new fragrance that is promptly imitated at a fraction of Chanel's price and cost. Chrysler creates a phenomenally successful line of "minivans," only to be pursued by minivans from every other major automaker. Some copyists even advertise that their products are as close as possible to the originals.

All of these forms of copying — and many more — are protected by federal and/ or state law. The reason is that copying serves two fundamental purposes. First, it facilitates price competition. If others were not permitted to offer the same product or service, competition as to price would be confused and blunted by distinctions among the goods or services offered. Where the competitor offers exactly the same thing, prices are driven down, and "efficiency" in the economic sense is maximized.

Second, copying transmits society's collective store of knowledge. We learn by imitation. Without copying, it would be necessary for everyone to "reinvent the wheel" before marketing a project, writing a play, performing an experiment, or undertaking any other creative activity. This would be inefficient and undesirable. The manufacturer of a screwdriver *must* start with the assumption that his goods should look and feel just about like the ones already on the market. If not, they might not fit the screws they are supposed to drive, and customers might not know how to use them.

Once one person has gotten something right, society derives no benefit from laws that require the next person to do it differently. Any other approach is inefficient at best dangerous at worst. We would be appalled if we went to an attorney for a will and were informed that it had to be prepared by someone who had never seen a will before, or if we were informed that our gall bladder operation would have to be performed by a surgeon who had never seen one removed before. Working from scratch creates "bugs." Yet that is exactly what "clean room" techniques require. It has been suggested that the OS/2 operating system contains many programming shortfalls precisely because it was created using "clean room" techniques that prevented its designers from avoiding their predecessors' mistakes.

For these reasons, the law has jealously guarded the right to copy. In 1910, Justice Holmes said that competitors enjoy "a right . . . to get whatever share they can in the popularity of [another company's] product by advertising that they are trying to make the same article, and think that they succeed." In 1989, Justice O'Connor observed in *Bonito Boats, Inc. v. Thunder Craft Boats, Inc.*, "imitation and refinement through imitation are both necessary to invention itself and the very life-blood of a competitive economy." Moreover, except for materials protected by patent or copyright, "[t]hat which is published may be freely copied as a matter of federal right."

Bonito Boat harkens back to a tradition that today's judges often forget — a historical and deep-seated mistrust of patents and copyrights as monopolies that threaten the right to copy. This tradition may have begun as far back as 1623 with the English "Statute of Monopolies," which was a Parliamentary effort to curb exclusive patents granted by the Crown. It was continued in 1710 by the first true copyright statute, the Statute of Anne, which restricted the rights of an unpopular Crown monopoly over printing known as the "Stationers' Company."

The American colonists shared this hostility and expressed it in such actions as the Boston Tea Party. Consequently, there was a strong sentiment among the Founding Fathers that any power in the federal government to grant monopolies, and, in particular, monopolies in the nature of patents and copyrights would be intolerable. The most notable proponent of this view was Thomas Jefferson, who considered exclusive statutory monopolies such as patents to be an "embarrassment," and who viewed freedom from monopolies as a right to be litanized alongside the freedoms of religion and the press.

To be sure, Jefferson eventually came around to the view that "[m]onopolies may be allowed to persons for their own productions & their own inventions in the arts," but only for limited times. Thence the current Constitutional provision, which empowers Congress "To promote the progress of science and the Useful Arts by securing for limited Times to Authors and Inventors the exclusive Right to their respective Writings and Discoveries."

Ignoring this tradition, judges often appear to view the right to copy as merely an exception to some presumed rule against it. In truth, copyright does not protect against all or even most copying, and copyright itself is but one small part of a much larger body of federal and state law that serves a variety of important policies. These policies include the provision of incentive and reward for invention, but they also include the avoidance of stifling monopolies and the preservation of competition.

When weighing the importance of these divergent policies as they apply to user interfaces, judges should remember that the fundamental rule is one that abhors monopolistic limitations on the right to copy. At base, the laws that allow patent-holders or copyright owners to monopolize their creations are very circumscribed exceptions to the general rule that protects a higher principle — the right to copy.

Fallacy No. 3: The difficulty and expense of creating an interface supports its copyrightability

Proponents of protection for user interfaces often say: "The developer expended substantial time and effort in creating an interface that helped to make his product a success. If others can imitate this interface at a fraction of the original developer's cost, there will be no incentive to create better interfaces, and society will suffer. Therefore, the creators of interfaces must be allowed to monopolize their creations." This line of reasoning rests on three fallacies: one philosophical, one legal, and one factual.

The philosophical error lies in the implicit assumption that copyright is a matter of natural right — the popular notion that, if you create something by your own labors, it is yours, and others may not use it without your permission. This argument has a powerful emotional appeal, but the "natural right" theory of intellectual property rights was rejected by Jefferson in favor of a "social and economic rationale" under which protection is granted by society as an inducement to new creation. Where protection would interfere with the creation of new works, it defeats the purpose and should properly be denied.

The fallacy of law is that the difficulty or expense of creating a thing makes it a proper subject of copyright or patent protection. There is no such legal principle. The most potent counter-example is discovery of a law of nature.

Surely the effort and creativity required to discover new laws of nature are unrivaled. Einstein's $E=mc^2$ is the most famous example, but millions of dollars and years of individual effort are commonly expended to make the most modest advance in scientific knowledge. Nevertheless, the law accords no protection whatsoever against the exploitation of that discovery by others. The reason is that such discoveries are simply too important to the common good to allow their monopolization by any one owner.

The fallacy of fact is twofold. First, it is wrong to assume that financial incentives are necessary or even sufficient to motivate creative effort. Scientists often devote their lives to discovery without the slightest hope that they will have exclusive rights in the laws of nature they publish. (We're not even being paid to write this!) On the other hand, works that are motivated solely by a need to make money (we call them "potboilers") are frequently of inferior quality and value to society at large.

Second, it is also wrong to assume that legal protection is necessary if one is to profit from an intellectual creation. Innovations such as the Federal Express method of delivery, and designs such as Parisian fashions or minivans, are neither patentable nor copyrightable. Nevertheless, they can be enormously profitable. One important explanation for this is lead time: The first person to bring a new product to the market has a jump on competitors, and this lead can be extended by brand identification and product improvements while the competitors are trying to field their first version of the product.

This is not to say that legal protection is never required for financial reward. A key determinant is whether the creator provides any benefit or value other than the intellectual creation itself. In the case of an original dress, the designer's trademark has a high value. In the case of a minivan, particular implementations seem to be as significant as the basic idea itself. In the case of Federal Express, the idea must be matched by near-perfect execution for the service to succeed.

On the other hand, once a book is published, the author has little else to offer a potential buyer; for this reason, copying of a book effectively eliminates the author's possibility of meaningful recovery. Similarly, an unlimited right to copy the programming code of an "off the shelf" computer program would probably deprive its owner of any meaningful recovery on his investment.

For present purposes, then, a vital question is whether the creator of a user interface is more like Chrysler with its minivan, or more like an author with his book when it comes to the need for legal protection in order to earn a living. The evidence seems strong that interface developers fall more into the Chrysler category. Like the overall concept of a minivan, the interface of a computer program is but one determinant of commercial success. The program must have features that consumers want, it must be relatively free of bugs, and it must be backed up with a credible and effective support staff. To name but a few other determinants of the commercial success of a computer program. Unlike the copyist of a book, the copyist of a user interface must add important new value to the underlying program in order to compete effectively with the creator of the interface.

The conclusion seems inevitable: Creators of interfaces will be — and indeed have been — able to profit handsomely, without any legal protection for the "look and feel" of their programs, just as Chrysler has been able to profit without any legal right to prevent other auto manufacturers from marketing products that "look and feel" very much like Chrysler's minivans.

Fallacy No. 4: The existence of alternative interfaces implies that each of them is copyrightable

As we have noted, the Copyright Act is supposed to contain a bulwark against harmful monopolies; the Act's provisions which withhold protection from such things as ideas or processes, and which limit protection to creator's "expression" thereof. Accordingly, the distinction between things that may and may not be protected by copyright is commonly referred to as "the idea/expression dichotomy." For example, if any portion of a spreadsheet's interface is held to be "expression" rather than "idea" or "process," the owner will be empowered to monopolize that portion.

If you think that the supposed bulwark may be difficult to maintain because this distinction is difficult for judges to draw, you are right. After a lifetime of unparalleled contribution to the law of intellectual property, Learned Hand declared that "no principle can be stated as to when an imitator has gone beyond the 'idea,' and has borrowed its 'expression.'" *Peter Pan Fabrics, Inc. v. Martin Weiner Corp.*, 274 F.2d 487, 489 (2d. Cir. 196). Benjamin Kaplan, the wisest of American copyright professors and himself an eminent jurist, referred to the distinction as "abracadabra." Nonetheless, court and commentators accept this dichotomy as law, discoursing learnedly and interminably on what constitutes the idea, and what the expression, of a screen display, or a pattern of keystrokes, and the other myriad elements of a program's interface.

The difficulty of resolving such arguments has led to the reliance on a particularly pernicious "test" for distinguishing ideas from expressions: the so-called "Doctrine of Merger," under which one asks whether there is only one way of doing whatever it is that the plaintiff has done. If so, then the "idea" and its "expression" are said to have "merged," and copyright protection is denied. If not, the plaintiff wins. Needless to say, the plaintiff almost always wins.

The problem with this bogus "doctrine" is that it begs the question: Is something that can be expressed in only one way necessarily an "idea" for purposes of protection? Sometimes yes, sometimes no. Consider "its spring and the world is mudluscious/the goatfooted balloon man whistles far and wee." Could anyone honestly say that he or she had found another way to express what e e cummings expressed in this poetry? Does the fact that the idea of this poetry can be expressed in only one way imply that it is solely an "idea" that may not be copyrighted? Of course not.

On the other hand, each expression of something that can be expressed in an unlimited number of ways is not necessarily "expression" for purposes of copyright protection. There are undoubtedly a vast number of ways of designing a dress or a building, or of structuring the input formats of a computer program, or of preparing an accounting form, or of writing a conditional sales agreement; yet the learned judges have decided that no one of these kinds of creation is entitled to copyright protection. The "Doctrine of Merger" is hopelessly inadequate to explain or elucidate any of these decisions.

The secret is that for most copyrighted works, it is impossible to speak intelligently about their "ideas" as distinguished from their "expressions." As Judge Kaplan observed, it is senseless to attempt to distinguish intelligently between the "idea" and "expression" of a work of modern music that is lacking in melody, or of an abstract painting that is lacking in representation. Not only is it impossible to make this distinction for many works, but it also is not necessary to do so. The Copyright Act does not state the "dichotomy"; it is entirely judge-made. While it may be a useful distinction for some works (the Doctrine of Merger is usually traced to a decision involving a jeweled bee pin) are likely to be required for most other works if courts are to succeed in implementing the underlying copyright and competitive policies.

A different vocabulary helps: focusing on the question of whether elements of an interface constitute "methods of operation" or "function" is probably more illuminating than asking whether they constitute "ideas." Better yet, though, the courts should confront the underlying policy questions directly.

The debate without the fallacies

As we have seen, the "idea/expression dichotomy," the emotional "natural rights" argument, and the argument that improvements and creativity require financial incentives are not useful tools in the debate over copyright protection for the user interface of computer programs. But if these are not useful tools, what are?

Courts should begin with a thoughtful consideration of the policies of the Copyright Act in particular, and the federal law of competition, monopolization and copying in general. There is nothing all that mysterious or difficult about these underlying policies or their application. One important policy, encountered in contexts as diverse as patent cases, trademark cases, and unfair competition cases, is the preservation of competition. Another is the encouragement of innovation.

However, if there is a cardinal rule that can be distilled from the patchwork of exceptions, judge-made rules, and constitutional policies that are incorporated into the Patent and Copyright Acts, it is this: Legal protection has been, and should be, granted only where it is necessary to provide a financial reward to the innovator. Thus, because a book, once published, can only provide recovery if there is protection against copying it, books have been and should continue to be protected. So also programming code, so also an "invention" as defined in the Patent Act. On the other hand, legal protection has been denied wherever the innovator can obtain a financial reward without it (as with business records), or where there is a substantial risk that protection would materially diminish competition (as with laws of nature and other "ideas"), or when: protection would conflict with other social goals such as computer literacy (as evidenced by the refusal to allow copyright protection for standard map symbols, formats, and designs).

Applying these general principles to an example of user interface, one must first ask whether, as a practical matter, the persons who create user interfaces will be prevented from obtaining any recovery for their labors without legal protection. The balance probably tips against protection in most cases. Interfaces are almost always designed in conjunction with the design of a program as a whole. The program will make money if it operates well, fills a market need, and is backed up by reliable delivery of updates and other services. If the interface is not protected, the creator's profits might not be as large as they would be if the interface were protected — but that is a good thing because monopoly profits are generally disfavored in a competitive economy.

The second inquiry is the effect of copyright protection on competition. Copyright protection for one novel does not threaten competition among novelists because readers are not reluctant to read novels having new characters and plots. By contrast, it seems virtually certain that copyright protection for interfaces favors monopolization by the most dominant software companies. The simple reason is that interfaces take time to learn, and once one learns a particular interface, one is reluctant to invest the additional effort required to learn another one. As a result, protection for the interface of a successful program creates a powerful barrier to entry.

The third policy consideration is the effect of protection on innovation. It is frequently argued that broad protection for software interfaces is valuable because it will compel programmers to invent completely new interfaces that will be better than the existing ones. Without the broad protection, the industry will stagnate at a lower level than it might otherwise have attained.

The famous example of Remington's "QWERTY" typewriter keyboard debunks this reasoning. Although QWERTY is demonstrably inefficient, it became the standard *without* reliance on legal protection; and it has survived challenges from demonstrably superior systems — such as the "Dvorak simplified keyboard" — largely because skilled typists are loath to relearn their skill. This proves two points. First, the lack of legal protection for a standard "user interface" does not discourage innovators from creating new and improved keyboard designs. Second, the existence of legal protection for an interface has little to do with the ability of its creator to earn a reward. QWERTY was never protected, but Remington and others made plenty of money selling typewriters. On the other hand, none of the patented or unpatented keyboard designs that followed QWERTY has achieved any commercial success.

Those who argue that broad protection favors innovation also assume that important innovations in software interfaces are revolutionary and not evolutionary in nature. This is wrong. It is impossible to point to a single element of any current mass-market program's interface that did not have a progenitor in one or more prior programs. Software interfaces are "user languages" — means of communication between programs and their users. Like other languages, they evolve over time, and each depends on an accumulation of conventions about meaning and syntax that were established by prior languages. Extending copyright protection to any one user language would prevent others from building on its conventions of meaning and syntax, and retard its evolutionary development.

For all these reasons, courts should not extend copyright protection to any part of a computer program that users would prefer not to relearn before buying a competitive product. Many user interface elements — command terms, syntax, organization of command terms in a menu, to name a few — fall into this category. By contrast, many other parts of computer programs — most notably the programming code itself — can be protected without serious harm to competition and innovation in the industry.

To make a meaningful distinction between what will foster innovation and what will not, courts must distinguish the needs of computer programmers and users from the needs of the authors and readers of more traditional literary works. Software is different from books, poems, and plays. A program is written in a different language from the language by which it "interfaces" with the user; a book or play is not. The purpose of a book is to be read and quoted; the purpose of software is to perform functions. A court that fails to accommodate these profound differences is bound to render bad decisions.

Knowledge of the industry must be combined with thoughtful and candid balancing of underlying policies. The Copyright Act gives courts extraordinary latitude to decide what should and should not be monopolized by copyright, particularly in the case of work as utilitarian as computer programs. Courts should seize this opportunity to fashion principles that will advance the science and art of computer programming. Only in this way can the constitutional purpose of copyright protection be achieved.

Novelty, Scope, and the Shared Geometry of Patent and Copyright Protection*

One of the most important developments in modern intellectual property law has been the extension of copyright to utilitarian works formerly considered the exclusive domain of patents. Copyright law and patent law are, at least superficially, radically different. Copyright gives no protection against independent creation; patent does. Patent requires novelty and nonobviousness; copyright does not. Patents are issued after an elaborate examination procedure; copyright arises automatically. Patents last for 17 years; copyright for 75 years or more.

On the face of it, the application of copyright and patent to the same subject matter creates a potential for inconsistency and conflict. The same invention that is not novel and, therefore, ineligible for patent protection might nevertheless be original and, therefore, eligible for the much longer duration of copyright protection. The same work that was not copied, and therefore not a copyright infringement, might nevertheless infringe a patent covering the same subject matter.

While Congress could, in principle, adopt a dual system of protection, and the Supreme Court has shown sympathy for overlapping methods of protection,[1] a dual system seems unwise in this case. Wholesale extension of copyright protection to non-novel utilitarian works would seem to threaten the fundamental patent principle that works that are known or used by others are in the public domain and should not be withdrawn from public availability.[2] It also creates a high risk that multiple parties will claim copyright for the same "invention." Patent resolves such conflicts through detailed rules governing priority of invention, but such rules are utterly lacking in copyright.

The apparent inconsistency would be eliminated if copyright and patent were not so different. In particular, if copyright had a novelty requirement, the

---

 Presented to Computer Law Association, November 5, 1990. The author gratefully acknowledges the assistance of Alexander H. Pyle and Susan Barbieri Montgomery in the preparation of this paper.

[1] See *Mazer v. Stein*, 347 U.S. 201 (1954) (copyright and design patents may cover same subject matter); *Kewanee v. Bicron Corp.*, 416 U.S. 470 (1974) (state trade secret laws not preempted by patent system). But cf. *Bonito Boats, Inc. v. Thunder Craft Boats, Inc.*, — U.S. —, 109 S. Ct. 971, 980 (1989) (state law prohibiting plug molding preempted by federal patent law).

[2] See generally 35 U.S.C. §102(a) (patent barred if it was known or used by others in the United States prior to invention by the applicant).

danger of withdrawing utilitarian works from the public domain and of conflicting claims to the same work would be eliminated.

The thesis of this paper is that the concept of novelty is fundamental to both copyright and patent law. Copyright has been able to avoid an explicit novelty requirement because of the nature of the subject matter to which it has traditionally been applied. This has had the desirable consequence of dramatically reducing the social cost of providing copyright protection. However, as copyright is intended to reach subject matter closer and closer to that of patent law, the benefit of enforcing a novelty requirement begins to outweigh its costs.

1. The economic and social basis for patent and copyright protection

The most often-cited justification for patent and copyright protection is that they provide incentives for inventors and authors to create products that are socially useful or desirable. Indeed, the U.S. Constitution authorizes exclusive rights in the nature of patent and copyright as a means to the end of "promot[ing] the Progress of Science and useful Arts." U.S. Constitution, art. I, sec. 8, cl. 8. The Supreme Court has endorsed this idea: "The economic philosophy behind the clause empowering Congress to grant patents and copyrights is the conviction that encouragement of individual effort by personal gain is the best way to advance public welfare through the talents of authors and inventors in 'Science and useful Arts.'" *Mazer v. Stein,* 347 U.S. 201, 219 (1954). Businesses might be less willing to make substantial investments in research and development if competing firms could copy their inventions as soon as they reached the market, or to pay authors large royalties if others could issue competing editions of the same book. Indeed, one study has suggested that the level of patent protection a country provides is linked with its level of economic growth. R. Rapp and R. Rozek, "Benefits and Costs of Intellectual Property Protection in Developing Countries," 7 (National Economic Research Associates, Working Paper #3, June 1990).

Providing an incentive to authors and inventors is not, of course, without cost. Creating property (or monopoly) rights in works of authorship and inventions is inefficient in an economic sense. For the period of the statutory grant, it drives their prices above what the price would be without the rights. This means that fewer of the public will be able to afford goods or services that embody the intellectual property, and resources will go to enriching the copyright and patent holders that might otherwise have been available for investment in productive resources. [3]

In addition, the copyright and patent systems have high "transactional" costs. Obtaining a patent is an expensive, time- and resource-consuming proposition. Enforcing one in the costs is still more costly. Under current law, obtaining a copyright has little marginal cost, but its enforcement can as expensive as enforcing a patent.

Finally, overly broad grants of rights can jeopardize rather than enhance future development. If Schoenberg could have prevented later composers from writing twelve-tone music, if Picasso and Braque could have prevented other painters from using cubist conventions, or if Joyce could have prevented other writers from stream-of-consciousness technique, the progress of modern culture would have been severely curtailed. Similarly, if the Wright Brothers could have used their patents covering the Flyer to prevent others from building flying machines, the history of modern aviation might have been stultified.[4]

In sum, both the copyright and patent are engaged in a balancing act — granting just the right amount of exclusive rights to create an incentive for individual effort without chilling future development. Both copyright and patent achieve this balance by defining an area that is open to all comers — the public domain.[5] As we will see, copyright identifies the public domain by careful definition of copyrightable and uncopyrightable subject matter. Patent law also defines patentable and unpatentable subject matter but focuses on the requirement of novelty. The question is why.

2. Definitions of subject matter

2.1 Copyrightable subject matter

The logic of the Copyright Act is like a Venn diagram in which the "universe" includes everything set down in a tangible medium of expression. Copyright

---

[3] See generally Breyer, "The Uneasy Case for Copyright: A Study of Copyright in Books, Photocopies, and Computer Programs," 84 *Harv. L. Rev.* 281 (1970).

[4] There is some basis for the belief that the development of aviation was indeed retarded by over-broad enforcement of patents granted to aviation's pioneers, such as the Wright Brothers and Glenn Curtis. See Merges & Nelson, "On the Complex Economics of Patent Scope," 90 *Columbia L. Rev.* – (1990).

[5] For an excellent discussion of the role of the concept of the public domain in copyright law, see Litman, "The Public Domain" (unpublished manuscript; Professor Litman teaches at Michigan state University).

protection extends to the whole universe except for the area within the universe carved out by the phrase "any idea, procedure, process, system, method of operation, concept, principle or discovery."[6] Copyright thus protects the interests of the public by defining what is not copyrightable, rather than by defining what is.[7]

Many decades of copyright adjudication, and repeated amendments to the Copyright Act, have produced a laundry list of things that are not copyrightable. Professor Litman listed them as follows:

> Copyright [does] not protect ideas, methods, systems, facts, utilitarian objects, titles, themes, plots, scènes à faire, words, short phrases and idioms, literary characters, styles, or works of the federal government.[8]

Although Litman refers to her list as a "hodge-podge,"[9] it is unified by the fact that, with the possible exception of works of the federal government, all of the items on the list are capable of use beyond the particular use to which the author put them. Thus, they are all relatively general in nature. Litman's list can therefore be understood as particular applications of Learned Hand's famous "abstractions test":

> Upon any work, and especially upon a play, a great number of patterns of increasing generality will fit equally well, as more and more of the incident is left out. The last may perhaps be no more than the most general statement of what the play is about, and at times might consist only of its title; but there is a point in this series of abstractions where they are no longer protected, since otherwise the playwright could prevent the use of his "ideas," to which, apart from their expression, his property is never extended.[10]

Hand's "test" contemplates a continuum of generality or abstraction, along which every element of every copyrighted work may be placed. One can

---

[6] 17 U. S. C.§102(b). See Hemnes, "The Adaptation of Copyright Law to Video Games," 131 *U. Pa. L. Rev.* 171, 209 (1982).

[7] By contrast, nothing is protected by patent until a patent is issued. 35 U.S.C. §§101, 111, 131.

[8] Litman, supra, unpublished manuscript at 33 (citations omitted).

[9] Id. at 34.

[10] *Nichols v. Universal Pictures Corp.*, 45 F.2d 119, 121(2d Cir. 1930), cert. denied, 282 U.S. 902 (1931).

visualize the particular types of uncopyrightable subject matter as points along the continuum:

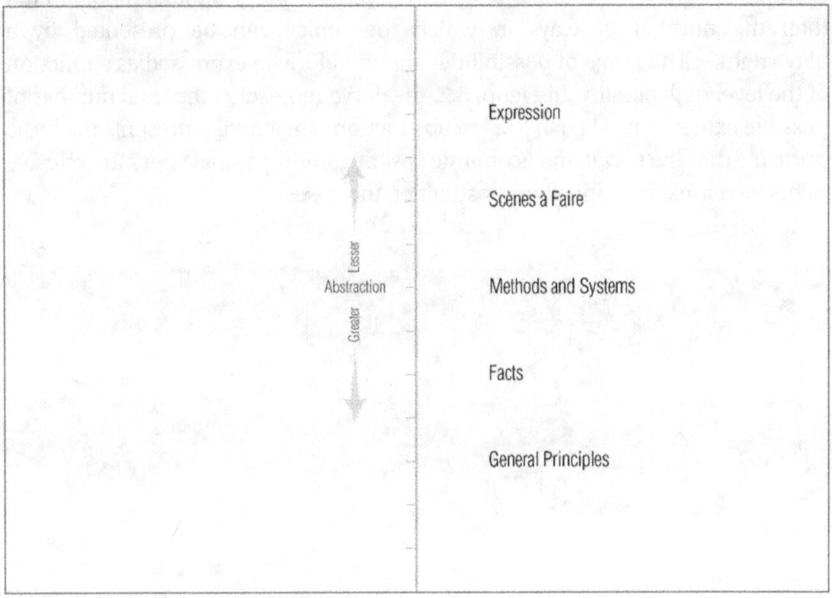

Figure 3.1 Abstraction Continuum

It is fairly obvious that copyright should not extend the full length of Figure 3.1. As one moves in the direction of increasing levels of abstraction, the scope of the copyright monopoly would increase. The social cost of the monopoly — its potential for interference with the creation of other works — increases with its breadth. At the same time, the odds that the thing the author claims to have created is truly original diminishes, and the social benefit of creating an incentive to create the thing, therefore, diminishes as well. At some point, the social cost exceeds the benefit, and, as Hand observed, copyright protection must be denied.

A second common test for copyrightable subject matter is commonly referred to as the "doctrine of merger." Where there is only one way of expressing something,[11] where the number of possible expressions is small[12], or where the

[11] *Herbert Rosenthal Jewelry Corp. v. Kalpakian*, 446 F.2d 738 (9th Cir. 1971). The author has questioned the validity of the *Kalpakian* case's holding; see Hemnes, "Three Common Fallacies in the User Interface Copyright Debate," 7 *Comp. Lawyer* 14 at n. 44.

expression is dictated by function,[13] copyright will be either denied or curtailed.[14] This test is closely related to Hand's abstractions test. As the level of abstraction increases, the number of possibilities decreases. To use Hand's example of a play, the number of general topics for plays is much more limited than the number of ways in which the topics can be presented by a playwright.[15] The range of possibilities can therefore be expressed as a function of the level of generality. In Figure 3.2, the curve represents the total number of possible expressions at each level of abstraction. The curve represents the basic principle that the social and economic cost of granting a single person exclusive rights increases dramatically as abstraction increases:

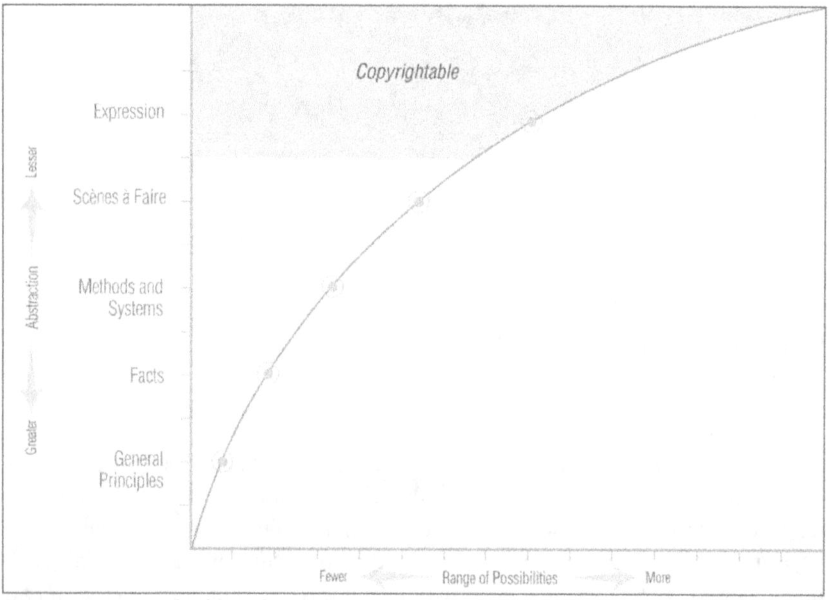

Figure 3.2 Copyrightable Subject Matter

---

[12] *Morrissey v. Procter & Gamble Co.*, 379 F.2d 675 (1st Cir. 1967) (sweepstakes instructions not copyrightable).

[13] *Kieselstein-Cord v. Accessories By Pearl, Inc.*, 632 F.2d 989 (2d Cir. 1980).

[14] The *Morrissey* case suggested that copyright protection might be limited to verbatim copying.

[15] Aristotle's *Poetics* catalogs a handful of general topics for drama; his categories hold largely true to this day.

2.2 Patentable subject matter

Although an "abstractions test" is not usually considered a feature of patent law, it is possible to create a very similar representation of patentable subject matter. Thus, it is said that patents are available for inventions, but not for discoveries or laws of nature.[16] Sufficiently high levels of generality therefore preclude patentability, just as they preclude copyrightability.

Unlike copyright, patent also requires a minimum level of generality. Trivial and useless improvements and variations are not patentable.[17] If I am the first person to print poems on mousetraps, or to paint them chartreuse, I cannot patent my invention. One can represent these principles as follows:

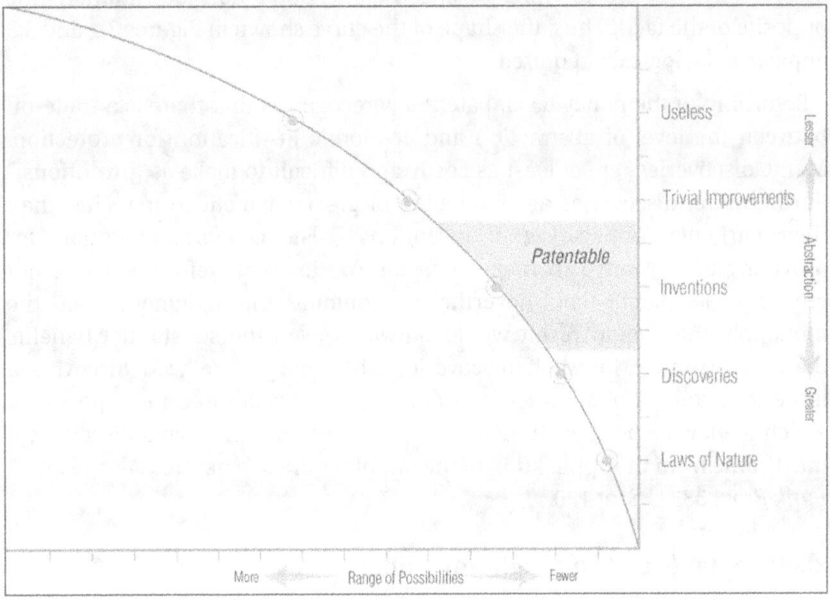

Figure 3.3 Patentable Subject Matter

[16] See, e.g., *O'Reilly v. Morse*, 56 U.S. (15 How.) 62 (1853); *Funk Bros. Seed Co. v. Kale Inoculant Co.*, 333 U.S. 127 (1948).

[17] See 35 U. S. C. §103 (a patentable invention must not be obvious to one ordinarily skilled in the art).

It should be noted that the assumption that there is a much larger number of possibilities at lower levels of generality has both an empirical and logical basis. At the highest possible level of generality, there are but a few basic laws of nature. For example, there are but four basic forces in nature, at least two of these seem to be manifestations of the same force, and physicists labor daily to reduce the remaining three to one. On the other hand, the number of practical applications of a basic force such as electromagnetism is very great. By the same token, the number of applications of a discovery exceeds at any time the number of discoveries. The fact that steam occupies 1670 times the volume of an equal mass of water is a single fact that provides the basis for all steam locomotion. Finally, the number of possible non-facts (i.e., the possible range of fiction) has to exceed the number of facts: for every fact that one can assert, it is possible to think of at least one other non-fact (namely, the opposite of the fact). Thus, the shape of the curve shown in Figures 3.2 and 3.3 appears to be logically required.

Returning to the policy level, Patent law recognizes that there is a trade-off between the level of abstraction and economic justification for protection. Many "discoveries" are at least as costly and difficult to make as "inventions." Furthermore, discoveries are frequently of greater benefit to mankind than their particular application in inventions.[18] The economic rationale for providing an incentive to make such discoveries is therefore equal, if not greater. The patent law nevertheless contains the judgment that the monopoly that would result would outweigh even the substantial benefits than an incentive for such discoveries would have. "He who discovers a hitherto unknown phenomenon of nature has no claim to a monopoly of it which the law recognizes. If there is to be invention from such a discovery, it must come from the application of the law of nature to a new and useful end." *Funk Bros.*, 333 U.S. at 130.

2.3 Patentable and copyrightable subject matter compared and combined

It is immediately apparent that the continua represented by Figures 3.2 and 3.3 have points of contact. What patent law calls "discoveries" is highly analogous to what copyright law calls "facts." Many patentable inventions are equivalent to uncopyrightable "methods of operation" and "processes"; indeed, this is probably the reason why they are deemed to be

[18] By analogy, creating an idea such as the sonnet form is arguably a more important development than any particular sonnet.

uncopyrightable.[19] The laws of nature that are out of reach of the patent laws are, in terms of generality, comparable to the grammatical rules and other general principles that are equally uncopyrightable. These shared points of reference create a scale that enables one to create a composite representation showing the subject matter of both patent and copyright law:

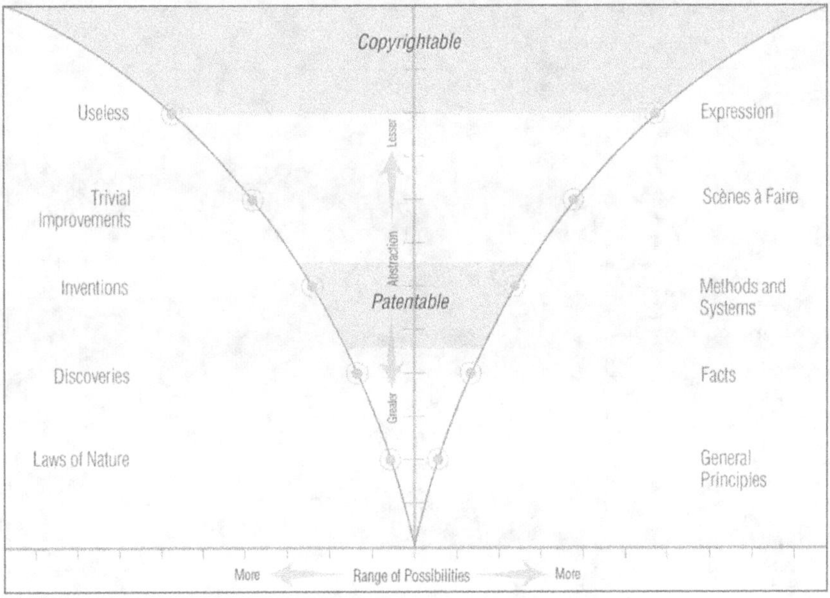

Figure 3.4 Copyrightable and Patentable Subject Matter Compared

This combined representation dramatizes several important points. First, the distinction between utilitarian and nonutilitarian works tends to run on a "north-south" axis rather than an "east-west" axis. That is, the more abstract elements of copyrightable works — methods, facts, words, and rules of grammar have nearly exact analogs in patent law, and are at least as "useful." A word, for example, is certainly as useful as the discovery that Mars has two moons. The figure thus suggests that copyrightable works do not exist in a different, nonutilitarian realm from patentable works. Instead, both cover the same realm of human endeavor; the difference is that copyright *protection* traditionally operates at a far lower level of generality than does patent law.

---

[19] See *Baker v. Selden*, 101 U.S. 99 (1879).

Second, the figure dramatizes the fact that copyright protection has traditionally been applied at a level of abstraction where the range of possible works is very large. In comparison, patents operate at a much higher level of abstraction and a correspondingly smaller range of possible invention. One can construct a further visualization representing a "cut" through the bottom of the area of copyright protection and another "cut" through the top of the area of patent protection:

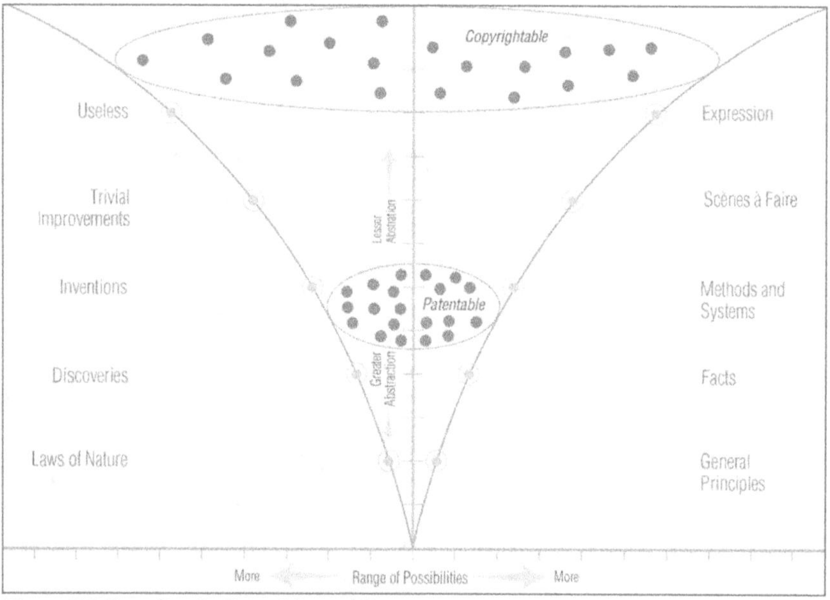

Figure 3.5 Crowding in Copyright and Patent

The shaded areas in Figure 3.5 represent areas of exclusive rights carved out by copyrights and patents. They are all about the same size, and there are about the same number of them at each level. The greater crowding shown at the patent level is an important feature, to which we will now turn.

2.4 Originality, novelty, and scope of protection

Thus far, we have examined similarities between copyright and patent law. Both carve out an area of public domain by reference to the level of abstraction of the work in which rights might be claimed. Both assume that as the level of abstraction increases, the number of possibilities diminishes. Both even identify some of the same elements of the public domain, most notably facts and basic laws and principles.

There are, however, very marked differences in both history and approach. The most notable of these are: i) patent requires novelty, while copyright requires only originality; ii) patent provides a remedy for independent creation of the same invention, while copyright does not; but iii) copyright provides a remedy for the creation of derivative works, while patent does not.

Figure 3.5, it is submitted, provides insight into these striking differences. Copyright has traditionally functioned at such a low level of abstraction that there is assumed to be a virtually infinite range of possible creations. On the other hand, patent law operates at a level of abstraction where there is a limited range of possible inventions. This simple difference has fundamental implications.

First, note that there is an inverse correlation between the level of abstraction and the odds that two persons will independently create the same thing. At the most general end of the scale — laws of nature, discoveries — there is believed to be a near certainty that two persons will eventually come up with the same idea or fact. Indeed, parallel discovery is very common in science. Simultaneous development of the calculus by Leibniz and Newton is perhaps the most famous example. At any particular time, certain discoveries seem ripe for the picking. Once Galileo had developed a workable telescope, the discovery of Jupiter's moons was inevitable — if Galileo had not happened to train his instrument on Jupiter, someone else surely would have.

On the other hand, at the least general end of the scale, the odds of independent creation of the same thing are virtually nil.[20] If Galileo hadn't lived, the odds seem good that by now, someone else would have discovered Jupiter's moons. If, on the other hand, James Joyce hadn't lived, the odds are at least equally good that no one else would have written *Finnegans Wake*. The odds are somewhat better, though, that others would have developed a "stream-of-consciousness" literary technique. The relation between the likelihood of independent creation and level of abstraction is shown in the following figure.

---

[20] This is the basis for Hand's famous "Ode to a Grecian Urn" example. *Sheldon v. Metro-Goldwyn Pictures Corp.*, 81 F.2d 49 (2d. Cir.), cert. den., 298 U.S. 669 (1936).

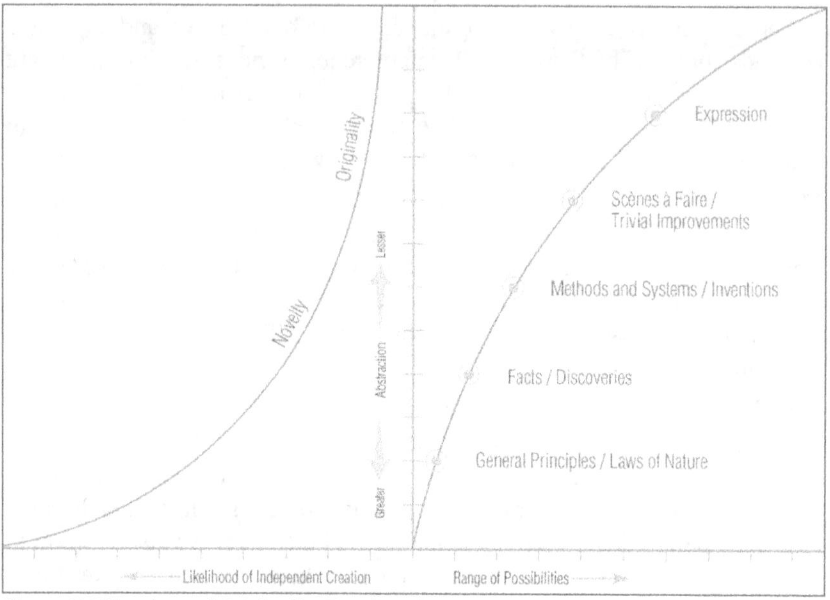

Figure 3.6 Novelty and Originality Compared

Patent operates at a level of generality at which there is at least a plausible possibility of independent creation of the same invention; copyright does not. This explains why patent law, but not copyright, has a strict novelty requirement. Where independent creation is possible, there must be a mechanism for deciding which of the multiple possible inventors will have the benefits of legal protection. According protection to more than one of them would dramatically reduce the incentive to create and produce a fertile area for inconsistent and conflicting claims of rights. According benefits to the first of them has the desirable effect of accelerating the speed at which inventions are made and brought into the patent system. Thus the patent requirement of novelty.

Compared to the copyright concept of originality, the patent's novelty requirement imposes a very high social cost. The issuance of a patent involves a costly and time-consuming examination process. Even when this cost has borne the fruit of a patent, the patent can be challenged at any time on the ground that the Patent Office made a mistake by failing to consider any preexisting invention. These costs are nevertheless necessary if the Constitutional mandate to grant only rights that will promote progress.

Progress surely would be retarded, not promoted, if exclusive rights were granted in inventions that existed already.[21]

One might inquire why the same should not also be true of copyright. Granting exclusive rights to an author for the recreation of an existing work would appear to be as pernicious as granting such rights to the second inventor. Arguably, therefore, the Constitution requires both copyright and patent to test for novelty.

The standard view is that copyright's originality test is not a test for novelty requirement.[22] On examination, though, one realizes that, at the level of abstraction at which copyright traditionally operates, the odds of independent creation are so unlikely that if two works are the same, one is presumed to have been copied from another. On the other hand, if one was not copied from the other, then it must be not only original but also new. Therefore, *at the level of abstraction at which copyright traditionally operates, a test for originality is equivalent to a test for novelty.* The copyright laws can therefore meet the constitutional requirement of novelty while sparing society the cost of an explicit novelty requirement.[23]

The different levels of generality at which copyright and patent law have traditionally operated also explain the difference in their remedies. The rights accorded by patent law extend to independent creation of the same invention for precisely the reason that independent creation is likely. Not providing a remedy would dramatically reduce the value of the patent grant, and would therefore diminish the incentive for new inventions.

Like the novelty requirement, the remedy for independent creation carries with it a high social cost. In particular, it imposes on the society at large the burden of searching the records in the Patent Office to ensure that one is not

---

[21] Granting such exclusive rights was one of the offenses of King George against the colonies that led to the American Revolution, and was one of the reasons that any grant of copyright or patent protection was originally opposed by Thomas Jefferson and others. See generally Hemnes, "Three Common Fallacies," supra.

[22] This is endorsed by none less than Learned Hand in the *Bleistein* case, noted above.

[23] Case law under copyright, particularly the seminal cases of *Learned Hand*, displays a marked effort to reduce the requirement of originality to the only necessary criterion for novelty at copyright's level of generality: that the copyrighted work was not copied from any other work. See, e.g., *Bleistein v. Donaldson Lithographing Co.*, 188 U.S. 239 (1903); *Jewellers' Circular Pub. Co. v. Keystone Pub. Co.*, 274 F. 932 (S.D.N.Y. 1921); *Hoague-Sprague Corporation v. Frank C. Meyer Co.*, Inc., 31 F.2d 583, 586 (E.D.N.Y. 1929) ("the originality required in case of copyright means little more than a prohibition of actual copying").

infringing the rights of another. Copyright is able to avoid this burden. Where independent creation is unlikely, providing a remedy for it would impose an impossible searching burden on society without significantly improving the rights of the copyright holder. The principle that the patent and copyright systems should achieve their effects at minimum social costs, therefore, implies that copyright need only remedy copying. Thus, copyright can achieve the social and economic purpose of increasing our collective store of works (which necessarily requires the creation of new, and not merely original works) without worrying about whether any particular work is, in fact, new.

Figure 3.5 also helps to explain why the scope of copyright protection for a particular work can be expanded virtually limitlessly without creating a risk of overlapping and contradictory rights. The history of copyright protection in the United States has been one of relentless expansion of the scope of protection. Originally, only literal copying was prohibited. Abridgment was considered a beneficial act that should not be within the control of the copyright owner. B. Kaplan, *An Unhurried View of Copyright,* 10–12 (1967). Translations were likewise considered to be outside the scope of copyright protection. See, for example, *Stowe v. Thomas,* 23 F. Cas. 201 (C.C. Pa. 1853). Since the latter part of the nineteenth century in the United States and Europe,[24] the scope of protection was expanded to include dramatizations and translations, works that are "substantially similar" as well as "derivative" works and new modes of exploiting works through, for example, electronic distribution channels. None of these changes in the law appear to have led to the development of overbroad monopolies.

There has not been an equivalent expansion in the scope of patent protection. Furthermore, the prerequisites for issuance of a patent have become more stringent. In the nineteenth century, for example, the *Hotchkiss* case[25] added to the novelty requirement the concept that is now incorporated into the Patent Act in the form of the nonobviousness requirement of Section 103. Furthermore, in a series of decisions, Judge Learned Hand and others consistently expanded the types of information that would constitute anticipation of an invention. *Metallizing Engineering Co., Inc. v. Kenyon Bearing & Auto Parts Co. Inc.*, 153 F.2d 516 (2nd Cir. 1946); *Application of Borst,* 345 F.2d 851 (C.C.P.A. 1965); *In Re Theis,* 610 F.2d 786 (C.C.P.A. 1979). Finally, the Supreme Court has repeatedly warned against the monopolistic dangers

---

24 Since 1886, the Berne Convention has established minimum rights for authors in member countries. See generally, S. Stewart, *International Copyright and Neighbouring Rights,* chapter 5 (1983).

25 *Hotchkiss v. Greenwood,* 52 U.S. (11 How.) 248 (1850).

of excessive patentization of industry. "Congress may not authorize the issuance of patents whose effects are to remove existent knowledge from the public domain or to restrict free access to materials already available. Innovation, advancement, and things which add to the sum of useful knowledge are inherent requisites in a patent system which by constitutional command must 'promote the Process of . . . useful Arts.'" *Graham v. John Deere Company of Kansas City*, 383 U.S. 1, 6 (1966). The Court reaffirmed the importance of limiting the scope of patent protection last year: "the efficient operation of the federal patent system depends upon substantially free trade in publicly known, unpatented design and utilitarian conceptions." *Bonito Boats, Inc. v. Thunder Craft Boats, Inc.*, ___ U.S. ___, 109 S. Ct 971, 980 (1989). Thus, while the Founding Fathers' concerns about the monopolistic propensities of copyright protection have given way to a concern to find improved ways of providing financial incentives and rewards for authors, their concerns in the sphere of patents have, if anything, intensified. The reason lies in the far greater risk for monopolization that is inherent in any grant of rights at a comparatively high level of generality.

3. Implications

If the foregoing analysis is correct, copyright and patent can be understood as the application of the same underlying social and economic policies to different paradigmatic subject matters. There is nothing particularly surprising about this conclusion. The Constitution treats copyright and patent in the same breath and applies the same standard to both of them: in each case, the rights may be granted for limited times, but only for the purpose of promoting the progress of their respective fields of endeavor.

In particular, the comparative simplicity of copyright's originality requirement can be understood as a collapsed version of the novelty requirement of patent law. Both require novelty; indeed, the Constitution would seem to mandate a novelty requirement, since offering a reward for the recreation of existing works would not promote progress. As applied to copyright's traditional subject matter, however, the novelty requirement is satisfied by the much simpler (and socially less costly) test of originality.

The differing scope of protection can also be explained. Copyright has been able to expand its scope of protection from verbatim copying to substantially similar works, translations and even derivative works because the field of traditional copyrightable subject matter is perceived to be virtually unlimited. If the limit is infinite, one can expand enormously without approaching the limit. On the other hand, copyright can avoid the costs of a remedy for independent creation because it would burden society without enhancing rewards for authors. The opposite has been true of patents. The courts have jealously guarded the limits on patentable subject matter, particularly as pertains to the novelty/nonobviousness requirement, but recognize a remedy for independent creation because it is the only realistic means of recovery for the inventor.

This paper began by noting that in recent years the subject matter of copyright has been relentlessly expanded into areas that were formerly the domain of patents. If the theory is correct, one would expect claims of copyright for comparatively abstract elements of copyrighted works to give rise to concerns about the novelty of the works and the scope of copyright protection for such works.

There are some intimations that this has begun to take place. To begin with, the courts' unwillingness to recognize copyright in scènes à faire seems motivated at least as much by a suspicion that the scene a faire is not original as by its high level of abstraction.[26] Also, where a work is utilitarian, the courts have grown restive with the bare originality requirement. One of the most telling cases is *Donald v. Zack Meyer's TV Sales and Serv.*,[27] in which the Fifth Circuit denied copyright protection for a conditional sale contract, quoting much older precedent to the effect that "originality . . . must have aspects of 'novelty' and be something more than a trivial addition or variation." One can only imagine that the court must have been greatly concerned with the possibility that one individual could "corner the market" on a form of conditional sales contract. Should others be required to use forms that would possibly be less enforceable?

Unfortunately, such clear thinking has been largely absent from cases dealing with the most utilitarian of copyrighted works — computer software. One sees occasional glimmerings of concern. In *Telemarketing Resources v. Symantec Corporation*,[28] District Judge Aguilar held that the plaintiff could not point to the defendant's use of pull-down windows as a point of similarity because "[p]laintiffs may not claim copyright protection of an idea and expression that

---

[26] See Litman, supra, at 26–28. See also Hemnes, "The Adaptation of Copyright Law to Video Games," supra, at 212–218.

[27] 426 F.2d 1027 (5th Cir. 1979), cert. den., 400 U.S. 992 (1971).

[28] Copr. L. Rep. ¶26,514 (N.D. Cal.1989).

is, if not standard, then commonplace in the computer software industry."[29] By and large, though, the courts have shown little sensitivity to the potential that copyright claims in software have for withdrawing standard computer programming techniques from the public domain.

The Constitutional and policy underpinnings of both copyright and patent protection strongly suggest that a novelty requirement is a hidden part of copyright law. For traditionally copyrighted works, the requirement of originality is a sufficient test for novelty. However, where copyright is asserted at patent-like levels of abstraction, a mere requirement of non-copying as a test for novelty is not enough to prevent the grant of rights to persons who did not add to society's storehouse of knowledge and know-how. Furthermore, the scope of protection accorded by the Copyright Act — particularly as it pertains to derivative works — may be so broad that it will inhibit others from making later contributions.

All of these are good reasons why CONTU's original recommendation that computer programs should be included in copyright should be reexamined. However, as a stop-gap, I would propose that consideration should be given to the following solution: copyright claims for a utilitarian work should be subject to the defense that the elements claimed to have been infringed are not novel or would be obvious to one ordinarily skilled in the art. In determining what is novel, courts should attempt to harmonize their decisions with those under the Patent Act. Furthermore, the Copyright Act should permit courts to consider the impact on the relevant industry in defining the scope of the copyright holder's rights.

This proposal would achieve the Constitutional purpose of rewarding only those works that advance progress at a minimum of additional social cost. It would not impose on copyright holders the burden of applications; it would not impose on the government the burden of a substantive examination process. The presumptive validity of copyright would remain. The concept of a utilitarian work is already in the Copyright Act; it would be further developed through the new, proposed provision. However, it would have the enormously desirable consequences of leaving standard programming and other techniques in the public domain, and thus avoiding head-on conflict

---

[29] Id. at 23,087. This sensible comment is of course entirely inconsistent with the copyright concept of originality, as enunciated by Judge Hand in *Bleistein*. It reflects, however, an appreciation for the fact that elements of a computer program like pull-down windows are subject to novelty concerns in a way that Keats's "Ode to a Grecian Urn" is not.

with the principles of patent law that would otherwise prevent the assertion of exclusive rights in creations already available to the public. It would also help tailor the scope of copyright in a manner that is more fitting to the restricted field of invention in which patent has traditionally operated.

Chapter 4

Private Law

"Software Revenue Generation in Network Environments" (1992)

"Restraints on Alienation, Equitable Servitudes, and the Feudal Nature of Computer Software Licensing" (1994)

"IP Boilerplate, Made Difficult" (2010)

"Intellectual Property Indemnity Clauses" (2013)

The last chapter observed that the software industry has prospered, despite the law's failure definitively to resolve the scope of intellectual property rights in software. One lesson to be learned is that certainty in property ownership rights may not be as important to economic activity as we like to think. Another is that uncertainty may, in some cases, actually be beneficial. One might think of property rights as having a core that is solid and well understood, surrounded by a penumbra that is much less certain.[1] In the case of computer software, and especially the algorithms that drive it and the user interfaces that allow us to interact with it, the fact that rights in the algorithms and user interfaces were never completely resolved provides a field in which innovators can encroach on the prior art more closely, while at the same time the early movers can assert rights more broadly if it is important enough for them to do so. If intellectually unsatisfactory, this may be quite beneficial practically.

For software, though, there was another factor that richly compensated for the lack of certainty in the underlying law. This was software licensing. Ubiquitous today, the concept of distributing a commercial product under a license was by no means obvious in, say, 1970. Distributing a product under license allows the producer to effectively write its own law regarding rights in the product, filling the void left where the underlying legal principles are unclear. The "Restraints on Alienation" and "Intellectual Property Indemnity Clauses" articles in this chapter provide snapshots of what lawyers were thinking of when they first developed the practice of software licensing. Both

[1] A related concept is Merges's discussion of the "waiver space" associated with intellectual property rights. See Merges, *Justifying Intellectual Property*, at 147–49.

articles consider the tendency for lawyers to go too far when they are given a chance to, in effect, write private laws favoring only their own clients.

There is a surprising parallel between real estate law and intellectual property law. It is usually said that intellectual property is a species of personal property. In fact, though, it has much more in common with real estate. Ownership of chattels is intrinsically limited by the fact that only one person can have possession of and use them at a time. That person is usually the owner; it might also be a lessee or bailee, but that increases the total number of persons involved with the chattel from one to two (owner plus lessee/bailee). Joint ownership is possible, if uncommon, but joint possession and use at the same time requires some considerable mental gymnastics, not to mention being highly unusual and rare.

Not so real estate and intellectual property. A single parcel of land or building can have, and often does have, numerous owners (partners, JV participants, members on an LLP, etc.), and several tenants and subtenants that is limited only by the available space and market demand. So also intellectual property: it can be co- or jointly owned; the number of licensees often numbers in the thousands; sublicensees and other incidental users — including the IP equivalent of squatters — abound. Like landlords, the owners of IP try very hard to control minutely the persons using their property and the uses to which the property may be put, and software licenses became as dense — and probably as infrequently read — as real estate leases.

The "Restraints" article raises an issue closely related to one decided by the Supreme Court during its 2017 term. The case before the Court, *Impression Products v. Lexmark International,* Inc.,[2] was a patent case in which the patentee, Lexmark, imposed a no-resale/no-reuse restriction on its patented ink cartridges. The question was whether the first sale "exhausted" the patent right, rendering the downstream limitation unenforceable by means of a patent infringement lawsuit (while preserving the possibility of a breach of contract action against the initial transferee). The Court held the patent right to have been exhausted by the first sale, essentially on the ground that any other holding would have upset the common law rule prohibiting downstream restrictions on alienation of chattels. The Court left open the possibility that a downstream restriction could have been enforced if the initial transaction had been a license of intellectual property rights as opposed to a sale of a chattel whose manufacture or use required exercise of such rights.

---

[2] No. 15-1189, 137 S. Ct. 1523 581 U.S.____ (2017).

Lexmark is written very much in the tradition of a common law court considering what rule would best facilitate commerce, citing the likes of Lord Coke and the embarrassment to commerce if one couldn't be confident that a purchased chattel could be resold. In other words, the instinct of commercial law, and commercial lawyers, is to make property as freely transferrable as possible. Restraints on alienation and servitudes clog up the mechanisms of commerce. Quite to the contrary, the instinct of intellectual property law and lawyers, vividly on display in the Federal Circuit's overruled decision in favor of Lexmark, is to give the intellectual property rights holder the greatest possible freedom in constructing, subdividing, and exploiting the intellectual property rights. In other words, restraints on alienation and downstream restrictions on the use of chattels are anathema to the common law, but the norm in the context of intellectual property licensing.

The situation is somewhat less clear when it comes to real property, where some downstream restrictions — servitudes — are permitted, while others are not. The "Restraints" article in this chapter concludes that an intellectual property licensor's ability to restrict downstream users of licensed products should not be subject to the near-total rejection of restrictions on the use and transfer of chattels, but should be subject to some of the same restrictions that originally arise in the context of servitudes on real property.

The last two articles in this chapter are more work-a-day pieces that have been included primarily for their value in describing some of the issues that lawyers struggle with in drafting and negotiating intellectual property licenses. The "Indemnity Clauses" article is perhaps the most valuable in this regard. The rising importance of intellectual property rights in general, and patent infringement claims, in particular, has stimulated a mighty effort to reallocate liability for infringement. In many cases, the effort is futile, bordering on the comical, as one sees huge corporations demanding that comparatively tiny and impecunious vendors grant blanket indemnity against third-party infringement claims, while the same large corporations themselves disclaim all liability for infringement when they are wearing their hats as vendors. The "Indemnity Clauses" article concludes with the novel suggestion that patent infringement lawsuits ought to be considered events of *force majeure* and treated as such in contract drafting. This makes so much sense that it is fair to say it will never be accepted in practice.

This chapter begins, though, with an article dealing with software revenue generation in network environments. This piece is fairly remarkable in predicting, in 1992, that the data generated over networks would become more valuable than the software that generates the data. I cannot claim to have anticipated the rise of Google, Facebook and Amazon, and the article erroneously labored over the question how one might charge for the use of computer software in network environments, but I was onto some of the radical changes in the industry that have replaced boxed software, floppy disks and "shrink-wrap" license agreements with the Cloud, "click-through" agreements and software-as-a-service. If the Restraints article pursued the similarity of software licenses to real estate, the Network article tended toward a view of software more as a service and as a means to the end of Big Data.

Software Revenue Generation in Network Environments*

I. Background: Unauthorized copying

In his book *Order Without Law: How Neighbors Settle Disputes,* Professor Robert Ellickson of Yale Law School convincingly defends the proposition that "[f]or a wide variety of reasons, legal interventions can flop."[1] Legal interventions are particularly unsuccessful when the rules of law are poorly communicated and understood, and the transaction costs of enforcing them are high.

Nowhere is this more true than in the area of computer software protection. It has been completely settled, at least since the adoption of CONTU's recommendations in 1980, that computer programs are copyrighted works, and that the unauthorized duplication and distribution of computer software programs is an infringement of copyright. Software vendors have been at pains to educate software users to this apparently simple fact, through agreements that reinforce the law's proscription on copying, by notices displayed on diskettes and computer screens when programs are "booted up," and by highly publicized lawsuits against infringers, many of which have been brought under the auspices of the Software Publishers' Association. Unsatisfied with the already draconian remedies for unauthorized copying contained in federal law,[2] the vendors have now prevailed on Congress to make the unauthorized duplication of multiple copies of computer software a felony punishable by up to 10 years' imprisonment.[3]

Nevertheless, nonsystematic unauthorized copying continues unabated. In the university setting, a refusal to share one's software with a friend is considered positively unneighborly. One of the reasons may be that the rules about authorized and unauthorized copying and distribution are poorly understood, even by intellectual property practitioners. Take a common, everyday transaction like the sale of a PC with a hard disk full of software. Is that okay? The most experienced copyright attorney could not give a simple

1 Robert C. Ellickson, *Order Without Law: How Neighbors Settle Disputes* (1991), 281–82.

2 These can include statutory damages of up to $100,000 per infringement, impoundment and destruction of infringing articles, attorneys' fees, actual damages, and criminal penalties. 17 U.S.C. §§503–506; 18 U.S.C. §2319.

3 18 U.S.C. §2319 (as amended Oct. 29, 1992).

answer.[4] In this context, the person who acquires a copy of a program can easily rationalize his or her action, and even the criminalization of unlawful copying and distribution is unlikely to carry much weight.

Even to the extent that it is understood, the prohibition against copying computer software is like the speed limit. A speed limit is a good idea; it saves lives and gasoline, but it is impossible to enforce where roads are designed for higher speeds, and cars are easily capable of attaining such speeds. So it is for copyright protection for computer software. It allows software vendors a recovery for their investment; it encourages the development of new software programs, but it is simply too easy and cheap to copy software for the law to be an effective deterrent. At most, the prohibition may inhibit some unauthorized copying — rather like the 55 mph speed limit may hold some drivers to 65, rather than 75 mph — but it surely fails to attain anything close to 100 percent compliance. The criminalization of software copying undoubtedly deters legitimate businesses from engaging in systematic duplication, but it is unlikely to prevent the wholesale loss of revenue through incidental, private copying of software programs.

In setting their hopes on the extermination of unauthorized copying, software vendors have undertaken a Sisyphus-like task. The moment they think they have it licked, something like network usage comes along, rolling their copy-based revenues downhill again.

II. Network licensing

At first glance, network use of software seems tailor-made to add to the vendors'·woes. To begin with, it exacerbates the definitional problem. Does it infringe a vendor's rights to access software over a network? If the sale of a PC loaded with software is a tricky question of arithmetic, the question of network use is a differential equation. The Copyright Act permits use of a single copy of a program on a single "machine."[5] Is the network as a whole a

[4] The answer depends in part on whether the user owns a copy of the program, which in turn depends on whether there is a license agreement covering the program and what that agreement says. If, as is likely, the license is a "shrink-wrap" version, there is the further question whether the agreement is enforceable, and whether it constitutes an "abuse" of the vendor's copyright. The answers to these questions could vary for each program that is loaded onto the PC's hard disk. It is wholly unrealistic to believe that any layperson would puzzle all this out before buying the thing, and equally unrealistic to believe that the seller would erase any of the software before selling it because he or she was unsure of his or her right to do so.

[5] See 17 U.S.C. §117.

single "machine"? The answer may vary, depending on whether the network operates by downloading the program from a "server" onto a "client" terminal. Questions of this type are regularly debated by intellectual property attorneys. The copyright laws cannot reasonably be expected to enforce a standard of behavior when the standard itself is the object of debate and controversy.

Worse yet, networks are veritable engines for the creation and distribution of unauthorized copies of software. Many Local Area Networks (LANs) permit "file transfer," through which software that is resident in one LAN-connected device is copied and transferred in its entirety to another LAN-connected device.[6] The other device could be a portable or home computer connected to the LAN via a modem, in which case the user can carry off a copy of the software after the copy is made.

Emerging networking technologies will undoubtedly magnify the problem. "Gateway" software permits LANs to be connected to other LANs, or to "wide area" networks (WANs) — that is, publicly available telephone and packet-switched lines.[7] Software of this type will make it possible to effortlessly make and keep a copy of a program that is accessible over a WAN. At present, the use of networks for software distribution might be inhibited by the substantial size of many programs. However, networks having gigabit-per-second capacities are under active consideration.[8] At those data rates, the network replication of the most complex software programs would be virtually instantaneous.[9]

Software vendors have responded defensively — or not at all — to these profound developments. They have lobbied for ever-harsher penalties for unauthorized copying of software, brought highly publicized lawsuits, and attempted to resolve the definitional problems by complicated license agreements covering the scope of the licensed rights, the uses permitted, and

---

[6] See Frederick L. Cooper and Walter Sapronov, "Software Protection and Pricing in a LAN Environment," 26 *Jurimetrics J.* (1986), 162, 164–65.

[7] Id. at 165.

[8] The Corporation for National Research Initiatives (CNRI) recently received an award from the National Science Foundation (NSF) and Defense Advanced Research Projects Array (DARPA) for testing leading to networks capable of operating with data rates of one gigabit (1,000,000,000 bits) per second.

[9] To appreciate the power of such a network, one might reflect that the software program being used to create this document occupies approximately five megabytes of memory. It could be transmitted over the proposed gigabit network in less than l/100 of a second.

the measure to be applied for purposes of pricing. These various approaches have resulted in user dissatisfaction ranging from outrage to mere annoyance.[10]

Most network licenses are a variant on one of two themes: counting noses, and licensing "sites." Nose-counting is usually accomplished using one of three models — per-CPU licenses (which one might aptly term node-counting), per-user licenses, and "concurrent use" licenses. Under the first model, one counts up the number of computers that are attached to the network and charges a fee for each[11]. This method has encountered objection from both the vendors' and users' points of view. Users complain that the system is inflexible,[12] does not accommodate use on portable computers that are not connected to the network,[13] and results in paying for many more copies of the program than are ever likely to be actually in use simultaneously.[14]

Users are equally unenthusiastic about per-user licenses. If anything, they exacerbate the problem of paying for more licenses than are needed at any one time. An organization that has, say, 50 persons and 30 computer terminals probably does not want to pay for 50 licenses.[15] There is also a question of whether the licenses follow individuals as they move to different departments, or even different corporate entities, within a large organization.[16]

The third license model, the concurrent-use license, is currently in vogue. It is analogized to a library having a limited number of copies of the program. Individuals within an organization may "check out" copies of a program for their network use. The number of programs that may be checked out at any one time is limited by agreement. The terms of the agreement may be enforced by "lock-out" devices in the operating system that prevent more than the agreed number of programs from being "checked out" at any one time.[17]

---

[10] A 1992 survey reported that 62 percent of Fortune 1000 respondents were unsatisfied with current means of software licensing. *See* Stephen N. Hollman et al., *New Approaches to Overcome the Inadequacies of Current Software Licensing in a Network Environment,* U.S.Cal. Computer L. Inst. 548 (1992).

[11] See Software Publishers Association 1992 Network License Survey 1. [hereinafter SPA Survey]; *supra* note 10, at 545; Cooper *supra* note 6. at 166; Raysman, *Licensing Issues in Network Environments.* 12 New Eng. Computer L. Inst., 339, 355–56 (1992) (Raysman 1992).

[12] SPA Survey, *supra* note 11, at 1; Hollman *supra* note 10. at 7.

[13] SPA Survey, *supra* note 11, at 1.

[14] Raysman, *supra* note 11, at 356.

[15] See id. at 356–57.

[16] SPA Survey. *supra* note 11, at 1.

[17] Id. at 1. 3; Raysman, *supra* note 11, at 358–59; Hollman, *supra* note 10, at 3.

The concurrent-use license addresses users' complaints about paying for more licenses than they need. On the other hand, it creates its own form of nuisance, and cost savings may be illusory. If, for example, a given user anticipates that, on average, 15 of its 20 terminals will be in use at any one time, it is statistically likely that there will be times when more than 15 are in use at once. Few things are more annoying or less productive than needing access to software on a network and being told that it is currently unavailable because too many copies are in use. The tendency, therefore, is to license the maximum number of copies likely to be needed at any one time-which recreates the problem of excess license fees for copies that are redundant the majority of the time.

Perhaps most importantly, all of the nose-counting methods[18] create a legal or a technological impediment to the full realization of the power of networks. Networks are designed for the rapid deployment of digitized information of all kinds — including software programs. Like the 55 mph speed limit, legal restrictions that limit users to less than networks are capable of are unlikely to be wholly effective.

One approach that attempts to avoid interference with the user's full utilization of LAN technology is the site or enterprise license. In a site license, the licensee is permitted to make and use as many copies of the licensed software as it wishes, so long as the copies do not leave a particular site. Enterprise licenses take this principle one step further by permitting use and copying within an entire corporate organization.

Site licenses are understandably popular with users for the obvious reason that they maximize the "resource sharing" feature of LANs.[19] On the other hand, site licenses shift the balance so far in favor of the user that they are disfavored by vendors[20] and are typically offered only to the largest of

---

[18] A further variant is the per-server license. This is practical where the network does not permit file transfer from the server to the client terminals. It is associated with slow performance when a server is used at or near its capacity. See Raysman, *supra* note 11, at 357–58; Hollman, *supra* note 10, at 164–65 (distinguishing remote log on from file transfer systems).

[19] See Cooper, *supra* note 6, at 164; Raysman, *supra* note 11, at 360. Site licensing has been endorsed as the "preferred solution" for network software licensing because it "removes from the manager the burden of proving license compliance." *Network Software Licensing* (Microcomputer Managers Ass'n White Paper Committee), Oct. 2, 1991, at 10.

[20] Raysman, *supra* note 11, at 360. The SPA Survey does not even acknowledge the possibility of site licenses.

licensees in exchange for very large up-front cash payments; that induce the vendors to overcome their misgivings. For a software vendor — whose profits depend on its ability to charge for copies of the software that are made and used — the thought of a customer having the right to make copies of its software is often too much of a risk to accept. Instead, vendors tend to hedge on the true site or enterprise license by limiting the number of copies that are permitted, by controlling the copying of documentation, and by other means.[21] Hollman notes that "[t]hese vendor controls and licensee monitoring do not comfortably lend themselves to application software usage in a network environment because of the substantial administrative responsibilities that devolve upon the licensee."[22]

III. Networks as a solution to the revenue problem

In each case described above (except the site or enterprise license), the fundamental problem is that the pricing mechanism is at odds with the inherent flexibility and utility of network-operated software. As Cooper and Sapronov note, the chief benefit of LANs is "resource sharing."[23] Of course, copying software and giving it to one's friends is also a matter of "resource sharing." To the vendor, there is little difference: in either case, two people are using the software, but only one paid the asking price.

The thesis of this article is that, in the long run, software vendors will not be able to realize adequate revenues through any means of licensing that involves counting the number of copies. It is simply too easy to make and use unauthorized copies. Indeed, technological improvements in networking are *designed* in part to facilitate the making and utilization of copies of software over the widest possible areas. A further thesis is that legal means of controlling software use are bound to fail if they are at odds with the inherent capabilities of the technology. On the other hand, a pricing mechanism that does not interfere with the utilization of the technology is more likely to be accepted.

One might draw an analogy to the telephone system. Not too many years ago, AT&T and its subsidiaries used their monopoly to control not only the

---

[21] Hollman, *supra* note 10, at 546.

[22] Id. at 552–53.

[23] Cooper, *supra* note 6, at 164. One might observe that there is a fundamental difference between software and other resources that are shared over a network. A printer, for example, by its nature, can only be used by one person at a time and cannot be duplicated effortlessly by the licensee. Not so the software program, which can be duplicated at an essentially nonexistent marginal cost and used simultaneously by as many persons as have access to a processing unit.

use of their network but also access to the telephones themselves. One never purchased a telephone; instead, they were all owned by the telephone company and installed in one's home or business[24] for a monthly fee. There was an additional fee for each phone installed.

Under this model, the telephone company's method of revenue generation was analogous to the prevalent methods of software revenue generation in the network environment. The telephone company "counted noses" (telephones). The basic monthly fee was calculated based on the number of telephones installed, plus a fixed fee for access to the network.[25] As in the case of software, it was not uncommon for people (especially students) to hook more phones onto the network than they had paid for. Although the telephone company could, in principle, police unauthorized connections by impedance checks, various subterfuges were available to defeat the policing — the easiest of which was to disable the extra telephones' ringers.

As long as Western Union was the only source of telephones in the country, the problem of unauthorized hookups was manageable because the telephone company controlled the manufacture of "copies" of its telephones. However, the breakup of the telephone company's monopoly made telephones freely available on the market and made it as impossible for the successor telephone companies to control the manufacture and distribution of telephones, as it is for a software vendor to control the manufacture and distribution of copies of their programs.

For present purposes, what is significant about this story is not that the telephone companies lost control over the manufacture and sale of telephones; it is that they have continued to earn substantial revenues off of their networks, notwithstanding the loss of revenue from telephone rentals. The reason is that telephones are useless if they are not connected to a network, and at the same time, the network provides a very effective means of revenue generation. Indeed, an argument can be made that it is in the telephone companies' interest to have as many telephones (and fax machines, and modems, and other data-generating units) as possible attached to their networks. By billing for network usage rather than for "data generation units," the telephone company has also achieved a higher degree of compliance with the basic premise of its operation. It is believed that far fewer people attempt to use the telephone network free of charge (through tampering or other

---

[24] There were also the equivalent of LANs, known as "private branch exchanges" (PBXs). See id. at 163.

[25] There were, of course, additional metered charges for long-distance calls.

means) than attempted to hook up unauthorized telephones under the prior billing system.

There may be a lesson in this for software vendors. When computers and software were first invented, all of them were stand-alone, and their output was inevitably on screens or in hard-copy form. Today, a very substantial portion of the data created by computer software finds its way onto a network, either as an endpoint or as a means toward the end of hard-copy distribution. As an example, this article is being written on a word processing program operating on a home computer. The next step, however, will be to bring a diskette into the office and load it onto the office LAN. Loading it onto the LAN is essential for editing by others in the author's office and for access to high-speed, high-quality printers of a type not commonly found in homes.

The proliferation of networks as the basic means of transmission of the data generated by computer software suggests that the software is becoming more like telephones: an instrumentality whose value inheres in its connection to a network. At the same time, there will always be many fewer networks than there are copies of particular software programs, just as there are many fewer telephone networks than there are telephones. One might therefore look to the networks as a logical focus for the capture of the value inherent in information generated by computer software.

For such an approach to be successful, however, it is critical that the system be able to monitor and bill users without inhibiting usage by imposing artificial barriers to the network's ability to make and distribute copies of programs. If the premises on which this paper is based are correct, it is likely that such a system would be better accepted by users, would not be subject to rampant efforts at evasion, and would, in the long run, capture revenue for software vendors more effectively than any system that depends on the fallacious assumption that a software vendor can control the number of copies of its software that are created.

There are a variety of means of accomplishing this result. One is simply to meter data flow over the network and bill the user in proportion to its use of the network, just as the telephone company does.[26] This would indirectly measure software use, although it would not (without more) distinguish which software is being used to generate the data. This simple model would work, however, if all of the software on a particular network came from the

---

[26] As with telephone services, there could be a "basic" monthly charge for use up to a given level of activity, with a surcharge for additional use.

same software vendor, and the vendor could establish a blended rate for the use of all of its programs.

A more complicated model would require the metering of individual program use by identifying which software program generated particular bits of data. This is, I am told, technologically feasible in a packet-switched network. Each program could be coded to leave a distinctive signature on bundles of data; the passage of those bundles through the network could be metered and would provide the basis for billing for the software usage.[27]

The third, and possibly most promising, model would adopt operating systems that monitor the usage of particular software programs, store the information in memory, and report it to the network upon log on or log off. The proprietor of the network would be billed by the software vendor for the amount of usage of each program.[28]

It has been objected that use-based systems of the type proposed will be unpopular with vendors because they generate a stream of revenues, rather than a larger amount of cash upfront for a fully paid-up license; and that users will not like them because they cannot predict their costs.[29] It is not clear, however, that such objections would, in fact, carry weight. Vendors could always charge an up-front fee to load their software onto a network in the first place. Thereafter, use-based charges would be analogous to charges for other utilities such as telephone and lighting. While not fixed in advance, they are highly predictable and do not represent a serious impediment to businesses' willingness to use such utilities. Indeed, the fact that the charges would go up and down with the intensity of use could be a strong selling point, since the intensity of use is likely to bear a direct relation to the user's overall level of business activity and revenues.

It would be possible to implement a charging scheme of the type described above under current law, simply by agreement between the parties. If software is to be used on a LAN, the vendor could require the user to agree to use an operating system that contained the monitoring capability described above, and collect its usage-based fees directly from the provider of the LAN. Ideally, the industry might develop a standard operating system object that would

---

[27] One technical difficulty with this model is that many programs are used interactively, with data generated (for example) by a spreadsheet program of one vendor being imported into a document being generated by another vendor's word-processing program.

[28] The author is indebted to Richard Binder of the Corporation for National Research Initiations for this suggestion.

[29] See. e.g., Hollman, *supra* note 10, at 553.

contain the monitoring capability to avoid conversion and compatibility problems. The LAN proprietor would be permitted to make an unlimited number of copies of the software, as long as the network refused access to any data, terminal or computer that did not receive a report in the required form from the metering software at the time of log-on or data transmission.

Looking to the future, one might envision WANs as mechanisms for capturing software revenues. Indeed, if one accepts the principle that in the future, the principal value of software will be the generation of data that flows over networks, WAN proprietors become natural "publishers" of computer software. Just as manufacturers of razor blades sell razors at little or no cost (making up their profit on the sale of the blades), WAN proprietors should be motivated to distribute copies of their software at a very low initial fee (and not to worry too much about unauthorized copying of the software), making their revenues instead on charges for the transmission of the data that the software generates.

For software vendors who are not the proprietors of WANs or LANs, one might consider federal legislation identifying a new right of the owner of copyright in a computer program — namely, the exclusive right to transmit data generated by the program over a network.[30] Vendors could license that right to the network proprietors, in exchange for the proprietors' agreement to collect payments from users of the network based on their software usage.

None of these schemes is entirely foolproof. It will always be possible to circumvent the system in some way or another. By analogy, one who charges a toll to use a bridge over a river will always lose revenue to persons who chose to use their own boats or to swim. However, it is believed that, by concentrating on networks as choke-points through which the bulk of valuable information will pass in the future, a proposal like the ones described above will capture more revenue than any of the current methods. It is also believed that it would not tempt circumvention because it does not interfere with one of the essential utilities of software: its ease of replication and use.

---

[30] Such a right is comparable to the exclusive rights to perform a copyrighted work publicly by means of transmission. 17 U.S.C. §101 (definitions of public performance, transmission program, and transmit);17 U.S.C. §106(4) . The difference is that the legitimate use of computer software does not usually result in public performance of the software itself; rather, it results (in the network environment) in the transmission of data that can be made to bear a distinctive signature of the computer program that generated it.

Restraints on Alienation, Equitable Servitudes, and the Feudal Nature of Computer Software Licensing*

Background: The development of the computer software license

A discussion of computer software licensing appropriately begins with the question of why a license is needed at all. The purchase or sale of a truck, a lathe, a set of instructional manuals, or a box of pencils does not require a complex legal document. At most, terms and conditions of sale are printed on the back of a purchase order or an invoice, and no one worries about them enough to hire a lawyer. Negotiations are usually limited to price, credit, delivery, and warranty terms. It does not take a lawyer to figure these out.

Why should software be any different? The license agreement immeasurably complicates what otherwise seems a simple, straightforward business transaction. From the vendor's standpoint, the license impedes sales; from the user's standpoint, the license frustrates purchases. For everyone involved, the license agreement dramatically increases transaction costs.

It is tempting to say that a license agreement is required because computer software is a type of intellectual property, while a truck and a lathe are not. But this answer is wholly inadequate. A book contains every bit as much "intellectual property" as a computer program, yet the purchase of a book is not conditioned on a "shrink wrap" license agreement.[1] For that matter, a truck or a lathe may embody patented inventions, the benefit of which ordinary people blithely buy and sell without the aid of license agreements every day of the week. Again, why should computer programs be any different?

The answer to this question is largely historical. At some point in the development of computer technology, perhaps during the 1960s, people came to see computer programs as having value independent of the hardware on which they operated.[2] This created a challenge for lawyers. If one represented a client, A,

---

* *71 Denver University Law Review* 577 (1994) (Symposium Issue: Software Issues in Computer Law). The author gratefully acknowledges the contributions of Mark Clark to the analysis presented in this article and the assistance of Daniel Schaeffer and Karen Cheyney in its preparation.

[1] A "shrink wrap" license agreement requires the consumer to abide by the terms of the license when he opens the protective packaging containing the software. Opening the packaging means that the consumer consents to the terms of the license. There are questions regarding the enforceability of such purported agreements. See *infra* note 26.

[2] *See* Robert W. Wild, Comment, "Computer Program Protection: The Need to Legislate a Solution," 54 *Cornell L. Rev.* (1969), 586, 587; 81 *Harv. L. Rev.* (1968), 1541, 1543–45.

who wanted to make his computer program available to B for a price, into what legal framework did this transaction fit? It wasn't exactly a sale or lease of the program because, in the typical case, A wanted to continue to use the program and to make the same program available to C, D, and E for a price as well.

The transaction was more like a sale of a copy of the program, akin to the sale of a copy of a book or a device embodying a patented invention. But this categorization had the difficulty that computer programs, unlike books, were not clearly protected by copyright in the 1960s and early 1970s.[3] Prevailing wisdom held that protection for computer software programs was precluded by the principle that mathematical formulas and algorithms were not patentable.[4] In the absence of clear copyright or patent protection, providing a copy to B would enable B to make other copies and sell or give them away to C, D, or E, destroying A's market.

Lawyers for software developers were therefore driven to the conclusion that trade secret law provided the only protection for their clients' programs.[5]

---

[3] For a discussion about the copyrightability of computer programs under the 1909 Copyright Act, see Note, *supra* note 2. The Copyright Act of 1976 extended protection to computer programs to an unspecified extent. *See* H.R. Rep. No. 1476, 94th Cong., 2d Sess. 54 (1976). It was not until 1980 that computer programs were definitively protected under copyright law: "Any lingering doubts as to the copyrightability of computer programs was dispelled by the Computer Software Copyright Act of 1980 which 'has the effect of clearly applying the 1976 law to computer programs'. . . ." 1 *Melville B. Nimmer & David Nimmer on Copyright,* §2.04[C], at 2-46.3 to 2-46.4 (1993) (footnotes omitted)(quoting H.R. Rep. No. 1307, 96th Cong., 2d Sess. 19 (1980)); *see* Computer Software Copyright Act of 1980, Pub. L. No. 96-517, §10, 1980 U.S.C.C.A.N. (94 Stat.) 3028.

[4] See *Parker v. Flook,* 437 U.S. 584, 585 (1978) (method for calculating "alarm limits" during catalytic conversion process held unpatentable); Gottschalk v. Benson, 409 U.S. 63 (1972) (method for converting binary-coded decimal numerals into binary numerals in a digital computer held unpatentable). This impediment was substantially eliminated by *Diamond v. Diehr,* 450 U.S. 175 (1981), which allowed patent protection for the process of curing synthetic rubber while not pre-empting the use of the mathematical formula embodied in the process. It is now widely believed that patent protection for software programs can be obtained by describing an invention that embodies a program to achieve a particular result. See John T. Soma, *Computer Technology and the Law,* §§2.02–2.03 (1983 & Supp. 1992). Thus far, however, there have been few court cases testing the validity of such patent claims. *Id.*

[5] See, e.g., *Cybertek Computer Prod., Inc. v. Whitfield,* 203 U.S.P.Q. 1020, 1022 (Cal. Super. Ct. 1977); *Amoco Prod. Co. v. Lindley,* 609 P.2d 733, 743 (Okla. 1980); see also Lester Horwitz & Ethan Horwitz, *Intellectual Property Counseling and Litigation,* §11.03[3][a] (1994) (Horwitz 1994); Wild, *supra* note 2, at 590–92; Note, *supra* note 2, at 1554–56. In the early days of computing, the majority of programs were protected by trade secret

Trade secrets partake of the plasticity of the common law. Anything can be a trade secret, as long as it is, in fact, maintained in secrecy and provides a competitive advantage to its owner.[6]

A trade secret may be disclosed to others without losing its protected status, as long as the persons to whom it is disclosed agree that they will not themselves disclose it.[7] This principle has the absurd implication that something can be a secret even if everyone knows it, much like in the story of "The Emperor's New Clothes."[8] This fiction nevertheless forms the basis in commerce for trade secrets, since, without it, the first disclosure would destroy the protected status of the secret.

So far, one might conclude that a software developer in 1970 could have simply required purchasers of copies of the program not to resell or otherwise disclose it to anyone else. This would protect the secret while giving the

---

law, if at all. Unlike copyrights and patents, trade secret protection has been analogized to a blanket, "protecting everything beneath it," including both ideas, and the expression of those ideas. Horwitz, *supra* §ll.03[3]; see also T. Buckman, Comment, *Protection ofProprietary Interest in Computer Programs,* 51 J. Pat. Off. Soc'y (1969), 135.

[6] See *Restatement of Torts,* §757 cmt. b (1939). Section 757 defines trade secret as follows:

> A trade secret may consist of any formula, pattern, device or compilation of information which is used in one's business, and which gives him an opportunity to obtain an advantage over competitors who do not know or use it. It may be a formula for a chemical compound, a process of manufacturing, treating or preserving materials, a pattern for a machine or other device, or a list of customers. It differs from other secret information in a business (see §759) in that it is not simply information as to single or ephemeral events in the conduct of the business, as, for example, the amount or other terms of a secret bid for a contract or the salary of certain employees, or the security investments made or contemplated, or the date fixed for the announcement of a new policy or for bringing out a new model or the like. A trade secret is a process or device for continuous use in the operation of the business. Generally, it relates to the production of goods, as, for example, a machine or formula for the production of an article. It may, however, relate to the sale of goods or to other operations in the business, such as a code for determining discounts, rebates or other concessions in a price list or catalog, or a list of specialized customers, or a method of bookkeeping or other office management.

[7] *Management Science of Am. v. Cyborg,* 6 Comp. L. Serv. Rep. 921 (N.D. Ill. 1978) (distribution to 600 licensees under confidentiality agreements did not destroy secret); *Data Gen. Corp. v. Digital Controls Corp.,* 297 A.2d 433, 436 (Del. Ch. 1971), *aff'd* 297 A.2d 437 (Del. 1972) (distribution to licensees under confidentiality agreements did not destroy secret).

[8] See, e.g., Amy Ehrlich, *The Random House Book of Fairy Tales 3* (1985) (adapted from original by Hans Christian Anderson).

purchaser the bargained-for use of the program. Still, no license would be required — only a simple nondisclosure agreement.

Lawyers for vendors perceived, however, that such an arrangement would violate an ancient tenet of the common law that "restraints on alienation" are generally unenforceable.[9] According to the United States Supreme Court, "[t]he right of alienation is one of the essential incidents of a right of general property in movables. . . ."[10] The Supreme Court could have included real estate and some intangibles as well. The right of alienation finds expression in such diverse places as the antitrust laws,[11] the Bankruptcy Code,[12] the Copyright Act,[13] patent law,[14] and Article 2 of the Uniform Commercial Code.[15] It serves a variety of societal interests, including: promoting free commerce in goods; avoiding resale price maintenance and other restraints of trade; preventing springing interests that could defeat the rights of an owner; providing creditors a means of recovery on debts; and promoting competition.[16] As the United States Supreme

---

[9] See Theodore F. T. Plucknett, *A Concise History of the Common Law* (5th ed., 1956), 528-29. Plucknett traces the principle of freedom of alienation to developments that occurred about the year 1200. Id.

[10] *Dr. Miles Medical Co. v. John D. Park & Sons Co.*, 220 U.S. 373, 404 (1911); see also *Meyer v. Estes*, 41 N.E. 683 (Mass. 1895); see generally *Beley v. Naphtaly*, 169 U.S. 353, 363 (1898); A. James Casner & W. Barton Leach, *Cases and Text on Property* (1st std. ed., 1951, & Supp., 1959), 1075–82 (citing cases); 61 AM. Jur. 2d *Perpetuities and Restraints on Alienation* §100 (198l) (citing cases).

[11] See *Dr. Miles Medical Co.*, 220 U.S. at 404.

[12] See 11 U.S.C. §365(f) (1) (1988) (authorizing trustee or debtor in possession to assign any executory contract that the Bankruptcy Code allows them to assume, notwithstanding any provision in the contract or applicable law that "prohibits, restricts or conditions the assignment of such contract.") There are some limitations on this power. See *infra* note 71.

[13] 17 U.S.C. §109(a) (1988) ("the owner of a particular copy . . . lawfully made under this title . . . is entitled, without the authority of the copyright owner, to sell or otherwise dispose of the possession of that copy. . . ."). Section 109 contains certain restrictions on the right of alienation, which are not here relevant.

[14] "[O]ne who buys patented articles of manufacture from one authorized to sell them becomes possessed of an absolute property in such articles, unrestricted in time or place." *Keeler v. Standard Folding Bed Co*, 157 U.S. 659, 666 (1895) (holding that purchaser of articles manufactured by patentee may resell the articles in a territory which the patentee had granted exclusive rights to another person).

[15] U.C.C. §2-403(1) (1978) ("A person with voidable title has power to transfer a good title to a good faith purchaser for value.").

[16] See, e.g., Casner & Leach, *supra* note 10, at 1080 (quoting *Meade v. Dennistone*, 196 A. 33 (Md. 1937) ("restraints take property out of commerce. . . .")).

Court stated in *Keeler v. Standard Folding Bed Co.*,[17] "[t]he inconvenience and annoyance to the public that an opposite conclusion would occasion are too obvious to require illustration."[18]

Software is ordinarily made available in the form of some moveable, tangible embodiment, such as diskettes or tapes. If A transferred title to these chattels to B, B could transfer good title in the chattels to a person who had not agreed to hold them in confidence, even if such a transfer violated an obligation owed by B to A.[19] Like the little boy in "The Emperor's New Clothes" who dared to say that the emperor had no clothes on,[20] the purchaser might lawfully tell the secret and thus destroy the basis for the developer's rights.[21]

To get around the conflict between the need for nondisclosure on the one hand, and the right of alienation on the other, lawyers invented the software license. The notion is to purport to give the user of the software none of the indicia of ownership. Lack of ownership avoids the "restraint on alienation" problem because the user never has more than a bailment of the copy of the software. Unless the bailee is a merchant who deals in goods of that kind,[22] a mere bailee does not have the power to transfer good title to a chattel.[23] Thus, carefully drafted software licenses never "sell" anything to the user, not even the copy of the program that is delivered to the user.[24]

---

[17] 157 U.S. 659 (1895).

[18] Id. at 667.

[19] See U.C.C. §2-403(1) (1978) ("A purchaser of goods acquires all title which his transferor had or had power to transfer. . . ."); see also *RCA Mfg. Co. v. Whiteman*, 114 F.2d 86, 89 (2d Cir ("Restrictions upon the uses of chattels once absolutely sold are at least prima facie invalid; they must be justified for some exceptional reason, normally they are 'repugnant' to the transfer of the title."), *cert. denied*, 311 U.S. 712 (1940).

[20] *See* Ehrlich, *supra* note 8, at 3.

[21] See *infra* Part II.B for a discussion of the question whether a purchaser of a copy could be held to his seller's agreement not to disclose it.

[22] See U.C.C. §2-403(2) (1978).

[23] Id.

[24] See Miles R. Gilbume & Ronald L. Johnston, "The Protection and Enforcement of Trade Secrets in Software and High Technology Information," in Daniel T. Brooks & Michael S. Keplinger, *Software Protection: Current Developments in Copyright and Patent Their Relationships to Trade Secret* (1982), 225, 239 ("[I]n light of policies against restraints on alienation, restrictions on use or disclosure of a licensed product are more likely to be enforceable than with respect to a sold product.").

With this addition, one has all of the ingredients of the classic software license.[25] The license recites that the licensed program is a valuable trade secret of the vendor, the use or disclosure of which without the vendor's permission would cause irreparable injury. Indeed it would: lawful disclosure by any licensee would break one link in the chain of nondisclosure obligations on which trade secret protection hangs. The license further recites that the vendor retains all right, title and interest in the copy of the program that is being provided to the user. This finesses the restraint on the alienation problem. The license permits the licensee to use the program, but only to the extent provided in the agreement. Finally, the agreement is signed by the licensee to ensure its enforceability.[26]

In most cases, the retention of "title" in the "licensor" is little more than a legal fiction. Although the license purports to create a reversionary interest in the licensor at the termination of the license, few if any copies of licensed software are ever returned to their licensors. Even when a license terminates, the license will ordinarily provide that the licensee may certify that it has destroyed all copies of the licensed program in its possession as an alternative to returning the program. In reality, there are very few instances in which this is actually done. Instead, the licensee assumes practical ownership of a copy, under the legal fiction that its possession is a mere bailment.

Once lawyers persuaded software developers that they could not sell their programs like books and instead had to demand that their customers sign onerous license agreements as a condition to accessing to the software, the floodgates were opened for lawyers to pile into the agreements all protections they could think of for their clients. Warranty disclaimers, limitations on liability, noncompetition covenants, and clauses indemnifying the vendor against third-party claims all seemed to be insignificant if the customer were already willing to sign a rather burdensome license agreement to gain access to the software.

---

[25] See *infra* Appendix for a representative computer software license agreement.

[26] "Shrink wrap" agreements included in the packaging of computer software are not signed; as a result there are nagging worries about their enforceability. At least one state has a statute that makes such agreements enforceable. See L.A. Rev. Stat. Ann. 51:1963–65 (West 1987). Portions of that statute, however, were found to be preempted by the Copyright Act. *Vault Corp. v. Quaid Software Ltd.*, 655 F. Supp. 750, 762–63 (E.D. La. 1987) (statute provisions allowing software licensor to prohibit acts of licensee which are permitted under §117 of Copyright Act were preempted and license provisions forbidding such acts were unenforceable), *aff'd*, 847 F.2d 255 (5th Cir. 1988).

The next section of this article will demonstrate that the software license recreated one of the most ancient forms of property ownership.

I. The feudal nature of software licensing

A. Characteristics of the feudal system

As we have seen, the computer software license was an effort to separate a right of possession from the right of alienation. The latter right was not always a feature of our law. In feudal times, title to real property could not be passed without the consent of the lord of whom it was held.[27] The chain of title descended vertically from the Crown, rather than temporally from one's predecessors in interest.[28] The Crown held all land as "lord paramount."[29] The Crown granted "tenures" in exchange for certain duties or services.[30] The grantee could grant "subtenures," also called "subinfeudations."[31] If he did, the grantee became a "mesne lord" with respect to persons holding of him.[32] Land so held of another was known as a "feud," "fief," or "fee." The process continued through the layers of society (sometimes seven or eight of them in all) until it reached the persons who actually created the avails of the land, the "tenants paravail."[33]

An important feature of the feudal system was the personal nature of the relation between lord and tenant or vassal. The relation was created through the ceremonies of "homage" and "fealty" by which the lord and tenant bound themselves to one another.[34] Vassals owed duties of military or other services (including in some cases payment of money) to their lords.[35] The lords also enjoyed the "incidents" of homage, relief, wardship and marriage, aids and

---

[27] Casner & Leach, *supra* note 10, at 251; Plucknett, supra note 9, at 539. This statement may represent Norman views imposed on a rather different English custom. Id. at 517, 539–40.

[28] There is some question whether "feudalism" as a unified doctrine ever existed throughout Europe. See, e.g., Plucknett, *supra* note 9, at 509 ("All these characteristics of feudalism . . . are subject to infinite variation in every quarter of Europe. . . .")

[29] Gleason L. Archer, *The Law of Real Property* (2d ed., 1927), 20.

[30] Id.; Herbert Thorndike Tiffany, *A Treatise on the Modern Law of Real Property and Other Interests in Land* (Carl Zollmann, abr. ed., 1940) at 13.

[31] Archer, *supra* note 29, at 20; Tiffany, *supra* note 30, at 14.

[32] Tiffany, *supra* note 30, at 14.

[33] Id.

[34] Id. at 18; *supra* note 9, at507.

[35] Casner &: Leach, *supra* note 10, at 253–54; Plucknett, *supra* note 9, at 531–32.

escheat.[36] The lords, in turn, owed duties of protection to vassals. Figure 4.1 summarizes the feudal system of land tenure.

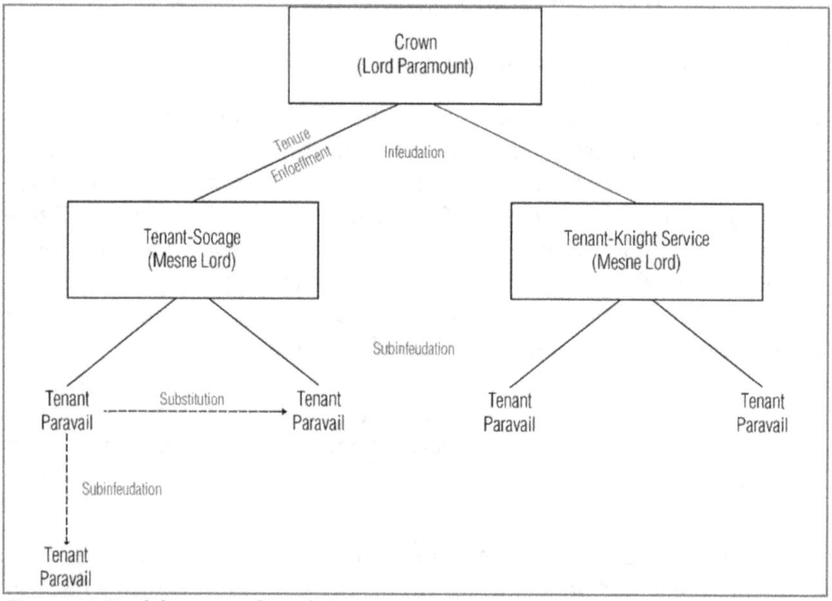

Figure 4.1 Feudal System of Land Tenure

There were two means of alienation in the feudal system.[37] One was the creation of subinfeudation.[38] A second was the substitution of one tenant for another.[39] Either of them was potentially damaging to the ability of the tenant's lord or lords to realize the value of the services and incidents that were due them. "In the case of substitution the incoming tenant might be poor, dishonest, or unfriendly. . . ."[40] Subinfeudation undermined the lord's ability to realize the value of the incidents of "wardships, relief, marriage and escheat."[41]

To prevent these threats to the lords' interests, the practice in Normandy was to require every subinfeudation and every substitution to be confirmed

---

[36] Casner &: Leach, *supra* note 10, at 254–56.

[37] See Plucknett, *supra* note 9, at 538; Casner &: Leach, *supra* note 10, at 259.

[38] See Plucknett, *supra* note 9, at 538; Casner &: Leach, *supra* note 10, at 259.

[39] See Plucknett, *supra* note 9, at 538.

[40] Id.

[41] Id. at 538–39; Tiffany, *supra* note 30, at 20.

by the tenant's lord and by every superior lord.[42] This requirement was never clearly adopted in England, at least concerning subinfeudation.[43] As a result, tenants in England were able to use subinfeudation to realize the value of their holdings, while defeating almost entirely the ability of their lords to realize more than nominal value from their seignories.[44] The nobility acted repeatedly to remedy the problem.[45] The third Great Charter (1217) stated, "No freeman henceforward shall give or sell so much of his land that the residue shall be insufficient to support the service due in respect thereof to the lord of the fee."[46] More importantly, the celebrated Statute Quia Emptores[47] abolished altogether the practice of subinfeudation of an entire fief.[48] In exchange, however, it ratified the process of substitution of one tenant for another.[49]

The Statute Quia Emptores has sometimes been cited as the wellspring for the common law's hostility to restraints upon alienation.[50] In fact, as we have seen, English law and practice had favored alienation to a greater extent than Norman law since a time that antedated the Magna Carta.[51] Furthermore, the Statute Quia Emptores actually abolished an important form of alienation —

---

[42] Plucknett, *supra* note 9, at 539–40.

[43] Id. at 540; Tiffany, *supra* note 30, at 19–20. Plucknett suggests that substitution without the lord's consent may have occurred in England, while Casner and Leach definitively rule it out. Compare Plucknett, *supra* note 9, at 540 with Casner & Leach, *supra* note 10, at 259.

[44] Plucknett, *supra* note 9, at 539. A tenant could, for example, deprive his lord of the value of the incident of wardship by selling the right to occupy his land for a substantial sum (none of which would go to the lord) and then subinfeud the purchaser for a nominal sum — "rose at midsummer." Id. If the tenant died leaving a minor heir, the lord could collect only the rose until the heir reached majority. Id.

[45] See id. at 540.

[46] Id. (quoting the third Great Charter (1217)); see also Tiffany, *supra* note 30, at 19–20. Although designed to protect lords against loss of rights through alienation, Plucknett and Tiffany agree that this clause had little effect. See Plucknett, *supra* note 9, at 540; Tiffany, *supra* note 30, at 20. In any event, it was superseded in 1290 by the celebrated Statute Quia Emptores, 18 Edw. 1, ch. 1 (1290) (Eng.). Id.

[47] 18 Edw. 1, ch. 1 (1290) (Eng.).

[48] Casner and Leach note that the prohibition on subinfeudations was achieved by interpretation of the statute, as it did not appear in the text. Casner & Leach, *supra* note 10, at 260.

[49] See Plucknett, *supra* note 9, at 540.

[50] See Archer, *supra* note 29, at 25.

[51] See Plucknett, *supra* note 9, at 539–41.

the practice of subinfeudation of the tenant's entire fief.[52] The Statute Quia Emptores did, however, expressly permit any tenant in fee simple to sell part or all of his tenancy by substitution without his lord's permission,[53] and without payment of any fee to the lord.[54] The substituted tenant or tenants would hold directly of the lord.[55] Although the substituted tenant might be less reliable than the one he had chosen, the lord always had recourse to his right of forfeiture if there were a default in the new tenant's rendering of service to the lord.[56]

The Statute Quia Emptores represented a significant step in the conversion of property from one in which the personal relationship of vassalage dominated to one in which the personal relationship took second place to ownership of the land itself.[57] By abolishing the creation of new enfoeffments, the Statute Quia Emptores led directly to the eventual abolition of the feudal system as a whole.[58]

B. Feudal characteristics of software licensing

The system of software distribution under license is analogous to the feudal system of land tenure. The computer program constitutes a trade secret owned entirely by the program's developer. The developer discloses the secret

---

[52] See Archer, *supra* note 29, at 25; Plucknett, *supra* note 9, at 540; Tiffany, *supra* note 30, at 20–21. Subinfeudation of a part of a tenancy, for example by the creation of a life estate or an estate for years, continued to be permitted. Tiffany, *supra* note 30, at 21.

[53] See Casner & Leach, *supra* note 10, at 260.

[54] See id.

[55] See Plucknett, *supra* note 9, at 540; Tiffany, *supra* note 30, at 20–21.

[56] Casner & Leach, *supra* note 10, at 253. By contrast, if a tenant subinfeuded his entire fief to another and then defaulted in his services to his lord, the fief would forfeit to the lord, but the lord would be bound by the terms of the subinfeudation. If the subinfeudation required only the payment of a "rose at midsummer," that is all the lord would receive. Plucknett, *supra* note 9, at 539. The fact that such an obvious ruse could be used to defeat the services due to a feudal lord suggests the view that the feudal system was never completely implemented in England.

[57] Casner & Leach, *supra* note 10, at 260.

[58] See Plucknett, *supra* note 9, at 540–41; Tiffany, *supra* note 30, at 21. The statute's prohibition against subinfeudation — which was probably intended to shore up the feudal system by protecting the incidents of lordships — actually contributed to its demise. The tenancies of mesne lords regularly terminated as a result of causes such as escheat (reversion to the lord for lack of a surviving heir). With no new infeudations being created, the feudal pyramid was inexorably flattened and, in the seventeenth century, it was abolished altogether. See Plucknett, *supra* note 9, at 540–41; Tiffany, *supra* note 30, at 21.

to distributors, who enter into a personal contract with the developer. The contract recites that the secret still belongs to the developer (licensor) and binds the distributors to maintain the secrecy of the program and to pay certain royalties or other amounts to the developer. The developer, in return, promises to defend the title to the software. The distributors — mesne lords, in feudal terminology — enter into sublicenses with end-users. These end-users —who derive benefit from the intellectual property as tenants paravail — bind themselves to the distributors on terms analogous to the distributors' contracts with the developer. Neither the distributor nor the end-user is permitted to alienate its rights, either by sublicense or substitution, without the consent of the licensor.

As in the case of feudal ownership of real property, the personal relationship between intellectual property licensor and licensee is considered a vital part of the relationship. Both copyright and patent licenses[59] have traditionally been considered mere covenants not to sue, personal to the named licensee, and not assignable by the licensee without the consent of the licensor.[60] There is a strong sense that persons who create copyrightable or patentable property select their licensees with care and should not suffer from having a different licensee imposed on them by assignment of the license. To bolster this principle, software licenses typically provide that they are personal in nature and not assignable or sublicensable without the consent of the

[59] United States law seldom distinguishes between the assignability of copyright licenses and patent licenses. For example, in *Harris v. Emus Records Corp.*, 734 F.2d 1329 (9th Cir. 1984), the court decided the transferability of a copyright license primarily by analogy with decisions relating to patent licenses. Id. at 1333–34. It cited only two cases regarding transferability of copyright licenses, both without discussion, and one of the cited cases was itself decided by reliance on patent decisions. Id. at 1333 (*citing Ilyin v. Avon Publications,* 144 F. Supp. 368, 372 (S.D.N.Y. 1956)) (copyright licensee had no right to assign its privilege)); cf. *Mills Music v. Cromwell Music,* 126 F. Supp. 54, 61–62 (S.D.N.Y. 1954) (deciding assignability of copyright license by analysis of whether contract involved "a relationship of personal credit and confidence." (quoting *Paige v. Faure,* 127 N.E. 898, 899 (N.Y. 1920))).

[60] *Harris,* 734 F.2d at 1333–34 (citing *Hapgood v. Hewitt,* 119 U.S. 226, 233 (1886)); *Unarco Industries, Inc. v. Kelley Co.*, 465 F.2d 1303 (7th Cir. 1972), *cert. denied,* 410 U.S. 929 (1973)) (holding that trustee in bankruptcy did not have power under prior law to transfer a nonexclusive copyright license, and relying on established patent authority); see *PPG Industries, Inc. v. Guardian Indus. Corp.*, 597 F.2d 1090, 1093–94 (6th Cir.), *cert. denied,* 444 U.S. 930 (1979); *llyin,* 144 F. Supp. at 372 (applying traditional approach); *Mills Music,* 126 F. Supp. at 61–62; see also 3 *Nimmer on Copyright, supra* note 3, §§10.0l[C][4], 10-02[B][4]; 3 Peter D. Rosenberg, *Patent Law Fundamentals,* §16.0l[l][b] (2d ed. 1991).

licensor.[61] Figure 4.2 summarizes the typical system of software usage. The parallels to the feudal system of land use are striking.[62]

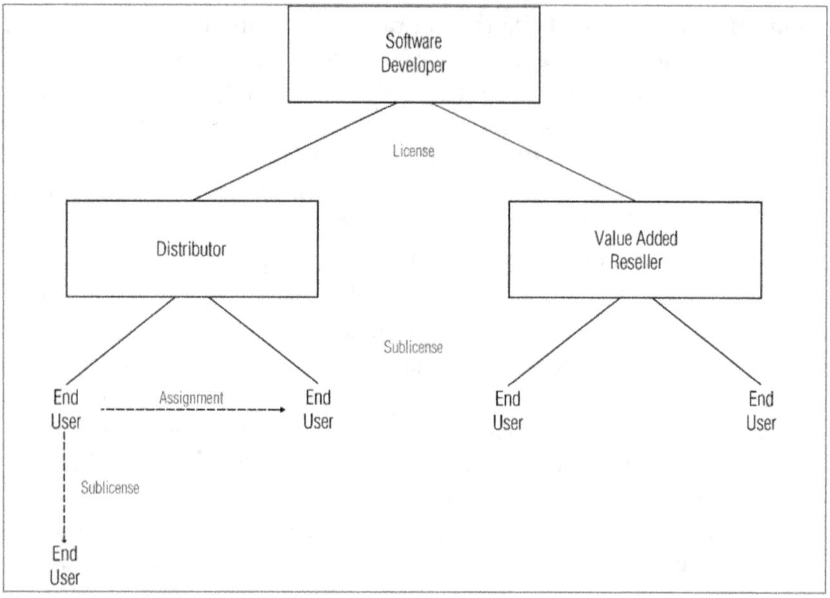

Figure 4.2 Feudal System of Software Licensing

If one accepts that modern software licensing has taken a form that is analogous to the feudal system of land tenure, it is worth inquiring whether the pressures that undid the feudal system might not have analogs at work in the context of software licensing. In particular, one would expect to find a growing tendency to consider licensed rights in computer software (or, for that matter, other embodiments of intellectual property) to be alienable property of the licensee, rather than a personal privilege granted to the licensee by the licensor. That would lead, in turn, to commercial resistance

---

[61] See *infra* Appendix, §3. There is a trend toward provisions allowing transfer of the licenses of "off the shelf" software. The implications of such transfer, and of transfers to which the licensor has not consented, are discussed later in this article.

[62] A further point of similarity is that the system of software licensing is, to a varying extent, a fiction that is only occasionally enforced in reality. Thus, for example, nonassignment clauses are frequently disregarded in practice, without any complaint from the licensors.

against restraints on alienation, and even cases holding that agreed-to restraint on alienation are unenforceable.

All three processes are already underway. To begin with, the traditional principle that a patent or copyright license is personal to the licensee is no longer followed in all jurisdictions.[63] The alternate line of authority springs from the decision of Justice Traynor in *Farmland Irrigation Co. v. Dopplmaier.*[64] Beginning with the observation that earlier federal common law limiting the assignability of patent licenses was not binding following *Erie R.R. Co. v. Tompkins,*[65] Justice Traynor found no reason to exempt patent licenses "from a general rule adapted to facilitate the freest possible transfer of valuable contract rights. . . ."[66] The court held that assignability should be determined by asking, as to each license, whether "the duties imposed upon [the licensee] may be of such a personal nature that their performance by someone else would in effect deprive the [licensor] of that for which he bargained,"[67] or whether "assignment would materially impair the [licensor's] chance of obtaining the performance he expected."[68]

The easiest case for permitting an unconsented assignment would be a reorganization of a business, in which the use of the licensed product by the successor in interest is in practical terms indistinguishable from that of the original licensee. For example, in *Synergy Methods, Inc. v. Kelly Energy Systems,*[69] Judge Pettine allowed the assignment of a technology license in connection with a merger.[70] A harder case occurs when the licensee is to perform substantial services on behalf of the licensor, as, for example, in the case of a distributorship agreement. The assignee might be less capable of performing these services than the original licensee was, thus depriving the licensor of the benefit of the bargain. Even this consideration might be overcome, however, in reorganization proceedings where the success of a debtor's reorganization might well depend on its ability to transfer valuable licensed rights to a

---

63 *See infra* notes 64–73 and accompanying text.

64 308 P.2d 732 (Cal. 1957).

65 304 U.S. 64 (1938).

66 *Dopplmaier,* 308 P.2d at 740.

67 Id.

68 Id. at 741.

69 695 F. Supp. 1362, 1366 (D.R.I. 1988) (quoting *Trubowitch v. Riverbank Canning Co.,* 182 P.2d 182, 188 (Cal. 1947) (Traynor, J.)) (validity of a transfer resulting from a change in the form of the licensee's business "depends upon whether it affects the interests of the parties protected by the nonassignability of the contract.").

70 *Contra PPG Industries, Inc. v. Guardian Indus. Corp.,* 597 F.2d 1090, 1093-94 (6th Cir.), *cert. denied,* 444 U.S. 930 (1979).

successor entity.[71] Thus, the bankruptcy court in *Matter of Sentry Data, Inc.*[72] held that a software distribution agreement was transferable without the licensor's consent because it was not personal in nature.[73]

At the same time that the personal nature of the license relationship has come under question, software licensees have bargained for, and won, more of the indicia of ownership. Today, it is common for a licensee to negotiate for a "fully paid up, royalty-free, perpetual" license to use a basic item of software.

---

[71] The Bankruptcy Code authorizes a trustee or debtor in possession to assign any executory contract that the Code allows them to assume, *"notwithstanding a provision in an executory contract or . . . in applicable law,* that prohibits, restricts or conditions the assignment of such contract," subject only to an obligation to provide "adequate assurance of future performance" to the other party. 11 U.S.C. §365(f) (1988) (emphasis added). The trustee/debtor-in-possession is barred from nonconsensual assumption of leases and licenses only to the extent that "applicable law excuses [the licensor] . . . from accepting performance from or rendering performance to an entity other than the debtor or debtor in possession, whether or not such contract . . . prohibits or restricts assignment of rights or delegation of duties." 11 U.S.C. §365(c)(l)(A) (1988). Therefore if a software licensee were in bankruptcy and the license were held not to be "personal" in nature, as seems quite possible, the licenses could be transferred without the licensor's consent, even if they contained antiassignment clauses. See, e.g., *In re Taylor Mfg., Inc.,* 6 B.R. 370 (Bankr. N.D. Ga. 1980).

There is authority in the First and Fifth Circuits, however, which holds that the Bankruptcy Code permits assumption and assignment in spite of "state laws that enforce contract provisions prohibiting assignment"; by contrast, laws "that forbid assignment even when the contract *is* silent . . . are to be heeded." *In re* Pioneer Ford Sales, Inc., 729 F.2d 27, 28–29 (1st Cir. 1984) (invalidating assignment of franchise agreement because state statute required franchisor's consent to transfer); accord In re Braniff Airways, Inc., 700 F.2d 935, 943 (5th Cir. 1983) (assignment of airline's airport lease disapproved without airport's consent because District of Columbia Code and FM regulations required such consent). The Sixth Circuit Court of Appeals held that a trustee or debtor in possession in bankruptcy has no greater power to transfer a copyright license than a licensee that is not in bankruptcy. *Harris v. Emus Records Corp.,* 734 F.2d 1329, 1334 (6th Cir. 1984). However, the vitality of the *Harris* decision is doubtful. It was grounded in limiting language that appeared in the old Bankruptcy Act but not in the current Bankruptcy Code. "Section 70(a) (5) of the Bankruptcy Act provides for the transfer of all assets which the bankrupt 'could by any means have transferred . . .' prior to the petition for bankruptcy." Id. at 1334.

[72] 87 B.R 943 (Bankr. N.D. Ill. 1988).

[73] Id.

Although it is probably unnecessary,[74] language of this kind increases the licensee's comfort level that the vendor's bankruptcy cannot trigger a forfeiture of the licensed rights, which may be vital to the operation of the licensee's business. Even if the vendor's pricing strategy contemplates a stream of payments rather than a single, up-front payment, the vendor can accommodate this request because it can tie a stream of payments to "updates" and "maintenance" of the software, rather than to the basic right to use it.

A factor contributing to vendors' tolerances for such perpetual licenses is the expanded scope of copyright and patent protection for software. The original justification for going to the trouble of a licensing agreement was to protect the software as a trade secret because other forms of protection were at best of doubtful validity through the early 1970s.[75] Since that time, the United States Copyright Act has been amended to extend copyright protection explicitly to computer programs;[76] the European Communities have adopted a Directive requiring all member states to protect computer programs under copyright;[77] and the courts, particularly in the United States, have gone overboard in their zeal to accord programs protection at least equal to that given books and other copyrighted works.[78] Furthermore, patents are

---

[74] Amendments to the Bankruptcy Code that were enacted in 1988 effectively prevent an intellectual property license from terminating the licensee's right. See Thomas M. S. Hemnes, "Computer Software Licensing After the Enactment of the Intellectual Property Bankruptcy Protection Act," *Computer Law,* No. 10 (Oct. 1988), 7, 9.

[75] See *supra* notes 3–5 and accompanying text.

[76] 76. 17 U.S.C. §117 (1988).

[77] Council Directive 91/250, art. 1, 1991 O.J. (L 122) 42, 44.

[78] See, e.g., *Whelan Assoc. v. Jaslow Dental Lab., Inc.*, 797 F.2d 1222, 1238–40 (3d Cir. 1986) (holding copyright extends to the "structure, sequence, and organization" of a program), *cert. denied,* 479 U.S. 1031 (1987); *Apple Computer, Inc. v. Franklin Computer Corp.*, 714 F.2d 1240, 1249 (3d Cir. 1983) (holding copyright protection extends to machine-readable code), *cert. dismissed,* 464 U.S. 1033 (1984); *Lotus Dev. Corp. v. Paperback Software Int'l,* 740 F. Supp. 37, 68 (D. Mass. 1990) (holding Lotus 1-2-3's user interface contains copyrightable elements). These cases have recently been questioned. The *Whelan* court's "structure, sequence, and organization" formula was not followed in *Computer Assoc. Int'l v. Altai, Inc.*, 775 F. Supp. 544, 559 (E.D.N.Y. 1991). *Lotus* arguably extends copyright protection beyond that given to books in *Baker v. Selden,* 101 U.S. 99, 107 (1879), which held that a method of double-entry bookkeeping, manifested in the forms, charts, and columns printed in a treatise, was not copyrightable. See also Ronald Abramson, "Why Lotus-Paperback Uses the Wrong Test And What the New Software Protection Legislation Should Look Like," *Computer Law,* No. 8 (Aug. 1990), 6–7; D. Lee Antton & Gary M. Hoffman,

increasingly perceived as available for computer software,[79] according rights that are arguably much deeper than those available under copyright.[80]

In the relaxed atmosphere encouraged by such broad noncontractual protection for software, it is easy to overlook the fact that a "fully paid up, royalty-free, perpetual" license is virtually indistinguishable from the sale of a copy. To return to the real estate model, a deed conveying the perpetual right to use a parcel is considered a conveyance of fee simple, and clauses in the conveyance purporting to restrict its alienation or attachment are void under the rule of the Statute Quia Emptores.[81] It seems likely that, given an appropriate case, a court would explode the fiction that a fully paid up, royalty-free, perpetual license is not a sale.

In the context of Article 2 of the Uniform Commercial Code, the fiction is regularly disregarded. In *Communications Groups, Inc. v. Warner Communications Inc.*,[82] the court held that installation by the plaintiff of its specially designed computer software involved a transaction of movable, tangible and identifiable products or "goods" under the U.C.C.[83] The court disregarded language in the agreement purporting to retain title in the licensor and characterizing the agreement as a "license," in part because the licensee paid a one-time perpetual license fee.[84] The court concluded that Article 2 of the U.C.C. governed the transaction.[85]

"Copyright Protection and Innovation: The Impact *of Lotus Development v. Paperback Software*," *Computer Law*, No. 8 (Aug. 1990), 1, 3.

[79] See Soma, *supra* note 4.

[80] Unlike copyright, patent protects against the independent creation of the same invention. Compare 35 U.S.C. § 271 (1988) (defining exclusive rights of patentee) with 17 U.S.C. § 106 (1988) (defining exclusive rights of copyright holder).

[81] Archer, *supra* note 29, at 113.

[82] 527 N.Y.S.2d 341 (N.Y. Civ. Ct. 1988).

[83] Id. at 345–46; see also *Advent Sys. Ltd. v. Unisys Corp.*, 925 F.2d 670, 675 (3d Cir. 1991) (computer software is a "good" within the meaning of the Pennsylvania version of the Uniform Commercial Code); *RRX Indus., Inc. v. LAB-CON, Inc.*, 772 F.2d 543, 546 (9th Cir. 1985) (computer software system was a "good" rather than a service, for purposes of the California Commercial Code). But see *United States v. Brown*, 925 F.2d 1301, 1307 (10th Cir. 1991) (computer program was intangible intellectual property, and as such, did not constitute goods, wares, merchandise, securities, or monies within the meaning of the National Stolen Property Act).

[84] *Communication Groups*, 527 N.Y.S.2d at 345. Oddly, the court reasoned that this made the transaction a lease, rather than a sale. In this regard, the court's reasoning was probably result-oriented. Notwithstanding the U.C.C.'s statement that it only applies to sales, courts have often applied it to leases where the lease has no termination date or the

If the license is merely a sale in disguise, then the clauses in the "license" agreement prohibiting subsequent transfer by the "licensee" are nothing more than unenforceable restraints on alienation.[86] Ironically, in adopting a feudal model for software licensing, lawyers for vendors thus sowed the seeds of its own demise. Just as the Statute Quia Emptores undermined the feudal system, its latter-day progeny, the Copyright Act, patent law, the common law, and the Bankruptcy Code,[87] lie in wait to challenge restraints on alienation imposed in a modern transaction, particularly if the transaction is a sale masquerading as a feoffment.

In at least one case, the restraints failed. In *First Nationwide Bank v. Florida Software Services,*[88] two software vendors had licensed computer software programs to two savings and loan institutions ("S&Ls").[89] The licenses were each for five years and required both up-front license fees and quarterly payments.[90] As is customary, the vendors' licenses required the licensees to hold the software in secrecy and confidence[91] and prevented the licensees from transferring or assigning their interests in the software, without the consent of the vendors.[92]

The S&Ls followed their own custom by becoming insolvent. Their assets were acquired by the plaintiff in the action, First Nationwide Bank, under procedures established by the Financial Institutions Reform, Recovery and Enforcement Act of 1989 ("FIRREA").[93] The licenses were in effect at the time of the acquisition, and First Nationwide continued to use the licensed software and make the quarterly payments through the end of the license terms.[94] The vendors objected to such use on the ground that it violated the anti-assignment

---

lessee has continued, uninterrupted use of the leased item at the end of the lease. See L. J. Kutten, *Computer Software: Protection/Liability/Law/Forms*, §1.11[2] (1993), 1–27.

[85] *Communication Groups,* 527 N.Y.S.2d at 345.

[86] See *supra* notes 9–17 and accompanying text.

[87] See *supra* notes 11–15 and accompanying text.

[88] 770 F. Supp. 1537 (M.D. Fla. 1991).

[89] Id. at 1539.

[90] Id. The court's opinion does not state whether the quarterly payments were for the right to use the software, for maintenance, or both.

[91] Id. at 1540. The court's opinion notes that the banks had access to the vendors' "trade secrets." Id.

[92] Id. at 1539.

[93] Act of August 9, 1989, Pub. L. No. 101-73, 1989 U.S.C.C.A.N. (103 Stat.) 183 (amending 12 U.S.C. §1821).

[94] 770 F. Supp. at 154-0. When the vendors refused to accept the quarterly payments, the bank started depositing them into the court. Id.

provision of the license agreements.[95] They rather ungenerously offered consent, however, if the bank paid additional license fees totaling almost $2 million (the original license fees had totaled about $750,000).[96]

The court refused to enforce the anti-assignment clause of the license agreements, on two grounds: 1) permitting the assignment did not "infringe on any substantive right of [the vendors]";[97] and 2) requiring the bank to pay an additional license fee "is contrary to the general contract principles of good faith and fair dealing."[98]

The "general contract principles of good faith and fair dealing" are not a satisfying explanation for the court's decision. The insolvent banks knowingly accepted licenses that were not assignable. Presumably, they might have bargained for assignable licenses and paid a higher price for the privilege of assignment. The court permitted them to transfer more rights than they had, without paying the toll that a right to transfer might have required. Does that order not violate the "principles of good faith and fair dealing" as least as much as the licensors' insistence on an arguably inflated transfer fee?

One might argue that the licensors sought to obtain, in effect, a windfall from the licensees' misfortune in becoming insolvent. However, this argument also falls short of the mark. It is the essence of contract law that one may insist on the benefit of a bargain, even if its enforcement results in an unexpected profit.

The court's comments only have force if one believes that the licensors did, in fact, receive the benefit of their bargains. As has been noted, the court based its conclusion on the finding that the use was permitted to the original licensees, and that there had been no disclosure beyond that permitted by the original licensees. In fact, there had been a new disclosure, even if access to the program following the reorganization was limited to the same employees who had access before. After the reorganization, those persons were employed by a new entity, First Nationwide, which therefore gained access to the programs to the extent that a corporation can ever have access to any form of information. However, it is clear that the court had in mind what one might call the "objective" extent of disclosure of the trade secrets — that is, how many people knew and used it — not the legal identity of the employer of those people.

---

[95] Id.

[96] Id. at 1539–40.

[97] Id. at 1541. To the extent that this conclusion requires an interpretation of FIRREA, it is beyond the scope of this paper

[98] Id. at 1542.

In other words, the court's result seems correct, and its comment about "good faith and fair dealing" appropriate, if one believes that the identity of the licensee is immaterial to the license transaction. As long as the licensee paid the homage the license required of it (i.e., did not exceed the licensee's scope of use and nondisclosure provisions), the licensor cannot complain if the homage is paid by original Licensee A or by Licensee B.

The elimination of the personal nature of the relation between lord and tenant was, as we have seen, one of the fundamental changes wrought by the Statute Quia Emptores. After the Statute Quia Emptores, a lord could not complain if the identity of his tenant changed.[99] So also, under the rule of *First Nationwide*, the identity of a software licensee is not a material part of the vendor's bargain.[100] It is the performance of the contract that counts, regardless of the identity of the person performing it

Under the Statute Quia Emptores, the substituted tenant held directly of the lord, who could, in turn, proceed directly against the substituted tenant for satisfaction of the terms of the fief. Whether a software vendor could proceed directly against the transferee of a licensee's rights was not resolved in *First Nationwide*. It is this question to which we now turn.

II. Alienation and equitable servitudes

The *First Nationwide* court was assisted in reaching its result because the assignment of the license did not result in any expansion of the software's use or disclosure of the vendors' trade secrets to individuals other than the ones who had access to the trade secrets under the original agreement.[101] By the time the case was decided, the licenses had expired, and the bank's respective obligation to comply with licenses was not at issue.[102] In many cases, these favorable conditions would not exist. Assuming that *First Nationwide* represents the vanguard of what might become a typical holding, the next question is whether restrictive covenants imposed on licensees might be enforceable against transferees of the software, even if clauses that prevent outright transfer are not. This question intertwines with the difficult issue of

---

99 See *supra* notes 49–57 and accompanying text.

100 See *supra* notes 88–98 and accompanying text.

101 *First Nationwide Bank v. Florida Software Serv.*, 770 F. Supp. 1537, 1540 (M.D. Fla. 1991).

102 Id. at 1541.

the enforceability of "equitable servitudes" on movable property.[103] If the licensor cannot enforce material terms of the license against the transferee, then the argument for enforcing the restraint on alienation is improved. At the same time, if the restraint on alienation fails, the argument for enforcing the servitude becomes more compelling.

For our purposes, an equitable servitude may be defined as any limitation or condition on the use of property short of a prohibition against its transfer or alienation.[104] Servitudes are very common in real estate, comparatively rare in the case of chattels, and ubiquitous in software licensing.[105] Virtually every software license imposes restrictions on the use of the licensed software.[106] At a minimum, the license will ordinarily require the licensee to hold the software in confidence, to make copies or derivative works only for specified purposes, and to restrict its use to certain computers and locations.[107]

Equitable servitudes have a considerably shorter history than restraints on alienation. Their origin is ordinarily traced to the 1848 case of *Tulk v. Moxhay*,[108] decided by the English Court of Chancery. In *Tulk v. Moxhay*, the plaintiff owned property in Leicester Square.[109] He conveyed the "Leicester Square Garden or Pleasure Ground" containing an "equestrian statue then standing in the centre thereof, and the iron railing and stone work round the same"[110] to one Elms, who covenanted that he and his heirs and assigns would maintain the Pleasure Garden and grant the plaintiff's tenants access to it.[111] The Pleasure Garden was eventually conveyed to the defendant, who

---

[103] Zechariah Chafee addressed the issue of the enforceability of "equitable servitudes" in two articles: Zechariah Chafee, Jr., "Equitable Servitudes on Chattels," 41 *Harv. L Rev.* 945 (1928) [hereinafter Chafee I]; Zechariah Chafee, Jr., "The Music Goes Round and Round: Equitable Servitudes and Chattels," 69 *Harv. L Rev.* 1250 (1956) [hereinafter Chafee II].

[104] See Chafee I, *supra* note 103, at 946–48.

[105] Based on personal knowledge and conversations with convey, assign, and commercial attorneys in author's law firm.

[106] In some cases, the licensors have attempted to extend the reach of their restrictive covenants very far indeed. In *Lasercomb Am. v. Reynolds*, 911 F.2d 970 (4th Cir. 1990), for example, the license agreement between a software developer and its licensee included a 99-year noncompetition provision that forbade the licensee from attempting independently to implement the idea which the developer's program expressed. Id. at 978.

[107] See, e.g., *infra* Appendix §3.

[108] 2 Ph. 774 (1848).

[109] Id.

[110] Id.

[111] Id.

proposed to build on it.[112] The Court of Chancery affirmed an injunction preventing Elms' successor from doing so.[113]

Tulk v. Moxhay exemplifies the basic requirements for equitable enforcement of servitude against a subsequent purchaser — that is, for the covenant to "run" with the land.[114] First, there must be notice of the servitude.[115] In real estate, notice is invariably satisfied by including the servitude in the deed, which is recorded and becomes part of the title record that a purchaser is assumed to have examined before purchasing the parcel.[116] Second, there must be a "dominant tenement" that benefits from the servitude, or at least a "scheme" from which the party seeking to enforce the covenant will benefit.[117] In *Tulk v. Moxhay,* the plaintiff owned several of the houses that formed Leicester Square, and the houses' occupants were entitled to use the Pleasure Garden under the terms of the servitude.[118] Their benefit from the servitude is obvious. Third, the servitude must satisfy some appropriate purpose appurtenant to the dominant tenement, and must not impose a "new and unusual" incident on land ownership.[119] This may be translated into a requirement that the servitude must be something of the sort

---

[112] Id. at 775.

[113] Id. at779.

[114] The precise holding of *Tulk v. Moxhay* was that equity would enforce a servitude that would not "run" with the land as a matter of law. Casner & Leach, *supra* note 10, at 1117 n.13. In England, covenants would "run" as a matter of law only if there were a tenurial relation between the original covenantor and covenantee. Charles M. Haar & Lance Liebman, *Property and Law* (2d ed., 1985), 9589. Under this rule, the covenant in *Tulk v. Moxhay* would not have "run" at law because it was contained in a deed conveying fee simple as opposed to a deed conveying a tenancy. This limitation is not applicable in the United States where, as has been noted, the feudal or tenurial system of land ownership was never effectively established. Thus, for example, in *Neponsit Property Owners' Ass'n v. Emigrant Indus. Sav. Bank,* 15 N.E.2d 793, 795 (N.Y. 1938), the court enforced a covenant contained in a deed that was not in the nature of a leasehold. Although technical differences between covenants running at law and at equity may remain, they are both beyond this Article's scope, and not immediately pertinent to the possible extension of the real property principles to the field of intellectual property licensing discussed in the text.

[115] See, e.g., *Smith v. Wedgwood Builders Corp.,* 590 A.2d 186, 189 (N.H. 1991) (notice requirement in statute not met). For these requirements, see generally Casner & Leach, supra note 10, at 1115–32.

[116] *Smith,* 590 A.2d at 190 (bona fide purchaser has duty to investigate).

[117] See *Werner v. Graham,* 183 P. 945, 947 (Cal. 1919).

[118] 2 Ph. at 774.

[119] *Norcross v. James,* 2 N.E. 946,949 (Mass. 1855).

that a purchaser of property might ordinarily expect to find, and not something that would impose an extraordinary or bizarre burden on the purchaser. In *Tulk v. Moxhay*, the obvious purpose was to enhance the value of properties in Leicester Square by preserving a park-like enclosure that the plaintiff's tenants could enjoy. Thus, one purchasing a park-like area in an otherwise residential neighborhood might reasonably expect that there is some reason why no one has previously built on the park. In later cases, particularly in the United States, this third requirement has been supplemented with the principle that the servitude cannot violate public policy.[120] Thus, for example, a servitude that prevents the sale of property to persons of a particular race is unenforceable.[121]

The law of equitable servitudes never found a stable home in the general law of chattels.[122] Attempted servitudes on chattels frequently took the form of manufacturers' efforts to control the price at which, or territories in which, articles of commerce could be sold by distributors and retailers.[123] Such restrictions were almost universally perceived as unlawful restraints on alienation.[124] Chafee argues convincingly that this rationale fails completely to appreciate the distinction between "conditions which totally restrain alienation by enabling the seller to recover the sold property" and those "which merely give the seller some measure of equitable control over its disposition in the hands of later owners, who never cease to retain the property."[125] Nevertheless, he concedes that there are significant differences between a servitude on a chattel and one on land.[126] The principal differences Chafee cites are these: (1) "Land remains in the same hands for comparatively long periods of time and is transferred after an elaborate investigation of the title, whereas chattels are ordinarily sold with rapidity";[127] (2) "restrictions on land [use] arise from the desire to protect a neighborhood as a rough unit . . . [for which there is no

---

[120] See, e.g., *Shelley v. Kraemer*, 334 U.S. 1, 21 (1948) (court would not enforce covenant that promoted racial inequality).

[121] Id. at 23.

[122] Chafee I, *supra* note 103, at 977–87, 1011–13 *passim*. Chafee pointed to "the [counter-vailing] economic claims of consumers and independent wholesalers and retailers, [and] the immense judicial labor required for a satisfactory development of the operation and limits of the proposed device." Id. at 1013.

[123] See id. at 980–82 (summarizing and citing cases).

[124] Id.

[125] Id. at 983.

[126] Id. at 985.

[127] Id.

analogue in chattels]";[128] and (3) restrictions on land "do not endure forever, but lapse when the preservation of the desired neighborhood standard can no longer be accomplished."[129] With chattels, it is very difficult to define a "dominant tenement" that is benefitted by the servitude. Chafee postulates that the manufacturer's business and marketing scheme should suffice to fill this role.[130] However, this consideration is probably more than counterbalanced by the fact that the benefit to the manufacturer is in direct conflict with the interest of distributors, retailers, and consumers in paying a lower price for the manufacturer's goods.[131] By contrast, many equitable servitudes on land are mutual in nature: all of the members of a neighborhood are both burdened and benefitted by the set of restrictions.[132]

The important question for our purposes is whether intellectual property licensing in general, and software licensing, in particular, is more like real property, where equitable servitudes are widely enforced, or chattels, where they are not. To analyze this question, it is useful to distinguish among the types of restrictions that software vendors commonly seek to impose on their licensees. Although a complete survey would be beyond the scope of this paper, it is possible to describe and analyze a few broad categories.

The first of these categories might be described as restrictions that are necessary to preserve the commercial value of the software. The most obvious are confidentiality obligations that are required to preserve trade secret protection for the licensed software.[133] There is a compelling argument that restrictions in this first category should "run" with the licensed right and be

---

128 Id.

129 Id.

130 Id. at 964, 986.

131 This interest forms the basis for the antitrust principle that resale price maintenance schemes are per se unlawful. See *Dr. Miles Medical Co. v. John D. Park & Sons Co.*, 220 U.S. 373, 408-09 (1911). Although Chafee questions the economic basis for this ruling, he seems ultimately to have resigned himself to the strength of the interests represented by "consumers and independent wholesalers and retailers." Compare Chafee I, *supra* note 103, at 988–995 with id. at 1013.

132 See, e.g., *Snow v. Van Dam*, 197 N.E. 224, 226 (Mass. 1935). The servitude *in Tulk v. Moxhay* was an exception to this principle, since it burdened only the Pleasure Garden parcel, while benefitting all of the other parcels on Leicester Square. Nevertheless, as the court noted in that case, "nothing could be more inequitable than that the original purchaser should be able to sell the property the next day for a greater price, in consideration of the assignee being allowed to escape from the liability which he had himself undertaken." 2 Ph. at 776–77.

133 See *supra* note 7.

enforceable against transferees of the original licensee who take with notice of them. In the first place, it is easy to determine a dominant tenement that is benefitted by the servitude: the vendor's trade secret.[134] Second, the vendor can easily provide for notice by including a simple statement on the diskettes or other media that contain the program, and by causing the program to display a proprietary rights notice when the software is first turned on. Third, the restriction is hardly novel or unexpected. It serves the appropriate purpose of preserving the value of the software not only for the vendor but for all of its other licensees. All licensees presumably paid for the right to use the software, and their investments would be made worthless if the software became freely available to the public without charge.

Restrictions on the scope of the licensee's use, such as limitations to use on a single central processing unit, or a network of defined location, should probably fall into the same enforceable category.[135] Again, such restrictions are entirely within the realm of what a purchaser of computer software would expect to find. Without such restrictions, every licensee would be entitled to unlimited use, and it would be impossible to establish a price for the software. Furthermore, restrictions on the licensee's scope of use are consistent with statutory limitations on the rights of the owner of a copy under the Copyright Act[136] and with the rights of the purchaser of a patented article under patent law.[137] Thus, to the extent that licensed rights become more freely transferable,

---

[134] Chafee argues that a patent or copyright should also provide a dominant tenement supporting a servitude. See Chafee I, *supra* note 103, at 998. But the courts have been less than enthusiastic in enforcing patentees' and copyright proprietors' efforts to create servitudes. Id. at 999–1005. There is, however, a distinctive difference between the confidentiality required to support a trade secret and the price, territorial and other restrictions attempted by patentees and copyright holders. Copyrights and patents arise by statute, and copyright holders or patentees will retain substantial rights even if restrictions on resale price or territory are not enforced. By contrast, a trade secret will lose its protected status if enforceable confidentiality obligations are not imposed on all who lawfully come into possession of the secret.

[135] A variation on such a restriction would be a license term that requires the licensee to pay an additional license fee for expanded use.

[136] 17 U.S.C. §109(b) (1988), *amended by* 17 U.S.C. §109(b)(l) (Supp. IV 1992).

[137] See Donald S. Chisum, *Patents: A Treatise on the Law of Patentability, Validity and Infringement* §16.03[2] (1991).

public policy, as adumbrated in the copyright and patent laws, would seem to support enforcement of the restrictions.[138]

Other covenants contained in many software licenses are more problematic. Suppose, for example, that the original licensee has agreed to cross-license its own technology to the software vendor, to assist the vendor in performing research and development, or to indemnify the vendor for claims of third parties to whom the licensee provides goods or services using the licensed software. Such covenants frequently form an important part of the bargain in licensing transactions, and it would be just as inequitable to allow a transferee of the licensed rights to take free of them as it would have been to allow the transferee of Elms' parcel to take free of the restrictions Elms had agreed to in *Tulk v. Moxhay.* On the other hand, covenants of this type are not usually essential to preserve the trade secret status or commercial value of the licensed software.[139] In addition, they are almost always novel, unpredictable, and unexpected, and a transferee's ability to meet such obligations is likely to be wholly different from that of the original licensee. If, for example, part of the consideration for the license was a cross-license from the original licensee, a transferee who was not a successor to the original licensee's business would probably lack the technology sought to be cross-licensed. In this event, the licensor would lose a fundamental part of the benefit of its original bargain.

Some novel executory obligations may fail for reasons of public policy. For example, the licensor in *Lasercomb America, Inc. v. Reynolds*[140] sought to prevent its licensee from competing with the licensed product for a period of 99 years.[141] The Fourth Circuit Court of Appeals found this burden so onerous that it refused to entertain the licensor's action for copyright infringement

---

[138] Another class of covenants that should probably "run" with the software are warranty limitations and limitations on liability. Subject to important public policy restrictions, such covenants (to the extent that they constitute covenants of the licensee at all) commonly "run" with chattels, as a result of the decline of privity of contract in the field of product liability. See, e.g., *Mass. Gen. Laws Ann.* ch. 106, §2-318 (West 1990). There is no reason to suppose that they should not also "run" with license software rights.

[139] See *supra* notes 5–8 and accompanying text (requirements for trade secret protection).

[140] 911 F.2d 970 (4th Cir. 1990).

[141] Id. at 973.

against the original licensee.[142] *A fortiori,* this restriction should not be enforceable against a transferee of the licensed software.

Even if restrictions falling into this third category do not violate an obvious public policy, there is nevertheless a strong argument that they do not meet the criteria for enforcement of an equitable servitude. This brings us back to the question with which we began this section of this paper. The *First Nationwide* court based its refusal to enforce a restraint on the alienation of licensed software rights on a finding that the transferee had complied with all material covenants of the software license.[143] This led to the question of whether the software licensors in *First Nationwide* could have enforced those covenants against the transferees if there had been a default. If the analogy to equitable servitudes on real property holds, the author concludes that restraints of the type imposed in *First Nationwide* would have been enforceable against the transferees, even in the absence of their express consent, as long as they had notice of the restraints. The restraints, which limited use of the software and protected against public disclosure, were typical, predictable, and essential to the protection of the licensed software rights.[144] The enforceability of the restraints supports the conclusion that the license should be transferrable because the licensor is no worse off after the transfer than it was before.

On the other hand, the analogy to equitable servitudes suggests that many complex and novel restrictions and covenants would not be enforceable against subsequent transferees. This, in turn, suggests that restraints on alienation of a license that contains such restrictions and covenants should be enforced. In such a case, the relation between licensor and licensee is truly personal in nature because no one but the particular licensee is likely to be in a position to satisfy the terms of the license. The software license then retains its tenurial quality. The licensee should no more be permitted to transfer its rights without the consent of the licensor than a twelfth-century tenant should have been able to transfer his land without the consent of his lord.

---

[142] Id. at 979. This rationale required an extension of very thin existing precedent, and has been justifiably criticized on the ground that "it permits the misuse defense to be collaterally asserted by a willful infringer not personally injured by the copyright holder's conduct." Philip Abromats, "Anticompetitive Software Licensing Restrictions as Copyright Misuse," 10 *Software Protection* 3 (1991). See also Christina Ambrosio & Roni Schneider, Note, "Copyright Misuse ... Getting Defensive: *Lasercomb America, Inc. v. Reynolds,*" 6 *J. Legal Comm.* 181 (1990).

[143] See *supra* notes 97–98 and accompanying text.

[144] See *supra* notes 90–92 and accompanying text.

It thus appears that the question of what rights in computer software should be freely alienable depends on the important measure on the question of whether the licensor can enforce the terms of the license against the transferee. If the traditional criteria for enforcement of an equitable servitude against transferees are met — the existence of a dominant tenement, notice, and absence of novelty[145] — then the terms should be enforceable against a transferee and the argument for enforcing a restraint against transfer fails. However, if the license imposes terms that are enforceable against the original licensee, but that otherwise do not meet the criteria for enforcement of a servitude, then the argument for enforcing the restraint is compelling.

Conclusion

We began this inquiry by asking why computer software is licensed at all. The explanation is that the practice arose at a time when the only effective means of protecting rights in software was by trade secret law, and most software was tailor-made for a particular application. To accommodate these facts, lawyers re-created a system of software exploitation that is surprisingly analogous to the feudal system of land tenure that existed in England and Normandy prior to the Statute Quia Emptores. In each case, the system is characterized by personal obligations flowing between the licensor (lord) and licensee (tenant) and restraints on alienation by the licensee (tenant) without the consent of the licensor (lord).

The feudal system of land tenure could not be sustained indefinitely. It was always partly fictional; it was inconsistent with English traditions that encouraged free alienability of land rights, and — to the extent that it had been required as a quasi-military means of securing land use — it became unnecessary as the legal framework for land ownership stabilized. The Statute Quia Emptores, which permitted alienation of tenure by substitution of a new tenant without the consent of the feudal law, both manifested and accelerated its demise.

Computer software licensing is following a very similar course. Originally justified by the necessity of protecting software as a trade secret, software licensing now appears to be both unnecessary, in light of expanding copyright and patent protection, and inconsistent with the general right of alienation that appears in the common law, the Copyright Act, patent law, the Bankruptcy Code, and the Uniform Commercial Code. Furthermore, the personal nature of software programming services has given way to

---

[145] See *supra* notes 104–132 and accompanying text.

widespread commerce in software as a basic commodity. These changed circumstances have placed pressure on restraints on alienation that are a hallmark of traditional software licensing.

To keep current with the changing environment, courts will need to address the question of whether, and to what extent, restrictive covenants, short of an outright prohibition on alienation, should be enforceable against transferees of licensed software rights. Real estate law governing the "running" of equitable servitudes provides a useful guide to the sorts of covenants that should be enforceable against transferees and those that should not. Where the material covenants in a license "run" under these criteria, there will be a strong argument against the enforcement of outright restraints on alienation. These will generally be circumstances in which the license does not impose restrictions on the licensee other than those affecting the scope of use, nondisclosure, and warranties' limitations. Where, on the other hand, the license imposes complex obligations such as cross-licenses, the covenants will not "run." In combination with covenants that do not "run," license terms limiting restraints on alienation should be enforced.

IP Boilerplate, Made Difficult*

This paper catalogs drafting problems caused by some standard boilerplate provisions in agreements governing rights in intellectual property. But an initial word of caution: not all problems need to be resolved. Negotiating and drafting an agreement is an exercise in modulating ambiguity and risk. The goal of a negotiation or drafting exercise is to achieve an acceptable level of risk for the client, not to eliminate every risk. Furthermore, ambiguity can help bridge the gap between opposing interests by deferring rather than accruing a definitive resolution. Therefore, the reader should use this catalog both as a precaution and as an opportunity when preparing the next IP agreement.

1. Clauses transferring rights in IP

> "A hereby transfers, sells, and assigns to B all of A's right, title, and interest in the patents, copyrights, and trademarks listed on Schedules A, B, and C"

Many uncertainties lurk within this apparently simple clause. Here are a few of the basic drafting concerns:

a. Do you really mean to assign *only* the IP interests listed on the schedules? What about unregistered copyrights and trademarks? Are they listed? And can they be listed? Everything fixed in tangible form is potentially copyrighted,[1] and everything capable of indicating origin could be or become a trademark.[2] Do you mean to capture those things, or not?

b. What about the goodwill associated with the trademarks? The blackletter law is that a trademark cannot exist independently of the goodwill associated with it, and assignment of a mark without the goodwill associated with it is therefore not only invalid, but threatens the validity of the mark.[3] This could be

---

 Paper originally presented to the Boston Chapter of the Copyright Society of the USA, spring 2010. The author gratefully acknowledges the assistance of Leon Schwartz in the preparation of this paper, as well as input from many colleagues who contributed their lists of most common drafting problems.

[1] *See* 17 U.S.C. §102; see also 1–2 Nimmer on Copyright §2.03.

[2] See 15 U.S.C. §1052; see also 1–1 Gilson on Trademarks §1.03.

[3] See 15 U.S.C. §1060; see also *Pepsico, Inc. v. Grapette Co.*, 416 F.2d 285, 288 (8th Cir. 1969).

good or bad, depending on whether you are representing the assignor or assignee.

i. Intent-to-use ("ITU") trademark applications are particularly problematic. In the case of an ITU, a mere recitation of goodwill is not sufficient. The assignment is likely to be found invalid unless it accompanies an assignment of the entire business or part of the business to which the mark relates.[4] This may or may not be possible, depending on the nature of the underlying transaction.

c. How about claims for infringement that arose prior to the assignment? If the claims are not specifically transferred, then they may remain with the assignor.[5] This could significantly diminish the value of the assignment to the assignee; on the other hand, the existing claims could be considered an asset of the assignor having value that should be included in the purchase price.

d. What about inchoate rights, such as the right to apply for a patent, or continuations, continuations-in-part, and divisionals that spin off of existing patents?

i. Continuations-in-part are especially problematic. Many assignment clauses mindlessly include them as standard boilerplate. However, a continuation-in-part will always contain new inventive material that is not covered by the original patent application. If you are representing the assignor, do you really mean to be giving away future inventions made by your client that happen to have an inventor in common with the assigned patents?

The foregoing issues are essentially questions of drafting. The simple assignment clause can implicate many substantive legal issues. Here are a few examples:

---

[4] *Mister Donut of America, Inc. v. Mr. Donut, Inc.*, 418 F.2d 838, 842 (9th Cir. 1969) ("The law is well settled that there are no rights in a trademark alone and that no rights can be transferred apart from the business with which the mark has been associated.").

[5] See *Chemical Foundation, Inc. v. E. I. Du Pont De Nemours & Co.*, 29 F.2d 597, 600 (D. Del. 1928); see also *Manning v. Miller Music Corp.*, 174 F. Supp. 192, 194-95 (D.N.Y. 1959).

e. State law quirks

i. Examples:

1. Illinois has a statute called the Employee Patent Act[6] under which an employee's assignment of inventions does not apply to an invention for which no employer equipment, supplies, facilities, or trade secret information was used and which was developed entirely on the employee's own time unless the invention (a) relates to the employer's business or actual anticipated research or development, or (b) results from any work performed by the employee for the employer.

2. In Pennsylvania, if you do not state consideration for employee invention assignment, the assignment of IP rights can carry an implied promise to continue employing the assignor for a "reasonable" period of time,[7] which, depending on value of property assigned, has sometimes been held to be a number of years.

   a. Note: this doesn't invalidate the assignment, but in an M&A transaction can create significant cost by adversely impacting the acquiror's ability to terminate one or more employees.

ii. Moral: IP assignments are largely governed by state law in the US. Therefore, check state law, especially if assignments from employees as part of their employment, are involved.

f. International quirks

i. Europe: compensation to employees for assignments of patent rights

---

[6] 765 ILCS 1060/1–3 (from Ch. 140, par. 301 to 303).

[7] *Harsco Corp. v. Zlotnicki*, 779 F.2d 906, 910 (3d Cir. Pa. 1985) ("It is the settled law of agency that if the agent or employee furnishes a consideration in addition to his mere services, he is deemed to have purchased the employment for at least a reasonable period of time where the duration of employment is not otherwise defined.").

1. Many European countries, notably including Germany [8] and France,[9] require compensation to employees for assignments to their employers of inventions made during the course of their employment. Other countries, including the UK,[10] Belgium,[11] and the Netherlands,[12] provide employee compensation only in exceptional circumstances.

2. Moral: When trying to capture rights in inventions made in Europe, investigate carefully the countries in which the inventions will be made and ensure that compensation requirements have been addressed. In many cases, this can be addressed in the employment or collective bargaining agreements with the employees by the inclusion of appropriate compensation clauses.

ii. India: "Magic Words" in copyright assignments

1. Indian copyright law includes several features that can surprise and harm one attempting to effect an assignment of copyright. An assignment should be made *after* the work is completed. The assignment must specify its geographical scope — typically, the assignee will want it to be worldwide — or it will be

---

[8] The German law, the Employees Invention Act of 1957 ("Arbeitnehmererfindergesetz"), requires disclosure by the employee and payment of "adequate" compensation by the employer. In addition, if the employer abandons patent protection for the invention the employer is required to so notify the employee to give the employee an opportunity to pursue the patent in his or her own name. The act applies to inventions made in Germany, regardless whether the inventor is a German national.

[9] Patent Act 1978 (France), codified in the Intellectual Property Code 1992. The French statute requires "additional" compensation for inventions made within the employee's scope of employment and "just" compensation for inventions outside the scope of the employee's normal duties.

[10] Patents Act 1977 (UK), Sections 40 to 42 require compensation if the patent has been of outstanding value to the employer and there is a disparity between the benefits received by employer and employee.

[11] There is no statutory provision in Belgium, but the courts can award compensation in exceptional cases.

[12] Patent Act 1955 (Netherlands), Article 12 provides for compensation if the inventor has not been compensated via salary, pecuniary allowance or extra remuneration.

deemed limited to India. It must recite that there is no obligation to exercise rights in the copyrighted work, on penalty of the risk of a reversionary interest in the assignor. Lastly, and most dangerously, it is deemed to be only for a five-year duration if it is not expressly made "perpetual."[13]

2. These quirks of Indian copyright law are of increasing importance, given the amount of software development being outsourced to India.

iii. Germany: Copyrights are nontransferable under German law.[14] Accordingly, an exclusive license is the closest one can come to an outright assignment of German copyright.

In addition to the foregoing drafting and legal issues, IP assignment provisions often implicate the following ancillary issues:

g. The missing or uncooperative inventor/developer problem

i. It is very common in performing due diligence on a target company to find that the chain of title for critical IP rights is not complete, especially with respect to patent rights in the United States and other jurisdictions (such as Germany)in which the patent right inheres in the first instance in the inventor/employee, not in the employer.

1. This is especially common with founders, who often fail to assign their rights to the companies they create

a. It is also common with employee inventors, who under the laws of the United States and other important jurisdictions, will own inventions

[13] Indian Copyright Act 1957 Section 19.

[14] Article 29 of the German Copyright Act (Urheberrechtsgesetz. UrhG) provides that "Copyright may be transferred by execution of a testamentary disposition or to coheirs as par of the partition of an estate. Copyright shall not otherwise be transferable." This principle seems to derive from the concept in German law that copyright is inherently bound to the personality of the author.

made in the course of employment absent an enforceable assignment to the employer.

b. It is equally common among third-party consultants engaged by the target company to create potentially patentable work product.

2. The only sound solution is to verify that all employees and consultants have entered into agreements enforceable within their jurisdictions to assign rights in their inventions or other work product (subject to specific concerns in specific jurisdictions of the type described immediately above).

h. The conflicting grant, license back, and field of use problem

i. In an effort to resolve conflicts between the rights of a company developing new technology and its vendors, the company will often agree to grant rights back to the vendors.

ii. Such grants need to be very carefully reviewed and constrained, as they can easily become a cloud on the company's title to its intellectual property.

iii. Field of use clauses often cause comparable issues. The field definitions are often vague and subject to dramatically differing interpretations.

2. Clauses regarding assignment of contracts

"This Agreement shall not be assigned in whole or in part without the express written permission of both parties [which shall not unreasonably be denied]"

What is the net effect of this provision?

i. What is an assignment?

Suppose you have a simple royalty-bearing nonexclusive IP license: A licenses B to use widgets in exchange for a royalty of Z on each widget used by B. Consider the following possibilities:

1. A assigns its general intangibles (including this license) to its bank in connection with A's line of credit with the bank.
2. A assigns its accounts receivables (including accrued royalties) to its bank in connection with A's A/R financing.
3. B assigns the license to C.
4. B assigns the license to C in connection with C's purchase of substantially all of B's assets.
    - Suppose C promises to pay the royalties to A,
    - Suppose A accepts C's payment of royalties following the "assignment,"
5. B merges with C.
6. B is a corporation, and C purchases all the shares of B.
7. B undergoes a reorganization in bankruptcy.

Which of these transactions would be effective without the consent of the non-assigning party? Although the matter is not completely free from doubt, there is a growing body of case law suggesting that possibilities 3 through 5 are all ineffective in the absence of consent of the licensor.[15] There is little doubt that if the IP involved were a patent, possibility 3 would violate the "blackletter" principle that patent licenses personal in nature and, therefore, not assignable without the consent of the licensor.[16] However dubious its intellectual underpinnings,[17] this principle is now leaking out of its patent origins into copyright and attenuated instances of "assignment." In *PPG*

---

[15] Many of the decided cases involve contracts that contain anti-assignment provisions, but the nonassignability principle is often stated in general terms.

[16] *Everex Sys. v. Cadtrak Corp. (In re CFLC, Inc).*, 89 F.3d 673, 679-80 (9th Cir. 1996).

[17] This principle is often associated with, and may in some way be derived from, the idea that a nonexclusive patent license is a "mere covenant not to sue." *Intellectual Prop. Dev., Inc. v. TCI Cablevision of Cal., Inc.*, 248 F.3d 1333, 1345 (Fed. Cir. 2001). One imagines that the authors of this principle were not acquainted with modern patent licenses, which can run to many dozens of pages with elaborate obligations running in both directions between the contracting parties.

Industries, Inc. v. Guardian Industries Corp.,[18] the Sixth Circuit held that as a matter of federal law, a patent license did not automatically vest in the surviving corporation after a statutory merger, despite language in the Ohio statute stating that it would automatically transfer to and vest in the surviving corporation.[19] Although the license in *PPG Industries* stated that it was "non-exclusive" and "non-transferrable," the court's dicta suggested that the transfer would be valid only if there were an "express provision" permitting transfer. So much for state corporate law governing mergers. In *Cincom Systems, Inc. v. Novelis Corp.*,[20] the same court applied the same principle to a computer software license that was tied to the use of the software on a particular computer. To reach this result, the court first extended the principle to copyright — as far as this author is aware, for the first time ever — on the ground of the "historic kinship between patent law and copyright law." The court then decided that a reorganization of the licensee, following which the software continued to be used on exactly the same computer, was a transfer. The net effect of this ruling was that the licensor, Cincom, received a windfall of over $450,000 by charging a second licensing fee for the use of the same software on the same computer for the same purposes it had originally licensed.

PPG Industries and *Cincom* clearly hold that case #5, above, is an impermissible assignment, at least in the face of anti-assignment language in the underlying contract. *A fortiori*, it seems inevitable that the same result would hold for case #4, where there is an actual assignment of contracts in connection with an asset purchase. Additional caselaw points to the extension of the *Cincom* principle to #7, as well as to trademarks.[21] It has not yet been expanded to cases #1, 2, and 6, but the trend seems clear that *any* change in the character or identity of the licensee potentially jeopardizes the underlying license.[22]

---

[18] 597 F.2d 1090 (6th Cir. 1979).

[19] Id. at 1095.

[20] *Cincom Sys. v. Novelis Corp.*, 581 F.3d 431 (6th Cir. 2009).

[21] *Baxter Healthcare Corp. v. Concepts, Inc.*, 69 F.3d 785 (7th Cir. 1995) (sales of stock do not constitute assignment); *Superior Bedding Co. v. Serta Associates, Inc.*, 353 F. Supp. 1143, 1149 (N.D. Ill. 1972) (anti-assignment clauses are standard in trademark licensing agreements, and are necessary to prevent licensor from losing trademark rights); *In re Alltech Plastics, Inc.*, 1987 Bankr. LEXIS 2259, 5 U.S.P.Q.2D (BNA) 1806 (Bankr. W.D. Tenn. Dec. 30, 1987) (where the debtor is becomes a shell corporation, assignment of license during reorganization is improper).

[22] *Perlman v. Catapult Entertainment (In re Catapult Entertainment), 165* F.3d 747, 751 (9th Cir. 1999) (A debtor in possession cannot assume a nonexclusive patent license, because under federal patent law such a license is personal and nondelegable).

It remains to be seen whether cases such as *Cincom* are one-way streets. If Cincom, the licensor, rather than Novelis, the licensee, had performed the corporate reorganization (as is often the case when, for example, the IP holdings of a corporation are consolidated into a single holding company), could Novelis have complained that the transfer violated the anti-assignment provision, excusing its further performance?[23] The argument would certainly be credible if, as is often the case, the license contained maintenance or warranty obligations that could be affected by the reorganization. Suppose Cincom pledged all its general intangibles, including the license, to a lender who then foreclosed, leaving the licensee to look to a new vendor to satisfy the licensor's obligations. Or suppose Cincom had filed for bankruptcy, assumed and assigned the license agreement to a new entity — potentially a competitor of Novelis. Could Novelis have escaped its license obligations in such cases? We do not yet know the answer to these questions in the abstract. However, if they are of concern in a particular instance, it is highly advisable to address them directly in the agreement. It is likely that a court would follow the parties' intent, as long as no strong public policy was violated.

A further puzzle arises if the anti-assignment provision contains the very commonly employed fudge that consent to the assignment "shall not unreasonably be withheld."[24] Had Cincom's license included this phrase, it would certainly seem "reasonable," on at least one understanding of that word, for Cincom to withhold consent to Novelis's reorganization on the ground that it reasonably preferred to collect another half-million dollars by not consenting. On the other hand, such an interpretation has such a self-serving circularity that it might be considered to have gutted the concept of "reasonableness" entirely. The simple truth is that no one drafting or agreeing to such a clause can have the slightest idea of how it might be interpreted in a disputed case; the clause is more properly understood as a right to plea for mercy from the other party to the contract.

The implication for the drafters of anti-assignment clauses is clear: beware what you wish for, and beware what you have agreed to. An IP licensor, careful to prevent its licensees from assigning their agreements under any

---

[23] The answer could depend on the terms of the anti-assignment provision. If it forbade assignment of "the agreement" it seems to apply equally to the licensor and licensee. If it only forbade assignment of "the licenses granted hereby" a credible argument could be made that it was intended to apply only to assignment by the licensee.

[24] *Taylor Equip. v. John Deere Co.*, 98 F.3d 1028, 1034 (8th Cir. S.D. 1996) (Suggests that the right to limit assignment retained by lincesor would be limited in the presence of a reasonableness clause).

circumstances, may discover that it has drafted a provision that interferes with a corporate reorganization, a statutory merger or a line of credit. An IP licensee is even more at risk. Anti-assignment clauses in key IP licenses regularly compromise corporate development strategies by precluding asset sales, mergers and acquisitions. They can severely impact the market value of the company or, in particularly egregious cases queer sale of a business altogether.

The only sensible solution in any situation involving a key IP license is to pay as much attention to the anti-assignment provision as one does to other critical features of the agreement. Reliance on "not unreasonably withheld" clauses should be avoided. Care should be taken to draft a provision that anticipates and provides for the possible transactions each party might want to enter into.

***

> "This Agreement may be assigned to the purchaser of substantially all the assets of the Licensor" — or — "A hereby consents to the assignment of Agreement X to B."

We come now to the next question: How should consent to an assignment be phrased? This question necessarily returns us to things we learned in the first year of law school, but may overlook in the urgent need to complete a deal. The assignment of contracts is a perennial subject that has troubled the common law for centuries. Corbin's one-volume treatise devotes no fewer than 93 pages to the topic;[25] Farnsworth refuses even to address the issue as a single topic, dividing it instead into two discrete subchapters, one on assignment[26] and the other on delegation.[27]

Here's a quick review: Contracts contain both rights and obligations. As a general rule, contractual rights are freely assignable, [28] with notable exceptions such as the "federal" prohibition on assignment of certain IP rights. An effective assignment of a contractual right divests the assignor of the right and vests the right in the assignee.[29]

---

[25] Corbin, *Corbin on Contracts* (1952), 783–876.

[26] Farnsworth, *Contracts* (4th ed., 2004), §§11.2 to 11.9 ("Farnsworth").

[27] Id. §§11.10 to 11.11.

[28] As Farnsworth observes, "Today most contract rights are freely assignable. If the law were otherwise, our modern credit economy could not exist." Farnsworth, §11.2 at 682.

[29] Id. §11.3 at 687.

Delegation of obligations is another matter entirely. It is one thing to say that if A promises to pay money to B, B can, by assignment to C, extinguish C's right to be paid by B and, at the same time, force A to pay money to C instead of B. It would be quite another thing to say that A can, by "assignment" to D, force B to accept D's promise to pay what A owed — D's credit may be worthless, which would leave B with no recourse for the debt. For this reason, the basic common law rule (also codified in the Uniform Commercial Code and contained in the Restatement [Second] of Contracts) is that delegation of a duty does not excuse the obligor's performance.[30] To discharge the delegating (assigning) party, a *novation* is required under which the obligee both agrees to accept performance by the delegate and discharges the delegating party from further obligations.[31]

The assignment provision quoted above fails to effect a novation. As a result, the original obligor under the IP agreement would remain secondarily liable for obligations under the contract if the assignee failed to perform them. Unless this is the intended result, a better-drafted clause would require the obligee to discharge the original obligor/assignor and to accept performance by the assignee in lieu of, and as full accord and satisfaction of, the original obligor's obligations under the agreement. Depending on the circumstances of the assignment, terms addressing continuing obligations that arose prior to the assignment should also be included. These will frequently include, as an example, warranties of performance and title.

3. Affiliates/subsidiaries clauses

> "A and its Affiliates/Subsidiaries grant to B and its Affiliates/Subsidiaries a license to [do whatever]"

The basic issue raised by this clause is temporal: the parties' "Affiliates" and "Subsidiaries" are likely to change during the course of the license. In *Imation v. Koninklijke Philips Electronics,*[32] Philips granted to Imation "and its SUBSIDIARIES a personal, non-exclusive, indivisible, nontransferable, irrevocable, worldwide, royalty-free license under PHILIPS LICENSED PATENTS." The "LICENSED PATENTS" were defined, in pertinent part, as patents that "are owned or controlled by the granting party or any of its

---

[30] See Farnsworth §11.10 at 718–19.

[31] Id. §11.11 at 726. The novation can be implied if the oblige accepts performance from the delegee without a reservation of rights against the delegating party. Id.

[32] *Imation Corp. v. Koninklijke Philips Elecs. N.V.*, 586 F.3d 980 (Fed. Cir. 2009).

SUBSIDIARIES such that such party or its SUBSIDIARIES now has or hereafter obtains the right to grant the licenses within the scope of this Agreement." "SUBSIDIARY" was defined as "any . . . form of business organization as to which the party now or hereafter has more than a fifty percent (50%) ownership interest." The term of the license was from the effective date of the agreement through the end of the patent term for each licensed patent.

Imation acquired new "SUBSIDIARIES" following the expiration of the term of the license. The issue was whether the license grant extended to those subsidiaries. The court analyzed this in rather metaphysical terms as a question whether the license grant should be construed as a single "unitary" grant or an agreement to grant multiple licenses over time. If the former, then the license would cover subsidiaries coming into existence following the term of the agreement, because they fell within the definition of "SUBSIDIARIES" (which specifically included the clause "now or hereafter"). If the latter, then the license would not cover the later-created subsidiaries because the separate grant to those subsidiaries would have fallen outside the term of the agreement.

The court held that the language of the grant, "agrees to grant *and does hereby grant,*" combined with other language in the contract that was inconsistent with a series of grants,[33] constituted a *present* grant in effect encompassing, *nunc pro tunc,* all of Imation's present and future subsidiaries. The court's reasoning suggests that the result could have been different if the words "and does hereby grant" were not in the granting clause.

For our purposes, the holding of this case is less important than the general caution it represents when dealing with related parties such as Affiliates and Subsidiaries. I would be willing to bet that the drafters of this agreement did not tarry long over either the terms of the granting clause or the open-ended definition of Subsidiaries. "Agrees to grant and does hereby grant" is a stock phrase, a sort of scene à faire, in license drafting. However, when combined with a definition of "Subsidiaries" that included future "Subsidiaries," it had an effect in this agreement that was evidently – judging from the existence of the litigation – unintended by the licensor.

There is no quick and easy solution to this sort of problem. The extension of licenses to affiliates and subsidiaries — not to mention joint venturers, consortia or others with whom one or the other parties to a license may be involved — requires careful consideration and oftentimes laborious negotiation

---

[33] For example, Article 3 of the agreement provided that the term of the licenses "shall commence on the effective date of the agreement."

and drafting. It is the beginning of a solution, however, to recognize the problem and to be prepared to deal with it in the course of each drafting exercise.

4. Joint ownership clauses

> "The Parties shall jointly own all rights in the technology created during the course of the Project defined herein"

Another all-too-common source of difficulty is the all-too-easy compromise of joint ownership of intellectual property.[34] Much as businesses are fond of referring to arm's length contractual relationships as "partnerships," they are also inclined to avoid disputes over IP rights by proposing joint ownership of IP generated during development projects, joint ventures and other multiple-party efforts. This leads to myriad drafting challenges.

Problem 1: Patent prosecution

As we all know, patents do not arise automatically. The patenting process entails not only substantial expense (which can increase dramatically if protection is sought in multiple countries) but also a substantial commitment of both management and technical resources. Any agreement providing for joint ownership of patentable technology must therefore provide a decision mechanism for questions such as the following:

- What inventions should be the subject of a patent application?
- How broadly should the claims be drafted, and how should the claims connect to the parties' business interests?
- What inventions are better protected as trade secrets or injected into the public domain?
- In which jurisdictions should patent applications be filed?

34 This section of this paper will focus exclusively on patents, copyrights and trade secrets, all of which are capable of being jointly owned. Joint ownership of trademarks is problematic because a mark is supposed to signify a single source. Addressing this issue is beyond the scope of this paper.

- How are the costs of the patent application paid and/or recovered?

There is no pat answer to these questions. In many cases, the easiest solution is to place both control of the process and its expense in the hands of one party. The Research Agreement form of the MIT Office of Sponsored Programs[35] is an example of this solution. Under this agreement, inventions made jointly by sponsor and MIT personnel are jointly owned, but MIT has a first right to file a patent application in the name of both parties. The expenses of prosecution are shared equally unless one of the parties declines to share in the expense, in which case the other takes over prosecution.[36]

The problem of control over the prosecution process is generally nonexistent for copyrights, as they arise automatically upon creation in all Berne Convention countries. An exception is, of course, the United States, where copyright registration is not mandatory but frequently highly desirable. An agreement providing for joint ownership of IP created during the course of a research or development agreement should address the issue of United States copyright registration in parallel with patent prosecution.

For trade secrets, there is no registration process, but parties jointly owning trade secrets need to consider their mutual confidential obligations carefully, since release by either party will destroy the value of the trade secret for the other party.

Problem 2: Exploitation and licensing of the jointly-owned IP

Assuming that jointly-owned patents, copyrights, or trade secrets are obtained, the next set of questions concerns exploitation, licensing and enforcement. The joint ownership agreement should address the following major issues:

- Do the joint owners have an equal right to exploit the IP, or does one or the other hold an exclusive field of use license?

---

35 See http://web.mit.edu/osp/www/MIT%20RESEARCH%20AGREEMENT%20FOR%20US%20SPONSORS%20033010%20OSP%20web%20sample.pdf.

36 This solution can be problematic if the parties' resources for and interest in broad international protection are not the same. The party with the greater interest in broad protection may wind up picking up the tab, but still sharing joint ownership of the resulting patents with the other party. As noted below, joint ownership of patents has divergent implications in various countries.

- Which of the joint owners has a right to grant licenses to third parties, and under what terms?
- How are proceeds of exploitation shared among the joint owners?
- Which of the joint owners has the right to pursue infringers? Who bears the costs of enforcement, and who is entitled to recovery of the proceeds?

On the first of these issues, the MIT Research Agreement provides an example of one sort of solution. It gives each party an "independent, unrestricted right" to license joint inventions to third parties "without accounting to the other party." Absent further agreement or understanding between the parties, such a provision substantially diminishes the value of the jointly-owned IP to either party, and one might question whether joint ownership of such IP is worth the trouble and expense. Under the MIT Agreement, the sponsor can "request" an exclusive license to MIT's joint interest, and one expects that this would often be the case.

If the jointly owned IP covers different forms of IP protection, the exploitation and licensing provisions need to be harmonized with divergent principles of law. In the United States, either joint owner of a patent can grant a license to a third party or otherwise exploit the patent without any duty to account to the other joint owner for the proceeds (i.e., there is no obligation to share proceeds).[37] The US rule for copyrights is just the opposite: joint owners of a copyright are obligated to account to one another for the proceeds of their exploitation of the work.[38]

Things get still more complicated in the international arena. In many countries, notably the UK and Germany, the consent of all of the joint owners of a patent is required for any license. In addition, the rule regarding duties to account varies from country to country. As an example, the rule in the UK regarding jointly owned patents is exactly the opposite the rule in the United States: the joint owners of a UK patent have a duty to account to one another for proceeds.

Enforcement implies a further set of complications. Because of the cost and risk involved in any infringement lawsuit, this topic needs to be carefully considered, often using terms covering costs, decision making, and control, that

---

[37] 35 U.S.C. §262.

[38] This is a judge-made right. See 1 Nimmer on Copyright §6.12[A].

parallel those governing patent prosecution. Both joint owners are likely to be considered necessary parties to any litigation, which tends to exacerbate the strains on the joint relationship. Can one of the joint owners prevent the other from bringing an infringement action against a third party for business reasons unrelated to the jointly owned invention? If not, is the other joint owner entitled to compensation for the lost opportunity? It should be noted that the ability and willingness to pursue litigation can be critical to a licensing strategy. For this reason, control over infringement claims is intimately connected to control over the licensing process for jointly owned IP.

Problem 3: Ancillary rights

A further issue that a joint ownership provision ought to address is that of ancillary rights. In the case of patents, this includes not only continuations, continuations-in-part, reissues and divisionals, but also improvements that are dominated by the original patents. Are some or all of these also jointly owned and subject to the same rules regarding exploitation? As noted above, continuations-in-part are a particularly troublesome issue that is often overlooked in drafting. A continuation-in-part can include completely new subject matter that may not have been jointly developed with the inventors of the original, underlying invention. Ownership clauses often toss in "continuations-in-part" as mindless boilerplate, but doing so can easily have the unintended consequence of granting joint rights to contracting parties for inventions the other parties had nothing to do with.

5. Integration clauses

> "This Agreement supersedes all prior agreements and negotiations between the parties [respecting its subject matter]"

This is yet another boilerplate clause often thrown into IP agreements without giving any thought to its actual implications. Several considerations need to be addressed before signing off on any such clause.

First, and most fundamentally, are there other agreements between the parties that ought to survive? Very often, the contracting parties will have begun their relationship with an NDA. In most cases, confidential information exchanged under an initial NDA ought to survive the execution of a subsequent license, development or other IP-related agreement. Depending on the interpretation of the clause "respecting its subject matter," the above clause could erase the NDA and its obligations. This could work, but only if the subsequent agreement included its own confidentiality clause and only if that clause captured not only confidential information exchanged under the new agreement, but also information disclosed under the original NDA.

Including a boilerplate integration clause in any agreement that is part of a series of related agreements can also cause problems, particularly with warranty and indemnity provisions. If the new agreement and prior agreements overlap regarding subject matter, an over-simple integration clause of the type provided above can inadvertently extinguish warranty and indemnity obligations arising under prior agreements.

Finally, the clause "between the parties" in this sample integration clause can be ambiguous. Suppose that there is an earlier agreement between parties A and B and that the later agreement is between parties A, B, and C. The earlier agreement was between *some* of the parties, but not all of them. Was this earlier agreement intended to be superseded? Or, to return to the previous discussion regarding mergers and acquisitions, suppose party B from the prior agreement subsequently merged with or was acquired by party C. If the subsequent agreement is between A and C, is it the intent of the parties to supersede the prior agreement between A and B, or not? All these issues need to be considered as possible elaborations on the standard integration clause.

6. Choice of law/forum clauses

> "This Agreement shall be interpreted and enforced under the laws of [US State]"

US attorneys suffer a parochial tendency to believe that we can impose our laws on agreements, and on parties to agreements, throughout the world if one of the parties to the agreement has a connection to the United States. This is often erroneous. Consideration should usually be given, at a minimum, to the jurisdictions in which work generating IP is being performed, and whether their laws would govern rights in the IP. As an example, the provisions of European laws referenced above,[39] providing for ownership of inventions created by employees and compensation to employee inventors, will not be superseded by a US choice of law. Also, the Indian requirements for copyright assignments will apply to any copyrightable material — notably computer software and entertainment properties – will prevail over contrary US law principles. These are but examples; it is probably fair to say that the IP laws of

---

[39] See notes 9, 10, 12, 13.

every jurisdiction contain some provisions that cannot be superseded by agreement and that are inconsistent with standard US practice.

7. UN Convention on International Sales of Goods

This should usually be disclaimed, even in software license and transfer agreements. There is a split on international authority, but some jurisdictions take the approach that CISG applies to software purchases, including the purchase of IP underlying the software. If CISG is not specifically disclaimed, it may be deemed adopted under the governing law jurisdiction that is has been selected under the specific contract. CISG is most remarkable for the fact that it has no parole evidence rule (and, in fact, has an anti-parole evidence rule); as a consequence (if not expressly excluded), one cannot be certain that the terms of what appears to be an unambiguous written contract are the final and binding terms.

The foregoing list is intended to highlight some of the more frequently overlooked subtleties in drafting IP agreements. There are, of course, many other ways to go astray, which might perhaps be reserved for next year's MCLE presentation.

Intellectual Property Indemnity Clauses*

I. Background

The practices associated with intellectual property indemnity can be traced in part to Article 2 of the Uniform Commercial Code.[1] At the dawn of the computer age, practitioners searched for legal models that they could use for transactions in intangible rights and products such as computer software. Although computer software did not fit easily into the "sale of goods" paradigm,[2] analogies to the familiar rules governing sales of goods were inevitable.[3]

Lurking in the lower reaches of Article 2 of the UCC, one finds an implied warranty of noninfringement in Section 2-312 (2):[4]

> Unless otherwise agreed, a seller that is a merchant regularly dealing in goods of the kind warrants that the goods shall be delivered free of the rightful claim of any third person by way of infringement or the like but a buyer that furnishes specifications to the seller must hold the seller harmless against any such claim that arises out of compliance with the specifications.

 The author gratefully acknowledges the assistance of Veronica Louie, Morten Boyd, Anthony Decicco, Andrew Lynn, and David Houlihan, as well as the editors of the Boston College Law School Intellectual Property and Technology Forum in the preparation of this paper.

1 For a summary of clauses found in typical indemnification agreements, and a summary of the pros and cons of each, see John Hutchins, "Anatomy of an Indemnification Provision: Identifying and Addressing Basic Indemnification Issues," AIPLA 2010 Annual Meeting Materials. See also John C. Miller, "40 Indemnification Clause Review Tips," *Cont. Mgmt.* (March 2007), 55–56.

2 The software industry settled on licensing, not sale, as its preferred model for software commercialization. Thomas M. S. Hemnes, "Restraints on Alienation, Equitable Servitudes, and the Feudal Nature of Computer Software Licensing," 71 *Denv. U. L. Rev.* 577 (1993–1994).

3 Indeed, there was a decade-long effort to adapt a revised UCC article perched between Article II and the non-UCC concept of an intellectual property license. See Maureen A. O'Rourke, "An Essay on the Challenges of Drafting a Uniform Law of Software Contracting," 10 *Lewis & Clark L. Rev.* (2006), 925, 926.

4 Uniform Commercial Code §2-312 (2). For a discussion of the application of this provision to IP licensing transactions, see G. Ross Allen, "The Basics of Indemnification," 21 *Intell. Prop. Litig.* (Spring 2010), 7, 8.

In the context of a sale of goods at the time Article 2 was drafted,[5] a noninfringement warranty made good economic sense. The only form of intellectual property likely to be of concern to the purchaser of goods was patent protection.[6] In the mid-twentieth century, when Article 2 of the UCC was adopted, patents were the disfavored stepchildren of the federal courts. A high percentage of patents were held to be invalid,[7] and the damages accorded to those found to be valid were often limited to a modest royalty.[8] Furthermore, patent rights are — as a rule — exhausted upon the first sale of a

---

[5] The Uniform Commercial Code's drafting commenced in 1942; the UCC was first published in 1952. See http://en.wikipedia.org/wiki/Uniform_Commercial_Code.

[6] Books could be considered an exception to this generalization. However, copyright covers only the right to reproduce and distribute a copyrighted work in copies; therefore, the purchaser of a copyrighted work may use it — i.e., read it — even if the work were distributed without permission of the copyright owner. See 17 U.S.C. §106. Therefore, the UCC's implied noninfringement warranty is quite unnecessary to the typical ultimate purchaser of a copyrighted work; it would only be important to persons higher in the distribution chain who need the right to redistribute the work.

[7] In a study, the PTO found that 70 percent of patents were held invalid in the courts of appeals during the period 1968–1977. "Patent and Trademark Office Study of Court Determinations of Patent Validity/Invalidity 1973–1977," 989 *Off. Gaz. Pat. & Trademark Office* 2 (979), available at http://ipmall.info/hosted_resources/ notices_reports/PTOin validitystudy.pdf.

[8] Section 284 of the Patent Act provides:

> Upon a finding for the claimant the court shall award the claimant damages adequate to compensate for the infringement, but in no event less than a reasonable royalty for the use made of the invention by the infringer. . . .

35 U.S.C. §284. In 1982, Congress created the Court of Appeals for the Federal Circuit by passing the Federal Courts Improvement Act. Pub. L. 97-164, Apr. 2, 1982, 96 Stat. 25. Well before 1982, in an opinion filled with hostility towards the patent "monopoly," the Supreme Court (Brennan, J.) held, *inter alia,* that the patentee could not recover more than nominal damages for contributory infringement if it already had been paid a royalty for the infringing product. Id. at 377–78. Between 1982 and 1989, reasonable royalty awards, accounted for 48 percent of patent damages awarded during these years. J. Shawn Mcgrath & Kathleen M. Kedrowski, *American Bar Ass'n, Trends In Patent Damages* 5 (2007), available at http://www.docs.piausa.org/ABA/07-06-01-ABA-Report-On-Patent-Damages.pdf. Enhanced damages accounted for only twelve percent of the damage awards in the same period, which thereafter increased by 175 percent over a ten-year period following establishment of the CAFC to make up 33 percent of patent damage awards between 2000 and 2006. Id.

product[9] , and far fewer patents were being issued.[10] Additionally, products were less complex, typically falling into only a single engineering domain, with correspondingly fewer points of intersection with issued patents. For all these reasons, the risk that the ultimate purchaser of a product would be sued for patent infringement was very remote, and even if the purchaser were sued, the damages would be only a tiny fraction of the purchase price — the average and median for all products was between 5 and 7 percent.[11]

In this context, a product manufacturer could provide an implied warranty of noninfringement with very little risk beyond whatever modest risk of infringement the manufacturer had already incurred by manufacturing the product itself.[12] Product purchasers did not typically insist on an indemnity beyond the implied warranty[13], perhaps because the risk was perceived as too remote to be worth worrying about.[14] The exhaustion doctrine would — in

---

[9] *Adams v. Burke,* 84 U.S. 453, 456 (1873) ("when the patentee, or the person having his rights, sells a machine or instrument whose sole value is in its use, he receives the consideration for its use and he parts with the right to restrict that use."); *Bloomer v. McQuewan,* 55 U.S. 539 (1852).

[10] By the end of 1982, the Patent Office had issued 4,370,711 utility patents in its history. United States Patent and Trademark Office, *U.S. Patent Activity: Calendar Years 1790 to the Present,* http://www.uspto.gov/web/offices/ac/ido/oeip/taf/h_counts.htm (last visited Mar. 19, 2013). It nearly eclipsed that number in the following 29 years, issuing 3,699,653 utility patents between 1983 and 2011.

[11] A survey conducted on behalf of the author of some 37 opinions awarding reasonable royalties on a percentage basis published prior to the establishment of the CAFC reveals a great deal of variance in reasonable royalty awards, which ranged from .75% to 25%, with median and average royalty rates of 5.34% and 6.65%, respectively. In the author's experience, royalties on manufactured products rarely exceed five percent.

[12] It is instructive that, according to this author's experience, standard practice at the time disclaimed the implied of merchantability and fitness in favor of more closely drafted express warranties, but almost always neglected to disclaim the implied warranty of noninfringement. It was simply not a point of concern.

[13] Support for this assertion is necessarily anecdotal. It is worth noting, however, that the no-IP indemnity rule still applies to nonwholesale purchases of chattels, which, in this author's experience, are rarely accompanied by a written agreement, much less an indemnity clause

[14] Indemnities generally provide fuller remedies than mere warranties. Warranties provide recovery for the difference in value between the product as sold and the product as delivered. U.C.C. §2-714. In the context of an infringement claim, this would be measured by the price of the royalty required to obtain a license to use the infringing item. See note [9] above. An indemnity, by contrast, would cover all losses occasioned by the infringement, usually including attorneys' fees and potentially including lost profits if there is an interruption in use. *See* Allen, *supra* note 5.

many cases — cause the claim to be made against the manufacturer rather than the user. Therefore, they would assume — probably quite rightly — that the manufacturer would "stand behind its product" and obtain the required license if an infringement claim were actually made.[15]

With this background, and without giving the matter too much additional thought, it did not seem unreasonable for the lawyers representing software and other technology providers to provide a warranty of noninfringement governing their clients' products as well. Such a warranty was certainly consistent with established practice as embodied in UCC Article 2. It, therefore, would have met the expectations of the marketplace. Furthermore, the risk of infringement liability seemed manageable. At that time, virtually no one believed that computer software would be patentable, and absolutely no one imagined that business methods would be patentable. The risks of trade secret or copyright infringement liability are more uniquely within the control of the software provider since each of them requires an element of intent or a near equivalent.[16] By adopting appropriate internal controls and standards, sometimes even including a "clean room,"[17] a software provider ought to be able to minimize its infringement risk.

As licensors, software providers had an additional consideration of the desire to control litigation concerning rights in the product. At that time, protection for

---

[15] Of course, if the original seller did not have the right to sell the product covered by a patent there would be no exhaustion, and the purchaser could in principle be sued for infringement. See *Quanta Computer, Inc. v. LG Elecs.*, Inc., 553 U.S. 617, 636 (2008) ("Exhaustion is triggered only by a sale authorized by the patent holder."). It is believed, however, that claims against end users were the exception rather than the rule, probably because the damages recoverable from the end user would have been limited to the royalty value of that person's use, whereas the recovery from the manufacturer would reflect the cumulative royalty value of sales to all end users. The *General Talking Pictures* case was an unusual exception in which the user was sued on the ground that the patentee's rights had not been exhausted by the first sale. *General Talking Pictures Corp. v. Western Electric Co.*, 304 U.S. 175 (1938), aff'd, 305 U.S. 124 (1938).

[16] To infringe copyright one must copy; independent creation of the same work never infringes. 17 U.S.C. §501. To misappropriate a trade secret one must be on notice of the existence of the secret and have entered into an express or implied agreement to protect it. U.T.S.A. §1.2.

[17] The "clean room" method may serve as a defense to infringement claims in trademark or copyright law. The method entails creating a new product from functional specifications by a team that does not have access to copyrightable material (e.g., computer code) of other products with similar functions. Duncan Davidson, "Common Law, Uncommon Software," 47 *U. Pitt. L. Rev.* (1986), 1037, 1097.

computer software was in a state of flux.[18] Copyright in computer software expanded in the years following the Copyright Act of 1976, but doubt persisted as to the extent of its protection. For instance, in following decades, the courts faced difficult questions regarding whether copyright protected operating systems that communicate only with machines[19] and whether it protected the "look and feel" of the user interface generated by the software.[20] These were considered weighty issues, going to the heart of the value represented by computer software. Accordingly, the software providers did not want to risk having them decided in litigation against their licensees, whose interest in broad protection would likely be less than the interest of the software providers.

In response to this concern, software providers migrated the infringement issue from the warranty clauses of software license agreements to indemnity provisions. As *quid pro quo* for indemnity, the licensor obtained prompt notice of the claim and full authority to defend or settle the case on behalf of the licensee. To mitigate their risk, most software licensors further provided that their obligation — and the licensee's sole remedy — was to (a) obtain for the licensee the right to use the licensed product; (b) modify the product to make it noninfringing; or — failing (a) or (b) — (c) to terminate the license and refund a pro-rated portion of the purchase price depending on how much of the license term had been exhausted at the date of termination.[21]

Clauses along these lines became a *de facto* standard in the software industry and persisted for many years. They were hardly perfect from the standpoint of licensees. Option (c) could be very detrimental in the case of software that was critical to a business; even if comparable noninfringing software were available, the end-user would be in the position of having to find, implement, and migrate all data or customizations to the new system. This could be expensive, risky, and time-consuming. If no comparable noninfringing software were available and the patentee refused to offer a license on commercially reasonable terms, a business that relied on the software could be crippled. Even option (b) could be problematic if the required modifications degraded functionality or compatibility. As a result, licensees with sufficient bargaining power would nibble at the edges of such

---

[18] For an example of how many issues were in the air at this time, see the author's effort to evaluate whether copyright would attach to video games. Hemnes, "The Adaptation of Copyright Law to Video Games," 131 *U. Pa. L. Rev.* 171 (1982).

[19] *Apple Computer, Inc. v. Franklin Computer Corp.*, 714 F.2d 1240 (3d Cir. 1983).

[20] This issue was never completely resolved. *Lotus Dev. Corp. v. Borland Int'l, Inc.*, 49 F.3d 807 (1st Cir. 1995), *aff'd per curium by an equally divided court*, 516 U.S. 233 (1996).

[21] For an example of one such clause, see Appendix B, Example 7.

indemnity clauses, sometimes allowing full refunds and often providing that (b) could only be exercised if functionality were not compromised. Nonetheless, the basic pattern — limited indemnity in exchange for control over litigation — became well fixed in many practitioners' minds.

As so often happens in the law, the basic practices that emerged in one field — the software industry — migrated to other industries as well. Intellectual property indemnification clauses were inserted into virtually any agreement in which the parties foresaw a risk of intellectual property infringement.

II. Destabilizing developments

The balance of power between technology vendors and consumers[22] represented by the "standard" IP indemnity clause was gradually but profoundly destabilized by the reforms in the patent system that followed the establishment of the Court of Appeals for the Federal Circuit ("CAFC") in 1982. Prior to the CAFC, the circuit courts of appeals had jurisdiction over patent appeals. To varying degrees, these courts were hostile to patents, which resulted in a surprisingly small percentage of litigated patents being enforced on appeal.[23] Patents were considered suspiciously anticompetitive,[24] and courts considered it their duty to limit the patents' anticompetitive impact. In the comparatively unusual instance when a patent was found to be valid and enforceable, the damages for infringement were generally measured in terms

---

[22] I will use the term "technology vendor" as a shorthand for the persons providing products, services or technology that may be subject to an intellectual property claim, and the term "technology consumer" or "customer" as a shorthand for the person obtaining such products, services or technology. In a particular case, the former will typically be a licensor or seller; the latter a licensee or buyer.

[23] *See* PTO study, *supra* note 7.

[24] *See, e.g.*, U.S. v. Line Material Co., 333 U.S. 287 (1948) (Douglas, J., concurring); Aro Mfg, Co. v. Convertible Top Replacement Corp., 377 U.S. 476 (1964).

of a reasonable royalty, which would typically be in the low single digits for manufactured articles.[25]

The exclusive jurisdiction over patent appeals accorded to the CAFC changed this pattern fundamentally. Populated by patent practitioners, the CAFC cast a kindly eye on patents, confirming the validity of patents two-thirds of the time.[26] The CAFC also dramatically expanded the scope for damages, permitting claims based not only on the potential profit of the patented product but also on profits from lost sales of ancillary products and enforcement of the statutory provisions permitting treble damages in cases of willful infringement.[27] Finally, the CAFC, with affirmance of the Supreme Court,[28] dramatically expanded the range of things that could be patented from the traditional subjects of mechanical devices, chemical compounds,

---

[25] See Jonathan E. Kemmerer & Jiaqing "Jack" Liu, "KPMG Advisory Paper: Profitability and Royalty Rates across Industries: Some Preliminary Evidence" 12 (2012), available at https://www.kpmg.com/Global/en/IssuesAndInsights/ArticlesPublications/Documents/profitability-royalty-rates- across-industries.pdf; note 11 *supra.* A common rule of thumb is that the total royalty burden on a product should not exceed 25% of the gross profit margin. See *Uniloc USA, Inc. v. Microsoft Corp.*, 632 F.3d 1202, 1311 *et seq.* (CAFC 2011) (acknowledging the 25 percent "rule of thumb" but finding it "fundamentally flawed" to determine a "baseline royalty rate"). However flawed the CAFC may find this rule of thumb, in actual licensing transactions, where one does not ordinarily have the rather expensive luxury of expert testimony and cross examination, it continues to reflect actual practice, and the total royalty burden on manufactured products rarely exceeds 5 percent. Royalties on products with lower production and distribution costs such as software can be higher, reflecting their much higher gross profit margin.

[26] See Matthew D. Henry & John L. Turner, "The Court of Appeals for the Federal Circuit's Impact on Patent Litigation," 35 J. *Legal Stud. Chicago* (June 2005), 4, 5 (Donald Dunner, Michael Jakes and Jeffery Karceski (1995) report that from 1982 to 1994, the CAFC found patents valid in 67 percent of adjudications).

[27] *Rite-Hite Corp. v. Kelley Co., Inc.*, 56 F.3d 1538 (Fed. Cir. 1995) (en banc) (extending scope of lost profit damages to include profits from sale of devices not covered by patent at issue); *Beatrice Foods Co. v. New England Printing & Lithographing Co.*, 923 F.2d 1576, 1578 (Fed. Cir. 1991) (recognizing damages for willful infringement may be enhanced). For an analysis of damage awards by year, concluding that they are not systematically "excessive," see Mazzeo, Hillel, and Zyontz, "Are Patent Infringement Awards Excessive?: The Data Behind the Reform Debate" (Working Paper, 2011), available at http://ssrn.com/abstract=1765891.

[28] *Diamond v. Chakrabarty*, 447 U.S. 303 (1980) (finding living, man-made micro-organism patentable subject matter); *Diamond v. Diehr*, 450 U.S. 175 (1981) (finding machine controlled by computer program patentable).

and industrial processes to include computer software,[29] forms of life,[30] and even business methods.[31]

The inexorable invasion of digital technology into all realms of human endeavor paralleled these legal developments. What had begun as something buried in the bowels of mainframe computers, with no intrinsic value other than to help operate and sell hardware, had morphed into something of global consequence known as "the Web," "the Internet," and "the Cloud." Large patches of this Cloud have been staked out with patent claims, permitting the patentees to charge tariffs for anyone passing over or through them.

In this context, the goods and services provided by giant corporations using digital technology became the targets of an increasing number of patent infringement claims. In these claims, damages would be calculated in millions of dollars due to the huge volume of business that had become dependent on the technology and increasing reasonable royalty awards by courts. Worse yet, a large corporation could face the possibility of an injunction against its use of critical technology if it did not settle. Technology-dependent enterprises found themselves enmeshed in patent infringement actions that almost always concerned technologies they had licensed from third parties. Patentees realized the enormous potential financial reward from suing the oftentimes large and well-heeled licensees and corporate customers rather than the frequently smaller and poorer technology licensors and providers.

Furthermore, from the patentee's standpoint, it made more sense to sue the corporate consumers of new technologies since they had a weaker incentive to defend vigorously than the licensors. Moreover, obtaining negotiated license agreements to settle their claims was evidence strengthening the

---

[29] *Arrhythmia Research Tech. v. Corazonix Corp.*, 958 F.2d 1053 (Fed. Cir. 1992).

[30] *Association for Molecular Pathology v. U.S.P.T.O.*, No. 2010-1406 (Fed. Cir. July 29, 2011).

[31] *State Street Bank & Trust Co. v. Signature Financial Group*, 149 F.3d 1368 (Fed. Cir. 1998). Patent protection for business methods was never fully accepted outside the United States and in the United States engendered such a fury of controversy that the CAFC was subsequently required to retrench. See *In re Bilski*, 545 F.3d 943 (Fed. Cir. 2008) (en banc). For summaries of international treatment of business method patents, see Robert E. Thomas & Larry A. DiMatteo, "Harmonizing the International Law of Business Method and Software Patents: Following Europe's Lead," 16 *Tex. Intell. Prop. L.J.* 1 (2007); Joy Y. Xiang, "How Wide Should the Gate of "Technology" Be?: Patentability of Business Methods in China," 11 *Pac. Rim L. & Pol'y J.* 795 (2002); Andre J. Porter, "Should Business Method Patents Continue to be Patentable?," 29 *S.U. L. Rev.* 225, 245–58 (2002).

patents' claim to validity.[32] Patentees, therefore, developed "roll-up" strategies in which they brought actions against the corporate consumers — not the producers — of technology and offered attractive settlements at amounts substantially lower than the likely cost and risk of litigation.[33]

A particularly striking example of the "sue the corporate customer, not the manufacturer" strategy is Innovatio IP Ventures' ongoing litigation against a host of hotels, coffee shops, and supermarkets that provide wireless network access to customers through devices complying with the 802.11 Wi-Fi standard. Innovatio claims that this technology infringes approximately 31 patents that it had acquired from Broadcom Corporation shortly before sending demand letters to the various merchants.[34] Manufacturers of wireless devices used by the defendants attempted to protect their hapless customers by filing actions for a declaratory judgment of noninfringement and accusing Innovatio of racketeering, based on Innovatio's alleged use of misleading demand letters and sham litigation tactics.[35] Thus far, the manufacturers have been less than completely successful in foreclosing the Innovatio lawsuits against their customers.[36]

---

32 See, e.g., John T. McNelis, "New Designs: Licenses May be Evidence of Nonobviousness of an Invention," *Daily J.*, 1998, at 1, 2, available at http://www.fenwick.com/docstore/Publications/IP/IP_Articles/New_Designs.pdf.

33 It has been observed that patent litigation is the "sport of kings." A fully litigated patent infringement case is unlikely to cost less than several million dollars. See Anne Louise St. Martin, J. Derek Mason, "Arbitration: A Quick and Effective Means for Patent Dispute Resolution," 12 *N.C. J.L. & Tech.* 301, 317 (Spring 2011) (putting the average cost of patent litigation with $1,000,000 to $25,000,000 in jeopardy at $2,500,000) (citing Am. Intell. Prop. L. Ass'n, *2009 Report of the Economic Survey* 29 (2009)).

34 See Dow Lohnes Intellectual Property, "The Essential Patent Blog, Catching up on . . . Innovatio IP Ventures, LLC's Litigation Activities," Jan. 3, 2013, http://essentialpatentblog.com/2013/01/catching-up-on-innovation-ip-ventures-llcs-litigation-activities/; Gregory Thomas, "Innovatio's Infringement Suit Rampage Expands to Corporate Hotels," *The Patent Examiner*, Sept. 30, 2011, http://patentexaminer.org/2011/09/innovatios-infringement-suit-rampage-expands-to-corporate-hotels/.

35 See *Motorola Solutions, Inc. v. In re Innovatio IP Ventures, LLC* (In re Innovatio IP Ventures, LLC Patent Litig.), No. 11 C 9308; Case No. 11 C 9309; Case No. 12 C 427, 2013 U.S. Dist. LEXIS 15968 (N.D. Ill. Feb. 4, 2013).

36 Id. In another example known to the author, a patent holding company sued a series of e-commerce sites, all of which were "upstream" in the value chain, as opposed to the vendor of the accused technology. Far greater amounts of money pass through the e-commerce sites than are paid to the technology vendor, making the damage calculation far more favorable to the patent holder. In such situations, the upstream technology customers have far less incentive to fight than the vendor, whose entire business model can be placed at risk.

As a result of these developments, the limited indemnity/defense of litigation solution that had emerged from early software licensing practice came under intense pressure. Scarred by the increase in patent infringement claims, licensees began to demand unlimited indemnity from all of their technology licensors, without the alternatives for licensors to (a) obtain a license from the patentee, (b) modify their technology, or (c) give a refund to the licensee.

Licensors, on the other hand, began to look for new ways to protect themselves against potentially ruinous infringement liability. For example, in one well-known case in the District of Massachusetts, Freedom Wireless sued Boston Consulting Group (BCG) for patent infringement in March 2000. A modestly-sized public company with a market capitalization of about $120 million at the time, BCG had provided software to major players in the telecommunications industry and indemnified them against infringement claims. When BCG lost the case, it suffered a jury verdict of $128 million, based largely on its technology's scope of use by its licensees. BCG eventually settled for $55 million[37] after it had spent $27 million defending the case.[38]

III. Current situation[39]

The net effect of these developments is a highly unstable environment that arguably serves the interests of neither new technology developers and providers nor their consumers. The outcome of negotiation often reflects bargaining power rather than a rational distribution of risk and reward between vendor and consumer.

It is very common for large enterprises with substantial leverage to insist on a blanket IP indemnity — with no restriction on liability — in all transactions. One suspects that the primary purpose of such clauses is to protect counsel from criticism. If the company is sued for infringement, the likely first question for its lawyers is, "Are we indemnified?" Nobody wants to be in the position of saying "No" or "Yes, but . . .", so the easiest solution is to establish a blanket policy in which all IP licenses must carry indemnification and the

---

[37] Additionally, the indemnitees paid another $32 million.

[38] See *Freedom Wireless, Inc. v. Boston Communs. Group, Inc.*, 390 F. Supp. 2d 63, 68 (D. Mass. 2005); Peter Lattman, "Big Win for Quinn Emmanuel in $55 Million Patent Settlement," WSJ Law Blog, http://blogs.wsj.com/law/2006/07/24/freedom-and-boston-communications-group-settle-big-win-for-quinn-emanuel/ (July 24, 2006).

[39] Appendix B provides examples of the highly variable clauses found in license agreements.

indemnification must not be subject to the limitations on liability that otherwise would limit the licensor's obligations.

If the licensor's resources are inadequate to defend a claim or pay an adverse judgment, this solution fails to achieve the purpose of shifting the licensee's risk, and it can be potentially fatal to the licensor. Furthermore, the licensor/technology provider is unlikely to be in a position to mitigate its risk. Whereas a computer software company formerly could mitigate risk through "clean rooms" and company policies, the cost of conducting a "freedom to operate" study to determine whether the new technology infringes any issued patents is so prohibitively high that none but the largest manufacturers ever attempt one. Furthermore, even the most thorough study will not uncover patent applications that are pending but not yet published. The sheer volume of published applications and issued patents, combined with the multiple fields of technology incorporated into many modern products, make a thorough search and review even of materials that are theoretically accessible virtually impossible to perform. For these reasons, the risk of infringement liability cannot be characterized fairly as a defect in a product that the licensor will not "stand behind"; [40]instead, its nature is similar to a business risk — akin to natural disasters or *force majeure* — that cannot be effectively avoided through any exercise of diligence.

The net effect of the blanket indemnity solution in situations in which the technology consumer is much larger than the technology vendor is to create the appearance, but not the reality, of a transfer of infringement risk. The large organization will still bear the risk of infringement liability regardless of the indemnity clause's content; at most, it will have the power to bankrupt its vendor if a third party makes an infringement claim. This may be inconsistent with the large organization's interest if the technology is important to its

---

[40] As an example, the author was representing a very small, privately owned design shop for consumer devices in its attempt to negotiate a license of one of its designs to a nationwide "big box" housewares chain ("Big Box"). Big Box, whose annual revenues total billions of dollars and who would have been capable of selling millions of dollars' worth of products based on the particular design, insisted on an uncapped indemnity from the design shop, including the usual provision that the licensor would not only indemnify but also defend Big Box and hold it harmless in the event of a claim. It did not matter that the design shop's resources would have been exhausted after the first couple of months of litigation nor that any measure of damages based on Big Box's sales would have immediately bankrupted the design shop. Big Box's policy was final, and it had to be implemented. When challenged, the attorneys for Big Box responded with the standard rhetorical question, "Isn't your client willing to stand behind his product?"

enterprise and cannot realistically be replaced or supported without the vendor's help.

At the opposite extreme, some vendors with great market power simply refuse to offer any IP warranty or indemnity and are able to do so because their licensees have no alternative to the technology.[41] Others devise new ways to create the illusion that they have provided indemnity for their products when, in fact, they are providing none. One finds, for example, clauses entitled "Indemnification" that begin with the usual IP indemnity and defense provisions but then add a list of exceptions, including such things as technology already in use at the time the patent is issued and patents known to the licensee. Read literally, the "already in use" clause says that if the licensed product already infringes at the time the license is granted (as it would in the case of any issued patent that reads on the product), then the indemnity would not apply, effectively shifting the burden of conducting a freedom to operate study on the licensee. The "known to the licensee" clause is also highly protective of the licensor. It would permit the licensor to escape indemnity liability by establishing that the licensee was aware of an infringed patent, even if the licensee had no idea that the patent read on the licensed technology. It is certainly possible to imagine another customer "checking the box" that there was an indemnity clause without realizing that the clause provided little or no protection.

Another gambit is to provide indemnity only for final judgments of infringement. In practice, judgments are rare; instead, the vast majority of cases are settled on terms that do not admit infringement even if they might require payment of substantial sums to settle the claim.[42] In such cases, the customer who has paid to make a claim go away — which will usually be the case if the patentee sets its settlement figure below the customer's realistic present value of risk — will be unable to recover the settlement amount from

---

[41] Microsoft is an exception, but it has dramatically beefed up its patent portfolio to back up its indemnity obligations. See Ina Fried, "Microsoft to back customers in infringement cases," CNET News, Nov. 10, 2004, http://news.cnet.com/Microsoft-to-back-customers-in-infringement-cases/2100-1014_3-5445868.html.

[42] See, e.g., Jay P. Kesan & Gwendolyn G. Ball, "How Are Patent Cases Resolved? An Empirical Examination of the Adjudication and Settlement of Patent Disputes," 84 *Wash. U.L. Rev.* 237, 273–74 (2006) (in a study including 5,071 infringement cases with identified outcomes, 66% ended in settlements, dismissals or consent judgments, while only 13 percent were decided on the merits).

the vendor because there was no final judgment of infringement.[43] While there may be negotiation as to whether the vendor pays the cost of settlement, the customer may conclude that payment is a better option than continuing to sustain the risks and burdens of ongoing litigation, even if the customer believes that the claim lacks merit. This will be particularly likely if the potential risks are great enough to require disclosure to investors.

One has also seen the development of gamesmanship regarding the interpretation of indemnity clauses when a claim is actually made. In a recent case, the customer/licensee received a letter claiming that the licensed technology infringed a series of patents.[44] The customer duly provided prompt written notice of the claim to the vendor. The vendor responded that its indemnification clause required there to be a "claim," which the vendor interpreted as requiring a lawsuit to have been filed.[45] The customer was then in the position of deciding whether to provoke a lawsuit in hopes of receiving indemnification or to settle without a lawsuit, typically for less than the matter could be settled after a lawsuit was filed.[46]

A final problem frequently encountered — but seldom resolved — concerns "mixed" technology. The typical indemnification clause will exclude the combination of the licensed technology with other technology not supplied by the vendor.[47] In contrast, the typical patent, if artfully drafted, will include claims not only for a core invention but also for the combination of the core invention with all the applications and product configurations that the patent drafter can imagine. Furthermore, many of the most important licenses concern "platform" technologies that, by their nature, are intended both to interoperate with technologies from other vendors and to provide a basis on

---

[43] The risk-benefit calculus could shift in the direction of litigation if the indemnitor is paying the cost of defense, but this will not be the case if indemnity only covers a final judgment.

[44] This itself was somewhat unusual — it is more common to receive a letter putting one on notice of a patent and offering a license, without actually claiming infringement.

[45] This position seems directly contradicted by the court's decision in *R. Bradley Maule v. Philadelphia Media Holdings, LLC, et al.*, No. 08-3357, 2010 U.S. Dist. LEXIS 23635 (E.D. Pa. March 15, 2010). *See* Appendix A.

[46] The recent cases of *Southern California Gas Co. v. Syntellect, Inc.*, No. 08cv941 BEN (NLS), 2011 U.S. Dist. LEXIS 33373 (S.D. Cal. March 28, 2011) and *Olaes Enters., Inc. v. A.D. Sutton & Sons, Inc.*, No. 09 Civ. 8680 (CM)(PED), 2011 U.S. Dist. LEXIS 67737 (S.D.N.Y. June 20, 2011) suggest that narrow readings of indemnity provisions may not be favored by courts if the indemnitee chooses to bring a claim against the sophisticated indemnitor. See the summary of these cases in Appendix A.

[47] See Appendix B, Example 7.

which the licensee can build its own applications and solutions. In this context, the exclusion of indemnity liability for all but the bare thing licensed becomes an exception that consumes the rule; virtually every infringement claim will involve such combinations that will be excluded from the scope of indemnification. Thus, the "check the box" mentality applied by many technology consumers — while draconian in its approach to total liability — often completely fails to realize that, in practice, its blanket indemnity will be washed out by its use of the licensed technology in combination with both its own additions and technology from other vendors.

In summary, current IP indemnification practices tend to advance appearance over reality. A more nuanced approach could both reduce transaction expenses and lead to a more realistic approach to infringement risks. There are some alternatives.

IV. A better approach[48]

Devising a solution to these dilemmas should begin with the consideration of what is actually at stake. Rather than thinking of intellectual property as an undifferentiated lump — "IP" — it is helpful to remind ourselves that "IP" comes in a variety of flavors, and each of them has unique characteristics that suggest different approaches to warranties and indemnification. One should also consider what arrangement would minimize the aggregate cost of the infringement risk.[49] Finally, we need to ask what arrangement is most likely to promote innovation and deployment of new technologies, which, after all, is the crux of intellectual property protection.

A full or even partial analysis of these issues is far beyond the scope of this paper, but the general issues are worth considering. It is fair to say that the current regime, focusing as it does on a crude mixture of moralizing ("Won't you stand behind your product?") and bargaining power ("Take it without an

---

[48] Robert E. Rudnick and Andrew M. Grodin review most of the clauses that can be considered from the standpoint of a technology vendor to mitigate its indemnification liability in "Drafting and Negotiating Defense and Indemnification Provisions," *Intell. Prop. Litig.* (Spring 2010), 9–12.

[49] This question lands one squarely in the middle of a complex question of law and economics, famously articulated by Calabrese and Melamed in the context of tort liability. Guido Calabresi, *The Costs of Accidents: A Legal and Economic Analysis* (Yale University Press, 1970); G. Calabresi and A. D. Melamed, "Property Rules, Liability Rules, and Inalienability: One View of the Cathedral," 85 *Harvard Law Review* 1089 (1972).

indemnity or find another product"), fails utterly to address these important questions.[50]

We now propose to apply these considerations to each species of intellectual property.

A. Trade secrets

First, consider trade secrets. Trade secrets can attach to any form of technology, from industrial methods to chemical formulas and computer software. To be protected as a trade secret, something must be actually maintained in secrecy and confidence, and it must be disclosed only to persons who have agreed to hold it in secrecy and confidence.[51] To misappropriate a trade secret, one must have either accessed it through improper means or violated an express or implied agreement to hold it in confidence. For these reasons, violation of trade secret rights cannot happen by accident, and it is reasonable to expect a technology vendor to have adopted policies and procedures that will keep track of its trade secret obligations and guard against misappropriation.

Furthermore, to the extent that trade secret misappropriation is a form of tort, it is possible to obtain insurance against liability that arises from employees' commission of such torts. The insurance would include limits on liability but would serve to mitigate — at least in part — the risk of indemnity liability to one's customers.[52] Finally, a licensee of technology misappropriated from a third party would have no liability to the third party unless the licensee continued to use it, without justification, after receiving notice of the

---

50 *Owens-Illinois, Inc. v. BTR plc*, No. 05 Civ. 2873 (LLS), 2010 U.S. Dist. LEXIS 64813 (S.D.N.Y. June 28, 2010) is an example of a case in which the court interpreted the scope of an indemnification provision in part in reliance on the economics of the situation, reasoning that the indemnity should not attach to a class of products sold after an acquisition when the acquirer was in a position to reap all the benefits of the sale. See Appendix A.

51 18 U.S.C. §1839.

52 See Kenneth J. Vanko, "Does a Trade Secrets Defendant Have Insurance Coverage?," http://www.non-competes.com/2011/08/does-trade-secrets-defendant-have.html (Aug. 18, 2011); Drew E. Pomerance, "Trade Secret Insurance," *California Lawyer*, Nov. 1999, http://callawyer.com/cleStory.cfm?qVersionID=184&eid=261413&evid=1 (insurance coverage for alleged trade secret misappropriation may exist in advertising injury provision of a comprehensive general liability policy).

misappropriation. Even in this case, damages would be limited to the period of use following notice.[53]

From the standpoint of cost and risk minimization, these factors generally support the conclusion that the risk of liability should fall primarily on the technology vendor. The vendor is in a position to reduce the risk by implementing practices and procedures designed to avoid trade secret misappropriation. The customer, on the other hand, is not in a position to mitigate the risk and must necessarily rely on the vendor to do so. Furthermore, the implicit cost to the vendor to provide indemnity against trade secret misappropriation claims is likely to be minimal, since the customer would have no liability until it is actually on notice that it is using infringing materials. From the standpoint of innovation, the marginal additional risk of indemnification liability could, in theory, chill innovation by the vendor. This, however, is likely outweighed by the comfort it provides to the customer and the low risk of actual liability requiring indemnification, both of which factors, in turn, facilitate the deployment of new technologies.

For all these reasons, there is a strong case that imposing some degree of indemnification liability on technology vendors for liability arising from misappropriation of trade secrets is reasonable because it will neither impose risks that the vendors cannot mitigate nor chill the creation and deployment of new technologies. Whether the indemnification liability ought to be capped and — if capped — at what level ought to reflect the relative sizes of the parties and their bargaining power in a negotiation.

B. Copyright

Copyright has some but not all of the characteristics of trade secret liability. Like trade secrets, copyright infringement requires the infringer to do something that the infringer can ordinarily identify as wrongful or possibly wrongful: copying, distributing, displaying, or performing somebody else's work without their permission. There are greyer areas here than in trade secret misappropriation, which include unconscious copying,[54] the creation of

---

[53] See, e.g., *FMC Corp. v. Spurlin*, 596 F. Supp. 609, 616 n. 18 (W.D.P.A. 1984) (citing Restatement of Torts §758 (1939)); *Vantage Point, Inc. v. Parker Bros., Inc.*, 529 F. Supp. 1204, 1210 n. 2 (E.D.N.Y. 1981); *IMED Corp. v. Systems Engineering Assoc. Corp.*, 602 So. 2d 344, 349 (Alabama 1992).

[54] *Bright Tunes Music Corp. v. Harrisongs Music, Ltd.*, 420 F. Supp. 177 (S.D.N.Y. 1976) (finding copyright infringement even though copying may have been subconscious).

works that are "substantially similar" to the original,[55] or the differentiation between idea and expression.[56] Nevertheless, the creative process will usually raise sufficient red flags in the minds of knowledgeable creators that they should know when to seek competent advice about what they may or may not do consistent with their copyright obligations. In addition, as already noted above, copyright provides no remedy for the mere use of a copyrighted work.

For this reason, a person who believes that a product has infringed his or her copyright is less likely to bring an action against ultimate users of the infringing work. Copyright law provides more draconian remedies than trade secret law, including statutory damages and attorneys' fees liability.[57] These, however, are reserved for cases of willful infringement and, therefore, can be mitigated by the technology vendor by policies prohibiting unauthorized copying, clean rooms and other actions within the vendor's control.[58]

In conclusion, some level of indemnity protection in copyright claims can also be justified for reasons very similar to those applicable to trade secrets. The vendor is in a position to mitigate the risk, the additional indemnification liability is probably marginal, and the comfort provided to end-users by the indemnity promotes technological deployment.

---

[55] *Selle v. Gibb*, 741 F.2d 896, 900 (7th Cir. 1984)(proving copyright infringement includes proof of substantial degree of similarity between the two works).

[56] *Nichols v. Universal Pictures Corp.*, 45 F.2d 119 (2d Cir. 1930) (determining protectable and nonprotectable portions of a play).

[57] Compare 17 U.S.C. §504 (allowing actual damages, lost profits, statutory damages as much as $30,000, as well as additional damages of twice the relevant license fees for the relevant year in certain circumstances) with U.T.S.A §3 (limiting damages to actual loss and unjust enrichment related to the misappropriation and exemplary damages not to exceed twice the award for actual loss in cases of willful and malicious misappropriation). Also compare 17 U.S.C. §505, which allows the court to assign reasonable attorney's fees at its discretion with U.T.S.A. §104, which requires bad faith or willful and malicious misappropriation before attorney's fees may be awarded.

[58] *See* 17 U.S.C. §504(c)(2) (permitting a court to increase statutory damage awards on evidence of willful infringement and reduce statutory damages where an infringer proves that he or she "was not aware and had no reason to believe that his or her acts constituted an infringement of copyright."); *Fitzgerald Pub. Co. v. Baylor Pub. Co.*, 807 F.2d 1110, 1114-17 (2d Cir. 1986) (discussing the "innocent infringer" defense as a means to reduce statutory damages).

C. Patents

1. Claims under patents known to the vendor

Patents inhabit a completely different property right and liability terrain. Most fundamentally, patents can be infringed unwittingly by a person who developed and sold a product in complete ignorance of the patentee's claims. By contrast, accidental infringement of a trade secret is impossible, and unconscious infringement of a copyright at least requires prior access to the infringed work[59] and can be completely avoided by "clean room" techniques.[60]

One must, therefore, begin by making a distinction between known and unknown patents. If the vendor is aware of the potential infringement claim, it may be in a position to mitigate the risk, whether through workaround solutions, licensing, or litigation. The vendor may also be able to reduce risk through the acquisition of defensive patents, although this would provide no benefit in the case of claims by nonpracticing entities ("trolls"). The possibility of mitigation should not, however, be overstated. Patent claims are notoriously difficult to interpret, and therefore, even for known patents, it is not always possible to avoid infringement with any degree of certainty.

To the extent that there is an unmitigable degree of risk of infringement, even for known patents, that risk must be multiplied by the damages that could be sustained (and indemnified) if the risk materializes. Unlike copyright, patent rights permit the patentee to prevent others from using or practicing the claimed invention. Furthermore, as discussed above, patentees are often motivated to bring infringement actions against end-users, particularly when the end-users are larger than the technology vendors and have less incentive to challenge the infringement claim or the validity of the underlying patent. The measure of damages in actions brought against an

---

[59] See, e.g., *Bright Tunes Music Corp. v. Harrisongs Music,* Ltd., 420 F.Supp. 177 (1976).

[60] See, e.g., *NEC Corp. v. Intel Corp.,* No. C-84-20799-WPG, at *44–*45 1989 U.S. Dist. LEXIS 1409 (N.D.CA Feb. 6, 1989) (use of clean room indicated that "copying clearly was not involved" in development of code sequence and that similarities were more likely the result of the use of the same product constraints); but see *Cadence Design Sys. v. Avant! Corp.,* 125 F.3d 824, 830–31 (9th Cir. 1997) (lower court erred in finding that clean room procedures "did not appear to be sufficient" but failing to determine whether these procedures were infringing or merited the issuance of a preliminary injunction). Clean room development is discussed in: *Sega Enterprises Ltd. v. Accolade, Inc.,* 977 F.2d 1510, 1526 (9th Cir. 1992); *Eng'g Dynamics Inc. v. Structural Software Inc.,* 89-1655, 1992 WL 409251 (E.D. La. Apr. 8, 1992) (clean room evidence relevant to the "access" prong of the infringement test).

end-user can be based on its size, revenues, and scope of use. As a result, it will bear no relationship to the size and resources of the technology vendors.[61] For these reasons, the measure of damages in patent infringement cases has a multiplier effect on the risk assumed by technology vendors via their indemnification obligations. This inevitably chills innovation by increasing its effective cost.

The fact that damages can be measured by the size of the user rather than the size of the vendor also implies that it is difficult to create a pricing model by which the vendor assumes the risk of infringement liability but shares the risk with its end users. Such a model would require the price to vary with the scope of the end user's use. This may be feasible for some products such as software licensed on a per-user or enterprise basis. In contract, the price per unit is never linked to the customer's size or the scope of the customer's use for other products such as hardware and other equipment items; at most, there may be an indirect relationship between the number of units purchased and the customer's size. Perpetual and "all you can eat" licenses are quite common, and their license fees bear no relationship to the size of the user or the scope of its use.

Furthermore, the vendor who attempts to defray its risk via pricing will be at a price disadvantage in comparison with competitors who are willing to absorb the risk. For these reasons, most technology vendors are not in a position to use pricing to spread the risk among all users of their technology. These factors create a particular disadvantage for the smaller or newer technology vendor since its larger or more established competitors might, by reason of their size, be able to accept the risk, and, by reason of their use of older technologies and command of a large defensive patent portfolio of their own, might actually be facing a much smaller risk.

A further complication present in the case of patents but absent from copyright and trade secret infringement issues concerns combinations of a sold or licensed device with third-party technology. If a person uses a product purchased or licensed from one vendor in combination with products purchased or licensed from other vendors, it is virtually impossible to imagine scenarios in which the combination would increase the risk of a third-party

---

[61] See *Georgia-Pacific Corp. v. United States Plywood Corp.*, 318 F. Supp. 1116, 1120 (S.D. N.Y. 1970) (factors for determining a reasonable royalty include, inter alia: the nature and scope of the license, commercial relationship between the parties, how the infringer uses the patented invention, portion of the infringer's realizable profit that should be credited to the invention).

trade secret or copyright infringement claim regarding the first vendor's product. By contrast, patent claims often cover systems and methods that encompass technology, products or services sourced from multiple vendors. The end-user of such a combined system would be liable for infringement, but the component vendors could also be liable on theories of inducement or contributory infringement.[62] If, as is often the case, the vendor of a component excludes indemnity for the combination of its product with other components, then the end-user, who may be using each component exactly as intended by the multiple vendors, may be left with no recourse. This result is difficult to justify since the end-user is not in a position either to mitigate the risk by workarounds or to defray it over the entire class of intended users via a pricing model.

On the other hand, if the vendor provides indemnification for combinations, its infringement risk will increase dramatically. This increases the cost of, and provides a disincentive for, innovation. In principle, it should be possible for a vendor to build the cost of indemnification into its price. In practice, however, this is rarely done. Furthermore, for the reasons described above, these factors tend to disadvantage the smaller vendor with newer technology, whose infringement risk is necessarily greater.

Despite these issues, one can make a reasoned case for technology vendors to assume indemnification liability with respect to patent claims based on patents known to the technology vendor. This may also apply to those claims concerning combinations of the technology vendor's technology with technologies sourced from third parties that fall within a range of use anticipated and intended by the vendor. For such claims, the vendor's ability to mitigate the risk and — at least theoretically — defray it through pricing may outweigh the marginal negative impact on innovation.[63]

---

[62] See *Akamai Techs., Inc. v. Limelight Networks, Inc.*, 692 F.3d 1301 (Fed. Cir. 2012) (induced infringement can be found when multiple parties enact separate steps of a method patent); *Centillion Data Sys., LLC. v. Qwest Communs. Int'l*, 631 F.3d 1279, 1285 (Fed. Cir. 2011) (customers' access requests of automated billing system constituted is an infringing use "as a matter of law"). But see *Quanta Computer, Inc. v. LG Electronics, Inc.*, 128 S. Ct. 2109 (2008) (doctrine of exhaustion applied to find no infringement when the method claim of a patent was substantially embodied in the components sold by the patent licensee).

[63] Some mitigation of the chilling effect of the indemnity liability might be found in caps on the indemnity liability, which would provide some protection against bankrupting the vendor, with consequent loss of its technology to the marketplace as a whole.

2. Claims under patents unknown to the vendor

A second — and in many cases, much larger — class of possible patent infringement claims arise from patents that are unknown to the vendor. One can subdivide this class into patents that are discoverable in principle and those that cannot be discovered through any effort of diligence. Unless the patent applicant authorizes earlier publication, patent applications remain secret for eighteen months from the date of application,[64] This period of confidentiality can be longer if the patentee is not seeking protection outside the United States. For this reason, even the most thorough and expensive "freedom to operate" search provides no guard against patents that are published after the search has been performed.

In regard to published applications and issued patents, it is theoretically possible to conduct a "freedom to operate" study that identifies potentially troublesome patents and patent applications. However, these studies are rarely performed for many compelling reasons. They can be extremely expensive. Depending on how densely patented the subject field of invention is, these searches could easily identify hundreds of possibly relevant patents and patent applications, each with multiple independent and dependent claims. The searches place the vendor on notice of all the identified patents,[65] which creates a risk of willful infringement with its concomitant risk of up to treble damages if the vendor is found later to have infringed one of the patents. This implies, in turn, a need to review each claim in each patent, which is a daunting and very expensive undertaking.

Furthermore, the results are inherently uncertain. Unpublished patents and patent applications may not be considered; the claims that will ultimately be issued on published patent applications cannot be known in advance. Even the interpretation and validity of their issued patents' claims is a highly subjective undertaking.

For these reasons, risk mitigation through workarounds or anticipatory licensing is not possible in those cases concerning patents unknown to the

---

[64] 35 U.S.C. §122; See also "Changes to Implement Eighteen-Month Publication of Patent Applications," 65 FR 57024-01 (2000).

[65] In general, a client will be deemed to be on notice of the patents its counsel uncovers in the course of such a search. See *In re* Seagate Tech., LLC, 497 F.3d 1360, 1371 (Fed. Cir. 2007) (willful infringement requires "that the infringer acted despite an objectively high likelihood that its actions constituted infringement of a valid patent" and the risk was "known or so obvious that it should have been known to the accused infringer.").

vendor. To an increasing extent, both vendors and technology consumers are therefore seeking more indirect means of mitigating their risk.

Some choose to mitigate risk by building or acquiring extensive patent portfolios.[66] Such portfolios provide some defensive strength against patent claims brought by operating companies, which may be exposed to infringement risk themselves, but they provide no protection against trolls. This strategy is very costly, with the acquisition price for large portfolios extending into the billions of dollars[67] and the cost of building large portfolios easily reaching into the many hundreds of thousands of dollars, which is far beyond the reach of smaller innovators.

A second growing strategy is to participate in patent pooling arrangements.[68] Acquiring a nonexclusive license from the pool eliminates the risk of infringing a patent within the pool. Depending on the nature of the pool, it may further provide some deterrent against an infringement action from an operating entity against participants in the pool.[69] Participation in the pool provides little protection against claims by nonoperating claimants, who have no need for the patents included in the pool.

---

[66] See, e.g., Oliver Herzfield, "Yahoo's Patent Litigation Plan Backfires," Forbes (May 7, 2012) http://www.forbes.com/sites/oliverherzfeld/2012/05/07/yahoos-patent-litigation-plan-backfires/ (Facebook's acquisition of over 750 patents from IBM, Phillips, and other sources was intended to support its infringement counterclaims in a 2012 lawsuit with Yahoo); Jia Lynn Yang, "Google Seeks to Buy Motorola Wireless," Washington Post, Aug. 16, 2011, A09 (Google's $12.5 billion acquisition of Motorola Mobility thought to be primarily driven by Motorola's more than 17,000 wireless technology patents); Andrew Pollack, "Medtronic to Pay $1.35 Billion to Inventor," *New York Times*, Apr. 23, 2005, C2 (Medtronic paid $800 million to acquire a patent portfolio in addition to $550 million to settle an infringement suit with the inventor).

[67] For example, Microsoft paid over $1.1 billion to acquire 800 patents and 300 licenses from AOL in a deal that analysts anticipated would close at $300 million. Thorold Barker, "Microsoft Goes Shopping at AOL," *Wall Street Journal*, Apr. 10, 2012, C10. Two weeks later, Microsoft would sell 650 of those patents to Facebook for $550 million. Jessica Guynn, "Facebook Buys AOL Patents from Microsoft for $550 Million," *LA Times*, http://articles.latimes.com/2012/apr/23/business/la-fi-tn-facebook-buys-aol-patents-from-microsoft-for-550-million-20120423 (Apr. 23, 2012).

[68] One might think of patent pools as a poor man's portfolio.

[69] Enforcement of pools of patents against nonparticipants raises antitrust concerns that are not pertinent to individually owned portfolios. See, e.g., Gilbert, "Antitrust for Patent Pools: A Century of Policy Evolution," http://elsa.berkeley.edu/users/gilbert/wp/patent_pools100302.pdf.

There is also the possibility of insurance. Insurance policies that provide limited coverage against infringement risk are available, and such policies can be written to include indemnification liability.[70] These policies can, however, be costly, and they will always include a retained or co-insurance amount and a liability cap.[71] No technology vendor's insurer would write the policy with uncapped indemnity liability for patent infringement claims.

In short, no current approach — not indemnification, not patent pooling nor insurance — effectively addresses the risks associated with claims under patents that are known neither to the technology vendor nor to the technology consumer. Infringement indemnification for such claims burdens the vendor without offering a means to mitigate its risk or spread it among the users of the technology. Building and acquiring patent portfolios is a strategy for large, well-heeled vendors and consumers that is rarely available for the smaller technology innovator or user. Patent pools provide limited risk mitigation and are more likely to be available to smaller players. However, they provide no protection against nonoperating entities while, at best, providing compromised defensive protection against operating entities. Finally, insurance is limited and expensive.

D. Patent infringement liability and *force majeure*

So far, we have considered the patent indemnification issue in terms of which party — the vendor or consumer — ought to bear the risk of unforeseen and unforeseeable patent infringement liability? There is, however, another model that is very accepted in commercial transactions, namely, events of "*force majeure.*"[72]

---

[70] Kim Cauthom, Tom Britven, & Tamara Turek, "Sharing the Risk: Patent Infringement Liability Indemnification and Insurance," *Intell. Prop. Litig.* (Spring 2010), 13–16.

[71] Id. Premiums can range from one to ten percent of the insured amount per year. Id.

[72] Here is a fairly typical example of a *force majeure* clause:

> No party shall be liable or responsible to the other party, nor be deemed to have defaulted under or breached this Agreement, for any failure or delay in fulfilling or performing any term of this Agreement, when and to the extent such failure or delay is caused by or results from acts beyond the affected party's reasonable control, including, without limitation: (a) acts of God; (b) flood, fire, earthquake or explosion; (c) war, invasion, hostilities (whether war is declared or not), terrorist threats or acts, riot or other civil unrest; (d) government order or law; (e) actions, embargoes or blockades in effect on or after the date of this Agreement; (f) action by any governmental authority; (g) national or regional emergency; and (h) strikes, labor stoppages or slowdowns or other industrial disturbances (collectively, a "Force Majeure Event").

For all the reasons discussed above, there can be little question that claims under patents unknown to either vendor or customer are beyond the reasonable control of either contracting party. Furthermore, a patent issued to a third party is indisputably the act of a governmental authority that prevents both parties from practicing the patented invention without the consent of the patentee. On their face, such patent claims are therefore events of *force majeure* that are beyond the control of either party and, therefore, ought to excuse both parties' performance.[73] If one applied the *force majeure* clause to such claims, both parties would bear the risk of infringement liability.

In practice, this question seldom arises because many contracts contain both a *force majeure* provision and a patent indemnification clause. In such cases, it seems likely that the *force majeure* clause would not impact the indemnification obligation because the government's grant of patent does not preclude performance of the indemnity obligation. It is worth asking, however, why patent infringement beyond both parties' control should be treated differently than other events (earthquake, hurricane, other government action, etc.) that are equally beyond both parties' control.

Force majeure clauses likely gained popularity to mitigate the harshness of the common law rule that an unconditional contractual obligation to do something is not excused by impossibility of performance if the obligor could have added an exculpatory clause.[74] However, even within common law, a range of events excuse performance even if the contract does not specifically enumerate them. These include, for example, the death or disability of a person whose performance was contracted for,[75] destruction, through no fault of the obligor, of a thing necessary for performance,[76] or—most relevantly—domestic governmental action that precludes performance.[77] The last of these rules rests on the proposition that "[t]he law does not require [a party] to disobey the law; and the state does not penalize him for yielding to its own commands."[78] In cases of such discharge, the risk of nonperformance

---

[73] Carefully drafted force majeure clauses address the effect of an event of *force majeure* in more detail. For example, in a contract for sale of goods the seller's obligation to pay should be excused if delivery of the goods is prevented by embargo, even though the embargo did not prevent payment.

[74] See E. Farnsworth, *Contracts* (4th ed., 2004), sec. 9.6 (hereinafter, *"Farnsworth"*).

[75] A. Corbin, *Corbin on Contracts* (1952), sec. 1334 (hereinafter, *"Corbin"); Farnsworth,* Sec. 9.5.

[76] *Farnsworth,* sec. 9.5; *Corbin,* secs. 1337, 1338, 1339.

[77] *Corbin,* 1343.

[78] Id.

falls on the obligee, while the obligor is subject to a duty of restitution for payment made prior to destruction of the necessary thing or other act creating impossibility.[79]

One might question whether the grant of a patent is equivalent to other government edicts prohibiting performance.[80] In principle, the patent holder can grant licenses permitting performance. In some cases, however, the patent holder may refuse to grant a license or conditions the license on terms that render performance impracticable or unprofitable. In these cases, performance will be rendered impossible without violating the law. If a license is available, the traditional common law rule states that the increased expense of obtaining the license will not discharge the obligation to perform.[81] However, more recent cases and the Commentary to UCC Sec. 2-615 have admitted the possibility that an extreme cost increase could justify nonperformance.[82]

Determining whether risks excuse an obligation is not easy. As Corbin observes, "the court must be alert to weigh any evidence to show a custom throwing the risk upon one party rather than the other, or to show that there was a mutual contemplation of its being borne by one of them."[83] A key factor is whether facts making performance more difficult or expensive "are such as are commonly foreseeable and in contemplation."[84] As Corbin observed, "[w]here neither custom nor agreement determines the allocation of risk, the court must exercise its equity powers and pray for the wisdom of Solomon."[85] To quote Farnsworth, "[t]he new synthesis candidly recognizes that the judicial function is to determine whether, in the light of exceptional

---

79 *Corbin,* Section 1337. As Corbin notes, either party can agree to assume the risk by promising indemnity. Id. The question, for our purposes, however, is whether it is reasonable to assume such a risk in the case of unforeseen or unforeseeable patent infringement.

80 One might argue a difference in that patent law provides only a private remedy for infringement: the state does not make patent infringement (unlike copyright infringement or trade secret misappropriation) a crime. But this seems a distinction without a difference: in either case, it is an act of state — the granting of a patent — that transforms otherwise lawful behavior into behavior that is subject to sometimes very onerous state-enforced sanctions in the form of injunctions and damages, which may even be trebled to punish willful infringement.

81 *Corbin,* sec. 1333.

82 *Farnsworth,* 9.6.

83 Corbin, Section 1333.

84 Id.

85 Id.

circumstances, justice requires a departure from the general rule that a promisor bears the risk of increased difficulty of performance."[86]

We do not consider what a court would hold in a case concerning a contract silent on the patent infringement issue, which rarely occurs in modern-day contracts. We do, however, consider whether it makes more sense to treat unforeseen and unforeseeable patent infringement liability by analogy to the *force majeure* model — in which parties typically expand the common law range of risks that excuse performance — rather than relying on the UCC Article 2 indemnification model. It seems that for such claims, *force majeure* makes much more sense.

As we have seen, the UCC's implied warranty of non-infringement,[87] and its sequelae in the contractual indemnification against unknowable infringement risks, rose in the context of a very different patent liability context. The Official Comment to Section 2-312 is instructive:[88]

> When the goods are part of the seller's normal stock, and are sold in the normal course of business, it is the seller's duty to see that no claim of infringement of a patent or trademark by a third party will impair the buyer's title.

The drafters of Article 2 thus understood patent infringement as a defect in title. There are, however, radical differences between infringement and title. Confirming title to chattels is relatively simple partly due to Section 2-403(1) of the UCC, which provides that a person with voidable title transfers good title to a good faith purchaser for value. Thus, if the seller purchased the chattel in good faith, he need look no further to confirm his good title to the chattel. By contrast, the good faith purchase of an infringing product provides no

---

[86] *Farnsworth*, sec. 9.6. Farnsworth proceeds to list four criteria: whether performance as agreed was rendered impracticable; whether the nonoccurrence of the event was "a basic assumption on which the contract was made"; whether the event was without the fault of the obligor; and whether the obligor has not assumed a greater obligation than the law imposes. Id. The second and fourth of these criteria would certainly not apply in the case of a contract in which the vendor agreed to indemnify for patent infringement. Our question, though, is not whether such indemnity should be enforced, but whether it is reasonable to agree to it in the first place, or whether the risk of unforeseen infringement ought more properly to be addressed in a *force majeure* clause.

[87] See text at note 4 above.

[88] UCC Sec. 2-312 (Official Comment 4).

protection against infringement liability.[89] Conversely, the good faith purchaser undoubtedly acquires good title, notwithstanding the risk of infringement. In short, infringement and title are two completely different concepts.

The Article 2 drafters also failed to appreciate the impossibility of determining whether goods are infringing. It is highly unlikely that a merchant such as Home Depot, Best Buy, NewEgg, or Amazon would diligently conduct "freedom to operate" studies on all the products on their shelves. Article 2 imposes an impossible warranty obligation on them, which naturally leads to indemnification demands against their suppliers. However, their suppliers are, as we have seen, equally unable to conduct the UCC's prescribed noninfringement diligence.

The very imperfect analogy between infringement and title might have been inconsequential at a time of slower technological development when patent infringement claims against end-users were rare, and patent infringement damages were limited.[90] However, things have changed markedly since Article 2 was first drafted and since its implied warranty of noninfringement morphed into a standard noninfringement indemnification. The pace of technological development has accelerated to the point where the "blind spot" between patent application filing and publication or issuance may include multiple product cycles. The range of patentable inventions has dramatically expanded. Furthermore, perhaps most importantly, the damage awards for patent infringement have multiplied.[91]

In this context, Farnsworth's comment that "the judicial function is to determine whether, in the light of exceptional circumstances, justice requires a departure from the general rule that a promisor bears the risk of increased difficulty of performance"[92] becomes directly relevant. If Section 2-312 of the UCC had been a contract at the time of its adoption, it would be reasonable for a court to conclude that the enormous changes in technology,

---

[89] Good faith purchase could, however, negate a claim for damages for willful infringement. See *SRI Int'l, Inc. v. Advanced Tech. Labs., Inc.*, 127 F.3d 1462, 1466-67 (Fed. Cir. 1997) ("the primary consideration [for willful infringement] is whether the infringer, acting in good faith and upon due inquiry, had sound reason to believe that it had the right to act in the manner that was found to be infringing."); *Paper Converting Machine Co. v. Magna-Graphics Corp.*, 745 F.2d 11, 20 (Fed. Cir. 1984) ("An increase in damages for willfulness . . . is generally inappropriate when the infringer mounts a good faith and substantial challenge to the existence of infringement.").

[90] See text at notes 22 to 25 above.

[91] See text at notes 26 to 31 above.

[92] See supra note 82 and accompanying text.

patentability and patent damages since its adoption represented exactly the kind of "exceptional circumstances" that would excuse the seller from its noninfringement warranty.

This result can be achieved privately by a simple disclaimer, supplemented by a *force majeure* clause that addresses unforeseen patent claims alongside other events that are beyond the reasonable control of either party. It may be worth noting that a distinction must be made between unusual or unforeseeable events, on the one hand, and foreseeable but unavoidable events, on the other. If one lives in an earthquake zone, one can foresee that an earthquake will likely occur, but one cannot predict exactly when or where. Similarly, for many industries in the current environment, all parties understand that patent infringement claims have a substantial probability of occurring. The problem is that it is not possible to predict exactly when and where these will occur. As a result, neither party in a transaction can position to mitigate the risk. Making matters worse, protective steps to mitigate infringement risk, such as a freedom-to-operate study, may actually increase the risk by placing one party on notice of potential claims and, therefore, subject to enhanced damage awards for willful infringement. In new areas of technology development, it becomes particularly difficult to mitigate risk, and patent infringement claims occur more frequently. Neither party can predict the nature of these claims or methods to avoid them.

If lawyers use the *force majeure* model as a starting point for discussion instead of Article 2's defect in title paradigm, negotiations can proceed in a far more positive direction. By definition, a *force majeure* event can be neither prevented nor avoided, and the risk falls randomly on either or both parties to a transaction. At the same time, *force majeure* clauses can create a framework in which each party helps to mitigate both its own and the other party's risk. It is very common, for example, for a *force majeure* clause to place some burden on the party seeking to excuse its performance to give prompt notice to the other party and to take steps to minimize, if possible, the impact of the *force majeure* event. The clause might, for example, require the technology vendor to attempt in good faith to obtain a license for some period of time following the claim and to refund either all or a *pro rata* portion of what had been paid if the license was not available on commercially reasonable terms.[93]

---

[93] By analogy to the common law of impossibility, when performance is excused by reason of illegality or other legally recognized frustrations of purpose, the party excused is ordinarily required to grant restitution to the other party. *Corbin*, Section 1478.

Thrusting the infringement risk on both parties would have other desirable effects as well. It would encourage both vendors and their customers to pursue insurance as a means of mitigating the risk, exactly as is done for events such as earthquakes and hurricanes.[94] If insurance against patent infringement claims were more widely accepted, and if the insurance were purchased by both vendors and consumers of technology, one can expect that the cost of such insurance would decline, just as the cost of health insurance is driven down if everyone, including healthy people, pays into the insurance pool. Furthermore, insurers are in the business of assessing risk and, in comparison with individual vendors or their customers, are in a far better position both to price the risk and to spread it among the population of people who could be sued.

One can also imagine the development of other models for risk mitigation if vendors and their customers accept that the indemnity is not working and that something better needs to be found. Vendors and their customers could create and pay into patent defense pools that would be available if a claim is made respecting the relevant technology. This would, in effect, create a mutual insurance company for the technology in circumstances in which ordinary insurance policies are either unavailable or prohibitively expensive. The securities markets, which are currently starved for credible investments, might also be tapped.[95] The scale of damages and expenses in patent

---

[94] At a more ambitious level, one might imagine a vendor and its customers paying into a patent defense pool that would be available to be tapped if a claim is made respecting the relevant technology. This would, in effect, create a mutual insurance company for the technology in circumstances in which ordinary insurance policies are either unavailable or prohibitively expensive.

[95] Due to the accelerating pace of weather-related disasters, there is an expanding market in insurance-linked securities, specifically targeting the "catastrophe bond market." See, e.g., "Swiss Re, Insurance-linked Securities Market Update" (July 2011), available at http://media.swissre.com/documents/ILS_Market_Update_July_2011.pdf; "Swiss Re Launches the First Catastrophe Bond Indices, Press Release" (June 28, 2007), available at: http://www.swissre.com/media/news_releases/swiss_re_launches_the_first_catastrophe_bond_indices.html. Some $3.8 billion was invested in insurance-linked securities during the first half of 2012 alone. "Swiss Re, Insurance-linked Securities Market Update" (July 2012) available at: http://media.swissre.com/documents/ILS_Market_Update_public_Version_F.pdf.

litigation,[96] and the correlative amounts that people would be willing to pay to insure against the risk, could easily support a market in insurance and insurance-linked securities. This market would require the parties to understand that indemnification clauses provide a false sense of security in many cases and are not equivalent to real policies of insurance.

Any or all of these initiatives would diminish the chilling effect that indemnity liability can have on vendors who wish to deploy new and innovative technologies, and would also diminish the chilling effect that the risk of patent liability has on technology consumers who would otherwise want to deploy innovation. They all depend, however, on a recognition that the indemnification model is not providing an effective solution.

Depending on the circumstances of the case, other arrangements might depart from the *force majeure* default setting. A vendor who puts a high priority on controlling the patent landscape for its field might choose to offer indemnification to ensure control in litigation over any patent that touches the vendor's core technology. On the other hand, a large technology customer using technology licensed from small vendors could conclude that funding and controlling the defense of infringement litigation serves its interests better since the vendors will not be able to offer an adequate defense.

Whereas it is undisputed that many technology consumers will nevertheless demand indemnity for unforeseen and foreseeable patent infringement, it is unclear whether this negotiation position serves these consumers' interest. The net effect of the indemnification can be to cripple or even extinguish the vendor if a claim is made. If the technology is important to the customer's business, keeping the vendor in business could have a much higher value than bringing an unsecured claim for damages in the vendor's bankruptcy proceeding. Particularly in cases in which the customer is much larger than

---

[96] These costs are likely to expand with the increase in suits brought by nonpracticing entities. Patent troll suits rose from 22 percent of patent infringement claims in 2007 to make up nearly 40 percent in 2011. Sara Jeuss, Robin Feldman, & Joshua Walker, "The America Invents Act 500: Effects of Patent Monetization Entities on Litigation," 11 Duke L. & Tech. Rev. (2012) 357, 377–78. In general, troll suits last longer and involve higher damage awards than suits brought by practicing entities. A 2011 Pricewaterhouse Coopers report places the median damage award in nonpracticing entity suits between 1995 and 2011 at $8 million, with an average length of 2.55 years. Chris Barry et al, "Pricewaterhouse Coopers, 2012 Patent Litigation Study 25" (2012), available at http://www.pwc.com/en_US/us/forensic-services/publications/assets/2012-patent-litigation-study.pdf. Meanwhile, suits involving practicing entities lasted 2.27 years with a median damage award of $5,222,748. Id.

the vendor and patent infringement liability can therefore far exceed the vendor's — but not the customer's — ability to pay, a solution in which the consumer assumes the risk but defrays it through some combination of insurance patent pool participation, and building its own patent portfolio, is more likely to provide real protection.

V. Conclusion

Few practitioners of intellectual property law — particularly those in the financial services, IT, and Internet spaces — can be wholly pleased with the current state of affairs. A patent system that works reasonably well to provide a reward for innovation in fields such as pharmaceuticals and chemicals that may be characterized by several common characteristics. In these fields, there are established routes for publication and searching. Furthermore, alternative means of rewarding innovation seem inadequate in the face of enormous investment and time to market. Additionally, in these fields where patent holders are almost always the product providers, becoming the pioneering firm on the market may trump long-term profit. Finally, the lexicon used in filing — and thus required for searching — is unstable and nonpracticing trolls exert an inordinate influence on costs and behavior through lawsuits that are, if not settled, decided by juries who lack the technical capability to assess relevant technologies.

The problems of indemnity provisions canvassed in this paper are but one symptom of this larger problem. The nation's patent laws attempt a one-size-fits-all solution to the challenge of incenting one person's innovation without, at the same time, deterring everyone else's. The deficiencies in the underlying law manifest themselves in contractual struggles over liability for infringement. What ought to be a discussion over a division of the rewards of innovation becomes a wrangle over distribution of the risks of being struck by the lightning of a patent troll's suit — something that is more in the nature of an event of *force majeure* than a manageable dimension of technological innovation and deployment.

A comprehensive solution to the underlying problem will be a long time coming. By expanding the opportunities for third parties to oppose the issuance of patents, the America Invents Act attempts to provide some protection against patents that are improvidently granted for pre-existing art.

It, however, retains the rather improbable theory that, with few exceptions,[97] incentives for innovation in all industries should be based on the same model. In an era of Congressional gridlock, the odds of a thoughtful and more comprehensive legislative solution seem remote at best.

In the meantime, privately negotiated redistributions of risks and rewards offer the only hope for improvement. Section 2-312 of the Uniform Commercial Code, in which all intellectual property claims are lumped together with defects in title, is not an effective starting point for discussion. A better approach distinguishes patent infringement claims not known to the vendor from all other intellectual property claims. As to the latter, imposing liability on the vendor via an indemnification provision represents a workable solution in many cases, although consideration must always be given to the vendor's realistic ability to make good on the indemnity and to careful drafting of the indemnification provision to address issues such as combinations and methods that are not within the vendor's control. As to the former, the better starting point is the concept of *force majeure*, with each party bearing the risk of a claim that neither can control or avoid. This would, in turn, encourage both technology vendors and their customers to pursue more realistic approaches to risk management than the frequently illusory protection afforded by vendor indemnification.

[97] There are some variations in the AIA. For example, the government may permit extensions of the patent term in the case of certain drugs or mandatory licenses in the case of patents having national security value. 35 U.S.C. §156; 28 U.S.C. §1498. Generally, however, the rules for liability and scope of a patentee's rights are uniform across all types of invention.

Appendix A

Summary of recent caselaw respecting indemnification clauses

***Southern California Gas Co. v. Syntellect, Inc.*, No. 08cv941 BEN (NLS), 2011 U.S. Dist. LEXIS 33373 (S.D. Ca. March 28, 2011):**

Southern California Gas (SCG) entered into a contract with Syntellect to purchase an automated interactive telephone system, which SCG could use for handling incoming customer phone calls. Two indemnity provisions were included in the contract, including an obligation that Syntellect defend and indemnify SCG in the event SCG was sued for IP infringement in connection with the automated interactive telephone system. SCG was later sued for patent infringement. SCG sued Syntellect to enforce the indemnity provision when Syntellect failed to provide a defense and indemnify SCG in its settlement with the third party. The contract specifically provided:

> Supplier shall indemnify, defend and hold Company, and its present and future direct or indirect parent company(ies), subsidiaries and affiliates . . . harmless from and against any and all claims, actions, suits, proceedings, losses, liabilities, penalties, damages, costs or expenses (including attorneys' fees and disbursements) of any kind whatsoever arising from (1) actual or alleged infringement or misappropriation by Supplier or any subcontractor of any patent, copyright, trade secret, trademark, service mark, trade name, or other intellectual property right in connection with the System, including without limitation, any deliverable, (2) Supplier's violation of any third-party license to use intellectual property in connection with the System, including, without limitation, any deliverable.

The court rejected a number of Syntellect's arguments as to why it should escape liability:

1. Syntellect argued that because the third party did not specifically name Syntellect or its software as the infringer in its complaint against SCG, the indemnity provision is not triggered. The court held that the indemnity provision does not require a third party specifically to name Syntellect or its product to trigger the indemnitor's duties.

2. Syntellect argued that SCG's own negligence extinguished its right to indemnity. The court held that the broad indemnity

provision does not extinguish Syntellect's liability even in cases where SCG is actively negligent. Nor does it extinguish Syntellect's liability even in cases where SCG is accused of patent infringement for its own acts.

3. Syntellect argued that California's UCC §2312(3) extinguishes SCG's right to indemnity because its software product merely complied with the specifications SCG furnished. The court held that §2312(3) does not apply because of the specific written indemnity provision in the agreement.

***Owens-Illinois, Inc. v. BTR plc*, No. 05 Civ. 2873 (LLS), 2010 U.S. Dist. LEXIS 64813 (S.D.N.Y. July 28, 2010):**

Owens-Illinois (Owens) purchased from BTR a group of food and beverage packaging companies under a Share Disposition Agreement, including Continental PET Technologies, Inc. (CPET). CPET manufactured plastic food and beverage containers and was developing a plastic beer bottle using material (CPTX-312) that could trigger patent infringement claims. BTR brought a summary judgment motion on the issue of whether the agreement required it to indemnify Owens for losses Owens sustained in connection with a patent infringement action that was brought against CPET by a third party. The agreement contained a noninfringement warranty and indemnification provision stating that BTR will indemnify Owens for "any actual Losses . . . relating to or arising out of (i) any breach of any representation or warranty made by Seller contained in this Agreement. . . ." Indemnifiable Losses include "any actual damages, claims, losses, charges, actions, suits, proceedings, deficiencies, interest, penalties, and reasonable costs and expenses (including without limitation reasonable attorneys' and consultants' fees). . . ." BTR's indemnification obligation was only triggered if Owen's losses exceeded $35 million. After the deal between Owens and BTR closed, CPET was sued for patent infringement. CPET then sublicensed rights to use the relevant patent with Chevron, an exclusive licensee.

Owens sent BTR notice of the patent infringement suit against CPET, but BTR did not participate in the suit. In a separate suit, a court held that Chevron did not have the rights to grant a sublicense to CPET. CPET and the third party then settled the matter in which CPET agreed to pay $25.1 million and execute a license agreement. Owens sought to enforce the indemnification provision in its agreement with BTR.

The court addressed the issue of whether BTR's IP representations and warranties covered CPET's sales of CPTX-312 containers, since those sales did not start until after closing. The court found that the CPTX-312 sales were not included because the warranty was limited to "all Intellectual Property necessary to operate the Packaging Business as currently conducted" and "the conduct of the business of the Packaging Companies as currently conducted." The court also reasoned that placing the risk of loss from the future sales on Owens was consistent because Owens would control the extent of those sales and reap all the profits. Furthermore, the court did not find that an obligation to indemnify for losses from manufacturing automatically created a promise to indemnify for losses from sales. Thus, the sale of CPTX-312 containers was not covered by the agreement's representations and warranties, relieving BTR from its indemnification obligation for losses arising out of the third party's claim for CPET's infringing sales.

Olaes Enters., Inc. v. A.D. Sutton & Sons, Inc., No. 09 Civ. 8680 (CM)(PED), 2011 U.S. Dist. LEXIS 67737 (S.D.N.Y. June 20, 2011):

OCC (counterclaim defendants) was sued by Olaes for copyright infringement predicated on the use in OCC-licensed products of certain artistic enhancements to OCC logos allegedly copyrighted by Olaes. In license agreements between OCC and its licensees, OCC warranted and represented that it owned certain "Property" it was authorizing the licensees to imprint on various consumer goods. The agreements also included indemnification provisions, which required OCC to indemnify the licensees for damages and reasonable legal expenses incurred in defending against a claim of the sort Olaes brought against the licensees. The licensees sought to enforce the indemnification provision against OCC. Although OCC said it would indemnify the licensees, hired attorneys and paid the licensees' legal bills, OCC reneged on the arrangement once a judge denied OCC's motion to dismiss Olaes' copyright claims. OCC argued that it had no obligation to indemnify as to what the licensees were imprinting on their merchandise because OCC had warranted and represented to the licensees only that no else could claim an interest in OCC's Property, which did not include the licensees' imprints. All of the licensees settled with Olaes and brought a renewed motion for indemnification.

The court found that OCC could not deny its contractual obligation to indemnify the licensees in connection with this lawsuit because of the following:

1. OCC represented to the licenses that they were free to incorporate the entire design provided by OCC into their licensed products.

2. OCC delivered the designs used by the licenses to those licensees in tangible or electronic format without copyright notice or other notice that would have identified Olaes as having any proprietary right in the designs.

Thus, the licensor led each licensee to believe the licensor owned the material that was provided for the licensees' use, making the representations and warranties applicable and triggering the licensor's indemnification obligation.

R. Bradley Maule v. Philadelphia Media Holdings, LLC, et al., No. 08-3357, 2010 U.S. Dist. LEXIS 23635 (E.D. Pa. March 15, 2010):

Gyro Advertising (Gyro) contacted Shannon Associates because it needed an illustration of a pig flying in front of the Philadelphia skyline for a PMH advertising campaign. Shannon Associates provided such an illustration to Philadelphia Media Holdings (PMH), a Gyro client. In a professional services agreement between Gyro and Shannon Associates, Shannon Associates agreed to provide and perform services and deliver deliverables for Gyro's benefit. The agreement contained a noninfringement warranty and an indemnification clause, which stated:

> Contractor shall defend, indemnify, and hold harmless Gyro and its officers, directors, shareholders, employees, representatives, agents, successors, and assigns from and against any and all losses, obligations, risks, damages, injuries, costs, settlements, liabilities, and expenses (including reasonable attorneys' fees), and against any and all claims, actions, suits, and proceedings, arising out of or relating to (a) any breach of Contractor's representations or warranties in this Agreement; (b) any breach of this Agreement by Contractor; (c) any fraud, negligence, willful misconduct, or violation of law by Contractor; and (d) any damage to property or injuries to persons, or other acts or omissions caused or contributed to by the Contractor or any of its Representatives, or anyone acting under the Contractor's direction or control or on the Contractor's behalf, in the course of performance under this Agreement.

R. Bradley Maule sued Gyro and PMH on the basis that the illustration infringed upon his copyrighted photograph. Gyro notified Shannon Associates of the suit, and Shannon Associates responded two months later that it did not have an obligation to indemnify based on the agreement (e.g., there had not yet been a breach), but that it would defend and indemnify

Gyro. Gyro rejected the offer for defense in the future because it believed the case was close to a settlement.

The court found that the language of the agreement was clear and unambiguous and that Shannon Associates was required to indemnify Gyro for the costs, attorneys' fees and the amount paid to settle the litigation. Shannon Associates warranted, represented and covenanted that the illustration did not "infringe any intellectual property rights of any person," and that neither the illustration nor "any use or exploitation by Gyro of the [illustration would] infringe any patent, copyright, trademark, trade secret, privacy, publicity, or other intellectual property or proprietary right of any person or entity." The court rejected Shannon Associates' argument that it was not obligated to defend and indemnify Gyro because a term such as "alleged" or "claimed" did not appear after "against any and all claims." The court held that such wording was not necessary before the term "breach" to trigger indemnification obligations because "claim" is defined as "to assert" or "a cause of action." Analyzing the two separately, the court found that Shannon Associates had a duty to indemnify and a duty to defend Gyro under the agreement.

Appendix B

IP Indemnification Clause Examples

Example 1:

Vendor, at its own expense, will indemnify Buyer against any claim, suit, action, or other proceeding brought against Buyer based on a claim that the Product(s) as delivered to Buyer infringes in any manner any patent right of a third party.

Example 2:

Seller will defend, indemnify and hold Buyer harmless against a third-party action, suit or proceeding ("Claim") against Buyer to the extent such Claim is based upon an allegation that a Product, as of its delivery date under this Agreement, infringes a valid United States patent or copyright or misappropriates a third party's trade secret.

Example 3:

INDEMNIFICATION. The term "***Claim***" means any claim, suit or action by any third party, and the term "***Losses***" means any damages awarded and fines assessed in any Claim by a court of competent jurisdiction or pursuant to an arbitration proceeding, any amounts due under Claim settlement, and any other costs or expenses incurred in complying with any injunctive or equitable relief or any settlement requirements.

a. Party Indemnification.

i. Indemnification by Party-1. Upon receipt of notice from Party-2 requesting Party-1 to do so, Party-1 agrees to indemnify, defend, and hold harmless Party-2 and its affiliates, subsidiaries, shareholders, members, directors, officers, employees, agents, and parents, from and against any Claim, and any associated Losses to the extent caused by violation of any patent, copyright, trademark, trade secret, or other intellectual property or proprietary right due to Party-1 providing the Deliverables (except to the extent a Claim is caused by Party-2's internally created specifications).

ii. Indemnification by Party-2. Upon receipt of notice from Party-1 requesting Party-2 to do so, Party-2 agrees to indemnify, defend, and hold harmless Party-1 and its affiliates, subsidiaries, shareholders, members, directors, officers, employees, agents, and parents, from and against any Claim, and any associated Losses to the extent caused by violation of any patent, copyright, trademark, trade secret, or other intellectual property or proprietary right to the extent caused by Party-2's internally created specifications or Party-2's use of the Deliverables.

b. Indemnification Procedures.

The term "***indemnifying party***" means the party assuming indemnification obligations under this Agreement, and the term "***indemnified party***" means all parties, including any third parties, which the indemnifying party agrees to indemnify under this Agreement.

i. **Notice**. The indemnified party must give the indemnifying party prompt written notice of a Claim, provided, however, that failure of an indemnified party to give prompt written notice does not relieve the indemnifying party from its indemnification obligations under this Agreement except to the extent the defense is materially prejudiced by the failure. When the indemnifying party receives notice of a Claim from an indemnified party, the indemnifying party agrees, at its sole cost and expense, to assume the defense of the Claim by representatives chosen by the indemnifying party. The indemnified party may participate in the defense of the Claim and employ counsel at its own expense to assist in the defense of the Claim, subject to the indemnifying party retaining final authority and control over the conduct of the defense.

ii. **Conduct of Defense**. The indemnifying party's defense attorneys must be reasonably experienced and qualified in the areas of litigation applicable to the defense. The indemnifying party has the right to assert any defenses, causes of action or counterclaims arising from the subject of the Claim available to the indemnified party and also has the right to settle the Claim, subject to the indemnified party's prior written consent to the extent the settlement affects the rights or obligations of the indemnified party. The indemnified party agrees to provide the indemnifying party with reasonable assistance, at the indemnifying party's expense, as may be

> reasonably requested by the indemnifying party in connection with any defense, including, without limitation, providing the indemnifying party with information, documents, records and reasonable access to the indemnified party as the indemnifying party reasonably deems necessary.

Example 4:

Vendor shall indemnify, defend, and hold harmless Buyer, its officers, agents, and employees against all losses, damages, liabilities, costs, and expenses (including but not limited to reasonable attorneys' fees) resulting from any judgment or proceeding in which it is determined, or any settlement agreement arising out of the allegation, that (i) Vendor's furnishing or supplying Buyer with parts, goods, components, programs, practices, or methods under this order constitutes an infringement of any patent, copyrights, trademark, trade name, trade secret, or other proprietary or contractual right of any third party, or (ii) Buyer's use of such parts, goods, components, programs, practices, or methods supplied by Vendor under this order for research use in the manner and for the purposes specified in the accompanying product literature constitutes and infringement of any patent, copyrights, trademark, trade name, trade secret, or other proprietary or contractual right of any third party, *provided that* the foregoing indemnity shall not apply to any new product made by Buyer with use of the products supplied by Vendor hereunder. The foregoing shall not apply unless Buyer has informed Vendor as soon as practicable of the suit or action alleging such infringement and tendered defense of the suit or action to Vendor. Vendor shall not settle such suit or action without the consent of Buyer (such consent not to be unreasonably withheld) unless such settlement does not require any payment of money or other consideration by Buyer. Buyer shall not settle such suit or action without the consent of Vendor unless Vendor has declined to defend Buyer in such suit or action. In any suit or action for which Vendor has accepted the defense of Buyer, Buyer retains the right to participate in the defense at its own expense, but shall permit Vendor to control the defense (subject to good-faith consultations with Buyer) and shall not confess judgment, admit liability, or take any other actions prejudicial to the defense of such suit or action.

Example 5 (Licensee friendly):

1.1 In the event a third party makes a claim against Licensee that the Products provided by Seller under this Agreement infringe such third party's IPR, Seller shall:

a. Procure an irrevocable release for the Licensee, free of cost to Licensee, from such alleged infringement claim(s) for past use; and

b. For continued use of the Products that are the subject of the infringement claim(s), do one of the following: (i) First, using commercially reasonable efforts, procure for Licensee a worldwide royalty-free license to continue to use the Products that are the subject of the infringement claim(s); and if unable to procure such right, (ii) modify or replace the Products so as to make such Products (while retaining the form, fit and functionality of such Products) noninfringing, to the satisfaction of such third party; and

c. Indemnify Licensee for all reasonable costs (including attorneys' fees) and damages (including redesign costs), if any, incurred by Licensee.

1.2 Where a third party has initiated a lawsuit or other similar proceeding (including the seeking of preliminary injunction) against Licensee based on an allegation that the Products infringe IPR of such third party, Licensee shall notify Seller of such occurrence as soon as commercially reasonable, and Seller shall assume and diligently conduct the defense of such lawsuit or other proceeding and pay all costs relating thereto, including attorneys' fees. If Seller fails to assume the defense within a period of thirty (30) days, Licensee may conduct the defense, and Seller shall reimburse Licensee for the costs incurred (including reasonable attorneys' fees).

1.3 Any settlement of the lawsuit or other proceeding referred to in section 1.2 shall be subject to Seller taking, at its own expense and costs, the measures set out in section 1.1.

1.4 In the event Seller is not successful in its defense, in whole or in part, in the lawsuit or other proceeding referred to in section 1.2, Seller shall:

a. Reimburse Licensee for any damages or costs awarded against Licensee related to the past use that is found to be infringing; and

b. Take, at its own expense and costs, one of the actions as defined in sections 1.1(a) and 1.1(b) to avoid future infringements, and

c. Indemnify Licensee for damages incurred, as defined in section 1.1(c).

1.5 Licensee shall, upon Seller's written request and at the expense of Seller, provide reasonable assistance to Seller to support Seller in the defense of the lawsuit or other proceeding referred to in section 1.2. In addition, Seller agrees to provide such reasonable assistance to Licensee, where Licensee undertakes to conduct the defense as provided in section 1.2.

1.6 Seller shall not be liable under sections 1.1 to 1.5, where the allegation or claim of infringement is based solely on one of the following:

a. The unauthorized or unforeseeable use by Licensee of the Products where the Products would not be infringing but for such unauthorized or unforeseeable use; or

b. The unauthorized alteration or modification of the Products by Licensee where the Products would not be infringing but for such unauthorized modification or alteration.

Example 6 (Licensee friendly):

1.1 **"Claim" and "Losses" Defined**. "Claim" means any demand, or any civil, criminal, administrative, or investigative claim, action, or proceeding (including arbitration) asserted, commenced or threatened against a Licensee entity or person employed or engaged by a Licensee entity. "Losses" means all judgments, awards, settlements, liabilities to third-party plaintiffs, damages awarded to third-party plaintiffs, liens and claims together with all related costs and expenses incurred by reason of a Claim, including reasonable attorneys' fees and disbursements, costs of investigation, litigation, settlement and judgment, and any taxes, interest, penalties and fines with respect to any of the foregoing to the extent Licensor breaches any of its obligations to defend Licensee under Section 1.2. "Losses" shall not include a claim by Licensee Indemnitees for consequential damages suffered by them directly (in contrast with amounts awarded to third-party claimants), whether in the nature of lost profits or punitive damages against Licensor.

1.2 **Indemnification**. Licensor will, at its sole cost and expense, indemnify, defend and hold harmless Licensee and its affiliates and subsidiaries, and their respective officers, directors, employees, contractors, agents, representatives, successors and assigns (collectively, "Licensee Indemnitees") from and against any and all Losses resulting from a Claim that any Product(s), Deliverable(s), works, information, material(s) and/or Services furnished by or on behalf of Licensor, or the use thereof by Licensee, constitutes an infringement, misappropriation or unlawful use or disclosure of any Intellectual Property Rights of a third party.

1.3 **Procedures**. Licensee agrees to give Licensor prompt written notice of any Claim for which a Licensee Indemnitee seeks indemnification, provided that any failure by Licensee to provide such notice will not relieve Licensor of its indemnification obligations except to the extent Licensor can demonstrate actual prejudice as a result of such failure. Within 30 days after receiving Licensee's notice of a Claim, but no later than 10 days before the date on which any formal response to a Claim is due, Licensor will notify Licensee in writing as to whether Licensor acknowledges its indemnification obligation and elects to assume control of the defense and settlement of the Claim (a "Notice of Election"). Licensor will have the right to conduct the defense of the Claim and, consistent with the rights of Licensee Indemnitees hereunder, all negotiations for its settlement, provided, however, that Licensee may participate in such defense or negotiations to protect its (or their) interests and that any settlement will be for the payment of money by Licensor and will not, without the prior written approval of Licensee, obligate or impose any liability on any Licensee Indemnitee in any way, including without limitation, to any determination or admission regarding any Licensee Indemnitee's interest. Licensee shall reasonably cooperate with Licensor's defense of any Claim and shall render an accounting of all amounts for which indemnification is sought. If Licensor does not deliver a timely Notice of Election, the affected Licensee Indemnitee(s) may defend and/or settle the Claim in such a manner as it (or they) may deem appropriate, at the cost and expense of Licensor, including payment of any settlement, judgment or award and the cost of defending or settling the Claim. Licensor will promptly reimburse the Licensee Indemnitee upon demand for all Losses suffered or incurred as a result of or in connection with the Claim.

1.4 **Corrective Actions**. Licensor will give Licensee prompt notice of any threat, warning or notice of any Claim asserted against Licensor that any Products, Deliverables, information, materials and/or Services furnished by or on behalf of Licensor, or the use thereof by Licensee, constitutes an infringement, misappropriation or unlawful use or disclosure of any Intellectual Property Rights of a third party. In addition to Licensee's other rights and Licensor's other obligations hereunder, if all or any part of a Product or Deliverable is, or in the opinion of Licensor's intellectual property counsel may become, the subject of any claim or suit for infringement of any Intellectual Property Right, Licensor may, and in the event of any adjudication that the Product or Deliverable, or any part thereof, does infringe or if the use of the Product or Deliverable, or any part thereof, is enjoined, Licensor will promptly (a) procure for Licensee, at no additional cost or expense to Licensee, the right to use the Product or Deliverable, or the affected part thereof, or (b) to the extent such option is not available to Licensor on commercially reasonable terms following commercially reasonable efforts to procure such right, replace, at no additional cost or expense to Licensee, the Product or Deliverable, or affected part thereof, with a modified or substituted Product or Deliverable or part, that does not violate any third party's Intellectual Property Rights and that is qualitatively and functionally at least the equivalent of the affected Product or Deliverable, or part thereof.

1.5 **Return**. If neither (a) nor (b) of Section 1.4 is available to Licensor on commercially reasonable terms following commercially reasonable efforts by Licensor, and Licensor has so advised Licensee, then Licensee may at its option surrender the Products and/or Deliverables, in whole or in part, and receive a full refund of the aggregate payments made by Licensee for or in respect of the returned Products and/or Deliverables, including amounts paid in respect of Services performed in relation to the returned Products and/or Deliverables.

Example 7 (Licensor friendly):

1.1 **Indemnification**. Subject to Section 1.2, Licensor shall, at its own expense, indemnify and defend Licensee against any claim by a third party that the Licensor Software as used in compliance with this Agreement infringes a valid U.S. patent issued prior to the Effective Date, Berne Convention copyright or U.S. trade secret (a "Claim"), provided that Licensee: (i) provides Licensor with prompt written notice of the Claim; and (ii) permits Licensor to exclusively defend, compromise, settle or appeal such Claim. Licensee shall provide Licensor with full information, assistance and cooperation, at Licensor' expense, to enable Licensor to defend, compromise, settle and/or appeal such Claim and shall not settle or compromise any Claim without Licensor' prior written consent. The provisions set forth in this Section1.1 shall not prohibit the participation of Licensee with Licensor in the defense or appeal of any Claim should Licensee choose to participate, at its own expense (such expense not being indemnified by Licensor) and with attorneys of its own choice, provided that Licensor shall have sole control and authority with respect to any such defense, compromise, settlement, appeal or similar action related to the Claim. Licensor shall pay any final award of damages assessed against Licensee resulting from a Claim defended by Licensor pursuant to this Section 1.1, including any awarded costs or attorneys' fees, or any settlement amount agreed to by Licensor.

1.2 **Exclusions**. Licensor shall have no obligation to Licensee under Section 1.1 if the alleged infringement or violation is based upon:

i. Use of the Licensor Software other than as set forth herein and in the then-current version of the Documentation;

ii. Any modification or alteration to or of the Licensor Software performed by anyone (including Licensee) other than Licensor or its subcontractors, agents or assignees;

iii. Licensor' compliance with Licensee's designs, specifications or instructions if Licensor is unable to follow such designs, specifications or instructions without infringement or violation;

iv. Combination, operation or use with software, hardware, information, data, or other materials, not approved or supplied by Licensor, if infringement (including, without limitation, contributory infringement) would have been avoided by use without such software, hardware, information, data, or other materials;

v. Use of a superseded or altered release of the Licensor Software if the infringement would have been avoided by use of the current unaltered release of the Licensor Software; or

vi. Use of the Licensor Software after Licensor's notice to cease use of the Licensor Software due to a claim of infringement.

1.3 **Remedies**. Notwithstanding anything to the contrary in the foregoing, should Licensee's right to continue to use the Licensor Software pursuant hereto be subject to a claim that it infringes or misappropriates a valid patent or copyright or other intellectual property right, or if

Licensor reasonably believes such a claim may arise, Licensor may fulfill its obligations under this Article 1 by, in Licensor' sole discretion and at no cost to Licensee:

i. Procuring for Licensee the right or license to continue to use the Licensor Software;

ii. Modifying the Licensor Software to render it noninfringing but substantially functionally equivalent to the Licensor Software prior to such modification; or

iii. If the alternatives described in clauses (i) and (ii) of this Section 1.3 are not commercially practicable, Licensor may terminate the License(s) to the Licensor Software, in which case Licensor shall refund to Licensee any fees paid under this Agreement by Licensee to Licensor for unused use of or support for the allegedly infringing Licensor Software. For the purposes of this Section 1.3(iii), the fees with respect to unused use of allegedly infringing Licensor Software that is licensed for a one-time or up-front License fee shall be the unamortized value of such one-time or up-front License fee actually paid by Licensee to Licensor under this Agreement for such allegedly infringing Licensor Software, as depreciated on a five-year straight line schedule beginning on delivery of such allegedly infringing Licensor Software to Licensee. Upon such refund, Licensee shall return such allegedly infringing Licensor Software, and Licensee's right to use such Licensor Software shall cease.

1.4 **Effect**. THIS ARTICLE 1 STATES LICENSOR'S AND ITS SUPPLIERS' ENTIRE LIABILITY AND CUSTOMER'S EXCLUSIVE REMEDY FOR INFRINGEMENT AND/OR MISAPPROPRIATION, WHETHER SUCH ACTION, CLAIM OR PROCEEDING IS BASED ON BREACH OF WARRANTY OR ANY OTHER CAUSE OF ACTION. EXCEPT AS STATED ABOVE, LICENSOR AND ITS SUPPLIERS DISCLAIM ALL INDEMNITIES, EXPRESS, IMPLIED OR STATUTORY FOR INTELLECTUAL PROPERTY INFRINGEMENT AND/OR MISAPPROPRIATION.

1.5 **Licensee Indemnity**. Licensee shall indemnify, defend and hold Licensor harmless from any claims and liability and any and all damages and costs (including reasonable attorneys' fees) arising out of: (i) Licensee's breach of any of its obligations under this Agreement;

(ii) any breach by Licensee of any third-party agreements relating to the Licensor Software; (iii) any claim related to Licensee's or Authorized Users' or any third party's use of the Licensor Software, except to the extent such claims are subject to Licensor' indemnity obligations under Section 1.1; and/or (iv) any claim that any materials, software, or other items provided to Licensor by Licensee infringes a third party's intellectual property rights.

Example 8 (Licensor friendly):

1.1 **Licensor Indemnification**. Licensor will defend at its own expense any action against Licensee brought by a third party to the extent that the action is based upon a claim that the Licensed Software infringes any US copyrights, US patents issued as of the Effective Date or that Licensor misappropriated any trade secrets recognized as such under the Uniform Trade Secret law in the development thereof, and Licensor will pay those costs and damages finally awarded (without right of appeal) against Licensee in any such action that are specifically attributable to such claim or those costs and damages agreed to in a monetary settlement of such action. If the Licensed Software becomes, or in Licensor's opinion is likely to become, the subject of an infringement claim, Licensor may, at its sole discretion and expense, either (a) procure for Licensee the right to continue using the Licensed Software; (b) replace or modify the Licensed Software so that it becomes noninfringing; or (c) accept return of the Licensed Software and give Licensee a refund for the License Fees paid by Licensee as further described below, less a reasonable allowance for the period of time Licensee has used the Licensed Software. If Licensee obtains a perpetual license to the Licensed Software, the refund shall be equal to the License Fees prorated over sixty (60) months. If, however, Licensee obtains a subscription-based license, the refund shall be equal to the balance of any License Fees pre-paid for the duration of the then-current subscription term. Notwithstanding the foregoing, Licensor will have no obligation under this Section 1 or otherwise with respect to any infringement claim based upon (i) any use of the Licensed Software, not in accordance with this Agreement; (ii) any use of the Licensed Software in combination with other products, equipment, software, or data not supplied by Licensor; (iii) any use of any release of the Licensed Software other than the most current release made available to Licensee; or (iv) any modification of the Licensed Software where the modification is the basis of the claim. THIS SECTION 1.1 STATES LICENSOR'S ENTIRE LIABILITY AND LICENSEE'S SOLE AND

EXCLUSIVE REMEDY FOR CLAIMS OF INFRINGEMENT OR MISAPPROPRIATION OF ANY INTELLECTUAL PROPERTY RIGHT.

1.2 **Licensee Indemnification.** Licensee will indemnify, defend and hold harmless, at its own expense, Licensor, its agents, employees and representatives from or against any and all damages, losses, claims, expense, costs (including attorney's fees and litigation costs) and other liability incurred by Licensor relating to any action against Licensor by a third party for the infringement of a copyright, patent, trademark or misappropriation of a trade secret relating to Licensee's use of the Licensed Software in an unauthorized manner. Licensee will pay those costs and damages finally awarded against Licensor in any such action that are specifically attributable to such claim or those costs and damages agreed to in a monetary settlement of such action. THIS SECTION 1.2 STATES LICENSEE'S ENTIRE LIABILITY AND LICENSOR'S SOLE AND EXCLUSIVE REMEDY FOR CLAIMS AND ACTIONS DESCRIBED IN THIS SECTION 1.2.

1.3 **Procedural Requirements.** Each party's indemnification obligations are conditioned on the other party (a) promptly notifying such party in writing of such action; (b) giving such party sole control of the defense thereof and any related settlement negotiations; and (c) cooperating and, at such party's request and expense, assisting in such defense. Notwithstanding the foregoing, Licensee shall not have any right, without Licensor's written consent, to settle any action if such settlement arises from or is part of any criminal action, suit or proceeding or contains a stipulation to or admission or acknowledgment of, any liability or wrongdoing (whether in contract, tort or otherwise) on the part of Licensor.

Example 9 (Negotiated variation of Example 8):

1.1 **Licensor Indemnification.** At its own expense, Licensor will defend at its own expense, indemnify and hold harmless Licensee and Affiliates (including the employees, officers, directors, agents and contractors of each) from any action brought against Licensee brought or Affiliates (including the employees, officers, directors, agents or contractors of each) by a third party to the extent that the action is based upon a claim that the Licensed Software infringes any US copyrights, US patents issued as of the Effective Date trademarks or that Licensor misappropriates any trade secrets recognized as such under the Uniform Trade Secret law in the development thereof, and Licensor will pay those costs and damages finally awarded (without right of appeal) against Licensee in any such action that are specifically attributable to such claim or those costs and damages agreed to in a monetary settlement of such action. If the Licensed Software becomes, or in Licensor's opinion is likely to become, the subject of an infringement claim, Licensor may, at its sole discretion and expense, either (a) procure for Licensee and Affiliates the right to continue using the Licensed Software as provided in this Agreement; (b) replace or modify the Licensed Software so that it becomes noninfringing but retaining similar functionality in all material respects; or, if neither of the foregoing options are commercially feasible, (c) accept return of the Licensed Software and give Licensee a refund for the License Fees paid by Licensee as further described below, less a reasonable allowance for the period of time Licensee has used the Licensed Software. If Licensee obtains a perpetual license to the Licensed Software, the refund shall be equal to the License Fees prorated over sixty (60) months. If, however, Licensee obtains a subscription-based license, the refund shall be equal to the balance of any License Fees pre-paid for the duration of the then-current subscription term, which will be a full refund during the first year and thereafter prorated over forty-eight (48) months. Notwithstanding the foregoing, Licensor will have no obligation under this Section 1 or otherwise with respect to any infringement claim to the extent it is based upon (i) any use of the Licensed Software not in accordance within violation of the terms of this Agreement; (ii) any use of the Licensed Software in combination with other products, equipment, software, or data not supplied by Licensor or referenced in the Documentation as necessary or authorized for the operation of the Software; (iii) any use of any release of the Licensed Software other than the most current release made available to Licensee at no additional charge with notice that use of such release is necessary to avoid such a claim and after a reasonable period of time to promptly install such release; or (iv) any modification of the Licensed Software by or on behalf of Licensee, except when done pursuant to instructions from or on behalf of Licensor, where the modification is the basis of the claim. THIS SECTION 1.1 STATES LICENSOR'S ENTIRE LIABILITY AND LICENSEE'S SOLE AND EXCLUSIVE REMEDY FOR CLAIMS OF INFRINGEMENT OR MISAPPROPRIATION OF ANY INTELLECTUAL PROPERTY RIGHT.

1.2 **Licensee Indemnification**. Licensee will indemnify, defend and hold harmless, at its own expense, Licensor, its agents, employees and representatives from or against any and all damages, losses, claims, expense, costs (including attorney's fees and litigation costs) and other liability incurred by Licensor relating to any action against Licensor by a third party for the infringement of a copyright, patent, trademark or misappropriation of a trade secret to the extent relating to Licensee's use of the Licensed Software in an unauthorized manner Licensee Data. Licensee will pay those costs and damages finally awarded against Licensor in any such action that are specifically attributable to such claim or those costs and damages agreed to in a monetary settlement of such action. THIS SECTION 1.2 STATES LICENSEE'S ENTIRE LIABILITY AND LICENSOR'S SOLE AND EXCLUSIVE REMEDY FOR CLAIMS AND ACTIONS DESCRIBED IN THIS SECTION 1.2.

1.3 **Procedural Requirements**. Each party's indemnification obligations are conditioned on the other party (a) promptly notifying such party in writing of such action; (b) giving such party sole control of the defense thereof and any related settlement negotiations; and (c) reasonably cooperating and assisting, at such party's request and expense, assisting in such defense. Notwithstanding the foregoing, each party shall not have any right, without the indemnified party's written consent, to settle any action if such settlement arises from or is part of any criminal action, suit or proceeding or contains a stipulation to or admission or acknowledgment of, any liability or wrongdoing (whether in contract, tort or otherwise) on the part of Licensor, the indemnified party or Affiliates (including the employees, officers, directors, agents or contractors of each).

Chapter 5

Quasi Property

"The Bankruptcy Code, the Copyright Act, and Transactions in Computer Software" (1988)

"Computer Software Licensing after the Enactment of the Intellectual Property Bankruptcy Protection Act" (1989)

As computer software gained commercial importance, the question naturally arose whether it could be considered a lendable asset, like real property, personal property, and accounts. The effort was closely related to the futile initiative, pursued over many years and with enormous vigor by many interested parties, to create an Article 2B of the Uniform Commercial Code addressing license transactions. After the draft Article 2B failed, it was rechristened UCITA, but unlike the UCC, which has been adopted with minor revisions in 49 states (Louisiana being the outlier), UCITA has been adopted by only two: Virginia and Maryland.

There is obviously something afoot here. While the UCC and the correlated Bankruptcy Code were successful in sweeping all manner of nonrealty property — goods, negotiable instruments, documents, securities, bank deposits, letters of credit, bills of lading, accounts, even leases — within the purview of commercial law, providing for their ownership, transfer, and hypothecation, the comparable effort with respect to intellectual property has been largely unsuccessful. The articles in this chapter address a narrow aspect of this failure, namely security interests in intellectual property and the closely related question of what happens when a technology company goes bankrupt. The impediments to effective security interests identified in the articles have a cascading effect: if a lender cannot reliably secure and foreclose on the asset, the asset becomes essentially worthless as collateral, and the "asset" loses its value to the borrower as a basis for financing.

A key problem addressed in these articles is the question of whether a license is an "executory contract" that can be "rejected" by a bankruptcy trustee. Ordinarily, the answer is yes under Section 365 of the Bankruptcy

Code.[1] Following rejection, the counterparty is left with an unsecured claim (usually worthless or nearly so) for damages caused by the rejection, and secured lenders are left with clear title to whatever assets would otherwise have been burdened by the executory contract. This is what happened in the celebrated 1985 *Lubrizol* case,[2] in which the debtor, a company called Richmond Metal Finishers, had granted a nonexclusive license to Lubrizol to use a proprietary metal finishing process. The debtor deemed the license to be burdensome and rejected it, stripping Lubrizol of its right to use the process. This was sufficiently catastrophic for Lubrizol that it took its complaint to the Fourth Circuit, where it lost, then to the Supreme Court, where it was denied certiorari, and finally to Congress, where it found relief in the enactment of an amendment to Section 365, the new Section 365n.[3] Section 365n allows the licensee of any intellectual property other than a trademark[4] to elect to retain its rights, notwithstanding rejection by the bankrupt. This is good news for licensees, but bad news for creditors, since it saddles the debtor's property with whatever awful licenses the debtor may have granted, likely getting the debtor into trouble in the first place. In other words, due to Section 365n, the intellectual "property" of the debtor becomes effectively co-owned with any licensees of that property.

In a very recent decision, *Mission Products Holdings, Inc. v. Tempnology, LLC*,[5] the Supreme Court held, in an 8–1 decision, that the rejection of a trademark license did not terminate the license, on the ground that rejection was a breach, not a rescission, of the underlying agreement. In effect, this holding implies that the Fourth Circuit's decision in *Lubrizol* was wrong and extends Section 365n of the Bankruptcy Code, where it expressly did not go — namely, to trademarks. In my judgment, the Supreme Court's decision in *Mission Products* was cavalier at best; wrong at worst. Section 365n includes detailed provisions respecting the obligations on a licensee following its election to retain a rejected license — including, among other things, the payment of royalties. The Supreme Court says nothing about these ongoing obligations of the licensee and disregards the manifest purpose of Section 365, which is to allow a debtor to disburden itself of unwanted executory

---

[1] 11 U.S.C. §365.

[2] *Lubrizol Enterprises, Inc.v. Richmond Metal Finishers, Inc.*, 756 F.2d 1043 (4th Cir. 1985), *cert. den.*, 475 U.S. 1057 (1986).

[3] Intellectual Property Bankruptcy Protection Act of 1987, 102 Stat. 2538 (100th Cong. 1988).

[4] The Supreme Court has just now extended the effect of Section 365n to trademarks. *Mission Products Holdings, Inc. v. Tempnology*, LLC, 587 U.S. (May 20, 2019).

[5] Id.

obligations. One can only imagine the impact the *Mission Products* holding will have on lenders who thought they had taken a security interest in a borrower's trademarks — suddenly, any licensee holds a right in the trademark that is effectively superior to that of the secured lender.

Section 365n and *Mission Products* implicate the larger question raised by the failure to subsume licenses under the UCC umbrella, namely whether and to what extent the honorific title "property" can fairly be applied to patents, copyrights, trademarks, and trade secrets at all. In his book *Justifying Intellectual Property,*[6] Professor Merges articulates a compelling case for the assignment of property-like rights to the products of intellectual endeavor. With sensitive reference to the philosophers of property, most notably John Locke, Immanuel Kant, and John Rawls,[7] Merges argues convincingly that the assignment of intellectual property rights is both fair to the creator and just when viewed from the standpoint of society.

It is, however, a peculiar form of property. A key factor is often the question of whether and to what extent the intellectual property can be effectively separated from its creator so that it can be bought and sold independently of the services of the creator. Another is to balance the interest of the public in the intellectual property against the interest of its creator. To take John Locke's and Merges's analyses, the individual mixes her labor with some publicly available resource and thus creates something new that becomes the individual's property by reason of the admixture of the individual's labor, which she owns, with the resource. So, for example, a sculptor adds his labor and creativity to base clay, producing a work that he owns, just as in Locke's hypothetical acorn gatherer combines his labor of gathering acorns lying on the ground, creating new value that the gatherer is justified in claiming as her own. Voilà: now we have property, a commodity susceptible to commercial

---

[6] R. Merges, *Justifying Intellectual Property* (Cambridge, MA: Harvard University Press, 2011).
[7] I take some pride in having had Rawls as a professor when I was an undergraduate. He was the preeminent philosopher of social justice of the twentieth century, but his character was as fine as his theory. I offer the following anecdote as proof. At the start of one of his classes on ethics (when his *Theory of Justice* was our text in manuscript form) he was giving the reading list. He said, toward the end, "And you probably should also read Kant's *Perpetual Peace.*" A hapless undergraduate raised his hand and asked, "Who is that author?" This of course provoked tittering among the grad students lining the front row of the class. Ignoring them, Rawls never batted an eye, and replied to the undergraduate with complete sincerity and respect, "That's Immanuel Kant, K-A-N-T." Another of Merges's intellectual locutors, Robert Nozick, was my thesis advisor. I submit this solely by way of personal justification for my presumptuousness in discussing Merges's book.

dealings! The sculpture, like the crops, can be bought and sold independently of the further efforts of the sculptor or farmer.

So far, so good, and we have no need for intellectual property law to permit the sculptor to sell his sculpture or the gatherer to sell her acorns. The sculpture and bag of acorns are, so to speak, old fashioned personal property. The law of personal property gives legal protection and recognition to the value that exists already in the physical object that results from the sculptor's or gatherer's labor, protecting it against, among other things, theft. But in the case of the sculpture, intellectual property law takes property rights a step further. Copyright law declares that the sculptor has created not just a sculpture (achievement enough in itself!) but a "work," which is a Platonic abstraction that is embodied in the sculpture as a "copy," but exists independently of the particular sculpture, hovering, one might say, above and beyond it. It is this Platonic form to which the intellectual property right attaches. One might say that intellectual property law, or in this case more precisely, copyright law, disaggregates the creativity from the clay, permitting an abstracted version of the creativity to be bought and sold independently of the base material with which it was originally combined.[8] Patent law employs the same intellectual magic, identifying an "invention" that is described by the "metes and bounds" of a patent's claims and exists independently of any particular embodiment. Put in Marxist terms, one might also say that intellectual property alienates the creativity from the object and from the object's creator, permitting the creativity to become an independent article of commerce. It achieves this result negatively by preventing others from duplicating the work or invention in copies or embodiments. Unlike old-fashioned property, though, the thing that is protected, this artificial construct, has no natural value that exists prior to and independently of the legal construct. Like a derivative security, IP is a highly artificial construct, but one that can generate enormous value.[9]

Secured lending and bankruptcy, which are the subject of this chapter, test the outer limits of the success of this legal project. The whole point of secured lending is to make it possible to sell something originally owned by the debtor independently of the debtor if the debtor defaults on the loan. And the whole point of a bankruptcy liquidation under Chapter 7 of the Bankruptcy Code is

---

[8] In many cases, and in Professor Merges's analysis, the "base material" is a further abstraction, namely the "public domain" on which every creator draws in producing something original.

[9] One can only imagine what Plato would think if he were told that we mortals found a way to buy and sell the eternal Forms.

to permit creditors to sell the debtor's assets without the debtor's consent or involvement.

Despite its evident value, intellectual property has never played the large role in financing that is played by real estate, accounts receivable, chattels, or other more traditional forms of property. There seem to be a couple of reasons for this. The first is seen in Section 365n of the Bankruptcy Code and in the recent *Mission Products* decision. Despite the ownership rights conferred on the creator or inventor by intellectual property law, there is, at least in the bankruptcy setting, a strong desire to allow the intellectual property to leak into the public domain through the rights of licensees who are dependent on the intellectual property for their livelihood.[10] When the IP proprietor is bankrupt, and the claimants are its creditors, not the original creator of the IP, rights in the intellectual property tend to collapse in the face of the hardship its enforcement could cause to others.[11]

A second and arguably more general reason is that, despite the law's effort to separate IP from its creator, IP is often too difficult to repossess and exploit in the absence of the creator.[12] This is particularly true of species of intellectual property such as computer software that must be constantly updated, debugged, and maintained to sustain its value. In many cases, the millions of lines of code in a commercial software product can only be maintained by the personnel who are intimately familiar with the code. Selling rights in the code to an entity that has never seen it before would be an exercise in futility, which is why any merger and acquisition transaction involving rights in software products will include "stay" provisions, ensuring that the individuals who know the code will be there to maintain it after the sale takes place. The conversion of many software "products" into "services" — "software-as-a-service" ' in a sense, proves the point that despite the precepts of intellectual property law, computer software is not quite property at all, or at least not in the sense that Locke's bag of acorns is.

The following chapter will consider another curious species of intellectual property: trademarks, which protect both their proprietors against poaching and the public against deception, while carving out a broad swath reserved to

---

10 One is reminded here of Locke's charity proviso, discussed by Merges in *Justifying*, p. 61 *et seq.*

11 Compulsory licensing under European patent law and "march-in" rights in the United States under the Bayh-Dole Act, 35 U.S.C. §203, are in the same vein: they tend to preserve the public's rights in intellectual property that is lying fallow.

12 The "moral" rights in copyrighted works, which in general are not alienable, are another example of the stickiness between authors and their works.

ordinary use through the doctrine of "fair use." And finally, in the last chapter, we will consider the related topic of whether personal data can be owned at all, and if so, by whom.

The Bankruptcy Code, the Copyright Act, and Transactions in Computer Software*

The Copyright Act of 1976 (the Copyright Act)[1] is an imperfect hybrid of new rights and old assumptions. The Copyright Act creates a radically new system of rights in which copyright is infinitely divisible and arises whenever pen is set to paper.[2] As a result, copyright inheres in a great many "works" — including the vast agglomeration of letters, memos, notes, proposals, computer programs, print-outs, reports, and what-not generated by our paper-intensive economy — that will never have titles and will never be registered with the Copyright Office. At the same time, section 205 of the Copyright Act assumes that any work in which copyright is transferred will have a title and a registration number.[3] Thus, subsequent transferees who take in good faith, without notice, and for valuable consideration prevail over prior transferees unless the work has been registered, the prior document of transfer recorded, and the work identified in the prior document by title or registration number.

Unfortunately, the requirements of section 205 are so little understood outside the traditional publishing and entertainment bar that many valuable copyright "transfers" are never recorded. Unrecorded transfers frequently include such fundamental commercial transactions as exclusive licenses, asset purchases, and security interests.

Thus far, few parties appear to have been harmed by a failure to record under section 205. Just as the first transferee may not realize that recording

---

1 17 U.S.C. §§101–810 (1982). Unless otherwise stated, all Copyright Act of 1976 citations refer to Title 17 U.S.C. §§101–810, codifying Pub. L. No. 94-554 (1976) (Title I of the 1976 Copyright Act).

2 17 U.S.C. §102(a) ("Copyright protection subsists . . . in original works of authorship fixed in any tangible medium of expression, now known or later developed, from which they can be perceived, reproduced, or otherwise communicated, either directly or with the aid of a machine or device.").

3 17 U.S.C. §205(c) (1982). Section 205(c) provides:

> Recordation of a document in the Copyright Office gives all persons constructive notice of the facts stated in the recorded document, but only if —
>
> (1) the document, or material attached to it, specifically identifies the work to which it pertains so that, after the document is indexed by the Register of Copyrights, it would be revealed by a reasonable search under the title or registration number of the work; and
>
> (2) registration has been made for the work.

would be advisable, the next transferee may not realize that he or she could challenge the earlier unrecorded transferee's rights. Thus, a commonality of error has protected most commercial transactions in copyrighted works from the problems inherent in the transfer recording provisions of section 205.

It is, however, unrealistic to suppose that this conspiracy of ignorance can last forever. As copyright protection for computer software has expanded, attorneys have begun to scrutinize transactions such as asset purchases and exclusive software licenses for compliance with the Copyright Act. Scrutiny is likely to be most acute whenever a software vendor has filed for bankruptcy. In bankruptcy proceedings, many parties are strongly motivated to maximize the estate of the debtor by challenging any transfer of valuable rights executed by the debtor prior to the filing of bankruptcy proceedings. In this climate, a failure to record under section 205 can have disastrous consequences for the software licensee.

This Article will explore the impact of the bankruptcy of a computer software vendor on transactions such as software licenses and asset purchases. Part I of this Article will show that the vendor's trustee can set aside many such transactions by combining the section 205 transfer recording provisions of the Copyright Act with the trustee's status as a lien creditor under the Bankruptcy Code's "strong arm clause" or by asserting the trustee's power to reject executory contracts under section 365 of the Bankruptcy Code.[4] Part II of this Article will address the means available for reducing the risks identified in Part I, including source code escrows and security interests. Part III of this Article will address problems in the registration of copyright in computer programs and propose statutory and regulatory reforms for providing more satisfactory long-term solutions.

This Article assumes that computer programs are intangible assets that vendors protect both as trade secrets[5] and as copyrighted works.[6] Additionally,

---

[4] 11 U.S.C. §§365, 544(a)(1) (1982). Unless otherwise stated, all Bankruptcy Code citations refer to Title 11 U.S.C. §§101–151326, codifying Pub. L. No. 95-598 (1978) (Title I of the Bankruptcy Reform Act of 1978), as amended by Pub. L. No. 98-353 (1984) (Bankruptcy Amendments and Federal Judgeship Act of 1984) [hereinafter 1984 Amendments].

[5] To date, most courts and commentators have permitted programs to be protected by trade secret law, despite their wide distribution. 2 R. Callman, *The Law of Unfair Competition, Trademarks and Monopolies* §14.16 (4th ed., 1982); see, e.g., *Data General Corp. v. Digital Controls*, 357 A.2d 105 (Del. 1975) (six thousand people with access to drawings that disclosed plaintiff's trade secrets); *Management Science America, Inc. v. Cyborg Systems, Inc.*, 6 Computer L. Serv. Rep. 921 (N.D. Ill. 1978) (computer software licensed to more than six hundred customers and disclosure of system's documentation to potential customers).

computer programs have a variety of forms which may be divided into two broad classifications. The first classification is source code, which is easily understood by humans and is indispensable in debugging and modifying programs. The second classification is object code, which cannot be understood by humans without difficulty and is not commonly used in debugging and modifying the programs.[7]

---

[6] Presently, it appears settled that copyright subsists in all computer programs that have been set down in any tangible medium of expression. See *Apple Computer, Inc. v. Formula Int'l Inc.*, 725 F.2d 521 (9th Cir. 1984); *Apple Computer, Inc. v. Franklin Computer Corp.*, 545 F. Supp. 812 (E.D. Pa. 1982), 714 F.2d 1240 (3d Cir. 1983), cert. dismissed, 464 U.S. 1033 (1984). For a thoughtful questioning of this holding, see Samuelson, "CONTU Revisited: The Case Against Copyright Protection for Computer Programs in Machine-Readable Form," 1984 *Duke L. J.* 663. See also Davidson, Protecting Computer Software: A Comprehensive Analysis, 1983 ARIZ. ST. L.J. 611, 675-93. The foregoing commentators distinguish software in its human and machine-readable manifestations, arguing that only the former should be copyrightable. Judge Newcomer took a different approach in *Apple,* 545 F. Supp. at 821, 824, where he reasoned that operating system programs (which primarily govern internal computer functions) are not copyrightable, although application programs (which primarily generate useful output) may be. In this article, unless otherwise indicated, it will be assumed that the vendor has not patented any process or apparatus which utilizes the licensed programs. For discussions of the patentability of such processes and apparatuses, see Kline, "Requiring an Election of Protection for Patentable/Copyrightable Computer Programs," 1985 *J. Pat. Off. Soc'y* 280 (Part I), 339 (Part 11); Davidson, supra, at 647–51; Rondau, "Protecting Computer Software: After *Apple Computer, Inc. v. Franklin Computer Corp.,*" 714 F.2d 1240 (3d Cir. 1983); "Does Copyright Provide the Best Protection?" 57 *Temp. L. Q.* 527, 529–32 (1984). Rondau finds patent law a questionable means of protecting computer software because the costly and time-consuming application procedure is unsuited to the pace of software development and because it is difficult to predict whether a particular program is patentable.

[7] The paradigmatic example of source code is the listing of instructions to be read by the computer's compiler or interpreter in a standard programming language such as BASIC. Source code may also include more generalized descriptions of the program's architecture such as flow charts and documentation that explain in detail the program's functions and logic. The paradigmatic example of object code is what comes out of the compiler: a series of 0s and 1s that directly represent the electrical charges or magnetic pulses that are manipulated to make a computer function. It is also commonly understood to include hexadecimal and other nonbinary numerical expressions of the program. But see Davidson, supra note 6, at 620–21 (distinguishing object and binary versions of a program, which arc in this article both classed as "object code").

I. Effect of bankruptcy proceedings on transactions in computer software

The filing of bankruptcy proceedings creates a new entity, the estate of the debtor.[8] The estate includes "all legal or equitable interests of the debtor in property as of the commencement of the case," "wherever located and by whomever held."[9] This includes tangible and intangible property, causes of action, and property recovered during the course of bankruptcy proceedings.[10] The estate undoubtedly includes copyrights and trade secrets.[11]

The estate of the debtor is administered by the bankruptcy trustee.[12] In the case of liquidation under Chapter 7, the trustee's central role is to marshal the debtor's assets in a way that will maximize the total value of the debtor's estate and permit its equitable distribution among the debtor's creditors.[13] In a Chapter 11 case, the trustee attempts to maximize the creditors' recovery by preserving the debtor's revenue-generating power as an ongoing business.[14] The trustee has unusual powers. Under Bankruptcy Code section 544(a), known as the "strong arm clause," the trustee may recover property transferred to others prior to bankruptcy. Under Bankruptcy Code section 365, the trustee may reject executory contracts, leaving the other party to the rejected contract with only an unsecured claim for any damages caused by the rejection. Both of these powers have serious implications for software transactions. We will consider the strong arm clause first.

---

[8] 11 U.S.C.A. §541 (West Supp. 1986).

[9] Id. §541(a)(l).

[10] H.R. REP. NO. 595, 95th Cong., 2d Sess. 368, reprinted in 1978 *U.S. Code Cong. & Admin. News* 5963, 6323; S. Rep. No. 989, 95th Cong., 2d Sess. 82–83, reprinted in 1978 *U.S. Code Cong. & Admin. News* 5787, 5868–69. See also *In re Golden Plan of California, Inc.*, 37 Bankr. 167, 169 (Bankr. E.D. Cal. 1984) (corporate name is "property of the estate").

[11] See, e.g., *In re Howley-Dresser Co.*, 132 F. 1002 (S.D.N.Y. 1904) (property of the estate includes copyright).

[12] In Chapter 11 cases, the trustee may be the debtor itself in the guise of the "debtor in possession" (a veritable sheep in wolf's clothing), an independent person appointed by the court or, in certain jurisdictions, by the United States Trustee. See 11 U.S.C. §§1101(a), 1104, 1501, 15103(a) (1982). The debtor in possession has the same powers as an independent trustee under both §§544(a)(1) and 365. Both will be referred to in this Article as the "trustee."

[13] See Jackson, "Bankruptcy, Non-Bankruptcy Entitlements, and the Creditor's Bargain," 91 *Yale L. J.* 857 (1982).

[14] See 6 Herzog and King, Collier on Bankruptcy, ¶8.05 (14th ed., 1981).

A. Bankruptcy code section 544(a)(1) as it affects copyright in computer programs

1. Effect of the strong arm clause on exclusive licenses and other copyright transfers[15]

Bankruptcy Code section 544(a)(1) provides that the trustee may avoid any transfer of property of the debtor . . . that is voidable by — (1) a creditor that extends credit to the debtor at the time of the commencement of the case, and that obtains, at such time and with respect to such credit, a judicial lien on all property on which a creditor on a simple contract could have obtained such a judicial lien. [16]

Section 101 of the Copyright Act of 1976 defines "transfer of copyright ownership" as including "an assignment, mortgage, exclusive license, or any other conveyance, alienation, hypothecation of a copyright or any of the exclusive rights comprised in a copyright, whether or not it is limited in time or place of effect, but not including a nonexclusive license."[17] The meaning of "transfer" for purposes of Bankruptcy Code section 544(a)(1) should be at least as broad as the Copyright Act's definition.[18] Accordingly, a wide variety of software transactions are "transfers" voidable by the trustee under Bankruptcy Code section 544(a)(1). These certainly include sales of rights in computer

---

[15] The discussion in Part I assumes that both the source and object code versions of the subject programs are transferred. The discussion in Part II addresses the effect in the more typical transaction where the vendee is given only object code, but has a contingent right to source code.

[16] Under §544, the trustee has other avoiding powers not immediately relevant. See 11 U.S.C. §544(a)-(b) (1982).

[17] 17 U.S.C. §101. This definition reflects the divisibility of a copyright under the Copyright Act. Under the Copyright Act of 1909, copyright was not divisible; under the new Copyright Act, it is infinitely divisible. H.R. Rep. No. 1476, 94th Cong., 2d Sess. 123, reprinted in 1976 *U.S. Code Cong. & Admin. News* 5659, 5738–39 [hereinafter House Report]; 3 M. Nimmer, *Nimmer on Copyright*, §§10.01–10.02 (1985). Note that the trustee, considered as hypothetical lien creditor, is a "transferee" because the trustee takes the debtor's copyright in the licensed software by "alienation or hypothecation."

[18] An exclusive license of one of the exclusive rights comprised in a copyright is traditionally treated as "property." *Goldsmith v. Commissioner*, 143 F.2d 466, 467 (2nd Cir. 1944), cert. denied, 323 U.S. 774 (1945). As such, it falls squarely within the Bankruptcy Code definition of "transfer," "every mode, direct or indirect, absolute or conditional, voluntary or involuntary, of disposing of or parting with property or with an interest in property." 11 U.S.C. §101(48). See 4 King, *Collier on Bankruptcy*, ¶544.02 (15th ed., 1985).

programs, such as the sales that occur when one company purchases another's software assets. They also include grants of security interests in software. Finally, and perhaps most surprisingly, they include exclusive software licenses.

The sale of an asset and the taking of a security interest are easily recognized transactions. An exclusive copyright license, on the other hand, is a broader concept than one might suppose. The Copyright Act provides no test for distinguishing between exclusive and non-exclusive licenses. The House Report indicates that a license limited to a particular time, place, or type of use is an "exclusive license" for purposes of the Act.[19] As one court put it, "[t]here appears to be no limit on how narrow the scope of exclusive rights can be yet still constitute a 'transfer of ownership,' provided the licensed rights are exclusive."

For this reason, many software licenses are likely to be considered "exclusive" licenses for purposes of the Copyright Act. If, for example, a software vendor granted to a bank a license to use its database management system and agreed with the bank that it would not license any other bank to use the same system during the period of the license, such an agreement would fall within the purview of "exclusive licenses" for purposes of the Copyright Act. Similarly, if the same software vendor modified its database management system for a particular customer and agreed with the customer that it would not provide the modified version to any other customer, that too would be considered an exclusive license for purposes of the Copyright Act. In contrast, "shrink-wrap" licenses of mass-market software seem clearly nonexclusive for purposes of the Copyright Act's definition.

Assuming that many software transactions transfer a part of the copyright in the subject programs, may a bankruptcy trustee for the vendor set aside such transfers? Bankruptcy Code section 544(a)(1) permits the trustee to avoid any transfer that is avoidable by a creditor who obtains a judicial lien. This leaves two questions: (1) could a creditor obtain a judicial lien on the copyright in the transferred programs; and (2) would such a lien enable the creditor to avoid the transfer?

The first question — whether, and to what extent, copyright can be obtained by "judicial lien" raises complex issues involving both federal and state law. The basic rule is that a trustee's rights and powers as a hypothetical lien creditor under section 544(a)(1) are determined by the state in which the

---

[19] See House Report, supra note 17, at 123; see also 3 M. Nimmer, *Nimmer on Copyright*, §10.02[A] (1982).

property in issue is located.[20] For intangible property, which has no "location," the law of the state in which the debtor is domiciled or has its principal place of business determines the issue.[21] While the authors have found no case expressly so holding, it seems likely that copyright falls within the purview of state laws permitting attachment of intangible property.[22] Furthermore, even if copyright does not fall within the scope of a particular state's judicial attachment provisions, the Bankruptcy Code defines "judicial lien" as including any "legal or equitable process or proceeding."[23] An author's ownership of copyright is undoubtedly subject to the powers of coercion of the state's courts in equity.[24] Thus, under the laws of most states, copyright is

---

20 *In re Ireland,* 14 Bankr. 849, 850 (Bankr. M.D. La. 1981); see Restatement (Second) of Conflict of Law §§6,222 comment b (importance of situs to determination of law governing interests in property).

21 *Gordon v. Holly Woods Acres, Inc.*, 328 F.2d 253, 255 (6th Cir. 1964); see *ABKCO Industries, Inc. v. Apple Films, Inc.*, 39 N.Y.2d 670, 675 (1976) (situs of intangible property for attachment purposes is place of business of party whose performance is required by contract that creates the intangible property). Similarly, consensual liens on general intangibles are governed by the law of the state in which the debtor is located, U.C.C. §9-103(3)(b) (1972), which is in turn defined by the Uniform Commercial Code as the debtor's place of business. Id. §9-103(3)(d).

22 For example, New York statutes provide for levy by order of attachment of any property, tangible or intangible, that could be assigned or transferred. *N.Y. Civ. Prac. L. & R.* §§5201(b), 6202, 6214(b) (McKinney 1978); see ABKCO Industries, 39 N.Y.2d at 673–74 (licensor's interest in license to promote and distribute film is attachable intangible property because it is assignable by licensor); cf. *Marshak v. Green*, 746 F.2d 927, 929 (2d Cir. 1984) (trademark divorced from its goodwill is not assignable and therefore not attachable property within the meaning of §5201(b)).

23 11 U.S.C. §101(27) (1982) ("'judicial lien' means lien obtained by judgment, levy, sequestration, or other legal or equitable proceeding."); see *In re H. & S. Transportation Co.,* 42 Bankr. 164 (Bankr. M.D. Tenn. 1984) (maritime lien created pursuant to federal statute is not avoidance by trustee under §544(a)(1) because it is obtained automatically and not by legal or equitable process or proceeding).

24 *Ager v. Murray,* 105 U.S. 126 (1882). In several early cases the Court suggested that copyright was not subject to seizure or sale by writ of execution because it is an incorporeal right "resting altogether in grant," *Stephens v. Cady,* 55 U.S. (14 How.) 528, 531 (1852); see also *Stevens v. Gladding,* 58 U.S. (17 How.) 447,451 (1855), but might be reached and applied pursuant to a creditor's bill if transfer was compelled in conformity with the then Copyright Act requirement of a writing signed by the proprietor of the copyright. Stephens, 55 U.S. (14 How.) at 531–32. Stephens and Stevens, however, concerned executions at law; whereas equity works in personam. A debtor's interest in patent or copyright, which cannot be taken at law, is assignable by the debtor and may be ordered sold or assigned by a court of equity in satisfaction of a judgment debt of the owner-debtor. Ager, 105 U.S. at 131–32. Copyright is reached not through seizure of

likely to be subject to taking by "judicial lien" within the meaning of the Bankruptcy Code, if not by legal attachment, then by equitable coercion. This conclusion appears to be supported by the Copyright Act of 1976 itself, which expressly recognizes that copyright is subject to transfers by operation of law,[25] and is consistent with the broad equitable powers conferred upon the Bankruptcy Court.[26]

---

property, but by exercise of equitable powers of coercion; the order to sell or assign is enforceable by contempt or by execution by an appointee of the court in the name of the debtor-owner. D. Dobbs, *Law of Remedies*, §1.3 (1973). The merger of law and equity is reflected in the definition of "judicial liens" subject to the trustee's strong arm powers, which is quoted in the preceding note.

[25] 17 U.S.C. §20l(d)(l) (1982) ("the ownership of copyright may be transferred . . . by operation of law"). However, the conclusion that copyright is subject to "judicial liens" is complicated by §20l(e), which protects authors against involuntary loss of rights in their works. Section 201(e) provides for involuntary transfers as follows:

> When an individual's ownership of a copyright, or of any of the exclusive rights under a copyright, has not previously been transferred voluntarily by that individual author, no action by any governmental body or other official organization purporting to seize, expropriate, transfer, or exercise rights of ownership with respect to the copyright, or any of the exclusive rights under a copyright, shall be given effect under this title except as provided under Title 11.

However, §201(e) probably does not prevent the trustee in bankruptcy form obtaining the status of a hypothetical lien creditor with respect to the typical software vendor/debtor's copyrights, for several reasons. First, §201(e) protects only "individual" authors. "Individual author" is not defined by the Copyright Act. However, the House Report explains the exemption as follows:

> The purpose of [§201(e)] is to reaffirm the basic principle that the United States copyright of an individual author shall be secured to that author, and cannot be taken away by any involuntary transfer. . . . Traditional legal actions that may involve transfer of ownership, such as bankruptcy proceedings and mortgage foreclosures, are not within the scope of this subsection; the authors in such cases have voluntarily consented to these legal processes by their overt actions — for example, by filing in bankruptcy or by hypothecating a copyright. House Report, supra note 17, at 124.

The legislative history and purpose of §201(e) strongly suggest that the section would not apply to works made for hire, if the employer/author is a corporation or business entity. Nothing in the statutory provisions for "work made for hire" suggest otherwise. See 17 U.S.C. §§101 (definition), 201(b) (employer for whom work is made is considered the author).

Second, §201(e) does not apply when any of the exclusive rights under a copyright have been transferred voluntarily prior to the filing of bankruptcy. Thus, the section would be unavailing in the common situation where an independent programmer has assigned rights in the program to the vendor prior to the initiation of bankruptcy proceedings.

If a judicial lien on copyright can be obtained within the meaning of section 544(a)(1), under the laws of the state in which a particular bankrupt vendor is domiciled, the question remains whether such a lien would prevail over an exclusive license or other software transfer. Priority between conflicting copyright transfers is governed by section 205 (e) of the Copyright Act. Under section 205 (e), the prior transfer prevails if it is recorded in the manner required to give constructive notice under section 205 (c) within one month of its execution[27] or prior to the subsequent transfer. A transferee is thus protected against the trustee's claim under section 544(a)(1) if the transfer is recorded prior to the filing of bankruptcy proceedings.[28]

If the transfer is not recorded, the trustee will prevail under section 205 (e) as a subsequent transferee if certain conditions are met.[29] The subsequent transfer to the trustee must be recorded, and it must be taken in good faith, for valuable consideration, and without notice of the exclusive license. A brief discussion of each of these requirements follows.

First, consider the recording requirement. The Copyright Act requires the prior transfer to be unrecorded and the later transfer to be recorded in order for the later transfer to prevail over the prior transfer. Read literally, this would require the trustee to race unrecorded transferees to file in the Copyright Office.

A strong argument can be made that this requirement cannot be applied literally to the bankruptcy trustee. First, there is no document to record. The

---

Third, and most importantly, §201(e) states an exception "as provided under Title 11." See supra. The quoted language was inserted by amendment pursuant to the Bankruptcy Reform Act of 1978. See Pub. L. No. 95-598, Title III §313 (1978). This reference to the Bankruptcy Code strongly suggests that a trustee's rights in the debtor's copyrights, under §544(a)(1) or otherwise, are not intended to be affected by §201(e). For all these reasons, §201(e) should not prevent a trustee from asserting rights under § 544(a)(1) in a bankruptcy software vendor's copyrights if the relevant state law permits a lien creditor to do so.

[26] 11 U.S.C. §105(a) ('the court may issue any order, process or judgment that is necessary or appropriate to carry out the provisions of [the Bankruptcy Code]'); see, e.g., *In re Virginia Block Co.,* 6 Bankr. 670 (Bankr. W.D. Va. 1980) (court exercises equitable powers under §105(a) to compel senior lienholder's marshaling of assets and foreclosure so as to satisfy its claim, if possible, without proceeding against jointly secured property).

[27] The one-month period is extended to two months if the execution of the transfer is outside of the United States. 17 U.S.C. §205(e) (1982).

[28] For a discussion of the problems associated with copyright registration and recordation of software licenses, see infra text accompanying notes 153–63.

[29] The Copyright Act does not specify which party prevails if the prior transfer has not been recorded, but the subsequent transferee fails to satisfy the criteria of §205(e).

"transfer" in bankruptcy proceedings is a statutory construct: the vesting in the trustee of the rights of a hypothetical lien creditor under section 544(a)(1). Second, requiring the bankruptcy trustee to file something in the Copyright Office (for example, a certified copy of the bankruptcy petition) is not necessary to give notice of the trustee's rights. Filing the bankruptcy petition creates nationwide notice of the existence of bankruptcy proceedings.[30] Third, requiring such recording would be inconsistent with the policy of giving the debtor (and its trustee) a "breathing spell from [its] creditors."[31] Finally, licensees are probably stayed from making their own filings after the bankruptcy proceedings are initiated.[32] For these reasons, the trustee should

---

[30] H.R. Rep. No. 595, supra note 10, at 331–32; S. Rep. NO. 989, supra note 10, at 49–51. Most bankruptcy judges would not be sympathetic with an interpretation that required trustees to make pro forma filings in the Copyright Office that served no substantive purpose at a time when they are very busy taking care of concrete details like payrolls, leases, utilities, and the other pressing concerns in the early stages of bankruptcy proceedings.

[31] S. Rep. No. 989, supra note 10, at 54.

[32] The filing of bankruptcy proceedings acts as an automatic stay against "any act to obtain possession of property of the estate or of property from the estate . . . [and] any act to create, perfect, or enforce any lien against property of the estate." 11 U.S.C. §362(a)(3)-(a)(4) (1982). Many other acts are also stayed. See generally id. §362(a). Whether the automatic stay applies to recording in the Copyright Office of an asset purchase agreement or exclusive software license will depend on whether the purchased or licensed software is considered "property of the estate" at a time subsequent to execution of the purchase or licensing agreement and prior to Copyright Office filing. "Property of the estate" is defined by the Bankruptcy Code as including "all legal or equitable interests of the debtor in property as of the commencement of the case." Id. §541 (a)(l); see also *United States v. Whiting Pools, Inc.*, 462 U.S. 198, 204 n.8 (1983) ("Congress intended to exclude from the estate property of others in which the debtor had some minor interest such as a lien or bare legal title . . . [but] not limit the ability of a trustee to regain possession of property in which the debtor had equitable as well as legal title"). The definition of "property of the estate" would appear to exclude an interest in copyright transferred by the debtor before the commencement of the case, if the transfer was valid under the Copyright Act. See *Butner v. United States*, 440 U.S. 48, 55 (1979) (state law determines a debtor's legal or equitable interest in property for purposes of §541(a)(1) unless some federal interest requires a different result); 17 U.S.C. §301 (1982) (federal preemption of matters within the scope of the Copyright Act). Transfer of copyright ownership is valid if it is evidenced by a written instrument, signed by the owner of the rights conveyed — regardless of whether or not the instrument is filed in the Copyright Office. See id. §204(a). All of which suggests that the automatic stay should not apply to the recording in the Copyright Office of an asset purchase or exclusive software license, so long as the purchase agreement has been validly executed and the purchaser or licensee has possession of the licensed programs

be deemed to have recorded its hypothetical lien for purposes of section 205 (e) of the Copyright Act.[33]

The second requirement under section 205 (e) of the Copyright Act is that the subsequent transferee must take "in good faith." Clearly, the Bankruptcy Code's hypothetical lien creditor is assumed to act in good faith.[34] A contrary assumption would eliminate much of the power of the "strong arm clause."

The third requirement under section 205 (e) of the Copyright Act is that the subsequent transferee must take "for valuable consideration." Bankruptcy Code section 544(a)(1) postulates that the hypothetical creditor "extends credit to the debtor at the time of the commencement of the case and . . . obtains, at such time and with respect to such credit, a judicial lien." This means there is valuable consideration for the creditor's claim against the debtor, but does it also mean that there is consideration for the lien (i.e., for the transfer)? Although no case directly supports this proposition and the Bankruptcy Code is ambiguous, a fair reading of section 544(a)(1) is that the hypothetical lien creditor status is intended to eliminate any defenses to the trustee's rights that might be available to any creditor that could be hypothesized,[35] including defenses based on a lack of consideration. For this

---

as of the filing of bankruptcy proceedings, unless recording is for the purpose of perfecting a security interest in the licensed programs. See infra text accompanying notes 154–63. On the other hand, §362(a) is interpreted very broadly as prohibiting any act that would dismember the estate or inhibit the orderly, equitable distribution of assets among creditors. *In re R.S. Pinellas Motel*, 2 Bankr. 113, 117–18 (Bankr. M.D. Fla. 1979). For example, a notice of termination of a licensing agreement, an act designed to obtain possession of intangible property of the licensee-debtor's estate, is within the scope of the automatic stay and thus has no force or effect after the commencement of the case. Id. at 118–19. The automatic stay meshes with Bankruptcy Code §547, under which the trustee may avoid transfers of property which improve the position of a creditor and are made within ninety days prior to filing, or one year prior to filing in the case of transfers to insiders. Both sections favor the equitable distribution of assets among creditors. H.R. Rep. No. 595, supra note 10, at 340–42; S. Rep. No. 989, supra note 10, at 49–51. For these reasons, one can argue that the automatic stay of §262 should be held to prevent the recording of software purchases and licenses following the filing of bankruptcy proceedings.

33 *Sampsel v. Straub*, 194 F.2d 228, 231 (9th Cir. 1951), cert. denied, 343 U.S. 927 (1952) (If state law requires a creditor asserting a judicial lien to file notice of the lien, under § 544(a) the trustee is deemed to have so filed); See 4 King, *Collier on Bankruptcy*, ¶544.02 (15th ed., 1985) (discussion of trustee's "ideal creditor" status under §544(a)(1).

34 *In re Waynesboro Motor Co.*, 60 F.2d 668, 669 (S.D. Miss. 1933); see 4 King, supra note 34, at ¶544.02.

35 See id. at ¶544.01–.02.

reason, the hypothetical lien creditor should be considered to have given valuable consideration for the transfer.

Section 205(e) of the Copyright Act finally requires the subsequent transferee to act "without notice of the earlier transfer." Bankruptcy Code section 544(a)(1) gives the trustee the avoiding power of a hypothetical lien creditor "without regard to any knowledge of the trustee or of any creditor."[36] Section 544(a)(1) is silent on the question of whether knowledge of the debtor should affect the trustee's rights. Our software transferor clearly had knowledge and notice of transactions it entered into prior to the filing of bankruptcy proceedings. If the transferor's knowledge were imputed to the Bankruptcy Code's hypothetical lien creditor, then the rights of the lien creditor might not prevail under section 205 (e) of the Copyright Act because the hypothetical creditor had "notice of the earlier transfer."

The better view is that the debtor's knowledge cannot be imputed to the trustee in his or her capacity as hypothetical lien creditor under Bankruptcy Code section 544(a)(1). The trustee has an "ideal" creditor's status; his status is derived from the Bankruptcy Code and not from actual creditors of the debtor. Accordingly, when faced with challenges to unperfected security interests, the trustee has the status of a lien creditor without notice for purposes of section 544(a) of the Bankruptcy Code, even if a particular creditor or the debtor had notice of a transfer.[37] Properly understood, the bankruptcy trustee is not a representative of the debtor but is instead a representative of the debtor's creditors.[38] If the debtor's knowledge were imputed to the trustee, then the trustee could not assert some rights, including the avoidance powers of a transferee without knowledge under

---

[36] The strong arm clause gives the trustee in bankruptcy the rights of a creditor who has complied with all legal and equitable requirements of a lien creditor. *In re Waynesboro Motor Co.*, 60 F.2d at 669.

[37] When the predecessor to §544(a) was first enacted in 1910, courts occasionally focused on the general principle that a trustee represents the (actual) creditors and failed to recognize the change created by the artificial status accorded the trustee under the strong arm clause. See, e.g., *Walton Land & Timber Co. v. Runyan,* 269 F. 128, 129 (5th Cir. 1920) (failure to accord trustee status of creditor without notice). It was difficult to dispel the former notice that a trustee was bound by the rights of actual creditors or to accept the possibility that distributees of the proceeds of recovery by the trustee should include creditors who could not have recovered under non-bankruptcy law. See 4B Moore, *Collier on Bankruptcy,* ¶70.53 (14th ed., 1978) (discussion of early problems arising with respect to actual notice under the strong arm clause).

[38] See generally Jackson, "Bankruptcy, Non-Bankruptcy Entitlements, and the Creditor's Bargain," 91 *Yale L. J.* 857 (1982).

section 205 (e) of the Copyright Act, which could be asserted by a creditor who did not have notice of the earlier transfer. This would put such a creditor in a worse position as a result of bankruptcy proceedings than the creditor would be in in the absence of the proceedings and damage the central function of bankruptcy proceedings: to provide an efficient and equitable clearing house for the creditors' claims.

For the foregoing reasons, the statutes, the legislative history, and precedent all support bankruptcy trustees for software vendors as having the power to avoid an unrecorded transfer of copyright in computer programs. It must be acknowledged, however, that strong equities favor the transferee. If the transfer occurred as part of a business acquisition, the purchaser may have made a substantial investment in the acquisition of an "asset." If the transfer is an exclusive license, the exclusive licensee may be heavily dependent on the licensed software. In either case, the transferee may have had no idea that the Copyright Act required recordation of the copyright "transfer" when he or she entered into the transaction. Confronted with such a sympathetic case, courts sometimes strain to soften the harsh impact of the strong arm clause.[39] A court could resolve any of the doubtful points (i.e., constructive recording by the trustee, consideration for the lien, or the trustee's insulation from the debtor's knowledge) against the bankruptcy trustee as a way of protecting the transferee against the harsh effects of avoidance under section 544(a)(1).[40]

---

39 It has been held, for example, that the trustee cannot use his or her statutory lack of knowledge to avoid the rights of holders of equitable interests in the debtor's real property. *McCannon v. Marston* (*In re Hotel Assocs., Inc.*), 679 F.2d 13, 17 (3d Cir. 1982). The *McCannon* court reasoned that while the words "without regard to any knowledge" in §544(a) address the concern that the trustee's personal knowledge should not affect the trustee's status as a hypothetical lien creditor under Article 9 of the U.C.C., the words should not be read to extinguish the rights of equitable owners in possession of real property nor the obligation of a potential subsequent purchaser (i.e., the trustee) to inquire into the possessor's claimed rights, equitable or legal, in the property in a state where clear and open possession of real property constitutes constructive notice of the rights of the possessor. Id. at 16–17. The court's holding, however, may be limited to the trustee's bona fide purchaser status under §544(a)(3) or to real estate transactions, for which the Bankruptcy Code makes special exceptions. See 11 U.S.C. §544(a)(3); *In re Hardway Restaurant, Inc.*, 31 Bankr. 322, 328 (Bankr. S.D.N.Y. 1983) (McCannon requires applying state law recognized constructive notice as a bar to the trustee's bona fide purchaser under §544(a)(3)).

40 Under the Bankruptcy Code, the court has the power to fashion equitable solutions for which there is no express provision if they are "necessary or appropriate." 11 U.S.C. §105(a) (1982).

Nevertheless, equally sympathetic unrecorded transferees have consistently failed to forestall loss of property under the strong arm clause. Examples include a lessor's interest in personal property subject to an unrecorded long term lease; a principal's claim to recover goodwill and customer information following termination of an unrecorded agency agreement; a purchaser's or creditor's interest in real estate subject to a deed; and a divorcee's interest in occupancy of property subject to a divorce decree that was not recorded in the Registry of Deeds.[41] These seemingly harsh decisions can be justified by the failure of the purchaser, secured creditor, or lessee to take steps readily available to it to protect its interest.[42] The software transferee's failure to record its purchase agreement or exclusive license can be similarly faulted.

For this reason, unrecorded software purchases and exclusive licenses should be voidable by a bankruptcy trustee under Bankruptcy Code section 544(a)(1), at least to the extent the transaction covers copyright in the subject programs.

---

[41] *Westberry Office Machine v. Hovis*, 35 Bankr. 8, 9 (Bankr. D.S.C. 1983) (fourteen-month rental of photocopier did not fall within the "temporary use" exception to state law rental agreement recording requirement); *Saint Paul Fire & Marine Insurance Co. v. Roy Dart Insurance Agency, Inc.* (*In re Roy Dart Insurance Agency, Inc.*), 5 Bankr. 207, 214–216 (Bankr. D. Ma. 1980) (agency agreement providing for transfer of goodwill and customer information to principal upon termination of agency created a security interest in "general intangibles" subject to U.C.C. filing requirements for perfection); *In re Anderson*, 30 Bankr. 995, 1002–06 (Bankr. M.D. Tenn. 1983) (recorded deed, having technically defective acknowledgments, failed to satisfy state filing requirements despite trustee's notice and the later filing of corrected deeds); *Lancaster v. Hurst* (*In re Hurst*), 27 Bankr. 740, 743–44 (Bankr. E.D. Tenn. 1983) (divorcee's conditional right under divorce decree to occupy ex-husband's property rent-free falls within state law filing requirement for perfection of instruments conveying any right of occupancy). Despite the sympathetic circumstances of the cited cases, and other similar cases, each court upheld the trustee's exercise of strong arm powers on the behalf of creditors because the party or parties claiming an interest had failed to meet the formal requirements for providing notice to potential creditors. See also infra text accompanying notes 95–100 (discussing the Fourth Circuit's recent comments on the inappropriateness of equitable arguments in bankruptcy proceedings).

[42] *In re DG & Assocs., Inc.*, 9 Bankr. 94, 97 (Bankr. E.D. Tenn. 1981) is an example of a particularly harsh application of §544(a)(1) A bank's perfected security interest in bankrupt's equipment, accounts receivable, and present and after acquired inventory was held to be rendered "unperfected" by the bank's failure to refile its financing statement upon learning of the debtor's pre-bankruptcy name change, despite the absence of an explicit statutory requirement of refiling when the debtor's name changes. The court was unconvinced by the bank's arguments in part because "[t]he bank could easily have filed and thereby given notice to subsequent parties." Id. at 97.

Following a section 544(a)(1) avoidance, the licensed copyright is recoverable by the trustee under the turnover provision of the Bankruptcy Code.[43]

2. Effect of the strong arm clause on nonexclusive licenses

For two reasons, a bankruptcy trustee cannot avoid nonexclusive copyright licenses. First, such licenses are not "transfers of copyright ownership" within the meaning of the Copyright Act.[44] Second, the Copyright Act expressly protects the interests of non-exclusive licensees against subsequent transferees of copyright. Section 205(f) provides that "[a] nonexclusive license, whether recorded or not, prevails over a conflicting transfer of copyright ownership if the license is evidenced by a written instrument signed by the owner of the rights licensed or such owner's duly authorized agent, and if . . . the license was taken before execution of the transfer." The trustee has the rights of a creditor holding a judicial lien on the copyright under Bankruptcy Code section 544(a)(1) and is, therefore, a transferee of a copyright by alienation or hypothecation under Copyright Act section 101.[45]

Thus, the trustee is a conflicting transferee for purposes of Copyright Act section 205 (f). Under section 205 (f), the rights of a nonexclusive licensee should prevail if the copyright in the licensed program is owned by the vendor, and the nonexclusive software license is signed by the vendor or its agent. There is no reason to suppose that this result would not be followed under section 544(a) (1) of the Bankruptcy Code. Hence, it appears that non-exclusive licenses of copyrights in computer programs are not voidable under section 544(a)(1).

B. Bankruptcy code section 544(a)(1) as it affects trade secrets contained in computer programs

The legal landscape changes dramatically when one considers the trade secret dimension of the licensed programs. Regardless of whether it is exclusive or nonexclusive, a trade secret license is a common law contract conferring on the licensee a right to use the secret under the terms of the

---

[43] 11 U.S.C. §542 (1982) ("Turnover of Property to the Estate"). See infra note 71.

[44] See 17 U.S.C. §101 (1983) (definition of "transfer of copyright ownership"); see also supra text accompanying note 17; cf. *Harris v. Emus Records Corp.*, 734 F.2d 1329, 1334 (9th Cir. 1984) (debtor/licensee's rights under a non-exclusive compulsory license do not pass to bankruptcy trustee because the licensee has no proprietary right nor transferable interest in copyright).

[45] See supra text accompanying notes 16–18.

license, highly analogous to a lease of personal property.[46] Because such a contract does not "transfer" any property, the trustee cannot claim that the trade secret license is voidable under section 544(a)(1).[47] Many trade secret licenses, however, are executory contracts subject to the trustee's power of rejection.[48] The trustee's exercise of the power of rejection is discussed in the following section of this Article.

C. Bankruptcy code section 365 as it affects software licenses

1. Definition of executory contract: *Lubrizol Enterprises v. Richmond Metal Finishers*

One of the trustee's most versatile tools is the power to accept or reject executory contracts. Section 365 of the Bankruptcy Code provides, with certain exceptions, that 'the trustee, subject to the court's approval, may accept or reject any executory contract or unexpired lease of the debtor.'[49] The court will approve either acceptance or rejection unless the trustee has failed to exercise "sound business judgment."[50] This standard gives the trustee a very wide latitude. In practice, the trustee may pick and choose among the

---

[46] See *Ruckelshaus v. Monsanto Co.*, 467 U.S. 986, 1001-05 (1984)) (owner of trade secret has property rights therein, which are comparable to rights in other intangible interests and protected by the taking clause of the fifth amendment); 1 Milgrim, *Milgrim on Trade Secrets*, §1.06 (1985) (licensor retains property right in licensed trade secret). A trade secret that a debtor is entitled to protect as property under applicable state law passes to the debtor's trustee in bankruptcy. *In re Uniservices*, 517 F.2d 492, 496 (7th Cir. 1975).

[47] By contrast, real property leases are often described as transfers of a limited property right creating an estate in the realty, and are voidable under §544(a)(3). See, e.g., *In re Belize Airways Ltd.*, 12 Bankr. 387 (Bankr. S.D. Fla. 1981) (unrecorded agreement of sublease is voidable under state recording statute); see also 2 King, *Collier on Bankruptcy*, ¶365.09 and 365.10; cf. *Library Publications, Inc. v. Medical Economics Co.*, 548 F. Supp. 1231 (E.D. Pa. 1982), aff'd mem., 714 F.2d 123 (3d Cir. 1983)) (exclusive license of copyright transfers a limited property right to licensee).

[48] Rejection of executory contracts is discussed in detail in the following two subsections of this Article. See infra text accompanying notes 50–102.

[49] 11 U.S.C. §365(a) (1982). Note that section 365 applies to Chapter 7 liquidation cases, and to Chapter 9, 11, and 13 reorganization cases. See id. §§103(a), 901(a) (1982).

[50] *NLRB v. Bildisco & Bildisco*, 465 U.S. 513, 523 (1984). As applied, this standard "requires that the decision be accepted by the courts unless it is shown that the bankrupt's decision was one taken in bad faith or in gross abuse of the bankrupt's retained business discretion." *Lubrizol v. Richmond Metal Finishers*, 756 F.2d 1043, 1047 (4th Cir. 1985). cert. denied, 106 S. Ct. 1285 (1986).

debtor's contractual obligations. The ones that burden the estate may be rejected, converting the debtor's executory obligations into unsecured indebtedness.[51] The ones that benefit the estate may be accepted, and their benefits made available to all of the debtor's creditors.[52]

The Bankruptcy Code provides no definition of the term "executory contract."[53] Nevertheless, legislative history and the policy of section 365 leave little doubt that many software licenses should be considered executory for

[51] Claims for damages caused by rejection of an executory contract are invariably treated as general unsecured claims, unless the contractual obligee has taken a security interest to secure the debtor's executory obligations. See 11 U.S.C. §502(g) ("A claim arising from the rejection, under section 365 . . . of an executory contract . . . shall be determined . . . the same as if such claim had arisen before the date of the filing of the petition"); see also 3 King, *Collier on Bankruptcy*, ¶502.07 (15th ed., 1985). The amount of such claim is determined by the court under §502(b).

[52] The trustee's option of assuming or rejecting executory contracts derives from a well-established principle of insolvency practice. Eighteenth-century English courts permitted trustees to abandon property "worthless or onerous" to the debtor estate, "including leases and other executory contracts," considerably before this "doctrine of abandonment" was codified in the English Bankruptcy Act. Countryman, "Executory Contracts in Bankruptcy: Part I," 57 *Minn. L. Rev.* 439, 440 (1973) [hereinafter Countryman I]. In the nineteenth century the United States Supreme Court incorporated English doctrine in its consideration of a case arising under the Bankruptcy Act of 1867. Id. American codification of the doctrine began in the Bankruptcy Act of 1935 with provisions explicitly limited to railroad reorganizations. See 49 Stat. 911 (1935), 11 U.S.C. §205 (1940). The Chandler Act amendments of 1938 extended the option to assume or reject executory contracts and unexpired leases of real property to trustees in straight bankruptcy cases through the addition of section 70(b) to the Act. 52 Stat. 873 (1938), 11 U.S.C. §110(b) (1940). Section 70(b) was the precursor of the 1978 Bankruptcy Code's §365. See 2 King, supra note 48, at ¶365.01–.02. The Code's §365 differs substantially from the former §706(b). See Quittner, "Franchises in Bankruptcy: Termination, Rejection and Assumption," 1984 *Comm. L. J.* 84. The 1984 Amendments have also affected §365; some of these changes will be discussed subsequently in this Article. For an overview of all of the 1984 Amendments' implications for §365, see Chatz & Schumm, III, "1984 Bankruptcy Code Amendments — Fresh from the Anvil," Aug./Sept. 1984 *Comm. L. J.* 317, 324–28. For a more detailed history of this doctrine, see Countryman I, supra, and Silverstein, "Rejection of Executory Contracts in Bankruptcy and Reorganization," 31 *U. Chi. L. Rev.* 467 (1964). (Countryman, Executory Contracts in Bankruptcy: Part I 1973) (Countryman, Executory Contracts in Bankruptcy: Part II 1974)

[53] The Commission on the Bankruptcy Laws of the United States, after a Congressionally authorized two-year study, recommended that "the term 'executory contract' should not be defined. Its general meaning is well understood, and any succinct statutory language risks an unintended omission or inclusion. Instead, the proposed Act should clearly indicate the treatment of certain incompletely performed agreements." H.R. Doc. No. 137, 93d Cong., 1st Sess. 198–99 (1973) [hereinafter Commission Report].

purposes of section 365 and, therefore, subject to possible rejection.[54] The House Report on the Bankruptcy Reform Act of 1978 states that although there is no precise definition of what contracts are executory [the term] generally includes contracts on which performance remains due to some extent on both sides. A note is not usually an executory contract if the only performance that remains is repayment. Performance on one side of the contract would have been completed, and the contract is no longer executory.[55]

The majority of courts have interpreted section 365 and its history as adopting Professor Vern Countryman's familiar definition of executory contract: "a contract under which the obligation of both the bankrupt and the other party to the contract are so far unperformed that the failure of either to complete performance would constitute a material breach excusing the performance of the other."[56] Courts that differ from the Countryman definition have either expanded the definition[57] or added a second step to the analysis.[58]

---

[54] Whether a contract is "executory" under the Bankruptcy Code is a question of federal common law. *In re Meadows*, 39 Bankr. 538, 540 (Bankr. W.D Ken. 1984). in contrast, the legal consequences of one party's failure to perform its remaining obligations under a contract is an issue of state contract law . . . a bankruptcy court should determine whether one of the parties' failure to perform its remaining obligations would give rise to a "material breach" excusing performance by other party under the contract law applicable to the contract under the choice of law rules of the state in which the court sits. *In re Cochise College Park*, 703 F.2d 1339, 1348 n.4 (9th Cir. 1983); accord *In re Alexander*, 670 F.2d 885, 898 (9th Cir. 1982).

[55] H.R. Rep. No. 595, supra note 10, at 347; see also S. Rep. No. 989, supra note 10.

[56] See, e.g., *In re Alexander*, 670 F.2d 885 (9th Cir. 1982); *In re Select-A-Seat Corp.*, 265 F.2d 290 (9th Cir. 1980); *In re Knudson*, 563 F.2d 916 (8th Cir. 1977); *In re Farrar McWill, Inc.*, 26 Bankr. 313 (Bankr. W.D. Ken. 1982); *In re Fashion Twenty, Inc.*, 16 Bankr. 784 (N.D. Ohio 1982); *In re Rovine*, 6 Bankr. 661 (Bankr. W.D. Tenn., 1980). Commentators generally agree that Congress intended to adopt the Countryman definition. See Cook, "Judicial Standards for Rejection of Executory Contracts in Bankruptcy Code Reorganization Cases," *1980 Annual Survey uf American Law* 691, and Quittner, supra note 53, at 84.

[57] The Tenth Circuit applied a "gloss" to Countryman's definition, which effectively expands it. The contract is executory when "neither party [has] completely performed and the obligations of each remain complex." *Workman v. Harrison*, 282 F.2d 693, 699 (10th Cir. 1960); *King v. Baer*, 482 F.2d 552, 557 (10th Cir. 1973), cert. denied, 414 U.S. 1068 (1973); see also *In re Harms*, 7 Bankr. Ct. Drc. (CRR) 671, 673 (D. Colo. 1981). The Tenth Circuit thus retains Countryman's requirement of bilateral nonperformance but removes the necessity of such nonperformance's resulting in material breach. *In re Harms* demonstrated the different results obtained by the two definitions. Debtor was sole general partner in several limited partnerships. Neither the limited nor the general

partners fully performed. Under *Countryman*, however, the partnership contract would not have been executory because under the terms of the partnership agreement failure of a limited partner to perform did not excuse the general partnership from performing. The limited partner would simply be forced to forfeit his partnership interest. Id. Because the general partner had many services left to perform and the limited partners were obligated to make substantial payments, the court did find the outstanding obligations of all parties complex, and therefore held the partnership contract executory. The *Harms* court's substitution of "complex" for *Countryman*'s requirement that outstanding obligations constitute "material breach excusing the performance of the other [party]," simply makes it easier for courts to find contracts executory. The Tenth Circuit test will thus increase, not decrease, the chances that software license agreements may be considered executory in the Tenth Circuit. The meaning of "complex" does not appear to be well developed, but both *Workman* and King focus on remaining detailed obligations that require additional expenditure of large sums of money. In *Workman* the court also contemplated the risky and speculative nature of the enterprise.

Some courts remove the bilateral nonperformance requirement entirely and state that "a contract is executory when something remains to be done by one or more of the parties." *In re American Magnesium Co.*, 488 F.2d 147, 152 (5th Cir. 1974); see *In re Brethren's Home*, 5 Bankr. Ct. Dec. (CRR) 658 (S.D. Ohio 1979) (where debtor nursing home owed ongoing obligations under resident patient's life care contracts and resident patients had completed performance by lump sum payment, life care contracts were nevertheless held executory). Despite the breadth of such holdings, the contract is generally not held to be executory where the debtor has no remaining performance obligations. See *H. K. Porter Co.*, 24 F. Supp. 766 (W.D. Penn. 1938) (where debtor had fully executed an assignment of rents to mortgage company to prevent foreclosure on his property, but mortgagee was still obliged to collect future rents, the contract, was not executory); *In re Horace Jones*, 8 Col. Bankr. 215 (M.D. Fla. 1976) (rejection of lease was not permitted, where the debtor landlord had no further duties to perform); see also Silverstein, supra note 53, at 475–76; Shanker, "The Treatment of Executory Contract and Leases in Bankruptcy Chapter X and Chapter XI Proceedings," 18 *Prac. Law.*, Apr. 4, 1972, 15, 28 ("[A] contract is executory only if there is future performance required on the part of the bankrupt.").

58 An alternative line of cases, following from *In re Booth*, 19 Bankr. 53 (Bankr. D. Utah 1982), potentially restrict the number of contracts that may be found executory. B. Weintraub & A. Resnick, "From the Bankruptcy Courts," 15 *U.C.C. L. J.* 273, 277 (1983). The Booth line of analysis treats the Countryman definition as a threshold inquiry "serv[ing] more as an 'exclusionary rule' than as the ultimate test of an executory contract." *In re Gladding Corp.*, 22 Bankr. 632, 635 (Bankr. D. Mass. 1983). As the Booth Court stated:

> [I]n the final analysis, executory contracts are measured not by a mutuality of commitments but by the nature of the parties and the goals of reorganization . . . it is the consequences of applying section 365 to a party, especially in terms of benefit to the estate and the protection of creditors, not the form of contract between vendor and vendee, which controls.

A recent example of the application of section 365 to technology licensing is *Lubrizol Enterprises v. Richmond Metal Finishers.*[59] The debtor, Richmond Metal Finishers (RMF), had granted Lubrizol a nonexclusive license to use a metal coating process owned by RMF. The license required RMF to notify Lubrizol of, and to defend, any patent infringement suit regarding the licensed technology and to indemnify Lubrizol for any losses resulting from misrepresentation or breach of warranty by RMF. It also required RMF to give Lubrizol the benefit of a "most favored nation" clause.[60] For its part, Lubrizol was required to pay royalties based on quarterly written reports delivered to RMF. The reports were subject to inspection by a certified public accountant.[61]

Like the district court, the Fourth Circuit found the license agreement to be executory under the Countryman test.[62] On the debtor RMF's side were the continuing obligations to defend infringement suits, to indemnify Lubrizol for certain losses, and to give Lubrizol the benefit of the "most favored nation" clause.[63] On Lubrizol's side were the obligations to account for and pay royalties, to make quarterly sales reports, and to keep books of account open to inspection by a certified public accountant.[64] The breach of any of these obligations would excuse performance by the other party.

Booth, 19 Bankr. at 56–57. Courts following the *Booth* line of analysis resist formalistic, automatic application of a rule in favor of an exercise of the bankruptcy court's equitable powers. See, e.g., *In re Adolphsen,* 38 Bankr. 776 (Bankr. D. Minn. 1983), aff'd, 38 Bankr. 780 (Bankr. D. Minn. 1983); *In re Cox,* 28 Bankr. 588 (Bankr. D. Idaho 1983); see also B. Weinstraub & A. Resnick, supra; but see *Shaw v. Dawson,* 48 Bankr. 857 (Bankr. D. N.M. 1985) (refusing to follow *Booth*). While these cases deal primarily with real estate contracts, the analysis suggests an alternative equitable argument for treating software licenses as not executory. Some courts may be willing to accept such an alternative in light of the relatively new and undefined legal nature of software copyright licenses.

59 756 F.2d 1043 (4th Cir. 1985), cert. denied, 106 S. Ct. 1285 (1986), rev'g *In re Richmond Metal Finishers,* 38 Bankr. 341 (Bankr. E.D. Va. 1984).

60 Under this clause, Lubrizol got the benefit of any lower royalty rate made available to another licensee. *Lubrizol,* 756 F.2d at 1045.

61 Id. at 1046.

62 The Fourth Circuit had recently adopted the Countryman test. See *Gloria Manufacturing Corp. v. Int'l Ladies' Garment Workers' Union,* 734 F.2d 1020, 1022 (4th Cir. 1984).

63 *Lubrizol,* 756 F.2d at 1046.

64 Id. In circuits which do not follow *Countryman,* a debtor's outstanding obligations to perform may well be enough to make a contract executory, even if the other party is obligated only to make payments. See supra note 58. A *Countryman* court might even be expected to reach a comparable result if the debtor's executory obligations constituted a significant impediment to the reorganization or liquidation of the debtor.

After finding the licensing agreement to be executory, the court addressed the question of whether its rejection would be "advantageous to the bankrupt."[65] The debtor's president testified that sale or further licensing of the technology, which was the debtor's principal asset, would be facilitated by stripping Lubrizol of its rights. Laboring under what the Fourth Circuit considered a "misapprehension of controlling law,"[66] the district court held that rejection could not deprive Lubrizol of its right to use the licensed technology and, therefore, "could not reasonably be found beneficial" to the debtor's estate.[67] The Fourth Circuit held otherwise. It stated that upon rejection, Lubrizol "could not seek to retain its contract rights in the technology by specific performance even if that remedy would ordinarily be available upon breach of this type of contract."[68] Worse yet, the court held that "Lubrizol [could] not rely on provisions within its agreement with RMF for continued use of the technology by Lubrizol upon breach of RMF," because section 365 (g) "provides only a money damages remedy for the nonbankrupt party," and "allowing specific performance would obviously undercut the core purpose of rejection under section 365(a)."[69] Based on its finding that rejection can "strip" the licensee of the technology, the court easily concluded that rejection passes the "sound business judgment" test.

In *Lubrizol,* the district court had reasoned that rejection of a nonexclusive technology license should not deprive the licensee of the right to use the technology because the license is comparable to a completed sale of property.[70] The court of appeals disagreed, arguing that "licensing agreements

---

65 In courts following the *Booth* line of analysis this question is merged with the question whether the contract is executory. See supra note 59.

66 *Lubrizol,* 756 F.2d at 1048; but cf. *In re Select-a-Seat Corp.*, 265 F.2d 290, 292 (9th Cir. 1980) (court allowed rejection of exclusive software license relying in part on fact that trustee had not attempted to deprive the licensee of right to use software).

67 *Lubrizol,* 756 F.2d at 1049. For this reason, the district court had disallowed rejection.

68 Id. at 1048.

69 Id.

70 38 Bankr. at 344; see supra text accompanying note 47. Rejection of the contract of sale under is not a right of rescission. *In re Murphy,* 694 F.2d 172, 174 (8th Cir. 1982). The trustee does not enjoy an equitable right to 'undo' the transaction by recovering property already delivered to the purchaser. To recover the sold goods, the trustee would have to rely instead on the avoidance powers of 11 U.S.C. §§544(a)–(b) (1982) (state law fraudulent conveyances), 545 (statutory liens), 547 (preferential transfers), 548 (fraudulent transfers), and 549 (post bankruptcy petition transactions), and the "recovery" or "turnover" rights under §§550 and 542. A trustee may recover property transferred, or the value of such property, if the transfer is avoided, id. §550(a), subject to limitations on recovery from subsequent third party good faith transferees, id.

are more similar to leases than to sales of property because of the limited nature of the interest conveyed."[71] The district court's "sale of property" analogy would have been compelling if an exclusive copyright license had been involved. Under the Copyright Act, the exclusive licensee does not have a mere contractual right to use property for a limited period of time. Instead, the exclusive licensee gains something comparable to title in a separable piece of the original copyright.[72] The licensee may register as the owner of the

---

§550(b). As discussed above, §544(a)(1) grants the trustee the rights of a lien creditor. It is unlikely that a lien creditor would have rights superior to a buyer in the ordinary course under the laws of any jurisdiction. See U.C.C. §9-307(1) (1978) (protecting buyers in the ordinary course against the holders of security interest. The right to recover property under §550 is limited to avoided transfers and the code provides no comparable rights for property delivered pursuant to rejected executory contracts. Upon filing of the petition, however, an entity, other than a custodian, having possession or control of property of the estate must turnover such property to the trustee. 11 U.S.C. §§542(a), 363(b)(l) (1982). Section 541 in turn defines "property of the estate" as including "all legal or equitable interest of the debtor in property as of the commencement of the case." ("Property of the estate" also includes certain property acquired by the trustee after the commencement of the case. See id. §541(a)(2)–(a)(7) (1982)). Where the debtor has legal title to the property, but no equitable right to immediate possession, §541(d) provides that the trustee gains no better title:

> The legislative history of [§541 (a)(l)] indicates that Congress intended to exclude from the estate property of others in which the debtor had some minor interest such as a lien or bare legal title . . . [but] not limit the ability of the trustee to regain possession of property in which the debtor had equitable as well a legal title.

United States v. Whiting Pools, Inc., 462 U.S. 198, 204 n.8 (1983). Under Article 2 of the Uniform Commercial Code, a seller has no right to repossession of goods following delivery, even if the buyer has failed to pay. See U.C.C. §§2-703–2-710 (1978). A fortiori, a seller that has breached the contract (including a trustee breaching by rejection) has no equitable interest in goods already delivered, even if the seller has purported to retain legal title. Such goods therefore are not "property of the estate" for purposes of section 541.

[71] *Lubrizol,* 756 F.2d at 1046, 1048.

[72] See 3 M. Nimmer, supra note 17, at §10.02. The Copyright Act defines "transfers" as including exclusive rights limited in time. See 17 U.S.C. §101 (definition of "transfer"). Modern real estate law (and other personal property law) generally disapprove "fee tails." *Merrill v. American Baptist Missionary Union,* 73 N.H. 414, 416 (1905) (conveyance in fee tail is not enforceable because tying up real estate indefinitely by entitlement is against state policy); see R. Cunningham, W. Stoebuck, and D. Whitman, *The Law of Real Property,* §2.10 (1984) (fee tail estate is regarded with hostility by courts and legislatures); 2 R. Powell, *Real Property,* ¶¶192, 198 (1983) (listing various state statutes that operate so as to convert fee tail to fee simple estate). As a result, title to copyright can be carved up in the dimension of time, whereas title to other property cannot.

exclusive right transferred,[73] much as if it were the original owner of that right, and, provided that it has registered, the licensee may sue in its own name for infringements of its exclusive rights.[74] Thus, the Copyright Act vests substantial indicia of ownership in the exclusive licensee.[75] In contrast, the technology license in *Lubrizol* was a trade secret license, which does not transfer any property right in the trade secret to the licensee.[76]

The Fourth Circuit's rejection of the sale of property analogy applies wherever a technology transfer does not involve an exclusive copyright license or patent assignment.[77] There is no basis in the Copyright Act, the Patent Act, or the common law of trade secrets on which to argue that a license is a

---

[73] 17 U.S.C. §408(a) (1982).

[74] Id.§501(b).

[75] Even if an exclusive copyright license thus seems protected against loss of right to use the licensed programs following rejection under §365, the license remains subject to avoidance under §544(a)(1) if it has not been recorded in the manner required by Copyright Act §205(c). See supra text accompanying notes 28–29. On the other hand, rejection of an exclusive license that has been recorded would split trade secrets rights in the licensed programs from copyright in the same programs. Under *Lubrizol*, rejection of the license would terminate the licensee's right to use the trade secrets, while §205(c) of the Copyright Act would permit the licensee to retain its portion of the copyright. The same splitting occurs where the trustee avoids an exclusive copyright license, but cannot avoid the trade secret license covering the same technology. For reasons already discussed, Copyright Act §301 appears to require the licensee to prevail under these circumstances. See supra text accompanying notes 47–48.

[76] 1 Milgrim, supra note 47, at §1.06 (a trade secret is property that is subject to assignment by sale, but a license only conveys the right to use the property; property right in the secret remains with the licensor). An exclusive license of patent is also distinguishable from an exclusive copyright license because an exclusive patent license does not convey a property interest in patent. An exclusive patent license, as opposed to an assignment of the whole patent, merely protects the licensee from a claim of infringement by the patent owner. *Western Electric Co. v. Pacent Reproducer Corp.*, 42 F.2d 116, 118–19 (2nd Cir. 1930), cert. denied, 282 U.S. 873 (1931); *Bell Intercontinental Corps. v. United States*, 381 F.2d 1004, 1010–11 (Ct. C1. 1967). Where a patent licensor cancels a licensing agreement, the license cannot be given effect for any purpose. *Krantz v. Van Dette*, 165 F. Supp. 776, 784 (D. Ohio 1958), aff'd, 272 F.2d 709 (1959).

[77] Comparable results are found in *In re J.H. Land and Cattle Co., Inc.*, 3 Collier Bankr. Cas. 2d (MB) 695 (Bankr. W.D. Okla. 1981) (permitting rejection of an oil and gas leasehold) and *O.P.M. Leasing Services, Inc.*, 23 Bankr. 104 (Bankr. S.D.N.Y. 1982) (requiring nondebtor equipment lessee to return equipment upon rejection of the lease). But see *In re Petur U.S.A. Instrument Co., Inc.*, 35 Bankr 561 (W.D. Wash.1983) (refusing to allow rejection of a technology license where rejection would ruin the licensee's business).

transfer of property rights.[78] It is, therefore, difficult to analogize such licenses to complete sales. *Lubrizol* falls squarely within the rule of cases holding, for example, that bankruptcy trustees may reject contracts as diverse as oil and gas leases,[79] franchises,[80] and equipment leases.[81]

The typical software license imposes on both the licensor and licensee far greater executory obligations than the technology license imposed on the debtor in Lubrizol. Even the most barebones software license requires the licensor to warrant title to the licensed software[82] and requires the licensee not to disclose the trade secrets contained in the software to any third party.[83] Most software licenses go much farther, as well. For example, the vendor usually agrees to maintain the software by debugging and updating it.[84] Therefore, most nonexclusive software licenses are executory and subject to rejection under section 365.[85]

---

[78] Unless, of course, the license is an exclusive copyright license. See supra text accompanying notes 71–77.

[79] *In re J.H. Land and Cattle Co.*, Collier Bankr. Cas. 2d (MB) 695.

[80] In re Fashion Two Twenty, 16 Bankr. 784 (Bankr. N.D. Ohio 1982).

[81] *O.P.M. Leasing Services*, 23 Bankr. at 104; but cf. In re Petur, 35 Bankr. at 561.

[82] The licensor's obligation to defend title is an executory obligation which, if breached, would excuse the licensee of its obligation to perform. See *O.P.M. Leasing Services*, 23 Bankr. at 117; Countryman, "Executory Contracts in Bankruptcy: Part II," 58 *Minn. L. Rev.* 479, 502 (1974) (discussing patent licenses). Many of the obligations in a software license, particularly those on the vendor, are contingent. Examples include warranties and an obligation to defend title to the licensed programs. But "contingency of an obligation does not prevent its being executory under §365." *In re G-N Partners*, 48 Bankr. 462, 465 (Bankr. D. Minn. 1985); see also *In re Sun Ray Bakery*, 5 Bankr. 670, 672 (Bankr. D. Mass. 1980) (where consignees had fully paid for exclusive distribution rights, the consignee's continuing obligation to distribute goods according to contract is a material performance obligation constituting an executory contract); *In re Fashion Two Twenty*, 16 Bankr. at 786 (franchisee's contingent obligations to maintain its business location, to push the franchisor's products and to purchase a minimum amount of products are unperformed obligations constituting an executory contract, despite franchisee's full performance of payment obligation).

[83] This assumes, of course, that the vendor protects its programs both under copyright and trade secret law. This is usually the case. See supra notes 6–7.

[84] Debugging, updating, and other maintenance often require day-to-day cooperation between vendor and customer. In finding a franchise agreement to be executory, the court in *In Re Rovine Corp.* emphasized that the agreement "required a continuing cooperative effort between franchisor and franchisee." 6 Bankr. at 666.

[85] See *In re Select-a-Seat Corp.*, 265 F.2d 290 (9th Cir. 1980) (holding an exclusive software license to be executory, although the terms of rejection allowed the licensee to continue to use the software on a nonexclusive basis).

2. Effect of rejection on right of licensee to use software

If a software license is executory, the question remains whether rejection by the trustee terminates the licensee's right to use the licensed software. The Fourth Circuit appeared to answer affirmatively in *Lubrizol*, but in a comparable case, *In re Select-A-Seat*,[86] the Ninth Circuit concluded that an exclusive software license was executory in part on the ground that the rejection would not deprive the licensee of the right to use the software on a nonexclusive basis.

Although the outcome may appear more humane than *Lubrizol*, *In re Select-A-Seat* is not a compelling contrary precedent. The Ninth Circuit did not consider whether the debtor could have abrogated the licensee's right to use the software if the debtor believed that termination of the licensee's right to use the software was supported by sound business judgment.

The *In re Select-A-Seat* court also failed to consider the implications of section 205 (e) of the Copyright Act.[87] Because the software license in *In re Select-A-Seat* was exclusive, it constituted a transfer of copyright in the licensed program.[88] If the transfer was recorded in the manner provided by section 205 (c) of the Copyright Act, then the purported rejection should not have been allowed because the licensee's acquisition of an exclusive right was protected against the trustee under section 205 (e) of the Copyright Act.[89] If, however, the transfer was unrecorded, then the debtor could have avoided the transfer under section 544(a)(1), extinguishing the licensee's right to use the licensed software. There is no basis for believing that the right of rejection under section 365 should not terminate the licensee's right to use in the same manner that the avoidance power under section 544(a)(1) can and does.

---

86 Id.

87 It is possible that *In re Select-a-Seat* arose prior to the Jan. 1, 1978, effective date for the Copyright Act. Section 30 of the Copyright Act of 1909, which was effective prior to that date, however, created the same relevant implications as §205(e). Assignments of copyright not timely recorded were void under the old Act as against subsequent takers for value, without notice, who have duly recorded. 17 U.S.C.A. App. §30 (West Supp. 1986) (former Title 17).

88 Even if the licensor had not registered the copyright, it could claim "automatic" protection of its copyright because the programs were works of authorship set down in a tangible medium of expression, which had not entered the public domain by publication without a copyright notice. 17 U.S.C. §102(a) (1982). Note that such publication would also have destroyed the programs' trade secret status.

89 For a discussion of the question whether the power to reject an executory contract permits the trustee to in effect avoid a duly recorded exclusive license, see infra text accompanying notes 116–19.

If it had been considering a nonexclusive software license, the *In re Select-A-Seat* court might have considered basing its holding on section 205 (f) of the Copyright Act. Section 205(f) provides that a nonexclusive copyright license prevails over a subsequent transferee if the license is in writing, signed by the copyright owner, and taken before execution of the transfer, or its recordation, in good faith, and without notice of the transfer.[90] As the bankruptcy trustee is a subsequent transferee,[91] does this mean that the Copyright Act protects the holder of a nonexclusive copyright license against loss of its right to use the licensed work following rejection of the license?

Again, it is necessary to reconcile the Copyright Act and Bankruptcy Code. Copyright Act section 205 (f) is plainly intended to protect nonexclusive licensees against persons who acquire copyrights in the subject work from their licensors. It is not intended to protect nonexclusive licensees against their own licensors. In the context of a section 365 rejection, the trustee is not asserting special status as a transferee from the debtor.[92] Instead, the trustee is exercising an option the debtor had all along: the option of defaulting. Section 365 does not create this option; it merely limits the remedies available to the non-bankrupt contracting party following default by the trustee. In practical terms, section 365 means that following rejection, the nonbankrupt licensee cannot assert equitable rights for specific performance[93] and can recover only monetary damages in the form of an unsecured claim against the debtor's estate.[94] Section 205(f) does not purport to regulate the circumstances under

---

[90] 17 U.S.C. §205(f) (1982)

[91] See supra text accompanying notes 30-44.

[92] Compare §544(a)(1), under which the trustee has the rights of a lien creditor. See supra text accompanying notes 16–44.

[93] *In re Waldron*, 36 Bankr. 633, 642 n.4 (Bankr. S.D. Fla. 1984); rev'd on other grounds 785 F.2d 936 (11th Cir. 1986), cert. denied sub nom. *Waldron v. Shell Oil Co.*, 106 S. Ct. 3343 (1986).

[94] See *Lubrizol*, 756 F.2d at 1048 ("Allowing specific performance would obviously undercut the core purpose of rejection under § 365(a)."); 2 King, supra note 48, at ¶365.08. Compare the Bankruptcy Code's remedies for rejection in two unique situations: where the nonbankrupt lessee or vendee is in possession of real property that is the subject of either lease or sale. In either situation, the nonbankrupt may choose to treat the lease or contract as "terminated" and assert a claim for damages, or the nonbankrupt may remain in possession, continue to make payments due and offset against such payments certain damages caused by the rejecting bankrupt. 11 U.S.C. §365(h)–(i) (1982). The difference in treatment of lessees of realty and lessees of personal property and licensees follows from the tradition that only the former creates an estate in the property. See 2 King, supra note 48, at 365.09–365.10; see also supra text accompanying notes 48, 71–77.

which a copyright licensor may terminate a nonexclusive license, nor does it regulate the licensee's remedies in the event of such termination. It should not, therefore, protect a nonexclusive software licensee from the risk of losing the right to use the licensed programs following rejection of the license by the vendor's trustee.

Lubrizol had urged affirming the district court for "policy considerations," including "serious burdens" on contracting parties and the "general chilling effect upon the willingness of such parties to contract at all with businesses in possible financial difficulty."[95] Indeed, there are some practical differences between certain types of technology licenses and other executory contracts. For example, it is not uncommon for software licensees to pay a lump sum upfront as the license fee, followed by smaller periodic payments thereafter as "maintenance" fees. In such a case, a transfer of the right to use appears to be "fully performed" upon execution of the license, while the maintenance obligations remain executory.[96] Furthermore, following installation of the licensed software, the licensee's business may become so heavily dependent upon its use that an abrupt termination caused by a bankrupt vendor's rejection could have catastrophic effects on the licensee.

Aside from the Copyright Act provisions discussed above, it is difficult to see why the plight of a terminated technology transferee is more troubling than that of, for example, a franchisee whose franchise agreement has been terminated by a bankrupt franchisor. The franchisee probably made a substantial upfront payment for the right to operate the franchise. Loss of the right to use the franchised name could be as catastrophic to its business as

---

[95] *Lubrizol,* 756 F.2d at 1048.

[96] A similar case occurs with the sale of goods under warranty where the sale (delivery and payment) is fully performed, but the obligations under the warranty remain outstanding. In such a case, the court may treat the warranty as an executory contract and allow rejection by the trustee without requiring the return of the goods. See, e.g., *In re Smith Jones, Inc.,* 26 Bankr. 289 (Bankr. D. Minn. 1982) (rejection of express written warranties of furnaces and air conditioners sold by debtor). If exclusive copyright licenses were treated similarly — as fully performed transfers of property coupled with outstanding maintenance obligations — then the effect of rejection would be limited to the maintenance obligations. In deciding to authorize the trustee's rejection of warranties, the *Smith Jones* court noted that other remedies for defective parts, available at common law or by statute, were not affected by rejection, and, furthermore, customers, by reason of rejection of the warranties, may have an immediate, estimatable claim for damages. Id. at 294. Because alternative rights to maintenance of licensed software are not available at common law or by statute, a software licensee's remedies would be limited to an unsecured claim for damages.

the loss of the right to use a program that controls the internal operation of a business would be to the software licensee. Nevertheless, it has been held that rejection of the franchise agreement terminates the franchisee's right to operate the franchise.[97] As the Fourth Circuit stated," [t]echnology licensees such as Lubrizol . . . share the general hazards created by section 365 for all business entities dealing with potential bankrupts."[98]

Yet, the Fourth Circuit's declaration that "under bankruptcy law such equitable considerations may not be indulged by the courts"[99] may be harsher than necessary. A better approach would be to adjust the trustee's remedy upon termination without jeopardizing the trustee's ultimate right to terminate the licensee's use of the technology. In the case of computer software, few programs are truly unique. If the effective reorganization of a bankrupt vendor required its trustee to terminate all existing licenses so that he or she could offer exclusive rights in the licensed programs, the court could allow the licensees a reasonable period of time in which to find and bring on line software from another vendor which would replace the functions of the software covered by the terminated licenses. The licensee should be permitted to use the licensed technology indefinitely only in the very unusual case where no comparable technology is obtainable on the market, and the licensee paid for the license in full prior to the filing of bankruptcy proceedings.[100]

---

[97] See *In re Fashion Two Twenty, Inc.*, 16 Bankr. 784 (Bankr. N.D. Ohio 1982). It could be argued that the franchisor has a more compelling business reason for terminating the franchisee's right to use than the technology licensor. In the franchise situation, a trademark or a system of trademarks is usually the central licensed asset. Multiple ownership of trademarks is disfavored because it tends to deceive the public as to the source of the products or services being sold. See 1 J. McCarthy, *Trademarks and Unfair Competition*, §16.14 (1984). Furthermore, use of a trademark by one not subject to license obligations regarding the quality and types of goods and services provided under the trademark tends to dilute its distinctive quality and diminish its value to the bankrupt franchisor's estate. On the other hand, an exclusive technology license can be much more valuable than a nonexclusive one. The ability of a bankrupt software vendor, such as RMF in *Lubrizol*, to offer an exclusive license to potential purchaser would be lost if any prior licensee retained the right to continue to use the licensed technology. The difference, if any, between the trademark license as a franchise and a technology license is, at most, one of degree, not one of kind.

[98] *Lubrizol*, 756 F.2d at 1048.

[99] Id.; but see supra note 41 (equitable powers of bankruptcy court) and note 66 (merger of equitable considerations and determination of executority).

[100] This may explain the result in *In re Petur*, 35 Bankr. 561 (Bankr. W.D. Wash. 1983). where there was evidence that termination of the technology license would ruin the licensee's business.

Thus, a trustee for a bankrupt software vendor may reject software licenses in exercise of his or her sound business judgment, and, upon rejection, the licensee's right to use the software may be terminated.[101] Accordingly, a skillful trustee can use rejection in two ways. First, the trustee can use the threat of rejection to persuade licensees that the terms of their licenses need revision: most likely, that the payments need to be increased. Alternatively, the trustee can reject all outstanding licenses and sell the programs to another vendor. Such a vendor would be free to renegotiate new license terms with the rejected customers of the bankrupt vendor. The customers' outrage at their treatment may be overcome by their need to continue operations that depend on the licensed programs. It is, in either case, very much a seller's market.

In sum, vendor bankruptcy presents the following threats to the software licensee. First, if the license is exclusive and recorded, the licensee's right to use may be protected, but the trustee can, nevertheless, reject any outstanding obligations under the license agreement, including debugging and maintenance. If the exclusive license is unrecorded, then, under Bankruptcy Code section 544(a)(1), the trustee can avoid it altogether. Second, if the license is nonexclusive, it is subject to rejection by the trustee. Rejection terminates the obligation to perform debugging and maintenance for the software and, under *Lubrizol*, extinguishes the licensee's right to use the licensed programs.

Part II of this Article discusses strategies for reducing these risks, including escrows, recordation, and security interests.

II. Source code escrows and security interests in software

A. Source code escrows

1. Description of escrow arrangement

Software users who are concerned about their ability to use, modify, and update licensed software in the event of vendor bankruptcy frequently request that the source code be deposited with an escrow agent. Banks, companies specializing in software escrows, and attorneys are commonly used as escrow agents.[102]

---

[101] This conclusion follows from the recent denial of Lubrizol's petition for certiorari. *Lubrizol Enterprises, Inc. v. Canfield*, 106 S. Ct. 1285 (1986).

[102] For a discussion of software escrows, see generally Nycum, Kenfield, and Keenan, "Debugging Software Escrow: Will It Work When You Need It?," 4 *Computer L. J.* 441 (1984) [hereinafter Nycum].

Under the typical escrow arrangement, the software vendor agrees to place the source code and any related documentation in the possession of the escrow agent for a period of time at least equal to the term of the underlying software license. The agreement may also require the vendor to make periodic deposits of source code incorporating enhancements in, updates to, new editions of, or other variants of the licensed software.[103]

The escrow agent is required to hold the source code in secrecy until it receives notice of an event requiring release, or until it returns the source code to the vendor upon the termination of the escrow. To obtain the source code from the escrow agent, a participating licensee must inform the escrow agent and the vendor that an event requiring release has occurred. For example, such an event might be the failure or refusal of the vendor to maintain or update the software. Upon receipt of such notice, the escrow agent is required to notify the vendor that it will release the source code to the licensee unless the vendor objects in writing within a specified period of time.[104] If the vendor objects, the escrow agent is directed to hold the source code until ordered to release it by a court or the vendor. If the vendor does not object, then the escrow agent is required to release a copy of the source code to the requesting licensee, retaining a copy for itself and other participating licensees.

The escrow agent's reasonable expenses are sometimes paid by the vendor and sometimes by the vendee. Either or both parties indemnify the escrow agent for any liability arising as a result of its performance of its obligations under the escrow. Some escrow agreements require arbitration of disputes over the existence of an event requiring release.

Upon release of the source code to a licensee, the escrow agreement usually gives the licensee rights and obligations respecting the source code similar to those which apply to the object code. These include, at a minimum, the right to use the source code to maintain the licensed programs, subject to the obligations not to disclose the source code to third persons and to return or destroy the source code upon the termination of the license.

The software escrow is a complex relationship that raises many practical and legal questions. How does the licensee determine what it is required to

---

[103] Exactly what further deposits are required depends on the terms of the underlying license. If, for example, the license does not cover future editions of the licensed programs, then the source code for such further editions would not need to be covered by the escrow agreement.

[104] The vendor might object on the grounds that no event requiring release has occurred or that the licensee is in default of its obligations to the vendor.

deposit? How does the licensee or licensor maintain the software? Of what use is the software escrow if every time there is an "event requiring release," the vendor objects to the release, and the dispute is shunted into interminable legal proceedings, during which the licensee is without effective maintenance and support? Examination of all of these issues is beyond the scope of this article. Instead, this article focuses on the question of whether a software escrow can be made to survive a vendor's bankruptcy proceedings.

2. Enforceability of escrows in bankruptcy proceedings: *In re Newcomb*

No reported case has yet addressed the enforceability of source code escrow arrangements in bankruptcy proceedings. One of the few cases that discuss escrows in the bankruptcy setting is *In re Newcomb* [105], but that case required the Eighth Circuit to address the enforceability of an escrow agreement in bankruptcy proceedings in the starkest possible terms. In *Newcomb,* the United States had recovered a judgment against Newcomb (the bankrupt) prior to the filing of bankruptcy proceedings. Newcomb appealed, depositing with a bank in escrow a sum sufficient to satisfy the judgment. The terms of the escrow were simple. If the judgment was affirmed on appeal, the United States got the money; if the judgment was reversed on appeal, Newcomb got the money. The appellate court affirmed,[106] but before the escrowed funds were paid to the government, Newcomb and his wife filed for bankruptcy.

The bankruptcy trustee filed a complaint for turnover of the escrowed funds, claiming: (1) the escrow agreement was an executory contract; (2) the transfer of the escrowed funds was preferential; and (3) the trustee's status as lien creditor under section 544(a) (1) was superior to any interest of the government in the escrowed funds.[107] The bankruptcy court ordered the funds turned over to the trustee, and the district court affirmed.

On appeal, the Eighth Circuit reversed in a brief opinion, which is nevertheless one of the most detailed to date addressing the enforceability of escrow arrangements in bankruptcy proceedings.[108] Considering whether the

---

105 *In re Newcomb,* 744 F.2d 621 (8th Cir. 1984), rev'g I*n re O.P.M. Leasing Services, Inc.,* 46 Bankr. 661 (S.D.N.Y. 1985).

106 *United States v. Newcomb,* 682 F.2d 758 (8th Cir. 1982).

107 *Newcomb,* 744 F.2d at 624.

108 Escrow arrangements are discussed in the context of §365 in several cases where a deed for land was placed in escrow and the executority of the real estate contract is at issue. See, e.g., *Shaw v. Dawson,* 48 Bankr. 857 (Bankr. D. N.M. 1985). The cases are generally inapplicable to escrow arrangements for copyrighted software because state law determines the effect to be given real estate contracts, and the decisions focus on

escrow agreement was an executory contract, the court held that at the time the bankruptcy petition was filed, the only remaining performance was the escrow agent's act of turning over the funds to the United States. The court found this insufficient to meet the Eighth Circuit's test for executority: whether "performance remains due on both sides at the time of the bankruptcy petition.'[109] The court opined that 'an escrow is something more than a contract — it is a method of conveying property."[110] Analyzing Missouri law in detail, the court found that the creation of an escrow transfers an equitable interest in the escrowed property to the ultimate grantee, while leaving legal title in the hands of the depositor. Legal title is conveyed to the ultimate grantee when and if the condition of the escrow is satisfied. [111]

The court found that both the creation of the escrow and the payment of the escrowed funds upon satisfaction of the condition of the escrow were "transfers" within the meaning of the Bankruptcy Code.[112] It concluded, however, that the second "transfer" would not deprive the estate of "anything of value" because the only interest in the escrowed funds remaining in the debtor was a contingent right to the funds if the court reversed the judgment for the United States.[113] Because the first transfer — the creation of the escrow — had been made more than 90 days before the filing of bankruptcy proceedings, it was not preferential under Bankruptcy Code section 547. The court therefore resolved the trustee's preference claim in favor of the United States.

---

whether such contracts are security devices in a particular state. Id., at 861. Compare *In re Simon* wherein the court held that funds placed in an escrow account with a mortgagee bank by a bankruptcy mortgagor prior to the filing of bankruptcy proceedings were not property of the estate, and thus not subject to the turnover provision, because the funds were no longer within the bankrupt's control. *In re Simon*, 167 F. Supp. 214, 215 (E.D.N.Y. 1958).

109 *Newcomb*, 744 F.2d at 624; see also supra note 59 (discussion of this alternative to the *Countryman* test).

110 *Newcomb*, 744 F.2d at 624. Similarly, some courts have recognized an escrow as a method of conveying and perfecting a security interest. See, e.g., *In re Copeland*, 531 F.2d 1195 (3d Cir. 1976); but see *In re Dolly Madison Indus., Inc.*, 351 F. Supp. 1038 (E.D. Pa. 1972), aff'd mem., 480 F.2d 917, 918 (3d. Cir. 1973).

111 *Newcomb*, 744 F.2d at 725–26. A majority of courts concur with the Missouri rule that delivery to an escrow agent transfers equitable title to the escrowed property and satisfaction of the conditions of an escrow agreement transfers legal title. See, e.g., *In re Missionary Baptist Found. of America*, 14 Bankr. Ct. Dec. 1252, 1254 (5th Cir. 1986) (Texas law); see also 28 *Am. Jur. 2D Escrow*, §10 (1963); 30A C. J. S. Escrows, §§9, 10 (1965).

112 *Newcomb*, 744 F.2d at 626. See 11 U.S.C. §101(48) (1982); see supra note 18.

113 *Newcomb*, 744 F.2d 627; compare 11 U.S.C. §541, discussed supra note 71 (bare legal title is not "property of the estate" for purposes of §541).

The *Newcomb* court rejected the trustee's third contention that its avoidance power under section 544(a)(1) took priority over the United States' interest in the escrowed funds. The court concluded that by the time the bankruptcy petition was filed, the condition of the escrow had been satisfied, and the debtor, therefore, had no interest in the escrowed funds to which a judgment lien could attach.[114]

Newcomb strongly supports the enforceability of an escrow arrangement in bankruptcy proceedings, at least when the escrow agreement is very simple and the escrowed property is not regulated by recording or title registration statutes. Under the *Newcomb* analysis, a bankruptcy trustee cannot recover escrowed property under sections 541 and 542, even if the escrow agreement is executory, so long as there is a possibility that an event requiring release could occur. Further, *Newcomb* squarely holds that the release of property (e.g., source code) from escrow is not a transfer which the trustee may avoid under Bankruptcy Code section 547 or 549. In contrast, any escrow deposit made within ninety days prior to the filing of bankruptcy proceedings may be preferential, depending on the circumstances of the deposit.[115]

3. Application of *In re Newcomb* to source code escrows

Newcomb's application to source code escrows may be problematic. The typical source code escrow agreement is considerably more complicated than the one-shot deal in *Newcomb*. A source code escrow usually requires the

---

114 Id. at 624. The court did not address whether the debtor would have such an interest if the condition were still unresolved on the date the petition in bankruptcy was filed. Its analysis of the preference issue, however, strongly suggests that § 544(a)(1) should not assist the trustee in this situation either. See supra notes 23–24 and accompanying text. Even if local law permitted a lien creditor to attach the bankrupt's contingent reversionary interest in the escrowed funds, it could attach no more of an interest than the bankrupt had: a contingent reversionary interest. See supra note 71. If the condition of the escrow were fulfilled, this interest would prove to be worthless.

115 A detailed discussion of the circumstances under which a trustee may avoid preferential transfers is beyond the scope of this article. In general, a transfer to one who is not an "insider" may be avoided if it is within ninety days of filing of the bankruptcy petition and it is not a "contemporaneous exchange for new value given by the debtor," 11 U.S.C. §547(c)(l) (1982), and not a payment of a debt in the ordinary course of business, id.§547(c)(2). See generally id. §547(c). Additionally, an attempt to perfect an interest by recording within 90 days of filing of the bankruptcy petition and more than ten days after the agreement was executed would probably be preferential even if the agreement creating the interest had been executed more than 90 days before filing. See id. §§547(c)(l)(B), (2)(B).

vendor to make an initial deposit of the then-current version of the source code for the licensed programs, followed by periodic deposits reflecting modifications and updates of the program. If bankruptcy proceedings are initiated respecting the vendor after the initial deposit is made, but before deposits of updates and modifications are made, the vendor's obligation to make such deposits would almost certainly be subject to rejection by the trustee under section 365,[116] even if the source code already deposited cannot be recovered by the trustee.

Applied to a source code escrow, *Newcomb* is unlikely to prove helpful in the section 544(a)(1) issue. Its finding that the debtor's contingent right to recover the escrowed funds cannot be used as a basis for avoidance of the escrow under section 544(a)(1) is based on the holding that the creation of an escrow is a "transfer" for purposes of the Bankruptcy Code. If it is also a "transfer" of copyright in the source code, it will be effective against the bankruptcy trustee only if it has been recorded in the manner required by Copyright Act section 205 (c).[117]

The recording problem of Copyright Act section 205 will not often arise because most escrow agreements do not purport to transfer copyright in the escrowed source code. Instead, they concern only the physical tapes, disks, documentation, or listings embodying source code. The agreement usually states that the licensee's right to use the source code following an event requiring release is governed by the same license agreement that governs the

---

[116] One unanswered question is whether this executory obligation means that the trustee can reject the escrow arrangement as a whole. The answer is probably "no." If the materials deposited into escrow are not "property of the estate," as Newcomb suggests, then the escrow arrangement becomes quite analogous to a sale of goods which are delivered in installments. The courts have held that such contracts are not executory with respect to delivered installments; the trustee cannot, by rejecting the contract, require the buyer to give back goods which have already been delivered. See *In re Perry*, 25 Bankr. 817, 819–20 (Bankr. D. Md. 1982). For these reasons, Nycum's proposal for a series of "mini-escrows," one for each successive deposit, is probably unnecessary to protect against loss of source code already deposited in escrow. Nycum, supra note 103, at 461. For most software vendors, such a series of mini-escrows is commercially impractical as well.

[117] Cf. supra note 116 (discussing preferential transfers when an interest is recorded within ninety days of bankruptcy). This article has already examined the Copyright Act's definition of "transfer" in detail. See supra text accompanying notes 15–20. It seems likely that any escrow purporting to cover copyright in the source code is a "conveyance, alienation or hypothecation" and therefore falls within the Copyright Act's definition of a "transfer."

licensee's original right to use the licensed programs in non-object code form. Thus, the typical source code escrow agreement will not itself conflict with section 544(a)(1), but its usefulness may depend on the continuing existence of the underlying license agreement.

The vulnerability of software licenses in vendor bankruptcy proceedings has been considered at length in this Article. If the license is exclusive and unrecorded, the vendor's trustee can probably avoid it under section 544(a)(1). If it is nonexclusive, the trustee can probably reject it under section 365. In either case, the escrow arrangement may well leave the licensee with possession of a copy of the source code, but without the benefit of the underlying license.

The possibility of a licensee gaining possession of a copy of the source code for a licensed program by exercising its rights under a source code escrow, while at the same time losing its license to use the program, raises a further issue at the copyright/bankruptcy boundary. Section 117 of the Copyright Act provides that the owner of a copy of a computer program copy acquires a transferable right to make a copy for archival purposes or adaptation in order to use the program on a "machine."[118] There is a strong argument that a licensee that gains lawful possession of a copy of the source code through an escrow arrangement is entitled to the benefit of section 117, and may therefore continue to use the program, despite avoidance or rejection of its software license. Note, however, that the rights of the owner of a copy under section 117 are strictly limited. In particular, they do not include the right to modify the program, other than for use on a single machine, or to make copies of it, other than for use on a single machine.

This suggests that a source code escrow may successfully protect the licensee against loss of the right to use licensed software in the event of vendor bankruptcy, but it may not protect the licensee's need to debug and modify the program using the escrowed source code. It is questionable whether a bankruptcy trustee would have either the resources or the inclination to police its rights to prevent such licensees from making debugged or modified versions of the program. If the trustee does not police such rights, the escrow may serve its purpose, partly by operation of law and partly otherwise.

In sum, source code escrows afford partial protection against the dangers of vendor bankruptcy. Source code deposits made more than ninety days prior to the filing of bankruptcy proceedings are likely to survive the trustee's claims and find their way into the possession of a licensee participating in the escrow arrangement. Under section 117, the licensee will acquire a right to use the

---

[118] 17 U.S.C. §117 (1982).

source code on a single machine. The licensee will not, however, retain any additional right to debug or modify the licensed programs using the source code, unless copyright in the licensed programs was also transferred to the escrow agent, and the transfer was recorded in the Copyright Office. Also, any versions of the source code which were not deposited with the escrow at least ninety days before the bankruptcy filing will be lost to the bankruptcy trustee.

B. Security interests in software

To the commercial lawyer, protecting the interests of a party dealing with a potential insolvent is simple: get a security interest whenever performance is not immediate. This section of the Article examines whether this proven method of protecting against the bankruptcy trustee is feasible in the software license context.

First, consider the advantages a security interest in software might afford a licensee when the software licensor files a petition in bankruptcy. Under the 'equality is equity' motto of bankruptcy,[119] ideal equality seems to require that all creditors share equally in the bankrupt's estate, without regard to their pre-bankruptcy status. Bankruptcy law, however, does not go that far.[120] Instead, bankruptcy law has been shaped by an early policy decision that security interests are valid property rights that should not be disturbed in bankruptcy proceedings.[121] Property of the estate administered by the trustee consists of whatever assets of the bankrupt remain after the secured creditors have taken their collateral.

A software licensee could avail itself of the protection of a security interest in several ways. The simplest situation would be as follows. A vendor licenses its customer to use a particular complicated program. Pursuant to the license agreement, the vendor provides the program to the customer in the form of object code, contained on a tape, and provides the customer with explanatory documentation. The license agreement also requires the vendor to provide extensive training to the customer as well as system debugging, enhancements, updates, and other maintenance over the term of the license agreement. To secure the vendor's obligations during the license, the vendor could grant the customer a security interest in the source code of the

---

119 See Jackson, supra note 13, at 859.

120 2 G. Gilmore, *Security Interests in Personal Property*, §45.2 (1965).

121 Id. A security interest is a property right and, as such, is no part of the bankrupt's estate. Id.; see also J. Maclachlan, *Law of Bankruptcy*, §150 (1965); 11 U.S.C. §506 (1982) (determination of secured status of creditor's interest).

program, including all enhancements, updates, and modifications in the program which the vendor is obligated to provide to the customer in object code form under the terms of the license. Additionally, the security agreement could include as collateral all of the vendor's rights, including both copyright and trade secret rights, in the programs. The security agreement would allow the customer to foreclose its interest in the source code and the collateral if the vendor defaults, and the default is not cured within an agreed-upon period after notice to the vendor.[122]

Using a security interest would solve the two fundamental problems of escrow arrangements in the bankruptcy context. First, a security interest would give the customer an interest in the vendor's source code, which is not subject to rejection by a trustee in bankruptcy, without at the same time giving the customer or an escrow agent possession of or title to the source code. This relieves the customer's concerns regarding potential rejection and avoids the necessity of transferring either title or possession of one of the vendor's most valuable assets to a third party in anticipation of a disagreeable contingency — the vendor's default. Second, a security interest would grant its holder a trustee-proof interest in updates and enhancements without any need for a series of transfers to the escrow agent. Moreover, the security interest arrangement can be made more simple than the typical escrow agreement.

One objection to the use of a security interest is that its foreclosure is more time-consuming than obtaining source code from an escrow agent. In practice, this is unlikely to be true because most escrow agreements include a waiting period during which the vendor may object to the release of the source code. Furthermore, it is unlikely that the vendor would permit its source code to be released by an escrow agent without a fight. Similarly, most security agreements contain provisions requiring the debtor to assemble the collateral and deliver it to the secured party upon the secured party's demand following default, but few

---

[122] In connection with such a security agreement, other parts of the contract between the vendor and the customer would require modification. For example, many licenses contain provisions requiring that the licensee not disclose even the object code to third parties, not compete with the vendor, and not modify the licensed software without the vendor's consent. Such licenses will further provide that such provisions survive any termination of the license agreement, even if caused by the default of the vendor. All of these provisions must be modified so that the customer would not incur liability to the vendor in the event of a foreclosure of its security interest in the source code. Alternatively, the security agreement could cover all of the vendor's rights under its license and other agreements relating to the source code, so that in the event of a foreclosure the rights of the vendor and the customer would effectively merge in the hands of the customer.

debtors comply with such a demand until compelled to do so either by the circumstances or by a court. In either case, the customer must assume that some court action will be required to wrest control of the program from the vendor or the vendor's trustee in bankruptcy.[123]

Another objection to the use of a security interest is that foreclosure of the security interest in the source code could be as costly as recovery of the source code from an escrow agent because a security agreement covering the source code would not prevent the vendor's trustee in bankruptcy from rejecting the underlying license. This objection is unsound. A secured party in possession may use or operate the collateral for the purpose of preserving its value or in a manner and to the extent provided in the security agreement.[124] Thus, a separate license is not required for the period between the time the licensee takes possession and the time the source code is either sold or retained in satisfaction of the vendor's obligations, if the security agreement provides for use during such period.[125] Furthermore, the security interest described above

---

[123] If the vendor is in bankruptcy proceedings, the customer/secured party can move for leave to foreclose its security interest under §362(d) of the Bankruptcy Code. Action on such a motion is usually quite prompt, at least in the bankruptcy courts with which the authors are familiar. Section 362(e) provides that the motion will be deemed allowed if the court does not otherwise order within thirty days of the filing of the motion. Because recovery of source code from an escrow agent would also be likely to require a §362(d) motion for relief from the stay, the delay in obtaining possession of the source code would probably be the same whether the customer holds a security interest or participates in an escrow arrangement in any case in which the software vendor is in bankruptcy proceedings. See Nycum, supra note 103, at 456.

[124] U.C.C. §9-207(4) (1978).

[125] It might be claimed that foreclosure on the source code would convey no right to use the object code. This is not itself a serious problem because object code can be generated from source code by using the appropriate compiler programs. To be safe, the security agreement could state that the secured party may generate object code during the period of the possession of the collateral following default.

In the present software marketplace, however, it would be unusual for the vendor's system designer or programmer to restrict the software to the use of standard compilers. More likely, enhancements or modifications of a compiler are used. Additionally, the compiler in its premodification form may have been licensed from a third party. In either case, the appropriate compiler may not be readily available to the licensee. Without the appropriate compiler the source code would be useless. Similarly, the licensee's ability to perform maintenance and updating depends on access to maintenance tools such as test programs and program specifications. Therefore, any security agreement should include the vendor's rights in documented source code, maintenance tools, and specialized compilers or assemblers. Additional useful information includes: description of program generation descriptions and locations of

covers not only the tangible embodiment of the licensed programs in source code form but also copyright and trade secret rights in the intangible programs themselves. Following foreclosure, no license from the vendor would be required because the vendor would no longer own the property being licensed.[126]

1. Priority with respect to lenders

Despite the legal advantages discussed in the preceding section of the Article, there are practical problems with having the customer licensee hold a security interest. The vendor may have already granted a security interest in the same collateral to a lender. In that case, granting the licensee a junior security interest in the same collateral would not ensure the licensee's access to it because the licensee's right to take possession of the collateral would be subject to the lender's prior security interest.[127]

The security interest also creates troublesome obligations in the event of default. Under Article 9 of the Uniform Commercial Code (the UCC), a foreclosing secured party must "dispose of any or all of the collateral in its then condition or following a commercially reasonable preparation or processing" and "apply the proceeds to the costs of such disposition and to the indebtedness, remitting any balance remaining either to the debtor or to the holders of junior security interests."[128] Selling the source code and rights in the programs to another vendor may be the last thing a licensee wants to do when there has been a default in the vendor's maintenance or other obligations. Article 9 provides that the secured party may propose to retain the collateral in satisfaction of the indebtedness.[129] This route extinguishes the licensee's claim for damages caused by the vendor's default, but in the

---

any programs or codes used by, but not owned by, the vendor; functional specifications for any development data bases; names and addresses of the system's programmers; and names and addresses of other users and licensees of the system. See B. Olson, *Client Alert: Trends in High Technology Asset Protection,* vol. I, no. 2 (1986).

126 See U.C.C. §9-504(1)(a) (1978) (secured party's right to sell, lease, or otherwise dispose of collateral following default).

127 The lender might be the first to foreclose its interest, in which case possession of the source code would never reach the licensee. Even if the lender chose not to foreclose its prior interest in the source code, the licensee's rights in the source code would remain subject to divesture at any time that the lender chose to assert its prior interest. U.C.C. §9-503 (1978); 9 R. Anderson, *Uniform Commercial Code,* §9-503:6 (3d ed., 1985).

128 U.C.C. §9-504(1) (1978). Section 9-507(2) provides tests for determining what is "commercially reasonable."

129 Id. §9-505(2).

bankruptcy setting, such a claim might not be valuable anyway. Of more concern is the right of the vendor, or its trustee, to require the foreclosing licensee to sell the collateral.[130]

2. Priority with respect to multiple licensees

A further problem is created by the fact that vendors frequently have multiple customers for the same piece of software. Security interests under Article 9 are by nature "first come, first served." The first licensee to perfect a security interest would have priority over subsequent licensees holding similar interests. Thus, the utility of the security interest as a means of protecting the interests of licensees does not extend beyond the first licensee taking such an interest. Furthermore, a security interest held by one licensee could create a strong disincentive for others to obtain rights in the same software from the vendor, because a foreclosure could threaten to replace the vendor with a new owner of rights in the licensed programs. Additionally, the existence of multiple financing statements filed with respect to a vendor could intimidate potential lenders.

The problem of multiple licensees should not, however, be exaggerated. Expensive software of the type with which this Article is primarily concerned is usually custom-fit for each licensee. To the extent that rights in and the source code for programs licensed to a particular licensee can be segregated from the vendor's other products, it is quite possible that many licensees will be the only persons claiming a security interest in that particular item of collateral.

While the existence of multiple financing statements is an unavoidable consequence of granting security interests to licensees, the problem of priority can be solved, at least if the number of licensees is not too large. The licensees could, for example, participate in an agreement under which the most senior interest holder would, upon foreclosure, distribute copies of the source code, grant licenses to the other licensees and condition any sale of rights in the programs on such licensees' right to retain a copy of source code and license for their own use.[131] Where the number of licensees is comparatively large or the licensees do not wish to enter into contractual

---

[130] Id. The right of the debtor to require a sale of the collateral can be waived after default, but not before. Id. §§9-505(2), 9-501(3). If, however, a sale is required and not waived by the trustee, the licensee may buy the collateral at a public or private sale. Id. §9-504(3).

[131] Of course, such a plan would place the junior licensees at the mercy of a trustee in bankruptcy for the foreclosing senior licensee. If the senior licensee were a financially responsible entity, this risk might be acceptable.

relationships among themselves, or the vendor does not want to reveal the identity of its licensees to the public at large,[132] granting security interests directly to licensees would probably not be feasible.

3. Secured source code escrows

A potential solution to the practical problems associated with multiple holders of security interests in source code is to grant the security interest to an independent third party, which could hold the interest in trust for the vendor's licensees. This could be viewed as a variation of the software escrow described above in which the escrow agent holds a security agreement in the source code and the vendor's rights in the licensed programs instead of (or in addition to) the source code itself. Such an approach would combine the simplicity and market acceptance of source code escrows with the protection against rejection by a bankruptcy trustee afforded by a security interest.

The solution might be structured around the standard software escrow. The vendor would enter into a master agreement with the escrow agent. Like the typical master escrow agreement, this agreement would require the vendor to make an initial deposit of source code and documentation covering the basic version of the licensed software, and would require the vendor to make periodic deposits reflecting pertinent enhancements and updates. Unlike the typical escrow agreement, however, the vendor would also grant to the escrow agent a security interest in the source code for the licensed programs and all of the vendor's rights in the licensed programs. The conditions permitting foreclosure of the agent's interest would be the same as the "events requiring release" under the standard escrow agreement: usually, the vendor's failure to provide updates, enhancements, debugging, or other maintenance. Licensees would execute contingent license agreements with the escrow agent, not with the vendor,[133] under which the escrow agent would agree to deliver to the licensees the source code for the licensed programs. The licensees would agree to hold the source code in confidence and to use it only for purposes within their license agreement for object code with the vendor.

---

132 Regardless of the vendor's desire, the identities of the licensees would nevertheless appear in financing statements and collateral copyright assignments filed by each licensee. See infra text accompanying notes 144–62 (for a discussion of filing to perfect security interests).

133 The security agreement could provide that after foreclosure the escrow agent would have the right to grant such licenses. See supra text accompanying notes 124–26.

The secured software escrow described above has the following advantages. It would protect the escrow against the dual dangers of rejection of the underlying license by a trustee in bankruptcy and failure of the vendor to make periodic deposits under the terms of the escrow agreement.[134] Also, it is a modest variation of the source code escrow, which is already in widespread use. For this reason, there is a better chance that the secured software escrow would be accepted by vendors and licensees than the more uncommon approaches, such as mini-escrows[135] or security interests granted directly to licensees.[136]

Perhaps the most important point is that the security interest would improve the escrow agent's (and indirectly the licensees') leverage in bankruptcy proceedings. Secured parties enjoy many special advantages under the Bankruptcy Code. Most important among them is the principle that the bankruptcy court must prohibit any use of property in which another entity holds a security interest unless there is "adequate protection" of the entity's security interest.[137] This requirement gives the escrow agent who holds a security interest considerably more leverage in bankruptcy proceedings than the escrow agent who does not hold such an interest. Compared with the ordinary software escrow, the secured escrow is therefore likely more protective of the interests of licensees in any situation in which the vendor's bankruptcy is a possibility.

The secured escrow does have some significant problems. The first problem would be the existence of a prior security interest held by a lender. Even if the lender has not taken an express interest in the vendor's source code, and in

---

[134] See supra text accompanying notes 117–18.

[135] See supra note 117.

[136] See supra text accompanying notes 123–27.

[137] 11 U.S.C. §363(e) (1982). In contrast, the interest of a party in an unsecured escrow agreement is afforded limited protection from the trustee's use of the property. If the trustee ultimately assumes the escrow agreement and the license, the licensee is entitled to "cure" of default, compensation for loss resulting from default, and adequate assurance of future performance as well as compensation for use of the property. Id. §§365(b), 363. If the trustee ultimately rejects the contract, the licensee is limited to compensation for use during the pendency of the petition and an unsecured claim for prepetition damages. See supra text accompanying notes 94–96; *Whitcomb & Keller Mortgage Co.*, 715 F.2d 375 (7th Cir. 1983). In *Whitcomb & Keller*, the bankruptcy court ordered the vendor to continue providing computer service to the bankrupt and to tum over master databases to a third party purchaser of the bankrupt's accounts receivable. Ultimately, the trustee was allowed to reject the computer service contract, and the vendor was limited to prepetition damages. Post-petition services were paid for out of administrative expenses in the amount contracted for.

the rights in the vendor's programs, blanket security agreements used by banks and other lending institutions invariably cover all of the debtor's "general intangibles." There is a good chance that "general intangibles" include software, including its source code.[138] Thus, some accommodation must be made between the lender and the escrow agent.

One approach is for the lending bank to act as the escrow agent as well. It is not uncommon for the same bank to be a secured lender to a debtor and also the indenture trustee for holders of the debtor's debentures. A bank may feel that the security of knowing that it will not be required to negotiate with an escrow agent exceeds the discomfort that such a dual role could occasionally cause. So long as the bank agreed that, if an "event requiring release" occurred, it would foreclose on the collateral (the source code and rights in the licensed programs) and provide a copy of the source code to the licensees, the interest of the licensees should be protected.

An alternative is to require any prior holder of a security interest arguably covering the source code and rights in the licensed programs to subordinate its interest to that of the escrow agent. Although this may seem unlikely, lenders already accept unsecured source code escrows, which certainly diminish the value of source code as collateral for indebtedness should an event requiring release occur.[139] Lenders also realize that their best security is a financially healthy debtor. A vendor that offers its customers a secured source code and program rights escrow could enjoy a competitive advantage over a vendor that does not. Lenders who understand the marketplace would be quick to accommodate such competitive needs.

A second problem with the secured escrow is foreclosure of the security interest by the secured escrow agent in the event of default. This article has observed that the vendor can require the foreclosing secured party to dispose of the source code in a "commercially reasonable manner."[140] The granting of rights in the source code to participants in the escrow arrangement could depress the market value of the collateral. The Official Comments to Article 9 recognize that circumstances exist where the otherwise valuable estate of a

---

[138] See infra text accompanying notes 146–49.

[139] If such an event occurs, the source code would be distributed among the vendor's licensees. Such distribution would threaten the source code's trade secret status and therefore diminish its value as collateral.

[140] See supra text accompanying notes 129–31. A secured party proposing to dispose of collateral in an unreasonable manner may be enjoined from doing so. U.C.C. §9-507(1) (1978). Section 9-507(1) further provides for damages where commercially unreasonable disposition has occurred.

bankrupt would have little or no resale value if the secured party is allowed to repossess and sell that part of the estate that the secured party holds as collateral.[141] In such a case, a bankruptcy court may exercise its equitable powers to control the manner of disposition, regardless of whether the disposition proposed by the secured party is commercially reasonable, in order to preserve the estate for the benefit of all creditors.[142] These risks can be diminished, but not eliminated, by restricting the rights of the licensees in the source code. Imposing the risk of liability for failure to sell in a commercially reasonable manner on the escrow agent might raise escrow fees to unacceptable levels. It probably would, however, solve the problem if the licensees indemnified the escrow agent for such liability. This would represent, at most, a fee for the source code.

4. Perfection of security interests in software

For a security interest in source code to work, the secured party must perfect its security interest in the source code and all the rights in the licensed program. Perfection of a security interest in the tangible embodiments of the source code should be a straightforward filing in which the financing statement would identify the embodiments as collateral.[143] Perfection of a security interest in the vendor's intangible property rights is more complicated. This Article has noted that a vendor will usually claim two sorts of rights in software: copyright and trade secret. Both copyrights and trade secrets fall within the Article 9 definition of "general intangibles."[144] A security agreement that grants a security interest in "general intangibles" probably

---

[141] U.C.C. §9-507, comment 1 (1978).

[142] See supra text accompanying notes 50–53; 11 U.S.C. §105(a) (1978) (general equitable powers of bankruptcy courts); §365(e)(1) (1978) (general unenforceability of executory contract clauses that ipso facto modify the contract upon insolvency or filing for bankruptcy).

[143] See U.C.C. §§9-302, 9-402(1). Alternatively, perfection of a security interest in the embodiments of the source code may be had by possession. Id. §9-305; *In re Copeland*, 391 F. Supp. 134 (D. Del. 1975). Aft'd, 531 F.2d 1195 (3rd Cir. 1976) (security interest perfected by secured party's escrow agent taking possession of the collateral).

[144] See supra note 5 and accompanying text. If patents are also involved, a security interest may be created and perfected in the patents. See, e.g., *In re Transportation Design and Technology, Inc.*, 40 U.C.C. Rep. Serv. 1393 (Bankr. S.D. Cal. 1985).

covers items such as copyrights and trade secrets,[145] but to avoid any doubt, the security agreement should identify the programs and expressly state that all copyright, trade secret,[146] and other rights of any and all description in such programs are covered by the security interest. Because trade secret status for any item, including a computer program, will depend on a supporting network of confidentiality agreements and other claims, sound drafting of the security agreement should also include an assignment of all contracts and claims supporting trade secret status for the licensed programs and related documentation.[147] The financing statement, on the other hand, would merely describe the collateral as "general intangibles."[148]

This article has already shown that all computer programs are subject to federal copyright protection from the time they are set down in a tangible medium of expression.[149] This protection applies regardless of whether the owner has registered its copyright claim with the Copyright Office,[150] and regardless of whether the owner has sought to protect its program as a trade secret. The question therefore arises whether a security interest in the

---

145 See U.C.C. §9-106 (1978) (definition of "general intangibles"); id., comment ("Examples [of 'general intangibles'] are . . . copyrights, trademarks, and patents"); see, e.g., *United States v. Antenna Systems, Inc.*, 251 F. Supp. 1013, 1016 (D. N.H. 1966) (confidential engineering concepts, ideas, and principles are "general intangibles" within the meaning of the Uniform Commercial Code).

146 See U.C.C. §9-110 (the requisite description of collateral is sufficient "if it reasonably identifies what is described"); cf. Antenna Systems, 251 F. Supp. at 1016 (failure to refer to "general intangibles" in security agreement).

147 For example, the security agreement should cover claims against third parties to whom the trade secret was disclosed under circumstances implying confidentiality. See Restatement of Torts, §757 comment b (1939); see generally *U.S.M. Corp. v. Marson Fastener Corp.*, 379 Mass. 90 (1971) (describing steps necessary to create trade secret status for industrial information).

148 See U.C.C. §9-402(1) (1978) and comments thereto (limited requirements of "notice filing"). Compare infra note 153 and accompanying text (notice provided by Copyright Office filing).

149 17 U.S.C. §101 (1982). See supra note 6.

150 Registration is not a precondition of copyright protection, unless registration is necessary to preserve a copyright otherwise invalidated by an omission of copyright notice. 17 USC. §§408(a), 405(a) (1982). Registration is, however, a prerequisite to suing for copyright infringement and failure to register does preclude certain statutory remedies for infringement that occurred prior to the date of ultimate registration. Id. §§41 l(a), 412(1). Deposit of copies in the Copyright Office, which is required within three months of first publication, is not a precondition of copyright protection. Id. §407(a).

copyright in computer programs should be perfected by filing in a state office[151] or by filing in the Copyright Office.

The Copyright Act provides for the filing of assignments and other "document[s] pertaining to a copyright" in the Copyright Office.[152] This would seem to include agreements creating a security interest in copyright,[153] and, in fact, such filings are increasingly common.[154] Furthermore, documents properly filed in the Copyright Office with respect to registered work are constructive notice to all persons of the contents of the documents,[155] thus serving a purpose analogous to that of a financing statement filed in a state office. On the other hand, the Copyright Act fails to specify whether or to what extent it governs or regulates security interests in copyrights.[156]

Whether filing a security agreement in the Copyright Office will perfect a security interest in copyrights is answered affirmatively in section 9-302 of the UCC. Compliance with the Copyright Office filing system is considered the equivalent of filing under Article 9 of the UCC, and a security interest in a copyright 'can be perfected only by compliance therewith.'[157] Thus, section 9-

---

[151] See U.C.C. §9-401 (1978) (place of filing) and §9-103 (1978) (place of filing in multi-state transactions).

[152] U.S.C. §205(a) (1982).

[153] Copyright Office regulations define "a document [pertaining] to a copyright" as "a document . . . [having] a direct or indirect relationship to the existence, scope, duration, or identification of a copyright, or to the ownership, division, allocation, licensing, transfer, or exercise of rights under a copyright. That relationship may be past, present, future, or potential." 37 C.F.R. §201.4(a)(2) (1986).

[154] "Note, Transfers of Copyright Under the New Copyright Act," 88 *Yale L. J.* 125 n.4 (1978).

[155] 17 U.S.C. §205(e) (1982). Copyright Office filing also satisfies a requirement for a copyright owner's recovery of certain statutory damages, which are conditioned on the infringer's knowledge or reason to know that it was infringing a valid copyright. Id. §504(c) (1982).

[156] While the Copyright Act regulates "transfers of copyright ownership" that include "mortgage . . . or any other conveyance, alienation, or hypothecation," 17 U.S.C. §101, the sections governing priority among conflicting transfers only cover conflicts in which at least one transfer is registered. Id. §205(e)–(f). Despite a proposal by the motion picture industry, Congress refused to enact a federal system of copyright mortgage foreclosure. See House Report, supra note 17, at 123.

[157] U.C.C. §9-302(4) (1978); see also id. §9-302(e) comment 8 (1978) ("Filing under [Article 9] is not a permissible alternative."). There is little case law on where to file to perfect a security interest in copyright. In the only case the authors found where the issue was raised, the failure to record in the Copyright Office was immaterial because there were no subsequent transfers in dispute. See *Bankers Capital Corp.*, 637 S.W.2d 424, 430 (Mo. App. 1982). A 1985 case addressing the question of where to file to

302 seems to spare holders of a security interest in copyright in licensed software the burden of having to file twice. Perfection of a security interest should be by Copyright Office filing.

Holders of security interests in copyright would nevertheless be well advised to comply with both Copyright Office and state filing systems. Copyright Office filing does not perfect the agent's security interest in either the tangible embodiments of the source code or in the vendor's trade secret rights in the source code. Furthermore, the effectiveness of Copyright Office filing has not been tested.[158] Finally, the scope of federal preemption does not extend to all aspects of a security interest in copyright. The Copyright Act does not establish priority in all circumstances,[159] and probably does not include sufficient provisions regulating the rights of parties and third parties to exclude security interests in copyright entirely from Article 9 of the UCC.[160] For these reasons, there is a consensus among commentators that holders of security interests in copyright should comply with both filing systems.[161]

Whether or not a secured party complies with both systems or files solely with the Copyright Office, compliance with Copyright Office filing regulations may be ineffective if the copyright is not registered. Part III of this Article discusses the specific requirements of copyright registration, including particularly the deposit requirement.

---

perfect a security interest in a patent noted that it was a case of first impression despite long coexistence of the UCC and the Patent Act. *In re Transportation Design and Technology, Inc.* 40 U.C.C. Rptr. Serv. 1393 (Bankr. S.D. Cal. 1985).

158 See supra note 158; compare *In re Transportation Design and Technology, Inc.*, 40 U.C.C. Rptr. Serv. 1393 (UCC filing perfects security interest in patent) with *In re Otto Fabrics, Inc.*, 55 Bankr. 654 (Bankr. D. Kan. 1985) (federal patent law governs perfection of security interest in patent).

159 See supra text accompanying note 157.

160 U.C.C. §9-104(a) (1978) and comment 1; see also *Republic Pictures Corp. v. Security-First National Bank of Los Angeles*, 197 F.2d 767 (9th Cir. 1952) (old Copyright Act preempts state secured transaction law only in the limited areas of recording and the effect of recording on priority); 1 G. Gilmore, *Security Interests in Personal Property*, §13.10 (1965).

161 See 3 Nimmer, *Nimmer on Copyright*, §10.05[A] (1985); Concoff, G., "Motion Picture Secured Transactions under the Uniform Commercial Code: Problems in Perfection," 13 *U.C.L.A. L. Rev.* 1214, 1215 (1966); "High-techs in Chapter 11 Can They Survive?: 2d Annual New England Bankruptcy Law Conference," 90–91 (MCLE, Inc., 1985).

III. Copyright act deposit and registration requirements as they apply to computer software

The foregoing analysis suggests that a purchaser or exclusive licensee of computer programs, or one holding a security interest in such programs, must record with the Copyright Office in order to protect itself against the bankruptcy trustee. Unfortunately, recordation creates more problems than it should.

Pursuant to Copyright Act section 205 (e), recordation of a program protects it against subsequent transferees such as a bankruptcy trustee if recordation is made "in the manner required to give constructive notice under subsection (c)." Subsection 205(c) requires registration of the program if recordation is to give constructive notice. Registration, in turn, requires a deposit, and the deposit creates a problem for computer software.

A. The section 408 deposit requirement

Under Copyright Act section 408, registration is made by "delivering to the Copyright Office the deposit specified by this section, together with the application and fee specified by sections 409 and 708."[162] The deposit generally consists of one or two complete copies of the work.[163] The Register of Copyright is authorized, however, to adopt regulations that "require or permit, for particular classes, the deposit of identifying material instead of copies."[164] Once deposited, the identifying materials are held in the Copyright Office or delivered by the Register of Copyright to the Library of Congress.[165] In either case, the original deposit or a facsimile reproduction is publicly available for inspection.[166]

Because most software vendors endeavor to protect their programs as trade secrets, they do not deposit complete copies of their programs pursuant to section 408(b). Instead, most vendors who register their copyrights avail themselves of Copyright Office Regulation 202.20(c)(2)(vii), which permits the deposit of "identifying materials" consisting of the first and last twenty-five

---

[162] 17 U.S.C. §408(a) (1982).

[163] Id. §408(b).

[164] Id. §408(c).

[165] Id. §704.

[166] The Copyright Office must retain the deposit or a facsimile of unpublished works for the term of the copyright and of published works for as long as practicable and desirable. Id. §704(d). All articles deposited in connection with completed copyright registrations and retained under the control of the Copyright Office are open to public inspection. Id. §705(b); see also Davidson, supra note 6, at 734–43.

pages of a visually perceptible copy of the program.[167] Unfortunately, a strict application of this regulation to most typical types of licensed computer programs is doubtful. By its own terms, the regulation applies only to a class consisting of works fixed or published only in machine-readable form. Most licensed software is fixed in a variety of forms, including both human-readable source code and machine-readable object code.[168] If all of these manifestations of the program are considered to be one "work," then the regulation would not apply because the source code version of the work is human-readable.[169] Thus, registration of the program under the Copyright Act and the regulations promulgated thereunder could only be accomplished by

---

[167] 37 C.F.R. §202.20(c)(2)(vii) and (vii)(A) provide in full:

> (vii) Computer programs and data bases embodied in machine-readable copies. In cases where a computer program, database, compilation, statistical compendium or the like, if unpublished is fixed, or if published is published only in the form of machine-readable copies (such as magnetic tape or disks, punched cards, or the like) from which the work cannot ordinarily be perceived except with the aid of machine or device, the deposit shall consist of:
>
> > (A) For published or unpublished computer programs, one copy of identifying portions of the program, reproduced in a form visually perceptible without the aid of a machine or device, either on paper or in microform. For these purposes, 'identifying portions' shall mean either the first and last 25 pages or equivalent units of the program if reproduced on paper, or at least the first and last 25 pages or equivalent units of the program if reproduced in microform, together with the page or equivalent unit containing the copyright notice, if any. If the program is 50 pages or less, the required deposit will be the entire work. In the case of revised versions of such works, if the revisions occur throughout the entire computer program, the deposit of the first and last 25 pages will suffice; if the revisions are not contained in the first and last 25 pages, the deposit should consist of any 50 pages representative of the revised material.

[168] See supra text accompanying note 7. The analysis in the text assumes that the software in question includes trade secrets and will therefore be considered "unpublished" by the vendor. A different conclusion might be reached for software published only in object code, such as mass-market programs sold pursuant to shrink-wrap agreement.

[169] In applying Regulation 202.20(c)(2)(vii), the Copyright Office has taken the position that source code best satisfies the "identifying portions" requirement. 48 Fed. Reg. 22951, 22952 (1983); Compendium II of Copyright Office Practices 806.12(a)(l) (1984). Thus, human-readable source code satisfies the deposit requirements for a class of work labeled "machine-readable works." The apparent inconsistency in the Copyright Office position offers little guidance to a court in choosing between the alternative views that source and object code of the program are either one "work" or a "work" and "derivative work." See infra text accompanying note 171.

depositing at least one complete copy of the work. Most vendors are reluctant to do this for fear of losing their trade secret protection for the program.

An alternate view is that the source and object code versions of a program are different "works," with the object code being a "derivative work" resulting from the "translation" of the source code into machine-readable form.[170] Applying this theory, a vendor might use the first and last twenty-five pages of object code as its deposit. Because object code is usually fixed only in machine-readable form, such a deposit would (on the separate works theory) be authorized by Regulation 202.20(c)(2)(vii).

If the separate works theory is accepted by the courts, registration of object code under Regulation 202.20(c)(2)(vii) followed by recordation of software licenses could be used to protect exclusive licensees and transferees of object code against a trustee's avoidance power under Bankruptcy Code section 544(a)(1), but it would not give any protection against the avoidance of source code licenses, transfers, and security interests.[171] Under section 103(b) of the Copyright Act, copyright in a derivative work "extends only to the material contributed by the author of such work, as distinguished from the preexisting material employed in the work."[172] Thus, if one considered object and source code versions of a program to be different works, registration of the first and last twenty-five pages of object code would be effective to register copyright in the object code, but not in the source code. Copyright in the source code (a separate work) would be left unregistered, and the recordation of a license or other document covering source code in whole or in part would not give constructive notice under Copyright Act section 205 (c) and, therefore, would not protect the

---

[170] The Copyright Act defines "derivative work" as "a work based upon one or more preexisting works, such as a translation, . . . or any other form in which a work may be recast, transformed, or adapted." 17 U.S.C. §101 (1982) (definition of "derivative work"). Copyright in the derivative work is distinct from copyright in the work from which it is derived, although the permission of the owner of the prior work is needed to create a derivative work. Id. §§103, 106.

[171] A software license will invariably cover object code, because without a right to use object code the licensed program cannot be used in connection with a computer. Source code might or might not be covered by a software license, but a contingent license to use source code will usually accompany any software escrow arrangement. See supra text accompanying notes 117–18.

[172] The "author" of object code is usually a computer program known as a "compiler." The fact that there is no human author tends to support the conclusion that the object code is not a separate, derivative work, but merely the original work "fixed" in a different manner, just as a motion picture on film can also be "fixed" on a video tape.

licensee (or other transferees) against a bankruptcy trustee's claims under Copyright Act section 205 (e) and Bankruptcy Code section 544(a)(1).

In practice, the dilemma created by the limitation of Regulation 202.20(c)(2)(vii) to works fixed or published only in machine-readable form is largely ignored. Most applicants follow the Copyright Office's lead[173] and submit source code to satisfy the 'identifying portions' requirement for deposit. However, the validity of this practice, as a means of protecting both source and object codes, has not been considered by any court.

In addition to Regulation 202.20(c)(2)(vii), the Copyright Office has adopted an informal procedure whereby it will accept object code under its "Rule of Doubt"[174] as a deposit for purposes of registration if the copyright owner informs the Copyright Office that the work is a trade secret. Using this procedure, a software vendor might attempt to register copyrights in the object code version of its programs, and the vendor's exclusive licensees could thereafter seek the safe harbor of recordation under Copyright Act section 205 (e) against the claims of a bankruptcy trustee.

As an alternative to Regulation 202.20(c)(2)(vii), owners of computer programs have increasingly requested permission for deposit of noncomplying identifying materials under the "special relief provisions of Regulation 202.20(d) in order to avoid making a deposit that reveals trade secrets."[175] Special relief is currently allowed by the Copyright Office in several alternative forms: the first and last 25 pages of source code with some parts blocked-out; at least the first and last 10 pages of source code, with no blocked-out portions; or the first and last 25 pages

---

173 See supra note 170.

174 See Copyright Office Circular No. R. 61; 48 Fed. Reg. at 22952. The "Rule of Doubt" means that the office has acknowledged that the application for registration has been filed and a deposit made, but takes no position as to whether or not the work contains original authorship subject to copyright protection. Id. The apparent purpose of this rule is to facilitate registrations of the object code version of computer programs while withdrawing from such registrations the benefit of §410(c) of the Copyright Act, under which a certificate of copyright registration constitutes prima facie evidence of the validity of the copyright and of the facts stated in the certificate. There is no statutory basis for "Rule of Doubt" registrations, nor are such registrations even supported by a formal regulation promulgated by the Copyright Office. For these reasons, the validity of a registration issued under the purported "Rule of Doubt" is doubtful. Its effect has never been considered by any court.

175 51 Fed. Reg. 34667, 34668 (1986). Regulation 202.20(d) provides in pertinent part: 'In any case, the Register of Copyrights may, after consultation with other appropriate officials of the Library of Congress and upon such conditions as the Register may determine after such consultation, . . . (ii) permit the deposit of incomplete copies.

of object code plus any 10 or more consecutive pages of source code with no blocked-out portions.[176] These alternatives allow owners to satisfy Copyright Office procedures without jeopardizing state law trade secret protection.

The question arises whether the deposit alternatives allowed as "special relief" constitute "identifying materials" within the meaning of Copyright Act section 408(c)(l). The same question arises with regard to the first and last twenty-five-page deposit authorized by Regulation 202.20(c)(2)(vii).[177] Source code (or object code) for any reasonably sophisticated computer program is typically hundreds, or even thousands, of pages long. One of the historical purposes of the deposit requirement for copyright registration is to create a public record of what the work is in which a copyright is claimed.[178] Therefore, the deposit of the first and last ten or twenty-five pages of a work that is several thousand pages long manifestly fails to achieve this purpose. Indeed, owners of computer programs who deposit their works make sure that nothing important appears in the few pages which are deposited. Under these circumstances, there would be no way for a person accused of infringement to determine whether the work introduced by the plaintiff into evidence is the same work as the one "registered," except by relying on the plaintiff's own testimony. Furthermore, the deposit fails to make the copyrighted work available for public inspection — a right usually thought to be the quid pro quo for the copyright monopoly.[179] For this reason, there is a very compelling

---

[176] 51 Fed. Reg. at 34668 (1986); see Compendium II of Copyright Office Practices 808 (1984). Proposed amendments to Regulation 202.20 include the three forms of "special relief" currently allowed and a fourth alternative for small programs of 25 pages or less. 51 Fed. Reg. at 34668–669. The proposed rulemaking codifies current practice with the additional requirement that a deposit include the page showing copyright notice and a statement as to the total number of lines in the program. Id.

[177] See supra note 168.

[178] *Merrill v. Tice,* 104 U.S. 557, 561 (1882) (deposits are quasi-records, kept for the purpose of public inspection and ascertaining the subject of the copyright); see also Samuelson, supra note 6, at 706–19 (public disclosure is a constitutionally mandated trade-off for the copyright monopoly).

[179] See supra note 179; but see *National Conference v. Multistate Legal Studies,* 692 F.2d 478, 484–87 (7th Cir. 1982). cert. denied, 464 U.S. 814 (1983) (deposit requirements are procedural only and not for the purpose of public disclosure of the copyrighted work). The Multistate court upheld Regulation 202.20(c)(2)(vi) as consistent with the Copyright Act and constitutional despite the fact that the regulation requires return of secured test deposits submitted for registration. The Copyright Office relied in part on the Multistate holding when it created the informal procedure for registering computer programs containing trade secrets. See "Notice of Inquiry Deposit of Computer Programs and Other Works Containing Trade Secrets," 48 *Fed. Reg.* 22951–54 (1983).

argument that the deposits authorized by Regulation 202.20(c)(2)(vii) and the informal rule for source code under Regulation 202.20(d) are invalid on the ground that they are inconsistent with the requirement of Copyright Act section 408(c)(1) that the deposit consist of "identifying material."[180]

It remains to be seen whether a bankruptcy court would hold that the trustee might avoid an exclusive software license if the vendor and its exclusive licensee had made a good faith effort to register the licensed programs and to record the license in a manner which is condoned by the Copyright Office, but which probably does not comply with the requirements of the Copyright Act. This issue reflects the conflict between the two radically different approaches taken by the Bankruptcy Code and the Copyright Act. In bankruptcy court, justice follows a very harsh logic. Bankruptcy judges have little sympathy with the defense: "But, your Honor, we assumed. . . ." If a secured lender files a financing statement identifying its collateral as inventory or equipment when it is really "general intangibles," such as copyright, this probably inadvertent mistake can cost the lender its secured status.

In contrast, in copyright infringement cases, courts frequently overlook technicalities which might deprive the copyright owners of the benefit of copyright protection.[181] The policy of the Copyright Act is, in part, to do away with an over-technical approach to matters such as the placement of the copyright notice.[182] Similarly, the Copyright Office has strained to accommodate the needs of owners of copyrights in computer programs, even at the expense of possibly violating the Copyright Act.

It seems slightly more likely that, at least at the district court level, the balance would fall on the side of an exclusive licensee which attempted in good faith to have the licensed program registered by the vendor and to record its license in the manner provided by Copyright Act sections 205(c) and (e). Such a result cannot be assured, however, and the weight of logic probably favors a contrary

---

180 By contrast, Regulation 202.20(c)(2)(viii), which applies to works such as textiles and fabrics, permits the deposit of "an actual swatch or piece of such material sufficient to show all elements of the work in which copyright is claimed." This gives potential infringers, defendants in infringement actions, and courts hearing such actions, a full opportunity to determine the similarity between the work registered and the allegedly infringing work, as well as providing public access to the copyrighted work.

181 See, e.g., *Midway Mfg. Co. v. Arctic Int'l.*, Inc., 547 F. Supp. 999, 1009 (N.D. Ill. 1981), aff'd, 704 F.2d 1009 (7th Cir. 1983), cert. denied, 464 U.S. 823 (1983) (holding that deposit of an audiovisual tape of the play of a video game is sufficient to register copyright in the computer program that operated the game).

182 House Report, supra note 17, at 143–44.

outcome. In a situation like this, old habits are of little assistance, and the first few cases of this type will permanently reshape the law.

B. The section 205 registration requirement

The conflict between Bankruptcy Code section 544(a)(1) and Copyright Act section 205 illustrates a second, and more fundamental, defect in the Copyright Act. Reflecting its heritage in laws that applied only to published works, section 205 of the Copyright Act works on the assumption that all copyrighted works can realistically be registered, and provides protection against subsequent transferees only where the transferred work has been registered. This may make sense for published works or for unpublished works that are destined for publication, but it produces absurd results when it is applied to other types of works subject to federal copyright law. Every piece of paper on which someone has written, every photograph, and every scrap of film on the cutting room floor is a "work" in which copyright subsists under the Act. This may seem academic, but it becomes very important in any transaction involving a purchase of assets where some of the assets consist of valuable intellectual property.

Suppose, for example, that a management consulting firm sold off a part of its business. The assets purchased would include a vast array of studies, reports, memoranda, computer programs, and other intangibles, the great bulk of which would not be registered with the Copyright Office. Must the purchaser insist on registration of all of these "works" to protect itself against a subsequent transferee or a trustee in bankruptcy?[183] The costs of such an undertaking could easily exceed the value of the transaction.[184] Yet such a result seems required by

---

183 Special relief might be sought by petitioning the Copyright Office under 37 C.F.R. § 202.20(d). The special relief might consist of an identification of the works en masse by the name of the transferor. Such relief, however, seems inconsistent with the requirement of Copyright Act§409(6) that the application for registration identify the works by title as well as by author. Furthermore, to the extent that the special relief would relate to the works only of the transferor, the question might arise whether it is a "class" of works for which the Register of Copyrights is authorized to accept deposits of identifying materials under § 408(c). Finally, it would be difficult to imagine what the identifying materials would be for such an unwieldy mass of paper, short of a laboriously compiled index or photocopies of the works themselves.

184 Indeed, in response to cases involving related works or parts of a work that are published separately, Congress sought to rectify administrative problems and ease the burden and expense to copyright owners created by the separate registration requirement. Section 408(c)(2) allows for a single registration for a group of works by the same individual author, all first published as contributions to periodicals within a

Copyright Act section 205. An analogy in the area of tangible property would require a purchaser of aggregates to register every rock, every pebble, and every grain of sand it is purchasing. The problem is that the Copyright Act gathered many works under its protective wing but only has the ability to deal with those works one at a time, rather than in groups.

C. Proposed legislative and regulatory solutions

1. Elimination of registration requirement

This Article suggests three solutions to the deposit and prior registration problems. The first and most extreme solution is to eliminate the requirement of copyright registration altogether, bringing the United States' law into conformity with the copyright laws of many other countries. This solution is the most intellectually satisfying. It would recognize that copyright law is not like patent law, where the scope of monopoly is determined by an agency of the government, but rather is more like federal antitrust law, where Congress has specified broad goals and created federal causes of action but left it to the courts to sort out the details. This approach was considered and rejected during the many years of deliberations, which ultimately led to the Copyright Act. Until the problems discussed in this Article cause a highly visible disaster, it is unlikely that Congress will enact such a sweeping change.

2. Elimination or modification of deposit requirement

Much less extreme, the second solution is to accommodate the registration of copyright in works, which are also protected as trade secrets. The Proprietary Rights in Software Committee of the American Bar Association proposed to solve this problem by eliminating the deposit requirement for computer programs altogether.[185] Alternatively, Copyright Act section 705(b) could be amended to exclude from public inspection articles deposited as unpublished

---

twelve-month period, to be effectuated by a single deposit, application, and registration fee. In providing for a single registration of a group of related published works, Congress recognized that "[i]n a number of cases the technical necessity for separate applications and fees has caused copyright owners to forego copyright altogether." House Report, supra note 17, at 154. What Congress failed to recognize or address are similar undesirable results involving unpublished groups of related works in the sale of assets. Additionally, §408(c)(2) does nothing to ease the burden and expense of depositing each related work or part of a work. See discussion supra note 185; see also infra text accompanying notes 191–93.

185 See Davidson supra note 6.

trade secrets.[186] Regulation 202.20 could be discarded. In its place, and if an appropriate amendment were made in section 705(b), the Copyright Office should adopt a regulation permitting the deposit of an entire work that the copyright holder treats as a trade secret in a way that will protect the work against disclosure to the public, whether under the Freedom of Information Act or otherwise.[187] This approach addresses the immediate problem of registering a computer program but does not solve the problem of protecting transferees of unregistered works against the rights of subsequent transferees, such as a bankruptcy trustee under section 205.

3. Revision of section 205 on model of uniform commercial code

The third solution attempts to reach a middle ground between the two solutions suggested above.[188] This approach would amend section 205 to make it work on the model of the UCC. Rather than identifying and indexing transfers by the title or registration number of the work, transfers could be identified and indexed by the names of the transferor and transferee. The document filed might be called a "transfer statement;" on the model of the UCC's financing statement, it would be required to include only a general description of the work or works transferred.[189] Further, the section 205 (c) requirement that the underlying work

---

[186] The Semiconductor Chip Protection Act of 1984 (Chip Act) and related Copyright Office regulations provide a possible model for excluding trade secrets from deposited materials available for public inspection. The Semiconductor Chip Protection Act of 1984, Pub. L. No. 98-620, §302, 1984 U.S. Code Cong. & Admin. News (98 Stat.) 3335 (codified at 17 U.S.C. §§901–14 (Supp. II 1985)). The Chip Act provides protection for a mask work in a semiconductor ship. A "mask work" is the series of related images representing the surface pattern on layers of a semiconductor chip. Id. §902(a)(l), 90l(a)(2). Regulations authorized by the Chip Act, allow for withholding of trade secrets from "identifying materials" for purposes of registration by means of "blocking out" such information on the deposit printout of a mask work. Id.§908(d); 37 C.F.R. §21 l.5(c).

[187] Deposit of the entire work might be resisted by the owners of valuable programs, for fear of "leaks" out of the Copyright Office. The American Bar Association committee suggests that such a deposit should not be required at all, apparently believing that problems of proof could be addressed in other ways. See Davidson, supra note 6, at 742.

[188] If this suggestion is followed, but registration is retained as a prerequisite to filing suit and other remedies under § § 411, 412, then the second proposal — clearly accommodating the need for registration of works which are also protected as trade secrets — should also be adopted.

[189] Cf. U.C.C. §9-402 (1978).

be registered could be eliminated.[190] Because only a brief description of the work transferred would be required, recording the transfer would not jeopardize any trade secret protection for the transferred works.

Under this proposal, a person acquiring all of the assets of a business could file a "transfer statement," identifying the transferred work as "all work of the transferor." A person acquiring an exclusive license to operate a computer program on a certain kind of central processing unit could file a "transfer statement" describing the "transferred rights" as "the right to operate the [name] database management system on an a [name] mini-computer." As under the UCC and real estate recording statutes, the burden would be on subsequent transferees to search the transfer records of their transferors and make an inquiry if it appeared that someone else might have filed comparable rights at an earlier date. The limited purposes of "notice filing" would thereby be served.

A system like the one proposed would not provide absolute title assurance, as it always depends on the quality of the original transferor's title.[191] But the current system does not provide absolute protection either. For example, it is only possible to search the Copyright Office records under the current system if one knows either the title or registration number of the subject work. This approach is defective because the same work (or at least works so substantially similar that one would constitute an infringement of the other) might take on various titles over time.[192] Furthermore, substantially similar works might be separately registered and have separate registration numbers. Moreover, there is always the problem that the original author of the work plagiarized it so that the apparently clean title shown on the Copyright Office records would be subject to an infringement action.

---

190 Cf. 17 U.S.C. §903(c)(l) (1984) (ownership, transfer, licensing, and recordation of a semiconductor chip mask work). Copyright Office recordation of signed documents pertaining to a mask work is constructive notice of the contents of the documents; registration is not a requirement for effective constructive notice.

191 Combining the two systems is a possibility. This would be similar to the dual system of registered and unregistered interests in realty that exists in some states, including Massachusetts. Thus, the holder of an exclusive right could "quiet title" by registering a previously unregistered work. Such a system could only be made to work if there was a formal proceeding in which others having arguably conflicting rights in the property could appear and object; it is doubtful whether such a system could be funded and made to work on a national scale through the Copyright Office.

192 See Note, supra note 156, at 131

A recordation system modeled after the UCC and title recording statutes (i.e., indexed by transferor and transferee, not by the identity of the property transferred) would eliminate the section 205 problems discussed in this Article and provide most of the "quiet title" advantages sought to be achieved by section 205.[193] Protecting exclusive licensees and asset purchasers against subsequent transferees such as a bankruptcy trustee promotes commerce in copyrighted works and diminishes the threat of inconsistency between copyright and trade secret protection for unpublished works. It also provides a solution to serious defects in source code escrows by providing an effective means of perfecting security interests in copyrighted works.

Until Congress enacts statutes adopting changes like those suggested in this Article, transferees will be subject to the mercy of the courts. As this Article has discussed, if the court is a bankruptcy court, its mercy may not always be tender.

---

[193] The current §205(e) makes it possible for any transferee to obtain protection against competing transfers by recording its transfer first (subject, of course, to the three or six-month waiting period). This is believed to provide reassurance to persons who spend large sums on acquired properties, such as motion picture producers and publishers. Alternatively, one could amend to provide that §205(e) applies only to transfers that take place after a work has been registered. The priority of a transfer occurring prior to registration should be governed by the simple rule of §205(f): the transfer is prior to any conflicting transfer if it is in writing and taken prior to the execution or recordation of the other transfer. Such a charge would dilute the 'quiet title' advantages of the current §205(e). The authors submit, however, that the implications of §205(e) described in this Article are so destructive of the quiet title of purchasers and exclusive licenses of the great mass of unregistered works that, on balance, security would be enhanced rather than diminished by the change.

Computer Software Licensing after the Enactment of the Intellectual Property Bankruptcy Protection Act*

On October 18, 1988, the "Intellectual Property Bankruptcy Protection Act"[1] became law. The result is an amendment to Section 365 of the Bankruptcy Code[2] that dramatically alters the balance of power between a bankrupt software licensor and its licensees.

The Act is a direct response to the celebrated case of *Lubrizol Enterprises v. Richmond Metal Finishers.*[3] As will be seen, the Act eliminated some of the uncertainties created by Lubrizol at the expense of creating a new set of uncertainties of its own.

This article will first describe the problems to which the Act responds, then how the Act works, and finally, some of the issues that practitioners will likely face in the new environment created by the Act.

The trustee's power of rejection

The basic purpose of bankruptcy proceedings is to provide an efficient and equitable clearing house for creditors' claims.[4] To this end, the Bankruptcy Code gives the bankruptcy trustee[5] extraordinary powers designed to maximize the value of the debtor's estate and then distribute that value

---

 The author gratefully acknowledges the assistance of Shing Hsieh and Susan Montgomery, as well as the thoughtful review of Marie Radcliffe, in the preparation of this article.

1 Pub.L. 100-506, 102 Stat. 2538 (1988) (hereinafter the "Act").

2 11 U.S.C. §365 (1982). Title 11 U.S.C. §§10–1330 is referred to throughout as the "Bankruptcy Code."

3 756 F.2d 1043 (4th Cir. 1985), *cert. denied,* 106 S.Ct. 1284 (1986), rev'g *In re Richmond Metal Finishers,* 38 Bankr. 341 (Bankr. E.D. Va. 1984).

4 See Jackson, "Bankruptcy, Non-Bankruptcy Entitlements and the Creditors' Bargain," 91 *Yale L. J.* 857 (1982).

5 After the filing of bankruptcy proceedings, the debtor's estate is administered by either a debtor in possession, an independent person (trustee) appointed by the bankruptcy court or, in some jurisdictions, by the United States Trustee. SH 11 U.8.C. 111101(1), 1104 (1982). All three have the same powers for purposes of the matters discussed in this paper, and all three will be referred to as the "trustee."

equitably among the creditors.[6] Among the more important of these is that of rejection under Section 365 of the Bankruptcy Code.[7] Section 365 makes it possible for a trustee to get rid of unprofitable contracts.[8] It is related to the trustee's more general power (and, indeed, responsibility) to "abandon" property that costs more to maintain than it is worth.[9]

Rejection cuts off the contractual obligee's right to obtain specific performance and thus converts the debtor's burdensome obligation to perform into a general unsecured claim which may be treated on a par with other unsecured claims.[10] If the trustee did not have the power to reject a burdensome executory contract, then an unsecured obligee under an executory contract would, in effect, be given a right to drain the debtor's assets to the detriment of other unsecured creditors. This would violate the bedrock principle of bankruptcy that "equality is equity."[11]

The trustee's power to reject a burdensome executory contract under Section 365 is thus central to the administration of a debtor's estate. Trimming the trustee's power makes it harder to administer the estate and reduces the recovery of unsecured creditors. Congress has been sparing in its grants of exceptions and limits.

Prior to the adoption of the Act, the only limits on the trustee's power of rejection were for real estate leases, timeshare interests, collective bargaining agreements and health, life and disability benefits. Under Section 365 (h)(1), a lessee or holder of a timeshare interest may elect to remain in possession of the leasehold or timeshare interest even if the lease or timeshare plan has been rejected by the trustee. Section 365(h)(2) requires the lessee or timeshare interest holder to continue to make payments as if the contract had not been

---

[6] For bankruptcy purposes, "equitable" distribution means distribution among creditors of a given "class" proportionately to the size of their claims. There are, roughly, three broad classes of creditors: those holding administrative claims (i.e., claims for debts incurred in administering the debtor's estate), those holding secured claims (which are in turn ranked in order of priority), and those holding general, unsecured claims.

[7] 11 U.S.C. §365.

[8] The debtor's estate includes not only tangible assets such as real estate and personal property, but also all of the debtor's contract rights. 11 U.S.C. §541(a) (1). Just as an old auto can be far more costly to maintain than it is worth, the cost of compliance with an im-provident contract can easily exceed its benefits.

[9] 11 U.S.C. §554. See also H.R. Rep. No. 100-1012, 100th Cong., 2d Sess. 2 (1988) (hereinafter "House Report").

[10] 11 U.S.C. §365(g); see 2 King, *Collier on Bankruptcy*, para. 365.08 (15th ed. 1988).

[11] *In re Teltronics, Ltd.*, 649 F.2d 1236, 1241 (7th Cir. 1981) (quoting *Cunningham v. Brown*, 265 U.S. 1, 13 (1924)).

rejected, subject to an offset for any reduction in value caused by the bankrupt's failure to meet Its continuing obligations under the rejected contract.[12] Section 1113[13] requires a process of negotiation before a collective bargaining agreement may be rejected, and limits the bases on which rejection can occur. Section 1114[14] provides similar protection for health, life and disability benefits.

Lubrizol Enterprises v. Richmond Metal Finishers

Lubrizol Enterprises v. Richmond Metal Finishers demonstrated that even a solvent client and an escrow agreement[15] are not proof against bankruptcy's dangers. The debtor, Richmond Metal Finishers ("AMF"), owned a proprietary metal coating process. AMF had granted Lubrizol Enterprises ("Lubrizol") a nonexclusive license to use the process.

---

[12] One is tempted to believe that the reason for this is that rejection of a lease or timeshare interest would impose an exceptional burden on the lessee or timeshare interest holder. It is certainly true that the Bankruptcy Code includes provisions designed to accommodate particular hardships, particularly if their sufferers are politically powerful. However, it would be a mistake to suppose that real estate lessees and timeshare interest holders are the only politically powerful groups potentially burdened by the trustee's power of rejection. Politically well-represented persons such as franchisees and oil and gas lessees have also felt the sting of Section 365. See, e.g., *In re Fashion Two Twenty*, 16 Bankr. 784 (Bankr. N.D. Ohio 1982); *In re J.H. Land and Cattle Co.*, 3 Collier Bankr. Cas. 2d 695 (Bankr. W.D. Okla. 1981). And yet the Bankruptcy Code makes no special provision for their protection.
A more nonpolitical rationale for the real estate lease and timeshare interest exceptions is that a leasehold or timeshare interest creates an estate in the realty and is thus a transfer of a limited property right. See, e.g., *In re Belize Airways Ltd.*, 12 Bankr. 387 (Bankr. S.D. Fla. 1981) (agreement of sublease). Just as a sale of personalty is complete upon delivery, notwithstanding any outstanding warranty obligations under the contract of sale, the existence of affirmative obligations on the lessor or timeshare interest seller do not negate the "transfer" of the leasehold or timeshare interest that occurs as soon as the period of the lease or timeshare plan has started to run.
The Senate Report analogized intellectual property licenses to real estate leases. S. Rep. No. 100-505, 100th Cong., 2d Sess. 4 (1988) (hereinafter "Senate Report"). While exclusive licenses of copyright are undoubtedly akin to transfers, see 17 U.S.C. §101 (definition of "transfer"), it is open to question whether ail intellectual property licenses should be so elevated.

[13] 11 U.S.C. §1113.

[14] 11 U.S.C. §1114.

[15] *Lubrizol* did not involve an escrow agreement, but an escrow would not have protected the licensee, for the reasons explained later in this paper.

After filing for reorganization under Chapter 11 of the Bankruptcy Code, AMF decided that it could fetch a better price for its technology if it "stripped" Lubrizol of its licensed rights. AMF therefore petitioned the bankruptcy court for leave to reject the nonexclusive license to Lubrizol under Section 365 of the Bankruptcy Code. Finding the license agreement to be "executory,"[16] the Fourth Circuit upheld the debtor RMF's right to prevent Lubrizol from using the technology following rejection of the license agreement.

The standard escrow — considered sufficient protection against a bankrupt licensor by many software licensees — would have been powerless to protect Lubrizol. Lubrizol already had access to the technology, but rejection cut off Lubrizol's right to use the technology. After *Lubrizol*, counsel for licensees began to imagine a situation in which the licensee obtains a copy of the source code from the dutiful escrow agent, only to find that rejection of the underlying license which permits the licensee to use the source code for updates and maintenance renders the source code of little use to the licensee.

Once the Supreme Court had denied *certiorari* in *Lubrizol*, Lubrizol and others formed the Bankrupt Licensors Coalition (the "BLC").[17] The BLC perceived that the only sure protection against the bankruptcy trustee's power to reject executory contracts would be an amendment to Section 365 of the Bankruptcy Code. Acting in association with the Computer and Business Equipment Manufacturers Association (CBEMA), the BLC persuaded Senators DeConcini and Heflin to introduce Senate bill 1626, entitled the "Intellectual Property Bankruptcy Protection Act of 1987." The original version of Senate bill 1626 proved unacceptable to representatives of the bankruptcy bar. Negotiations led to a substantially revised version, which won the support of the National Bankruptcy Conference and, with minor revisions, was eventually enacted.

The following sections of this paper will describe how the Act works, some drafting tactics to take full advantage of the Act and various situations in which the Act may have unintended and potentially harmful consequences.

---

[16] See infra text accompanying notes 21–25. Under the license, RMF Indemnified Lubrizol for Infringement claims and agreed not to grant more favorable licensing terms to anyone else; Lubrizol agreed to pay RMF royalties based on sales of products made using the licensed process.

[17] The name of the organization was ironic, for a coalition of bankrupt licensors BLC is not; it is a coalition of licensees worried about protecting themselves against the possibility that their licensors might go bankrupt.

I. How the Act works

A. Situations in which the Act applies

As already noted, the Act is an amendment to the Bankruptcy Code. Section 1(a) of the Act adds a definition of "Intellectual Property" to Section 101 of the Code.[18] Section 1(b) of the Act adds a new Subsection (n) to Section 365 of the Bankruptcy Code.[19] The rights and obligations under the new Section 365(n) apply only if there is "an executory contract under which the debtor is a licensor of a right to intellectual property." Virtually every word of this phrase is laden with specialized meaning.

B. "Executory contract"

For Section 365 (n) of the Act to apply, there must be an "executory contract" between the debtor and the licensee. Neither the Act nor any other provision of the Bankruptcy Code defines the term "executory contract."[20] A majority of courts have interpreted the term as adopting Professor Vern Countryman's definition: "a contract under which the obligations of both the bankrupt and the other party to the contract are so far unperformed that the failure of either party to complete performance would constitute a material breach excusing the performance of the other."[21] Courts that differ from the Countryman definition have either expanded it to include contracts that Countryman would not consider to be executory[22] or added a second step to the analysis.[23]

---

[18] 11 U.S.C. §101.

[19] 11 U.S.C. §365.

[20] See H.R. Doc. No. 137, 93d Cong., 1st Sess. 198-99 (1973) (executory contract is not defined in the Bankruptcy Code); House Report at 4 (the Act does not affect determination of whether a contract is executory).

[21] Countryman, "Executory Contracts and Bankruptcy: Part 1," 57 Minn. L. Rev. 439, 460 (1973). This is the test that was used by the Fourth Circuit in the Lubrizol case. See Lubrizol, 756 F.2d at 1045. *See also Gloria Manufacturing Corp. v. Int'l. Ladles Garment Worker's Union,* 734 F.2d 1020, 1022 (4th Cir. 1984); *In re Alexander,* 670 F.2d 885 (9th Cir. 1982); *In re Select-A-Seat Corp.,* 625 F.2d 290 (9th Cir. 1980); *In re Knudson,* 563 2d 916 (8th Cir. 1977). See also House Report at 2.

[22] See, e.g., Workman v. Harrison, 282 F.2d 693, 699 (10th Cir. 1960); King v. Baer, 482 F.2d 552, 557 (10th Cir. 1973), cert. denied, 414 U.S. 1088 (1973).

[23] See, e.g., *In re Booth,* 19 Bankr. 53 (Bankr. D. Utah 1982). The tests for an executory contract are described in greater detail in Hemnes and Montgomery, "'The Bankruptcy Code, The Copyright Act, and Transactions In Computer Software," 7 *Computer/Law Journal* 327, 343–45 (1987) (hereinafter, "Hemnes and Montgomery").

Regardless of the definition employed in the particular jurisdiction, it is highly likely that virtually all computer software licenses will be deemed to be executory for purposes of Section 365 of the Bankruptcy Code.[24]

C. "Licensor of a right"

The second requirement for Section 365(n) to apply is that the debtor must be the "licensor of a right to intellectual property." Like the concept of an "executory contract," the concept of a "license" is not defined in the Bankruptcy Code or the new Act. The legislative history of the Act — particularly the fact that it is intended to reverse *Lubrizol*[25] — suggests at the very least that the Act should cover a license of the type involved in *Lubrizol* (i.e., a nonexclusive grant of a right to use intellectual property in exchange for royalties). It is equally clear that sponsors of the legislation believed that it would also cover exclusive licenses.[26]

On the other hand, the Act probably was not intended to apply to transfers of intellectual property rights.[27] A difficult question may therefore arise where an agreement that is styled a "license" or "grant of rights" is, in effect, a transfer of some or all of the "licensor's" rights in the intellectual property. Many standard book publishing contracts take this form. Also, many software licenses contain elements of exclusivity. Under the Copyright Act, a license containing any element of exclusivity is a transfer of a "piece" of the Copyright.[28] Are exclusive copyright licenses therefore unprotected under the Act?

The purposes of the Act strongly suggest that exclusive computer software licenses should be protected as "licenses," notwithstanding their characterization as "transfers," under the Copyright Act. It seems likely that this reading would be followed, at least in situations that resemble the *Lubrizol* evil to which the Act was addressed. On the other hand, an exclusive grant of all of the licensor's rights of the type found in book publishing contracts should probably fall outside the Act's reach.

D. "Right to intellectual property"

The final precondition for Section 365(n) to apply is that the license must grant a "right to Intellectual property." As originally proposed, Senate bill 1626

---

[24] See Hemnes and Montgomery, *supra* note 23, at 349.
[25] See House Report at 6; Senate Report at 5.
[26] See House Report at 6.
[27] Publishing contracts frequently take this form.
[28] 17 U.S.C. §101 (1982) (definition of "transfer").

defined intellectual property as Including "inventions, designs, works of authorship, mask works, protected information, trademarks, trade names, service marks, and other products of intellectual or creative effort now or hereafter protected by applicable nonbankruptcy law." In the Act, the catholic nature of this original definition has been reduced to a list of items:

1. Trade Secret;
2. Invention, process, design, or plant protected under Title 35;
3. Patent application;
4. Plant variety;
5. Work of authorship protected under Title 17; or
6. Mask work protected under Chapter 9 of Title 17

all "to the extent protected by applicable nonbankruptcy law."[29]

The most conspicuous omissions from this list are trademarks and trade names. These had been included in the original version of Senate bill 1626. The original bill's provisions regarding trademarks were, however, wildly inconsistent with basic principles of trademark protection — for example, the concepts that a trademark is intended to identify a single source and that trademark licensing relationships are largely dependent on the control of the quality of the products sold by the licensee.[30] As a result, the U.S. Trademark Association successfully objected to the inclusion of trademarks in the bill.

E. Effect of Act prior to rejection of executory intellectual property licenses

Although the Act was principally designed to solve problems created by the rejection of intellectual property licenses, it has important consequences immediately upon the filing of bankruptcy proceedings involving a licensor of intellectual property. Under Section 365(n)(4)(B), the licensor shall "non [*sic*; read "not"] interfere with the rights of the licensee as provided in such contract, or any agreement supplementary to such contract, to such intellectual property

---

[29] 11 U.S.C. §101(52).

[30] See Senate Report at 5.

(including such embodiment), including any right to obtain such intellectual property (or such embodiment) from a third entity."[31]

Read literally, Section 365(n)(4)(B) seems to tell the trustee of a bankrupt software vendor that he must stand idly by while the source code for the debtor's computer program goes out the window of an escrow agreement. However, it is difficult to believe that a bankruptcy court would actually give it such an interpretation. While the trustee is prevented under the terms of Section 365(n)(4)(B) from interfering with the "rights of the licensee," the trustee must surely have a right to contest in litigation the question whether such rights exist or not. Under this circumstance, it must be possible for the trustee to "interfere with" the release of the source code. Otherwise, the terms of the escrow would become a nullity upon the filing of bankruptcy proceedings.

Section 365(n)(4)(A) also requires a trustee for the licensor to take certain affirmative actions pending the rejection of an executory contract. In particular, the first part states:

> (4) Unless and until the trustee rejects such contract, on the written request of the licensee the trustee shall —
>
> (A) to the extent provided in such contract or any agreement supplementary to such contract —
>
> (i) perform such contract; or
>
> (ii) provide to the licensee such intellectual property (including any embodiment of such intellectual property to the extent protected by applicable non-bankruptcy law) held by the trustee. . . .

Note that the trustee is obligated to perform the contract or provide certain intellectual property or embodiments to the licensee only "to the extent provided in such contract or any agreement supplementary to such contract." Section 365(n)(4) thus appears to invite the drafting of "ipso facto" clauses that take effect upon the filing of bankruptcy proceedings by the licensor. On the other hand, Section 365(b)(2) makes such clauses unenforceable to take full advantage of Section 365(a)(4) without violating Section 365(b)(2); it will be highly advisable to include in any license agreement a provision specifically stating that if the licensor fails to perform its obligation, whether

[31] 11 U.S.C. §365.

as a result of bankruptcy proceedings or for any other reason, the licensor shall provide to the licensee source code, documentation, compilers and all of the other items that otherwise would be provided to the licensee in the event of a release under the terms of an escrow agreement.

If the license agreement has been drafted to include obligations of the type required by Section 365(n)(4)(A), a difficult question of interpretation remains. Suppose, for example, that the agreement exactly tracks the language of that section, and that the licensee serves on the trustee a written request for the trustee to perform the contract. Can the trustee be obligated under this circumstance to perform the contract, or can the trustee instead opt to provide to the licensee intellectual property under Section 365(n)(4)(A)(ii)?

It seems likely that the trustee would have the option of providing the intellectual property under Section 365(n)(4)(A)(ii). The reason is that any contrary result would allow the licensee to impose affirmative executory obligations on the bankrupt licensor.[32] Depending on the nature of the license agreement, these obligations could be quite onerous. They might, for example, include an obligation to expend resources in the development of new programs, updates, enhancements, or the like. If the licensee could obtain specific performance of such obligations, it would create in the hands of the licensee a super-priority over the assets of the bankrupt licensor. This would be highly unfair to the licensor's secured and unsecured creditors.

One might argue that the licensor has the option of rejecting the contract and thus terminating his or her obligation to perform under Section 365(n)(4)(A). Read in this way, Section 365(n)(4) could be seen as an inducement for the trustee to make an early decision whether he or she wants to assume or reject the executory contract. While this interpretation is plausible (and not inconsistent with the intentions of the proponents of this legislation), the more reasonable interpretation would seem to be to give the trustee an option of either performing under the contract or providing intellectual property to the licensee.

The question remains what the trustee is obligated to do under Section 365(n)(4)(A)(ii) and its sister provision, Section 365(n)(3)(A). Both sections require the trustee to "provide to the licensee" intellectual property. Does "provide" mean "transfer?" Suppose, for example, that the license agreement required the debtor to transfer all rights in the licensed works (including patents and copyrights) to the licensee in the event of the licensor's failure to perform.

---

32 Both the Senate and House reports emphasize that the Act is not intended to impose affirmative executory obligations on the trustee. See Senate Report at 9; House Report at 7.

Would this be enforceable under the provisions of Section 365(n)(4)(A)(ii) or 365(n)(3)(A)? Read literally, the clauses would seem to require this conclusion. However, such a reading could produce highly anomalous results in situations to which the Act was probably not intended to apply.

The most alarming of such possible situations is an asset purchase transaction. Imagine, for example, a situation in which party A agrees to sell certain intellectual property to party B. Pending the sale, A licenses B to use the intellectual property. If A goes bankrupt prior to the closing date, could B contend that it is entitled to specific performance of the transfer of the intellectual property under the terms of the asset purchase agreement? To require specific performance of the intellectual property part of an asset purchase agreement under circumstances in which the transferor is bankrupt would be potentially devastating to the transferor's secured and unsecured creditors. Furthermore, the situation just described is certainly not a core example of the injustices created by *Lubrizol* that the Act was intended to rectify.

The more reasonable interpretation of Section 365(n)(3)(A) is that the word "provide" does not mean "transfer." While the Senate Report is silent on the issue, the House Report strongly suggests that the language in Section 365(n)(3)(A) means the provision of a limited right in the nature of license to use the subject intellectual property.[33] This legislation history, combined with the purpose of the Act, strongly suggests that this interpretation should be given to Section 365(n)(4)(A) as well.

F. Effect of Act following rejection of executory intellectual property licenses

We finally come to the provisions of the Act that represented the principal focus of its drafters. Section 365(n)(1) creates in the licensee a right to make an election upon the rejection of an executory intellectual property license by a trustee for the licensor. Three issues that will arise under this provision are: (1) what justifies rejection; (2) how and when the right of an election may be exercised; and (3) what the status of the intellectual property license is following a rejection and election to retain rights. This article will address each of these in order.

---

[33] See House Report at 8 ("The licensee is protected by being able to retain the ability to use the licensed intellectual property . . .").

1. Rejection

The Act gives the licensee a right of election after the trustee has rejected the intellectual property license. Rejection is a right that arises under Section 365 (a).[34] Note that under Section 365(a), the trustee may only reject an executory contract "subject to the court's approval." Bankruptcy courts generally follow one of two rules in determining whether to allow rejection of an executory contract or not. The first, and probably more common of these, is known as the "sound business judgment" test. This was the test applied in *Lubrizol*.[35] As the name implies, it permits rejection of an executory contract wherever the rejection would be in the business interest of the debtor.

The second and somewhat more restrictive test applied to the rejection of an executory contract requires the court to balance the benefit to the debtor against the harm which rejection could cause to other contracting parties. A good example of the application of this balancing test is a case decided by Judge Wolf in the District of Massachusetts, *Infosystems Technology, Inc. v. Logical Software, Inc.*[36]

The Act does not purport to choose between or to amend either of these tests. However, the Act may make it easier to reject intellectual property licenses in jurisdictions that apply the balancing test. The reason is that the Act dramatically reduces the harm that rejection could cause to an intellectual property licensee. For this reason, the balance is likely to shift in favor of rejection more often.

2. Nature of the licensee's options

As noted, Section 365(n)(1) permits the licensee of a rejected intellectual property license to "elect" either (A) "to treat such contract as terminated," or (B) "to retain its rights . . . under such contract."[37] Under either option, the licensee may assert a claim for any damages caused by the rejection.[38] The

---

[34] 11 U.S.C. §365(a).

[35] 756 F.2d at 1048–49.

[36] No. 87-0042, *slip op.* (D. Mass. June 25, 1987), *aff'g* 166 Bankr. 683 (Bankr. D. Mass. 1986). See also *In re Huang*, 23 Bankr. 798, 801-802 (Bankr. 9th Cir. 1982); *In re Meehan*, 59 Bankr. 380, 385 (E.D. N.Y. 1986); *In re Midwest Polychem*, 61 Bankr. 559, 562 (Bankr. N.D. 111. 1986); *In re Chipwich*, 54 Bankr. 427, 431 (Bankr. S.D. N.Y. 1985); *In re Turbo Wind*, 42 Bankr. 579, 584–85 (Bankr. S.D. Calif. 1984); and *In re Petur*, 35 Bankr. 561, 563–64 (Bankr. W.D. Wash. 1983).

[37] See House Report at 8.

[38] Id. Senate Report at 10.

House Report indicates that the election must be for the entire remaining duration of the contract.[39] The Act is silent on the method by which the licensee may make such an election.[40] Since no leave of court or other formal action appears to be required, it is presumably sufficient to notify the trustee or debtor in possession that the licensee wishes to make this election. Under Section 365(n)(2), a licensee electing to retain rights is obligated to make "all payments with respect to such rights due under such contract with respect to the rights retained for the duration of such contract." and is deemed to have waived "any right of set off it might have with respect to such contract" and any claim it might otherwise have under Section 503(b) of the Bankruptcy Code for certain administrative expenses related to performance under the contract.[41]

Because of the obligations to pay and the waivers contained in Section 365(n)(2), there would be some temptation to delay in making an election to retain rights. However, the right to continue to use intellectual property under Section 365(n)(4)(B) terminates upon rejection of the contract by the trustee. Thus, once the contract is rejected, the trustee can force the licensee either to make an election to retain rights, which then subjects it to the obligations and waivers contained in Section 365(n)(2), or to treat the rejection as a termination of the agreement under Section 365(n)(1)(A).

It is possible to imagine further issues arising concerning the nature of the licensee's right of election. The Act permits "the" licensee to elect to retain rights under a rejected intellectual property license. What if a particular license agreement grants rights to more than one licensee? May each such licensee independently elect to retain rights under the agreement, or must they all act in concert? Alternatively, suppose that the license covers various items of intellectual property. May the licensee pick and choose among those items of intellectual property, retaining some while permitting others to lapse?

Neither the Act nor its legislation history provides any guidance on these issues. They will remain to be resolved by the courts in the context of particular license agreements.

3. The status of license after exercise of the licensee's option to retain rights

Perhaps the most troubling question of interpretation under the new Act is the status of a rejected license agreement after a licensee has elected to retain rights under Section 365(n)(1)(B). As already noted, the Act requires the

---

39 See House Report at 9.

40 See HouseReport at 7.

41 11 U.S.C. §503.

licensee to make all payments with respect to such rights due under such contract "with respect to the rights retained" for the duration of such contract.[42] The Act is silent, however, with respect to all other conditions and obligations that are imposed either on the licensor or the licensee under the terms of the executory intellectual property license. These would include such important provisions as confidentiality obligations imposed on the licensee of a trade secret,[43] obligations on the licensee to cross-license its own intellectual property back to the bankrupt licensor, obligations or conditions applicable to a distributor/licensee with respect to minimum sales, territorial restrictions, or the like, and myriad other provisions that are commonly combined with intellectual property licenses.

The House Report states, "A licensee that retains its rights under a rejected contract remains bound by the other obligations or duties required under the contract, except for those so directly related to obligations or duties that the licensor has been freed from by rejection as to make it inequitable to bind the licensee to them."[44] Presumably, the House Committee derived this conclusion from the election required by Section 365(n)(1). The licensee can elect to treat the rejection as a termination or retain rights, but not both. Thus, the Committee may have reasoned that a licensee who elects to retain rights under section 365(n)(1)(b) cannot, at the same time, assert that the rejection is a termination that excuses the licensee's performance.

There are several problems with this analysis. In the first place, it ignores Section 365(g), under which the rejection of a contract constitutes breach of the filing date of bankruptcy proceedings. The Senate Report states that the Act "leaves unaffected the licensee's rights under Section 365(g), so that a general claim for damages . . . can be asserted by the licensee."[45] One might contend that allowing the licensee to use the debtor's Section 365(g) breach as an affirmative defense against payment and other performance obligations would be tantamount to allowing an offset on administrative claims, both of which are waived under Section 365(a)(2)(c). But even If this were the case,

---

[42] This provision will presumably require the court to allocate the amounts payable under the contract between those that are due "with respect to the rights retained" and all other amounts.

[43] Both the House and the Senate believed that the licensor's right to petition the bankruptcy court for a confidentiality order under Section 107 of the Bankruptcy Code would be sufficient to protect the confidentiality of any licensed technology. See House Report at 7; Senate Report at 5.

[44] See House Report at 7.

[45] See Senate Report at 10.

the trustee will surely default in fact - or fail to satisfy conditions on the licensee's obligations - when he or she refuses to perform affirmative obligations under the rejected license agreement. Should not that breach or failure of condition excuse the licensee from further performance?

It would probably be fair to say that the proponents of this legislation believed, somewhat naively, that the right to use licensed technology and the concomitant obligation to pay for such use could be surgically removed from a complicated license agreement without doing violence to the parties' other rights. The reality, in the judgment of this writer, is likely to be much harsher. Where a licensor has rejected a contract, and the licensee has elected to retain rights in the intellectual property covered by the contract, it is quite likely that the licensee will assert as an affirmative defense against both the licensee's further performance and the payment of amounts that would otherwise be owing under Section 365(n)(2)(B) that the licensor is in default of its obligations of the contract and that the default excuses the licensee's obligations to perform. There was testimony on this issue before the House Subcommittee. Proponents of the legislation plainly wanted to leave the door open for the licensee to make such an argument.[46]

The result of the legislation, in many cases, will be a situation in which the licensee can continue to use licensed technology, can obtain possession of such valuable property such as source code for the technology and will claim not to have to pay a penny or perform any other obligation in return. A bankruptcy court's only means of considering this result will be to, in effect, redraft the contract for the parties, and even this extraordinary remedy is not clearly mandated by the Act.

II. Drafting tips

The Act places a premium on the careful drafting of intellectual property licenses. Under Subsections 365(n)(3) and (4), the licensee can require the licensor's trustee to perform his or her obligations under a license pending assumption or rejection of the contract and to disclose or turn over such indispensable items as source code and documentation, but only "[t]o the extent provided" in the license. In the case of a source code license, these provisions should not present any special difficulties, since the license would already require the licensor to disclose or turn over source code and

[46] Hearing on H.R. 4657, a Bill to Amend the Bankruptcy Laws with Respect to Rejection of Intellectual Property Licenses, 100th Cong., 2d Sess. (June 3, 1988) (statement of Marilyn Shea-Stonum).

documentation. However, where source code is to be provided only in the event of a licensor default, or where the licensor has continuing maintenance or development obligations that will generate new intellectual property to be handed over to the licensee from time to time during the course of the license, the license should specifically require disclosure of source code, documentation, or new developments by any bankruptcy trustee or in the event of a default. Anything less explicit would seem inadvisable.

A second important drafting implication is that any substantial continuing payment obligations should, wherever possible, be included in a separate maintenance or update agreement, in which they would be tied to the licensor's obligation to maintain the licensed software or other technology, and not to the licensee's right to use the licensed product.[47] If possible, the basic right to use the product can be tied to any initial up-front payment, making the licensed rights "fully paid up."

Finally, anyone counseling a software vendor whose software will be repackaged by an OEM or value-added reseller, or otherwise sublicensed, will need to exercise special care to protect the vendor's rights in the licensed software and any payments due for its use. As noted below, the operation of the Act will otherwise create a situation in which the ultimate consumers can continue to use the software, but the vendor cannot continue to receive payments from the bankrupt middleman for use by such consumers.

III. Traps for the unwary

A. Strong-arm clause

The Act is not a cure-all for licensor bankruptcy proceedings. While the Act swings the balance of equities very radically in favor of licensees, the trustee for the licensor retains substantial powers under the Bankruptcy Code that are unaffected by the Act.

Among the most important of these powers is the trustee's right to avoid transfers of property under the "strong-arm clause."[48] Section 544 provides that the trustee may

---

[47] Such license-splitting is already advisable as one possible means of avoiding a finding that the license agreement Is executory and therefore subject to the trustee's right of rejection under Section 365.

[48] 11 U.S.C. §544(&) (1).

> avoid any transfer of property of the debtor . . . that Is voidable by — (1) a creditor that extends credit to the debtor at the time of the commencement of the case, and that obtains, at such time and with respect to such credit, a Judicial lien on all property on which a creditor on a simple contract could have obtained such a Judicial lien. . . .

It has already been noted that under the definitions of the Copyright Act, any license that contains an element of exclusivity constitutes a transfer of copyright.[49] Under Section 205 of the Copyright Act,[50] a copyright transfer is subject to the rights of subsequent transferees if it is not recorded with the Copyright Office. It is quite likely that the bankruptcy trustee would be considered such a subsequent transferee under the strong-arm clause.[51] The Act was not intended to diminish the trustee's powers under the strong-arm clause.[52] Thus, it is quite likely that an unrecorded exclusive license of property that is protected by copyright (e.g., computer software) is subject to avoidance by a trustee in bankruptcy under the strong-arm clause, notwithstanding the protection that the Act may give the licensee against a rejection of the same license under Section 365 of the Bankruptcy Code.

B. Sublicenses

The Act creates new risks for persons who permit their software to be sublicensed. Suppose, for example, that A is a software vendor, B is a value-added reseller, and C is one of B's customers. A grants B a license to sublicense A's software in connection with B's sale of product to people like C. B goes bankrupt.

Nothing in the Act states that the sublicensee's right to retain applies only to intellectual property owned by the bankrupt licensor. Thus, the Act allows C to retain its rights in the software licensed to C by B, even though that software is owned by A. Upon retaining its rights in the licensed software, C would be obligated to make payments related to its use of the software.[53] In the typical value-added reseller situation, these payments would be owing to. B. The Act does not require B to remit any sums to A. If B rejects its license agreement

---

[49] See supra notes 12 and 28.

[50] 17 U.S.C. §205.

[51] See Hemnes and Montgomery at 332–341.

[52] See Senate Report at 11.

[53] Subject of course to the possible affirmative defense that such payments are not required If B is materially in breach of its obligations to C under license agreement. See text accompanying note 46.

with A, A will have nothing more than an unsecured claim against B's estate for any amounts that are owing to A by B. Furthermore, A's software could be in jeopardy if restrictions on C's use or disclosure of the software are made in the sublicense agreement because an action to enforce such restrictions would be subject to the affirmative defense that B is in breach of its obligations to C.

Counsel for persons in A's position will need to take special care to minimize the risks described above. One means of doing this may be to require a separate license agreement between A and C that would permit A to enforce rights against C directly in the event of B's bankruptcy or other default.

C. Research and development agreements; cross licenses

Another type of transaction that the Act is likely to complicate, rather than simplify, is a transaction in which two or more parties cross-license technology to one another. Such agreements are quite common in connection with research and development projects.

Suppose, for example, that A and B cross-license certain technology to one another for the purpose of performing research and development, with the understanding that any product developed by either with the use of part of the other's technology will be licensed back to the other party. One of the two parties — call it B — goes bankrupt. If B attempts to reject its joint development agreement with A, A could elect to retain its rights in the technology that B is obligated to license to A. Under the Act, A must make any payments due to B for the right to use the technology. However, in the circumstances described above, no payments are owing to B. Instead, A must compensate B with a license-back of any developments made by A. This license-back is not explicitly protected by the Act. A would certainly complain that it should be excused from making the license-back on the ground that B's rejection of the contract and failure thereafter to perform is a material default.

A bankruptcy court might avoid inequity in these circumstances by construing "payments" in Section 365(n)(2)(B) as including benefits of all kinds flowing to the licensor in exchange for the rights enjoyed by the licensee. Such a reading finds some support in the legislative history. The House Report, for example, indicates that "royalty payments" (a term not found in the Senate version as finally enacted) should be construed by looking "to the substance of the transaction and not the label."[54] However, the example given in the House

---

[54] See House Report al 9.

Report (payments based on the licensee's sales of end products) clearly contemplates money payments, rather than payments in kind.

Unless and until the courts determine that nonmonetary "payments" are also covered by Section 365(n)(2)(B), parties might avoid this issue by including clauses that liquidate the value of their mutual executory obligations. When both parties are performing, the liquidated "payments" could be offset against one another, and the obligation to pay the liquidated amounts would arise only when there has been a rejection followed by an election to retain rights.

D. Security interests in intellectual property

The Act tends to weaken the value of intellectual property as security for loans. Suppose, for example, that A agrees to sell certain assets and to license other assets to B, including all rights in certain patented inventions and copyrighted works. A files a bankruptcy petition before the closing date, and B thereafter demands, pursuant to Sections 365(n)(1)(B) and 365(n)(4), that A "provide to" B the patents and copyrights required to be transferred under the terms of the asset purchase agreement.[55]

Are B's rights under the Act superior to the rights of persons holding perfected security interests in A's patents and copyrights? This question highlights the ambiguous nature of the Act's definition of intellectual property. The Act says that B, the licensee, can require A to "provide" to B "intellectual property," which includes A's "inventions" and "works of authorship." Does that include the patents and copyrights that protect the inventions and works of authorship? Or does it include merely an embodiment of the patent and a copy of the copyrighted work?[56] The former would seem to provide the licensee too much, and the latter too little. On the first interpretation, the Act would give each licensee the equivalent of a first priority security interest in the copyrights and patents covering any item of intellectual property required to be provided to the licensee. This would essentially eliminate intellectual property as a source of collateral for borrowing. On the latter interpretation, the licensee might be left with a copy of the subject intellectual property, but an insufficient right to use it.

---

[55] Note that B can elect to retain rights that are subject to a contingency, such as the closing. See Senate Report at 8 ("It is Important to note that the amendment, when referring to retention of rights under 'such contract,' deliberately omits the phrase 'the term of which had commenced' appearing in the somewhat parallel subsection 365(h) In connection with leases and time share plans.")

[56] The Senate bill had explicitly included patents and copyrights, but these were deleted in the final version of the Act.

What the Act was probably meant to say is that B can require A to "provide" copies of embodiments of the intellectual property,[57] together with a right to use such copies.[58]

E. Licenses of technology; licenses of trademarks or trade names

It has already been noted that trademarks, which were originally included in the Act, have now been deleted altogether. Suppose that A licenses B to make a patented product and requires B to use a certain trademark in connection with all sales of the product. A petitions for bankruptcy and rejects the contract, and B elects to retain its rights in the patented invention. Under the Act, B cannot elect to retain rights in its trademark. Can A then terminate B's retained right on the ground of B's failure to comply with its obligation to use the licensed trademark? If B's only obligation once it has retained rights in the patented product is to continue to make any payments that are owing to A, the answer to this question would seem to be "no."

Alternatively, can A enforce against B the obligation to continue to use the trademark in connection with a licensed product? This is a harder issue, since enforcing such an obligation is not directly inconsistent with the purposes of the Act. However, as has repeatedly been noted above, the Act is silent on the question of what ancillary obligations survive an election to retain rights under the license agreement.

Questions of this type will be particularly acute in any circumstance involving the bankruptcy of a franchisor. If the franchisor licensed proprietary information or patented inventions to its franchisees, the Act permits the franchisees to retain rights in that property following rejection of their franchise agreements. Can the franchisees thereafter advertise their own brand of hamburgers and french fries as made using the bankrupt's "secret process?"

IV. Conclusion

The Act undoubtedly achieves its primary purpose protecting intellectual property licensees against termination of their rights by bankrupt licensors. This should dramatically simplify many transactions of the type that now

---

57 See Senate Report at 9–10 (using an obligation to turn over a prototype as an example of the right afforded by Section 365(n)(1)(B)).

58 See House Report at 7 ("the debtor/trustee will essentially have no obligation to the licensee after rejection other than to turn over existing technology and permit the licensee to use the technology") and 8 ("The licensee is protected by being able to retain the ability to use the licensed intellectual property. . .").

require the parties to perform legal somersaults such as escrow agreements, trust relationships and security interests in order to avoid the risks created by *Lubrizol*. The Act thus facilitates the direct licensing of intellectual property in two-party transactions.

At the same time, however, the Act will require other parties to learn new maneuvers in order to minimize risks created by the Act itself. These risks are likely to be the most acute in the financing of intellectual property licensors and in multiple-party situations involving cross-licenses. As a result, the Act will chill secured and unsecured lending to intellectual property vendors and transactions that involve multiple-tiered licenses and cross-licenses of technology.

Chapter 6

Paradise Lost

"How Can You Find a Safe Trademark?" (1985)

"The Qualified Privilege to Use a Competitor's Trademarks in Comparative Advertising" (1988)

For many technology companies and their counsel, trademarks are the Cinderellas of intellectual property law. A techie believes that it's the genius of his or her invention that builds value, not its name. That is, until the fairy godmother of public opinion dresses the product in a lustrous brand (see Apple), winning the hand of the market prince.[1] What a trademark is, and how rights in it are acquired deserve more serious attention than they are sometimes accorded.

Trademarks are yet another oddity of property law. They are said to be owned by their "users" or "registrants," and yet they are intended for the benefit and protection not only of these proprietors but also of the public, who relies on them as indicators of origin. And their value to their proprietors can evaporate into thin air if the public uses them too much as the ordinary terms to describe a type of product. Thus have been lost to ordinary language words such as aspirin, cellophane, escalator, and thermos. In trademarks, it seems, ordinary language again has the final say.

The articles in this chapter were published at a time when the only means of acquiring rights in a trademark in the United States was to use it. Remedies for infringement could be enhanced through federal or (to a much lesser extent) state registration, but the law's common law roots — protecting the goodwill arising from custom and trade and providing priority of rights to the first user — remained very much in place.[2]

This changed fundamentally in 1988 when the Lanham Act was amended to provide for applications for registration based on a "bona fide intent to use" a

---

[1] Not so for companies in the household product and fashion industries, where the value of marks such as Crest®, Dove, and Polo Ralph Lauren are fully appreciated in distinguishing otherwise largely fungible products.

[2] See T. McCarthy, *McCarthy on Trademarks*, §1:19.50.

mark.[3] In a vestige of the old law, and for somewhat antiquated constitutional reasons,[4] use in commerce was still required as a precondition to federal registration, and a prior user retained some limited priority over a subsequent filer, but priority of rights in a mark now and for the first time in US jurisprudence could arise from a mere filing. Almost overnight, the practice changed, with trademark practitioners scrambling to get "intent-to-use" applications on file and pondering whether and when one could have a "bona fide intent" to use multiple variations on a mark for the same product.

By moving away from a concept of rights arising from use to a concept of rights arising from compliance with a bureaucratic procedure — filing — the United States brought its law into closer alignment with the law of most of its trading partners. This reflected a sea change in US statutory intellectual property law that culminated during the course of the years represented by these collected articles.

Letters patent issued by the English Crown were anathema to North American colonists, who justly reviewed them as monopolistic and antithetical to the burgeoning commercial opportunities on the west side of the Atlantic.[5] At the time of the Constitutional Convention, it was doubted whether the central government should have *any* authority to issue patents or copyrights at all. At the urging of no less than Thomas Jefferson and James Madison, the Constitutional Convention grudgingly added a clause to Article 1, Section 8, of what became the US Constitution, empowering Congress to "promote the Progress of Science and useful Arts, by securing for limited Times to Authors and Inventors the exclusive Right to their respective Writings and Discoveries." The key phrase was "for limited Times," which was intended to correct the perpetual monopolies to which favorites of the English Crown were habituated.

---

[3] Trademark Law Revision Act of 1988, 102 Stat. 3935 (Pub. Law 100-667, 100th Congress).
[4] In 1879 the Supreme Court had held the 1870 Trademark Act unconstitutional because the sole basis for federal regulation of trademarks was the Commerce Clause of the Constitution and the Act did not require use in interstate commerce as a precondition to federal registration. "The Trademark Cases: *U.S. v. Steffens, U.S. v. Wittemann,* and *U.S. v. Johnson,*" 100 U.S. 82, 25 L.Ed. 550 (1879). Subsequent caselaw has greatly attenuated the use-in-commerce requirement. See *Christian Faith Fellowship Church v. Adidas AG,* 841 F.3d 986 (Fed. Cir. 2016).
[5] The First Charter of Virginia (1606) was in fact letters patent granting the colonists (the "patentees") exclusive rights in the colony's lands and their proceeds, in perpetuity. See Yale Law School, Lillian Goldman Law Library, *The Avalon Project,* "The First Charter of Virginia; April 10, 1606," https://avalon.law.yale.edu/17th_century/va01.asp.

The first Congress enacted federal copyright and patent laws. The Copyright Act of 1790[6] was ruthlessly parochial: only citizens of the United States were eligible for copyright protection under the Act. The Patent Act of 1790[7] permitted any "person" to apply for a patent, but in 1793 Congress realized its mistake and amended the Act to provide that only US citizens could apply.[8] These limitations reflected the national practice of enthusiastically appropriating, without compensation, inventions that had been made outside the United States, especially in England.[9] Bounties were actually posted for the disclosure of English trade secrets. US publishers also pirated the works of authors such as Charles Dickens, whose books were copied just as soon as a sailing ship or steamer could deliver them to New York publishers.[10] As a developing country, the United States was more than happy to ride on the coattails of England, its erstwhile sovereign, without paying for the ride.[11]

The latter part of the nineteenth century saw important initiatives in the internationalization of intellectual property law. The Paris Convention, providing for "national treatment" (meaning that foreigners and natives get treated equally) of trademarks and patents, was first adopted in 1883,[12] and the Berne Convention, providing minimum standards for copyright protection, was accepted in 1886.[13] The United States acceded to the Paris Convention in 1887 but resisted accession to the Berne Convention for another century.

---

6 1 Stat. 124 (1st Congress 1790).

7 1 Stat. 109 (1st Congress 1790).

8 1 Stat. 318 (3d Congress 1793).

9 See generally Charles R. Morris, "We Were Pirates, Too," *Foreign Policy*, Dec. 6, 2012, https://foreignpolicy.com/2012/12/06/we-were-pirates-too/.

10 The International Copyright Act of 1891 recognized for the first time the copyrights of noncitizens, as long as the copies of their works were "manufactured" in the United States.

11 In contrast with statutory law, the common law in the United States was always international in nature, drawing heavily on English precedent. In the United States of the early to mid-nineteenth century, it was quite routine for our common law judges to look to and rely on English precedent. Lord Coke's opinions were considered with great attention by US jurists such as Joseph Story; to this day *Hadley v. Baxendale*, an English case from 1854, is fundamental precedent for the measure of damages in a common law breach of contract case brought in the United States. So also the US common law of trademarks is closely related to the English common law concept of "passing off." One imagines that English precedent is easier to follow when it protects US rather than English rights.

12 See World Intellectual Property Organization, "Paris Convention for the Protection of Industrial Property," https://www.wipo.int/treaties/en/ip/paris/.

13 See World Intellectual Property Organization, "Berne Convention for the Protection of Literary and Artistic Works," https://www.wipo.int/treaties/en/ip/berne/.

Accession to the Berne Convention and the adoption of an intent-to-use system for trademark registration in the United States, both in 1988, were part of a much larger wave of internationalization of intellectual property protection late in the twentieth century. The first manifestation was the Patent Cooperation Treaty (1970),[14] providing a unified process for international patent filings, although the substantive review remains in the hands of each member country. Another was the success of the Madrid Protocol (1996),[15] which for the first time captured major countries such as the United States, England and Japan within the ambit of the Madrid Agreement (1891),[16] which provides an international system of trademark registration procedure (although substantive review remains at the national level, as it does for patents under the Patent Cooperation Treaty). And of course, any consideration of internationalization of intellectual property law would be incomplete without mention of the advances made in the European Union to create a consistent system for all manner of intellectual property and related rights: patent (European Patent Convention, 1973, effective 1977), trademark (CTM created, 1996), copyright (Directive, 2001), database (Directive, 1996) and, perhaps most importantly in the current climate, personal data protection (Directive, 1995, followed by General Data Protection Regulation, which became effective in May 2018).

Much of the impetus for internationalization of intellectual property rights in the late nineteenth century came from Europe. The great treaties were named for the European cities of their birth — Paris, Berne, and Madrid — and the Paris and Berne Conventions were administered in large measure in that most neutral of all countries, Switzerland. The United States was a somewhat reluctant Johnny-Come-Lately, reflecting its nineteenth-century status as a rapidly developing economy eager to build on the technological advances of the Old World without paying for them.

Not so the push for internationalization in the late twentieth century, when the United States became alarmed at what it perceived as the theft of US technology in other countries, particularly those in the Far East. In the early 1990s, during the "Uruguay Round" of negotiations under the General

---

[14] See World Intellectual Property Organization, "PCT — The International Patent System," https://www.wipo.int/pct/en/.

[15] See World Intellectual Property Organization, "Madrid — The International Trademark System," https://www.wipo.int/madrid/en/.

[16] World Intellectual Property Organization, "Madrid Agreement Concerning the International Registration of Marks," https://www.wipo.int/treaties/en/registration/madrid/.

Agreement on Trade and Tariff, the Clinton Administration mounted a vigorous, but not to say adamant, argument for international recognition of intellectual property rights, especially copyright and patent[17], leading in 1994 to the Agreement on Trade-Related Aspects of Intellectual Property Rights (known as the "TRIPS accord"). Meanwhile, developing nations (no longer the United States!) complained that broad intellectual property protection under TRIPS could prejudice their access to important technologies.[18] The shoe was now most definitely on the other foot.

Viewed from the developing nation standpoint, intellectual property law has been a handmaiden of imperialism. The great European conventions of the late nineteenth century came at the high water mark of European colonialism when the extension of European civilization and its technology were viewed — at least in Europe — as a boon to the "lesser" world outside Europe. So also in the late twentieth century, when the Soviet Union had collapsed, it seemed — at least to Americans and perhaps also to Europeans — that democracy and freedom, spearheaded by the United States and its digital technologies, would initiate a new, long era of peace and prosperity. In each case, technology and its protection by law seemed to be one of the jewels in the crown of a brave new world.

How sadly and how quickly were these hopes dashed. Riding the heels of the nineteenth century's technological revolutions — steam power, railroads, the telephone, the telegraph, the transatlantic cable, to name a few — came the First and then Second World Wars, which employed the nineteenth century's technology to industrialize killing. And now, early in the twenty-first century, the late twentieth century's dream of a global community linked by the digital revolution has disintegrated into digital communities detached by hate and division.

---

[17] The irony of this turnabout was of course lost on nearly everyone in the United States, but not on many in the developing world who wanted to appropriate US technology just as the United States, when it was a developing nation, took advantage of European, and especially English, technologies — without paying for them.

[18] In the Doha Declaration, the World Health Organization recognized the concern of developing countries that TRIPS not be used to preclude access to affordable medication protected by patents. See https://www.who.int/medicines/areas/policy/doha_declaration/en/.

We worship technology's power, but forget that power corrupts.[19] In the concluding chapter of this book, we will consider whether and how the pervasive, intrusive, and seductive digital Argos distorts our senses of security and identity. And we will consider yet again the nature of property, and whether the facts comprising personal identity are no more subject to ownership "in gross" than the words comprising a trademark.

[19] Shoshana Zhuboff, *The Age of Surveillance Capitalism* (New York: Hachette), 2020. More on this in the following chapter.

How Can You Find a Safe Trademark?*

When selecting company and product names, executives like to think in marketing terms. How will the name sound, and what will it suggest to potential customers? Many months can go into selecting just the right name. But such efforts can turn into legal nightmares if companies ignore trademark law. This has become extremely complex in recent years, thanks in large measure to heightened competition in most business areas, so selecting a company or a product name not already in use has become increasingly difficult. Executives must be prepared to do extensive trademark searches and possibly alter names they have become fond of. They must also, the author says, turn away from descriptive and highly suggestive names and use logotypes to give distinction to names settled on.

All business owners must select names for their fledgling enterprises. For many owners, the selection process is easy. Some sell to middlemen or manufacturers who add brand names to the products. Others rely on word of mouth and acquaintances as marketing tools. A descriptive company name — Boston Sand and Gravel — or perhaps a surname coupled with a descriptive name — Perini Construction Company — is usually more than adequate from both marketing and legal standpoints.

For other starting businesses, though, selecting a distinctive and protectible brand name is much more difficult. The choices can be vital for products or services targeted at consumer markets, whatever they may be — dish soaps, cosmetics, convenience stores, personal computer software. Any business that expects to rely on mass marketing — whether in trade journals, in newspapers, or on television — must have an appealing name to distinguish its products from those of its competitors.

This article is intended for the entrepreneur who will operate in this second sort of marketing environment, one in which brand identification may be difficult to achieve, essential to preserve, and potentially even fatal if lost.

Basic marketing considerations

For brand names, two basic models exist. One places the entire marketing effort on the trademark and none whatsoever on the name of the supplier or the manufacturer. Ovaltine, for example, is probably known to most people in

---

the United States as the mark for a chocolate-flavored mix. But how many people know who makes Ovaltine? Spending money to educate the public about the source of Ovaltine would be wasteful or perhaps even detrimental. Procter & Gamble uses the same strategy. It makes little effort to connect its brands Ivory, Lilt, Tide, Crisco, and Zest with its corporate identity.

The other model is at the opposite extreme, where manufacturers concentrate their marketing efforts almost entirely on their company names. Hewlett-Packard, Mercedes Benz, and IBM are examples. Mercedes Benz identifies its products solely by model numbers and letters. IBM, which uses numbers for its mainframe computers, chose a very descriptive trademark (or "mark," as we commonly say) for its microcomputer product — PC, short for personal computer. Hewlett-Packard has evidently chosen to do without a mark for its microcomputer. Stressing high quality, reliability, and service, these manufacturers sell a limited variety of premium-priced products. They emphasize the products' sources rather than their special identities.

In variations on these basic models, some companies emphasize both their company names and individual names for each product — Kellogg's Rice Krispies, Lotus 1-2-3. Others, such as Sears, have families of product names for different classes of products.

The typical start-up need not be concerned about diversification. It has one product and may be content to give its company the same name as its product. The key is to find at least one name for the product, and possibly a second name for the company, that will serve as an effective marketing tool and at the same time provide a haven from trademark infringement.

(For the sake of convenience, I refer to "trademarks" and "products," although the same principles usually apply to services and their marks. I also occasionally refer to the "names" for products, although it is technically more accurate to say that companies have names, whereas the words that are used to designate the origin of products and services are marks. See the accompanying glossary for more information on these technicalities.)

Avoiding the pitfalls

"I formed a corporation under the name Mustang, Inc., and I therefore have a right to use Mustang as my brand name." This kind of reasoning is the commonest trademark trap. Both business owners and their corporate counsel fall into it. Against a prior user, the approval of a corporate name affords *no protection whatsoever.* The courts have held again and again that a company that has used a name or a mark and has made a large investment in it may compel a later user of a similar name engaged in a similar business to change even its corporate name.

A simple example will show the basis for this principle. Mustang is a famous trademark of Ford Motor Company. The name Mustang, Inc., is presently available as a corporate name in Delaware. Would anyone suppose that if I formed a Delaware corporation under this name, I would be entitled to begin to manufacture automobiles and call them Mustangs? The answer is that I could form the corporation, but as soon as I started in the business of automotive manufacturing, Ford could obtain an injunction compelling me to give up all use of the corporate name in connection with such manufacturing.

In general, the person who is first to use a mark or a name has priority over all others who choose to use it for similar goods, regardless of whether they have set up corporations or not. Even the federal registration of a trademark offers no protection against the prior user of a similar mark for similar goods unless the registration has been in effect and unchallenged for five years or more.

Following five simple rules will help the entrepreneur avoid the pitfalls often encountered in selecting a trade name or a trademark.

Rule 1: Never select a corporate name or a mark without first doing a trademark search

The only reasonably thorough method of identifying prior users of trade names and trademarks is a trademark search. In comparison with the cost of changing an established mark, the cost of doing a search is minuscule.

A well-equipped law firm can, almost instantaneously and at little expense, search federal registrations of trademarks on the Dialog database service. Firms specializing in trademark searches will perform more thorough research at a cost of about $150 to $500 per mark. A listing of trademark-searching companies is in the Yellow Pages for any major metropolitan area. Thomson & Thomson, Inc., of North Quincy, Massachusetts, Trademark Service Corporation of New York City, and CompuMark U.S. of Arlington, Virginia, are a few firms specializing in searches.

The search usually takes about a week. A reasonably complete trademark search should uncover registrations, both federal and state, of marks that are similar to the mark being searched and used in connection with similar products. It should also supply information from trade directories, telephone directories, and computerized databases about companies with trade names and unregistered marks similar to the mark being searched. The information in a trademark search is invaluable in determining whether another company has preempted a certain word, phrase, or symbol.*

However exhaustive it may be, a trademark search can never entirely eliminate the risk of an unregistered prior use. Also, no economical means of searching the availability of a corporate name covers all 50 states. A demonstration of the uncertainties entailed in trademark selection is the National Broadcasting Company's adoption of an "N" logo a few years ago. The mark turned out to be very similar to a logo that a public television station in the Midwest had previously adopted. After considerable embarrassment, the network settled the dispute over rights to the mark. This outcome is, though, the exception that proves the rule: a trademark search reduces but does not eliminate the likelihood of such embarrassment.

Experience teaches another important lesson about searching names and marks. Never search them one at a time. Some 600,000 trademarks and service marks are registered or pending with the United States Patent and Trademark Office. A good dictionary has only about 150,000 entries, and fewer than 5,000 words are in everyday use. The chance of finding a trouble-free name or mark on the first try, or even on the second try, is therefore small. Searching marks one at a time can prove time-consuming and discouraging.

A much better method is to begin with a dozen or so possible names or marks. Ask your trademark counsel to do a preliminary screening search covering only federal registrations of the marks. Counsel should be able to do this in a day. This screening search will usually eliminate all but a handful of them. Then have a trademark-searching firm search the remaining ones or, if resources are limited, the most desirable of the remaining ones. There is a fair chance that this procedure will produce a reasonably risk-free mark after only one or two rounds.

Searching several marks as a group not only saves time but also serves an important psychological purpose. Company names and marks are especially emotional things. Otherwise, hard-headed businesspeople tend to fall in love with them as soon as they are chosen. When the search turns up bad news (as it does more often than not), the businessperson's judgment about the risk of adopting the mark is likely to be colored by a fondness for the name or mark. An owner can avoid this problem by not becoming attached to a mark before the search.

---

* Of course, as of the publication of this collection, most initial searching takes place online. Comprehensive searches ordered from searching firms remain indispensable in higher-stakes settings.

The emotional nature of an entrepreneur's choice of a company name or trademark sometimes prompts the following attitude: "My attorney says I could get in trouble using this mark, but it's an attorney's job to be pessimistic. I took a long time to think this mark up and I like it. I'm going ahead and using it anyway."

Executives often underestimate the possibility that a prior user may sue to compel them to change their trade names or marks. They erroneously believe that by changing the spelling of a word or making small changes in a phrase, they may avoid infringement. Easy Pickins is a registered trademark for shoes and socks, and one might imagine that spelling the words another way — for example, E-Z Pikkins — would avoid infringement liability. This is not the case. A name or a mark can infringe on another if they are merely similar in sound, appearance, or meaning. The two marks E-Z Pikkins and Easy Pickins, are identical in sound. If used in the same geographical area in connection with similar goods or services, the later user would certainly infringe on the prior user's rights.

Executives also reason that differences between products will protect them. For example, an entrepreneur might want to market a modem for personal computers under the mark Hookup. He might find a prior user of the same mark for another PC peripheral device — perhaps a printer. Faced with the prior user, many business people decide that no one would confuse a modem with a printer and that there is, therefore, no likelihood of confusion between the two marks.

A court would almost certainly disagree. The fact that the two products are targeted at the same market — owners of personal computers — and that they move in the same channels of commerce — computer stores, computer mail order houses — would be enough to convince most courts that a likelihood of confusion exists about the source of the goods. Confusion about the source is the touchstone for trademark infringement. The likelihood of such confusion leads to a finding of infringement and the troubles that that implies: an injunction against further use, payment of damages for unauthorized use, and the necessity of finding a new mark.

Rule 2: If your attorney says you have a potential problem with a mark, trust that judgment

Attorneys don't like to give their clients bad news. If trademark counsel can find a way to justify your use of a mark despite some prior use, counsel will surely do so. But if the lawyer says you may encounter legal action if you adopt a particular mark, do not underestimate the risks involved. The more successful your mark is, the more tempting a target your company becomes for a suit by a prior user. Even the news that others seem to have gotten away with the use of equally similar marks should not be very comforting: the prior user might not have become aware of these usurpers or might have decided that they were too insignificant to be worth suing.

Incidentally, prior users who acquiesce to others using similar marks can "dilute" their rights to the marks and weaken their claims. The concept of trademark dilution is beyond the scope of this article. It is a matter that experienced trademark counsel should assess and base on a thorough trademark search and a knowledge of the law in the pertinent jurisdictions.

Should your trademark come under attack, the process can be very costly, amounting to hundreds of thousands of dollars in legal fees and lost marketing opportunities. If you lose, your business may have to change its trademark or company name. For a young venture, in particular, such costs can be devastating.

Not surprisingly, many business people — especially those at advertising agencies — believe that they will have difficulty penetrating a market if they do not choose a name that immediately identifies what the product is or what its qualities are.

Here is the law: a word or a combination of words that describe a product will not be protected as a trademark and cannot be registered on the Principal Register of the United States Patent and Trademark Office unless it has acquired "a secondary meaning." A descriptive word or phrase is said to have acquired a secondary meaning if, through long and exclusive use by one person, it has come to be associated with that person so that it indicates the source of goods and not merely their type.

(There are two federal registers — the Principal Register and the Supplemental Register. Registration on the Principal Register but not on the Supplemental Register grants prima facie evidence of rights to the mark, constructive nationwide notice of such rights, incontestability of trademark rights after five years, and standing to prevent the importation of infringing goods. The Supplemental Register is a repository for marks that, usually because of descriptiveness, cannot be registered on the Principal Register.)

Although purely descriptive words are not protected, the law will protect a word or a phrase that merely suggests a product or the qualities of a product. Examples of suggestive marks abound: Spic and Span, S.O.S., When It Rains It Pours. Predicting where the courts and the Patent and Trademark Office will draw the line between descriptiveness and suggestiveness, however, is very difficult. Some examples appear in table 6.1. [1]

Table 6.1 Protected and unprotected marks

Suggestive	**Descriptive**
protected	unprotected
Arch Rest (shoes)	After Tan (suntan lotion)
Holeproof (hosiery)	Breakfast Bread (bread)
Hour After Hour (deodorant)	Brilliant (flour)
Mr. Clean (cleaner)	Driverless (car rental)
Roach Motel (insect trap)	Faultless (bread)
Rusticide (rust remover)	5 Minute (glue setting in five minutes)
Soft Smoke (smoking tobacco)	Homemaker (calendar)
U-Drive-It (car rental)	Security (tires)
Wearever (cooking utensils)	Snap (ginger ale)

As you can see from the table, it is not easy — indeed, I would say it is usually impossible — to predict with confidence where the line will be drawn in a particular case. Some marks, such as Cyclone, clearly fall toward the suggestive end of the spectrum because they do not directly mention or even hint at the product (fences). Others (for instance, Breakfast Bread) fall near the opposite extreme. The great majority, though, fall into a very gray area.

A recent example of the risks of descriptive and suggestive marks is Miller's use of Lite for beer. The Miller Brewing Company had registered the mark Lite for its low-calorie beer and brought an infringement action against G. Heileman Brewing Company to compel it to stop using the word *light* on labels for its low-calorie beer. Miller lost, the court of appeals commenting that "the word *light*, including its phonetic equivalent *lite*, being a generic or

[1] These lists are based on similar but much more comprehensive lists appearing on pages 17–66 of Rudolf Callman's treatise, *The law of Unfair Competition, Trademarks and Monopolies,* fourth edition (Wilmette: Callaghan & Co., 1983) and on pages 448–449 and 499–502 of J. Thomas McCarthy's *Trademarks and Unfair Competition,* second edition (Rochester: The Lawyers Cooperative, 1984).

common descriptive term as applied to beer, could not be exclusively appropriated by Miller as a trademark, despite whatever promotional effort [Miller] may have expended to exploit it."[2]

In a later action, the same court ordered the cancellation of Miller's registration of the trademark Lite.[3]

The alternative is to choose a mark that does not describe or suggest the nature or qualities of a product in an obvious way. From a legal standpoint, coined terms like Kodak and Exxon are ideal, but suggestive terms are also acceptable as long as their connection to the product is imaginative, as Tide's is, and not direct or obvious, as Lite's is.

Rule 3: Seek a coined or a fanciful name or mark before you settle for a descriptive or a highly suggestive one

At first blush, we might question whether a nondescriptive mark could ever serve a useful marketing purpose. Consider, though, the marketing power of famous marks like Apple, Kodak, Exxon, Lotus, and Cadillac. From a marketing standpoint, there is no risk that advertising efforts spent on a coined or a fanciful word or phrase will spill over to benefit the competitors' products. From a legal standpoint, the advantages are even clearer. Coined or fanciful words and phrases are the darlings of trademark law. They are said to be "strong" marks because the courts will grant them much broader protection than other marks.

Finding an appealing nondescriptive mark is not as difficult as it might seem, and, once you find one, it can bring satisfying results. I suggest that you look for words or phrases with agreeable emotional connotations but nothing to do with your product. Try names of English places for anything associated with fine products — Sussex, Canterbury, Southwick, Hampshire. (Beware, though: many of these are already in use as marks.)

Mythological names, which can enable you to sneak a suggestive element into an otherwise fanciful mark, are another good source. The software company Whitesmiths, Ltd. (which in itself is a very appealing choice of company name — a whitesmith is a metal finisher, a craftsman) chose Idris as a mark for one of its software products. Idris is the name of a Persian god of toolsmiths and craftsmen and also a mythological Welsh giant. The word

---

[2] *Miller Brewing Co. v. G. Heileman Brewing Co.*, 561 F. 2d 75, 81(7th Cir. 1977).

[3] *Miller Brewing Co. v. Jos Schlitz Brewing Co.*, 605 F. 2d 990 (7th Cir. 1979).

is rare and memorable, and it contains hidden connotations of strength and craftsmanship.

Other very appealing words can be found in botany (Lotus, Apple) and astronomy (Quasar, Pulsar, Sun). Zoological names are also good — Impala, Cougar, even Elephant (this is a mark for computer memory disks, steel wool pads, and sporting goods, among other things). Last, try names of famous authors, historical figures, or works of art. How about Pushkin as a mark for typewriters, or Iliad as a mark for a word-processing program (if these are available)?

If you cannot give up the idea of a descriptive or a highly suggestive name or mark, use the next rule.

Rule 4: Whenever marketing or other considerations dictate the use of a name or a mark that is highly suggestive of the product, select a distinctive logotype for the descriptive or suggestive words

The name Digital Equipment Corporation, for example, directly suggests the company's principal product — digital computers. Other companies have names that include the word *digital* or words based on the formative *digi.* Indeed, currently, there are 83 federal registrations and applications for federal registration of marks that include *digital* and 422 that include *digi.* Digital Equipment Corporation, however, almost always displays the word *digital* in a well-known logotype consisting of lower case letters, each of which is embedded in a separate, contrasting-color rectangle. Another example of the same principle at work is the famous script that unmistakably associates the letters *GE* and the descriptive "general electric" with the venerable company of that name.

The selection of a distinctive logotype helps solve the two fundamental problems associated with descriptive names and marks. From a marketing standpoint, dollars spent on advertising the logotype will be less likely to benefit competitors with similar names but dissimilar logotypes. From a legal standpoint, the courts will grant only narrow protection at best to the descriptive name, but they will grant broad protection to the distinctive logotype.

Rule 5: Avoid abbreviations and acronyms wherever possible, and when no alternative is acceptable, select a distinctive logotype in which the abbreviation or acronym appears

You might wonder, "Why not just use the first letters of our corporate name as our trademark, as GM, GE, and IBM do?" Consider the following facts. There are 26 letters in our alphabet. There are 676 (26 x 26) combinations of 2 letters each, 17,576 (26 x 26 x 26) combinations of 3 letters each, and 456,976 (26 x 26 x 26 x 26) combinations of 4 letters each. There are, at the same time, more than 16,792,000 businesses in the United States. Of these, more than 400,000 are corporations with revenues in excess of $1 million. There simply are not enough letters and combinations of letters to go around.

Nevertheless, many business owners insist on selecting a highly descriptive name for their companies, and an abbreviation or acronym made up of the first letters of the words in their company name as their trademark. The result is predictable: a proliferation of two-, three-, and four-letter marks and trade names, many of which have been registered but few of which are genuinely distinctive.

Anyone who practices in the field of trademark law sees an additional, equally predictable result: frequent claims of trademark infringement that sap the clients' resources and are unusually difficult to resolve without litigation. Who can say, for instance, whether "XYZ" infringes on "YXZ" or "XYZZ"? Reasonable men grow hot over questions like this one. It sometimes takes an expensive lawsuit to settle the question, with an outcome that may be to no one's liking.

Costs vs. benefits

Selecting and protecting trade names and trademarks is not easy. The law governing rights to trade names and marks is quite complex. Furthermore, the cost of making a bad choice can be very high. Thus the executive planning to enter a market in which brand identification is important should budget a significant amount of time to selecting the brand name or mark and a significant amount of money to trademark searches, filing fees, and attorneys' fees.

As I noted earlier, a trademark search costs between $150 and $500, depending on how thorough you want it to be. This rate is per mark. Thus, if you search four marks, the searches will cost between $600 and $2,000. Your trademark counsel should review the searches and consult with you about them. The lawyer's fee at current rates will add another few hundred dollars to the search fee for each mark.

Most searches require follow-up work to learn details about the reported companies. Investigate these companies to see if they provide products or services similar to those with which the proposed mark will be used. While the trademark counsel can do the checking, you will save money if you do it yourself.

Once a mark is selected, and in use, a state registration is inexpensive to obtain. The filing fees are usually less than $50 per mark per class. (For purposes of registration, marks are grouped into classes of goods and services. A registration is accomplished class by class, and fees for registration are calculated class by class. If, for example, a mark is used for an ice cream shop and also for T-shirts sold in the shop, registration could probably be obtained in three classes — one for food, another for retail food selling services, and a third for clothing.)

The application is simple to prepare. Rarely does the state office in which it is filed examine it in detail. You get what you pay for, however: state registration has very limited value in protecting trademark rights.

Federal registration is much more valuable, but it is more difficult and costly to obtain. (You can apply for federal registration only if the mark is used "in commerce," that is, across state lines.) The current filing fee is $175 per mark per class. The Patent and Trademark Office is much pickier than state offices about the technical requirements for the application (for example, the drawing of the mark must be in India ink or its equivalent), and it reviews the marks thoroughly. On the initial filing, 91 percent of the applications for federal registration are not accepted. The applicants are obliged to respond to the examining attorney's objections, which are sometimes easy to overcome but can require the assembly of detailed and costly evidence such as survey results. In a few cases, the objections have been fatal.

Applications for federal registration are also subject to "opposition" and "interference" proceedings, in which the applicant is pitted against another person claiming ownership of a similar mark for similar goods. Although the initial application can be prepared and filed at a modest expense — well under $1,000 — a difficult or a contested application can cost many thousands of dollars to pursue to a conclusion. The process also takes a long time; a period of one to two years is typical.

It is possible to avoid all the expenses I have described if you are willing to accept the risk of changing your name or mark. But consider what you would pay for the right to use marks like Coca-Cola, Cheerios, Sony, Toyota. One day your mark might be as valuable as these, and you don't want to have a lingering doubt about whether you own it.

This article only scratches the surface of trademark law and marketing strategy. International protection of marks, for example, is based on very different principles — it emphasizes registration rather than use — and many of the considerations that apply to the selection of marks in the United States must therefore be revised in the international arena. In trademark law, then, there's much more to a name than usually meets the eye.

Glossary

Trade name: A name by which a legal entity does business or is known to the public, suppliers, and creditors. For corporations, the trade name is usually identical to the corporate name. For sole proprietors, partnerships, and joint ventures, the trade name is often completely different from the name of the underlying entity. Sam Spade, for example, might decide to call his business Personal Investigations. His trade name would be "Personal Investigations," but the name of the legal entity carrying on this business would be "Sam Spade" (sometimes referred to as Sam Spade doing business as Personal Investigations).

A legal entity can have any number of trade names. For example, Sam Spade might also operate a garden tool business under the trade name "Sam's Spades." The underlying legal entity is the same in either case — Sam Spade himself. Other examples: General Motors Corporation, Foley, Hoag & Eliot (a trade name of a common law general partnership), Coopers & Lybrand (a trade name of another common law general partnership).

In the United States, no formal action is required to adopt a trade name, except that in some jurisdictions, one must file a document giving notice to creditors and others of the identity of the underlying business entity.

Corporate name: A name given to a corporation when it is formed. Each corporation can have only one official name. It is the name under which the corporation has a legal existence distinct from that of its shareholders, officers, and directors and under which the corporation may enter into contracts, may sue, and may be sued. The appropriate office of the state in which the corporation is formed will approve the name only if it is not already being used in that state.

The name will not be approved if it is already used by another corporation formed under the laws of that state or by a corporation formed elsewhere but formally qualified to do business in that state. In some states, such as Massachusetts, the state officer also determines whether the proposed name is the same as any trademarks registered in that state. Corporate names can be reserved in advance of use for periods of one to six months, depending on the state in which they are to be used. Examples: General Motors Corporation, Digital Equipment Corporation, General Mills, Inc., and International Business Machines Corporation.

Trademark: A word, symbol, combination of letters or numbers, or other device such as distinctive packaging used to identify the goods of one company and to distinguish them from the goods of other companies. A trademark performing the same function in the case of services is referred to as a "service mark." Trademarks and service marks are referred to collectively as "marks."

A single business entity can have any number of trademarks and service marks. A mark can be the same as the business entity's official name (usually omitting "Inc.," "Corp.," or the like), but it can also be completely different. Chevrolet, Buick, GM, and GMC are all trademarks of General Motors Corporation. Apple IIe, Applesoft, and MacIntosh are all trademarks of Apple Computer, Inc. Decmate is a trademark of Digital Equipment Corporation, and Cheerios is a trademark of General Mills, Inc.

In the United States, unlike most foreign countries, marks cannot be reserved in advance of use. Instead, rights arise through use, and the courts will protect the right of the prior user against all subsequent users of the same or confusingly similar marks for the same or similar products or services, at least within the original user's geographical area of use and what is referred to as the original user's "zone of natural expansion." Even federal registration affords no protection against a prior user unless the registration has been in effect and unchallenged for five years.

Copyright: A statutory right that protects against reproducing literary and other works, but that generally does not protect against copying trademarks. Trademarks are protected by an entirely separate body of law — the law of unfair competition — and are registered through an entirely different system of registration, as described in the accompanying article.

Generic term: A term naming a product or a service without indicating its source. Generic terms are not subject to exclusive use by any one person. Unlike a generic term, a mark can always be thought of as an adjective modifying the word *brand.* Thus we have Sanka brand decaffeinated coffee and Chevrolet brand motor vehicles.

Marks are frequently used as names, and rights to them are not lost unless they become the commonplace terms for types of products and not merely for the products of a particular manufacturer. General Motors can call vehicles built by its Chevrolet Motor Division "Chevrolets" and not worry about the mark becoming generic — nobody uses "Chevrolet" to refer to anything other than vehicles built by that motor division. General Foods has to worry about losing rights to "Sanka," however, and Xerox Corporation has to worry about losing rights to "Xerox" because people commonly use those words to refer to products of the same type made by other companies. Many of today's generic terms were once valuable trademarks — aspirin, escalator, cellophane, kerosene, and yo-yo, for example.

Trademark registration: In the United States, marks may be registered in the United States Patent and Trademark Office under legislation known as the

Trademark Act of 1946 (also known as the Lanham Act) as well as under various trademark registration statutes in the 50 states. The symbol ® may only be used for marks registered with the United States Patent and Trademark Office. Registration on the Principal Register of this office confers important benefits: prima facie evidence of the registrant's rights in the mark, constructive national notice of such rights, the right to object to the importation of infringing articles, and incontestability of one's rights to the mark after five years of unchallenged registration.

Most foreign countries have their own trademark registration systems. An international agreement known as the Paris Convention confers limited rights to register a mark in all signatory countries once the mark has been registered in one signatory country. Under what is called the Madrid Arrangements, there is also a system of international registration for domiciliaries of countries that are party to the arrangements. The United States is a party to the Paris Convention but not to the Madrid Arrangements.[4]

[4] This omission was rectified in 2002 when the United States finally ratified the treaty, over a century after its first adaptation. —TH

The Qualified Privilege to Use a Competitor's Trademarks in Comparative Advertising*

Introduction

Is it a good idea to engage in comparative advertising from a marketing perspective?

1. ***The Downside Risk.*** Some years ago, a heated advertising war was waged for a piece of the nonaspirin analgesic market. Aspirin — a substance akin to the leaves of willow trees — was first introduced in the late nineteenth century by the Bayer Company. It was the only widely used nonprescription analgesic for many years. In 1955, McNeil Laboratories introduced TYLENOL in the form of an elixir for children. Adult strength TYLENOL was introduced six years later, in 1961.

By 1975, TYLENOL had captured over 10 percent of the analgesic market, representing about $50 million annually. Its principal competitor, Bristol Myers' DATRIL, had an essentially insignificant market share. Bristol Myers then launched its first direct advertising campaign against TYLENOL. It claimed that the products were "the same," and that DATRIL cost $1.85 per 100 tablets, against $2.85 for TYLENOL. In response, and at the cost of $20 million, Johnson & Johnson (successor to McNeil) attempted to make Bristol Myers' advertising invalid by dropping the price by 30 percent. J & J also attacked the DATRIL ads with networks and with self-regulatory bodies. Eventually, the DATRIL ads had a woman saying, "I buy whichever one costs less. Compare prices and save money."

The aspirin manufacturers shortly thereafter began running ads attacking TYLENOL in an effort to protect their market shares. The onslaught included ads by Sterling (Bayer) saying, "Makers of TYLENOL, shame on you." ANACIN spent an estimated $10 million over the first six months of its campaign, which was challenged by J & J in court on the ground that it created a false impression that ANACIN works faster than TYLENOL. One year later, the first national TV ad for DATRIL was announced, several years ahead of its planned schedule.

The result of all this? By 1978, TYLENOL had the highest share of the market ever, about 24 percent. DATRIL had a measly 1 percent or less, and the others had all lost market share.

2. ***The Upside Potential.*** In other cases, comparative advertising can be spectacularly successful, at least in the short run. WENDY'S is reported to have increased its sales by 20 percent in a one-month span by comparing its burgers with the BIG MAC and the WHOPPER. See Gallo, "False and Comparative Advertising under Section 43 (a) of the Lanham Trademark Act," *Communications and the Law*, February 1986, at 5.

3. ***The Moral of the Story.*** Comparative advertising breeds litigation and, even when pursued with a vengeance by several competitors against the same target, it can sometimes backfire. These facts should be kept in mind when advising clients at the fringes of what is permissible and what is not.

What is the matter with a comparative advertisement?

1. There are many potential causes of action for comparative advertisements that violate one or more of the rules that are described in this paper. The possible causes of action are cataloged in Appendix A.

2. The more basic question is why all comparative advertising is not actionable on the grounds of misappropriation or trademark dilution.

a. Misappropriation

i. The typical comparative advertisement starts with what a consumer knows about a competitor's product, and the ad then tells the consumer that the advertiser's product is in some way a better buy. The product that serves as the basis of comparison is almost invariably better known than the one advertised, and it almost invariably enjoys substantial market penetration and good will. At bottom, therefore, virtually every comparative advertisement attempts to ride on the coattails of the goodwill associated with a competitor's product.

ii. Riding on another's coattails has been held to be actionable as unfair competition at common law. The law of unfair competition reached a high-water mark in the celebrated case of *International News Service v. Associated Press*, 248 U.S. 215 (1918). While the *I.N.S.* case was decided as a matter of "federal common law" and is, therefore, itself of questionable vitality following *Erie R. Co. v. Tompkins*, 304 U.S. 64 (1938), the theory continues to enjoy substantial vitality in some jurisdictions, notably New York. See *Metropolitan Opera Ass'n, Inc. v. Wagner-Nichols Recorder Corp.*, 101 N.Y.S.2d 483 (Sup. Ct.), *aff'd*, 107 N.Y.S.2d 795 (App. Div. 1951); Goldstein, "Federal System Ordering of the Copyright Interest," 69 *Colum. L. Rev.* 49 (1969); but also see *United States Golf Association v. St. Andrews Systems, Data-Max, Inc.*, 749 F.2d 1028, 1034-1040 (3d Cir. 1984) (discussing the extent to which courts have limited *I.N.S.*).

b. Trademark Dilution

   i. A successful comparative advertisement will not only ride on the coattails of the "benchmark" product; it can (but will not necessarily) tend to take the shine off of the benchmark product's reputation.

   ii. While such tarnishment probably is not actionable at common law, 23 states have enacted "antidilution" statutes that aim to provide a remedy. They include major commercial centers such as New York, California, and Massachusetts.

In spite of the possible causes of action outlined above, the law in the United States has generally permitted direct product comparisons

1. The seminal case is *Saxlehner v. Wagner*, 216 U.S. 375 (1910), in which Justice Holmes wrote, "The defendants have a right to tell the public what they are doing and to get whatever share they can in the popularity of the plaintiff's product by advertising that they are trying to make the same article, and think they succeed."

2. The tradition of *Saxlehner v. Wagner* was revitalized by two important decisions handed down in the 1960s.

   a. *Smith v. Chanel, Inc.*, 402 F.2d 562 (9th Cir. 1968) (perfumer selling product simulating unpatented formula of CHANEL No. 5 perfume had right to use CHANEL trademark to inform public truthfully of that fact).

   b. *Société Comptoir de L'Industrie Cotonniere Etablissements Boussac v. Alexander's Department Stores, Inc.*, 299 F.2d 33, 36 (2d Cir. 1962) (where defendant used plaintiff's registered trademarks DIOR and

CHRISTIAN DIOR in tags hung on defendant's line of clothing which read "Original by Christian Dior-Alexander's Exclusive-Paris-Adaptation," court found no trademark infringement or false advertising, since there was no proof of likelihood of "confusion of source" or other misrepresentation by defendant's advertising).

3. For a recent case in the same tradition, see *Saxony Products, Inc. v. Guerlain, Inc.*, 513 F.2d 716 (9th Cir. 1975). The defendant marketed a line of "LIKE PERFUMES," including one called "FRAGRANCE S" under the slogan, "If you like SHALIMAR, you'll love FRAGRANCE S." Guerlain, the makers of the much better-known and more expensive SHALIMAR, sued. The Ninth Circuit held for the defendant on the ground that the defendant "could use Guerlain's trademark . . . to apprise consumers that FRAGRANCE S is "LIKE" or "similar to" SHALIMAR, so long as they were, in fact, similar, and there was no reasonable likelihood that consumers would be confused as to the origin of FRAGRANCE S.

4. There has thus arisen a conditional or qualified privilege to use another's trademark for purposes of product comparisons, despite the tendency of such advertising to misappropriate the goodwill of the other's product and possibly to tarnish the reputation of that product at the same time. The rationale for the privilege is that the potential harms are outweighed by the benefits to the public that result from price competition and dissemination of information. The balance of this paper will outline the limits and contours of this conditional privilege.

The conditional privilege to use another's mark for purposes of product comparisons

Historical overview

1. Despite the liberality of the courts' attitude toward product comparisons, the widespread use of such advertising in the United States mass media has a comparatively recent heritage, and it has only recently reached a crescendo in fields such as soft drinks (COKE v. PEPSI) and, especially, in the field of computers and related products, such as software and peripherals.

2. Prior to 1971, competitors were usually not named in advertisements. The other brand was referred to as "Brand X," or "the leading brand." At that time, the general feeling in the advertising industry was that naming a competitor would give him free publicity and/or evoke sympathy for him. See Thomson, "Problems of Proof in False Comparative Product Advertising: How Gullible Is the Consumer?," 72 *Trademark Rep.* 385, 386 (1982). In addition, "Advertisers

were reluctant to use it, and voluntary codes generally opposed comparisons. The major obstacle for televising comparative television commercials was the networks' refusal to air such advertisements." J. J. Boddewyn and K. Marton, *Comparison Advertising: A Worldwide Study* 11 (1978) (hereinafter "Boddewyn & Marton").

3. This traditional reluctance to engage in direct product comparisons was undermined by two developments: (a) further erosion of the causes of action that would be available where a competitor uses one's trademarks without permission, and (b) the influence of the Federal Trade Commission in encouraging such advertising.

Influence of the Federal Trade Commission

1. FTC jurisdiction over comparative advertisements encompasses statements which have the capacity to deceive consumers and to materially affect their purchasing decisions. These two elements comprise the FTC action in a nutshell. See generally, C. McManus, *The Law of Unfair Practices* 350 (1983).

2. In 1971, the Federal Trade Commission began encouraging advertisers to use comparisons "so they could make more meaningful promotional claims a benefit for consumers." Giges, "Comparative Ads: Better Than . . . ?," *Advertising Age*, September 22, 1980, at 59. The agency advocated the technique as "an effective way to present product information on which consumers can base more rational purchase decisions." Id. at 59. The Federal Trade Commission's view was that "Consumer benefits accrue because the public generally fares best when competition is strongest." Id. at 59. The networks agreed to air comparative advertisements on a one-year trial basis, which subsequently became permanent. Since that time, their use has grown exponentially. See Boddewyn & Marton, *supra*, at 11.

First condition on the exercise of the privilege: There must be no passing off

1. *Oral-B Laboratories v. Mi-Lor Corp.*, 810 F.2d 20 (2d Cir. 1987). The *Oral-B* case involved a relatively small manufacturer which marketed its toothbrushes in a package "confusingly similar to . . . the Oral-B toothbrush trade-dress," and used a label stating "COMPARE WITH ORAL-B" without stating that ORAL-B was a competing company. The Second Circuit affirmed the restraint of the packaging as well as the district court's prohibition of references to ORAL-B on MI-LOR's packaging and distinguished cases such as *Société Comptoir* because products in those cases were "already designed in a way that avoided a likelihood of confusion." The court stated that if MI-LOR

designed a toothbrush package "completely different from ORAL-B's," using comparative advertising would not be as likely to cause confusion.

2. At one extreme, and arguably representing the more mainstream approach, one finds the 1983 case of *Wendy's International, Inc. v. Big Bite, Inc.*, 576 F. Supp. 816 (S.D. Ohio). The defendant Big Bite aired a mildly satirical TV ad showing LITTLE WENDY, a trademark of the plaintiff, enjoying a Big Bite burger and saying, "Ain't no reason to go any place but Big Bite," which paraphrased a Wendy's slogan. The parties introduced conflicting survey evidence that suggested that between 3.3 percent and 53 percent of the persons surveyed who had seen the ad believed that Big Bite was somehow affiliated with Wendy's. The court seemed to find that at least 7 percent were confused, translated that percentage into numbers of burger eaters, and found for the plaintiff. Many courts are willing to protect a small minority of consumers, even at the expense of the more general interest in lifting legal restrictions on advertising.

3. At the opposite end of the spectrum is a 1985 case from the Central District of California, *Sykes Laboratory, Inc. v. Kalvin*, 610 F. Supp. 849 (D. Cal. 1985). The plaintiff marketed a popular nail-hardening product called "Sykes Perfect Nail." The defendant marketed low-cost beauty products under the "brand" name "the Generic Brand." One of these was described on its packages as "The Generic Brand Version of Sykes 'Perfect Nail.'" The box also stated, "Our company is not connected in any way with the name brand company or its suppliers." No survey evidence was introduced. Relying on the seminal 1968 decision of the 9th Circuit in *Smith v. Chanel*, the court found that Sykes had not infringed the plaintiff's rights. The court said: "If they have taken a 'free ride' on plaintiff's name without causing confusion or deception, then they have taken that to which they were legally entitled." *Sykes*, 610 F. Supp. at 855.

4. A great deal depends on the context in which the marks or slogans are used. Where it is clear that the defendant has taken reasonable steps to inform consumers as to the source of the product, the courts generally allow the comparison. Where it seems that the defendant is trying to leave some doubt as to source in the minds of the consumers, a ruling favoring the plaintiff is more likely. The leading cases are in the fields of laxatives, food processors and perfumes, of all things.

a. *G.D. Searle & Co. v. Hudson Pharmaceutical Corp.*, 715 F.2d 837 (3d Cir. 1983). This was an action brought by the manufacturer of the well-known laxative METAMUCIL against a company that sold the same product, psyllium hydrophilic mucilloid, under the trademark REGACILIUM. The defendant had for years advertised its product as "equivalent to METAMUCIL." In 1980, it changed its packaging in a way that Hudson admitted was intended to "knock-off the container utilized by the national equivalent METAMUCIL." Id. at 841. The Third Circuit affirmed the district courts order permanently enjoining the use of the new packaging, but permitting the defendant to continue to advertise its product as the "equivalent of METAMUCIL."

b. *Cuisinarts, Inc. v. Robot-Coupe International Corp.*, 509 F. Supp. 1036 (S.D.N.Y. 1981). The plaintiff was a former distributor of food processors made by the defendant and sold under the plaintiff's trademark CUISINART. After the termination of the distributorship, the defendant began to sell food processors under the mark ROBOT-COUPE, using the slogan "ROBOT-COUPE — IT'S PRONOUNCED ROBO-COOP (It Used To Be Pronounced Cuisinart)." The court found that this slogan created the false and misleading impression that the ROBOT-COUPE food processors came from the same source as the CUISINART ones, and enjoined the defendant's use of the phrase "It used to be pronounced Cuisinart," among other things.

c. *Calvin Klein Cosmetics Corporation v. Parfums de Coeur, Ltd.*, 824 F.2d 665 (8th Cir. 1987). The defendant marketed an OBSESSION smell-alike under the mark CONFESS, using the predictable slogan, "If you like OBSESSION you'll love CONFESS." The Eighth Circuit affirmed in part the district court's order preventing the defendant from using packaging that did not adequately distinguish the sources of OBSESSION and CONFESS, but the court permitted the defendant to continue to use the "like/love" slogan.

d. *Calvin Klein Cosmetics Corp. v. Lenox Laboratories, Inc.*, 815 F.2d 500 (8th Cir. 1987). The court of appeals here reversed the district court's entry of a preliminary injunction, commenting:

> *A realistic evaluation of consumer confusion must attempt to recreate the conditions in which buying decisions are made, and the court should try to determine not what it would do, but what a reasonable purchaser in market conditions would do.*

Id. at 504. The court of appeals also noted that the district court had failed adequately to take into account the "strong public interest in lowest possible prices . . . [and in] avoiding monopolies and in encouraging, not stifling, competition." Id. at 505.

e. *Charles of the Ritz Group, Ltd. v. Quality King Distributors, Inc.*, 636 F. Supp. 433 (S.D.N.Y. 1986) (holding that the phrase "IF YOU LIKE OPIUM, YOU'LL LOVE OMNI" created a likelihood of confusion as to source where "The use of the slogan on the tab appears to be a deliberate attempt to have the consumer identify the OMNI product as originating from the same source as OPIUM," and where there was survey evidence to the effect that 34 percent of consumers surveyed incorrectly identified a package of OMNI as a package of OPIUM).

Second condition: No gratuitous or bad taste disparagement

1. In general, references to competitors' products must be in good taste; humor must not be too bawdy; and the unauthorized user of the other's mark must be perceived as having acted in good will.

a. Disclaimers of affiliation are helpful. See *Sykes Laboratory, supra.*

b. Humor is always risky, especially if it is off-color (see cases cited below).

c. The comparison must be perceived as fostering some socially desirable goal such as price competition. See *Smith v. Chanel, supra.*

2. Examples:

a. *Dickes v. Fenne*, 1640, March 59, Jones W. 444, 82 Eng. Rep. 233. The defendant, a brewer of beer, told customers of the plaintiff, "that he would give a peck of malt to his mare, and she should piss as good beer as Dickes doth brew." These acts were held not actionable absent an allegation of special damages by the plaintiff, such as loss of customers, on the ground that the "words are only comparative and altogether impossible [as well]," and "where one says of a lawyer, that he had as much law as a monkey that the words were not actionable, because he hath as much law and more also. But if he had said, that he hath no more law than a monkey, the words were actionable."

b. *Girl Scouts of USA v. Personality Posters Mfg. Co.*, 304 F. Supp. 1228 (S.D.N.Y. 1969) (no infringement by contraceptive ad showing pregnant Girl Scout with slogan "Be Prepared").

c. *Chemical Corp. of America v. Anheuser-Busch, Inc.*, 306 F.2d 433 (5th Cir. 1962), *cert. denied,* 372 U.S. 965 (1963) ("Budweiser" mark infringed by parody of slogan "Where there's life ... there's bugs").

d. *Coca-Cola Co. v. Gemini Rising, Inc.*, 346 F. Supp. 1183 (E.D.N.Y. 1972) (trademark infringed by poster substituting "Cocaine" for "Enjoy Coke" in a registered logo).

e. *L.L. Bean, Inc. v. Drake Publishing Inc.*, 625 F. Supp. 1531 (D. Me. 1986) (feature in *High Society* magazine entitled "L.L. Beam's Sex Catalogue" held actionable under the Maine antidilution statute; injunction entered following summary judgment for the plaintiff), *rev'd,* 811 F.2d 26 (1st Cir.), *cert. denied* and *appeal dismissed,* 107 S. Ct. 3254 (1987) (because Bean's mark was used solely for noncommercial, editorial, and artistic purposes, application of Maine's antidilution statute was barred by First Amendment).

f. *Tetley, Inc. v. Topps Chewing Gum, Inc.*, 556 F. Supp. 785 (E. D. N. Y. 1983) (Petley Flea Bags not enjoined under the New York antidilution statute where the plaintiff had offered no proof that its mark was truly distinctive or that the parody would result in images of impurity in the minds of the plaintiff's consumers).

g. *Dallas Cowboys Cheerleaders, Inc. v. Pussycat Cinema, Ltd.*, 467 F. Supp. 366 (S.D.N.Y. 1979), *aff'd,* 604 F.2d 200 (2d Cir. 1979) (defendant's further publication of pornographic movie entitled "Debbie Does Dallas" and featuring actresses dressed as Dallas Cowboys cheerleaders enjoined under the New York antidilution statute).

h. *Lucasfilm Ltd. v. High Frontier*, 622 F. Supp. 931 (D. D.C. 1985) (trademark law does not apply to noncommercial use of common words "star wars" by political groups, and such use did not infringe film maker's well-known mark).

i. *Toho Co. v. Sears, Roebuck & Co.,* 645 F.2d 788, 793 (9th Cir. 1981) (use of "Bagzilla" mark on garbage bags not "unsavory or degrading").

j. *Jordache Enterprises, Inc. v. Hogg Wyld, Ltd.*, 828 F.2d 1482 (10th Cir. 1987) ("Lardashe" designer jeans for larger women held unlikely "to create in the mind of consumers a particularly unwholesome, unsavory, or degrading association with plaintiff's name and marks").

k. *Pillsbury Co. v. Milky Way Productions, Inc.*, 215 U.S.P.Q. (BNA) 124, 8 *Media L. Rep.* (BNA) 1016 (N.D. Ga. 1981) (*Screw* magazine held in contempt for violating TRO by republishing picture of "Poppin' Fresh" dough boy and dough girl in a depraved context which was held to violate Georgia's antidilution statute).

l. *Edgar Rice Burroughs, Inc. v. High Society Magazine, Inc.*, 7 *Media L. Rep.* (BNA) 1862, 1864 (S.D.N.Y. 1981) (magazine enjoined from further distribution of issue containing 10-page pictorial entitled "Monkeying Around with Tarzan and Jane" on grounds of infringement, dilution, and "unwholesome setting").

3. ***A Word to the Wise:*** Certain cases that were overtly decided on grounds of "likelihood of confusion" are better harmonized if viewed as decided *sub silentio* on grounds of taste or decorum. Compare *Universal City Studios, Inc. v. Casey & Casey, Inc.*, 622 F. Supp. 201 (D.C. Fla. 1985), *aff'd* 792 F.2d 1125 (11th Cir. 1986) (decorous depictions of "Miami Mice" on defendant's tee-shirts held unlikely to cause confusion as to source) with *Original Appalachian Artworks, Inc. v. Topps Chewing Gum, Inc.*, 642 F. Supp. 1031 (N.D. Ga. 1986) (GARBAGE PAIL KIDS bubblegum cards enjoined *inter alia* on trademark and unfair competition grounds due to the likelihood of confusion as to source with CABBAGE PATCH KIDS dolls).

Third condition: Facts must be material, accurate, and substantiated

So far, we have considered whether the mere use of a competitor's trademark, name, or product in a comparative advertisement is actionable. The general answer is "No, unless. . . ." The next question is whether trouble avoided on the issue of trademark use can be rediscovered on the matter of product claims, explicitly comparative or otherwise.

It has already been observed that, since the early 1970s, the FTC has taken the lead in encouraging comparative advertising. Since the early 1980s, the FTC has further encouraged resolution of disputes about accuracy through counter-advertising, rather than through lawsuits.

Equally significant in these contexts are the informal dispute resolution methods offered by the networks and the National Advertising Division of the Council of Better Business Bureaus. These dispute resolution procedures, as well as formal litigation, were used extensively in connection with the TYLENOL/DATRIL controversy.

A set of guidelines drawn up by the National Broadcasting Company ("NBC") provide a very helpful checklist for assessing comparative ads. See Appendix D (NBC Guidelines for Comparative Advertising Challenge Procedure).

1. What is not a fact: Puffing is OK.

   a. General, laudatory statements about the superiority of one's own products are protected. Mere expressions of opinion such as "The Finest" or "The Best" are "distinct from a statement of fact which, if not true, is likely to deceive." *In re National Executive Search, Inc.*, 76 F.T.C. 962, 977 (1969).

   b. *Carlay Co. v. Federal Trade Commission*, 53 F.2d 493, 496 (7th Cir. 1946) (the representation that a car could go an "amazing distance" without oil is "nothing more than a form of 'puffing' not calculated to deceive").

   c. The theory is that consumers are used to this sort of thing, so that ordinary boasting about one's product will not be taken literally. You don't have to go around saying, "our motor oil will go a reasonable distance, considering its price," or "this chess playing program is sort of like playing with Karpov, at least if he's having a bad day." See *Data Cash Systems, Inc. v. JS&A Group, Inc.*, 223 U.S.P.Q. (BNA) 865 (N.D. Ill. 1984).

   d. As Professor Prosser puts it in *Prosser on Torts* (3d ed.) at page 739:

      The "puffing" rule amounts to a seller's privilege to lie his head off, so long as he says nothing specific, on the theory that no reasonable man would believe him, or that no reasonable man would be influenced by such talk!

   e. An illustrative (if unauthoritative) catalog of examples of what is permissible puffing and what is not is found in the case of *Metro Mobile Courts, Inc.* v. *NewVector Communications, Inc.*, 643 F. Supp. 1289, 1292-1294 (D. Ariz.), *rev'd without opinion*, 803 F.2d 724 (9th Cir. 1986). The case involved advertisements run by a cellular telephone company. The following statements were found to be puffing:

- We ask you: Would you prefer to do business with the phone company with the best technology, lower rates, and better customer service? Or with someone who can claim none of the above?

- Better coverage. Metro Mobile's vast system is state-of-the-art Motorola switching equipment, locally situated. (This was found to be puffing, despite the fact that there existed a more advanced Motorola switching system.)

- You'll get better coverage and higher quality voice transmissions too.

The following statements were found to be actionable falsehoods:

- If you use our competitor's system, however, you're in for some hard times. Lower power, older equipment, and non-state-of-the-art technology make for bothersome transmission problems. (The competitor was, in fact, operating at the highest power allowed by law.)

- When you take a good look at Metro Mobile's cellular coverage area versus our competition's coverage area, we start looking very big . . . Metro Mobile will keep you talking longer, farther and clearer. (The competitor's coverage area was in fact larger.)

2. Statements of fact

a. Statements of fact about the advertiser's own product are actionable under Section 43 (a) of the Lanham Act, and related state and common law doctrines, if they imply a misleading or inaccurate comparison between the advertised product and its competitors.

i. The classic case is *Coca Cola Co. v. Tropicana Products, Inc.*, 690 F.2d 312 (2d Cir. 1982), where Bruce Jenner squeezed orange juice into a carton of Tropicana while saying that it is "pure, pasteurized orange juice as it comes from the orange." Coca Cola, the manufacturer of Minute Maid Orange Juice, challenged the ad under section 43(a) of the Lanham Act. The court found the statement inherently false; pasteurized orange juice doesn't come out of oranges. Also, the stuff was actually heated to over 200 degrees and sometimes frozen.

ii. The criteria for such an action under Section 43 (a) of the Lanham Act are found in *Skil Corp. v. Rockwell International*, 375 F. Supp. 777, 783 (N.D. Ill. 1974):

- Did the defendant make false claims about its own product? (False claims can be made through misleading statements, partially correct statements, or omissions. Misleading comparisons are actionable under Lanham Act §43(a), but false statements about the *competition*'s product are not, although they may be actionable under other theories.)

- Did the ads mislead or have a tendency to mislead a "substantial segment of the audience?"

- Is the deception material, that is, likely to influence the purchasing decision?

- Were the statements made in interstate commerce?

- Is the plaintiff likely to be injured, either by direct diversion of trade or by lessening of its good will?

iii. *U-Haul International, Inc. v. Jartran, Inc.*, 522 F. Supp. 1238 (D. Ariz. 1981), *aff'd*, 681 F.2d 1159 (9th Cir. 1982), held the following statements to be untrue and therefore actionable by Jartran's competitor U-Haul in an action brought under section 43(a) of the Lanham Act and related statutory and common law causes:

- Only Jartran can rent you trailers designed for the times. (U-Haul was also found to rent trailers "designed for the times" in terms of aerodynamic efficiency and small size.)

- Jartran guarantees you 10 MPG or more. (Jartran made no such guarantee, and some of its vehicles were certain to deliver less than 10 MPG.)
- Greater stability and safety.
- Exceptional and superb road stability.
- The court also found, based on survey evidence, that the statements "Many rental trucks average 5 MPG" and "Jartran guarantees you 10 MPG or more" were understood by consumers as stating an implied comparison with U-Haul, which was misleading and therefore actionable.

iv. Claims of uniqueness are always risky because they imply a comparison with all competitive products. The classic case is *Fedders v. FTC*, 529 F.2d 1398 (2d Cir. 1976), *cert. denied*, 429 U.S. 818 (1976), where a claim of "reserve cooling power" was held deceptive when the Fedders air conditioners didn't do anything their competitors didn't do under extreme conditions. See generally Note, "The Law of Comparative Advertising: How Much Worse Is 'Better' than 'Great'?," 76 *Colum. L. Rev.* 80, 97–111 (1976).

3. Statements of fact must be substantiated, even when they do not imply a comparison with competing products.

a. In a 1972 case involving claims concerning the Unburn sunburn lotion, the FTC first articulated the concept of "reasonable basis" for advertising claims. See *In Re Pfizer, Inc.*, CCH *Trade Reg. Rep.* para. 20,056 (FTC 1972). The Commission held that it was an unfair practice to make an affirmative product claim that a lotion instantly solved sunburn without a reasonable basis for making the claim.

b. Under the *Pfizer* doctrine, a determination of deceptive advertising based on inadequate substantiation consists of two stages: (1) what substantiating evidence constitutes a reasonable basis for making a product claim and (2) did the respondent in the case produce such evidence. See also *Litton Industries, Inc. v. FTC*, 676 F.2d 364, 373 (9th Cir. 1982); Scammon and Semenick, "The FTC's 'Reasonable Basis' For Substantiation of Advertising: Expanded Standards and Implications," 12 *J. of Advertising* 8 (1983); Note, "Unfairness in Advertising: *Pfizer, Inc.*," 59 *Va. L. Rev.* 324 (1973).

c. The courts are particularly sensitive to claims which imply surveys or studies. It is easy to fall into the trap of thinking that an advertisement is okay if it can be proven to be true at a later date. However, this is not generally sufficient. Whenever an ad implies that it is based on some study or survey, the study or survey must exist at the time the ad is placed and must support the proposition stated in the advertisement.

4. Comparisons — whether direct or indirect between an advertised product and its competitors — must fairly compare qualities or features that a reasonable person would take into consideration in making the buying decision.

a. As stated in the NBC guidelines, "The property being compared must be significant in terms of value or usefulness of the product or service to the consumer."

b. The issues of relevance and fair reporting of test results were litigated endlessly in a series of cases involving comparisons between the off-the-shelf analgesics ibuprofen and acetaminophen. See, for example, *American Home Products Corp. v. Johnson & Johnson*, 654 F. Supp. 568 (S.D.N.Y. 1987), where the court found certain advertisements to convey a misleading impression of the side effects caused by the three major pain killers.

i. As Judge O'Connor said, "Small nations have fought for their very survival with less resources and resourcefulness than these antagonists have brought in their epic struggle for commercial primacy in the [over-the-counter] analgesic field. "*American Home Products Corp. v. Johnson & Johnson*, 654 F. Supp. at 571–72.

c. In *In re American Home Products Corp.*, 3 *Trade Reg. Rep.* para. 19,673 (June 1971), the FTC sanctioned American Home Products

> ("AHP") for its commercial showing the superiority of BLACK FLAG ANT AND ROACH KILLER over competing products in killing all types of roaches, because the AHP commercial used a type of roach known to be resistant to the active ingredient in the competitive product. See also *Litton Indus. Inc. v. FTC*, 676 F.2d 364 (9th Cir. 1982) (FTC required Litton to report test results accurately).

5. Price comparisons are especially risky, both legally and as a practical matter. They invite price wars, and if they are too specific, they can be rendered actionable at the discretion of your competitor, simply by changing his price.

Chapter 7

The Gingerbread House

"The Current State of Privacy and Security Laws Affecting US Businesses" (2004)

"The Ownership and Exploitation of Personal Identity in the New Media Age" (2012)

Privacy/security law was not defined as a legal specialty when the first of these articles was written in 2004, but it has become the focus of whole departments at law firms and corporations today. I'd like to think that we were a bit ahead of the curve. For the most part, the article was a compendium of the then-current law both in the United States and in Europe, but it did include some interesting predictions, including the observation that, at the federal level, concerns over individual privacy would take a "back seat" to security concerns, while the opposite would be true at the state level. We also foresaw an increasing divide between privacy protection laws in Europe and in the United States, which narrowed only recently.

The second article raises the question of who owns the facts that, when assembled, make up one's identity? This article argues that people don't and can't control most facts about themselves. It goes against the grain of most current legislation. Overwhelming public pressure, combined with hostility and suspicion directed toward Silicon Valley giants Google, Facebook, and Twitter, has motivated governments to enact measures that treat facts about a person as something the individual is entitled to control. Facts about one's self become, in this legislation, a species of property, without quite being called that.

As of this writing, the most notorious of the new legislation is the General Data Protection Regulation of the European Union[1] (GDPR), with the

[1] General Data Protection Regulation (EU) 2016/679. Earlier US legislation such as the Health Insurance Portability and Accountability Act of 1996 (HIPAA), Pub. L. 104-191. 110 Stat. 1936 (1996). Gramm-Leach-Bliley Act, Pub. L. 106-102, 113 Stat. 1338 (1999). and the Children's Online Privacy Protection Act ("COPPA"), Pub. L. 105-277, 112 Stat. 2681 (1998) had focused on specific and particularly sensitive categories of personal data, namely health, finance, and protecting children.

California Consumer Privacy Act in 2018[2] (CCPA) close on its heels. Expanding on the earlier Data Protection Directive, the GDPR states six basic principles, all of which purport to give individuals more control over the "processing" of their "personal data." Understanding and applying GDPR requires one to master a new lexicon in which words we thought we had understood — "personal data," "data subject," "controller," "processor," "processing," and others — breach every previous levy of meaning. Harking back to the discussions of ordinary language, in earlier chapters of this book, the words in GDPR are like little wheelbarrows that strain to carry the heavy burden of their definitions. In applying GDPR, one cannot use these as words in the ordinary sense, but only as placeholders for the lengthy recitations in GDPR's definitions, and one is constantly flipping back to those definitions to decide whether something is or is not covered.

The GDPR definition of "processing" starts modestly enough with "any operation or set of operations which is performed on personal data or on sets of personal data." This predictably includes collection, transmission, and dissemination of personal data, but immediately overflows its banks to reach "restriction, erasure, or destruction."[3] Suppose, for example, someone mistakenly sends you an email, and you decide the right thing to do is to erase it. Well, then, you've "processed" the email both by collecting it and by erasing it. In doing that, you need to heed the six GDPR Principles, at the risk of stiff penalties — not to mention public opprobrium.[4]

The definition of "personal data" is, if anything, broader still. Under GDPR, "personal data" means anything that can be associated with an identified or identifiable individual. "Personal data" includes not only obvious things like name, email address, or likeness; it also means information that, standing alone, doesn't identify anybody, but that could, with some effort, identify an

---

[2] AB-375, Title 1.18.5 (2018), Cal. Code §1798.100 et seq.

[3] Here's the full definition: "'processing' means any operation or set of operations which is performed on personal data or on sets of personal data, whether or not by automated means, such as collection, recording, organisation, structuring, storage, adaptation or alteration, retrieval, consultation, use, disclosure by transmission, dissemination or otherwise making available, alignment or combination, restriction, erasure or destruction." GDPR Art. 4(2).

[4] In fairness to GDPR and its supervisory authorities, if "you" are an individual managing your own email account, the risk of an enforcement action is about zero; but if "you" are a business managing its handling of personal data, then actions as simple as receiving, storing, and deleting emails need to be thought through and justified under the GDPR principles.

individual when combined with other information.[5] In the case of *Breyer v. Germany*, the Court of Justice for the European Union found that a dynamic IP address (the transitory name of a particular computer when it is connected to the Internet) can be considered "personal data" because it could, in principle, be traced to an individual through the Internet Service Provider (ISP) used by the individual to access the Internet and the website proprietor. In that case, the Federal Republic of Germany had the power to obtain the required information from the ISP.[6] The fact that the Federal Republic of Germany had not, in fact, done such tracing was deemed irrelevant. It was sufficient that the tracing might have been done. Therefore, the consent of the unnamed hidden user of the ISP was required to "process" the dynamic IP address.[7] Under such rulings and the GDPR's sweeping definition, virtually anything that could be associated with an individual, whether posted by the individual or captured by a website or otherwise, becomes "personal data" that is subject to the "fundamental rights" that GDPR accords the "data subject." This includes Facebook posts, "likes," vacation pictures, references in third-party news articles, cross-references in scholarly journals — for want of a better word, everything that points to, comes from, or can be associated directly or indirectly with, an individual.

GDPR's ambitions extend beyond the mere borders of the European Union. To begin with, it applies to the "processing" of "personal data" by persons "within the Union," regardless of whether they are citizens, permanent residents, or merely passing through.[8] And GDPR's grasp extends not only to persons in the EU but to anyone offering ("targeting") goods or services to persons in the EU, or "monitoring" the "behavior" of persons in the EU. This means you, Google and Facebook, but it also includes any more modest soul

---

[5] Here's the full GDPR definition: "'personal data' means any information relating to an identified or identifiable natural person ('data subject'); an identifiable natural person is one who can be identified, directly or indirectly, in particular by reference to an identifier such as a name, an identification number, location data, an online identifier or to one or more factors specific to the physical, physiological, genetic, mental, economic, cultural or social identity of that natural person." GDPR Art. 4(1).

[6] The case was actually decided under the directive that was precursor to GDPR, Directive 95/46/EC (1995), but there is little doubt that the result would be the same under GDPR.

[7] The irony that such consent could be obtained only by first violating the privacy of the individual, who would otherwise have been unknown to the website operator, was apparently lost on the CJEU.

[8] GDPR, Art. 3.

located outside the EU who regularly sells to or attempts to sell goods or services to persons in the EU.

As noted, GDPR lays down six principles for the "processing" of "personal data." The data must be processed "lawfully, fairly and in a transparent manner"; be collected for "specified, explicit and legitimate purposes"; be "minimized" to what is necessary for the legitimate purposes; be accurate and kept up to date; be deleted when no longer necessary to the purposes; and be secured against unlawful access. These are the primary responsibility of the data "controller," defined as the person who determines the "purposes" and "means" of the processing.[9] If the data controller engages someone else to help with the data, the other person becomes the data "processor," for whose actions the controller is generally responsible but who has their own obligations under GDPR obligations as well.[10]

The data controller may process the personal data only if the data subject has provided "freely given, specific, informed, and unambiguous" consent or if the processing is necessary for at least one of five enumerated purposes: (i) the performance of a contract; (ii) compliance with a legal obligation; (iii) protecting the "vital interests" of a "natural person"; (iv) the performance of a task in the "public interest" or the performance of an "official duty"; or (v) the "legitimate interests" of the controller or another person — unless, in the latter case, the interests are overridden by the "interests or fundamental rights and freedoms" of the data subject, especially if the subject is a child.[11] It was a good day for lawyers when this regulation was enacted. Applying these categories requires learning, skill, imagination, and daring, and the penalties for processing data in violation are draconian — 10,000,000.00 euros or 2 percent of the previous year's turnover of the offending party, whichever is greater, depending on the offense.[12] Legal advice about GDPR merits many billable hours at high hourly rates.

Articles 12 to 22 of the GDPR are devoted to the rights of data subjects. These include the details of what information is collected, who is collecting it, who has access to it, how it is used, and to whom it might be transferred. These details will be familiar to anyone who has taken the trouble to actually

---

[9] GDPR, Art. 4 (7); Art. 5(2).

[10] See, e.g., GDPR, Art. 32, 33.

[11] GDPR Art. 6(1).

[12] GDPR Art. 83(4).

read a privacy policy on a website.[13] The data subject has a right, among other things, to access his or her data, to correct it if it is erroneous, to transfer the data from one controller to another, to restrict processing, to object to automated processing, and, most curiously, to require erasure of the data (the "right to be forgotten").[14]

Enforcement of the GDPR is primarily in the hands of "supervisory authorities" established in each member state.[15] Some of the supervisory authorities, notably those in Spain and the Republic of Ireland, have been very aggressive in their enforcement activities. Individual data subjects also have direct rights of action against controllers and processors.[16] And, perhaps most importantly, GDPR requires controllers to integrate compliance with GDPR into their operations,[17] known generally as "privacy by design." This requirement, combined with the draconian penalties for noncompliance, place data controllers on the front line of GDPR enforcement, which is undoubtedly a fundamental intent of its drafters.

Many of the principles of the GDPR have become models for enactments in other jurisdictions, most notably (at least in the United States) California, which enacted the California Consumer Privacy Act ("CCPA") in 2018. Making matters still more challenging for practitioners in this field, CCPA's vocabulary is just close enough to GDPR to create a kind of verbal interference pattern between

---

[13] Under GDPR such information must be provided in a "concise, transparent, intelligible and easily accessible form." GDPR Art. 12(1). It is debatable whether these goals can ever be attained.

[14] This is but one of the many respects in which the Regulation assumes a digital world that ceased to exist decades ago. It seems to assume that removing somebody's data is like deleting a file from a personal computer that is not connected to the Internet, much less the "cloud." Most computer programmers will tell you that "erasing" all personal data that has been captured by a sophisticated database is virtually impossible. Another example is the Regulations' bifurcation of data "Controllers" and "Processors." According to the Regulation, a "Controller" "determines the purposes and means of the processing of personal data," while the "Processor" "processes personal data on behalf of the Controller. Everybody prefers to be a "Processor" so you can blame the "Controller" if something goes wrong, and if you can't avoid being the "Controller" you want to impose an draconian data-processing agreement on the servant/Processor, requiring the Processor to do exactly what you require. Just try that if you are some little guy engaging Amazon Web Services as your "Processor." Despite the Regulation's bifurcation, AWS is going to determine how it processes your data and is not going to assume responsibility if something goes wrong.

[15] GDPR Art. 51.

[16] GDPR Art. 79.

[17] GDPR Art. 24

the two. CCPA concerns itself with "personal information"; GDPR with "personal data." The two categories overlap, but not entirely; among other things, CCPA-brand "personal information" does not include "publicly available information," whereas GDPR-brand "personal data" does. A "controller" in GDPR is comparable to a "business" in CCPA, except that, among other things, a GDPR controller can be a nonprofit entity, but a CCPA business cannot be. And so on throughout the statute and Regulation. The near-misses between these provisions, and the similar variances in the privacy provisions of many other states and countries, create no end of challenges for any enterprise attempting to operate and comply in multiple jurisdictions.

Although we are in the early days of plenary GDPR-type regulation (as of this writing, GDPR has been in effect only two years, and CCPA just took effect), it is worth considering what has driven the impetus for such regulation and whether it seems poised to achieve its stated objectives.[18] Consider first GDPR's dual principles of "transparency" and "control." Recital 7 of the GDPR states, "Natural persons should have control of their own personal data." Really? It is not at all clear what "control" over "personal data" actually means. If you walk through a mall, window shop down a street, or *faire les courses* in one of the charming outdoor markets in France, you have no "control" over any number of basic facts about yourself that are there for the world to see: your race, what you look like, how tall you are, whether you are fit or overweight, about how old you are, your sex,[19] physical disabilities if you have them, even your name if you happen to run into someone you know. An astute observer can also glean additional information just by the way you dress, the way you carry yourself, whether you are with a partner, whether the partner seems the same sexual orientation: all manner of information about you is there for the world to see. If you stop to consider a purchase or buy something, still more information spills out of your behavior: what interests you, what things you actually purchase. What persons observing you make of it, and how merchants may use it to affect their sales, is utterly beyond your control, short of becoming a hermit or wearing a disguise. This simple observation was at the heart of the personal identity article I published in 2012. Basic facts about one's self are, in a fundamental sense, public property and not subject to any criteria of ownership, including "control."

---

[18] The GDPR and the EU's earlier data protection directive have three stated and somewhat contradictory objectives: protecting fundamental data protection rights of individuals in the EU, facilitating the free flow of data within the EU, and harmonizing data protection law within the EU. GDPR Art. 1.

[19] Or at least your sexual appearance.

It is submitted that the current public outrage over "invasions" of privacy, and the resulting push to control personal information despite its inherently public nature, cannot be explained solely on the basis of practical and legal worries over having our passwords hacked or our identities "stolen." It has a deeper social and psychological dimension. The "problem," if there is one, is that people surfing the Internet do not realize that they are in a space as public as an open-air market and are shocked and demand a remedy when they discover that they are.[20] Surfing the Internet, posting or reading a post on Facebook, and making a purchase on Amazon all *feel* like private acts because they are typically done in the "privacy" of one's home, sitting at one's desk. When we discover that Mark Zuckerberg, Jeff Bezos, and the companies they control have eavesdropped on us, we are as outraged as if a Peeping Tom had watched through the bedroom window, peering into the private selves that we have revealed in our intimate relation with our computer screens.[21] The problem is not helped by the fact that virtually every social media website has something called a "privacy" policy that actually says (although not quite so candidly): "Beware! You're entering a glass house! We can see what you're doing here and sell what we see to others!" Adding to the deception, social media sites routinely and sanctimoniously promise that they will "respect" your privacy and include "privacy" settings in their apps.[22] And there is a further problem: nobody reads the policies, and the longer and more detailed they are, the less likely they are to be read and understood by the data subject. So today, people feel they are being exposed and violated by social media, and they want the law to do something about it: to give them "control" over their personal information and what others

---

[20] The parallels between social media sites and stores, malls, airports, and other public-seeming places are all the more striking when one realizes that both are under surveillance by their proprietors from the moment either is entered until one leaves. See "In Stores, Secret Surveillance Tracks Your Every Move," *New York Times*, June 14, 2019, https://www.nytimes.com/interactive/2019/06/14/opinion/bluetooth-wireless-tracking-privacy.html.

[21] I say "we" but I, like many in my generation, do not post on Facebook or Instagram or elsewhere and cannot fathom why the younger generations do. It is as if everyone had been given a little diary, in which they can record their doings, but unlike the diaries of old these modern ones are instantly published for part or all of the world to see. Are these diaries at all? Or advertisements for the self? "This is me; please watch me!"

[22] Interestingly, the Facebook policy dated April 19, 2018 is reached by clicking on the word "Privacy" on the right of the Facebook landing page, but the pages reached by such a click are called "Data Policy," and do not purport to protect the user's "privacy" at all. See https://www.facebook.com/privacy/explanation. The disclosures provide, in reasonably understandable English, considerable detail about the data Facebook collects and what it does with the data.

do with it. GDPR's twin principles of "transparency" and "control" are thus an attempt to use the law to solve something that is at base a psychological problem: the dilemma between wanting to be seen (via social media postings) and to control what others see.[23]

Both issues were in play in the recent *Vectaury* decision by the French data protection authority, CNIL.[24] *Vectaury* considered a species of "real-time bidding" ("RTB"), which is a fundamental element of Internet commerce and is expected to have generated in the United States some $23 billion in advertising revenues in 2018 alone.[25] In a typical RTB set-up, a "publisher" of content and advertisements (basically, this can be anybody with a webpage, but more paradigmatically, the big players like Google and Facebook) allows advertisers to bid to place advertisements on the publisher's "inventory" of ad placements (i.e., places where an ad can appear on the webpage when it is opened). The advertisers are provided with detailed personal information about the person accessing the website; in fact, the advertising term "inventory" can be more properly understood as an individual visiting a webpage at a particular moment, and what the "publisher" is really selling is direct access to a specifically identified or identifiable and electronically described person. Translated into normal English, the electronic auctioneer running the bidding is putting an individual, Joe, on the auction block saying, "Here's Joe; here's what he's interested in; here's some demographic information about him; here's his recent or not so recent browsing history: What's it worth to you to show him your ad right now, while he's standing here in front of you?" The bidding commences, and access to Joe is sold in some millionths of a second to the highest bidder. It is fair to say that the vast majority of Joes don't know they are being put up for auction in this way, and

---

[23] One might also argue that the unconsented use of facts about one's self constitutes a misappropriation, something like infringement of the right of publicity, but in this case by someone who is not a public figure. This argument runs up against the fact that persons using free social media, a browser, or online sales sites like Facebook, Google, and Amazon are in fact being compensated for the use of their personal data by the free-of-charge access they receive to the sites. They just don't understand or see it that way; perhaps they believe that services of this kind are free of charge, like using a publicly supported road (for which they of course pay taxes). The "fee," as in the case of taxes, is not as direct and therefore hidden from ordinary public view.

[24] Decision No.MED-2018-042 of 30 October 2018 giving notice to the company Vectaury.

[25] Statista, "Real time bidding digital display advertising spending in selected countries in 2014 and 2018 (in billion U.S. dollars)," https://www.statista.com/statistics/377658/rtb-digital-display-ad-spend-selected-countries/.

it is not difficult to understand why this process has captured the attention of supervisory authorities in the EU.

Vectaury offered a software platform to developers of applications for mobile devices, permitting their apps to track the devices' (and therefore their users') locations. This information was then transmitted back to Vectaury, which combined it with other data captured by the apps to run an RTB auction for its "inventory" of advertising spaces, targeted at the mobile devices' peripatetic users as they ambled through the streets of Paris (or wherever). Vectaury relied on the data subjects' consent to process their location data, requiring persons downloading apps containing the software to click through a series of "Accept," "Refuse," and "Manage Consent" options that were based on the Interactive Advertising Bureau's "Transparency and Consent Framework."

CNIL found, among other things, that the disclosures lacked the "transparency" required by GDPR and that Vectaury could not pass off the requirement of obtaining "freely given, specific, informed and unambiguous" consent via contract to the app developers. Regarding "transparency," CNIL found that references to the purpose of "personalization" featured in Vectaury's consent management system was barely comprehensible and failed the criterion of transparency. Translated, Vectaury's disclosure of the purpose for which it collected personal information was "collection and processing of information regarding your use of this service for the purpose of sending you advertisements and/or of the personalized content in other contexts, for example on other sites or applications. In general, the content of the site or the app is utilized to make deductions concerning your interests, which will be useful in the context of later selections of advertisements and/or content."[26] CNIL found, reasonably enough, that in addition to being incomprehensible to the ordinary person, the disclosure covered too large a number of situations and, in light of the complexity of the terms used, was not

26 Here's the original French: "*collecte et traitement d'informations relatives à votre utilisation de ce service afin de vous adresser ultérieurement des publicités et/ou du contenu personnalisé dans d'autres contextes, par exemple sur d'autres sites ou applications. En général, le contenu du site ou de l'application est utilisé pour faire des déductions concernant vos intérêts, ce qui sera utile dans le cadre de sélections ultérieures de publicité et/ou de contenu.*"

adequately adapted to the ordinary person downloading the app.[27] Because the disclosure was inadequate, it was impossible for a person to provide "specific, informed and freely given" consent.

A further lack of transparency was found in Vectaury's failure to advise the person downloading a Vectaury-charged app of the identities of the entities that would be bidding on the Vectaury inventory. CNIL declared that GDPR required Vectaury to disclose the identities of all of the entities to whom the personal data would be disclosed even though GDPR would also allow disclosure only of the "categories" of recipients.[28] In any RTB auction, this could be hundreds if not thousands of entities, and their identities can change minute to minute. Full compliance with this requirement is quite literally impossible — it would require updating each time a bidder was added or deleted, and seeking consent to the disclosure of personal data to each one each time advertising "inventory" was put up for "bid."

The decision sent shock waves through the RTB industry. Things have only gotten worse for the industry since then. By now, complaints about RTB advertising have been lodged with the supervisory authorities in Ireland, Belgium, the Netherlands, Spain, and Poland; more are expected to be filed in the future. The more recent complaints focus on the security of personal data that is widely disseminated through the RTB process: is it really possible for the "publisher" of advertising "inventory" to ensure the security of the personal data it provides to potentially thousands of bidders?

It is worth asking, will these enforcement proceedings under GDPR actually serve the principles of transparency and control? Let's suppose *Vectaury* were fully implemented, with one-by-one "acceptance" clicks on the location and other personal information being collected and the identities of the entities to whom it will be provided for RTB purposes. Would that do the trick? Or does it

---

[27] No kidding. On the other hand, could it have been made more comprehensible to the ordinary person and at the same time sufficiently comprehensive to satisfy CNIL? Lawyers struggle every day to put their clients' privacy policies into simple English (or French or German or any other language) without their becoming either overly simplified or excruciatingly detailed. One imagines that a person downloading the Vectaury-fueled apps could provide "freely given, specific, informed and unambiguous" only if she had been given a textbook on RTB, supplemented by a discussion of artificial intelligence and the operation of the "cloud," and then passed a test confirming her mastery of the technology before clicking "Accept."

[28] GDPR Art. 13, 14. The zealotry that European data protection authorities bring to their jobs, exemplified in this expansion of the more limited GDPR requirement, is truly remarkable.

open a Pandora's box of questions that the individual could never answer — who is Vectaury, who are all of these advertisers and others getting access to my personal data? How reliable are they, and do they have the institutional and technical ability to ensure the security of the data they receive? A private equity firm performing diligence on Vectaury before investing millions of dollars would be hard-pressed to run these questions to ground, much less an individual who just downloaded an app that used Vectaury's software. Most people will click "Accept" because they want the app, without having any answers to the underlying questions that would have to be answered actually to exercise "control" over their data. The analogy to "click-wrap" license agreements, agreed to by virtually everyone who wants or needs the relevant software, is inescapable.[29]

A strong argument can be made that the specificity required by GDPR is actually inimical to the goal of transparency.[30] "Privacy" policies that provide excruciatingly detailed disclosures about what is being collected and how it is being used are unlikely to be read and understood. Much more likely, like the click-through license agreement, the users will impatiently click "Accept, Accept, Accept," in their haste to download the app and start using it. Everyone on social media lives in a glass house with a little sign on its door that says, in effect: This Is a Glass House; We Can See You! And We Can Tell Others What We See — And Charge Them For It![31] Oh, of course, the sign also says that your privacy will be respected — meaning, quite simply, that "We" will only tattle to the people we choose and will get very angry with anyone who tries to peer into our glass house for their own commercial purposes. But the sign is rarely read before entering the glass house, overtaken by the potent desire to see and be seen. The glass house owners have learned to dole out little rewards for our revelations — beeps, clicks, "likes," that train us like B. F. Skinner's pigeons to peck away at our and others' posts to get these little serotonin rewards. Social media is like the gingerbread house in "Hansel and Gretel," luring them in to be fattened with personal information and then devoured.

---

29 See footnote, pages 186 and 195 above.

30 "Clear and conspicuous" notices provided under the Gramm Leach Bliley Act are considerably less detailed, and arguably more effective, than those required by GDPR. See, e.g., the current Citibank notice at http://www.citibank.com/citigoldinternational/homepage/resources/pdf/privacynot_en.pdf. See generally https://www.ftc.gov/tips-advice/business-center/guidance/how-comply-privacy-consumer-financial-information-rule-gramm.

31 I refer of course to "Terms and Conditions" and "Privacy Policies" associated with every social media site.

Here, the analogy of warning labels on tobacco products is strong.[32] If the goal is to warn and educate, shorter is better than longer, and the pictures of diseased lungs of the type found in New York, Canada, and Europe are more effective than words.[33] The implication of the tobacco warning labels, at least, is that GDPR is barking up the wrong tree: if we really want to alert people to the privacy risks of using a site, something pithy is better than the full disclosure contemplated by GDPR — something along the lines of, "USING THIS SITE EXPOSES YOUR PERSONAL DATA TO PEOPLE AND COMPANIES YOU DON'T KNOW!" perhaps combined with a picture of someone running naked through a mall chased by photographers.

The goal of control is another matter altogether. As noted above, most of the basic facts about a person are utterly outside of their control. Attempting to reimpose "control" in the electronic context seems both futile and, in many cases, unwise. Furthermore, most people who are at all active online freely publicize a wealth of personal information, whether through Facebook, LinkedIn, professional organizations, churches, or any number of other networking sites. GDPR places companies collecting or processing such information in the absurd position of being required to safeguard personal data that the data subjects have made no effort to control, actually have no right to control as a matter of copyright law,[34] and in many cases, have actually affirmatively disseminated.[35] In one sense, GDPR casts its net much too broadly — imposing substantial social costs to try to "control" facts like name, profession, or email address, that the individual has voluntarily

---

[32] There is a further parallel to the tobacco industry, which is that we now understand that social media sites are addictive and are in fact designed to be so. There are dozens of articles on this topic. As examples, see Göran Wågström, "Is Social Media Addiction Worse Than Cigarettes?," *Forbes*, Nov. 21, 2018, https://www.forbes.com/sites/forbestechcouncil/2018/11/21/is-social-media-addiction-worse-than-cigarettes/#edc09c25d64c; and Wikipedia, "Social media addiction," https://en.wikipedia.org/wiki/Social_media_addiction (and cites therein).

[33] See Hammond, Fong, McDonald, Brown, and Cameron, "Graphic Canadian Cigarette Warning Labels and Adverse Outcomes: Evidence from Canadian Smokers," *American Journal of Public Health*, Oct. 10, 2011, https://ajph.aphapublications.org/doi/ref/10.2105/AJPH.94.8.1442.

[34] It is axiomatic that copyright confers no rights in facts. *Feist Publications v. Rural Telephone Service Co.*, 499 U.S. 340 (1991).

[35] By contrast, the Gramm-Leach-Bliley Act, which remains one of the cornerstones of personal data protection at the federal level in the United States, requires the financial institutions it regulates to protect only "nonpublic" information about individuals. 15 U.S.C. §6801(a).

disclosed any number of times and that, as a matter of copyright law, are in the public domain once they have been published. Other facts — that a person is a bad credit risk, or a molester, or a fraudster, or has a communicable disease — are important for others to know, and should not be subject to the GDPR "right to be forgotten." GDPR Art. 17(3) permits the data controller to balance a request for erasure against public interests such as freedom of speech, public health, and scientific research. This places a substantial burden on platforms like Google and Facebook to make this judgment, at the risk of a lawsuit or enforcement proceedings if their judgment is questioned, and one might well ask whether one wants the likes of Mark Zuckerberg making such judgments on our behalf. [36]

Sarah Igo's excellent book, *The Known Citizen*,[37] which should be required reading for anyone practicing in the privacy field, chronicles the evolution of the concept of a right to privacy from its genesis in the *Harvard Law Review* article by Warren and Brandeis in 1890[38] to the present day. For Warren and Brandeis, it meant protection of nineteenth-century gentlemen against intrusions into their private family lives by the burgeoning tabloid press.[39] Initiatives like GDPR and CCPA seem an effort to translate the Warren/Brandeis concept of privacy into the Internet world. They want to remake an individual's digital life as their little castle, guarded against the prying eyes of social media companies just as Warren and Brandeis wanted to guard their Victorian homes against the intrusions of the tabloid press. One suspects, though, that they will be no more successful in controlling the dissemination of personal data over the Internet than Warren and Brandeis were in controlling the intrusions of the tabloid press, which today is as alive and well as it was in their day.

At this point, there is no empirical evidence addressing the question of whether detailed disclosures will achieve GDPR's twin principles of

---

36 See, e.g., *NT1 and NT2 v. Google and the Information Commissioner*, [2018] EWHC 799 (QB).

37 Sarah Igo, *The Known Citizen* (Cambridge, MA: Harvard University Press, 2018) (hereinafter "*The Known Citizen*"). Igo's book traces the meaning of the word "privacy," demonstrating convincingly that it has no stable meaning but instead evolves with social context, exactly as we would expect.

38 *The Known Citizen* at 34-43. See S. Warren and L. Brandeis, "The Right to Privacy," 4 *Harvard L. Rev.* 193 (1890).

39 *The Known Citizen* at 34-42. Since then it has morphed through successive stages, including concerns over government tracking using the newly-christened and ubiquitous social security number, wiretapping, birth control, the census, government surveillance, and finally, the desire to display one's self but to control exactly what is seen. Id. et seq.

transparency and consent/control. Nor do we know what their cost might be in terms of degradation of the Internet experience, or imposing fees and paywalls on websites that are currently supported by the sale of personal data to generate advertising revenue. It seems reasonable to speculate that some few people will actually read the detailed disclosures and learn something from them, and a subset of those people may exercise some "control" over the use of their personal data. It seems equally likely that, at least from a "transparency" standpoint, the public will be much more efficiently educated about the use of their data by the publicity attendant on data breaches and scandals. GDPR is likely to enhance this education function at least as effectively by its requirement that data breaches be notified to the data subjects[40] as through its requirements for detailed descriptions in privacy policies that virtually no one reads.

GDPR is great business for lawyers, but one is left wondering if its benefits justify the high costs of compliance. One is also left wondering whether regulators would be better advised to focus on the security and management of information such as financial records, health information, and the identities of children, which is essentially what existing US legislation does.[41] For the time being, though, we are stuck with GDPR, which is spreading like a virus throughout the globe, and we must struggle to square the circle of its requirements of transparency and consent.

Another of the six GDPR principles is data security. There is no question that data breaches are a serious concern, especially when they concern financial or other personal information that can be used to commit crimes, and that companies processing such data have been less successful than one might hope in preventing breaches. This is something that has been much more visible in the United States than in Europe. US law had required notification of data breaches since 2003,[42] but there was no EU-wide notification requirement until GDPR took effect in May 2018.[43] It remains to be seen whether the breach notification requirements of GDPR, its draconian penalties for breach and its thorough-going requirements for security by both "controllers" and "processors" will harden the keepers of personal data against attacks. Judging from the amount of legal effort being put into "Data

---

[40] GDPR Art. 33, 34.

[41] See note 6 above.

[42] California was the first state to mandate notification of data breaches, by a law that took effect July 1, 2003. Cal. Civil Code Sec. 1798.82. Since then comparable laws have been enacted in all 50 states.

[43] The Netherlands has had a more limited breach notification requirement since 2016.

Processing Agreements" and other documents attempting to impose liability and risk throughout the data processing stream, the privacy bar, at least, believes that GDPR will have some effect in improving the security of personal data against attack.

Any discussion of privacy would be grievously incomplete without consideration of a security problem of a different and much more dangerous character — namely extremism, terroristic violence, and political manipulation. Here "security" takes on a different meaning. It is not the security of personal information against unconsented use and disclosure; it is the security of persons and the society against hostile and sometimes lethal attacks. Here we find extremists who want their information to be seen so that it can accumulate and proliferate. The algorithms of Google, Facebook, and Twitter are extremists' favored tools of recruitment: they aggregate mutually reinforcing posts and disaggregate conflicting posts that might otherwise dilute their messages. Legislation like GDPR and CCPA is of no help here; indeed, it is counterproductive to the extent that the proponents underlying vile posts can hide who they are and even demand to be "forgotten."[44] GDPR and CCPA make social media, as the "controller" of personal data, responsible for its safekeeping but never for its content.

Finding a solution to this problem is of far greater urgency than legislation like GDPR and CCPA that try to give individuals "control" over their personal data. To date, no solution has been found short of state control in authoritarian countries. Social media companies and other Internet service providers occupy a unique and privileged space. The Communications Decency Act of 1996, passed in the hey-day of Internet enthusiasm under the Clinton Administration, exempts "interactive computer service[s]" from characterization as the "publisher" or "speaker" of posted third-party content, effectively removing responsibility for torts such as libel and defamation based on user content.[45] It also exempts Internet service providers from liability for taking down material they consider offensive. What this means in effect is that a Facebook, a Twitter, or a Google can leave up any post regardless of how dangerous it may be, but can also take it down if they

---

[44] GDPR Recital 16 states that GDPR does not apply to "activities concerning national security," and Recital 19 excludes processing of personal data in connection with criminal law enforcement, which is, however, governed by Directive (EU) 2016/680.

[45] 47 U.S.C. §230. Whether this would also exempt the platforms from liability for negligence in the posting of harmful information has not, to the knowledge of this author, been tested.

choose to. In Europe, the e-Commerce Directive of 2000[46] provides comparable protection for information "intermediaries."

These provisions were enacted at a time of what might, in retrospect, be called Internet euphoria, when the Internet promised a panacea for communication, knowledge transfer, and effortless commerce. Google had just been founded in 1998; Mark Zuckerberg hadn't yet enrolled at Harvard; 9-11 hadn't happened; even the dot-com bubble hadn't yet burst. The laws were intended to, and did, clear the way for the Frankensteinian social media we have today, from Facebook, Instagram, YouTube, and Twitter at the high end, to dregs like Gab at the bottom.

Some major players have begun to assert some control over hateful content on their platforms. Google recently announced a new policy regarding political advertisements, and Twitter allegedly has a plan to ban such ads.[47] In general terms, the Google policy limits the extent to which such advertisements can be narrowly targeted and prohibits "demonstrably false" advertising. In announcing the policy, Google's spokesperson stated that "no one can sensibly adjudicate every political claim, counterclaim, and insinuation, and we expect that the number of political ads on which we take action will be very limited."[48] And Facebook, which garnered $887 million in advertising revenue on political advertisements since May 2018,[49] has thus far failed to place any limits on political ads. Little wonder, given its revenues. In the end, the Internet giants are defeated by their own business models and algorithms, not to mention right-wing politicians who bray about every effort that appears selectively to take down right-wing extremism[50] — for the obvious reason that this is where much extremism resides.

By now, the evidence is overwhelming that the bright light of day promised by the Internet at the end of the twentieth century, originally conceived as Brandeis's disinfecting sunlight, shines as brightly on, and nourishes as

---

[46] Directive 2000/31/EC of the European Parliament and of the Council of June 8, 2000, on certain legal aspects of information society services, in particular electronic commerce, in the Internal Market ("Directive on Electronic Commerce").

[47] See https://support.google.com/adspolicy/answer/6014595?hl=en. See also "Google Changed Its Political Ad Policy," *New York Times*, Nov. 22, 2019 (Op Ed by Kara Swisher).

[48] Quoted in "Google announces new political ad policies that limit targeting but not all lies," *Washington Post*, Nov. 20, 2019.

[49] See https://www.businessinsider.com/trump-other-advertisers-spending-most-on-facebook-political-ads-2019-11.

[50] See "Conservatives Say Google and Facebook Are Censoring Them. Here's the Real Background," *Washington Post*, August 1, 2019.

steadily, the worst impulses of human nature. The algorithms of Google, Facebook, Twitter, and others are the extremists' favored tools of recruitment: they aggregate mutually reinforcing posts and disaggregate conflicting posts that might otherwise dilute the extremists' messages, and the platforms themselves are intentionally designed to concentrate viewing.[51] The halting half-measures taken by a limited set of social media to identify and stop harmful posts have done little to stem the tide of extremism washing through their systems.

At a minimum, the exclusion of liability provided by the Communications Decency Act and e-Commerce Directive ought to be reconsidered. Imagine how much more serious social media would become if victims of attacks could bring private tort actions against the platforms that negligently fostered the attackers. This might provide a measure of protection to individuals who are injured by doxing, by cyber-bullying, or by terrorist attacks that could have been prevented had the terrorists' posts and warnings been identified and either suppressed or reported to authorities by the social media.[52]

Admittedly, tort liability of the type precluded by the Communications Decency Act would do nothing to the political misuse of social media, where the First Amendment would surely trump any tort liability.[53] There, another option might be to try to apply something like the fairness doctrine to social media algorithms, requiring contrasting information to be searched and displayed equally with congruent information, or providing a legal remedy

---

51 See Kevin Roose, "The Making of a YouTube Radical," *New York Times*, June 8, 2019, https://www.nytimes.com/interactive/2019/06/08/technology/youtube-radical.html.

52 Would it be too much to say that we now realize that social media are dangerous instrumentalities and should be treated as such? The common law provides strict liability, irrespective of negligence, to people who use explosives and other abnormally dangerous devices. Restatement of Torts (Second) §520 provides strict liability (irrespective of negligence) for activities that are "abnormally dangerous," considering the following factors: "(a) existence of a high degree of risk of some harm to the person, land, or chattels of others; (b) likelihood that the harm that results from it will be great; (c) inability to eliminate the risk by the exercise of reasonable care; (d) extent to which the activity is not a matter of common usage; (e) inappropriateness of the activity to the place where it is carried on; and (f) extent to which its value to the community is outweighed by its dangerous attributes." Factors a, b, c, and (arguably) e are certainly present in the case of social media. Are they outweighed by the widespread use of social media and its value to the community (factors d and f)? It seems likely that a court would hold so, unless one limited the "activity" to the use of social media by extremists, in which case the balance would clearly shift in the direction of strict liability.

53 New York Times v. Sullivan, 376 U.S. 254 (1964).

when a site fails to do so. The fairness doctrine began in 1949 and was a creature of a time when there were but a handful of television and radio channels, which were considered a limited public resource and were required by the FCC to use their licenses to serve the community generally by presenting opposing views. How quaint! The doctrine was upheld against First Amendment attack by the Supreme Court in 1969 in the 8–0 decision in *Red Lion Broadcasting v. FCC*,[54] but it was discarded in 1987, during the Reagan era, on the ground that it inhibited the free speech protected by the First Amendment by discouraging controversial broadcasting and that it was unnecessary in light of the proliferation of media outlets. The theory of the doctrine's opponents was that the doctrine would "stifle the growth of dissenting views and, in effect, make free speech less free."[55] The inevitable result? The current compartmentalization of information in the likes of Fox News and MSNBC and far more radical channels distributing complete hogwash to their devoted viewers and listeners. Speech, in its aftermath, is certainly unrestrained, but actual discourse and the competition of ideas is lost. To quote Jonathan Swift, "Falsehood flies, and the truth comes limping after it."

One might argue that in today's social media, a tiny handful of companies are in much the same position as the handful of television and radio networks that exited in 1949.[56] Internet algorithms are driven by affinities: if you like this, you'll like that, making mutually supportive expression aggregate and contrasting expression separate. Could the algorithms be rewritten so that visiting one posting would introduce you to a conflicting posting? This seems technically feasible, and YouTube has now amended its algorithms to offer mainstream news to alt-right viewers,[57] but in the absence of law or regulation requiring the posting of conflicting views, it is hardly likely to dilute the concentration that YouTube's algorithms continue to promote. Furthermore, all points of view are not equal — there are some that cause real harm, and it is hardly in the society's interest to expose them in the interest of fairness or balance. And there is credible research suggesting that the exposure to conflicting information tends to reinforce contrary preconceptions. Google's initiative in limiting the extent to which political ads can be selectively

---

[54] 395 U.S. 367 (1969).

[55] See, e.g., Adam Thierer, "Why the Fairness Doctrine Is Anything but Fair," Heritage Foundation, October 29, 1993, https://www.heritage.org/government-regulation/report/why-the-fairness-doctrine-anything-fair.

[56] See "Big Tech Isn't Going Anywhere," *NY Times Supplement*, Nov. 17, 2019, p. 38.

[57] See Roose, "The Making of a YouTube Radical," https://www.nytimes.com/interactive/2019/06/08/technology/youtube-radical.html.

targeted might help a bit — particularly if it were also adopted by other dominant platforms, notably Facebook — but a convincing solution to the political and social risks posed by the Internet in general and by social media, in particular, that is consistent with the freedom and openness of liberal democracies has yet to be found.

I remain convinced that the opinions expressed in the personal identity article are valid, however much they may be at odds with the seemingly inexorable thrust of modern regulation of personal data. I also believe that the predictions in the much older 2004 paper on privacy law that efforts to enhance "privacy," in the sense of protection against unwanted intrusions in one's life, will be overtaken at the federal level by the acute need to protect against danger to our physical safety.[58]

---

58 This essay was completed prior to the coronavirus epidemic of 2020, which raises another contradiction between personal safety and privacy. If an individual tests positive for a communicable and potentially deadly disease, be it coronavirus, measles, SARS, or worse, the society's interest in protecting the community through quarantine far outweighs the individual's interest in protecting such medical information. In this context the "right to privacy" seems a luxury good, like chocolate in wartime.

The Current State of Privacy and Security Laws Affecting US Businesses[•]

Introduction

Rapid technological development, the press of commercial competition, the global reach of the Internet and the imperatives of security in the post-9/11 world have tied privacy law into a Gordian Knot. The crux of the problem is to reconcile an individual's expectation and need for privacy with society's need for security and the marketplace's demand for information. Competing solutions at the state, federal and international levels further complicate the policy dilemmas.

This article summarizes the major privacy laws that impact US businesses. We will see that United States privacy law and policy is an extraordinarily confused field, with radically different approaches used in a multiplicity of state and federal statutes, regulations, and enforcement policies. We will briefly contrast this situation with the more uniform regime in the European Union and conclude with some prognostications about the future.

Key factors at play in privacy laws

"Opt-in" v. "Opt-out"

Several themes pervade the various legislative and industry initiatives in this area. One of the most fundamental is "opt-in" vs. "opt-out." In an "opt-in" system, individuals must affirmatively consent to the collection and use of their personal data. This approach has been taken by several states and by the EU. In an "opt-out" system, personal information may be collected and used without an individual's affirmative consent, but the collector must give notice of the collection and afford an individual the right to "opt-out" from this collection. US regulation and business interests favor this approach.[1]

Industry-specific v. Information-specific

A second theme is regulation by industry vs. regulation by class of data. Federal privacy regulation is typically industry-specific. As an example, Gramm-Leach-

---

[•] Thomas Hemnes, Stella Cramer, Gina Perini, Ken Holston, Summary for clients, Foley Hoag, November 17, 2004.

[1]For example, the Gramm-Leach-Bliley Act, 15 USC §6801 et seq ("GLB").

Bliley Act (GLB) pertains solely to financial institutions.[2] The EU, some states, and proposed federal legislation favor information-specific solutions. As an example, the Data Protection Directive (1995)[3] ("Data Protection Directive") defines minimum levels of protection depending on whether data is "sensitive personal information" or merely "personal information," regardless of the industry or purpose for which the information is collected and used.

Preemption v. Minimum standards

A third theme is preemption vs. minimum standards. The Fair Credit Reporting Act[4] (FCRA), a fundamental item of US personal information legislation since its enactment in 1970, is preemptive legislation. It establishes a country-wide, uniform rule for the disclosure of credit information among affiliates that preempts all state laws of the same subject matter, thus prohibiting states from enacting more strict privacy laws.[5] By contrast, GLB and the EU Data Protection Directive are minimum standard provisions. US states and EU members are free to adopt laws that are more protective of personal data, so long as the minimum standards are met.

Self-regulation v. Legislation

Yet another theme is self-regulation contrasted with government regulation or legislation. The online industry has promoted self-regulation initiatives such as the "TRUSTe" seal or "trustmark." The theory is that the marketplace will favor companies that voluntarily adopt minimum privacy principles, as evidenced by a compliance mark. Although many companies have voluntarily acceded to these programs, and the FTC has occasionally enforced the voluntarily adopted principles, they have not stemmed the tide of new legislation and regulation. The authors believe that the topic is simply too important, too politically charged, and too closely related to commercial and

---

[2] The definition of financial institution for purposes of GLB has been broadly construed (for example, under the FTC Privacy Rule, 16 CFR Part 314), but it is nonetheless a limitation of GLB that it does not encompass persons collecting personal data who do not fall within that broad definition.

[3] 95/46/EC.

[4] 15 USC §1681 et seq.

[5] The FCRA was set to expire on January 1, 2004, but Fair and Accurate Credit Transactions Act of 2003, signed into law on December 4, 2003, removed the sunset provision. PL 108-159, sec. 711. Among other things, it preempted still more protective California legislation.

governmental concerns to be left for long to self-regulation. We, therefore, expect this dimension to become less important over time.

Privacy vs. Security

There is lastly the question of privacy vs. security. The events of 9/11 resulted in new security legislation, most notably the USA PATRIOT Act,[6] hastily passed one month after 9/11. Statutes expanding government surveillance powers have typically included balancing provisions recognizing the privacy rights of individuals. The Wireless Communications and Public Safety Act [7] ("911 Act") is an example. While expanding the use of wireless as an emergency location device, it prohibits sharing location information with persons not providing emergency services.

Similarly, the Communications Assistance for Law Enforcement Act ("CALEA")[8] expands a telecommunication carrier's duty to effect court-approved electronic surveillance but also defines the warrant requirements for such surveillance. Ironically, therefore, security legislation has catalyzed the development of US privacy law. We expect this trend to continue in the future.

Federal Law

Privacy and security provisions inhabit a myriad, cluttered landscape of federal statutes; it is not our purpose to catalog all of them. Instead, we summarize the federal statutes that impact a wide range of business operations in the United States.

Federal Trade Commission Act[9]

The Federal Trade Commission ("FTC") Act does not directly legislate privacy issues.[10] Rather, through the use of its enforcement tools, the FTC has been influential in the development and enforcement of privacy policies. The FTC

---

[6] Public Law 107-56 (2001).

[7] Public Law 106-181.

[8] Public Law 103-414, 108 Stat 4279.

[9] 15 USC §41 et seq.

[10] However, some federal statutes do. Please refer to the section below for details.

encourages companies to adopt privacy statements.[11] If a website does have a privacy policy and the company responsible for that website breaches that policy, the FTC may launch investigations to establish whether that company is committing "unfair and deceptive acts" in breach of Section 5 of the FTC Act.[12]

The FTC brought several enforcement actions under this section. In *FTC v. Toysmart.com*,[13] Toysmart's privacy policy promised that personal data would never be shared with third parties. When Toysmart ran into financial difficulties, it offered its customer lists for sale. The FTC alleged that offering its customer lists for sale was a deceptive practice. Under the settlement agreement, Toysmart agreed to file a bankruptcy order prohibiting the sale of the lists as a stand-alone asset. The lists were to be sold only as part of a package including the entire website, only to a buyer in a related market and only to a buyer that agreed to abide by the Toysmart privacy policy.

In *Liberty Financial Companies Inc.*,[14] the company operated an investment website called "Young Investor" directed at children and teenagers. The FTC alleged that the website falsely represented that personal information would be maintained anonymously. Contrary to this representation, the company, in fact, maintained identifiable personal information about children and their families' finances. The FTC required Liberty Financial to enter into a consent order that prohibited such misrepresentations in the future and required Liberty Financial to post a privacy notice on its website directed at children and to obtain verifiable parental consent before collecting personal information from children.

In *ReverseAuction.com, Inc.*,[15] the company advertised, offered, and promoted an auction service on the Internet. It also registered as a user of

---

[11] "Protecting Consumers' Privacy: 2002 and Beyond." Remarks of FTC Chairman Timothy J. Muris at the Privacy 2001 Conference, Cleveland, Ohio, October 4, 2001. US federal legislation does not generally require a company to have a privacy statement on its website. The FTC has considered recommending legislation requiring adherence to four fair information practices: "notice" of website information practices; allowing users "choice" as to how personal information is used; allowing users "access" to personal data; and ensuring "security" against unauthorized use. FTC chairman Muris, in his speech on October 4, 2001, stated that he did not see a need for additional legislation.

[12] Section 5(a) of the FTC Act, 15 USC §45(a)(1).

[13] *FTC v. Toysmart.com, Inc.* (District of Massachusetts) (Civil Action No. 00-11341-RGS) (July 10, 2000). The FTC also alleged that Toysmart infringed COPPA. See COPPA discussion below.

[14] FTC Docket No. C-3891 (Aug. 12, 1999). The FTC had two other complaints, but they are not relevant for the purposes of this article.

[15] FTC File No. 002-3046 (Jan. 6, 2000).

eBay (a well-known Internet auction site) and agreed to comply with eBay's user agreement. It managed to obtain the email addresses, eBay user identification names and eBay feedback ratings of eBay-registered users. Using this information, it sent unsolicited emails informing eBay users that their eBay user id was about to expire and promoting the ReverseAuction website. The FTC alleged that ReverseAuction had violated the eBay user agreement. This agreement prohibits an eBay user from using other eBay users' personal identification information to send unsolicited commercial email. The parties settled, with ReverseAuction agreeing, amongst other things, not to falsely represent that: (1) user ids of any other internet company are about to expire; (2) an internet company provided ReverseAuction with personal information of its users; or (3) that any internet company agreed to the dissemination of unsolicited email to the users of that company. ReverseAuction then had to send an email to all users (who had registered with ReverseAuction as a result of the unsolicited email), notifying them of what ReverseAuction had done illegally and offering to cancel the registration of these users. It also had to place a notice on its website and notify its users of its privacy practices on its website.

In *Eli Lilly and Company* (Lilly),[16] Lilly, a pharmaceutical company, operates the Prozac.com website and other websites that collect personal information from visitors. Lilly offered its users a personalized service to email them reminders about their medication. When the prozac.com reminder service terminated, Lilly sent an email to all 669 subscribers in which all of the subscribers were listed in the "to" box of the email, therefore disclosing to each individual subscriber the email addresses of all of the other subscribers. The FTC alleged that Lilly's promises in its privacy policy to protect the privacy and confidentiality of customers were deceptive, as it had failed to maintain appropriate internal procedures to protect sensitive information. The FTC consent order requires Lilly not to misrepresent the extent to which it maintains privacy or confidentiality of any personal information and to maintain a security program as defined in the order.

More recently, in *Guess.com, Inc.*,[17] the FTC turned its sights to the veracity of security policies of websites. It charged that, contrary to its security claims, the well-known clothing and accessories marketer, Guess, Inc., made its customers' personal information, including credit card numbers, vulnerable to the attacks of hackers because it did not use reasonable and appropriate

---

[16] FTC Docket. No. C-4047 (April 10, 2002).
[17] FTC File No. 022 3260 (August 5, 2003).

security measures to prevent such information from being accessed at its website. The FTC entered a settlement consent order with Guess that prohibits the company from misrepresenting the extent to which it maintains and protects the security of customer personal information collected and requires that Guess maintain a security program in accordance with specifications set out in the consent order.[18]

Fair Credit Reporting Act (1970)[19]

The Fair Credit Reporting Act (FCRA, 1970) is the well-known federal legislation that requires "consumer reporting agencies" (CRAs) to adopt reasonable procedures to meet the "needs of commerce for consumer credit, personnel, insurance and other information in a manner that is fair and equitable to the consumer, with regard to confidentiality, accuracy, relevancy and proper utilization of this information in accordance with the requirements of the Act."[20] It gives consumers the right to examine and correct their credit records. Enacted in 1970, it is one of the earliest pieces of federal legislation to address the control and management of sensitive personal information directly. For this reason, it has become a basic feature of the privacy landscape in the US. The Fair and Accurate Credit Transaction Act of 2003 (FACTA) amended the FCRA and, most notably, extended the preemptions contained in the 1996 amendments to the FCRA, which were scheduled to expire January 1, 2004.[21] FACTA also amended FCRA by expanding its reach to encompass identity theft, mandating free credit reports annually and requiring the disclosure of credit scores.[22]

Scope: Consumer reporting agencies

The FCRA is a typical example of the current regime of federal regulation of personal information policy in the United States. Its reach is limited to CRAs and, in certain situations, those who use credit reports produced by CRAs or

---

[18] See also *In the Matter of Microsoft Corporation,* FTC File. No. 012 3240 (Dec. 24, 2002) in which the FTC brought charges against Microsoft for false security and privacy promises. The FTC has brought other enforcement actions as well. For example, in *Geocities,* FTC Dkt. No. C-3849 (Feb. 12, 1999) the FTC brought an enforcement action against the proprietor of a website that misrepresented the purposes for which it was collecting personal information from children and adults.

[19] 15 USC §1681 et. seq. The FCRA was recently extended. See Note 5 above.

[20] 15 USC §1681(b).

[21] PL 108-159. Signed into law on December 4, 2003; see also note 5 above.

[22] Ibid.

who supply information to CRAs.[23] Thus, it is typical of industry-specific, as opposed to information-specific, legislation.

Privacy policy

The FCRA does not require CRAs to maintain a privacy policy. The FCRA does, however, set out standards on the collection, use and communication of the consumer reports by CRAs; a selective summary of some of these requirements follows.

Disclosure to third parties

A CRA may only disclose a consumer report in the circumstances listed in the FCRA.[24] These circumstances include disclosure: (1) to a person that the CRA has a reason to believe has a legitimate business need for the information; (2) in connection with a business transaction initiated by the consumer; or, (3) to review an account to determine whether the consumer continues to meet the terms of the account.[25] As an example, a service provider may wish to verify a new user's credit history and assess how large a deposit to require before activating the service. The FCRA permits the service provider to get this information from a CRA without the consumer's consent.

Consumer access

Every CRA, on a request by a consumer, must clearly and accurately disclose to the consumer:[26] (1) all information on the consumer's file at the time of the request (except for information on credit scores or other predictors on the consumer); (2) sources of information (except for sources acquired solely for preparing an investigative report[27]); (3) identification of each recipient of the consumer report, during the 1 year period preceding the date of the consumer's request (2 years for employment purposes); (4) dates, original payees and amounts of checks on which an adverse characterization is based;

---

23 The FCRA defines a CRA as "any person, which for monetary fees, dues, or on a cooperative nonprofit basis, regularly engages in whole or in part in the practice of assembling or evaluating consumer credit information or other information on consumers for the purposes of furnishing consumer reports to third parties, and which uses any means or facility of interstate commerce for the purpose of preparing or furnishing consumer reports. 15 USC §1681 a(f)

24 15 USC §1681(b).

25 15 USC §1681(b)(3)(F).

26 15 USC §1681(g).

27 See section below for more on "identity theft."

(5) a record of all inquiries received in the 1 year period preceding the date of the consumer's request that identified the consumer in connection with a credit or insurance transaction not initiated by the consumer; and (6) if the consumer requests the credit file and not the credit score, a statement that the consumer may request and obtain a credit score.

A written summary of the consumer's rights under the FCRA is to be included with this disclosure.[28] If contacted by a consumer who believes he or she was the victim of identity theft, the CRA must provide the consumer with a summary of rights of identity theft victims.[29] A new disclosure right added to the FCRA by FACTA extends the disclosure obligation of CRAs to credit scores, as specified.[30]

Notice to Consumer

The consumer is entitled to be notified of certain disclosures and use of his information. For example, CRAs are required to give notice to consumers of disclosure of certain information for employment purposes that is likely to have an adverse effect on the consumer's ability to obtain employment.[31] Also, persons preparing investigative reports on a consumer are also subject to certain disclosure requirements.[32] Finally, the FACTA amendments require notice to the consumer when any financial institution that extends credit and regularly furnishes information to a CRA furnishes negative information about credit extended to a customer to a CRA.[33]

Reporting of adverse decisions taken by third parties based on consumer reports is likely to be relevant to a wide variety of businesses. If a user of a report takes adverse action based on information in a consumer report, it is to provide notice to the consumer of this adverse action and to give details to the consumer of the CRA that provided the consumer report to the user and of the consumer's right to obtain a copy of the report.[34] Also, if a user of a report denies credit to a consumer or a charge for credit is increased, based on other information received from a third party (not a CRA) that impacts, for example,

---

[28] 15 USC §1681(g)(c).

[29] 15 USC §1681g(d)(2). A new requirement of the 2003 amendments, this is to be prepared by the FTC in consultation with the Federal banking agencies and the national Credit Union Administration. 15 USC §1681g(d)(1).

[30] 15 USC §1681g(g).

[31] 15 USC §1681(k).

[32] 15 USC §1681(d).

[33] 15 USC §1681s-2(a).

[34] 15 USC §1681(m).

the consumer's creditworthiness, general reputation or personal characteristics, then if the consumer requests reasons for this adverse action within 60 days of learning of the action, the user must disclose the information to the consumer.

Identity theft

FACTA creates an identity theft[35] regime that imposes obligations on CRAs, resellers and users of consumer credit information relating to fraud alerts, summary of rights, blocks on information, prevention of repollution of CRA files, and notice by debt collectors with respect to fraudulent information. In accordance with the provisions of the Act, consumers may request a "fraud alert" be placed in their file with the CRA.[36] Once the fraud alert is placed,[37] users of credit reports must use reasonable means to verify that the identity of all persons making requests in connection with the alerted credit report. Furnishers of information to any CRA also have new duties under FACTA and are required to avoid reporting inaccurate information to CRAs.[38]

Furnishers are required to have in place reasonable procedures to respond to any notification that it receives from a CRA relating to information resulting from identity theft so as to prevent the furnisher from refurnishing the blocked information. Furthermore, once a furnisher has received an identity theft report from a consumer, it may not furnish such information to a CRA unless it subsequently knows or is informed that the information is correct. Relatedly, debt collectors acting on behalf of creditors once notified that any information relating to a debt that person is attempting to collect may be fraudulent or the result of identity theft, must notify the creditor of the allegation.

---

[35] Identity theft is defined as "a fraud committed using the identifying information of another person, subject to such further definition as the Commission may prescribe, by regulation." 15 USC §1681a(q)(3).

[36] 15 USC §1681(s)(f); 15 USC §1681a(q)(4) defines identity theft report as having "the meaning given that term by the rule of the Commission, and means, at minimum, a report: (A) that alleges an identity theft; (B) that is a copy of an official, valid report filed by a consumer with an appropriate Federal, State or local law enforcement agency, including the United States Postal Inspection Service, or such other government agency deemed appropriate by the Commission; and (C) the filing of which subjects the person filing the report to criminal penalties relating to the filing of false information if, in fact, the information in the report is false."

[37] The FACTA charges the FTC with preparing a model summary of rights of consumers with respect to the procedures for remedying the effects of fraud or identity theft. 15 USC §1681g(d).

[38] 15 USC §1681s-2(a); The sale or transfer of debt caused by identity theft is also prohibited. 15 USC §1681m(b)(f).

Accuracy of information

Certain obsolete information is generally prohibited from consumer reports, including bankruptcies that predate the report by more than 10 years; civil suits, judgments or records of arrest that predate the report by more than 7 years or until the governing statute of limitations has expired.[39] When a CRA prepares a consumer report, it must follow reasonable steps to ensure the maximum possible accuracy of the information.[40]

If a consumer challenges the accuracy of a consumer report, the CRA is required, free of charge, to conduct a reasonable investigation and record the current status of the information or delete the item from the file within 30 days (this period may be extended) from the date of receiving the notice from the consumer, unless the CRA has reasonable grounds to believe the dispute is irrelevant. If, after investigation, the information is found to be inaccurate, the CRA must delete or modify the information, as appropriate.[41] This reinvestigation requirement applies to resellers as well.[42]

"Opt-out"

CRAs, as well as other persons making consumer reports, may share certain information with affiliated companies.[43]

The FCRA excludes from the definition of a "consumer report" certain information that is communicated between affiliates. A CRA preparing a report can communicate to persons related by common ownership or affiliated by common corporate control information relating solely to transactions or experiences between the consumer and the CRA.

A CRA may also share other information with an affiliate so long as it is clearly and conspicuously disclosed to the consumer that the information may be so shared beforehand, and the consumer is given the opportunity to "opt-out" of such information sharing.

An affiliate may not use the information described above to make a solicitation for marketing purposes to a consumer unless this use has been

---

39 15 USC §1681(c).

40 15 USC §1681(e)(b).

41 15 USC §1681(i).

42 15 USC §1681(i).

43 15 USC §1681 a(d)(2). "person" is defined as "an individual, partnership, corporation, trust, estate, cooperative, association, government or governmental subdivision or agency, or other entity." 15 §USC 1681a(d).

clearly and conspicuously disclosed to the consumer, and the affiliate has provided the consumer with an opportunity and simple method to "opt-out" of the solicitation.[44] This "opt-out" election is valid for 5 years but does not apply to those situations where there is a preexisting business relationship between the consumer and the person making the solicitation.[45]

Preemption

The FCRA preempts inconsistent State law concerning disclosures to affiliates.[46] Pursuant to FACTA's amendment to FCRA, preemption in this and other existing subject areas is permanent.[47] This continued preemption of more restrictive state laws, such as those in California described below, has provided substantial comfort to CRAs by ensuring that they can share personal information with all of their affiliated entities, subject only to the provisions of the FCRA, and without the risk of violating conflicting state law provisions.

Medical information

While the FCRA, as amended, generally facilitates the unconsented to exchange of personal information among affiliates, it does provide more robust protection for medical information. Under the 2003 amendments to the FCRA,[48] CRAs may not furnish a report containing medical information about a consumer for employment purposes or in connection with a credit or insurance transaction without the consumer's permission. The 2003 FCRA amendments further prevent a creditor from obtaining or using medical information in determining a consumer's eligibility for credit. A Medical Information Provider, defined as a person who provides medical services, products or devices or who furnishes medical information as a

---

[44] Sec. 624. Affiliate Sharing.

[45] A pre-existing business relationship between a person and the consumer includes: a financial contract between a person and a consumer; the purchase, rental or lease by a consumer of that person's goods or services; a financial transaction during the 18-month period immediately prior to the solicitation; an inquiry by the consumer regarding a product or service offered by that person during the 3 months immediately prior to the solicitation; or any other customer relationship defined in the regulations implementing this section.

[46] 15 USC 1681(t)(b)(2).

[47] 15 USC 1681.

[48] 15 USC 1681b(g).

primary business to a CRA, must notify the government of its status as such a provider.[49]

Children's Online Privacy Protection Act (COPPA)[50]

The Children's Online Privacy Protection Act became law in 1998, and the FTC rule promulgating regulations required under COPPA came into effect on April 21, 2000 (FTC Rule)[51]. This was a response to widespread concerns about the use of the Internet to collect information about children. Because of this focus, it is much more protective of the child's interest, and much less sympathetic to the interests of businesses operating over the Internet, than are most other examples of federal legislation. As such, its features may be harbingers of more stringent privacy protections that may eventually find their way into more general legislation.

Scope

Under COPPA, an operator of a website or online service directed at children or any operator with actual knowledge that it is collecting personal information from a child is prohibited from collecting this information in a manner that violates the FTC Rule.[52] A child for these purposes is an individual under the age of 13.[53] An operator means any person who operates a commercial website on the Internet or commercial online service and collects or maintains a user's personal information or on whose behalf this information is collected or maintained.[54]

On its face, COPPA appears to be another example of privacy legislation targeted at a particular industry segment. It is noteworthy, however, that the industry segment is defined in part on the basis of the type of information collected, and not by reference to any independent industry definition. In effect, therefore, COPPA regulates the collection of a type of information – namely, information about children under the age of 13, which brings it closer to a general privacy statute than, for example, FCRA (discussed previously) or Gramm-Leach-Bliley (discussed below).

---

49 1681s-2(a). This new component of the FCRA will take effect March 4, 2005.

50 15 USC §6501 et seq.

51 The FTC Children's Online Privacy Protection Rule (16 CFR Part 312).

52 15 USC §6502 (a)(1).

53 15 USC §6501(1); FTC Rule §312.2.

54 15 USC §6501(2)(A).

Violation of the FTC Rule is treated as a violation of a rule defining an unfair or deceptive act or practice prescribed under section 57a(a)(1)(B) of the FTCA.[55] The FTC has pursued a number of actions, the first action being against Toysmart in the case discussed above. One of the FTC complaints, in this case, alleged that Toysmart collected names, email addresses and ages of children under 13 without notifying parents or getting their consent, which was in breach of COPPA. The district court order required that Toysmart immediately delete or destroy all information collected in violation of COPPA.[56]

In another enforcement action, American Pop Corn (APC) was required to pay $10,000 in damages to settle FTC charges that it collected personal information from children without parental consent from its "Jolly Time" website.[57] It had also conditioned participation in certain prize offers by requiring the children to provide more information than was necessary to participate in the activity. APC had stated in its privacy policy that it would notify parents whenever individuals under the age of 18 registered at its site and that the parents would have the option to invalidate registration, but it did not actually contact the parents as promised, and so was in breach of its privacy policy. J. Howard Beales, Director of the FTC's Bureau of Consumer Protection, said in a press release that "the civil penalty of US $10,000 reflects the relatively small number of violations in this case . . . but we hope it sends a strong message to operators of websites directed to children: we intend to enforce COPPA vigorously."[58]

Most recently, the FTC challenged a company's method of obtaining parental consent in accordance with COPPA.[59] The FTC entered into a consent order with both Mrs. Fields Cookies and Hershey's Foods Corporation after it charged that the companies violated COPPA by not obtaining parental consent or verifying the validity of parental consent before collecting information about children under the age of thirteen through their websites. Mrs. Field's paid a fine of $100,000, and Hershey paid $85,000, the largest COPPA civil penalties to date.

---

[55] 15 USC §6502(c).

[56] See reference at footnote 12 above.

[57] FTC File No. 021 3026 (February 13, 2002).

[58] FTC Press Release, February 14, 2002.

[59] FTC Press Release, February 27, 2003; see also FTC Civil Action No. 4:CV03-35 - Hershey and FTC Civil Action No. 2:03 CV205 JTG- Mrs. Fields.

Privacy policy

The operator of a website subject to COPPA is required to post a notice on the homepage of its website or online service and at each area where it is collects personal information from children: (1) what information it collects from children, (2) how it uses that information, and (3) its disclosure practices for that information.[60]

The FTC has promulgated guidelines[61] to aid persons attempting to comply with the FTC Rule. Under the guidelines, a privacy policy must: be written clearly; describe the site's practices completely and accurately; include contact information for the collector; explain the types of personal information that it collects; state whether it collects the information passively or actively; state how it will use that information; state whether it discloses the information to third parties and if it does, the types of businesses the third parties are in, the general purposes for which they will use the information and if the third parties have agreed to maintain the confidentiality, security and integrity of the personal information; inform parents that they can consent to the collection and use of their children's personal information without disclosure to third parties; explain that website operators cannot condition a child's participation in an activity on a child providing more personal information than is reasonably necessary for the activity; inform parents that they can review their child's personal information and have it deleted and refuse to permit any further collection and show parents how to make this request.

"Opt-in"

Express consent is required from parents prior to the collection, use or disclosure of a child's personal information. Parents can require an operator to provide, upon a parent's request, a description of the specific types of personal information collected on their child, to forbid the future use or maintenance or future online collection of information from that child and, upon the parent's request, to provide to the parent any personal information collected from that child.[62]

---

[60] 15 USC §6502 (b)(1)(A)(i).
[61] "You, Your Privacy Policy and COPPA - How to Comply with COPPA," issued by the FTC.
[62] 15 USC §6502(b) (1)(A) and (B).

Preemption

COPPA provides that "no state or local government may impose any liability for commercial activities by operators in interstate or foreign commerce with an activity covered by this chapter that is inconsistent with COPPA."[63] However, states are given authority under the statute to enforce compliance with the Act with respect to the entities in their jurisdiction.[64]

Gramm-Leach-Bliley Act (1999) (GLB)[65]

Enacted on November 12, 1999, GLB is one of the first items of federal legislation to mandate the creation of privacy policies by institutions that collect, use and disseminate personal information.

Scope: Financial institutions

Like the FCRA, GLB is directed to one specific industry, the US financial services industry.[66] For the purposes of this article, we are considering the privacy provisions of GLB only. GLB provides that it is the policy of Congress that each financial institution has "an affirmative and continuing obligation to respect the privacy of its customers and to protect the security and confidentiality of customers' nonpublic personal information".[67] GLB lists the agencies or authorities that are to establish appropriate standards for financial institutions. These agencies and authorities are subject to GLB jurisdiction and are to prescribe regulations necessary to carry out the purposes of subchapter 1 (disclosure of nonpublic personal information ("NPI")) of GLB.[68] Subchapter 1 limits the circumstances when a financial institution may disclose NPI about a consumer to nonaffiliated third parties and requires a financial institution to disclose to all of its consumers its privacy policies and practices for information sharing with affiliates and nonaffiliated third parties. The FTC enacted the "Privacy of Consumer

---

[63] 15 USC §6502(d).

[64] 15 USC §6504(a).

[65] See footnote 1 above for reference.

[66] GLB is in fact a comprehensive revision of the federal scheme for regulation of the delivery of financial services; its primary goal was to allow financial institutions, insurance and investment companies to merge to become "one stop shops."

[67] 15 USC §6801(a).

[68] 15 USC §6804(a)(1).

Financial Information: Final Rule" (Privacy Rule), which became effective on November 13, 2000, and required full compliance by July 1, 2001.[69]

Under GLB, a financial institution (FI) is broadly defined as an entity "the business of which is engaging in financial activities," as described in Section 4(k) of the Bank Holding Company Act.[70] The Privacy Rule applies to an institution that is significantly engaged in these activities. The Privacy Rule gives examples of FIs, such as: a retailer extending credit by issuing its own credit card directly to consumers; an automobile dealership that, as a usual part of its business, leases automobiles on a nonoperating basis for more than 90 days; a check-cashing business; a business that operates a travel agency in connection with financial services; and mortgage brokers.[71] An FI does not, according to a recent Federal court opinion, include lawyers.[72] The FTC has jurisdiction over a FI only in the event that the FI in question is not subject to the enforcement authority of another agency listed in the Act.[73]

Privacy policy

Under GLB, FIs may not directly or through any affiliate disclose to a nonaffiliated third party any NPI of a consumer unless it has provided the consumer with a notice that complies with GLB.[74] Under GLB, FIs are required to disclose their privacy policies at the time of establishing a customer relationship with a consumer and then no less than annually for a continuing

---

[69] 16 CFR Part 313.

[70] 12 USC 1843(k).

[71] 16 CFR Part 313, 313.3(k)(2). Refer to this section for more examples.

[72] In *New York State Bar Ass'n v. Federal Trade Comm'n*, F. Supp.2d, 2003 WL 21919841 (Aug 11, 2003), the U.S. District Court for the District of Columbia issued a preliminary ruling that the FTC may have acted beyond its authority and engaged in arbitrary and capricious action when in an April 2002 letter it determined that lawyers are covered by the privacy notification mandates of the GLB Act. The court denied the FTC's motions to dismiss complaints by the ABA and the New York State Bar Association that challenge the FTC's position that the GLB Act's privacy rules extends to lawyers who provide legal services in areas of practice including real estate settlements, tax planning, and tax preparation. While the court only refused to dismiss the complaints, the opinion stated that it appeared that Congress did not intend for the privacy provisions of the GLB Act to apply to attorneys.

[73] 15 USC §6805(7). These agencies include Federal banking agencies (eg Office of the Comptroller of the Currency, Board of Governors of the Federal Reserve System) and other Federal regulatory authorities (eg National Credit Union Administration, Securities and Exchange Commission). The agencies were all to issue rules to implement subchapter 1.

[74] 15 USC §6802(a).

relationship with a customer.[75] The policy needs to be clear and conspicuous, in writing or electronic form or any other form permitted under the regulations prescribed under GLB, stating the FI's policies and practices.[76] The information to be included in the policy includes: the policies and practices of the FI concerning disclosure of NPI to nonaffiliated third parties (including the categories of person to whom NPI is or may be disclosed); the policies and practices of an FI concerning disclosure of NPI of persons who are no longer customers of the FI; the categories of NPI that are collected by FI; the policies that the FI maintains to protect the confidentiality and security of NPI; and any disclosures required under the FCRA concerning disclosures to affiliates.[77]

The notice must also include details of the consumer's right to "opt-out."

"Opt-out"

GLB is an "opt-out" statute. It provides that a FI may not disclose to a nonaffiliated third party any NPI unless: (i) the FI has given the consumer a privacy notice meeting the requirements summarized above and informing the consumer that the information may be disclosed to a third party; (ii) the consumer is given the opportunity before the information is disclosed to direct it cannot be disclosed to a third party; and (iii) the consumer is told how to exercise this option.[78]

There are exceptions to the notice and "opt-out" requirements, in particular when disclosure of NPI is necessary: to effect, administer or enforce a transaction requested by the consumer; to protect the confidentiality or security of the FI's records on the consumer, or to protect against fraud.[79]

---

[75] 15 USC 6803(a). The frequency of disclosure depends on whether an individual is a customer or a consumer. A customer is entitled to receive an FI's privacy notice automatically, consumers however are only entitled to receive a privacy notice if the company shares the consumer's NPI with companies not affiliated with it. A consumer is an individual who has obtained a product or service from an FI for personal or family reasons, a customer is a consumer that has an ongoing relationship with an FI. See 15 USC §6809 (9) and the brief from the FTC website "In Brief: The Financial Privacy Requirements of the Gramm-Leach-Bliley Act". Any reference to consumer in this article includes customers for the purposes of GLB.

[76] USC §6803(a)(1) to (3).

[77] This is the "opt out" requirement that is considered above at Section 3.2(g). The other requirements are listed in USC 15 §6803(b).

[78] 15 USC §6802(b)(1).

[79] See 15 USC §6802(e) for a list of general exceptions.

There is also an exception in which the FI must give notice to the customer if it provides NPI to its third-party service providers or the service providers of other financial institutions with which the FI has entered into a joint marketing agreement, subject to certain conditions that are listed in the Act.[80]

Preemption

GLB preempts state law to the extent that the state law is inconsistent with GLB, and then only to the extent of the inconsistency. State laws are not considered inconsistent where the protection provided under state law is more protective than provided under the privacy provisions of GLB. The FTC, after consultation with any other agencies that have jurisdiction, has the authority to determine this issue. States are therefore free to develop more protective laws regarding the collection and dissemination of personal information.[81] Many states have, in fact, done so (see below). In this regard, GLB is analogous to the EU's Data Protection Directive, which establishes minimum privacy standards on a pan-European basis, but leaves EU member states free to adopt their own more protective personal privacy laws.

Health Insurance Portability and Accountability Act (HIPAA)[82]

Unlike GLB, HIPPA is an example of information-specific legislation. It concerns the use of a patient's "protected health information"[83] by health care providers (hospitals, physicians), health insurers and health care clearinghouses. Most relevant health providers are required to comply with the rule implementing this legislation (HIPPA Privacy Rule)[84] from April 14, 2003.

Patients are guaranteed access to their medical records and are given certain controls over how their PHI is used and disclosed. Under the HIPAA Privacy Rule, patients are to give specific authorization before their PHI is disclosed in non-routine circumstances, for example, where it is not used for a patient's

---

80 15 USC §6802(b)(2).

81 15 USC §6807(a) and (b).

82 Public Law 104-191.

83 Protected health information is defined as "individually identifiable health information" that is (1) transmitted by electronic media; (2) maintained in electronic media; or (3) transmitted or maintained in any other form or medium. "Individually identifiable health information" is widely defined to include information on (1) the physical or mental health or condition of an individual; (2) the provision of health care services; or (3) payment for the provision of health care services. 45 C.F. R. §164.50.

84 45 CFR Parts 160 to 164.

treatment, such as being given to an employer or for marketing purposes.[85] PHI generally can be used or disclosed for treatment, payment purposes or health care operations without written patient consent. Entities covered by the legislation need to provide details of their privacy practices and patients' privacy rights to patients.

The HIPAA Privacy Rule does not supersede state privacy laws that offer more stringent privacy protections. States are free to enact laws that provide greater protection than HIPAA. A state law can meet the "more stringent requirement" among other ways, by prohibiting the use or disclosure of PHI permitted by HIPAA, providing the individual with greater access or rights to PHI than HIPAA, allowing greater information to be provided to an individual regarding disclosure and rights and remedies, and having a more narrow scope or duration. Very large numbers of state laws, for example, those covering mental health, HIV infections, AIDS information and the subpoenaing of patient records, are not preempted by HIPAA.

Electronic Communications Privacy Act (ECPA)[86]

The ECPA is another example of information-specific federal legislation. This act concerns itself with electronic communications in general and codifies the warrant requirements for the interception of electronic communications and creates privacy protection for stored electronic messages.

Title I of the Act concerns communication streams (communications while in transit) for both voice and data and prohibits: the interception of this type of communication; the disclosure of intercepted communications; use of intercepted communications; and intentional use of interception devices. It permits system operators to intercept, disclose and use these interceptions for the purposes of their business or pursuant to a warrant to assist in law enforcement.[87]

Title II concerns stored information, and it protects stored wire and electronic communications and transactional records. It prohibits unlawful

---

[85] The final rules for consent and authorization were recently issued by the Bush Administration. 67 Fed. Reg. 53181-53273.

[86] USC 18 §2701 et seq.

[87] 18 USC 2518.

access and disclosure.[88] Importantly, according to a recent court decision, inadvertent collection of website visitor data does not violate the ECPA, which only prohibits the "intentional" interception of information.[89] However, this inadvertent collection might be the basis of a negligence action.[90]

State laws

In response to public pressure, the states have been exceedingly active in their adoption of privacy protection legislation. By one count, some 5,000 privacy bills have been proposed in the various states, and many have been enacted.[91] As a result, businesses in the United States must cope with a patchwork of state legislation concerning privacy. Legislation in large states such as California is particularly important since it can easily become a de facto national standard.

Inconsistency with GLB

Several states have laws that provide higher standards of protection than GLB, including, in some cases, an "opt-in" rather than an "opt-out" approach. That is, if a financial institution wishes to disclose nonpublic personal information about its consumers to non-affiliated third parties, it is required to have the consumer's express consent prior to disclosure. GLB only supersedes a state law to the extent that it is inconsistent with GLB.[92] If the FTC determines that a state law provides greater protection than GLB, the state law is preserved.[93] Interested parties may petition the FTC for a determination. The states that have petitioned the FTC for a determination include Connecticut, Illinois, New Mexico, North Dakota, and Vermont. The FTC has posted on its website the determinations for Connecticut, Illinois, North Dakota, and Vermont. It

---

88 Title II has been relied on by plaintiffs in a recent case concerning privacy and the use of cookies: *In re Doubleclick Inc.*, 154 F. Supp. 2d 497 (2003). In this case the plaintiffs argued that placing cookies on their hard drives amounted to unauthorized access as defined under Title II of the Act (18 USC §2701(a)). However, Doubleclick successfully argued that it fell within the exception at 18 USC §2701 (c)(2) where conduct has been authorized by a user concerning a communication intended for that user.

89 *In re Pharmatrak Inc.*, No. 00-11672-JLT (D. Mass. Nov. 6, 2003).

90 Ibid.

91 Thibideau, Patrick. *FTC Eyes Telemarketing As Privacy Heats Up.* Computerworld, December 9, 2002, https://www.computerworld.com/article/2578080/ftc-eyes-telemarketing-as-privacy-heats-up.html.

92 15 U.S.C. §6807(a).

93 15 U.S.C. §6807(b).

has concluded that a Connecticut statute that prohibits the disclosure of "financial records" unless authorized by the customer is consistent with GLB. In reaching this conclusion, the FTC found that compliance by Connecticut financial institutions with both federal and state law requirements is not impossible, and so there is no "inconsistency" between that state and federal law. The FTC also found that a North Dakota privacy statute that prohibits FIs from disclosing customer information without the customer's express consent or "opt-in" was not inconsistent with GLB because it provided for an exemption from its state law requirements if the FI complies with GLB. Thus, a North Dakota FI is able to simply comply with the federal requirements or, if it does not fall under the exemption, must follow the state law "opt-in" requirements.[94]

California

As noted, legal developments in California often become the de facto standard for businesses operating across the US.

The California Financial Information Privacy Act (known as SB 1) requires financial institutions to provide a specified written form to a consumer relative to the sharing of the consumer's nonpublic personal information.[95] A consumer would also be able to instruct a financial institution not to share his nonpublic personal information with affiliates or nonaffiliated financial companies that a financial institution has contracted with to provide financial products and services. Permission of the consumer would be required before a financial institution could share the nonpublic personal information with other nonaffiliated companies. However, the extension of FCRA's preemption power by the FACTA amendments[96] nullifies the sections of the California Act related to information sharing among affiliates.

California has also imposed additional obligations on CRAs to accept "security alerts" from consumers and to impose a "security freeze" on the release of any information from a consumer's file held by a CRA.[97] However, it is unclear

---

[94] See letters from FTC to the Connecticut Commission of the Department of Banking, June 7, 2002, https://portal.ct.gov/DOB/Legal-Resources/Legal-Resources/FTC-Response-to-Banking-Department-Re-Connecticut-Privacy-Laws, and to the North Dakota Commissioner of Department of Banking and Financial Institutions, June 28, 2001, referenced at https://www.ftc.gov/news-events/press-releases/2001/06/north-dakota-financial-privacy-law-not-preempted.

[95] SB 1, Chapter 241, California Statutes of 2003. Effective July 1, 2004.

[96] See note 21 above for reference; see also FCRA section above.

[97] See Section 1785.15, and 1785.11.1 to 1785.11.6 of the California Civil Code.

whether this statute has now been preempted by the FCRA, as neither the FCRA nor FACTA requires any conduct with respect to a security freeze, thus, arguably, allowing the states to regulate in this area. Because the security freeze does not relate to the content of the credit report (which is preempted under FCRA[98]) but instead is a requirement restricting access to the report.

A new law, the California Database Protection Act (CDPA), came into force on July 1, 2003, requiring state agencies or businesses conducted in California that own or license computerized data that includes personal information to immediately disclose any breach of security to any California resident whose unencrypted personal information was or is reasonably believed to have been acquired by an unauthorized person.[99] An aggrieved customer can pursue a private right of action to recover damages.[100] Because most companies do not segregate their data regarding California consumers, the CDPA has the potential to have a national impact. Indeed, US Senator Diane Feinstein introduced a bill on June 26, 2003, called the "Notification of Risk to Personal Data Act," which is modeled on this California law and would place similar standards to those in California on a national level.[101]

In an effort to limit the increasing incidence of identity theft, another law came into effect in California on July 1, 2002, restricting the disclosure of social security numbers (SSN) by any person or entity.[102] It requires the transmission of SSN via the internet to be encrypted, and it prohibits private companies from publicly posting or displaying SSN; requiring an individual to use his SSN to access an Internet website (unless another authentication device is required to access the website), and printing an individual's SSN on any materials sent to an individual unless state or federal law requires otherwise.[103]

California has also recently enacted privacy legislation in other areas as well.[104] The Online Privacy and Disclosure Act imposes an obligation on every commercial website operator doing business in California to maintain the privacy of Californian residents and to notify them of its privacy policies and

---

98 15 USC 1681(t)(b)(2); section 625(b)(1)(E).

99 Sections 1798.82 and 1798.29 of the California Civil Code.

100 Section 1798.84 of the California Civil Code.

101 S 1356 IS. The bill was referred to the Committee on the Judiciary and on November 4, the Subcommittee on Terrorism, Technology and Homeland Security held hearings.

102 Section 1798.5 of the California Civil Code.

103 This law does not apply to local or state agencies, but SB 25 (California) proposes to extend the prohibition on the public posting or display of SSNs to state and local agencies.

104 Please refer to the website of the California Department of Justice for a description of California privacy laws as of publication of this book, https://oag.ca.gov/privacy.

practices where the operator collects personally identifiable information of a Californian resident.[105] Also, SB-27 requires a business that discloses a customer's personal information, including information related to income or purchases, to a third party for direct marketing purposes to provide the customer within 30 days of that customer's request with the names and addresses of those who received the information.[106]

Minnesota

Minnesota has passed one of the most sweeping privacy laws in the nation. Under the Minnesota law, which took effect in March 2003, all Internet service providers (ISPs) who provide services to consumers in Minnesota may disclose personally identifiable information only in certain, limited circumstances,[107] or where the consumer has given its consent.[108] The request to disclose must reasonably describe the types of persons to whom the information may be disclosed and the anticipated uses of the information. The Minnesota statute requires ISPs to take reasonable steps to maintain the security and privacy of a consumer's personally identifiable information. Consumers may bring individual enforcement actions and are entitled to damages greater than US $500 or actual damages, but no class actions may be brought.

Federal legislative privacy proposals

On-line Privacy Act (Hollings Privacy Proposal S 2201)

Scope

This Bill was considered by a number of Senate Committees and placed on the Senate Legislative calendar under General Orders, in 2002. A spokesperson from Senator Hollings' Washington office stated that the Bill might be reintroduced in the second session of the 108th Congress. It extends privacy legislation in the US dramatically by covering all data (as opposed to

---

[105] AB No. 68, Chapter 829, California Statutes of 2003.

[106] SB 27, Chapter 505, California Statutes of 2003. The requirements become effective January 1, 2005; also, as such information sharing relates to affiliates parties the FCRA preemption issue discussed above may be at issue.

[107] Chapter 395-S.F. No. 2908.

[108] Other circumstances are: where the disclosure is incident to the ordinary course of business of the ISP; to another ISP for the purposes of reporting or preventing violations of the published acceptable use policy or the customer service agreement of the ISP; if the consumer has consented to the disclosure; or if required by law.

classes of data covered by, for example, GLB) collected by ISPs, online service providers and those who use information from these sources. It covers personally identifiable information (PII) collected online only. Different levels of compliance are required for different levels of data, as follows.

Privacy policy

A provider cannot collect PII online unless it provides clear and conspicuous notice to the user disclosing: the specific types of information to be collected; methods of collecting and using the information collected; all disclosure practices of that provider, including whether it will be disclosed to third parties; and the user is to be informed if there are any changes to the privacy policy.

"Opt-out" and "Opt-in"

Sensitive PII (that is PII concerning health, political party affiliation, race, religious beliefs, sexual orientation, social security number and sensitive, financial information) cannot be collected or disclosed unless the user has expressly consented to the disclosure and the use of that information, prior to or at the time of collection.

Non-sensitive PII (that is, all other PII other than sensitive PII) cannot be collected or disclosed or otherwise used by an operator unless it provides "robust" notice in addition to "clear and conspicuous notice," and the user is given the opportunity to "opt-out".

Operators are to provide users with reasonable access to the information and with a reasonable opportunity to suggest corrections.

Enforcement

If PII is disclosed by an operator in breach of the Act or the security, confidentiality or integrity of PII is compromised, and there is disclosure of that information, the provider is to inform the user. Violation of this Act is an "unfair and deceptive act" for the purposes of the FTCA. A user can bring private actions for certain breaches.

Preemption

The Act proposes to preempt State statutes covering the same subject matter but not common law.

Consumer Privacy Protection Act (2003) (Stearns, HR 1636)

Scope

House of Representative Committees considered this Bill in 2002. It was reintroduced to the 108th Congress in March 2003 and then referred to the House Subcommittee on Commerce, Trade and Consumer Protection. It applies to the collection of PII from consumers only and applies to information collected on and offline, in contrast to the Holling's Privacy proposal that only covers online personal information.

Privacy policy

Data collection organizations (DCO) are to establish a privacy policy covering the collection, sale, disclosure and use of consumer PII. It is to be "clear and concise" and provided to consumers at the time of collection of the data. Consumers are to have the opportunity to prevent the sale and disclosure of PII to any DCOs that are not "information sharing partners" of the DCOs. Privacy policies are to be free of charge and accessible.

Enforcement

The FTC can more aggressively facilitate consumer access to information regarding identity theft. Senior management officials of all companies collecting PII are to approve information security programs. The FTC is the primary enforcement agency of the act. Private causes of action are barred. The Bill mandates ADR or arbitration for resolving disputes. It also mandates the creation of a self-regulatory organization.

Social Security On-line Privacy Protection Act (HR 70 IH)

This bill was introduced by Representative Frelinghuysen on January 7, 2003, and referred to the House Subcommittee on Commerce, Trade, and Consumer Protection. The bill would seek to regulate the use by interactive services of social security account numbers and related personably identifiable information.

Self-regulation

In the absence of general federal legislation, members of the online industry have "clubbed" together to put in place a voluntary initiative in the US. The most visible example is the "TRUSTe" seal program, where a branded seal or logo is awarded with a "sealmark" indicating websites that comply with the "TRUSTe" privacy principles, consumer resolution process and monitoring of the website by TRUSTe. If a website has a "trustmark," this signifies that the website will disclose what personal information is being collected, how it is used, who it is shared with, who collects it, the user's options, the website's security procedures and how the users can correct information. "TRUSTe" periodically updates its license agreements with companies that certify or annual recertify, and in December 2002, it made the requirements of its trustmark program more stringent by prohibiting companies from changing a consumer's privacy preferences for 12 months and tightening "opt-out" requirements so that it is easier for customers to prevent the sharing of their personal information.

Network Advertising Initiative ("NAI"), together with the FTC, has developed the NAI principles concerning the notice that NAI members must provide consumers with concerning the use of cookies. This is more relevant to Internet access and websites, but this may also be relevant in the wireless environment.

Security

Communications Assistance for Law Enforcement Act (CALEA)[109]

The aim of this Act is to ensure that law enforcement agencies can conduct interception. Telecommunication carriers are to ensure their systems can: isolate the content of targeted communications transmitted by a carrier within its area of service; isolate information associated with targeted communications (for example, origin and destination of communication, call identifying information); and carry out intercepts without the target being aware of the interception. If carriers comply with industry standards for surveillance capabilities, they are deemed to be in compliance for the purposes of CALEA. Where industry standards are nonexistent or deemed deficient, the Federal Communications Commission ("FCC") can establish standards by rules. Any such FCC rule must be reasonable in terms of the cost and impact on privacy.

USA PATRIOT Act[110]

Enacted in law in the very early aftermath of the September 11th terrorist attacks on the World Trade Center and the Pentagon, the PATRIOT Act makes important amendments to surveillance laws, among other types of law, and has a heavy impact on privacy rights. In the field of telecommunications, for example, the Act increases the number of surveillance obligations a carrier will need to

---

[109] See footnote 7 above for reference.

[110] See footnote 5 above for reference.

comply with. For example, pen/trap orders[111] were only valid in the federal district where they were granted. Now federal courts may approve universal jurisdiction in the US for them.[112] Section 206 expands orders under the Foreign Intelligence Surveillance Act (1976) to include roving surveillance.[113] The definitions of "pen registers" and "trap and trace devices" are amended to include equipment that monitors and addresses routing information for Internet communications. Section 222 preserves the position on technical mandates and other requirements on service providers to provide technical assistance to the authorities.

Beyond the realm of telecommunications, the customer identification program (CIP) of the Act requires the financial services industry to verify the identity of any person seeking to open an account, to maintain records of the information used to verify a person's identity and determine whether a customer is on any government list of known or suspected terrorists or terrorist organizations.[114] In accordance with the PATRIOT Act, the US Treasury has released final regulations created to prevent the funding of terrorist activities and money laundering. Banks and other financial institutions had until October 1, 2003, to comply with the federal regulations, which require them to put in place processes that allow for a risk-based identification of all new customers.[115] Importantly, under the rules, financial institutions need to verify the identity only of new customers.

Wireless Communications and Public Safety Act[116]

This Act, known as the "911 Act," covers four specific areas. It requires the FCC to designate 911 as the universal emergency number for wireless providers, and the FCC is to support states in rolling out an emergency communications

---

[111] Pen registers and trap and trace devices record/decode various types of dialing and signaling information used in processing and routing a communication, such as the signals that identify the digits dialed (outgoing) or the originating number (incoming). Monitoring content requires additional authorization.

[112] USA PATRIOT Act, Section 216.

[113] Authorized investigators can intercept all of a suspect's electronic communication or wire regardless of where the suspect is.

[114] USA PATRIOT Act, Section 326.

[115] US Treasury Press Release: *Treasury and Federal Financial Regulators Issue Final Patriot Act Regulations on Customer Identification* (April 30, 2003) at https://www.federalreserve.gov/boarddocs/press/bcreg/2003/200304302/default.htm.

[116] See footnote 6 above for reference.

network. It equates liability protection from technical failures on wireless users and providers with that of wireline providers and users.

Wireless providers are prohibited from sharing location information in non-emergency situations to third parties unless disclosure is expressly authorized by the user ("opt-in") (47 USC §222(f)). It provides immunity for emergency medical service providers and emergency dispatch providers.

The FCC has also issued the "Wireless E911 rules" to improve the reliability of the E911 wireless services by providing emergency personnel with location information. These rules are divided into two phases. Phase I required carriers, when a call is made, to transmit the phone number of the wireless handset and the location of the handset's cellular base station to a designated emergency service provider. Phase II requires the carriers to implement more precise location technology and is scheduled to be completed by December 31, 2005.

European Union (EU) Privacy Law

EU Data Protection Directive (1995)[117]

Any survey of privacy protection laws affecting United States businesses would not be complete without reference to the EU Data Protection Directive. The Directive not only affects persons doing business in the EU, but it also significantly restricts the cross-border transfer of personal information to jurisdictions outside the EU. In this way, it has direct relevance to the many businesses that operate both in the EU and in the US and that wish to collect and utilize personal information across the international borders.

In contrast to the position in the US, the Directive applies to the processing of all forms of personal data (online and offline), and it prevents disclosure of personal data to countries where personal data is not equally protected.[118] There is an "opt-in" requirement for the processing or transfer of sensitive personal data.[119] "Opt-out" is required for the processing of all other personal

---

[117] See footnote 3 above for reference. The EU Directive has also become a model for some other jurisdictions. For example, Hong Kong has adopted a "Personal Data Privacy Ordinance" that is based largely on the Data Protection Directive. The guidelines require data collectors to have a privacy statement on their website and to use encryption technology for sensitive data. There is also a voluntary anti-spamming code in place in Hong Kong that companies can subscribe to, if they so choose. If they do so, they will be entitled to use a particular logo indicating that they have adopted this practice.

[118] Article 25 of the directive.

[119] Article 8 of the directive.

data.[120] Also, each Member State is required to have a regulator to enforce the protection of personal data legislation.

This directive required all EU Member States to implement its obligations under their own laws by October 1998. The EU Commission issued its first report on the implementation of the directive on May 5, 2003.[121] According to this report, while all of the fifteen Member States have implemented national laws in accordance with the Directive, not all completed such implementations by the deadline nor have all completed the procedural process to formally notify such implementations.

The United States is not a country in which personal data is protected to the extent required by the EU Directive. For this reason, any transfer of personal data to the United States from an EU country would violate the Directive. This creates an obvious problem for any company doing business both in the EU and in the US; it also creates a problem for companies in the United States who wish to provide to European customers any services (for example, investment or portfolio management services) operated from servers located in the United States.

To alleviate this problem, a set of "Safe Harbor Principles" have been adopted as a result of negotiations between the US Department of Commerce and the European Commission.[122] Under these principles, US organizations can choose to participate and comply with the requirements of the principles. The requirements include EU-based principles for notice, choice, onward transfer, access, security, data integrity, and enforcement. Companies must "self-certify" with the US Department of Commerce that they meet these requirements. Alternatively, in certain circumstances, model clauses that have been approved

---

[120] Article 7 of the directive.

[121] COM (2003) 265 Final, at https://eur-lex.europa.eu/LexUriServ/LexUriServ.do?uri=COM%3A2003%3A0265%3AFIN%3AEN%3APDF. This report stated, among many other things, that "only few Member States implemented the Directive on time. Most Member States only notified implementing measures to the Commission in the years 2000 and 2001, and Ireland has still not notified its recent implementation." [As of the publication of this collection, the Directive has of course been superseded by the General Data Protection Regulation, which can be found at www.gdpr-info.eu. —TH]

[122] European Commission Decision c. (2000) 2441.

by the European Commission can be used in contract documentation[123] or consent of a consumer can be obtained to the transfer.[124]

In the experience of the authors, few businesses in the United States self-certify under the safe harbor rules[125]; the vast majority prefer to thrust the burden of compliance on their European customers by requiring them to obtain their customers' consent to the transfer of information out of the EU. One might question whether, in the long run, this will not place the United States at a competitive disadvantage, particularly in fields such as financial services, where the collection and maintenance of sensitive personal information is a fundamental part of the service to be provided.

Conclusion

Current US privacy policy is piecemeal and haphazard. Federal and state legislative and regulatory initiatives have accumulated into a web of overlapping and sometimes conflicting provisions that make for hazardous navigation by businesses in a wide range of industries. The future of the data protection law in the US will be interesting to watch. Clearly, there are a number of growing tensions between the contrasts in different approaches to this protection that may need to be resolved. Within the US itself, there is tension between the divergent approaches at the state and federal levels, between "opt-in" and "opt-out." between industry-specific and information-specific legislation, and between privacy and security. Complicating matters still further is the EU Directive, which affects any US business that needs access to personal information about Europeans, whether to do business in Europe directly or simply to offer information-based services to European customers.

---

123 European Commission Decision 2001/497/EC and EC Decision 2002/16/EC.

124 Article 26 of the directive. The Directive on Personal Data in the Electronic Communication Sector (COM/2000/385) was adopted on July 12, 2002. It introduces some significant new privacy protections and replaces the Telecommunications Data Protection Directive (97/66/EC), which applied the general principles set out in the Data Protection Directive as specific rules for the telecommunications sector. It is to be implemented in the national law of EU Member States by October 31, 2003. It also introduces significant new privacy protections in the areas of e-mail spamming, cookies, use of location data and security.

125 As of January 29, 2004, only 449 U.S. businesses had self-certified to the safe harbor list through the U.S. Department of Commerce. [As of the publication of this collection, the safe harbor has been replaced by the Privacy Shield. See www.privacyshield.gov. —TH]

There is no question that a single, uniform approach at the federal level would greatly simplify the compliance problems faced by businesses. However, it is much less clear that such legislation would adequately protect the privacy concerns of many citizens. If one were to generalize from the current patchwork of federal and state legislation, one would conclude that, in general, federal legislation has been dominated by concerns over security and uniformity, while state legislation has focused almost exclusively on the privacy rights of the individual. Any movement in the federal direction would be likely to continue this theme, with individual privacy rights taking a back seat to security and business needs. Ironically, in the international context, the federal approach is more likely to exacerbate the gap in privacy protection between the United States and Europe, while states' concerns would tend to narrow the divide.

There is no obvious or immediate solution to these tensions. In the current political climate, it is quite unlikely that the United States Congress would be disposed to look to the EU model for anything, including personal data protection; it seems equally unlikely that the EU would soften its rules in consideration of US concerns. Similarly, the extraordinary number of privacy bills introduced in state legislatures in the United States, fueled perhaps in part by growing concern over problems of identity theft, suggests that state privacy initiatives will continue unabated at the state level, while security and large business concerns will continue to dominate dialogue at the federal level.

The authors believe that this confusing and contradictory process is not only costly and difficult for businesses to comply with, but also fuels general anxiety over the security of personal information. Compared with an individual in Europe, an individual in the United States has no simple baseline assurance about the security of his or her personal information, and has a growing apprehension that the situation has slipped badly out of control. Identity-theft advertisements, intended to offer protective services to consumers, actually tend to reinforce the belief that they cannot protect themselves. Notices that are required for particular industries, such as the HIPPA-mandated notices everyone now receives in connection with medical procedures, lead naturally to the question of what is happening to personal information in contexts where no such notice is given. All of these lead to a growing lack of confidence in the security of the system, which in the long run, seems likely to be harmful both to individuals and to the businesses attempting to serve them.

Comprehensive solutions are unlikely to emerge at the state level, but at the same time, the federal government has shown itself generally disinclined to give privacy concerns the same weight as other, competing interests. In the international sphere, therefore, we expect that the United States will lag its European rivals for some years to come in according comprehensive privacy protection to its citizens. Whether this will harm United States businesses will depend to a large extent on the relative importance the public accords its privacy values.

The Ownership and Exploitation of Personal Identity in the New Media Age*

Introduction

The layperson thinks of property in binary terms: a thing is mine, or it is not. This probably stems from a very primitive, tactile sense of possession — if it's in my hand, I've got control over the thing, and I can prevent you from using it, which makes it mine.[1] Among children, disputes over ownership are resolved this way, and a tug of war resolves ownership by resolving possession. For a child, possession is ten-tenths of the law.[2]

As lawyers, we are trained and accustomed to thinking of property in a somewhat more nuanced way — as a "bundle of rights."[3] A child's ownership of a baseball bat gives her the right to possess it, to autograph it, to burn it, to sell it, to play baseball with it (subject, of course, to the rules of the game), but not the right to hit someone with it or to smash a window with it. Ownership of real estate is even more constrained by rule, regulation, and custom.[4] But the binary underpinnings remain: as to each right in the bundle, either I own it, or I don't; either I have the right to exclude others from its use, or I don't.[5] Some of the rights may be linked; others may be divisible, but each of them is

---

 Originally published in 12 J. Marshall Rev. Intell. Prop. L. 1 (2012). Reprinted with permission. The author gratefully acknowledges the insights and assistance of Gina Perini, Veronica Louie, Tristan Walsh and the editorial staff of the *John Marshall Review of Intellectual Property Law* in the preparation of this article.

1 See Robert P. Merges, *Justifying Intellectual Property* (Cambridge, MA: Harvard University Press, 2011), 100. ("The very definition of a property right is a claim 'good against the world,' often described as a 'right to exclude others from the particular legal interest involved. . . ."). I recommend to the reader Robert Merges's excellent disquisition. Id.

2 One easily overlooks how potent such memories and images can be in our more adult conceptions.

3 See Michael A. Heller, "The Boundaries of Private Property," 108 *Yale L. J.* 1163, 1192 n.150 (1999) (documenting broad use of the "bundle of rights" metaphor in US cases since 1940); Van Lindberg, *Intellectual Property and Open Source*, 3rd ed. (Sebastopol, CA: O'Reilly Media, 2008), 17 (describing property as a collection of independent rights, which "may be individually sold, licensed, given away, or destroyed").

4 See Heller, *supra* note 3, at 1173–74 (1999) (discussing the bevy of modern rules and regulations affecting real property).

5 See Michael A. Carrier, "Cabining Intellectual Property Through a Property Paradigm," 54 *Duke L. J.* 1, 52 (2004) (positing that the right to exclude is the most fundamental property right).

thought of as mine or not.[6] The "bundle of rights" phrase itself calls to mind an image of a bundle of sticks held in the hand, rather like the arrows held in the claw of the American Eagle. "I've got them; they're mine; you're excluded."

We have even extended this binary conception into the realm of intellectual property,[7] which, by its nature, is not capable of physical possession.[8] By federal statute, and indeed by the Constitution, patents and copyrights have an owner — the inventor or author — who holds in his hand the bundle of rights defined by the statute.[9] Those rights fundamentally permit the owner to exclude use by others.[10] By common law and state statute, trade secrets are much the same: they are owned by the person to whom they provide a competitive advantage.[11] The only difference is that they can slip through the owner's fingers rather easily if they are disclosed without restriction.[12] Patents, copyrights, and trade secrets are capable of joint ownership,[13] but that only means that more than one person or entity is on one side of the binary line; the whole world is on the other side.

---

6 John Page, "Grazing Rights and Public Lands in New Zealand and the Western United States: A Comparative Study," 49 *Nat. Resources J.* 403, 404–05 (2009) ("This fragmentation allowed society to treat private property rights as severable, such that the hallmark rights . . . are distinct 'sticks.' This notion of property as a divisible and relative bundle of rights has specific resonance in relation to private rights in public land."). Of course, there is the possibility of joint ownership, where two or more persons share ownership as against the rest of the world. See generally *United States v. Craft*, 535 U.S. 274, 279–82 (2002) (describing the three principal notions of joint ownership in US law).

7 Lindberg, *supra* note 3, at 17 (applying the "bundle of rights" paradigm to intellectual property).

8 Xuan-Thao N. Nguyen, "Holding Intellectual Property," 39 *Ga. L. Rev.* 1155, 1185 (2005).

9 See U.S. Const. art. I, §8, cl. 8 (guaranteeing authors and inventors exclusive rights to their writings and discoveries); 35 U.S.C. §261 (2012); 17 U.S.C. §201; *Beech Aircraft Corp. v. EDO Corp.*, 990 F.2d 1237, 1248 (Fed. Cir. 1993) (stating patent rights initially vest in the inventor).

10 17 U.S.C. §106; 35 U.S.C. §271.

11 Restatement (First) of Torts §757 (1939) ("A trade secret may consist of any formula, pattern, device or compilation of information which is used in one's business, and which gives him an opportunity to obtain an advantage over his competitors who do not know or use it.").

12 See *Ruckelshaus v. Monsanto Co.*, 467 U.S. 986, 1002 (1984) (stating that one may extinguish one's right to a trade secret either by publicly disclosing it or by failing to take reasonable measures to maintain its secrecy).

13 17 U.S.C. §201(a) (providing that authors of "a joint work are co-owners of copyright in the work"); 35 U.S.C. § 116 ("When an invention is made by two or more persons jointly, they shall apply for patent jointly . . .").

Trademarks are different. In the first place, they cannot be owned "in gross" — no one can control all uses of a word or symbol;[14] the rights of the owner are necessarily linked to the use to which the mark is put.[15] Furthermore, it is said that trademark law is intended to protect the rights of the consumer against confusion as well as the rights of the provider against misappropriation.[16] Ultimately, trademarks are intended to function as signposts, guiding the consumer to the source of goods or services.[17] Trademark infringement is misdirection[18] — a harm to the consumer — as much as it is misappropriation[19] — a harm to the provider. The law recognizes that both consumers and producers derive value from trademarks, and therefore attempts to balance the interests of both constituencies.[20] If one defines property as a bundle of rights, each of which is capable of ownership as against the world,[21] one might even question whether trademarks should be considered a species of property at all[22] — quite ironically, because in many cases (Coca Cola, McDonald's, Levi's) they might be considered the most valuable assets of their putative owners.[23]

---

[14] Jonathan D. Robbins, *Advising eBusinesses* §2:40 (2012).

[15] See *Time, Inc. v. Petersen Publ'g Co.*, 173 F.3d 113, 118 (2d Cir. 1999); 15 U.S.C. §1125 (2012). Where rights are defined by registration, the registration will be limited to defined uses or classes and the rights are subject to forfeiture if not actually used within a period of time following registration. *Id.* § 1127.

[16] 1 J. Thomas McCarthy, *McCarthy on Trademarks and Unfair Competition*, 4th ed. (Thomson Reuters, 2012), §2:2; see also *Two Pesos, Inc. v. Taco Cabana, Inc.*, 505 U.S. 763, 781–82 (1992) (explaining trademarks have a dual purpose to protect consumers and legitimate business interests).

[17] See 1 McCarthy, *supra* note 16, §2:2.

[18] Id. §2:33.

[19] Id. §2:30.

[20] Id. §2:33.

[21] Id. §2:14.

[22] See Kenneth L. Port, "The Congressional Expansion of American Trademark Law: A Civil Law System in the Making," 35 *Wake Forest L. Rev.* 827, 834 (2000) (claiming it is more convincing to speak of trademarks as property in civil law jurisdictions than in the UnitedStates).

[23] See *Jacob Siegel Co. v. Fed. Trade Comm'n*, 327 U.S. 608, 612 (1946) (stating that trade names are valuable corporate assets).

I begin with the question: can we understand personally identifiable information (PII)[24] as property in this context? Does it fall within the binary ownership framework we apply to patents, copyrights and trade secrets,[25] or is PII more akin to trademarks, where rights are in some sense shared between the original creator and the world at large?[26] There is no doubt that PII has high value, particularly as it flows through the channels of electronic commerce, and most particularly as it is pooled into what is dubbed Big Data.[27] Ironically, though, we will see that it attains and holds this value without having become property in any traditional sense of the word. We will also see that when it is collected to form an image of a person, it is not owned

---

24 PII is defined variously by the plethora of laws and regulations addressing it. The EU Data Protection Directive, Directive 95/46, of the European Parliament and of the Council of 24 October 1995 on the Protection of Individuals with Regard to the Processing of Personal Data and on the Free Movement of Such Data, 1995 O.J. (L 281) 31 (EC), defines "personal data" as "any information relating to an identified or identifiable natural person ("data subject"); an identifiable person is one who can be identified, directly or indirectly, in particular by reference to an identification number or to one or more factors specific to his physical, physiological, mental, economic, cultural or social identity. *Id.* art. 2(a). For purposes of U.S. government agencies, the U.S. Department of Commerce has published a Guide that defines personally identifiable information as "any information about an individual maintained by an agency, including (1) any information that can be used to distinguish or trace an individual's identity, such as name, social security number, date and place of birth, mother's maiden name, or biometric records; and (2) any other information that is linked or linkable to an individual, such as medical, educational, financial, and employment information." Erika McCallister et al., U.S. Dep't of Commerce, "Guide to Protecting the Confidentiality of Personally Identifiable Information (PII)" (2010); see also "Personally Identifiable Information (PII)," U.S. Gen. Services Admin., http://www. gsa.gov/portal/content/104256 (defining personally identifiable information as "information that can be used to distinguish or trace an individual's identity, either alone or when combined with other personal or identifying information that is linked or linkable to a specific individual").

25 See Carrier, *supra* note 5, at 53 (claiming the bundle of rights theory is predominate).

26 See, e.g., "Who, What, Why: In Which Countries Is Coca-Cola Not Sold?," BBC News Magazine, Sept. 11, 2012, http://www.bbc.co.uk/news/magazine-19550067?print=true (describing the relationship between Coca-Cola and consumers in light of the worldwide recognition of the Coca-Cola mark).

27 See Ann Cavoukian and Jeff Jonas, "Privacy by Design in the Age of Big Data," Senzing.com, June 8, 2012, 3, https://senzing.com/privacy-design-era-big-data/ (warning of the potential for misuse of personally identifiable information compiled in "big data" systems).

by that person at all. In other words, the playground paradigm for property ownership founders in the realm of New Media.[28]

I. The elements of value

One might think of these issues by analogy to a watershed. The vast aggregations of information that flow through the Internet, the value of which is pooled and captured along the way in servers and databases that throw off value like hydroelectric stations, all begin with tiny droplets of information generated by individuals and their individual transactions. It is worth asking, as to each of these droplets, what bundle of rights attach to it, and whether anyone "owns" the individual elements of that bundle.

A. Basic facts about individuals

One begins with information that defines who an individual is: name, sex, address, social security number, date of birth, place of birth, citizenship, telephone number, and facial and characteristics of appearance.[29] Who owns this information? It would be tempting to say that this information is owned by the particular individual to which it relates. Such a conception would fit neatly into an intellectual property scheme in which an original owner licenses or assigns rights to the next person in the "chain of title," who then licenses or assigns the information downstream into the large, valuable pools of data that can be exploited for value.[30] Reinforcing this conception, companies such as Facebook purport to acknowledge that their

---

[28] See "Definition of: New Media," PCMag.com, http://www.pcmag.com/encyclopedia_term/0,2542,t=new+media&i=47936,00.asp (defining new media as "forms of communicating in the digital world, which includes publishing on CDs, DVDs and, most significantly, over the Internet[,]" and as "[t]he concept that new methods of communicating in the digital world allow smaller groups of people to congregate online and share, sell and swap goods and information").

[29] See *supra* note 24 and accompanying text. Information of this kind is regulated as "personal information" or "personal data" under the data protection laws of most major jurisdictions. Id.; see also, e.g., 201 *Mass. Code Regs.* 17.02 (2012); Cal. Civ. Code §1798.80(e) (West 2012).

[30] Patricia Mell, "Seeking Shade in a Land of Perpetual Sunlight: Privacy as Property in the Electronic Wilderness," 11 *Berkeley Tech. L J.* 1, 71 (1996); see also Vera Bergelson, "It's Personal but Is It Mine? Toward Property Rights in Personal Information," 37 *U. C. Davis L. Rev.* 379, 412 (2003) (noting that the value in something like an individual's name comes from a third party collecting and organizing that name among a list of others).

users "own" the personal information they provide.[31] This, however, is not the case. One searches the laws of the United States[32] or Europe[33] in vain for any statute or principle respecting personal identity that is analogous to §201(a) of the Copyright Act — "Copyright . . . vests initially in the author . . . ."[34] — or §261 of the Patent Act — "[P]atents shall have the attributes of personal property."[35] Nothing in the law says that you own the fact that you are yourself — your identity.[36]

---

[31] See "Information We Receive About You," Facebook, https://www.facebook.com/about/privacy/your-info#usernames (last visited Oct. 14, 2012) ("While you are allowing us to use the information we receive about you, you always own all of your information.").

[32] See, e.g., 5 U.S.C. §552a (2012) (providing an example of a United States law regarding the sensitivity of one's personal information, but not providing for private ownership over that information). The Privacy Act of 1974 was a very early federal regulation respecting personal information. *Id.* It applies only to federal agencies, requiring them to give notice when they collect personal information, to give individuals access to personal information collected by agencies, and a right to correct such information when it is incorrect. Id.; see also "E-Government Act of 2002," Pub. L. No. 107-347, 116 Stat. 2899 (requiring, among other things, federal agencies to develop Privacy Impact Assessments regarding their collection and retention of personal information).

[33] This paper will be largely limited to US and UK/EU law, although the laws of most developed countries are analogous.

[34] 17 U.S.C. §201.

[35] 35 U.S.C. §261.

[36] See Mell, *supra* note 30, at 26–41. Patricia Mell acknowledges this fact, but argues that the law must extend the concept of property to encompass identity in the form of an electronic persona or personae. Id. In her view, the "fee simple" in each collection of electronic facts comprising an image of a person — a persona — should be owned by the individual, forcing others with an interest in those facts, the government, the public, commercial institutions to bargain with the individual for rights of use. Id. This is a sweeping and bold assertion, highly protective of the individual, but one that has not gained traction in the sixteen years since her publication. Identity, however, by its nature, cannot enjoy the exclusionary rights associated with all forms of property.

The European Personal Data Protection Directive[37] ("EU Directive") is instructive in this regard. Article 7 provides that personally identifiable data may be "processed"[38] only when one of the following circumstances obtains:

- the data subject has given his consent
- the processing is necessary for the performance of or the entering into a contract
- processing is necessary for compliance with a legal obligation
- processing is necessary in order to protect the vital interests of the data subject
- processing is necessary for the performance of a task carried out in the public interest or in the exercise of official authority vested in the controller or in a third party to whom the data are disclosed
- processing is necessary for the purposes of the legitimate interests pursued by the controller or by the third party or parties to whom the data are disclosed, except where such

[37] Directive 95/46, of the European Parliament and of the Council of 24 October 1995 on the Protection of Individuals with Regard to the Processing of Personal Data and on the Free Movement of Such Data, 1995 O.J. (L 281) 31 (EC) [hereinafter EU Directive]. The European Commission recently proposed amendments to the Directive. "Commission Proposes a Comprehensive Reform of Data Protection Rules to Increase Users' Control of Their Data and to Cut Costs for Businesses," *Europa Press Releases Rapid* (Jan. 25, 2012), http://europa.eu/rapid/pressReleasesAction.do?reference=IP/12/46&format=HTML&aged=0&langua. ge=en&guiLanguage=en. The proposed amendments are controversial in several respects, and have been criticized by the United States Department of Commerce. See Dep't of Commerce, *Informal Comment on the Draft General Data Protection Regulation and Draft Directive on Data Protection in Law Enforcement Investigations* 1 (2012).

[38] EU Directive, *supra* note 37, art. 2(b). For purposes of the EU Directive, "processing" includes "any operation or set of operations which is performed upon personal data, whether or not by automatic means, such as collection, recording, organization, storage, adaptation or alteration, retrieval, consultation, use, disclosure by transmission, dissemination or otherwise making available, alignment or combination, blocking, erasure or destruction[.]" Id.

> interests are overridden by the interests for fundamental rights and freedoms of the data subject[39]

What is noteworthy for our purposes is that, under the EU Directive, "processing" personal data, which includes collecting, using and disclosing, is generally permitted as long as the purpose is "legitimate" and does not violate "fundamental rights and freedoms."[40] The individual *can* give her consent, but it is not *required.*[41].The person collecting and using the personal data, even in the EU, does not need the individual's consent to do so.[42]

An individual thus has no general right to exclude others from knowing the basic elements of her personal identity.[43] She does, however, have some control over these basic elements of personal identity. She can change her address or telephone number,[44] with a bit more difficulty change her name,[45] and with considerably more difficulty, change her citizenship or social security number.[46] But it is very difficult to change one's facial appearance[47] and literally impossible to change one's date and place of birth or age,[48] however much one might want to do so. Under Article 12 of the EU Directive, the data subject also has the right to access all data processed about her and the right to demand the rectification, deletion, or blocking of data that is

---

39 Id. art. 7.

40 Id. art. 7(f).

41 Id. art. 2(h).

42 Id. art. 7 (providing disjunctive conditions for making data processing legitimate).

43 See id.

44 See, e.g., "Change of Address—Online Forms," USA. Gov, https://www.usa.gov/moving#item-37197; "Change Your Phone Number on Sprint.com," Sprint, http://support.sprint.com/support/article/Change_your_phone_number_on_sprintcom/case-ib376964-20090701-102238?INTNAV=SU:AL:MVT (last visited Oct. 16, 2012).

45 See, e.g., 735 ILL. Comp Stat. 5/21-101 (2007).

46 See, e.g., "N-400 Application for Naturalization," U.S. Citizenship and Immigr. Services, https://www.us-onlineimmigration.org/forms/n-400-citizenship-application; "Identity Theft and Your Social Security Number," U.S. Soc. Security Admin. (Oct. 2012), http://www.socialsecurity.gov/pubs/10064.html#a0=5&new= (follow "Should you get a new Social Security number" hyperlink) (explaining the conditions and requirements for obtaining a new Social Security Number).

47 *See Clinical Policy Bulletin: Face Transplantation,* Aetna, http://www.aetna.com/cpb/medical/data/800_899/0819.html (last modified Sept. 2, 2011).

48 See, e.g., "Corrections to Birth Records, Ill. Dep't of Pub. Health, http://www.dph.illinois.gov/topics-services/birth-death-other-records/birth-records/correct-birth-certificate (explaining that amendments to birth records are only permissible to correct mistakes).

incomplete, inaccurate, or is not being processed in compliance with the data protection rules.[49]With considerable variation, depending on the jurisdiction of residence, she can also have certain elements of this information — notably a telephone number[50] or a social security number[51] — withheld from the public at large.

Furthermore, she can prevent others from pretending to be her.[52] But at the base, she cannot prevent third parties from possessing and using the most fundamental pieces of information about her: those pieces that define who she is, at least for the purpose of identifying her.[53] That is, one might say, information that the individual does not own, any more than one owns one's personal appearance. One can marginally influence it and mold it, but in the end, it is others who see it and identify us by it. And they have a perfect right to do that; if people had no right to identify one another, all commerce — indeed all human interaction — would be impossible. You have to know with whom you are dealing.[54]

Basic information about individuals has some value in the marketplace.[55] Facebook recently acquired Face.com,[56] creators of a facial recognition software product, suggesting that Facebook sees value in the ability to

---

[49] EU Directive, *supra* note 37, art. 12. This principle has no general application under United States law, but some specific manifestations in places such as the Fair Credit Reporting Act. See 15 U.S.C. §§1681–1681x (2012).

[50] See 47 C.F.R. §51.217(c)(iv) (2012) ("A [local exchange carrier] shall not provide access to unlisted telephone numbers, or other information that its customer has asked the LEC not to make available, with the exception of customer name and address").

[51] In many jurisdictions, publishing of social security numbers is prohibited. See, e.g., *Mich. Comp. Laws* §§ 445.81–.87 (2012); *Ariz. Rev. Stat. Ann.* §44-1373 (2012).

[52] Identity Theft and Assumption Deterrence Act of 1998, 18 U.S.C. §§1001, 1028. A closely analogous concept is the right of a celebrity to control use of his or her identity for personal gain (the "right of publicity"). See, e.g., *Cal. Civ. Code* §3344 (West 2012).

[53] See, e.g., *Cal. Civ. Code* §1798.83(d)(1)(A); EU Directive, *supra* note 37, art.2(b).

[54] See 18 U.S.C. §1028. Here again the analogy to trademarks is instructive. Trademark law protects the interest of the public in knowing the source or origin of goods and services. 15 U.S.C. §1127. Identity law, if we may call it that, protects the interest of everyone in knowing whom they are dealing with. See 18 U.S.C. §1028.

[55] 2 McCarthy, *supra* note 16, §11:32 ("Even for noncelebrities, there exists a marketplace for the use of the identity of ordinary people in advertising.").

[56] Lauren Indivik "Facebook Acquires Face.com," *Mashable Bus.* (June 18, 2012), http://mashable.com/2012/06/18/facebook-acquires-face-com/.

recognize individuals by their appearance.[57] My age, my sex, where I live, my telephone number, what I do for a living — all of these narrow somewhat the goods or services I might be interested in buying, and at least permit a merchant to avoid wasting money trying to sell me things I am highly unlikely to buy.[58] But when combined with other facts about me, as well as my purchasing and lifestyle habits, the information can become considerably more valuable, and also considerably more subject to potential abuse.[59] We now turn to these other bits of information.

B. Sensitive facts about individuals

The EU Directive, implementing legislation in the member states, and United States state and federal law, all identify categories of information about the individual that are considered particularly sensitive and subject to special protections.[60] While the exact types of information that are considered sensitive vary from jurisdiction to jurisdiction,[61] there is an international

---

57 Samantha Murphy, "Facebook's Facial-Recognition Acquisition Raises Privacy Concerns," *Mashable Soc. Media* (June 25, 2012), https://mashable.com/2012/06/25/facebook-facial-recognition-privac/.

58 See Fed. Trade Comm'n, "FTC Staff Report: Self-Regulatory Principles for Online Behavioral Advertising," at i (2009), https://www.ftc.gov/sites/default/files/documents/reports/federal-trade-commission-staff-report-self-regulatory-principles-online-behavioral-advertising/p085400behavadreport.pdf (citing benefits of behavioral advertising).

59 See *Jacobs v. Nat'l Drug Intelligence Ctr.*, 423 F.3d 512, 518 (5th Cir. 2005) (explaining that the primary purpose of 5 U.S.C. §522a(b) is to prevent publicizing information that is detrimental to a person's character or reputation).

60 See EU Directive, *supra* note 37, art. 8 (prohibiting the use of "data revealing racial or ethnic origin, political opinions, religious or philosophical beliefs, trade-union membership, . . . and health or sex life"); Data Protection Act, 1998, c. 29, §2 (Eng.) [hereinafter Data Protection Act] (implementing the EU Directive and further protecting personal data regarding the commission of a crime or related proceedings); 815 *Ill. Comp. Stat.* §530/5 (2012) (restricting the collection of personal information including an individual's first and last name in conjunction with Social Security number, driver's license number, state identification card number, or financial account information, such as bank or credit card number, access code, and password); 42 U.S.C. §1320d-6(a) (2012) (protecting individually identifiable health information); 5 U.S.C. §552a(a)(4) (defining records about individuals that government agencies may not disclose).

61 Compare EU Directive, *supra* note 37, art. 8. (deeming information about racial or ethnic origin, political opinions, religious or philosophical beliefs, trade-union membership, and health or sex life sensitive information), and Data Protection Act, *supra* note 60, §2 (deeming the same in addition to criminal history), with 815 *Ill. Comp. Stat.* §530/5 (prohibiting the collection of first and last names in conjunction with a

consensus that two categories of information — information that could be used for purposes of unlawful discrimination and financial information — deserve special attention and protection.[62]

1. Information subject to potential abuse

Information in the category of being subject to potential abuse always includes information about an individual's health, which is universally considered sensitive and subject to special protection.[63] It may also include information about religion, political affiliation, marital status, and sexual orientation, among other categories.[64] Article 8 of the EU Directive defines this as "data revealing racial or ethnic origin, political opinions, religious or philosophical beliefs, trade-union membership, and the processing of data concerning health or sex life."[65] The United Kingdom implementing legislation, the U.K. Data Protection Act of 1998,[66] expands this definition slightly, defining "sensitive personal data" as data about the individual's racial or ethnic origin, political opinions, religious or similar beliefs, trade union membership, physical or mental health or condition, sexual life, or criminal history.[67] Several states in the U.S. have adopted legislation that similarly regulates "sensitive personal information," typically protecting information relating to an individual's physical or mental health.[68] At the U.S. federal level, there is no general regulation of sensitive personal information falling into this category, but the Health Insurance Portability and Accountability Act

---

Social Security number, driver's license or state identification number, or financial account number), and 5 U.S.C. §552a (prohibiting government agencies from disclosing information about citizens related to "education, financial transactions, medical history, and criminal or employment history and that contains his name, or the identifying number, symbol, or other identifying particular assigned to the individual, such as a finger or voice print or a photograph").

[62] See, e.g., EU Directive, *supra* note 37, art. 8 (defining sensitive personal data); Title VII of the Civil Rights Act of 1964 §703(a), 42 U.S.C. §2000e-2(a) (making it unlawful for employers to discriminate based on "race, color, religion, sex, or national origin"); 815 *Ill. Comp. Stat.* §530/5 (protecting personal financial information).

[63] See, e.g., 42 U.S.C. §17935.

[64] See Data Protection Act, *supra* note 60, §2.

[65] EU Directive, *supra* note 37, art. 8.

[66] Data Protection Act *supra* note 60.

[67] Id. §2.

[68] See, e.g., *Tex. Bus. & Com. Code Ann.* §521.002(a)(2)(B) (West 2012).

("HIPAA")[69] provides a broad definition of health-related information that is subject to strict standards regarding safety and disclosure.[70]

Article 8 of the EU Directive requires member states to prohibit the "processing" of any such sensitive personal information entirely, unless the processing is for one of a limited set of permitted purposes.[71] This brings sensitive personal data closer to the exclusionary right of a property owner, but not the whole way.[72] Although the purposes for which sensitive personal data may be processed without the individual's consent are substantially narrower than those applicable to personal information generally,[73] they are broad enough that it would be difficult to say that an individual owns his sensitive personal data.[74] As an example, the permissible purposes for which basic personal information may be processed include "performance of a contract."[75] This is not a permissible purpose with respect to sensitive personal data, but meeting one's obligations under employment law is a permissible purpose for processing sensitive personal data.[76] It is also permissible to process personal data for purposes of delivering health services.[77]

United States law regarding sensitive personal information is fundamentally different.[78] There is no general prohibition on its collection or dissemination;[79] instead, laws tend to focus on the misuse of such information for discriminatory purposes.[80] Thus, it is quite legal in the United

---

[69] Health Insurance Portability and Accountability Act of 1996, Pub. L. No. 104-191, 110 Stat. 1936.

[70] Health Insurance Portability and Accountability Act of 1996, Pub. L. No. 104-191, sec. 262, §§1171–77, 110 Stat. 1936, 2021–29 (codified as amended at 42 U.S.C. §§1320d–1320d-6 (2012)).

[71] EU Directive, *supra* note 37, art. 8.

[72] Compare Data Protection Act, *supra* note 60, §10 (allowing individuals to preclude others from obtaining, recording, holding, or operating on personal data, subject to a few exceptions), with 35 U.S.C. §154(a)(1) (2012) (granting patent owners the unqualified right to exclude all others from "making, using, offering for sale, or selling the invention").

[73] See EU Directive, *supra* note 37, art. 8.

[74] See id. art. 7 (giving reasons why processing of personal data may be necessary even without the consent of the data subject).

[75] Id. art. 7(b).

[76] Data Protection Act, *supra* note 60, §7.

[77] Id. §41C.

[78] See 5 U.S.C. §552a(b) (2012); 18 U.S.C. §1028.

[79] See 5 U.S.C. §§552a(a)(7), (b); 18 U.S.C. § 028(a).

[80] See 5 U.S.C. §552a(f); 18 U.S.C. §1028(a).

States to maintain and sell a database listing Democrats or Republicans or Mormons or Native Americans.[81] There is not even a hint in our law that such information is private or belongs to the individual.[82] On the other hand, if one used such a database as a criterion for hiring or firing, one could violate a wide variety of anti-discrimination laws.[83]Health information is an exception; "Protected Health Information" is regulated in a manner that is more closely analogous to the European model: HIPAA features enhanced notice requirements, as well as the requirement that "Covered Entities" (generally, health care providers and insurers) obtain consent before using or disclosing protected health information for any purpose other than treatment, payment, or other health care operations.[84]

In either case, a fundamental part of the rationale for these controls is that sensitive personal information is easily subject to abuse or misuse, both by governments and by private employers, neighbors, or others.[85] Thus, the United States and the EU share a similar goal in regulating this type of information, but the means they employ to reach that end are quite different. The EU focuses on both the collection and use of such data;[86] 86 the U.S. focuses on its misuse.[87]

---

[81] See 5 U.S.C. §§552a(a)(7), (b).

[82] See Samuel D. Warren and Louis D. Brandeis, "The Right to Privacy," 4 *Harv. L. Rev.* 193, 216–17 (1890). In a back-handed way, United States law does recognize that some facts ought not to be collected and released, but the focus there is more typically on the means for capturing the information — "invasion" of privacy — than on the nature of the facts themselves. Id. In the United States, if a person posts embarrassing photos or videos on the Internet, he cannot complain about somebody else collecting and storing the information they contain. In Europe, this would be illegal if the data controller's use of the information did not fall into a narrow set of exceptions. *See* EU Directive, *supra* note 37, art. 7.

[83] See 42 U.S.C. §2000e-2(a) (2012) (prohibiting employers from discriminating on the basis of "race, color, religion, sex, or national origin"); 42 U.S.C. §12112(a) (prohibiting employment discrimination based on disabilities).

[84] See 45 C.F.R. §164.508.-6.

[85] See *Jacobs v. Nat'l Drug Intelligence Ctr.*, 423 F.3d 512, 518 (5th Cir. 2005) (stating that the primary purpose of 5 U.S.C. §522a(b) is to prevent unauthorized publication of information that is detrimental to character reputation).

[86] EU Directive, *supra* note 37, art. 7; see also Data Protection Act, *supra* note 60 ("An Act to make new provision for the regulation of the processing of information relating to individuals, including the obtaining, holding, use or disclosure of such information.").

[87] See 5 U.S.C. §552a(b); 18 U.S.C. §1028.

2. Financial information

The second broad category of information singled out for special protection is financial information.[88] Here, United States and European law are more closely allied.[89] For example, financial information does not fall within the United Kingdom's definition of sensitive personal information,[90] and the processing of financial information is therefore not subject to the special limitations that apply to the processing of sensitive personal information.[91] At the same time, analogs to the general EU Directive principles appear in the Fair Credit Reporting Act (FRCA),[92] the Gramm-Leach-Bliley Act (GLB),[93] and various state laws designed to protect financial information and provide a remedy if it is improperly disclosed.[94] FCRA permits an individual to gain access to information about his credit record and insist on the correction of erroneous information.[95] GLB requires financial institutions to adopt policies informing consumers of their policies respecting the consumers' financial information that the institution collects, protects, and uses.[96] It also gives consumers the right to opt-out of information sharing beyond the collecting institution.[97] In these respects, both FCRA and GLB effectively incorporate, with respect to credit and financial information, principles that are given

---

88 15 U.S.C. §6801 (2012).

89 See Virginia Boyd, "Financial Privacy in the United States and the European Union: A Path to Translating Regulatory Harmonization," 24 *Berkeley J. Int'l L.* 939, 968–69(2006).

90 Data Protection Act, *supra* note 60, §2.

91 Id. §7.

92 Fair Credit Reporting Act, 15 U.S.C. §§1681–1681x.

93 Gramm-Leach-Bliley Act, Pub. L. No. 106-102, 113 Stat. 1338 (1999) (codified as amended in scattered sections of 12, 15 U.S.C.).

94 See, e.g., 201 Mass. Code Regs. 17.01 (2012) (governing the security of, among other things, financial information). Similar laws exist in many other jurisdictions, in some cases mandating security measures and in other cases mandating disclosure and remediation following an unauthorized breach of security. See 15 U.S.C. §§6801, 6803, 1681g(d).

95 15 U.S.C. §§1681g, 1681i. In this respect, the FCRA implements one of the basic principles of the EU Directive, but only with respect to the very narrow category of credit information. See 15 U.S.C. §§1681g, 1681i.

96 Gramm-Leach-Bliley Act, Pub. L. No. 106-102, §§501, 503, 113 Stat. 1338, 1436-37, 1439 (1999) (codified as amended at 15 U.S.C. §§6801, 6803 (2012)).

97 Id. §502, 113 Stat. at 1437–39 (codified as amended at 15 U.S.C. § 6802).

much more general application under the EU Directive,[98] with one important difference: GLB gives only an opt-out right, whereas the EU Directive and implementing legislation in member states, generally requires opt-in before personal information can be disseminated outside of the information controller and processors providing services to the controller.[99]

C. Behavioral facts about individuals

Thus far, we have discussed what one might consider comparatively static elements of personal identity. There is, however, a far more dynamic category of personal information that may have less potential for abuse than the static categories, but far more potential for commercial exploitation, particularly when it is combined with basic elements of personal identity. This category comprises the transactions and other electronic behaviors that are effected, recorded, confirmed, or stored electronically, often via the Internet.[100]

Information cascades from every transaction on the Internet, rushing effortlessly over international boundaries and transactions. Take this personal account as an example: My wife and I sent our daughter a Mother's Day present, a basket of fruit. To do this, we logged onto the Web from where we were at the time — England — and searched Google for companies delivering fruit. We visited two different websites for fruit delivery. After scrolling through their respective offerings, we decided on a fruit basket from Edible Arrangements and ordered it to be delivered on Mother's Day to our daughter, paying with a credit card via PayPal. We promptly received an email

---

[98] Compare EU Directive, *supra* note 37, art. 6 (requiring Member States to provide adequate safeguards for all personal data), and EU Directive, *supra* note 37, art. 12 (guaranteeing individual's the right to obtain and challenge all personal data relating to the individual), with 15 U.S.C. §6803 (requiring financial institutions to implement and disclose privacy policies), *and* 15 U.S.C. §§1681g, 1681i (permitting individual's to gain access to financial and credit information, and to challenge erroneous information).

[99] EU Directive, *supra* note 37, art. 7.

[100] See Steven C. Bennett, "Regulating Online Behavioral Advertising," 44 *J. Marshall L. Rev.* 899, 908–09 (2011) (discussing efforts on the part of various agencies to regulate online behavioral advertising). "Behavioral advertising," which targets individuals based on their browsing and transactional behavior, has spawned a growing legal literature. See, e.g., Dustin D. Berger, "Balancing Consumer Privacy with Behavioral Targeting," 27 *Santa Clara Computer & High Tech. L. J.* 3, 41–43 (2011) (discussing FTC self-regulatory principles regarding behavioral targeting in advertising); Matthew S. Kirsch, "Do-Not-Track: Revising the EU's Data Protection Framework to Require Meaningful Consent for Behavioral Advertising," 18 *Rich. J. L. & Tech.* 2, 24–38 (2011) (giving an overview of the EU's Data Protection Initiative and its impact on behavioral targeting).

confirmation of our order, including not only our email address but also our daughter's address and what we sent her as well.

By then, we had left a sizeable trail of valuable information that was originated in England, ran through the servers of British Telecom, then through the servers of Google/U.K., then to the servers of the ISP providers to Edible Arrangements and Edible Bouquets, and finally to the databases of Edible Arrangements and Edible Bouquets.[101] The information included PII about us: our name and address, the fact that we travel, the fact that we have a daughter, our means of payment, and even the different options we considered before landing on our selection of Mother's Day present. If we had used a mobile device, we also would have transmitted real-time information about our whereabouts, our peripatetic habits, and even our in-person shopping habits that made no use of the Internet whatsoever.[102] Like Hansel and Gretel, mobile devices leave a trail of locational breadcrumbs behind their users.[103] These crumbs are eagerly snatched by the device and service providers, who can associate them with mapping information to provide real-time advertisements and information to their users.[104] We also left a deposit of valuable information about our daughter: her name and address and the fact that she is a mother, both of which suggest targeted marketing and sales efforts that would be impossible without access to such information.

There is no doubt that companies assiduously track behavioral information. "Real-time ad bidding" — associating online advertisements with browsing history — is fundamental to the business models of companies such as Google and Amazon,[105] and Facebook recently announced a service it calls "Facebook

---

[101] See "Fact Sheet 18: Online Privacy: Using the Internet Safely," *Privacy Rts. Clearinghouse*, https://www.privacyrights.org/fs/fs18-cyb.htm#Internet_Service (last updated Oct. 2012).

[102] Melissa Loudon, "Mobile Surveillance — A Primer," Mobileactive.org, June 10, 2009.

[103] Id.

[104] See Quentin Hardy, "Head to Head Over Mobile Maps," *New York Times*, June 18, 2012, at B1. Service and device providers such as Google and Apple compete aggressively to capture the value of mapping and location information. See id.; Danielle Kucera, "Apple to Feature Yelp Check-Ins Within IPhone Maps App," *Bloomberg*, June 25, 2012, https://www.bloomberg.com/news/articles/2012-06-25/apple-to-feature-yelp-check-ins-within-iphone-maps-app. Steven Duque, "Twitter Places: To Check-in or Not to Check-in?," *Wall St. Cheat Sheet*, June 19, 2010, http://stevenduque.com/2010/06/geo-local-to-check-in-or-not-to-check-in/ (providing insight into the economic potential and social costs of location-driven services such as Foursquare and Twitter Places).

[105] Eric Savitz, "Facebook Exchange and the Rise of Real-Time Ad Bidding," *Forbes*, June 14, 2012, https://www.forbes.com/sites/ciocentral/2012/06/14/facebook-exchange-and-the-rise-of-real-time-ad-bidding/.

Exchange" that uses cookies Facebook places on browsers to target ads to Facebook users.[106] A recent study concluded that, since November 2010, behavioral tracking has increased by 400 percent.[107] The study found that, on average, a visit to a website triggers fifty-six (!) instances of data collection.[108]

Who owns this information? In the United States, end customer lists are considered a classic example of a trade secret,[109] and there is very little doubt that the customer lists of the Edible Arrangements company, and of the franchisee we chose to make and deliver the fruit, would be considered trade secrets that are owned by those companies.[110] There is also very little doubt that any additional information they can glean from my Web visit — what options I considered, how long I was on the site, how I paid, to whom the fruit was delivered, where I was when I placed the order — would be included in the information that they could protect as their trade secrets.[111] On the other hand, these facts are not quite theirs: I am perfectly free to disclose this information, and I just did. It is the aggregation of information about customers that US law would protect against unauthorized disclosure (more

---

[106] Douglas MacMillan and Jonathan Erlichman, "Facebook to Debut Real-Time Bidding for Advertising," *Bloomberg*, June 14, 2012, https://www.bloomberg.com/news/articles/2012-06-13/facebook-to-debut-real-time-bidding-for-advertising. A Facebook user cannot opt-out of the cookies Facebook uses for this purpose. Id. The only way to avoid the collection and use of this data is to disable the cookies on third-party websites or on the user's browser, either of which would substantially degrade the browsing experience by requiring the user to re-input basic information every time a page is visited. Id.

[107] Elinor Mills, "Behavioral Data Tracking Rising Dramatically (Q&A)," Cnet News, June 19, 2012, http://news.cnet.com/8301-1009_3-57456273-83/behavioral-data-tracking-rising- dramatically-q-a/.

[108] Id.; see also Bethany Rubin Henderson, "Hey That's Personal! When Companies Sell Customer Information Gathered Through the Internet," 14 *Bus. L. Today* 13, 13 (2004) (claiming the majority of companies collect "personally identifiable information from onlinevisitors").

[109] *Kewanee Oil Co. v. Bicron Corp.*, 416 U.S. 470, 474–75 (1974); see also 18 U.S.C. §1839 (2012) (including a compilation as a type of protectable trade secret); Cal. Civ. Code §3426.1(d) (2012) (defining a trade secret as any information having economic value derived from its secrecy). California is one of forty-seven states to have adopted the Uniform Trade Secrets Act definition of trade secrets. Cal. Civ. Code §3426.1(d).

[110] See *Kewanee Oil*, 416 U.S. at 474–75.

[111] Julie A. Katz, "To Be a Trade Secret or Not To Be a Trade Secret: Practical Considerations when Protecting IP Assets, in IP Value 2012: Building and Enforcing Intellectual Property Value: An International Guide for the Boardroom," 53 (10th ed., 2012), available at https://hbfiles.blob.core.windows.net/files/301c95d7-8588-43ca-bff0-bd7ef86556bd.pdf.

on this later).[112] In the United States, Edible Arrangements and its franchisee are generally free to store and use the information about my transaction, and make money by selling it to third parties.[113] Also, on the U.S. end, PayPal would be considered a financial institution for purposes of GLB, and their possession of my credit card and other financial information would be governed by the GLB principles.[114] They must have a privacy policy that I have been made aware of and must give me an opt-out right before they can sell information about me to third parties.[115] Not surprisingly, PayPal has all of these in place;[116] they have clearly given some attention to the rules and regulations in this regard. Among other things, their policy gives information about the "cookies" they leave on my computer when I do business with them,[117] which of course, is another species of personal information that my transaction generated.

The Electronic Communications Privacy Act[118] makes it a crime to intercept my electronic communications while in transit,[119] and the Stored Communications Act[120] makes it a crime to access, without authorization, the Internet systems through which my wife and I placed our order.[121] The United

---

112 *Hamilton-Ryker Grp., LLC v. Keymon*, No. W2008-00936-COA-R3-CV, 2010 WL 323057, at *15–16 (Tenn. Ct. App. Jan. 28, 2010).

113 15 U.S.C. §6802. There is in fact a very robust market in the U.S. for customer information of this kind.

114 15 U.S.C. §6809(3)(A). The GLB defines "financial institution," by reference to 12 U.S.C. §1843(k), to mean any institution in the business of engaging in activity that is (A) "financial in nature or incidental to such financial activity" or (B) "complementary to a financial activity and does not pose a substantial risk to the safety or soundness of depository institutions or the financial system generally." Id.; 12 U.S.C. §1843(k); see also Mark Silbergeld, Consumer Fed'n of Am., *CFA Handbook: Federal and State Legal Protections of Consumers' Financial Information Privacy and Security*, 4–5 (2009).

115 15 U.S.C. §§6803, 6802(b) (2012). PayPal in fact adopts an opt-in policy respecting sales of personal information it collects to third parties. "Privacy Policy," PayPal, https://www.paypal.com/us/webapps/mpp/ua/privacy-full.

116 Id.

117 Id.

118 Electronic Communications Privacy Act of 1986, Pub. L. No. 99-508, 100 Stat. 1848 (codified as amended in scattered sections of 18 U.S.C.).

119 18 U.S.C. §2511.

120 Stored Communications Act, 18 U.S.C. §§2701–12. This statute has assumed several names by different commentators. Orin S. Kerr, "A User's Guide to the Stored Communications Act, and a Legislator's Guide to Amending It," 72 *Geo. Wash. L. Rev.* 1208, 1243 n.1 (2004). I've chosen the simplest.

121 18 U.S.C. §2701.

States does not otherwise significantly regulate the collection and retention of information about my transactions, but it does impose some regulations on what can be done with the information.[122] Under the CAN-SPAM Act of 2003,[123] online advertisers must provide an option by which the recipient can opt-out of receiving future email advertisements.[124] Under the Telephone Consumer Protection Act of 1991,[125] a U.S. vendor is required to obtain prior consent before it can send a marketing text to a mobile phone.[126]

On the English end, it is unlikely that my web surfing or transaction information was captured and maintained by British Telecom[127] or Google/U.K. longer than necessary to complete the transaction. That is because I did not opt-in to permit them to do so, and therefore, they likely

---

122 Paula Selis et. al., "Consumer Privacy and Data Protection: Protecting Personal Information Through Commercial Best Practices," 2 (2002), available at https://agportal-s3bucket.s3.amazonaws.com/uploadedfiles/Home/News/Press_Releases/2002/PrivacyPolicy1.pdf ("In the United States there is no comprehensive privacy law that addresses the collection or use of personal information."). Although there are few laws on the books, the digital advertising industry has published self-regulation guidelines about online behavioral targeted advertising. Am. Ass'n of Adver. Agencies, et al., "Self-Regulatory Principles for Online Behavioral Advertising" (2009), referenced at https://www.ftc.gov/public-statements/2009/02/concurring-statement-commissioner-jon-leibowitz-ftc-staff-report-self. Also, the Obama Administration, the FTC, and various members of Congress have proposed variations on a "Privacy Bill of Rights." The White House, "Consumer Data Privacy in a Networked World: A Framework for Protecting Privacy and Promoting Innovation in the Global Digital Economy" (2012). Fed. Trade Comm'n, "Protecting Consumer Privacy in an Era of Rapid Change: Recommendations for Businesses and Policy Makers" (2012).

123 Controlling the Assault of Non-Solicited Pornography and Marketing Act of 2003, 15 U.S.C. §§7701–13 (2012).

124 Id. §7704(a)(5).

125 47 U.S.C. § 227.

126 Id. §227(b)(1)(A)(iii). Although not explicit in the statute, the FCC has clarified that §227(b)(1)(A)(iii) includes text messages in addition to voice calls. See Rules and Regulations Implementing the Telephone Consumer Protection Act (TCPA) of 1991, 68 Fed. Reg. 44,144, 44,165 (July 25, 2003) (to be codified at 47 C.F.R. pts. 64 & 68). The CAN-SPAM Act also requires prior consent if the message uses an Internet address that includes an Internet domain name (usually the part of the address after the individual or electronic mailbox name and the "@" symbol). 15 U.S.C. §7712.

127 See Directive 2002/58, of the European Parliament and of the Council of 12 July 2002 on Privacy and Electronic Communications, 2002 O.J. (L 201) 37 (EC) [hereinafter E-Privacy Directive]. The E-Privacy Directive prohibits, among other things, traffic and location data about subscribers and users from being used for marketing or other purposes without the individual's consent. Id. arts. 6, 9.

could not establish a legitimate reason to retain the information under the data protection principles of Article 7 of the EU Directive.[128] In other words, the potentially valuable information about me and my transaction has, at least in principle, evaporated on the European side of the Atlantic before it can be used.[129] If the facts were reversed, so that I was placing an order from the United States to a vendor in England, the resulting rights would have been quite different. Without my express consent, the English vendor could not have retained records about my transaction longer than required to complete the transaction, could not have sold it to third parties, and could not have used it to make sales to me in the future.[130] Like the US vendor, if the English vendor sent me commercial emails, it would be required to give me an opt-out right under the EU Directive on Privacy and Electronic Communication. (E-Privacy Directive)

On the other hand, Google/US could and undoubtedly would capture all the information about my Web surfing exercise, selling that information to its advertisers so that they can target ads to me the next time I log on to Google to do some fruit or Mother's Day shopping.[131] The value of this information in Google's hands — or Facebook's, or Amazon's — is directly measured by the lofty heights of their market capitalizations.[132] They are, in other words, profiting from my identity — who I am, what I'm interested in, what I buy — and I do not have any right to claim royalties on their profit.[133] In the United States, this information about me is, in some important sense, theirs, not mine.[134] In England, it is a little less theirs, but hardly more mine.[135]

---

128 EU Directive, *supra* note 37, art. 7.

129 Id.

130 Data Protection Act, *supra* note 60, §4, sch. 1.

131 John F. Tanner & Mary Anne Raymond, Principles of Marketing ch. 3 (Flat World Knowledge ed., 2010), *available at* http://catalog.flatworldknowledge.com/bookhub/2030?e=fwk-133234-ch03#fwk-133234-ch03 (discussing consumer behavior and how they make buying decisions).

132 See, e.g., Erin Carlyle, "Larry Page's Fortune Up As Google Overtakes Microsoft in Market Cap," *Forbes*, Oct. 1, 2012, https://www.forbes.com/sites/erincarlyle/2012/10/01/larry-pages-fortune-up-as-google-overtakes-microsoft-in-market-cap/.

133 See Bergelson, *supra* note 30, at 383.

134 See sources cited *supra* note 109. The fact that a company holds the aggregated information about a customer compiled into a customer list as a trade secret indicates an ownership right in that information. See *Hamilton-Ryker Grp., LLC v. Keymon*, No. W2008-00936-COA-R3-CV, 2010 WL 323057, at *15–16 (Tenn. Ct. App. Jan. 28, 2010).

II. Digital identity

One might think of a person's digital identity by analogy to a pointillist painting. Thousands upon thousands of tiny bits of digital information about an individual, including what we have called basic facts, sensitive facts, and transactional facts, can be assembled to form a picture of the individual: his likes, dislikes, predispositions, resources; and in fact, any facet of his personality that has had contact with the Internet.[136] The picture may vary, depending on the interest of the digital assembler of information and the access of that person to the individual's digital life,[137] but it will be a picture of identity nonetheless.

Who owns these pictures? We have already noted that the individual pieces of digital information are not owned, in any ordinary sense, by the individual generating them.[138] But what about the pictures as a whole? Who owns them? In some sense, the individual certainly created them, particularly as they relate to transactions effected on the Internet or information posted on the Internet. Does that mean that the individual owns them?[139]

Here we encounter something more closely akin to traditional notions of property rights, and the answer is a bit surprising. In Europe, the Database Directive,[140] adopted by the European Commission in 1996, requires member

---

135 See Kirsch, *supra* note 100, at 7–9. Not surprisingly, there are proposals to require consent before information about one's online behavior can be tracked for commercial purposes. See id. at 17–21.

136 See Erica Newland, "Disappearing Phone Booths: Privacy in the Digital Age," Center for Democracy and Tech. (May 2012), https://www.cdt.org/files/pdfs/Privacy-In-Digital-Age.pdf (cataloguing various types of data capable of being tracked by third parties).

137 See Mell, *supra* note 30, at 6.

138 Bergelson, *supra* note 30, at 383; see also Laura A. Heymann, "The Law of Reputation and the Interest of the Audience," 52 *B. C. L. Rev.* 1341, 1342 (2011).

139 I propose this question in part to test the theses that property rights either flow from the efforts of the individual, see John Locke, *Two Treatises of Government*, 314 (Peter Laslett ed., Cambridge Univ. Press, 1988 [1690]), or manifest individuality and thus promote individual autonomy, see Immanuel Kant, *The Metaphysical Elements of Justice*, 56 (John Ladd ed. & trans., Hackett Publ'g Co., 1999) (1797); MERGES, *supra* note 1, at 31–33, 68–77 (discussing the property concepts of John Locke and Immanuel Kant). What could be more personal, or more the product of my individual efforts, than my identity? Should it not, then, be my property?

140 Directive 96/9 of the European Parliament and of the Council of 11 March 1996 on the Legal Protection of Databases, 1996 O.J. (L 77) 20 (EC) [hereinafter Database Directive].

states to provide protection for databases.[141] U.K. regulations implementing the Database Directive expressly state that "[a] property right ('database right') subsists, in accordance with this Part, in a database if there has been a substantial investment in obtaining, verifying or presenting the contents of the database."[142] Similarly, the United States Copyright Act provides copyright protection for compilations so long as there is copyrightable authorship in their selection or arrangement.[143]

Therefore, the compilations of facts that comprise a person's digital identities are subject to ownership, but the owner is not the person; it is the compiler![144] Quite remarkably, the individuals who generate the information that comprises their digital identities do not own the databases, and therefore, in a very real sense, do not own their own identities.[145] Their identities, the images of which can vary from compiler to compiler, are owned by the companies who assemble the information into something useful and saleable.[146] The companies and enterprises that gather the information,

---

141 See id. art 7. The European Commission published a report in 2005 questioning whether the Database Directive had been effective, but no further action has been taken to amend or improve it. First Evaluation of Directive 96/9/EC on the Legal Protection of Databases (Dec. 12, 2005), available at https://publications.europa.eu/en/publication-detail/-/publication/5e9c7a51-597c-11e8-ab41-01aa75ed71a1 (updated).

142 The Copyright and Rights in Databases Regulations, 1997, S.I. 1997/3032, art. 13 (Eng.).

143 17 U.S.C. §103 (2012).

144 Id. To continue the analogy to Pointillism, Seurat surely owned copyright in his paintings, but not in the individual points of color of which they were composed. See generally Bergelson, *supra* note 30, at 404 (cataloguing court decisions acknowledging property rights of compilers of personal information). There is, of course, also the possibility that someone could be his own compiler, creating in effect a digital self-portrait. The personal pinboards created by users of www.Pinterest.com are an example. See "What is Pinterest?," Pinterest, http://pinterest.com/about/ The individual Pinterest user creates his or her own profile of preferences by "pinning" images from other Pinterest pinboards or from other websites. Id.

145 Dan Gillmor, "Google+ Forces Us to Question Who Owns Our Digital Identity," *The Guardian,* July 13, 2011, https://www.theguardian.com/commentisfree/cifamerica/2011/jul/13/google-plus-online-identiy.

146 Selis et. al., *supra* note 122, at 9 ("A consumer's personal information has the potential of being bought and sold like any other valuable commodity.").

package it, and make it available for exploitation and sale, often as an aggregation of individual compilations, own it and can profit from it.[147]

The conclusion that one does not own one's own identity might seem jarring at first.[148] On further reflection, though, one realizes that the lack of ownership over one's digital identity is not very different from one's identity outside of the digital space.[149] Identity is an edifice built out of facts about one's self that are known to others — basic facts, sensitive facts, historical facts, genetic facts, relational facts, transactional facts. These facts can be influenced by the individual, but they are not owned by the individual, either individually or in the aggregate.[150]

Think of identity as reputation. Do I own my reputation? I have a reasonably broad opportunity to mold my reputation by word and deed, and I have legal redress if my reputation is unfairly tarnished,[151] but if I have committed a

---

[147] See Tanzina Vega & Edward Wyatt, "U.S. Requests Tougher Rules on Data Sales," *New York Times*, Mar. 26, 2012, at A1. One can distinguish aggregations of facts about a single individual from aggregations of facts about multiple individuals, but the legal principles attaching to these aggregations are not different. See 17 U.S.C. §103. People commonly focus on the second of these, and much of what is referred to as "Big Data" resides in such multiple-individual aggregations. See *supra* note 27. On the other hand, it is the aggregation of facts about particular persons that delivers real marketing value — who is this person? How old is she? How much money does she have? Where does she live? Where is she now? What does she typically like to buy? See Clair Cain Miller and Somini Sengupta, "In Mobile World, Tech Giants Scramble to Get Up to Speed," *New York Times*, Oct. 23, 2012, at A1 ("[M]obile provides huge opportunities for these businesses, industry analysts say. That is largely because people reveal much more about themselves on phones than they do on computers, from where they go and when they sleep to whom they talk to and what they want to buy.").

[148] See sources cited *supra* note 30. Indeed, this legal fact seems to have inspired legal scholars such as Mell and Bergelson to exert enormous efforts to propose legal property rights in PII or identity or both. See id.

[149] See *Gill v. Hearst Publ'g Co.*, 253 P.2d 441, 444 (Cal. 1953) ("Consistent with their own voluntary assumption of this particular pose in a public place, plaintiffs' right to privacy as to this photographed incident ceased and it in effect became a part of the public domain").

[150] See *supra* note 82 and accompanying text.

[151] See *Barrows v. Wareham Fire Dist.*, 82 Mass. App. Ct. 623, 627 (2012) ("[T]he gravamen of the tort of defamation does not lie in the nature or degree of the misconduct but in its outcome, i.e., the injury to the reputation of the plaintiff."). The remedy, of course, lies in the tort of defamation. *Restatement (Second) of Torts* §558 (1977). There are well-known differences between the United States and the U.K. in the scope of this tort, driven largely by First Amendment considerations in the United

crime or a fraud, the people I deal with are entitled to know that and to protect themselves accordingly.[152] If, on the other hand, I have behaved in an exemplary fashion — paying my debts, respecting others, honoring contracts, avoiding litigation — others are entitled to know that as well. The individual might not want everyone to know the bad things, but the individual cannot, in general, prevent it. One's reputation is, to a large extent, the product of one's actions and initiative, but it is not, as a result, one's property.[153] It is, in a sense, community property.[154] The individual builds it, at least in part, but the community members can then use it — or decide that it would be unfair or unjust to use it — whether the individual wants them to or not.[155]

States that do not apply in the U.K. See Doug Rendleman, "Collecting a Libel Tourist's Defamation Judgment?, "67 *Wash. & Lee L. Rev.* 467, 478–80 (comparing U.S. and U.K. defamation laws); compare *N.Y. Times Co. v. Sullivan*, 376 U.S. 254, 269–71 (1964) (discussing that there must be a freedom to speak openly, especially in debates and criticism, even when that speech may not have been proven to be true), with Defamation Act, 1996, c. 31 (Eng.) (discussing the law of defamatory statements without making reference to any right or freedom to speak openly regardless of the context in which the defamatory statements were made).

152 See Sandra D. Scott, "What Is a Police 'Investigative Report'?," 51 J. *Mo. B.* 83, 84 (1995) (discussing one State's policy of informing the public about crimes in the community). In the U.K., evidence about criminal prosecutions is considered sensitive personal information and is therefore subject to special protections. Data Protection Act, *supra* note 60, §2. With the exception of juvenile crimes, there is no comparable principle in the U.S. See, e.g., *Hodge v. Jones*, 31 F.3d 157, 166 (4th Cir. 1994) ("[C]riminal records are matters of public record, easily obtained upon request, and . . . there is no automatic right to expunction thereof"); Joanna S. Markman, "*In Re Gault*: A Retrospective in 2007: Is It Working? Can It Work?," 9 *Barry L. Rev.* 123, 127 & 141 n.29 (2007) (discussing the confidentiality of juvenile records).

153 Heymann, *supra* note 139, at 1342. This conception diverges sharply from John Locke's view that the admixture of personal effort with raw material justifies property rights, or even Immanuel Kant's conception of property as the manifestation of individual liberty. See Merges, *supra* note 1, at 31–33, 68–77.

154 Heymann, *supra* note 139, at 1342 ("[R]eputation is a social creation dependent on intergroup communication."). Note in this connection that one's identity can be ascertained and owned by anyone who has the ability and takes the trouble to assemble the relevant facts. See 17 U.S.C. §103. Like any other compilation of data, another person can access the same or similar data and assemble its own compilation, without infringing the property rights of the first compiler. Id. An image of one's identity can be owned by anybody taking the trouble to compile it. *Id.*

155 See Heymann, *supra* note 139, at 1342. Merges struggles a bit to bring intellectual property within John Rawls's framework for a just society. Merges, *supra* note 1, at 102–05 (discussing John Rawls, *A Theory of Justice* (Harv. Univ. Press, rev. ed., 1999)). It is far

We can also return here to the analogy to trademark law. Trademark rights attach to the "good will" associated with a vendor and its products.[156] The good will of a business is listed as one of its assets;[157] indeed, it may be the business's largest asset, but it is utterly reliant on the public's perception of the business.[158] By change of heart, or even by generic use, the public at large can destroy this "asset," and the business has no legal recourse whatsoever.[159]

We might also return to our watershed analogy. No one owns the raindrops falling on the watershed, but when value is created by damming streams of information, that value can be owned and exploited by the persons building and running the dams. Eventually, of course, the information returns to the oceanic public domain.

A. The exploitation of identity

If it is jarring to consider that one's digital identity is owned by others, not by one's self, it is still more disturbing to consider what the owners might do with their information. It is one thing for Amazon to keep track of the books you bought and to use that information to identify other books you might like to buy. This is not too different from the proprietor of a local bookstore (if there remains one that has not yet been put out of business by Amazon) telling you that he just got in a book by an author he knows you will like. This is good customer service, as long as it is not too insistent. It would be quite another thing for the local bookseller to ring up his friend, the kitchenware merchant across the street, and tell him you just bought a cookbook that requires a particular utensil that the merchant might want to sell to him. The latter has

---

easier to bring the non-property concept of identity/reputation proposed in the text within the framework of what persons in the "original position" would agree upon. They could well agree, for example, that the community ought to have ready access to most reputational facts, but that it would be unwise to permit the free exchange of sensitive personal information that is subject to misuse, or that could easily be used to the disadvantage of the least fortunate in society (Rawls' Second Principle). Id. at 104.

156 Heymann, *supra* note 139, at 1343.

157 See 1 McCarthy, *supra* note 16, §2.19.

158 See id.

159 See 15 U.S.C. §1064 (2012) (allowing a petition to be filed for the cancellation of a registered trademark if it becomes the generic name the public uses for a good or service).

the feel of an invasion of privacy.[160] This is, of course, exactly what Amazon is doing all the time,[161] and in important part, what legislatures and regulators react to with the plethora of privacy laws we have today.[162] The problem is not that the bookseller or Amazon have and own information about your purchase. The problem is what they do with it.[163]

One sees a somewhat different issue in Facebook's "Sponsored Stories" service. In this service, Facebook features in advertisements the name and picture of Facebook friends who click a button to show they "like" something, charging a fee to the provider of the thing that was "liked."[164] Facebook does not share its revenue with the person doing the "liking."[165] This prompted a class action lawsuit, which Facebook settled by agreeing to give notice to its users that their preferences would be exploited in this way, coupled with an opt-out right.[166] The problem here cannot be considered an invasion of privacy. Surely the people who tap "like" intend for their positive response to

---

160 The Fair and Accurate Credit Transactions Act of 2003 (FACTA), an amendment to the Fair Credit Reporting Act, prohibits companies from using certain credit information received from an affiliate to market goods or services to a consumer, unless the consumer is given notice, a reasonable opportunity to opt-out, and a simple and reasonable method for opting-out (the FTC Affiliate Sharing Rule). Fair and Accurate Credit Transactions Act of 2003, Pub. L. No. 108-159, sec. 214, §624, 117 Stat. 1952, 1980–82 (codified as amended at 15 U.S.C. §1681s-3); see also "FTC Approves Affiliate Marketing Rule Regarding Use of Consumer Information," Fed. Trade Commission, Oct. 23, 2007, http://www.ftc.gov/opa/2007/10/affiliate.shtm.

161 Nick Eaton, "Suit: Amazon Fraudulently Collects, Shares Users' Personal Info," SeattlePI.Com, https://www.seattlepi.com/business/article/Suit-Amazon-fraudulently-collects-shares-users-1040886.php.

162 See, e.g., Do Not Track Me Online Act of 2011, H.R. 654, 112th Cong. (2011); Commercial Privacy Bill of Rights Act of 2011, S. 799, 112th Cong. (2011); BEST PRACTICES Act, H.R. 611, 112th Cong. (2011); Consumer Privacy Protection Act of 2011, H.R. 1528, 112th Cong. (2011); Do-Not-Track Online Act of 2011, S. 913, 112th Cong. (2011); Do-Not-Track-Kids Act, H.R. 1895, 112th Cong. (2011).

163 Hardly a day goes by without a new revelation about the use of personal information or the unauthorized disclosure of sensitive personal information. See, e.g., Natasha Singer, "You For Sale," *New York Times*, June 17, 2012, at BU1 (raising concerns about Acxiom gathering personal information from customers and selling it to marketers for targeted advertising when there have been multiple security breaches).

164 "Daily Report: What's Behind Facebook's Sponsored Stories," N.Y. Times Bits, June 1, 2012, https://bits.blogs.nytimes.com/2012/06/01/daily-report-whats-behind-facebooks-sponsored-stories/.

165 See id. The quid pro quo is the free service provided by Facebook to its users.

166 Somini Segupta, "To Settle Lawsuit, Facebook Alters Policy for Its Like Button," *New York Times*, June 22, 2012, at B2.

be known at least by their "friends," even if they have not read the fine print of Facebook's terms of use. The problem is more directly related to the exploitation of a person's identity for profit, which squarely implicates state right of publicity laws that generally require consent before a person's name or image can be used for commercial purposes.[167] It is worth noting that Facebook did not agree to discontinue the Sponsored Sites service.[168] Its settlement simply made it clearer to Facebook users that one of the quid pro quos for their free Facebook service was, in effect, a license to use their names and likenesses for commercial purposes.[169] If a person pays with anything other than cash, there is also the question of whether the vendor has safeguarded the credit card or bank information. Security breaches are distressingly common. In June of 2012, the FTC filed a complaint against Wyndham Hotels for security lapses that allowed hackers to access sensitive financial information of more than 600,000 individuals over a three-year period.[170] In the same month, LinkedIn, eHarmony, and Last.fm were all hacked, resulting in the release of millions of users' passwords,[171] and just three months before, the credit card processor Global Payments reported that some 1.5 million Visa and MasterCard account numbers had been stolen by hackers.[172] Even breaches of less sensitive information, such as that of Epsilon in which the email addresses of millions of individuals were inadvertently disclosed, are disturbing and potentially harmful to individuals.[173]

Many of the laws respecting PII can thus be understood as limitations on the ownership rights of, and the creation of liability for, the persons, or rather

---

[167] 4 Louis Alatman and Malla Pollack, *Callmann on Unfair Competition, Trademarks & Monopolies* §22:32 (4th ed., 1981).

[168] See Segupta, *supra* note 167.

[169] Id.

[170] "Complaint for Injunctive and Other Equitable Relief," *Fed. Trade Comm'n v. Wyndham Worldwide Corp.*, No. 12-cv-01365 (D. Ariz. June 26, 2012), available at http://www.ftc.gov/os/caselist/1023142/120626wyndamhotelscmpt.pdf. The gravamen of the complaint, which alleged losses to customers exceeding $10 million, id. ¶2, was that Wyndham's privacy policy misrepresented its data security precautions, which, it turned out, had essentially nil with personally identifiable financial information stored in plain text. Id. ¶¶24, 40.

[171] Sara Yin, "Last.FM Joins eHarmony, LinkedIn to Celebrate Breach Week," SecurityWatch, June 7, 2012, https://in.pcmag.com/opinion/84902/lastfm-joins-eharmony-linkedin-to-celebrate-breach-week.

[172] Brian Krebs, "MasterCard, VISA Warn of Processor Breach," Krebs on Security, March 30, 2012, https://krebsonsecurity.com/2012/03/mastercard-visa-warn-of-processor-breach/.

[173] See, e.g., Singer, *supra* note 164.

businesses, that assemble and own collections of PII. One might analogize the collections of PII that comprise one's digital identities to dangerous instrumentalities.[174] It is okay to build and own them; indeed, their creation represents the generation of an important new form of wealth in the Internet Age, but the use of such information must be regulated to avoid harm or unlawful exploitation. The www.pleaserobme.com episode is an example. The pleaserobme.com website scraped Twitter messages that had been pushed through the Foursquare social media site to provide a real-time list of people who were not at home.[175] The site apparently intended to raise awareness of the vulnerabilities created by location information, but its potential for abuse is obvious.[176] Facebook offered, for one day, a service called "Find Friends Nearby" that allowed Facebook users to see which friends were nearby.[177] It took the service down because of very real concerns over stalking.[178]

That this is the case is manifest in the basic principles of privacy legislation as diverse as the EU Directive, the Fair Credit Reporting Act, HIPAA, Gramm-Leach- Bliley, and the Massachusetts Data Security Regulations. In each case, the assembly of personal information about individuals is not prohibited.[179] Quite to the contrary, such assemblies are affirmatively encouraged, particularly in the areas of financial services and health care, because the information can greatly improve the efficient and effective provision of

---

174 See *Stecyk v. Bell Helicopter Textron*, No. 94-CV-1818, 1998 U.S. Dist. LEXIS 609, at *15 n.4 (E.D. Pa. Jan. 26, 1998) (defining a dangerous instrumentality as "anything which has the inherent capacity to place people in peril, either in itself (e.g. dynamite), or by a careless use of it (e.g. boat)").

175 See Caroline McCarthy, "The Dark Side of Geo: PleaseRobMe.com," Cnet News, Feb. 17, 2012, https://www.cnet.com/news/the-dark-side-of-geo-pleaserobme-com/.

176 Id.

177 See John D. Sutter, "Facebook Quietly Unveils 'Stalking App,'" CNN Tech, June 29, 2012, https://www.cnn.com/2012/06/25/tech/social-media/facebook-find-friends-nearby/index.html. The service was aptly dubbed "the stalking app" by the blog ReadWriteWeb. Id.

178 Id.

179 EU Directive, *supra* note 37, art. 6 (stating that personal data "must be . . . collected for specified, explicit, and legitimate purposes"); 15 U.S.C. §1681(b) (2012) (stating the Congressional purpose of the FCRA is to require consumer reporting agencies to collect information "in a manner which is fair and equitable to the consumer"); 45 C.F.R. §164.502 (2012) (setting forth permissible uses of medical information, under the assumption that such information should be collected); 15 U.S.C. §6802 (setting forth obligations of financial institutions in handling consumer information, under the assumption that such information should be collected); 201 Mass. Code Regs. 17.01–.05 (2012) (providing conditions for ownership of nonpublic information).

financial and health services.[180] The use of the information, however, is regulated and controlled once assembled.[181]

The regulations and controls fall into two broad classes: (1) requirements for the security of such information, particularly when it falls into the "sensitive" categories mentioned above, and (2) regulation over the dissemination of such information to third parties. In the first of these categories, one finds the example of the Massachusetts Data Security Regulations, which directly specify minimum security standards to preclude the unauthorized disclosure of PII,[182] HIPAA, which mandates a variety of security standards for health information,[183] and the payment card data security standard ("PCI DSS"), which is enforced through contracts among payment card companies, banks, and merchants.[184] Laws that require prompt notice of the unlawful disclosure of personal information fall into the same category.[185]

The second class of control over the use of PII held by third parties inheres in the variety of conditions that we have already seen on the use and distribution of PII. These include the almost universal requirement that individuals be provided with notice of the uses to which their PII will be put and the requirement that there be a division between opt-in and opt-out requirements for the use or disclosure of that information.[186] One might consider these requirements as something falling at least partly into the realm of consumer education for the digital age. It is not so much that the collection and exploitation of consumer information is an inherently obnoxious activity — we consider it good service to know one's customers and to endeavor to respond to them personally — but that the facility with which such information can be collected and disseminated for profit comes as a great and sometimes

---

[180] See 45 C.F.R. §164.502; 15 U.S.C. §6802.

[181] See, e.g., 42 U.S.C. §1320c-9 (regulating disclosure of personal information possessed for medical purposes).

[182] 201 Mass. Code Regs. 17.03–.04.

[183] 45 C.F.R. §164.306.

[184] See "PCI SSC Security Standards Overview," PCI Security Standards Council, https://www.pcisecuritystandards.org/security_standards/ .

[185] See, e.g., Cal. Civ. Code §§1798.80–.84 (West 2012) (explaining the California breach notification law); N.Y. Gen. Bus. Law §§ 899-aa(3)–(4) (McKinney 2012) (explaining the New York data breach notification law); Tex. Bus. & Com. Code §521.053 (West 2012) (explaining the Texas data breach notification law); 815 Ill. Comp. Stat. 530/5 (2012) (explaining the Illinois data breach notification law). Breach notification is also required by HIPAA and its implementing regulations. See 45 C.F.R. §§164.404–.405 (2012).

[186] See, e.g., 15 U.S.C. §6802(a)–(b) (2012).

unpleasant surprise.[187] Notice at least diminishes the surprise. It also provides a basis for consent where laws, such as the right of publicity, require it.[188]

All of these restrictions can be understood as limitations on the uses to which the owner of the collections of PII that we are referring to as "digital identity" can put that information. This is analogous to the limitations that are imposed on the owners of a wide variety of other types of property, particularly when the property is capable of causing harm.[189] If, for example, you own a car, you must register it to drive on the public roads, drive on the proper side of the road, use your turn signals before you turn, and not exceed the speed limit.[190]

B. Countervailing considerations

Let us take stock in where our reasoning has brought us. Digital identity comprises a collection of thousands of facts about a person, and that person does not own those facts.[191] The facts can be assembled in many ways, each giving a somewhat different picture of the person — an image, as it were, in a different light or from a different direction. The law gives the assemblers of those facts, not the individual, ownership of those digital images.[192] There is a somewhat uncertain right to complain about it if some of the facts comprising the image are untrue[193] or if their use offends policy,[194] but one cannot, in

---

[187] See, e.g., Miguel Helft, "Critics Say Google Invades Privacy with New Service," *New York Times*, Feb. 13, 2010, at B1 (describing public backlash after release of "Google Buzz," a service that used email and chat data to automatically publish users' contacts without notice or consent).

[188] See *Jones v. Corbis Corp.*, 815 F. Supp. 2d 1108, 1111 (C.D. Cal. 2011) *aff'd*, No. 11-56082, 2012 WL 2884790 (9th Cir. July 16, 2012) ("Notices are sometimes posted at these events stating that celebrities entering the red carpet consent to being photographed and recorded, and also to having their name or likeness used in connection with the event."); Cal. Civ. Code §3344 (prohibiting the use of a person's identity without that person's prior consent, and not requiring the consent to be in writing).

[189] See, e.g., 18 U.S.C. §923 (imposing a federal licensing requirement on gun ownership and limiting the use of guns even after they are licensed).

[190] See, e.g., 625 Ill. Comp. Stat. 5/11-100 to 1516.

[191] See Bergelson, *supra* note 30, at 403 ("Currently, neither property nor torts theory recognizes individuals' rights in their information.").

[192] See *supra* notes 180–182 and accompanying text.

[193] See, e.g., 5 U.S.C. §552a(d) (2012); 15 U.S.C. §§1681g, 1681i.

[194] See, for example, *Biddle v. Warren Gen. Hosp.*, 715 N.E.2d 518, 523 (Ohio 1999), for a discussion of numerous jurisdictions that have recognized a common law tort for the unauthorized disclosure of confidential medical information.

general, complain about the assembly of the images as a whole. At the same time, the law imposes some rather strict limits on what the assembler can do with these images.[195] One might say that these assemblies of facts are dangerous instrumentalities, and the misuse of them can give rise to both strict liability and liability for negligence if they are not used carefully.

Is this a reasonable outcome? Many scholars argue that there should be property rights in identity.[196] Robert Merges, for example, cites the development of a right of publicity as an example of the creation of property rights.[197] In its original form, the right of publicity attaches to what one might call a persona: an artifice built around a person as a result of fame, notoriety, and in many cases, the efforts of teams of publicists.[198] Fair enough. If a public persona is as much the creation of a work as is a character in a novel, why should the persona not have the same level of protection, more like a copyrighted work, and less like a trademark? This point can be taken, but at the same time, it does not equate to saying that facts about the person behind the persona also belong to him or her, nor that a construct built of those facts should belong to him or her. And, in fact, persons who have property-like

---

[195] See, e.g., 201 Mass. Code Regs. 17.03–.04 (2012) (requiring any entity that deals in personal information to implement robust, multi-faceted security measures to protect that information).

[196] See Sarah Ludington, "Reining in the Data Traders: A Tort for the Misuse of Personal Information," 66 *Md. L. Rev.* 140, 143–46 (2006) (discussing data trading and the debate among academics about protecting personal information through property rights).

[197] Merges, *supra* note 1, at 96–101.

[198] 1 Melville B. Nimmer and David Nimmer, *Nimmer on Copyright,* §1.01[B][1][c] ("The 'work' that is the subject of the right of publicity is the persona, i.e., the name and likeness of a celebrity or other individual.") (emphasis in original). The right of publicity is currently a state law-based right. Nineteen states recognize the right by statute: California, Florida, Illinois, Indiana, Massachusetts, Kentucky, Nebraska, Nevada, New York, Ohio, Oklahoma, Pennsylvania, Rhode Island, Tennessee, Texas, Utah, Virginia, Washington, and Wisconsin. "Statutes," Right of Publicity, http://www.rightofpublicity.com/statutes. Twenty-one states have recognized the right by common law (though it has been replaced by statute in some states): Alabama, Arizona, California, Connecticut, Florida, Georgia, Hawaii, Illinois, Kentucky, Michigan, Minnesota, Missouri, New Hampshire, New Jersey, Ohio, Pennsylvania, South Carolina, Texas, Utah, West Virginia, Wisconsin. 1 J. Thomas McCarthy, *Rights of Publicity and Privacy* §6.3 (2d ed., 2012); see also "Restatement (Third) of Unfair Competition," §§46–49 (1995) (discussing the right of publicity and its protection through statutory and common law and mentioning several states that use the common law right of publicity protection).

rights in their public personas have virtually no ability to exclude third parties from facts about their real selves.[199]

State laws protecting the "right of publicity" present a higher obstacle to this response because they are not typically limited to famous people; instead, they typically attach to the use of *any* person's name or likeness for commercial purposes.[200] This does not, however, establish that individuals own their digital identities. In the first place, publicity laws are almost always applied to the use of persons' names and likenesses as endorsements in advertisements;[201] they are not applied or understood to apply to the more indirect use of information about a person for other commercial purposes. Furthermore, their reach is limited to names and likenesses, and does not extend to transactional information about individuals.[202]

In recognition of the limitations of privacy and publicity law, two scholars — Vera Bergelson and Patricia Mell — argue at great length, and with impressive thoroughness, that a property right should attach to personal information, in

---

199 See *Midler v. Ford Motor Co.*, 849 F.2d 460, 462 (9th Cir. 1988) ("The purpose of the media's use of a person's identity is central. If the purpose is 'informative or cultural' the use is immune; 'if it . . . merely exploits the individual [it is not].'" [quoting Peter L. Felcher and Edward L. Rubin, "Privacy, Publicity, and the Portrayal of Real People by the Media", 88 *Yale L. J.* 1577, 1596 (1979)]).

200 See *N.Y. Civ. Rights Law*, §51 (McKinney, 2012) (regulating use of "any person['s]" identifying features); Cal. Civ. Code §3344 (West 2012) (proscribing use of "another's" identifying features); *Doe v. TCI Cablevision*, 110 S.W.3d 363, 369 (Mo. 2003) (stating the elements of a common law cause of action for violation of the right of publicity as follows: "(1) [t]hat defendant used plaintiff's name as a symbol of his identity (2) without consent (3) and with the intent to obtain a commercial advantage"). But see Ind. Code §32–36-1-6 (2012) (limiting regulation to people whose identifying features have "commercial value").

201 See I. J. Schiffres, Annotation, "Invasion of Privacy by Use of Plaintiff's Name or Likeness in Advertising," 23 A.L.R.3d 865 §2[a] (1969). This is what got Facebook into trouble with its Sponsored Stories service. See *supra* notes 165–170.

202 See *N.Y. Civ. Rights Law*, §51 (providing relief for the use of a person's "name, portrait, picture, or voice" without consent); Cal. Civ. Code §3344 (holding a person liable for damages for the unauthorized use of another's "name, voice, signature, photograph, or likeness"); Ind Code §32–36-1-6 (defining "personality" to mean a "person whose name, voice, signature, photograph, image, likeness, distinctive appearance, gestures, or mannerisms has commercial value" (numbering omitted)).

the Bergelson case,[203] or to "electronic persona" in the Mell's case.[204] At the risk of injustice by brevity to Bergelson's extended analysis, one might summarize that she believes that a tort remedy for invasion of privacy is inadequate and that the transaction costs of requiring data compilers to obtain the permission of their data subjects are not worse than the transaction costs of the subjects trying to prevent the compilations. She believes that, at bottom, it is unjust for third parties to profit from the individuality of the persons whose personal information resides in the third parties' databases:

> In a nutshell, the suggested legal regime would give individuals property rights in their personal information. They would own this information during their lifetime, subject to a (i) non-exclusive automatic inalienable license to the original collector and (ii) limited non-exclusive automatic license to the general public. This way, friends of, say, Robert Bork would be free to talk, and newspapers free to write, about movies he watches or books he reads, but a video- or bookstore would not be free to reveal his customer record even in the heat of his nomination campaign.[205]

Bergelson's qualifications (i) and (ii) on the individual's "property" interest in her personal information are so broad as to make one wonder whether it is a property interest at all.[206] If Robert Bork's friends and newspapers can trade in the same information that is in the possession of the bookstore, can it reasonably be said that the information belongs to him? Bergelson may be unhappy about the bookstore's disclosure of information about Bork's purchases and may want to create a remedy for it, but if the information were really his, it should not matter who had misappropriated it — the friend, bookstore or newspaper.

Bergelson's analysis also conflates the assembly of information that constitutes one's digital identity with the bits of information that go into that

---

203 See generally Bergelson, *supra* note 30 (arguing that individuals should have property rights in their personal information). Bergelson lists works that have focused on the social utility of granting individuals property rights in personal information. Id. at 383 n. 16. She also discusses defining rights to personal information based on torts or property. Id. at 414–19.

204 Mell, *supra* note 30, at 68–70.

205 Bergelson, *supra* note 30, at 442.

206 Bergelson distinguishes her property interest from the "fee simple" proposed by Patricia Mell. Id. at 438; Mell, *supra* note 30, at 76.

assembly. She dislikes the fact that persons putting together the assembly can profit from it, whereas the individuals cannot.[207] In effect, she reasons that if there is a property interest in the collection of data, then there ought to be a property interest in the individual bits of data it comprises.[208] But this may prove too much. Copyrights are granted in collections of facts, none of which individually are subject to ownership, whether via copyright or otherwise.[209]

Mell's position is bolder. While Bergelson acknowledges the right of the "first collector" to information about an individual, Mell wants even the first collector to be required to obtain the individual's consent to collect the information:

> The persona should be viewed as property, the ultimate "ownership" or "fee simple" of which resides in the individual. The rights of any other entity (i.e., any group, class, association or government) that might obtain, access, make use of or disclose the persona would be subordinate to those of the individual. As with other forms of property, the individual's right to restrict the use of his persona by others would vary depending upon the reason for the use.[210]

Fortunately, her definition of "persona" is limited to "a personal information file electronically stored, which, by virtue of at least one 'identifier,' relates the personal information to a specific person."[211] Were it not for this, she would have created a property interest in others' memories and diaries. She was also writing before the advent of iPads, iPhones, Droids, the Cloud, and the myriad other new electronic devices by which memories and images are stored these days.[212] Putting these anachronistic considerations aside, her conception, like Bergelson's, upends the basic principle that people who collect facts own their collections, whether the facts are human, botanical, zoological, commercial,

---

207 Bergelson, *supra* note 30, at 383 ("[O]n the one hand, [individuals] are powerless to prevent [their information's] unauthorized dissemination, and on the other, they are excluded from its profitable commercial exchange.").

208 Id. at 419 (quoting Alice Haemmerli, "Whose Who? The Case for a Kantian Right of Publicity," 49 *Duke L. J.* 383, 418 (1999)).

209 Feist Publ'ns, Inc. v. Rural Tel. Serv. Co., 499 U.S. 340, 344–45 (1991).

210 Mell, *supra* note 30, at 76.

211 Id. at 4.

212 See, e.g., Michael Chertoff, "Cloud Computing and the Looming Global Privacy Battle," *Washington Post Opinions*, Feb. 9, 2012, http://www.washingtonpost.com/opinions/cloud-computing-sets-stage-for-a-global-privacy-battle/2012/02/06/gIQAhV2V2Q_story.html (describing the impact of cloud computing on the issue of digital privacy).

or of any other nature.[213] The nasty fact is that other people can learn things about us, and we cannot easily make them forget or keep quiet about what they learn. The best we can do is to try to restrain abuses that are not justified by legitimate interests.

One must also return to the distinctions between the rights of privacy and publicity, on the one hand, and a property right in personal identity on the other. There is no question that the rights associated with PII are almost universally identified with a right of privacy — the right not to have unconsented intrusions into or publications of one's personal affairs.[214] In cases such as Facebook's Sponsored Stories service, they are also associated with the right of publicity — the right not to have one's name or likeness used in advertisements without consent.[215] As discussed above, the history of the development of the law of privacy and publicity, as manifest in the current regulation of PII, has not required the creation of an individual's property right, either in PII or in assemblies of PII comprising his digital identity.[216]

It is well known that the concept of a right of privacy, now manifest in all of the laws surveyed in this paper, was first elaborated by Louis Brandeis and Samuel Warren in their celebrated law review article, "The Right to Privacy."[217] In their article, Brandeis and Warren considered and then rejected whether the right to privacy is a species of property:

> These considerations lead to the conclusion that the protection afforded to thoughts, sentiments, and emotions, expressed through the medium of writing or of the arts, so far as it consists in preventing publication, is merely an instance of the enforcement of the more general right of the individual to be let alone. It is like the right not be assaulted or beaten, the right not to be imprisoned, the right not to be

---

[213] *Feist*, 499 U.S. at 345.

[214] See *Restatement (Second) Torts* §652A (1977). William L. Prosser identifies four species of privacy claims, which eventually found their way into the Restatement: false light, intrusion upon seclusion, public disclosure of embarrassing facts, and the appropriation of a name or likeness. William L. Prosser et al., *Prosser and Keeton on Torts*, 851–68 (5th ed., 1984).

[215] See *Fraley v. Facebook, Inc.*, 803 F. Supp. 2d 785, 806 (N.D. Cal. 2011).

[216] See Mell, *supra* note 30, at 8.

[217] Warren and Brandeis, *supra* note 82. The authors were motivated to propound their privacy thesis by "recent inventions and business methods" that "call attention to the next step that must be taken for the protection of the person." Id. at 195. They were concerned about photography and unscrupulous newspapers. Id. Imagine their shock if confronted with the Internet!

> maliciously prosecuted, the right not to be defamed. In each of these rights, as indeed in all other rights recognized by the law, there inheres the quality of being owned or possessed — and (as that is the distinguishing attribute of property) there may be some propriety in speaking of those rights as property. But, obviously, they bear little resemblance to what is ordinarily comprehended under that term. The principle which protects personal writings and all other personal productions, not against theft and physical appropriation, but against publication in any form, is in reality not the principle of private property, but that of an inviolate personality.[218]

It is worth noting that, in 1890, Brandeis and Warren were not even comfortable with the notion that copyright is a species of property.[219] They were, of course, writing at a time when the only protection for unpublished works was the common law right of first publication,[220] and it is easy to understand how they perceived a parallel between that right — really, a right to prevent disclosure — and a right of privacy. Statutory copyright has, since then, subsumed the common law right within the larger rubric of copyright ownership,[221] which, as we have seen, arguably has more of the characteristics of property ownership.[222] One might imagine that 120 years from now, the privacy rights associated with some of the personal information that comprises one's digital identity will have grown into something closer to a property right in one's identity, and there are certainly forces pushing in that direction, but it has not happened yet.

One might also consider whether the emergence of "identity theft" laws[223] disproves this thesis.[224] If something is capable of being stolen, and if one can

---

218 Id. at 205.

219 Id. at 200–04.

220 See *Caliga v. Inter Ocean Newspaper Co.*, 215 U.S. 182, 188 (1909) ("At common-law, the exclusive right to copy existed in the author until he permitted a general publication. Thus, when a book was published in print, the owner's common-law right was lost. At common-law an author had a property in his manuscript").

221 See 17 U.S.C. §106(2012).

222 See 17 U.S.C. §201.

223 See, e.g., 18 U.S.C. §1028.

224 See generally Jennifer Lynch, "Identity Theft in Cyberspace: Crime Control Methods and Their Effectiveness in Combating Phishing Attacks," 20 *Berkeley Tech. L. J.* 259, 259–60 (2005) (explaining that phishing e-mails ask the recipient to verify personal information on a fake website, acting as the real business with the real account, in order to "steal her identity," suggesting that the identity was owned in the first place).

remedy the theft, does this not imply that it was owned in the first place?[225] The answer is likely no, and the proof is in the more ancient laws against fraud.[226] Fraudsters have been around for a very long time and have run out of town on rails when they are uncovered.[227] Persons who steal identity in the electronic age have democratized fraud, and have brought the harm to bear more directly on the persons whose identities have been misappropriated, but the crime is essentially the same.

And, in effect, it proves my point: You cannot make yourself into somebody that you are not, and you cannot prevent people from knowing who you are.

III. Some modest proposals

The collection and exploitation of PII continues to attract intense legislative and regulatory attention. The Appendix to this article catalogs bills pending in the U.S. Congress alone as of November 2012. Many dozens of bills are pending in state legislatures across the country, and the Information Commissioners of Europe proliferate their own interpretations, and reinterpretations, of the European Directives and implementing legislation.[228]

Recent initiatives of the Federal Trade Commission (FTC) and the White House bear special mention. The White House published a white paper in February of 2012, proposing a Consumer Privacy Bill of Rights, enforceable industry codes of conduct, effective enforcement by the FTC, and global harmonization of privacy laws.[229] In March of 2012, the FTC published its

---

[225] Bergelson, supra note 30, at 404. Bergelson acknowledges that despite the name "identity theft," what the laws "really aim at is future crime (e.g., theft, fraud) the commission of which is facilitated by identity theft." Id. She points out that as long as there is no "intent to commit [a] future crime, an unlawful use or transfer of identifying information does not constitute a theft of identity," which suggests that the identity of a person is not truly owned. Id.

[226] See, e.g., *Commonwealth v. Boynton*, 2 Mass. (1 Tyng) 77, 79 (1806) (finding defendant liable for common law fraud for counterfeiting the signatures of a bank president and cashier). Naturally, this is long before any identity theft laws were in place, yet pretending to be someone, albeit through signature, was still unlawful. Id.

[227] See Mark Twain, *Huckleberry Finn*, ch. 17 (The Duke and the Dauphin).

[228] To catalog all the pending legislation, regulations and initiatives would convert this essay into a compendium.

[229] The White House, "Consumer Data Privacy in a Networked World: A Framework for Protecting Privacy and Promoting Innovation in the Global Digital Economy," 1–3 (2012) [hereinafter White House White Paper].

report entitled "Protecting Consumer Privacy in an Era of Rapid Change."[230] The Report proposed a "Privacy Framework" comprising three elements: "Privacy by Design," "Simplified Choice," and "Greater Transparency."[231] For the most part, the FTC's framework was consistent with the White House's "Bill of Rights." Both call for greater individual control, transparency, simplified choice, improved security, and a reasonable connection between the information collected and the context in which it is collected.[232] The FTC also recommends enactment of "Do Not Track" legislation that would provide consumers a means of preventing behavioral tracking.[233]

If one were to risk an overgeneralization, the FTC and White House proposals are, in comparison with their European counterparts, more concerned with the education of consumers as to how their information is collected and used and less with limits over the actual collection and use of the information. This is, of course, consistent with the more *laissez faire* attitude that the United States takes to commerce in general.[234] It also, though, reflects the underlying reality that the collection and exploitation of personal data in the United States ran well ahead of the public's understanding of it,[235] whereas in Europe, the EU Directive both educated the public at an earlier date and restrained some of the most aggressive marketing efforts one commonly sees in the United States.[236] Nevertheless, services like Amazon, Facebook, and Twitter that depend on the exploitation of personal data for their commercial success are hugely popular on both sides of the Atlantic.[237]

The White House and FTC got it about right to the extent that they emphasize education over control. For many, Internet commerce is like visiting a foreign country, where the customs and etiquette are new and often disconcerting. To complicate matters further, the inhabitants of this country are making up their customs as they go along, and the pace of innovation,

---

230 Fed. Trade Comm'n, "Protecting Consumer Privacy in an Era of Rapid Change: Recommendation for Businesses and Policymakers" (2012) [hereinafter FTC Report].

231 Id. at vii–ix.

232 See FTC Report, *supra* note 231, at vii–ix; "White House White Paper," *supra* note 230, at 1–2.

233 See FTC Report, *supra* note 231, at 4. Do-not-track bills were filed in both the House and Senate in 2011. See Appendix.

234 Jack Ewing, "U.S. Growth Is Tepid, but It's the Envy of Europe," *New York Times*, Apr. 28, 2012, http://www.nytimes.com/2012/04/28/business/global/28iht-econ28.html?_r=0.

235 See A. Michael Froomkin, "The Death of Privacy?," 52 *Stan. L. Rev.* 1461, 1502 (2000).

236 See Chertoff, *supra* note 213.

237 See Pingdom Team, "The Top Countries on Facebook," Royal Pingdom, Aug. 12, 2010, http://royal.pingdom.com/2010/08/12/the-top-countries-on-facebook-chart/.

particularly in the realm of the collection and use of PII, has outpaced the development of shared expectations as to what is acceptable and what is not. A great deal of mischief has been caused by the tendency of companies like Amazon, Facebook, and Twitter to be cagey about their collection and exploitation of PII, leading to surprise and outrage when the facts come to light.[238] To the uninitiated, they seem to have put their feet on the table during dinner without first considering alternative postures or begging the pardon of their dinner mates. In a sense, these companies and their customers are making up a new culture as they go along, and it is not at all surprising that the process causes considerable anxiety and misunderstanding.[239] A guidebook, with information about what to expect in terms of the collection and use of personal information, is important. Many of the recommendations of the FTC's framework and the White House's Bill of Rights can be understood and applauded in this context.

There is, however, a risk of regulatory overreaction to this collision of cultural expectations. Thanks to the collection of personal information and the assembly of digital identities, consumers obtain better, more personal service than would be possible without it.[240] Consumers can be spared many irrelevant advertisements with which they would be bombarded, commercial television-wise, if the information were not collected, and in the end, it is the exploitation of such information that makes so many free Internet services possible.[241] The assembly of such information both creates enormous new wealth for the companies that compile it and facilitates economic activity for

---

[238] See, e.g., Tony Romm, "Kindle Fire Sparks Lawmaker Privacy Worries," Politico, Oct. 16, 2011, http://www.politico.com/news/stories/1011/65978.html.

[239] See Natasha Singer, "U.S. Is Tightening Web Privacy Rule to Shield Young," *New York Times*, Sept. 28, 2012, at A1. This report indicates that public complaints regarding misuse of children's information have prompted the FTC to move "to overhaul" the Children's Online Privacy Protection Act in order to expand the scope of information subject to parental consent requirements. Id.

[240] William McGeveran, "Disclosure, Endorsement, and Identity in Social Marketing," 2009 *U. Ill. L. Rev.* 1105, 1114–15 (2009).

[241] See id. (discussing Google, which is a free website, and its paid search advertising based on a user's search inquiries or on the content of a user's email exchanges).

all the other enterprises that take advantage of the information.[242] One does not want to kill the goose laying these golden eggs.[243]

Beyond the economic risk, and from the author's parochial standpoint as an intellectual property lawyer, one must consider whether proposals for the creation of new property rights in personal data can be reconciled with long-established principles of intellectual property law that define the public domain. Without a rich source of raw material in the public domain, the creation of new inventions and works of authorship would be curtailed.[244] Surely no one imagines that an individual should be able to prevent an author from using facts about the individual's life to create a biography, but how does one distinguish this from the assembly of a digital identity by a company like Amazon? The biographer, like Amazon, wants to use the information for her own benefit and to sell the information to third parties to earn a profit. Can one make a reasoned distinction between the two activities? In a sense, Amazon's activity is more benign because it is quite unlikely to use the information in a way that would offend the individual. Furthermore, if there are "bad facts" about an individual — that he doesn't pay his debts, that he has committed fraud — should he be able to suppress this information because it is his "property"?

This inquiry brings one to an area in which regulation seems appropriate. There are compelling public policy reasons why certain types of information should not inform certain decisions. Race and religious affiliation are perhaps the most obvious examples. Making decisions about the extension of credit, employment, housing, lodging, transport, access to health services, and other

---

242 Ann Bartow, "Our Data, Ourselves: Privacy, Propertization, and Gender," 34 *U.S.F. L. Rev.* 633, 647–48 (2000).

243 The recent about-face by the U.K. Information Commissioner on the subject of cookies exemplifies avoiding the risk of over-reaction. See Charles Arthur, "Cookies Law Changed at 11th Hour to Introduce 'Implied Consent,'" *The Guardian*, May 25, 2012, http://www.guardian.co.uk/technology/2012/may/26/cookies-law-changed-implied-consent. The Information Commissioner had adopted regulations that, on their face, would have required prior consent before any cookie could be placed on an individual's computer. Id. This would have made use of the Internet enormously inconvenient, as each visit to a website would have to have been treated as a first visit as if one were required to pretend one did not know someone one had met many times before. Id. Under pressure from industry the Commissioner relaxed the regulations to permit Internet interactions to proceed more "normally." Id.

244 A. Samuel Oddi, "The Tragicomedy of the Public Domain in Intellectual Property Law," 25 *Hastings Comm. & Ent. L. J.* 1, 11 (2002).

universal needs on the basis of race or religion is, and should be, illegal.[245] This is not because an individual owns the fact that she is of a particular race or religion; it is because discrimination based on race or religion is heinous for more general social and historical reasons.[246] On the other hand, it is obvious that some products and services are more appropriately advertised to members of a particular religion or race, and maintaining such information for this purpose provides a valuable service — one probably does not want to try to sell crucifixes to Muslims, and Muslims would probably prefer to be spared crucifix promotions. In other words, it is the use of such information, not its assembly and distribution, that merits legal control.

We come then to a modest proposal: Wherever possible, regulate and provide a remedy for the potential misuse of PII as opposed to its assembly and benign exploitation. Section 604(g) of the FCRA is an example of such regulation.[247] It generally prohibits service providers from obtaining and using medical information in connection with any determination of the consumer's eligibility, or continued eligibility, for credit.[248] On the other hand, the statute contains no prohibition on creditors obtaining or using medical information for purposes that are not connected to a determination of the consumer's eligibility, or continued eligibility for credit.[249] One can imagine myriad purposes for obtaining such information, not the least of which is the provision of effective medical treatment.

The FCRA takes this a step further in placing the burden on Consumer Reporting Agencies—companies in the business of assembling credit-related information — of policing the limitations on the use of the Consumer Reports they assemble and sell.[250] This approach, which has withstood some forty years of enforcement and development and supports a highly viable industry, could be generalized to include all aggregations of PII that contain information capable of misuse. To use the analogy made earlier in this paper, such aggregations can be considered a modern form of "dangerous instrumentality."[251] Like dynamite, they have many viable purposes, but the

---

[245] See U.S. Const. amend. XIV, §1; 42 U.S.C. § 3604 (2012) (proscribing housing discrimination specifically).

[246] See *Brown v. Bd. of Educ.*, 347 U.S. 483, 492–93 (1954).

[247] 15 U.S.C. §1681b(g) (2012).

[248] Id.

[249] Id.

[250] Id. §1681(b).

[251] See *supra* notes 175–179 and accompanying text.

person creating and selling these aggregations of PII should bear responsibility for policing their potential for misuse.

This rationale extends as well to laws and regulations, placing responsibility on the data aggregators for unauthorized disclosure and for correcting erroneous information upon notice from a consumer. In fairness to legislatures and regulators, many existing and proposed regulations fall into these well-justified categories. One such regulation is the proposed Data Accountability and Trust Act of 2011,[252] which would, among other things, require businesses possessing electronic data to establish security procedures, and to have procedures for verifying and correcting the data.[253] Another example is the proposed Data Security and Breach Notification Act of 2011,[254] which would require security measures and notification in case of a breach.[255]

On the other hand, proposed regulation that prohibits the collection of certain types of information entirely, or permits it only with prior consent, seems overbroad.[256] For example, the proposed Geolocation and Privacy Surveillance Act of 2011[257] and proposed Location Privacy Protection Act of 2011[258] would both require prior express consent to the collection of geolocation information.[259] Another example is the proposed BEST PRACTICES Act of 2011,[260] which would, among other things, require prior consent to collect sensitive personal information.[261] It is not easy to understand how or why a person can legitimately prevent people from knowing his race or that he is walking through a particular mall at a particular time. These facts would be obvious to everyone else in the mall.

On the other hand, the use of that information to, for example, rob his home when he is not there, seems legitimately actionable. Again, it is the use, not the information itself, which deserves regulation. Put another way, the

---

252 H.R. 1841, 112th Cong. (2011).

253 Id. §2.

254 S. 1207, 112th Cong. (2011).

255 Id. §3.

256 See Clair Cain Miller and Somini Sengupta, "In Mobile World, Tech Giants Scramble to Get Up to Speed," *New York Times*, Oct. 23, 2012, at A1 ("[J]ust last week, European regulators warned Google to amend its privacy policy that allows it to gather information about people across diverse Google products, from Gmail to YouTube.").

257 S. 1212, 112th Cong. (2011).

258 S. 1223, 112th Cong. (2011).

259 S. 1212 §2; S. 1223 §3.

260 H.R. 611, 112th Cong. (2011).

261 Id. §103.

appropriate question of public policy concerns the use of the information, not its ownership.

Conclusion

There is something fundamental at work in the tug of war over the ownership of personal identity. On the one hand, everyone craves a measure of recognition; on the other hand, we morbidly fear exposure. When Brandeis and Warren wrote their classic article on privacy, photography was the new technology, and tabloid journalism was apparently the new business method.[262] They lived in Boston, a large city by nineteenth-century standards,[263] and a person living there could probably enjoy a measure of anonymity if he chose to. They saw the new technology and journalism as a threat to that "right to be left alone" and reacted against it with high Victorian umbrage.[264]

One imagines that if they had lived in a smaller place, their expectations for privacy would have been very much diminished. In small communities, everyone tends to know quite a lot about everyone else, for better or worse. Some of this knowledge is accurate; much of it is probably exaggerated through gossip and hearsay, but it is an inevitable fact of small-town life.[265] Indeed, it is one of the reasons many people flee small towns when they can.[266] Despite Brandeis's and Warren's perceived evils of photography and tabloid journalism, a measure of anonymity could be found for many years after 1890 in a big country with big cities, like the United States. Their concern was with what

---

[262] Warren and Brandeis, *supra* note 82, at 195 ("Instantaneous photographs and newspaper enterprise have invaded the sacred precincts of private and domestic life; and numerous mechanical devices threaten to make good the prediction that 'what is whispered in the closet shall be proclaimed from the house-tops.'").

[263] Samantha Barbas, "Saving Privacy from History," 61 *DePaul L. Rev.* 973, 983–844 (2012); see also John S. Billings, Dep't of the Interior, "Vital Statistics of Boston and Philadelphia Covering a Period of Six Years Ending May 31, 1890," at 1 (1895), available at www.census.gov/prod/www/abs/decennial/1890.html (reporting Boston's population in 1890 at 448,477).

[264] Warren and Brandeis, supra note 82, at 196 ("The press is overstepping in every direction the obvious bounds of propriety and of decency.").

[265] See A. G. Sulzberger, "In Small Towns, Gossip Moves to the Web, and Turns Vicious," *New York Times*, Sept. 20, 2011, at A1 ("In the small towns nestled throughout the Ozarks, people like to say that everybody knows everybody's business — and if they do not, they feel free to offer an educated guess.").

[266] See id. (chronicling one woman's strong desire to leave her small town after becoming the subject of a negative and untrue internet posting that caused friends and family to alienate her).

happens behind closed doors in peoples' homes, not the question of whether what one does outside of the home is subject to scrutiny.[267]

Now, in the early twenty-first century, privacy law abounds in all the major markets.[268] And the reason is obvious: With the Internet, there is no place to hide and no place where one can be anonymous and still engage in commercial life at all. People are somewhat shocked to discover that the Internet has made life in the biggest city as claustrophobic as the smallest of small towns. Just as the butcher, baker, and liquor store owner in a small town will know what consumers eat and drink, will know how much of each, and can gossip freely about consumption habits, and just as the members of a church or synagogue or social club will know an uncomfortable amount about a person's family and its travails, online vendors and social networks will have and may even share a comparable volume of information about a person.[269]

It is not clear that this is an altogether bad thing; on the contrary, as evidenced by Facebook, Twitter, Foursquare, Pinterest, and myriad other social networking sites, people actively seek it.[270] Where, in the past, young people fled small towns to find the anonymity of the big city, today they flee the anonymity of the big city to find recognition in the small towns represented by their friends on networks like Facebook.[271] The difference is that Big Brother, in the person of the collectors of online data, is watching in a way that was never the case in a small town. The same personal information that binds friends becomes more dangerous in the hands of an anonymous corporation or anonymous government agency that can exercise enormous power over the individual.[272]

---

[267] Warren and Brandeis, *supra* note 82, at 215 ("The general object in view is to protect the privacy of private life, and to whatever degree and in whatever connection a man's life has ceased to be private, before the publication under consideration has been made, to that extent the protection is to be withdrawn.").

[268] See *supra* Part I.B.

[269] See Fed. Trade Comm'n, "Privacy Online: Fair Information Practices in the Electronic Marketplace," at iii (1998).

[270] Lim Yung-Hui, "1 Billion Facebook Users on Earth: Are We There Yet?," *Forbes*, Sept. 30, 2012, https://www.forbes.com/sites/limyunghui/2012/09/30/1-billion-facebook-users-on-earth-are-we-there-yet/ (estimating how long it will take for Facebook to officially surpass one billion users).

[271] See Clive Thompson, "I'm So Totally, Digitally Close to You," *New York Times*, Sept. 7, 2008, at MM42.

[272] See, e.g., "FTC Announces Settlement With Bankrupt Website, Toysmart.com, Regarding Alleged Privacy Policy Violations," Fed. Trade Commission, July 21, 2000, http://www.ftc.gov/opa/2000/07/toysmart2.htm.

And so, regulation over the collection and dissemination of such information is both appropriate and inevitable. If successful, it protects against misuse of a person's information, particularly sensitive personal information, and also protects against the dissemination of false or misleading information about that person. Protection against, and remedies for, misuse of personal information should not, however, be confused with ownership of the collections of personal information that comprise identity. This is because, by engaging in commerce or social media, a person is making himself known to others, and others deserve to know whom they are dealing with in both personal and commercial affairs.[273]

Identity and the personal information on which it is built are thus inherently relational in nature. It is the opposite of anonymity, and one cannot have it both ways: You can achieve anonymity by refusing to interact with others, but once you begin to interact, you necessarily lose your anonymity and gain an identity in others' perceptions of you. At that point, your identity is not, and by necessity cannot be, your private possession.

---

[273] But see Assemb. 1844, 2011–12 Leg., Reg. Sess. (Cal. 2012) (prohibiting California employers from requesting their employees' username and password to social media accounts, and making it unlawful to discriminate against those who fail to comply).

Appendix

Bills pending in U.S. Congress as of November 1, 2012

Commercial Privacy Bill of Rights Act of 2011 (S. 799)

- Would require commercial entities that use or collect data to implement security measures to protect information and provide users with notice on their collection practices

- Entities must allow users to opt-out of collection of personally identifiable information and unique identifiers and allow users to access and correct data

- Entities may collect only as much information as necessary to process or enforce a transaction

- Authorizes FTC and state AGs to enforce penalties

Do-Not-Track Online Act of 2011 (S. 913)

- Gives the FTC the authority to propose and enforce standards of a Do Not Track mechanism

Do-Not-Track Me Online Act (H.R. 654)

- Gives the FTC the authority to establish online opt-out mechanisms for users to prohibit collection or use of "covered information"

BEST PRACTICES Act (H.R. 611)

- Advertisers must obtain expressed, written consent to collect "sensitive information," including race, ethnicity, sexual orientation and income

- Requires opt-in consent before a company may disclose information to a third party

- Requires companies collecting personal data to disclose practices and explain options to consumers in timely, easy to understand notices

Consumer Privacy Protection Act of 2011 (H.R. 1528)

- Would require entities to notify consumers that their personally identifiable information may be used for a purpose unrelated to the transaction

- Entities would be required to establish a privacy policy, make it readily available to consumers and notify consumers about changes in their privacy policies

- Entities must give consumers ability to opt out of the sale or disclosure of their information to any organization that is not an information-sharing partner

Geolocational Privacy and Surveillance Act (S. 1212)

- Would prohibit companies from collecting or sharing geolocation information without user consent

Location Privacy Protection Act of 2011 (S. 1223)

- Would require covered entities to offer prior notice and obtain expressed consent from consumers in order to track and collect GPS information

Electronic Communications Privacy Act Amendments Act of 2011 (S. 1011)

- Would update the ECPA to restrict third-party access to GPS information

- Would require authorities to obtain a warrant before accessing an individual's email, digital communications or geolocation information

Data Security and Breach Notification Act of 2011 (S. 1207)

- Requires businesses and NPOs that store personal information to implement reasonable security measures and alert consumers when data has been compromised

- In the event of a breach, affected individuals would be entitled to free credit monitoring for two years

Data Breach Notification Act of 2011 (S. 1408)

- Requires federal agencies and persons engaged in interstate commerce in possession of personally identifiable information to provide notice for any breach of such information

Personal Data Privacy and Security Act of 2011 (S. 1151)

- Would require financial firms, retailers, and federal agencies to guard private information, investigate possible breaches, and notify consumers if their information may have been compromised

Personal Data Protection and Breach Accountability Act of 2011 (S. 1535)

- Would require interstate companies that handle PII on 10,000 or more U.S. persons to provide notice and remedies to consumers in the event of breach

- Holds companies accountable for preventable breaches

- Enhances criminal and civil penalties against unauthorized collection or use of PII

SAFE Data Act (H.R. 2577)

- Would require businesses to notify consumers and the FTC within 48 hours of containing and assessing a breach

- Would entitle affected consumers to two years of free credit monitoring

Digital Accountability and Trust Act (DATA) of 2011 (H.R. 1841)

- Would require FTC to create regulations requiring businesses that own or possess electronic data containing personal information to establish data- security practices and procedures

- Authorizes FTC to require a standard method or methods for destroying obsolete non-electronic data

- Requires information brokers to submit their security policies to the FTC in conjunction with a breach or on FTC request

- Requires FTC to audit security practices of information brokers in the event of a breach

- Requires information brokers to establish procedures to verify the accuracy of information that identifies individuals and to allow consumers to access and correct data

Afterword

This book covers 45 years, during which the world changed profoundly. In 1974 there was no Internet, no World Wide Web, no Facebook, no personal computer, no cable TV, no cellular phones. The geopolitical structure was essentially what had been set by Roosevelt, Churchill, and Stalin at Yalta in 1945: two great blocs locked in a cold war that retarded economic globalization and ensured large-scale stability and ideological hegemony within their spheres. By 2020 all this had changed. Digitization had revolutionized communications and data accumulation. The Soviet Union and its bloc had collapsed; there was an intense period of internationalization and globalization, now followed by an equally intense period of xenophobia. China awoke from its thousand-year slumber to become a dominant powerhouse of international capitalism run by an authoritarian regime calling itself "Communist," putting the lie to the Western conceit that economic and political liberty must be linked.

The book chronicles the efforts of the law to cope with these changes. My focus throughout has been on what one might call the machinery of the law. We first considered the workings of the lawyers and judges who operate this machinery, in the context of the economic changes that infiltrated hide-bound institutions like the business law firms in which I've spent my career. Next came a consideration of the moving parts in the law's machinery — namely, words: What are they? How do they work? How do lawyers and judges use them? We then saw how words failed us when a vocabulary derived from sculpture serving as a lamp base tried and failed to grapple with computer games and programs. Chapter 4 had lawyers to the rescue, as they wrote contracts to fill the voids left in judicial opinions protecting computer software. This, as Rob Merges points out in his Foreword, is where a lot of law is actually made but is also overlooked by the Academy's concentration on judicial opinions and famous public cases. The next chapter reminds us that the edifice of intellectual property that lawyers and judges built so laboriously is something of a Potemkin village, which collapses when confronted with the stark reality of a bankruptcy proceeding and the need for licensees to use intellectual "property" even though someone else "owns" it. Chapter 6 returns to the social context of globalization in the context of another species of intellectual property, trademarks, which share the curious nature of something owned by one person but relied upon and used by many others. And finally, we came to that new species of intellectual quasi-property, personal data, which pushes the boundaries of what might be considered "property" at all.

Has the book fulfilled the promise of its title, to describe "how law works?" Well, it tells a fair amount about what lawyers do when they are working at the law and trying to apply it to new situations and their clients' needs. It ventures some speculations about the inner workings of the law and its uneasy relation with its own language. It offers some observations about the law's remarkable adaptability and ability to bridge differences, often through the manipulation and redirection of language. And it suggests, rightly I think, that the law sometimes works well and sometimes rather poorly.

I like to think that the cover art, a remarkable etching by my friend and college classmate Joe Moore, aptly captures the whole thing: some large thoughts, never quite complete; some littler ones, more nearly complete; a few definite points; and all of it intersecting and diverging as one follows each line of thought.

I am grateful to you, my reader, for having traveled this journey with me. Looking back on it, I hope to have been a reasonably informed time-travel tour guide, observing and commenting on the law and lawyers hard at work to adapt the law to the emerging digital age. Perhaps I have stimulated a thought or two along the way, and if I've managed to amuse like those Duck Boat narrator/drivers showing visitors the sights in Boston, so much the better.

Thomas Hemnes

Table of References

Cases

Statutes

Other Authorities

Rules

Constitutional Provisions

Selected Bibliography

Abramson, Ronald, "Why Lotus-Paperback Uses the Wrong Test and What the New Software Protection Legislation Should Look Like." *7 The Computer Lawyer 6* (August 1990).

Allen, G. Ross. "The Basics of Indemnification." *21 Intell. Prop. Litig. 7* (Spring 2010).

Ambrosio, Christina, and Roni Schneider. "Copyright Misuse . . . Getting Defensive: *Lasercomb America, Inc. v. Reynolds." 6 J. Legal Comm. 181* (1990).

Antton, D. Lee, and Gary M. Hoffman. "Copyright Protection and Innovation: The Impact of *Lotus Development v. Paperback Software*," *Computer Law* 1, no. 8 (1990).

Archer, Gleason L. *The Law of Real Property.* 2nd ed. Boston: Suffolk Law School Press, 1927.

Askin, Frank, "Police Dossiers and Emerging Principles of First Amendment Adjudication." *22 Stan. L. Rev. 196* (1970).

Austin, John L., *Philosophical Papers.* Edited by J. Urmson and G. Warnock. 3rd ed. Oxford: Oxford University Press, 1979.

Barbas, Samantha. "Saving Privacy from History." *61 DePaul L. Rev. 973* (2012).

Bartow, Ann. "Our Data, Ourselves: Privacy, Propertization, and Gender." *34 U.S.F. L. Rev. 633* (2000).

Beard, Mary. *How Do We Look: The Body, the Divine, and the Question of Civilization.* New York: Liveright Publishing (2018).

Bender, David. *Bender on Privacy and Data Protection.* New York: Matthew Bender (2019).

Bennett, Steven C. "Regulating Online Behavioral Advertising." *44 J. Marshall L. Rev. 899* 908–09 (2011).

Bergelson, Vera. "It's Personal but Is It Mine? Toward Property Rights in Personal Information." *37 U. C. Davis L. Rev. 379* (2003).

Berger, Dustin D. "Balancing Consumer Privacy with Behavioral Targeting." *27 Santa Clara Computer & High Tech L. J. 3* (2011).

Black, Hugo. "The Bill of Rights." *35 N. Y. U. L. Rev. 865* (1960).

Brennan, Jr., William J. "The Supreme Court and the Meiklejohn Interpretation of the First Amendment." *79 Harv. L. Rev. 1* 5 (1965).

Breyer, Stephen. "The Uneasy Case For Copyright: A Study of Copyright in Books, Photocopies, and Computer Programs." *84 Harv. L. Rev. 281* (1970).

Buckman, T. "Comment, Protection of Proprietary Interest in Computer Programs." *51 J. Pat. Off. Soc'y* 135 (1969).

Calabresi, Guido. *The Costs of Accidents: A Legal and Economic Analysis.* New Haven: Yale University Press, 1970.

Calabresi, Guido, and A. D. Melamed. "Property Rules, Liability Rules, and Inalienability: One View of the Cathedral." *85 Harv. L. Rev. 1089* (1972).

Callman, Rudolf, *The Law of Unfair Competition, Trademarks and Monopolies.* 4th ed. St. Paul, MN: Thomson/West, 1982.

Carrier, Michael A. "Cabining Intellectual Property Through a Property Paradigm." *54 Duke L. J. 1* 1 (2004).

Casner, A. James, and W. Barton Leach. *Cases and Text on Property.* Boston: Little Brown, 1951.

Cauthorn, Kim, Tom Britven, and Tamara Turek. "Sharing the Risk: Patent Infringement Liability Indemnification and Insurance." *Intell. Prop. Litig.* (Spring 2010).

Cavell, Stanley. *Must We Mean What We Say?* (New York: Charles Scribners Sons., 1969).

Chafee, Zechariah. "Book Review." *62 Harv. L. Rev. 891* (1949).

Chafee, Zechariah. "Equitable Servitudes on Chattels." *41 Harv. L. Rev. 945* (1928).

Charee, Zechariah. *Free Speech in the United States.* Athenium, 1941.

Chafee, Zechariah. "Reflections on the Law of Copyright" (pts. 1 & 2). *45 Colum. L. Rev. 503* (1945).

Chafee, Zechariah. "The Music Goes Round and Round: Equitable Servitudes and Chattels." *69 Harv. L. Rev. 1250* (1956).

Chisum, Donald S. *Chisum on Patents: A Treatise on the Law of Patentability, Validity and Infringement.* New York: Matthew Bender, 1991.

Concoff, G. "Motion Picture Secured Transactions under the Uniform Commercial Code: Problems in Perfection." *13 U.C.L.A. L. Rev. 1214* (1966).

Cooper, Frederick L., and Walter Sapronov. "Software Protection and Pricing in a LAN Environment." *26 Jurimetrics J. 162* (1986).

Corbin, Arthur L. *Corbin on Contracts.* St. Paul, MN: Thomson/West, 1952.

Countryman. V. "Executory Contracts in Bankruptcy: Part I." *57 Minn. L. Rev. 439* (1973).

Countryman, V. "Executory Contracts in Bankruptcy: Part II." *58 Minn. L. Rev. 479* (1974).

Currie, R., and D. Crampton, D. *Conflict of Laws: Cases – Comments – Questions.* St. Paul, MN: West Academic Publishing,1968.

Davidson, Duncan. "Protecting Computer Software: A Comprehensive Analysis." *1983 Ariz. St. L.J. 611* (1983).

Davidson, Duncan. "Common Law, Uncommon Software." *47 U. Pitt. L. Rev. 1037* (1986).

Dumbauld, Edward. *The Bill of Rights and What It Means Today.* Norman, OK: University of Oklahoma Press, 1957.

Dvorak, A., N. Merrick, W. Dealey, and G. Ford. *Typewriting Behavior.* New York: American Book Company, 1936.

Ehrlich, Amy. *The Random House Book of Fairy Tales.* New York: Random House, 1985.

Ellickson, Robert. *Order Without Law: How Neighbors Settle Disputes.* Cambridge, MA: Harvard University Press, 1991.

Emerson, Thomas. *Toward a General Theory of the First Amendment.* New York: Random House, 1966.

Farnsworth, E. Allan. *Contracts.* 4th ed. New York: Aspen/Wolters Kluwer, 2004.

Frantz, Laurent B. "The First Amendment in the Balance." *71 Yale L. J. 1424* (1962).

Freund, Paul. "Constitutional Dilemmas." In *On Law and Justice.* Cambridge, MA: Harvard University Press, 1968.

Fried, Charles. "Two Concepts of Interests: Some Reflections on the Supreme Court's Balancing Test." *76 Harv. L. Rev. 755* (1963).

Gilbert, Stuart. *James Joyce's* Ulysses*: A Study.* New York: Penguin/Random House, 1955.

Gilburne, Miles R., and Ronald L. Johnston. "The Protection and Enforcement of Trade Secrets in Software and High Technology Information." In Daniel T. Brooks and Michael S. Keplinger, *Software Protection: Current Developments in Copyright and Patent and Their Relationships to Trade Secrets* (1982).

Gilmore, Grant. *Security Interests in Personal Property.* Boston: Little Brown & Co., 1965.

Haar, Charles M., and Lance Liebman. *Property and Law.* 2nd ed. Boston: Little Brown, 1985.

Heller, Michael A. "The Boundaries of Private Property." *108 Yale L. J. 1163* (1999).

Hemnes, Thomas M. S. "Computer Software Licensing After the Enactment of the Intellectual Property Bankruptcy Protection Act." *Computer Law* 7, no. 10 (Oct. 1988).

Hemnes, Thomas, "Restraints on Alienation, Equitable Servitudes, and the Feudal Nature of Computer Software Licensing," *71 Denv. U. L. Rev. 577* (1994).

Hemnes, Thomas. "Three Common Fallacies in the User Interface Copyright Debate." *7 Comp. Lawyer 14* (1990).

Hemnes, Thomas, and Susan Montgomery. "The Bankruptcy Code, The Copyright Act, and Transactions In Computer Software." *7 Computer Law Journal 327* (1987).

Henry, Matthew D., and John L. Turner. "The Court of Appeals for the Federal Circuit's Impact on Patent Litigation." *35 J. Legal Stud 85* (2005).

Horwitz, Ethan, and Lester Horwitz. *Intellectual Property Counseling and Litigation* §11.03[3][a] (LexisNexis, 1994).

Igo, Sarah. *The Known Citizen.* Cambridge, MA: Harvard University Press, 2018.

Jackson, Thomas. "Bankruptcy, Non-Bankruptcy Entitlements, and the Creditor's Bargain." *91 Yale L. J. 857* (1982).

Jeuss, Sara, Robin Feldman, and Joshua Walker. "The America Invents Act 500: Effects of Patent Monetization Entities on Litigation." *11 Duke L. & Tech Rev. 357* (2012).

Kalven, Jr., Harry. "The *New York Times* Case: A Note on 'The Central Meaning of the First Amendment'." *1964 Sup. Ct. Rev. 191* (1964).

Kant, Immanuel. *Critique of Pure Reason.* Translated by N. K. Smith. New York: Macmillan & Co., 1929 [1781].

Kant, Immanuel. *Foundations of the Metaphysic of Morals.* Translated by Lewis White Beck. New York: Liberal Arts Press, 1959 [1785].

Kaplan, Benjamin. *An Unhurried View of Copyright.* New York: Columbia University Press, 1967.

Kaplan, Benjamin, and Richard Field. *Materials for a Basic Course in Civil Procedure.* 3rd ed. St. Paul, MN: Foundation Press, 1973.

Kesan, Jay P., and Gwendolyn G. Ball. "How Are Patent Cases Resolved? An Empirical Examination of the Adjudication and Settlement of Patent Disputes." *84 Wash. U.L. Rev. 237* (2006).

Kirsch, Matthew S. "Do-Not-Track: Revising the EU's Data Protection Framework to Require Meaningful Consent for Behavioral Advertising." *18 Rich. J. L. & Tech. 2* (2011).

Kline, Michael. "Requiring an Election of Protection for Patentable/Copyrightable Computer Programs." *1985 J. Pat. Off. Soc'y 280.*

Koch, Adrienne. *Jefferson and Madison: The Great Collaborators.* New York: Oxford University Press, 1950.

Koch, Adrienne, and William Peden. *The Life and Selected Writings of Thomas Jefferson.* New York: Random House, 1972.

Kutten, L. J. *Computer Software: Protection/Liability/Law/Forms.* Deerfield, IL: Clark Boardman Callaghan, 1993.

Levy, Leonard. *Legacy of Suppression.* Cambridge, MA: Belknap Press of Harvard University Press, 1960.

Lindberg, Van. *Intellectual Property and Open Source.* 3rd ed. Sebastopol, CA: O'Reilly Media, 2008.

Locke, John. *Two Treatises of Government.* Edited by Peter Laslett. Cambridge: Cambridge University Press, 1988 [1690].

Lynch, Jennifer. "Identity Theft in Cyberspace: Crime Control Methods and Their Effectiveness in Combating Phishing Attacks." *20 Berkeley Tech. L. J. 259* (2005).

Markman, Joanna S. "In Re Gault: A Retrospective in 2007: Is It Working? Can It Work?" *9 Barry L. Rev. 123* (2007).

McCarthy, J. Thomas. *McCarthy on Trademarks and Unfair Competition.* 4th ed. Toronto: Thomson Reuters, 2012.

McGeveran, William. "Disclosure, Endorsement, and Identity in Social Marketing." *2009 U. Ill. L. Rev. 1105* (2009).

Meiklejohn, Alexander. *Free Speech and Its Relation to Self-Government.* New York: Harper Brothers, 1948.

Mell, Patricia. "Seeking Shade in a Land of Perpetual Sunlight: Privacy as Property in the Electronic Wilderness." *11 Berkeley Tech. L. J. 1* (1996).

Merges, Robert. *Justifying Intellectual Property.* Cambridge, MA: Harvard University Press 2011.

Miller, John C. "40 Indemnification Clauses Review Tips." *Cont. Mgmt.* 55/56 (2007).

Murphy, Paul L. *The Meaning of Free Speech.* Westport, CT: Greenwood Publishing Company, 1972.

Nelson, Richard. "On the Complex Economics of Patent Scope." *90 Colum. L. Rev. 839* (1990).

Nimmer, Melville B., and David Nimmer. *Nimmer on Copyright.* New York: Matthew Bender, 1963–2019.

Note, "Computer Programs and Proposed Revisions of the Patent and Copyright Laws." *81 Harv. L. Rev 1541* (1968).

Note, "Judicial Review of Military Surveillance of Civilians: Big Brother Wears Modern Army Green." *72 Colum. L. Rev. 1009* 1047 (1972).

Note, "The Chilling Effect in Constitutional Law." *69 Colum. L. Rev. 808* (1969).

Note, "The First Amendment and the 'Abridgeable' Right of Self-Expression." *72 Colum. L. Rev. 1249* (1972).

Note, "The First Amendment Overbreadth Doctrine." *83 Harv. L. Rev. 844* (1970).

Note, "The Speech and Press Clause of the First Amendment as Ordinary Language." *87 Harv. L. Rev. 374* (1973).

Note, "Transfers of Copyright Under the New Copyright Act." *88 Yale L. J. 125* (1978).

Nycum, Susan, Dexter Kenfield, and Margaret Keenan. "Debugging Software Escrow: Will It Work When You Need It?" *4 Computer L. J. 441* (1984).

Oddi, A. Samuel. "The Tragicomedy of the Public Domain in Intellectual Property Law." *25 Hastings Comm. & Ent. L. J. 1* (2002).

O'Rourke, Maureen A. "An Essay on the Challenges of Drafting a Uniform Law of Software Contracting." *10 Lewis & Clark L. Rev.* 925 (2006).

Page, John. "Grazing Rights and Public Lands in New Zealand and the Western United States: A Comparative Study." *49 Nat. Resources J. 403* (2009).

Plato. "The Republic." Translated by Paul Shorey. In *Plato: The Collected Dialogues,* edited by Edith Hamilton and Huntington Cairns. Princeton, NJ: Princeton University Press, 1961.

Plucknett, Theodore F. T. *A Concise History of the Common Law.* 5th ed. Indianapolis: Liberty Fund, 1956.

Porter, Andre J. "Should Business Method Patents Continue to be Patentable?" *29 S.U. L. Rev. 225* (2002).

Posner, Richard. "The Law and Economics Movement." *The American Economic Review* 77, no. 2 (1987).

Prosser, J. W., and W. P. Keeton. *The Law of Torts.* 5th ed. St. Paul, MN: West Publishing Co., 1984.

Quittner, Arnold. "Franchises in Bankruptcy: Termination, Rejection and Assumption." *1984 Comm. L. J. 84.*

Rawls, John. *A Theory of Justice.* Cambridge, MA: Harvard University Press, 1971.

Raysman, Richard. "Licensing Issues in Network Environments." *12 New Eng. Computer L. Inst., 339* (1992).

Rendleman, Doug. "Collecting a Libel Tourist's Defamation Judgment?" *67 Wash. & Lee L. Rev. 467* (1964).

Rilee, Edward. "The Protection of Property Rights in Computer Software." *19 Pub. Ent. Advert. & Allied Fields L.Q. 265* (1980).

Robbins, Jonathan. *Advising eBusinesses.* Deerfield, IL: Clark Boardman Callaghan, 2012.

Rosenberg, Peter D. *Patent Law Fundamentals.* 2nd ed. Deerfield, IL: Clark Boardman, 1991.

Rudnick, Robert E., and Andrew M. Grodin. "Drafting and Negotiating Defense and Indemnification Provisions." *Intell. Prop. Litig.* (Spring 2010).

Samuelson, Pamela. "CONTU Revisited: The Case Against Copyright Protection for Computer Programs in Machine-Readable Form." *1984 Duke L. J. 663* (1984).

Schwartz, B. *The Bill of Rights: A Documentary History.* New York: McGraw-Hill, 1971.

Silbey, Jessica. *The Eureka Myth.* Stanford, CA: Stanford University Press, 2015.

Silverstein, Lee. "Rejection of Executory Contracts in Bankruptcy and Reorganization." *31 U. Chi. L. Rev. 467* (1964).

Sommer, Henry J., and Richard Levin. *Collier on Bankruptcy.* 15th ed. New York: Matthew Bender/Lexis Nexis, 1985.

Spivack, Peter G. "Does Form Follow Function? The Idea/Expression Dichotomy in Copyright Protection of Computer Software." *35 U.C.L.A. L. Rev. 723* 741 (1988).

St. Martin, Anne Louise, and J. Derek Mason. "Arbitration: A Quick and Effective Means for Patent Dispute Resolution." *12 N. C. J.L. & Tech. 301* 317 (Spring 2011).

Thomas, Robert E., and Larry A. DiMatteo. "Harmonizing the International Law of Business Methods and Software Patents: Following Europe's Lead." *16 Tex. Intell. Prop. L. J 1* (2007).

Tiffany, Herbert Thorndike. *A Treatise on the Modern Law of Real Property and Other Interests in Land.* Abridged by Carl Zollmann. Chicago: Callaghan & Co., 1940.

Tindall, William. *A Reader's Guide to Finnegans Wake.* Syracuse, NY: Syracuse University Press, 1969.

Warren, Samuel, and Louis Brandeis. "The Right to Privacy." *4 Harv. L. Rev. 193* (1890).

Wild, Robert W. Comment, "Computer Program Protection: The Need to Legislate a Solution," *54 Cornell L. Rev* (1969) 586–87; *81 Harv. L. Rev.* (1968), 1541, 1543–45.

Williston, Samuel. *Williston on Contracts.* 4th ed. Edited by Richard Lord. Rochester, NY: Lawyers Cooperative Publishing/Thomson Reuters, 2003–2019.

Wittgenstein, Ludwig. *Philosophical Investigations/Philosophische Untersuchunen.* 4th ed. Translated by G. E. M. Anscomb, P. M. S. Hacker, and Joachim Schulte. Hoboken, NJ: Wiley Blackwell, 2009 [1953].

Xiang, Joy Y. "How Wide Should the Gate of 'Technology" Be?: Patentability of Business Methods in China." *11 Pac. Rim L. & Pol'y J. 795* (2002).

Zhuboff, Shoshana, *The Age of Surveillance Capitalism.* New York: Hachette, 2020.

Index

A

B

C

D

E

F

G

H

I

J

K

L

T

U

V

W

X

www.ingramcontent.com/pod-product-compliance
Lightning Source LLC
LaVergne TN
LVHW050805220926
848485LV00013B/1433/J
* 9 7 8 1 6 2 2 7 3 8 2 6 7 *